EARNINGS MANAGEMENT
Emerging Insights in Theory, Practice, and Research

Springer Series in Accounting Scholarship

Series Editor:

Joel S. Demski
Fisher School of Accounting
University of Florida

Books in the series:

EARNINGS MANAGEMENT
Emerging Insights in Theory, Practice, and Research

Joshua Ronen
New York University

and

Varda (Lewinstein) Yaari
Morgan State University

 Springer

Joshua Ronen
Stern School of Business
New York University
West 4th Street
New York, NY 10012

Varda Yaari
Earl G. Graves School of Business & Management
Morgan State University
1700 East Cold Spring Lane
Baltimore, MD 21251

Series Editor:

Joel S. Demski
Fisher School of Accounting
University of Florida
PO Box 117166
Gainesville FL 32611-7166

Library of Congress Control Number: 2007931882

ISBN: 978-0-387-25769-3   e-ISBN: 978-0-387-25771-6

Printed on acid-free paper.

9 8 7 6 5 4 3 2 1

springer.com

To Ruth, Tavy, and Asaf
For Uzi, Hila, Linor, and Rona

Contents

Introduction

> Historically, bubbles are followed by crashes, which in turn are
> followed by punitive legislation. The 1999–2003 era is fully
> consistent with this pattern.... (Coffee, 2003a, p. 46) ...During
> the collapse of the high tech bubble in 2000 and 2001, publicly
> held firms audited by the Big Five fell by over $1 trillion in
> market value. (Coffee, 2003a, p. 66)

The accounting scene in the United States changed dramatically at the
beginning of the twenty-first century. The prosperity of the late-twenty-
century stock markets attracted small investors as well as large ones. Lynn
Turner, (2001b), cites a 2000 study that finds that in 1998, some 43.6% of
the adult population owned shares (84 million shareholders).

> These stockholders come from all walks of life, young and old, rich
> and not so rich. ... And interestingly, half of those stockholders have
> income of less than $57,000 and only 18 percent have family incomes
> that exceed $100,000. **Indeed, the average stockholder today is the
> average American who lives next door, is your aunt or uncle, a
> close friend or family member.** (Turner, p. 1, emphasis added)

With the bursting of the Internet bubble in 2000, the previously bullish
stock markets became bearish, and the ugly truth eventually caught up
with companies that allegedly tried to obscure unpleasant reality in their
accounting reports. The first big scandal occurred in 2000, when Xerox
revealed that it had overstated profits by $1.4 billion over a 4-year period.
Unfortunately, Xerox was not an isolated instance. Twenty large and
highly publicized scandals followed between October 2001 and the enactment of Sarbanes-Oxley Act of 2002, including those involving World-
Com, Adelphia, Tyco, and Global Crossing (see figure 1 in Cohen, Dey,
and Lys, 2005a). The corporate meltdowns in the wake of the scandals
caused hundreds of millions of dollars in losses to investors. The largest
collapse was that of WorldCom in May 2002, with estimated losses ap-
proximating $180 billion.

Besides accounting scandals, the current era is marked by the fall of the
audit firm that prepared Enron's financial statement, Arthur Andersen
LLP. Andersen, which was the fifth-largest accounting firm in the world,

collapsed because the company's Dallas office shredded documents pertinent to the Congressional investigation of Enron's bankruptcy.[1] These scandals shook the faith of investors in the integrity of the capital markets. The government stepped in through the enactment of the Sarbanes-Oxley Act of July 2002,[2] which is implemented by rules laid down by the Security and Exchange Commission (SEC) and strengthened by rule-making in individual states (see the Introduction to Part 2).

The Demand for Earnings Management Research

The new environment raises a host of questions that are of concern to academics, regulators, and practitioners. In this book, we restrict our attention to those that are concerned with firms' *earnings management* practice. Earnings management can be loosely defined as a strategy of generating accounting earnings, which "is accomplished through managerial discretion over accounting choices and operating cash flows" (Phillips, Pincus, and Rego, 2003, p. 493). Earnings management is an umbrella for acts that affect the reported accounting earnings or their interpretation, starting from production and investment decisions that partly determine the underlying economic earnings, going through the choice of accounting treatment and the size of accruals when preparing the periodic reports, and ending in actions that affect the interpretation of the reported earnings, such as presenting non-GAAP earnings (commonly known as pro forma earnings) and asking the auditor who prepares an opinion casting doubt on the firm's ability to remain a "going concern" not to use the term (Butler, Leone, and Willenborg, 2004, footnote 2).

The accounting debacles of the current era have driven demand for two types of research. The first strand—as exemplified by, Healy and Palepu (2003),[3] Coffee (2003a),[4] and Ronen (2002a,b,c)[5]—makes suggestions for

---

[1] On October 16, 2001, Enron Corp. announced that it was reducing its after-tax net income by $544 million and its stockholders' equity by $1.2 billion. On November 8, Enron reduced stockholders' equity by an additional $508 million by restating its previously reported net income for the years 1997–2000. Within a month, equity was lower by $1.7 billion (18% of the $9.6 billion previously reported on September 30, 2001). On December 2, 2001, Enron filed for bankruptcy under Chapter 11 of the United States Bankruptcy Code.

[2] The official title of the Act is the Public Company Accounting Reform and Investor Protection Act of 2002.

[3] Healy and Palepu argue for transforming the audit committee of the board of directors into a "transparency" committee that provides investors the information

improvements. The second strand attempts to make sense of the earnings management phenomenon (e.g., Demski, 2002; Coffee, 2003b; Dechow and Schrand, 2004; Erickson, Hanlon, and Maydew, 2004; Yaari, 2005; Ronen, Tzur, and Yaari, 2006; Ronen and Yaari, 2007). According to these researchers, if we know why earnings management takes place, and how it is achieved, we will be able to uproot it. Erickson, Hanlon, and Maydew (2006) elaborate on the demand for this sort of research:

> Some of the largest alleged accounting frauds in history occurred in the last several years, leading to the well-known upheaval in the accounting industry and sweeping legislative and regulatory changes. These events have left legislators, regulators, practitioners, and academics searching for answers about the causes of these alleged frauds. **Understanding the underlying forces that gave rise to the alleged frauds is a necessary precursor to effectively preventing future occurrences.** Many have suggested that the explanation lies in the incentives and opportunities for personal gain faced by executives. (p. 113, emphasis added)

Understanding earnings management may also reveal that not all earnings management is bad, so taking action to uproot the undesirable variety runs the risk of "throwing the baby out with the bath water." As Arya, Glover, and Sunder (2003) observe

> [A]ccounting research shows that income manipulation is not an unmitigated evil; within limits, it promotes efficient decisions. Our argument, admittedly controversial, **is worth airing**: earnings management and managerial discretion are intricately linked to serve multiple functions; accounting reform that ignores these interconnections could do more harm than good. (p. 111, emphasis added)

From the first strand, we choose to focus on Financial Statements Insurance (FSI); see Parts 2 and 3. We follow the second strand of research comprehensively. Of course, restatements and earnings management had

---

required to understand a firm's strategy, from vision and mission down to objectives, success factors, and risks.

[4] Coffee points to gatekeepers in the stock market as the parties to be blamed for the accounting scandals because they failed in their function of diminishing the asymmetry of information between management and outsiders. He suggests a penalty system that increases the cost of collusion between gatekeepers and management.

[5] In these studies, Ronen proposes restructuring the audit industry by letting auditors be hired by insurance companies that undertake to insure the quality of financial statements. See Ronen (2002a,b,c), Ronen and Berman (2004) and Dontoh, Ronen, and Sarath (2007).

been taking place long before the turn of the century,[6] and research on earnings management started some time ago as well. The first author of this book, Joshua Ronen, collaborated with Simcha Sadan in 1981 on a book that studied whether companies removed volatility in their series of reported incomes—intertemporal smoothing—and whether they signaled value to investors by choosing to present a material transaction in operating income or in extra ordinary items—classificatory smoothing. The earliest studies cited in Ronen and Sadan's book are two papers that appeared in *The Accounting Review*: Hepworth (1953), and Gordon (1964).[7]

The following subsection describes the progress of research on earnings management since the 1980s. We refer the reader, who is interested in earlier research, to the surveys in Ronen, Sadan, and Snow (1977), Ronen and Sadan (1981), and Stolowy and Breton (2000).

Historical Perspective: The Milestones

The accounting field and the research on accounting have been marked by a few events that have had a major impact on our knowledge and understanding of earnings management. We divide these milestones into theoretical research contributions, empirical research contributions, and regulatory innovations.

On the theoretical front, new insights have been provided by the penetration of game-theory tools into accounting, including studies by the following:

- Lambert (1984), examines real smoothing, a strategy whereby management uses its flexibility in making investment and production decisions to reduce the variability of the firm's total value. Lambert models real smoothing as the outcome of the principal–agent relationship between the owners and the manager.

---

[6] The "hall of infamy" for the late twentieth century includes Waste Management, Microstrategy, Rite Aid, Cendant, Sunbeam, Oxford Health, McKessom HBOC, and others. Accounting and Auditing Enforcement Release No. 1405 (SEC, June 19, 2001) states the following:

In February 1998, Waste Management announced that it was restating its financial statements for the five-year period 1992 through 1996 and the first three quarters of 1997 (the "Restatement").

[7] An excerpt from *Journal of Corporate Communications* (August, 22, 2002) cites accounting scandals in the 1930s.

- Dye (1988), rationalizes the internal and external demand for cosmetic earnings management. The internal demand follows from the principal–agent relationship between the firm's owners and the management, and the external demand follows from the capital market's need to price the firm.
- Dye (1985a), Arya, Glover, and Sunder (1998, 2003), and Ronen and Yaari (2002), challenge the applicability of the Revelation Principle. The Revelation Principle is a game-theory tool that states that whatever the equilibrium of a game in which players have private information, there is no loss of generality in restricting analysis to another equilibrium in which players reveal the truth. The Revelation Principle puts a question mark on the value of a formal analysis of earnings management.
- Sankar (1999), Ronen and Yaari (2001, 2002), and Ronen, Ronen, and Yaari (2003), among others, examine the effect of earnings management on the magnitude of the earnings response coefficient, voluntary disclosure, and the demand for additional information.

In empirical research, shifting attention to instances when management may demand earnings management has been fruitful. The following are noteworthy:

- Healy (1985), shows that compensation contracts may induce management to take measures to decrease reported income when it cannot increase its bonus, thus hoarding reported income.
- Schipper (1989), provides a discussion of the different definitions of earnings management (see our Chap. 2) and critically summarizes recent empirical developments. Her commentary appeared after a *Journal of Accounting Research* conference, Studies on Management's Ability and Incentives to Affect the Timing and Magnitude of Accounting Accruals. The most cited paper from this conference in the earnings management literature is by McNichols and Wilson (1988), on manipulation of the bad-debt expense (see Chap. 11).
- Jones (1991) separates discretionary accruals from non-discretionary accruals when she examines the demand of regulators for the earnings numbers during import relief investigations; the same approach to detecting earnings management has been examined further by Dechow, Sloan, and Sweeney (1995), Bartov, Gul, and Tsui (2000), Dechow and Dichev (2002), Kang (2005), Kothari, Leone, and Wasley (2005), Ye, (2006), Yaari, DaDalt, Ronen, and Yaari (2007).

At the regulatory level, we find the following significant developments:

- The 1998 "Numbers Game" speech by the then chief commissioner of the Securities and Exchange Commission, Arthur Levitt, Jr., which foreshadowed the subsequent regulatory measures to improve the quality of accounting earnings, including SAB 99 (materiality), SAB 100 (timing and recognition of restructuring), and SAB 101 (revenues recognition.)
- The Sarbanes-Oxley Act of 2002, which created the Public Company Accounting Oversight Board, an independent body responsible for the issuance of audit and ethics standards that effectively replaced self-regulation of accountants.
- Increased monitoring of accountants and accounting statements, including augmentation of the SEC staff by about 800 people at the time this is being written.

Our purpose in this book is to provide a comprehensive view of earnings management and to inspire further research. Although there are already a few literature reviews (e.g., Schipper, 1989; Healy and Wahlen, 1999; Stolowy and Breton, 2000; McNichols, 2000; Beneish, 2001; Fields, Lys, and Vincent, 2001), we believe that the breadth of our coverage will provide readers with an integrated view of the subject. We focus on later contributions, as the bibliography tops 2,000 items.

The Plan of the Book

The book is divided into four parts: the conceptual framework, the accounting scene and the findings of empirical research, theoretical contributions, and the design of the empirical research.

In Part 1, we explain the focus on earnings by consumers of financial information, which in turn explains the demand for earnings management. We present and discuss the definition of earnings management.

Part 2 contains a review of the accounting scene, the key players, and the earnings management incidents that are associated with them. We divide the participants into three major categories: management, other stakeholders (such as shareholders, debtors, employees, customers, and suppliers), and gatekeepers, who provide monitoring value (such as analysts, boards of directors, auditors, and the press). As examples of our analysis, we associate management with firms' managing earnings in order to increase the value of management's compensation, creditors with inducing firms to manage earnings in order to not violate debt covenants, and analysts with firms' motivation to meet or beat market expectations.

We discuss in Part 3 the theoretical contributions to the literature, dividing them according to the patterns of earnings management behavior:

- Truth-telling (and truth-revealing)—the choice of accounting treatment is neutral.
- Smoothing—dampening the fluctuations in the series of reported earnings by inflating low earnings and deflating high earnings. The outcome is that in the long run, the average reported income equals the average economic income but with smaller variability of the series of reported incomes.
- Income-maximizing and income-minimizing behavior, and *taking a bath*. The firm inflates, deflates, or super-deflates earnings (writing off assets, providing for expected future costs, and generally "clearing the deck").[8]

In Part 4, we describe the empirics of the earnings management literature. We start with the accrual process because a great deal of research examines the management of accruals. Understanding what accruals management is in turn requires familiarity with the unmanaged accruals process. We also review the progress of the research on earnings management that started with Ronen and Sadan (1981) and ended with the 1991 Jones model. The last chapter in this section contains a discussion of the modifications to the Jones model and alternative tests of earnings management.

Acknowledgments

We are grateful to our colleagues for their valuable input and inspiring discussions: Bill Baber, Sudipta Basu, Donald Byard, Masako Darrough, Salma Ibrahim, Joseph Kerstein, Joseph Tzur, Jimmy Ye, Amir Ziv. Likewise, we appreciate the helpful comments of our Ph.D. students: Nana Amoah, Loretta Baryeh, C.J., Alina Lerman, Arthur Wharton, and Jan Williams. We are indebted to our editor, Harry Butler, and we are particularly thankful for

---

[8] Mulford and Comiskey (2002, p. 15), define "taking a bath" as follows: "A wholesale write-down of assets and accrual of liabilities in an effort to make the balance sheet conservative so that there will be few expenses to serve as a drag on future earnings."

the valuable help and support of our families: Ruth, Tavy, and Asaf Ronen, and Uzi, Hila, Linor, and Rona Yaari. The second author also acknowledges a research grant from Morgan State University.

We hope that this book will serve to introduce our readers to the accounting scene and to the players and their incentives, as well as the interactions among the participants. We also hope that the book will inspire new ideas. The feedback received so far indicates that there is a good chance of accomplishing these goals, and so we wish the readers a fruitful and enjoyable reading.

We appreciate feedback from the readers: jronen@stern.nyu.edu and vardayaari@gmail.com.

Part 1

In the Introduction, we described the evolution of earnings management culminating in the recent accounting scandals. But before we delve into the details of the why, the how, and the impacts of earnings management, we ask, and attempt to answer the question of whether and why earnings are important. And in the same vein, we address the importance of the distinction between managed and unmanaged earnings. In Chapter 1, we discuss the different streams in accounting thought that explain why earnings are important. In Chapter 2, we present and discuss the definition of earnings management and how it is implemented.

1 The Importance of Earnings

In this chapter, we investigate the question of why earnings are so important that they are the object of management and manipulation. In the following chapter, we define earnings management formally. Until then, we define it loosely as deliberate actions to influence reported earnings and their interpretation.[1] For some readers, the importance of earnings is trivial because they are trained to regard earnings as the ultimate performance measure. There is evidence, however, that other financial statements' components might be more important than earnings in certain industries. Other performance measures are revenues, earnings before interest and taxes (EBITA); capital expenditures; balance sheet items such as assets and debt; cash flows from operations; or various non-financial performance measures. For example, Francis, Schipper, and Vincent (2003), identify often-used performance metrics from careful reading of the Standard and Poor's Industry Surveys, as given in Table 1.1.

Table 1.1 The prevalence of the performance measures in specific industries

Performance measure	Industry
Earnings	Communications equipment, computers, semiconductors, diversified-financial services, managed health care, household durable goods and investment services
Earnings before interest and taxes (EBITA)	Oil and gas equipment and services, healthcare facilities, and telecommunications
Cash flows from operations	Chemicals, industrial metals, and paper and forest products

---

[1] The definition includes interpretation because we also consider pro forma earnings as a form of earnings management. Even if the GAAP earnings are unmanaged, the non-GAAP earnings affect the interpretation of the GAAP earnings.

Performance measure	Industry
Non-financial measures	Airline industry (revenue per passenger mile, cost per available seat mile, and load factor) homebuilding (value of new orders and value of order backlog) retail restaurants (same store sales)

We contend that earnings are the ultimate object of managing the accounting numbers and dedicate the rest of the chapter to presenting the scholarly explanations for their importance. The understanding why earnings, specifically, are managed is critical for both the analytical and empirical research. The analytical models derive earnings management from modeling of variables that are specified by the researcher. Understanding why earnings are important dictates the choice of these variables. We discuss the analytical research in Part 3. The empirical research formulates and examines empirically testable propositions. Again, understanding why earnings are important is crucial for formulating hypotheses, choosing controls, and constructing samples. To illustrate, consider Palmrose and Scholz's (2004) finding that the single largest item in restatements is revenues. If revenues were the object of earnings management, and earnings were affected as a by-product of managing revenues, then the empirical design ought to focus on revenues and not earnings. We discuss the design of empirical research in Part 4.

1.1 The Dual Role of Accounting

At a first glance, earnings are important because accounting information in general is. The traditional view on the value of accounting information is that this information has a dual role: informativeness and stewardship (Ronen, 1979; Gjesdal, 1981; Dye, 1988; Antle and Demski, 1989; Antle, Demski, and Ryan, 1994; Natarajan, 1996, 2004; Rajan and Sarath, 1996; Narayanan and Davila, 1998; Sunder, 1997, 2002; Bushman, Engel, Milliron, and Smith, 2000; Lambert, 2001; Baldenius, Melumad, and Ziv, 2002; Christensen and Feltham, 2002, 2005; Baldenius and Ziv, 2003; Christensen and Demski, 2003; Feltham, Indjejikian, and Nanda, 2006).

The informativeness role arises from investors' demand for information to predict future cash flows and assesses their risk (see Statement of

Financial Accounting Concept No. 1, AICPA, 1994; and AIMR, 1993).[2] A rich literature illustrates this informativeness empirically by finding an association between earnings and stock price. We have no ambition to cover this literature, but as an example, consider Francis, Schipper, and Vincent (2003). They find that reported earnings numbers are more closely associated with prices than cash flows, sales, and other financial statements' data.

The stewardship role of accounting comes from the separation between ownership and management in public firms, which puts the manager in a position of a steward to shareholders. Since managers act as self-interested individuals, goal congruence between the shareholders and managers is no longer assured. For shareholders, the remedy is to demand information to monitor the manager after he has acted and to provide him with incentives that align his interests with their own, before he acts. As Watts and Zimmerman (1978, p. 113) state, "one function of financial reporting is to constrain management to act in the shareholders' interest."

The dual role of accounting provides a partial explanation to the prominence of earnings. Apart from the fact that the focus on shareholders and management ignores other stakeholders, such as suppliers, employees, regulators, etc. (see e.g., Tirole, 2002), the usefulness of earnings as an informative signal is dubious. The *informativeness* is questioned by the facts that the street prefer pro forma earnings over Generally Accepted Accounting Principles (GAAP) earnings (see, e.g., Bradshaw and Sloan, 2002; see also Chap. 2), and the association between earnings and stock price has been decreasing over time. Specifically, the Earnings Response Coefficient (ERC), which measures the weight of earnings in price movements, has been on the decline (see Sinha and Watts, 2001; Dontoh, Ronen, and Sarath, 2003, and the citations therein). With regard to *stewardship*, the increase in equity-based compensation in managers' incentives package has decreased the relative weight of earnings in their rewards (Murphy, 1999; Bushman and Smith, 2001).[3] To the extent that earnings are but one

---

[2] The AIMR's report, p. 97, states, "Financial statements are prepared and disseminated to provide the information that free financial markets need to operate."

[3] Furthermore, some criticize earnings, as a mechanism to induce management to act in the interests of shareholders, for inducing short-term thinking that focuses on quarterly performance and sacrifices the long-term well-being of the firm. This point is crucial when one notes that the horizons of shareholders vary from short run (such as day traders) to long run (such as value investors). As anecdotal evidence, consider the report of A.R. Sorkin (New York Times, 8/8/2004, Kissing the Public Goodbye) on the decision of the controlling family of Cox Communications, a cable company, to go private:

component affecting the price, the decreasing weight of earnings casts doubt on the motivation to manage earnings from a cost–benefit perspective. In other words, if the weight of earnings is small, then the benefit might be too small to justify the large costs associated with providing earnings and managing earnings.

We now turn to the scholarly explanations for the value of earnings.

1.2 The Value Relevance of Earnings

Since the producers and reporters of the accounting information are firms, it is natural to explore the importance of earnings from the perspective of the theory of the firm. Although we would like to have a single, comprehensive definition, this is not the case, probably because of the limitations of modeling: Bainbridge (2002), states,

> If scholarship is to transcend mere description, it must be situated in a model that guides analysis. Inevitably, however, the limits of human cognition require us to adopt models that make simplifying assumptions. (p. 1)

We identify three main approaches to the definitions of the firm that have shaped accounting theory.

- The costly contracting approach;
- The decision-making approach;
- The legal approach.

A basic cornerstone of all these approaches is that the public firm is characterized by separation of ownership from control; shareholders own and management controls. There is a conflict of interests between the firm's management and shareholders, and all behave rationally, where rationality is equated with pursuing self-interest in the opportunistic sense.[4]

"What's so hot about saying hasta la vista to ticker symbols?
Cox and others contemplating such a move seem to be fed up with all those pesky shareholders, **quarterly earnings targets** and second-guessing research analysts." [Emphasis added]

[4] Kreps (1990), discusses the distinction between utility maximizing and opportunistic behavior:

> To distinguish simple self-interest from opportunism, think of a completely honest individual who would never break her word or misrepresents what she knows, but who still seeks to maximize her own welfare. This is self-interest, as compared to an opportunistic individ-

The recognition that management, not the owners, makes most of the firm's decisions motivates the conflict of interests between the two parties. The decisions made by the management do not necessarily coincide with the wishes of shareholders. Being rational, each party takes actions that he considers to be beneficial to him personally, without necessarily taking into account any benefits to the other.

Despite their similarities, each approach is distinct in two respects. The first concerns the extent to which the audiences of the accounting earnings, henceforth "outsiders," know the firm's true economic earnings without relying on the accounting numbers. If the accounting numbers convey no new information, earnings are unlikely to be valuable. The second difference concerns the power of distant shareholders and other outsiders to carry out a given decision. They may not make the right choice because they are powerless to do so. This perspective implies that even when accounting numbers convey useful information, they still may not matter because they have no economic consequences.

Figure 1.1 classifies the three approaches according to two lexicographic criteria: knowledge and power.

The costly-contracting approach assumes full knowledge (and implicitly assumes power). Its main difference from the other two approaches, the decision-making approach and the legal-political approach, is that the latter adopts an "information perspective" (Healy and Palepu, 1993) whose basic tenet is the existence of information asymmetry between management and other stakeholders, with management having superior information.

The difference between the decision-making approach and the legal-political approach lies in their assumption about the shareholders. The former considers shareholders to be powerful but not knowledgeable. Under the latter, the shareholders have a problem monitoring management because they have neither the knowledge nor the power required for this task.

---

ual who would break his word or engage in misrepresentation under the right circumstances. Moreover, our use of the term "opportunism" is stretched to mean that it is opportunistic to refuse to divulge information that you hold and another lacks when the other person asks you to give up that information. (p. 745)

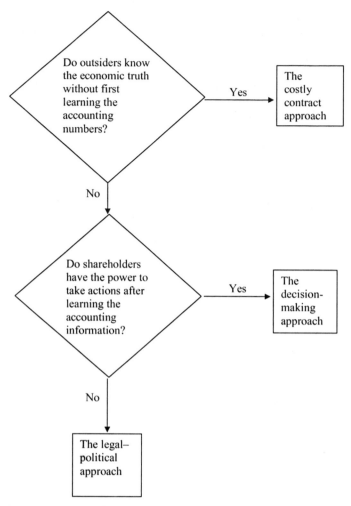

Fig. 1.1 The three different approaches that explain the importance of earnings

1.2.1 The Costly-Contracting Approach

1.2.1.1 The Approach

The firm is defined as a nexus of contracts (Coase, 1937).[5] Contracts are made between the firm and outsiders, such as lenders, and between the firm and insiders, such as management and other employees.

---

[5] The notion that the firm is a nexus of contract predates the Rochester school of thought. It is now known as the "Carnegie school." For a further discussion, consult Sunder (1999).

The raison-de-être for formally written contracts (instead of oral understandings) is the conflict of interests among the contracting parties. For example, lenders prefer that firms not pay out dividends to shareholders before they collect the principal. Employees prefer to have more perks, while owners prefer that they have fewer.

Given the conflict of interests between management and shareholders, it seems logical to consider earnings as a performance measure to enable shareholders to monitor management. Specifically, accounting numbers serve as a basis for the contracts that make up the firm. They are used because they are mutually observable, thus making possible the design of contracts that are enforceable by an outsider to the contract, an arbitrator or court. If the contracting parties know the underlying economic events and they use the accounting numbers only as a language to measure and specify the performance of the firm, then accounting numbers have no more intrinsic value than the particular language (e.g., English or French) in which the contract is written.

When are the accounting numbers valuable? They are valuable only when contracts do not adjust optimally to changing economic circumstances or when the adjustment is costly and the contracting parties prefer to avoid it. Consider, for example, a contract between a firm and its lenders. The debt contract specifies a few covenants, one of which dictates that the firm cannot pay dividends to its shareholders if its earnings are lower than a threshold number K. Consider a case in which earnings drop not because economic conditions deteriorate but because the Financial Accounting Standard Board (FASB) issues a new measurement rule that reduces reported earnings. This number has economic consequences, as it can stop dividend payments to shareholders. If, however, a firm that reaches this threshold renegotiates the debt contract so that the lenders adjusts the level of K downward, then, obviously, the new measurement rule has no economic repercussions.

Watts and Zimmerman (1990). State,

> An important reason that the information perspective failed to generate hypotheses explaining and predicting accounting choice is that in the finance theory underlying the empirical studies, accounting choice *per se* could not affect firm value. **Information is costless and there are not transaction costs** in the Modigliani and Miller (1958) and capital asset pricing model frameworks. Hence, if accounting methods do not affect taxes they do not affect firm value. In that situation there is no basis for predicting and explaining accounting choice. **Accounting is irrelevant**. (pp. 132–133, emphasis added)

The combination of two conditions, *incompleteness* and *opportunism*, renders contracts imperfectly adjustable to changing economic circumstance and hence lends importance to accounting financials.[6] It is impossible to design a truly *complete* contract, by which we mean one that specifies all future contingencies. So, realistically, contracts are *incomplete*, as some future contingencies are unforeseen by the boundedly rational parties to the contracts. The fact that contracts are incomplete is not in itself sufficient to render accounting numbers valuable because contracting parties could constantly revise the contract to reflect changing circumstances. If, in addition, the parties to the contract behave opportunistically, then one of them might refuse to adjust the contract. For example, suppose that two contracting parties of a joint venture agree that when earnings are high, 90% of the profits are awarded to A, and when they are low, 90% are awarded to B. They sign the contract assigning $20M as the cutoff between high and low earnings. Now, suppose that due to unforeseen change in economic conditions, the cutoff changed to $22M. If earnings are $21M, economically, 10% of the profits ought to be distributed to A while legally, A reaps 90% of the profits. Clearly, A prefers not to adjust the cutoff in the contract.

At first glance, the costly-contracting theory seems to be limited to contracts that exclude a sufficiently flexible menu of renegotiation options, whereas renegotiation in fact is quite a spread phenomenon. If options granted to management are "not in the money," because the share price fell after they were awarded, the board of directors may readjust the terms of the compensation. If the firm technically defaults on a debt contract, its creditors may issue a waiver, and if the firm fails to repay a loan, its creditors may renegotiate the lending contract or even exchange debt for shares.[7] Hence, another variation of the costly-contracting approach is that the contracting activity as well as renegotiation is costly, and these costs can be reduced by having a better, more efficient, set of accounting measures.

---

[6] Transaction-cost economists argue that a given transaction is made by an organization structured as a firm rather than by a series of open market transactions because the firm can do it at a lower cost. The recognition of the importance of *opportunism* and *the incompleteness of contracts* for the cost of transactions is attributed to Williamson (1985), and other transaction-cost economists.

[7] Asquith, Beatty, and Weber (2005), study bank debt contracts (as distinguished from public debt) that include performance pricing. Performance pricing clauses link the interest rate spread to the borrower's future performance. Specifically, if its credit quality improves (worsens), the interest rate goes down (up). Hence, performance pricing is an example of a renegotiation-proof contract since the renegotiation of the contract prompted by a change in the credit quality is already built into the contract.

Lambert (2003), states,

> In the late 1970s, a new perspective on the role of accounting num-
> bers emerged based on contracting theory. ...[E]ven sophisticated par-
> ties are limited in their abilities to write complicated contracts that in-
> corporate   numerous   performance   measures   and   numerous
> contingencies. Disciplining managers via the corporate governance
> process can also [be] a costly and time consuming process. Under
> such a viewpoint, **a small number of good summary measures is ex-
> tremely valuable because it saves on contracting costs, which,
> broadly defined, can be quite substantial.** (p. 389, emphasis added)

That is, accounting numbers matter because better measurement of future contingencies reduces the scope of the incompleteness of the contract
and thereby reduces the need for costly renegotiation.

This perspective on the value of accounting numbers can explain a
number of phenomena. Beatty, Ramesh, and Weber (2002), for example,
study the cost of flexibility in preparing the accounting numbers that borrowing firms are willing to incur in covenant calculations. (Debt contracts
include debt covenants based on accounting numbers.) They document
rate charges that were 84 (71) basis points lower when voluntary (mandatory) accounting changes were excluded. This finding indicates that borrowers are willing to pay for flexibility that would enable them to avoid
breaching debt covenants in the future.

The importance of accounting numbers for contracting also explains the
difference in the stock market's reaction to recognition of a transaction as
an expense in the income statement rather than disclosure in a footnote to
the financial statements. These two modes of revelation transmit the same
information, but they differ in their effect on the accounting numbers used
as a basis for the formal contracts of the firm with its constituency. Notable cases are the expensing of stock-based compensation (Espahbodi,
Espahbodi, Rezaee, and Tehranian, 2002) and the write-down of assets
(Aboody, 1996). (For further discussion, consult Hirshleifer and Teoh,
2003, and their discussant, Lambert, 2003.)[8]

The proponents of the *positive accounting theory* are closely associated
with the costly-contracting approach (Watts and Zimmerman, 1978, 1986,
1990). While we focus on formal contracts that are designed by the parties
that are expected to execute the contract, the positive accounting theory
recognizes that contracts can encompass cases such as tax collection and

---

[8] Hirshleifer and Teoh explain the importance of accounting numbers that are not
associated with actual cash flows by non-rationality of some of the traders. The
fact that form matters to decision making is substantiated by research based on
experimental evidence (see e.g., Frederickson, Hodge, and Pratt, 2006).

regulated industries. The contract between the firm and the regulators is a social contract. That is, although nobody has a formal written contract with regulators specifying that in return for taxes the person will get security and education, everyone pays taxes and expects federal and state services in return. The problem with such a social contract is that a dissatisfied customer cannot stop paying taxes; he can only hope for a change in government.

1.2.1.2 The View of Earnings Management

The costly-contracting approach implies that earnings management is an opportunistic behavior that is meant to pursue some target number determined by the formal contracts signed between the firm and its constituency. For example, a firm that is close to the threshold earnings specified by the debt covenants in its contracts with its lenders is likely to manage earnings upward to avoid breaching the covenants.

In Chap. 2, we present a definition of earnings management that is based on the informativeness of managed earnings for their audience. The scholars associated with the costly-contracting approach are likely to favor a definition such as this: "earnings management is the choice of accounting treatment that is either opportunistic or economically efficient." (see e.g., Watts and Zimmerman, 1990; Fields, Lys, and Vincent, 2001.) When earnings management maximizes the firm's value, it is considered economically efficient. When it does not maximize the firm's value, earnings management is opportunistic.

The limitation of the costly-contracting approach from an earnings management perspective is that earnings management phenomena are limited only to circumstances in which contracts either are not adjusted to changing economic conditions or are costly to renegotiate. Interestingly, the likelihood that contracts adjust to accounting choices is very small for social contracts that involve regulators since government employees have weak incentives to initiate adjustments. Jones (1991), writes,

> Managers have greater incentives to make income-decreasing accounting choices if they believe that the regulators do not completely adjust for these choices. Neither the public nor the regulators are necessarily thought to be "fooled" by the accounting numbers reported by domestic producers. Instead, the regulators may be "captured" or may simply not regard "undoing" the reported numbers to be cost effective. (p. 198)

1.2.2 The Decision-Making Approach

1.2.2.1 The Approach

The decision-making approach recognizes that the firm is a legal fiction. To the extent that it is a nexus of contracts, these contracts are designed endogenously by individuals (Jensen and Meckling, 1976). Hence, the focus ought to be on the decision makers who design these contracts. Sunder (1996), states,

> In contract model of organizations, we assume that the participating individuals pursue their respective self-interest. They cooperate in functioning of the organization only to the extent that they find such cooperation to be in their interest. **Organization itself does not need to have an objective, only the participating individuals do.** (p. 4, emphasis added)

The decision-making approach views the firm as a social enterprise whose output results from the interactions of many decision makers, who settle their relationships either through formal, written contracts, or through informal, implicit ones.[9] Consequently, the task of a student of a firm's behavior is to locate the key decision makers within the firm and identify their stake in the social outcome. From this perspective, the question why earnings are important to the firm ought to be rephrased to ask why earnings are important to the decision makers who have the authority to determine these figures.[10]

The decision-making approach is imbedded in game theory. Chronologically, it appeared before the costly-contracting approach, being inspired by the mathematical models of rational choice developed by von Neumann and Morgenstern, Savage, and others. Its focuses on a single decision maker whose preferences are summarized by a utility function

---

[9] Sunder (1996), states,

> It is often convenient to think of a firm or an organization as a set of contracts among people. I use the word contract loosely; instead of being a written or legally binding arrangement, a contract being only a mutual understanding or expectation among the participants about the behavior of one another. (p. 2)

[10] In numerous applications, what we have labeled the Rochester school and the decision-making schools can be combined if we recognize the decision makers as those who sign and carry out contracts. However, when earnings in general and earnings management are involved, each school propounds a different philosophy that yields a different explanation why earnings are valuable.

that ranks alternative outcomes (e.g., each employee prefers a higher salary to a lower salary). Each decision maker is rational, in that his chosen action maximizes his expected utility.

A decision d_i^* is optimal for decision maker i if it maximizes his expected utility EU_i, when he has to select a decision d_i from a feasible decision set D_i, knowing that the combination of his decision, d_i, and other pertinent decision makers decisions', d_{i-1}^*, will result in awarding him his share of the social outcome, s_i:

$$d_i^* \in \underset{d_i \in D_i}{\arg \max} \ E_{s_i} U_i(s_i | d_i, d_{i-1}^*) \tag{1.1}$$

The decision maker's share, s_i, depends in part on the actions taken by other decision makers. Observe, for example, a CEO who knows that the reported earnings, which he can affect by actions he has the authority to take, determine the stock price. The stock price affects the value of his stock options, but the stock price is determined not by him, but in the stock market by analysts, investors, market makers, and regulators.

The emphasis on optimal decisions[11] implies that any accounting number that provides *information* that is relevant for making a decision is valuable. (The converse is also true; an accounting signal that has no incremental information content is not valuable.) In particular, calculation of the expected utility requires understanding s_i, how to take expectations of U_i, and how the response of other decision makers affects s_i (see Christensen and Feltham, 2002).

Earnings, in particular, are valuable in making decisions that require estimating future earnings, such as valuing the firm, or that require assessing risk, such as investing in, or lending to, an enterprise. Moreover, since earnings and other financial accounting information are public, they determine not just what a given decision maker knows, but what he thinks that others know, what he thinks that others know that he knows, ad infinitum (Sunder, 1996, 2002). This infinite hierarchy of beliefs is the *common knowledge* structure of the game, which is likely to affect the social outcome through its effect on the players' mutual expectations.

Several features distinguish the decision-making approach from the costly-contracting approach. First, the decision-making approach assumes

---

[11] Amershi and Sunder (1987), explain why rational managers make foolish choices. Managers, who are motivated to maximize shareholders' value, may have the wrong model of investors' valuations. The stock price, which is supposed to correct managers' erroneous conjectures, often fails to do so because it is too noisy to allow managers to learn about their mistakes.

that the decision makers are not fully informed, which creates demand for the information in the accounting numbers.[12] Second, the decision-making approach allows for *implicit contracts*. How does such an implicit contract affect the optimal action? The answer is given by game theory. The assumption that decision makers are rational implies that each player can form correct expectations (Kreps, 1990) and therefore act optimally. The collection of all players' optimal actions yields an equilibrium, where one definition of an equilibrium is that the players choose strategies such that no player wishes to deviate unilaterally.[13] Then, the actions chosen are "self-enforcing contracts," and expectations are fulfilled without explicit contracts. Furthermore, repeated relationships between the firm and its stakeholders may lead to implicit contracts that are based on tacit cooperation under the threat that deviant behavior will be punished in the next round by the party that suffered from the deviation. Scott (2003), summarizes the importance of implicit contracts:

> Earnings management incentives also derive from **implicit contracts**, also called relational contracts. These are not formal contracts, such as the compensation and debt contracts just considered. Rather, they arise from continuing relationships between the firm and its stakeholders (shareholders, employees, suppliers, lenders, customer) and represent expected behaviour based on past business dealings. For example, if the firm and its manager develop a reputation for always meeting formal contract commitments they will receive better terms from suppliers, lower interest rates from lenders, etc. In effect, the parties act *as if* such favourable contracts exist. In terms of … game theory…, the manager and the firm's stakeholders must trust each other sufficiently that they play the cooperative solution rather than the Nash equilibrium.[14] (p. 378, emphasis added)

---

[12] Note that contracts are commitment to prespecified action. Hence, a contract that has earnings-based contingencies specifies actions long before the information contained in earnings is disclosed. There is no meaningful learning here. For the decision-making school, information is mostly acquired first, before a decision is made. Hence, different information content yields different actions with different cash flow effects.

[13] In the language of game theory: If formal contracts cannot be written, the game is a non-cooperative one (Harsanyi and Selten, 1988). It is solved by Selten's (1965), perfect Nash equilibrium, wherein the game tree is broken into subgames, and the choice is optimal in every subgame.

[14] Bowen, DuCharme, and Shores (1995), is an example that illustrates earnings management for implicit contracting purposes. In this study, the choice of accounting techniques is motivated by the intensity of the need for a favorable reputation with the firm's stakeholders.

1.2.2.2 The View of Earnings Management

The emphasis on the value of earnings for decision making implies that earnings management is innocuous when decisions based on managed earnings are the same as those based on unmanaged earnings. This can happen when players undo the accounting numbers to learn the underlying economic performance. Such a procedure, however, requires that all participants have the correct model of the magnitude and direction of the attempt at earnings management. A firm then will manage earnings only as a best response to others' expectations because if it does not manage earnings when expected to do so, it is effectively punished by the response of its audience. For example, if outsiders expect the firm to inflate profits by 10%, and a firm decides to report the truth, then its truthful report will be discounted by 10%, with the dire consequence of having a lower market price. This is the well-known "signal jamming" dynamic (Stein, 1989; Dye, 1988). Elitzur (1995), applies this dynamic to explain the role of accounting regulation. It determines the earnings management opportunities and what the market knows about them.

Given the billions of dollars of losses by investors in the recent accounting scandals, treating earnings management as innocuous is somewhat hard to swallow. The above argument is based on market participants' perfectly predicting the earnings management attempt. Still, within the game-theoretic framework, this assumption can be relaxed. Consider, for example, Ronen and Yaari (2002), on the effect of Rule 10b-5 of the 1934 Securities and Exchange Act on incentives for voluntary disclosure. We assume that investors do not observe economic earnings and that the firm's report is imperfectly audited. That is, there is some positive probability that the auditor will not detect the truth. Hence, a good-performance report can represent either a firm that reported the truth or a firm that successfully managed the report. Because it is unable to distinguish between the two types, the market discounts the report. Yet the value of the firm that misrepresents is still overestimated because the market puts some weight on the belief that the report could be true.[15] Consequently, oppor-

---

[15] A short numerical example explains the verbal argument. Suppose that the value of a firm with good performance is 1 and the value of a firm with bad performance is 0. Denote the price of the firm by P. If there is only one firm in the market telling the truth, the market price is

P(good performance) = 1; P(bad performance) = 0

The differing market price implies that when performance is bad, the firm has incentives to misrepresent (1 > 0).

tunistic earnings management might take place whereby poor-performance firms mask their results by pooling with (pretending to be) firms performing well.

The assumption that all players are rational limits the scope of earnings management. To the extent that earnings management is harmful, the parties that are harmed by it will take actions to deter it, unless the costs overwhelm the benefits. Ronen and Yaari (2007, p. 1), ask,

> [S]ince shareholders and managers act as principal and agent, why don't the former design a truth-inducing contract if earnings management is so harmful[?]

Our answer is based on the fact that managers have limited liability that bounds their compensation from below. Because limited liability renders the penalties that are required to induce a truthful report too costly, a contract that induces earnings management may be preferable.

1.2.3 The Legal-Political Approach

1.2.3.1 The Approach

The legal-political approach is the most recent, expressed in studies by Hart (1995a,b, 2001), La Porta, Lopez-De-Silanes, and Shleifer (1999a), Bebchuk, Kraakman, and Triantis (2000), Bebchuk and Hart (2001), Bebchuk (2002, 2005a, b), Bebchuk, Fried, and Walker (2002), Bebchuk and Fried (2003, 2004), Monks and Minow (2004), and Niskanen (2005).

To the extent that the firm is a nexus of contracts, this approach emphasizes the contract between management and shareholders, regarding contracts with other stakeholders as subordinate to this contract. Niskanen (2005), states,

---

If, however, the firm tried to misrepresent and it is known that the a priori chance of good performance is 80% and the auditor detects the truth with probability of 75%, the market price by Bayes' rule is

$P(\text{good performance}) = \beta \times 1 + (1-\beta) \times 0 = 0.94,$

where β is the marginal probability of observing good performance:

$$\beta = \frac{0.80}{0.80 + 0.20 \times (1 - 0.75)} = 0.94, \text{ and } \quad 1-\beta = \frac{0.20 \times (1 - 0.75)}{0.80 + 0.20 \times (1 - 0.75)} = 0.06.$$

The price now discounts a report of good performance because the marginal probability of getting such a report is $0.80 + (1-0.80) \times (1-0.75) > 0.80$, reflecting the chance that the auditor may not detect a bad performance. Still, the market price exceeds the poor performance value of zero.

> [Regarding the] view that corporate managers should also be accountable to other "stakeholders" affected by their decisions —such as employees, creditors, the local community, the environment, etc. ... I am wholly unsympathetic with this view. ... Although I recognize that a corporation's contracts with these other constituencies are not complete, they are *far* more complete than the open-ended contract with shareholders. Good managers will pay attention to the interests of the several types of stakeholders to the extent that this attention is consistent with the interests of the general shareholders. But making corporate managers accountable to multiple constituencies would substantially increase managerial discretion, increasing the prospect that they would not serve any constituency very well. (pp. 337–338)

As with the previous two approaches, the legal-political approach recognizes the conflict of interests between managers and shareholders. Specifically, the firm is a collection of assets that generate cash flows, but the rights to the cash flows in a typical management-controlled firm do not belong to those who have the right to decide how to manage these assets. Management possesses these decision rights. Its mission is to take actions to manage the firm's resources and assets in order to generate a stream of earnings that justify holding the firm's shares to shareholders and doing business with it to other parties. The parties with rights to the cash flows are largely understood (at least by the US model) to be shareholders who hold common stock. Legally, they are residual claimants, which implies that they are not guaranteed any cash.

The distinction between the two groups is important because of the inherent conflict of interests between them. Both parties pursue their own self-interest, and there is no a priori guarantee that these interests are aligned. Shareholders would like to earn a return on their investment and make efficient portfolio decisions, while managers are concerned with their compensation, promotion, tenure, and reputation. Thus, for example, although investors would like to know of poor performance as early as possible, management would prefer to postpone the bad news in order to get a high salary (or just to earn a reprieve until the tide changes) since their tenure and compensation are tied to performance.

This conflict of interests, however, is not sufficient to give rise to earnings management if the owners can effectively direct managers. Legally, owners have little real power over decisions that affect their share of the firm. For example, hostile takeover has been considered a mechanism to discipline management (e.g., Becht, Bolton, and Roell, 2003). While hostile takeover was quite prevalent in the eighties of last century, it dwindled with state legislation that allowed firms to adopt legal provisions that increased the cost of a takeover and made it prohibitively costly to the raiders, provisions that are known as "poison pills" (see e.g., Holmström and Kaplan, 2001). Other examples are that shareholders have no say over dividends payment. This is the decision of the board (Bebchuk, 2005a), that represents shareholders' interests. But shareholders have little power over the nomination of directors.[16] Robert Monks, a shareholder activists states, "the American shareholder cannot nominate directors, he cannot remove them, he cannot—except at the arbitrary pleasure of the SEC—communicate advice to them. Democracy is a cruelly misleading word to describe the situation of the American shareholder in 2006" (The Economist, March 11, 2006, p. 70). The former chief commissioner of the Securities and Exchange Commission (SEC), Mr. Donaldson, proposed change in the rules that will enhance the power of shareholders over nomination of directors (Release No. 34-48626). But succumbing to pressure from the bosses in America (i.e., management), the proposed rules have been put on hold indefinitely. For more examples, consult Bebchuk (2005a). Bebchuk (2005a, p. 842), summarizes, "The corporate laws of both the US and the U.K. start with the same basic principle: Even though they are the ones supplying the funds, shareholders do not necessarily have the power to order the directors to follow any particular course of action."

The legal weakness of shareholders vis-a-vis the board implies that shareholders' welfare depends on other elements of the governance system, where governance loosely defined as "the set of complementary mechanisms that help align the actions and choices of managers with the interests of shareholders" (Core, Guay, and Larcker, 2003, p. 27). For example, disappointed owners can sue the firm, which is a value-decreasing event that may lead to management's dismissal (see Chap. 3). Hence, two features of the shareholders–manager situation contribute to shareholders' inability to induce decisions that maximize their own utility. One is poor governance. The other is information. That is, shareholders need information to monitor management and the board with the limited tools in their possession. If they are unhappy with management's performance, they might try to form a coalition with other shareholders to replace the incumbent team (e.g., DeAngelo, 1988b; Bebchuk, 2005b).

---

[16] Bebchuk (2005b), examines whether shareholders propose a slate of directors as an alternative to incumbent management's slate of nominations and whether they are successful. The rule is that the group that gets the majority of votes wins. He finds that the scope of this phenomenon is small, and wins are scant. We note that if there is no alternative slate, directors can be nominated with the majority of the votes in the shareholders meeting against them because only votes in favor of the nominated directors are counted.

Earnings are summary information. As such, they have the added benefit that of conveying valuable information without requiring shareholders
to learn the firm's operation in detail, a process that would be costly and
cumbersome, and that might expose proprietary information to competitors.

At first glance, it seems that the difference between the decision-making
approach and the legal-political approach is slight. By adding costs to
governance structure, the same predictions can be made under both approaches. The truth of the matter, however, is that these two approaches
differ in their characterization of the information asymmetry between
shareholders and management: The decision maker faces uncertainty, but
he anticipates what he does not know, while investors under the legal-
political approach are ignorant. Hence, accounting information is more
valuable under the legal-political approach. Furthermore, unlike the decision-making approach, the legal system postulates that shareholders cannot
design contracts that prevent management from using discretion over financial reporting to promote self-interest at their expense. As Hermalin
and Weisbach (2003, p. 10) observe,

> In most large corporations, the shareholders are too diffuse, ration-
> ally plagued by a free-rider problem, and, for the same reason, too
> uninformed to set managers' compensation.[17]

1.2.3.2 The View of Earnings Management

Since owners are outsiders who rely on accounting information from insiders—management and boards of directors—to make decisions, both
value-enhancing and opportunistic earnings management make sense under the legal-political approach. Value-enhancing earnings management is
a way for managers to establish rapport with owners by signaling value-
relevant information without getting into too many cumbersome details.
Securing the goodwill of the owners is valuable.

Opportunistic earnings management is likely because of the conflict of
interest between shareholders and management and because, in general,
those possessing private information makes it easier to use it to the advantage of its holder at the expense of others. The message of the legal-
political approach regarding opportunistic earnings management is simple.
Either the legal system needs to be changed or it is an indication of poor
governance or poor information (in contrast to the game-theoretic approach, in which earnings management is taken into account by rational

---

[17] This picture seems to go under change as the SEC is proposing better disclosure
rules of management's compensation.

shareholders when they evaluate the firm's value and management's performance).[18]

We conclude with the following observation. There is also international evidence on the importance of governance and information to earnings management. Leuz, Nanda, and Wysocki (2003) in their study of earnings management in 31 countries in the 1990–1999 period find that firms in countries with developed equity markets, dispersed ownership structures, strong investor rights, and legal enforcement engage in less earnings management. They interpret this result as indicating that earnings management is used by insiders to mask poor performance so that outsiders will not challenge their private control rights. Wysocki (2004), examines earnings management and tax compliance and finds that a legal system with better investor protection laws and higher quality of accounting standards can mitigate earnings management and increase corporate tax compliance.

1.3 Summary

In this chapter, we present the three approaches that prevail in the literature to answering the question of why earnings are important. This question lays the foundation for the study of earnings management, because if earnings were not important, then what we label as earnings management might be something else altogether.

We present three approaches: the contracting approach, the decision-making approach, and the legal approach. The costly-contracting approach highlights the importance of formal contracts. Earnings and other accounting numbers provide summary statistics that are valuable for designing efficient contracts, given that contracts fail to specify all future contingencies. When an unforeseen contingency does occur, the contracting parties may be stuck with the old contract. In such a situation, earnings change from means to ends, and firms may manage earnings to comply with figures specified in their contracts.

---

[18] Empirically, small or young firms frequently suffer from poor transparency because they usually have a greater degree of information asymmetry than large or old firms (Bhushan, 1989). Earnings management has been shown to be more active when information asymmetry is more severe (Richardson, 2000; Gu, Jevons Lee, and Rosett, 2003). Yet even for small firms, there are variations in the quality of governance. For example, Hochberg's (2005) examination of the role of venture capitalists in newly public firms finds that venture capitalists reduce the scope of earnings management.

The decision-making approach regards earnings as providing valuable information for making decisions. If all stakeholders are fully rational, earnings management cannot take place without explicit or implicit consent from investors. Hence, either earnings management is innocuous because the managed report reveals the truth or it distorts the truth, but the resulting damage is less than the cost of eliciting truth.

The legal-political approach recognizes that shareholders lack tools to control management effectively. Earnings numbers are a valuable performance measure that summarizes the activities of the firm and allow shareholders to make better use of their limited set of tools. Earnings management in the good sense—providing a signal on future value—is an efficient means to bridge the information asymmetry between management and shareholders without getting into details. Earnings management in the bad sense—distorting the truth—is the result of poor governance.

2 Definition of Earnings Management

It is always difficult to frame a useful definition for a broad subject. Precise definitions are likely to be inadequate at best, and often positively misleading. (Paton, 1922, p. 3)

In this chapter, we introduce a formal definition of earnings management and compare it to alternative definitions. Given the generality of the term, we expand the definition by an examination of the means to manage earnings. We conclude with a thorough presentation of earnings management achieved by supplying pro forma earnings with GAAP earnings.

2.1 Definition

Table 2.1 summarizes the different definitions of earnings management, classifying them as white, gray, or black. Beneficial (white) earnings management enhances the transparency of reports; the pernicious (black) involves outright misrepresentation and fraud; the gray is manipulation of reports within the boundaries of compliance with bright-line standards, which could be either opportunistic or efficiency enhancing.

Table 2.1 Alternative definitions of earnings management

White	Gray	Black
Earnings management is taking advantage of the flexibility in the choice of accounting treatment to signal the manager's private information on future cash flows	Earnings management is choosing an accounting treatment that is either opportunistic (maximizing the utility of management only) or economically efficient	Earnings management is the practice of using tricks to misrepresent or reduce transparency of the financial reports

White	Gray	Black
Ronen and Sadan (1981), Demski, Patell, and Wolfson (1984), Suh (1990), Demski (1998), Beneish (2001), Sankar and Subramanyam (2001) [a]	Fields, Lys, and Vincent (2001), Scott (2003) [b]	Schipper (1989), Levitt (1998), Healy and Wahlen (1999), Tzur and Yaari (1999), Chtourou, Bédard, and Courteau (2001), Miller and Bahnson (2002) [c]

[a] "...under [the information perspective of earnings management],... managerial discretion is a means for managers to reveal to investors their private expectations about the firm's future cash flows." (Beneish, 2001, p. 3)

[b] "The push for increased transparency in financial reporting and corporate governance serves the shareholders only up to a point. Beyond that, managerial inhibitions induced by a lack of privacy can damage the interests of shareholders.... That earnings management reduces transparency is a simplistic idea. (Arya, Glover, and Sunder, 2003, p. 111)

Earnings management occurs "when managers exercise their discretion over the accounting numbers with or without restrictions. Such discretion can be either firm value maximizing or opportunistic." (Fields, Lys, and Vincent, 2001, p.260, citing Watts and Zimmerman, 1990)

"**Earning management** is the choice by a manager of accounting policies so as to achieve specific objective." (Scott, 2003, p. 369)

[c] "By "earnings management" I really mean "disclosure management" in the sense of a purposeful intervention in the external financial reporting process, with the intent of obtaining some private gain (as opposed to, say, merely facilitating the neutral operation of the process)." (Schipper, 1989, p. 92)

Earnings management is "the practice ... [of reaching] a desired number instead of pursuing some sort of protocol to produce a number that gets reported without regard to what some analysts predict that you will report." (Miller and Bahnson, 2002, p. 184)

Given our discussion of the three strands of thought on the value of earnings and the consequent demand for earnings management in Chap. 1, the definition in the literature that best describes earnings management seems to be the following:

> *Definition:* **Earnings management** occurs when managers use judgment in financial reporting and in structuring transactions to alter financial reports to either mislead some stakeholders about the underlying economic performance of the company or to influence contractual outcomes that depend on reported accounting numbers.[1]

This definition captures both the costly-contracting approach (earnings management is used to influence contractual outcomes) and the informa-

---

[1] Healy and Wahlen (1999, p. 368).

tional approach (earnings management is used to mislead stakeholders) that are outlined in Chap. 1. Like others, this definition points to management as the party responsible for making those decisions that fall under the umbrella of earnings management. It also captures the connotation of opportunistic manipulation of earnings.

There are, however, two weaknesses to this definition. First, it does not set a clear boundary between earnings management and normal activities whose output is earnings. Dharan (2003, p. 1), expresses this concern as follows:

> A related issue for financial analysts, investors and corporate executives is how to distinguish between earnings manipulation that ultimately proves to be fraudulent and the day-to-day struggles of managers to keep costs within budgets or to get revenues to meet desired sales targets.

Second, not all earnings management is misleading. Investors, for example, prefer to separate persistent earnings from one-time shocks. Firms that manage earnings in order to allow investors to better distinguish between the two components do not distort earnings. On the contrary, they enhance the informational value of their reported earnings.

We therefore offer an alternative definition of earnings management.

> Earnings management is a collection of managerial decisions that result in not reporting the true short-term, value-maximizing earnings as known to management.
>   Earnings management can be
>   Beneficial: it signals long-term value;
>   Pernicious: it conceals short- or long-term value;
>   Neutral: it reveals the short-term true performance.
>   The managed earnings result from taking production/investment actions before earnings are realized, or making accounting choices that affect the earnings numbers and their interpretation after the true earnings are realized.

This definition has three parts. The first measures earnings against the short-term truth as it is known to management. The second attaches subjective value to earnings management. The third describes in a broad sense how earnings management is achieved.[2] The combination of the first and the third parts of the definition captures what Schipper (1989), dubbed the "economic income perspective."[3]

---

[2] Note that our definition captures both that earnings measure economic truth and that they convey information to the audience (Demski and Sappington, 1990, 1992).

[3] The first part of our definition seems to capture what practitioners consider earnings management, although they do not use the term. Schilit (2002), for

Our definition relies on the premise that there exists an earnings number (the "short-term truth") that is objective, neutral, and value-maximizing (for the firm) in the short run. We emphasize the short term because earnings are reported for a quarter or a year. The advantage of this premise is twofold. First, it confers the ability to distinguish income-increasing from income-decreasing earnings management. The former reports earnings that are higher than the truth, while the latter reports earnings that are lower than the truth. Consider, for example, Table 2.2 (adapted from Dechow and Skinner, 2000).

Table 2.2 The different shades of earnings management

Reporting type	Accounting choices
Within GAAP	
"Conservative accounting"	• Overly aggressive recognition of provisions or reserves • Overstatement of restructuring charges and asset write-offs
"Neutral accounting" (not earnings management)	• Earnings that result from neutral operations
"Aggressive accounting"	• Understatement of the provision for bad debts • Drawing down provisions or reserves in an overly aggressive manner
Violates GAAP	
"Fraud"	• Recording sales before they are "realizable" • Overstating inventory by recording fictitious inventory

Earnings management tactics are spread across decisions that yield "conservative" earnings, that is, earnings that are deflated (relative to the

example, defines financial *shenanigans* as the "actions or omissions intended to hide or distort the real financial performance or financial condition of an entity" (p. 1). O'Glove (1987), refers to the *quality* of earnings, illustrating this concept with a simple example: "Suppose a company reported $2.00 per share earnings, and you dissect the number. Do you think the chief executive officer had any reason to understate the figure, that it really was $2.50? No reason at all. But he might have inflated the $2.00 from $1.50 to make his regime look better than it should" (p. xii). McBarnet and Whelan (1999), are concerned with *creative accounting*, in contrast to having accounts that comply with accounting standards or with company law.

truth); decisions that yield "aggressive earnings" , that is, earnings that are inflated; and fraudulent reports that violate GAAP.

The second advantage of the premise is that it recognizes that the short-run truth may obscure the long-run truth. To illustrate, suppose that the firm's persistent earnings are 100 and, due to a one-time surge in demand, the true earnings rise in this quarter to 120. Clearly, the short-term truth is different from the long-term truth.

We restrict our attention to the truth as it is known to management because we cannot rule out the possibility that management does not know the truth. This does not negate the information asymmetry pecking order in Chap. 1, which postulates that management has superior information. Thus, if the truth is x but management believes it to be x', then reporting x' does not constitute earnings management, but reporting x does.

Part 2 deals with the difficulty that arises from the positive connotation of truth. Defining earnings management as a non-truth-telling strategy marks it as pernicious.[4] Yet earnings management can be neutral, or even beneficial. Earnings management is valuable when, for instance, it conveys forward-looking, value-relevant information, by removing some of the noise in a truth-telling report of short-term earnings. For example, Gul, Leung, and Srinidhi (2002), find that managers of firms with greater investment opportunities use earnings management to signal future opportunities for growth. Earnings management can be innocuous if the receiver of the report is able to undo it to learn the underlying truth. Suppose that it is well understood that a change in depreciation policy is a means to boost earnings until the bad time passes. Then, when the firm changes a depreciation policy and publicizes it, the reader can undo the change to calculate the underlying truth.

Pernicious earnings management fits with the general conception of earnings management as misrepresentation (Demski, 2003). This is the case, for example, when the firm attempts to mask poor performance and mislead the audience, as with WorldCom, and many other firms whose bankruptcies was preceded by *restatements* of previously reported earnings.

Note that our definition excludes circumstances in which the reports reveal the short-term truth but the audience interprets the report differently. This is the case, for example, when the audience cannot distinguish between firms that report the truth and firms that attempt to pool with them.

---

[4] The connotation of pernicious earnings management is that it is immoral even when it does not involve fraud (Bruns and Merchant, 1990; DePree and Grant, 1999; Kaplan, 2001a, b; Shafer, 2002; Carpenter and Reimers, 2001; Fischer and Huddart, 2005).

To illustrate, consider an example drawn from Christensen and Demski 2003, chapter 14). The revenue-generating process for a given customer is a four-event/date sequence:

1. locate a potential customer,
2. make a sale,
3. expect a possible return from the customer, and
4. collect a payment.

By the revenue-recognition principle, a firm cannot recognize a sale if collection is not expected to occur with high probability. Hence, recognition of a sale at the date of event 2 implies one of two situations: either the firm honestly recognizes the sale, expecting the deal to go through, or the firm suspects that the sale may be reversed on Date 3 but decides to use an aggressive recognition strategy. Observing a Date-3 event of a return does not refute either possibility.

Consider a reader of the financial reports that are publicized after Date 2 and before Date 3. Suppose the reader believes that 80% of the firms in the industry are honest and that 20% are aggressive. Let the gross sale be $100. If the probability of a return and non-collection of the sale's revenues by a non-aggressive firm is 5%, the expected value of the sale is $95. If, however, the probability of return and non-collection is high, say 90%, then the expected value of the sale is reduced to $10. Suppose that all firms report $95 revenue. Unable to distinguish between the two types of firms, the reader makes his own prediction on the value of the sale. By Bayes' formula, the expected value of the sale is a weighted average of $95 and $10; the precise figure is 76 (= 0.80 × 95 + 0.20 × 10). Thus, a firm may be honest, but its sale will still be discounted because of the reader's skepticism. By dissociating what the firm chooses from the reader's interpretation of the report, our definition makes it easier to separate truth-telling from earnings management. To emphasize, we exclude truthful revelation that is discounted by the audience from our definition of earnings management; that is, we do not treat such instances as manifestation of earnings management.

[a] "under [the information perspective of earnings management],… managerial discretion is a means for managers to reveal to investors their private expectations about the firm's future cash flows." (Beneish, 2001, p. 3)

[b] "The push for increased transparency in financial reporting and corporate governance serves the shareholders only up to a point. Beyond that, managerial inhibitions induced by a lack of privacy can damage the interests of shareholders…. That earnings management reduces transparency is a simplistic idea. (Arya, Glover, and Sunder, 2003, p. 111)

Earnings management occurs "when managers exercise their discretion over the accounting numbers with or without restrictions. Such discretion can be either firm value maximizing or opportunistic." (Fields, Lys, and Vincent, 2001, p. 260, citing Watts and Zimmerman, 1990)

"Earning management is the choice by a manager of accounting policies so as to achieve specific objective." (Scott, 2003, p. 369)

[c] "By 'earnings management' I really mean 'disclosure management' in the sense of a purposeful intervention in the external financial reporting process, with the intent of obtaining some private gain (as opposed to, say, merely facilitating the neutral operation of the process)." (Schipper, 1989, p. 92)

Earnings management is "the practice ... [of reaching] a desired number instead of pursuing some sort of protocol to produce a number that gets reported without regard to what some analysts predict that you will report." (Miller and Bahnson, 2002, p. 184)

2.2 The Methods to Manage Earnings

The "how to" part of earnings management includes many variations. As Bruns and Merchant (1990), Ayres (1994), Francis 2001, and others note, earnings are known to be managed through the following:

- A choice from a menu of treatments that are accepted under GAAP, such as LIFO versus FIFO for inventory valuation (Hughes, Schwartz, and Fellingham, 1988; Neill, Pourciau, and Schaefer, 1995), depreication (Neill, Pourciau, and Schaefer, 1995; Bishop and Eccher, 2000), the full cost method versus the successful effort method in the oil and gas industry (Malmquist, 1990; Zeff, 1993; Aboody, 1996),[5] and revenue recognition policy (Bowen, Davis, and Rajgopal, 2002).

- A decision on the timing of the adoption of a new standard (e.g., Ali and Kumar, 1994, on the timing of the adoption of SFAS 87; Lehavy and Revsine, 1994; Smith and Rezaee, 1995; Amir and Livnat, 1996; Amir and Ziv, 1997a, on the adoption of SFAS 106; Balsam, Haw, and Lilien, 1995, on 11 major promulgations out of 96 standards that were issued by FASB between 1973 and 1989), a decision whether to write the transition effect of a new standard on the income statement or as a retroactive adjustment to stockholders' equity on the balance sheet

---

[5] The difference between the two methods is the timing of recognition of the costs of acquisition, development activities, and exploration for oil and gas. Under the full cost method, all these costs are capitalized; if the well is dry, the successful effort method expenses all costs immediately. (Of course, if exploration costs exceed the net present value of the future revenues from proven oil and gas reserves, an immediate loss must be recognized under the full cost method.)

(Balsam, Haw, and Lilien, 1995; Amir and Ziv, 1997a, b), and a decision not to implement a new standard on the grounds of immateriality (Gilkeson and Stengel, 1999).

- A judgment call when GAAP requires estimates, such as depreciation (Bishop and Eccher, 2000), the allowance for bad debt (McNichols and Wilson, 1988), assets valuation (Easton, Eddey, and Harris, 1993), pension accounting (Asthana, 1999; Brown, 2004; Bergstresser, Desai, and Rauh 2005; Hann, Lu, and Subramanyam, 2007) and asset write-offs (Strong and Meyer, 1987; Elliott and Shaw, 1988; Elliott and Hanna, 1996; Francis, Hanna, and Vincent, 1996; Rees, Gill, and Gore, 1996; Bunsis, 1997; Alciatore, Dee, Easton, and Spear, 1998; Bartov, Lindahl, and Ricks, 1998: Alciatore, Easton, and Spear, 2000; Black, Carnes, and Richardson, 2000; Burgstahler, Jiambalvo, and Shevlin, 2002; Riedl and Srinivasan, 2006).
- A classification of items as above or below the line of operating earnings (or earnings from continuing operations) in order to separate persistent earnings from transitory earnings (e.g., Godfrey and Jones, 1999; Dye, 2002; Lin, Radhakrishnan, and Su, 2006; McVay, 2006), such as the use of restructuring charges (Elliott and Shaw, 1988; Elliott and Hanna, 1996; Hwang and Ryan, 2000; Bens and Johnson, 2006).
- Structuring transactions to achieve desired accounting outcomes, such as Xerox' use of a Portfolio Asset Strategy to sell the lease contracts of its Brazilian subsidiary after capital leases were discontinued in favor or operating leases. (Revenues from operating leases are recognized only when rent payments are due.)[6]   Additional examples within the boundaries of GAAP include issuing costly contingent convertible debt that under SFAS 128 has no effect on diluted earnings per share until the contingencies are fulfilled (Marquardt and Wiedman, 2005); designing mergers to qualify for the pooling method (Aboody, Kasznik, and Williams, 2000; Ayers, Lefanowicz, and Robinson, 2002);[7] conducting transactions with related parties (Gordon and Henry, 2005). For example, Refco alledgely, parked 430 million dollars of accounts receivable at Liberty, a comapny that is affiliated with Refco's CEO, Mr. Phillip Bennet.

---

[6] See, Civil Action No. 03-CV-0671(DLC) COMPLAINT SECURITIES FRAUD.

[7] A related accounting choice concerns the treatment of in-process research and development costs in acquisitions accounted for by the purchase method. Levitt (1998), and then Press and Dowdell (2004), claim that firms manage earnings by writing these charges off instead of capitalizing them (to be amortized thereafter).

- Timing the recognition of revenues and expenses through, for example, timing the sales of assets in order to smooth earnings (see Bartov, 1993; and Gunny, 2005) and deciding whether to capitalize expenses, such as brand name costs (Muller, 1999).
- A real production (Lin, Radhakrishnan, and Su, 2006; Roychowdhury, 2006; Zang, 2007) and investment decision (Bens and Monahan, 2005), such as reducing research and development expenditures (Baber, Fairfield, and Hagard, 1991; Hansen and Hill, 1991; Bushee, 1998; Darrough and Rangan, 2005; Gunny, 2005; Singer, 2007; Zang, 2007) and affecting selling and adminsitrative expenses (Gunny, 2005; Lin, Radhakrishnan, and Su, 2006; Zang, 2007).
- Managing the transparency of the presentation. See, for example, the reaction of select analysts and Wall Street reporters to Enron's footnote disclosures of its SPE (Smith and Emshwiller, 2003).[8] See also Riedl and Srinivasan (2006), on the choice between presenting special items in a separate line in the income statement and presenting them in a footnote.
- Managing the informativeness of earnings through various means, such as reporting comprehensive income on the statement of equity rather than on the performance statement (Lee, Petroni, and Shen, 2006), and subtracting small expenses from GAAP earnings to present pro forma earnings, as discussed below.

We have no ambition to provide a comprehensive list of what companies do to manage earnings under each category, as that lies beyond the scope of this book. Nevertheless, it is worth noting that revenue recognition seems the largest single account subject to earnings management as indicated by anecdotal evidence, by an examination of restatements and of enforcement cases of the Security and Exchange Commission (Dechow, Sloan, and Sweeney, 1996; Bonner, Palmrose, and Young, 1998; PricewaterhouseCoopers, 2000[9]; Turner, 2001b; Anderson and Yohn, 2002; Wu, 2002; Palmrose and Scholz, 2004), and by an analysis of the frequency of situations in which auditees put pressure on auditors to acquiesce in the auditees' wishes (Nelson, Elliott, and Tarpley, 2003). Coffee (2005, p. 10). reports that the SEC study of all its enforcement proceedings over the

---

[8] Note that other authors (Hirst and Hopkins 1998; Maines and McDaniel, 2000; Hirst, Hopkins, and Wahlen, 2004; Hunton, Libby, and Mazza, 2006), establish a positive association between truth revelation and the transparency of the presentation.

[9] In the year 2000, for example, 66% of all cases filed under allegations of accounting fraud involve revenue recognition.

1997–2002 period finds that 126 out of the 227 "enforcement matters" were alleged "improper revenue recognition. "

Given that the auditee typically wishes to inflate earnings, a few known ways to manipulate revenues include the following:

- Recording contingent sales with right of return as sales;
- "Channel stuffing";
- "Bill-and-hold" transactions; and
- Violating quarter cutoff rules.

Recording contingent sales is self-explanatory. Since not all risks are passed to the buyer, recognition of contingent sales violates the revenue recognition principle. Channel stuffing is an example of the restructuring of transactions. To boost sales in the current period, the firm offers customers excessive discounts to induce buyers to make early purchases. Bill-and-hold sales are virtual transactions, as nothing much happens besides recording a bill of sale. The seller continues to hold the merchandize, and the buyer is not expected to pay. Violating quarter cutoffs refers to the practice of recognizing revenues before the quarter in which they are earned, such as recording revenues in advance of the actual shipment of merchandize to the customer.

2.3 Managing GAAP Earnings Through Pro forma Earnings

One method of earnings management is to break away from GAAP earnings by reporting pro forma earnings. Non-GAAP earnings exclude items that are classified as either "non-recurrent" or "non-cash," such as special items (mostly restructuring costs), amortization of goodwill before SFAS 141, and losses. Until March 2003, firms did not have to reconcile non-GAAP earnings with GAAP earnings. Our knowledge of the composition of the difference between them thus depends largely on voluntary disclosure by the firms. Bhattacharya, Black, Christensen, and Larson (2003), for example, report that the list of "adjustments"[10] by firms that made such

---

[10] Doyle, Lundholm, and Soliman (2003, p. 147) state,

> We decompose the difference between GAAP earnings and pro forma earnings (i.e., the exclusions) into two parts special items and other exclusions. Special item exclusions are relatively easy to identify, with the most common example being a restructuring charge.... The most easily recognizable "other exclusion" is the amortization of goodwill, but there are many others

disclosures includes the following items: depreciation and amortization expenses, stock compensation-related charges, merger costs, research and development, gains/losses, extraordinary items or discontinued operations, and adjustments for the number of shares used to calculate EPS. On a case-by-case basis, Doyle, Lundholm, and Soliman (2003), report that, unlike GAAP earnings, the adjustments might be inconsistent across firms and across time for the same firm. The research has consistently shown that pro forma earnings are different from GAAP earnings and analysts earnings (Gu and Chen, 2004; Bhattacharya, Black, Christensen, and Mergenthaler, 2007). DiGabriele and Eisner (2005), and Bryan and Lilien (2005), illustrate how negative earnings per share (EPS) calculated for GAAP earnings become positive when projected for pro forma earnings.

There is evidence that publication of pro forma earnings rose steadily before the implementation of section 401(b) off the Sarbanes-Oxley Act (e.g., Bradshaw and Sloan, 2002; Bhattacharya, Black, Christensen, and Larson, 2003; Bhattacharya, Black, Christensen, and Mergenthaler, 2004) and decreased thereafter (Heflin and Hsu, 2005; Nichols, Gray, and Street, 2005; Entwistle, Feltham, and Mbagwu, 2006; Marques, 2006).

Disclosure of pro forma earnings instead of GAAP earnings smacks of pernicious earnings management. After all, why should a firm disclose non-GAAP earnings if its GAAP earnings are favorable? As anecdotal evidence, consider the example of Kodak in Bryan and Lilien, 2005. They report that Eastman Kodak (EK) had "actual earnings" of $0.78 per share for the quarter ending December 31, 2004. Since analysts' consensus estimate was $0.65, Kodak had a positive surprise of $0.13, as compared to GAAP diluted EPS from continuing operations of —$0.04. The stock price rose on the day (and in the days after the multiple announcements of negative earnings, accounting errors, and weaknesses in internal control).

The profile of a typical firm reporting pro forma earnings seems to justify this concern. Ciccone (2002); finds that firms attempt to present a picture that is healthier than the GAAP truth. For example, they report pro forma profits to offset the impact of GAAP losses. Firms also use pro forma earnings to reduce volatility (see Ciccone, 2002, table 4). In the highest volatility portfolio in Ciccone's 1990–2000 sample, the average volatility of pro forma earnings is almost half the average volatility of

---

that are more difficult to identify. Some examples are the exclusion of operating losses from stores scheduled to be closed in the future (The Great Atlantic and Pacific Company, fourth quarter of 1998), the exclusion of stock compensation expense (Amazon, fourth quarter of 2001), the exclusion of in-process R&D charges (AT&T, third quarter of 1999), and the exclusion of legal settlement costs (General Motors, third quarter of 2001).

GAAP earnings. There is also a large difference between average pro forma earnings per share ($0.65), and average GAAP earnings per share ($0.05) in the subset of firms with high volatility of earnings. Hsu (2004), shows that the gap between GAAP and pro forma earnings is lower when non-recurrent items on the income statement increase earnings. Bhattacharya, Black, Christensen, and Mergenthaler (2004), find that the pro forma firms are significantly less profitable and have higher debt levels and higher market-to-book ratios, and Lougee and Marquardt (2004), note that firms with negative earnings surprises are more likely to release pro forma earnings information.[11] Frankel, McVay, and Soliman (2006), show that weak governance in terms of independence of the board leads to the removal of value-relevant items from GAAP earnings, especially when in doing so the firm meets the expectations of the market. Doyle, Lundholm, and Soliman (2003), find that stock returns for firms with large exclusions are up to 45% lower than stock returns for firms with small exclusions over a 3-year period after the pro forma earnings release. Bhattacharya, Black, Christensen, and Mergenthaler (2007), observe that trades of less sophisticated investors, as evidenced in the relative small size of their trades, indicate that they are more likely to use pro forma earnings than sophisticated traders, who seem to ignore them. In short, "pro forma firms" have stronger incentives not to reveal GAAP earnings.

It is little wonder that the press and regulators condemn the practice. Turner (2001b) states,

> A more recent recommendation for the Commission to consider came in the May 28, 2001 edition of Barron's. The article, in discussing earnings releases, appropriately stated:
> There's a flavor of performance measurement for practically every company that doesn't look too hot when measured in old fashioned earnings. The dot-coms were notorious for their promotion of "pro forma" earnings; ultimately, what passed for performance turned out to be a pipe dream. That didn't stop firms in other industries from adopting their own pro forma earnings management. The corporate architects of financial reporting are now building their own Tower of Babel.
> Barron's is right in noting pro formas are often used by companies with performance and business issues to mask their real earnings. In fact, the Washington Post has aptly defined pro forma earnings as "hypothetical" earnings.

Yet is reporting pro forma earnings nothing more than pernicious earnings management? The view that firms attempt to inflate performance is inconsistent with the fact that some firms report non-GAAP earnings that

---

[11] See the discussion of debt as a motivation for earnings management in Chap. 3.

are lower than their GAAP earnings. For example, 30% of the firms in the hand-picked sample of Bhattacharya, Black, Christensen, and Larson (2003), and 7% of the loss firms in the sample of Ciccone (2002), had higher GAAP profits. One explanation, provided by Lougee and Marquardt (2004), is that pro forma earnings sometimes could be used in beneficial earnings management because firms with low quality GAAP earnings can thus signal value. Evidence on the value of pro forma earnings is also provided in Bradshaw and Sloan (2002), Bhattacharya, Black, Christensen, and Larson (2003), and Frankel and Roychowdhury (2006), and their neutrality in affecting investors' beliefs in Johnson and Schwartz (2005).

We note that there is evidence that the market prefers non-GAAP earnings. Financial analysts and institutional investors prefer pro forma earnings because they exclude transitory items (Bradshaw and Sloan, 2002). Abarbanell and Lehavy (2002), report that there are certain items that analysts do not attempt to predict, and pro forma earnings are more closely related to analysts' definition of earnings. To wit, in the commercial database of I/B/E/S, actual earnings coincide with pro forma earnings and not with GAAP earnings (see also Gu and Chen, 2004). Bhattacharya, Black, Christensen, and Larson (2003), find that the pro forma earnings of over 65% of firms in their hand-collected sample coincide with the I/B/E/S numbers, and the median difference is but one cent.

Managers respond to pressure from "the street" and report pro forma earnings that do not contain transitory earnings (for a survey of management's motivation, consult Bowen, Davis, and Matsumoto, 2005, footnote 2). Doyle, Lundholm, and Soliman (2003), who check 50 random press releases of 1999 fourth-quarter earnings announcements, find that in 48 cases the I/B/E/S earnings per shares were featured in the press release; in the other two cases, all the exclusions necessary to reconcile GAAP earnings to the actual earnings per I/B/E/S were shown in the lead paragraph.

The Sarbanes-Oxley Act of July 2002 changed the rules of the game for pro forma earnings. Section 401(b) specifically directed the SEC to issue regulations to ensure that "publicly disclosed pro forma financial information, now known as non-GAAP financial measures, not be materially misleading and be accompanied by a reconciliation to the related financial statements presented in accordance with GAAP." In 2002, the SEC issued Regulation G, which requires all firms that publicize non-GAAP earnings after March 28, 2003, to produce concurrently the GAAP earnings and a reconciliation between the two. Nichols, Gray, and Street (2005), and Kolev, Marquardt, and McVay (2007), find that fewer firms now issue pro forma earnings, but those that do exclude GAAP items appear to have a stronger performance.

Regulation G raises two questions: first, will firms still use pro forma earnings as an earnings management strategy? Second, what type of earnings management is likely to take place when it is made in the open? The answer to the first question focuses on the presence of small, unsophisticated investors (see, e.g., the theoretical study of Hirshleifer and Teoh, 2003; the experimental study of Frederickson and Miller, 2004; Elliott, 2004; Dilla, Janvrin, and Jeffrey, 2006; the empirical studies of Allee, Bhattacharya, Black, and Christensen, 2006; Bhattacharya, Black, Christensen, and Mergenthaler, 2007). The less sophisticated will be impressed by non-GAAP information, especially when such earnings are higher and their presentation emphasizes them relative to the GAAP earnings. Some of the bias in perception, however, can be mitigated if the readers are willing to invest time (Dilla, Janvrin, and Jeffrey, 2006).

The second question is answered by the research that examines the use of non-GAAP earnings to influence the market's interpretation of the GAAP earnings. Elliott (2004), and Allee, Bhattacharya, Black, and Christensen (2006), examine whether the firm presents GAAP earnings before or after pro forma earnings. Bowen, Davis, and Matsumoto (2005), check the emphasis on pro forma versus GAAP by examining the headline, the first paragraph, and the rest of the release when companies voluntarily disclose both earnings figures. These studies also establish that firms use pro forma earnings to present their performance in a favorable light. Kolev, Marquardt, and McVay (2007), find an improvement in the quality of pro forma earnings post SOX, but it seems that firms now attempt to mask their exclusions by classifying more items as special.

2.4 Summary

This chapter concludes the first part wherein we presented the answers to the question of why earnings are the statistics that is managed and the definition of earnings management. Our definition of earnings management allows distinguishing between earnings management activities and managing earnings as part of normal operational decisions. We recognize that earnings management could be beneficial, neutral, or pernicious.

Part 2

In Chap. 2, we presented the definition of earnings management and discussed the main ways it is done. In this chapter, we use the definition by further exploring the different phenomena that are characterized by earnings management. We have identified 13 specific cases of earnings management, and we discuss each below.

Our classification revolves around the key players on the financial accounting scene, which can be grouped into three main categories: management, plain-vanilla users, and gatekeepers or monitors. Management reports earnings, users use earnings as an input to their decision making, and gatekeepers provide valuable signals to other users regarding the credibility and the informational value of the reported earnings (Coffee, 2002, 2003a, b). We associate with each player the earnings management events that seem most closely related to their decisions. As an example, consider analysts, who, in their capacity of gatekeepers, shape the market's expectation about future earnings. Firms might manage earnings to meet the expectations of the analysts, in order not to disappoint the market.

The Players

The accounting scene and the interactions between management and the firm's other constituencies are illustrated in Figure 1.

Figure 1 shows the main players: the manager, the users, and the gatekeepers. The firm is a principal-agent contract between management and the board of directors. The board sets the management's compensation. In Figure 1, we put management above the board. Optimally, the opposite should be the case. Cynthia Glassman, a commissioner of the Securities and Exchange Commission, states,

> In the U.S., management, the board of directors and the shareholders form a corporate decision-making hierarchy. Management is at the bottom of the hierarchy. Though some CEOs don't always seem to realize this, it's true. Nevertheless, management gets to make the vast majority of the decisions. Everything from business strategy and its

implementation down to the color of the wallpaper in the office hall-
ways is the province of management. Management's responsibility,
and it's a big one, is the day-to-day running of the corporation.

REGULATORS AND THE LEGAL SYSTEM

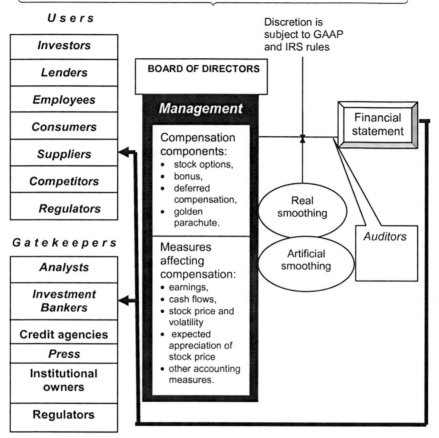

Fig. 1 The accounting scene and the relationships between management and other
stakeholders

The financial report is an outcome of management's actions, and it is an
input into the decision making of users and gatekeepers. More important,
the latter two groups take actions based on the financial reports that affect
the performance measures on which management's compensation is based.
For example, creditors use earnings to decide the firm's ability to pay back
loans, and their decisions determine the interest expenses in the income
statement and the capital that can be raised to finance investments. Gate-

keepers are dispersed in the diagram because they include the auditor, who participates in the preparation of the accounting reports (on the *upper right side* of the diagram); the board of directors, which monitors management as a representative of shareholders' interests (in the *center* of the diagram, just *below* management), and other gatekeepers that are external to the firm, such as analysts, institutional shareholders, investment bankers, credit agencies, and the press (in the *lower left corner* of the diagram).

Finally, note the dual role of regulators. On one hand, they are users. On the other hand, regulators determine the rules of the game. For example, Altamuro, Beatty, and Weber (2005), find that firms were less successful in meeting earnings benchmarks (see Chaps. 4 and 5) after being required to comply with SEC's Staff Accounting Bulletin (SAB) No. 101 that allows recognition of revenues only after the earnings process is complete. The legal system is an important component of the infrastructure of the accounting reporting system, and it can help or hinder attempts by users to affect the scope of earnings management.[1]

A crucial set of constraints that distinguishes the accounting scene in the twenty-first century has been shaped by the Sarbanes-Oxley Act (SOX), officially known as the Public Company Accounting Reform and Investor Protection Act of 2002.

The Sarbanes-Oxley Act

Knowledge of the legal system is important to understand the accounting scene. Since July 2002, the legal framework in the United States has included the Sarbanes-Oxley Act (SOX), in addition to the rules of the Securities and Exchange Commission (SEC), the listing requirements of the stock exchanges, the codes of conduct of the corporations, and state laws.[2]

---

[1] In his discussion of the optimal infrastructure of financial accounting reporting, Ball (2001), states,

> [P]erhaps most important of all [is] establishing an effective, independent legal system for detecting and penalizing fraud, manipulation, and failure to comply with standards of accounting and other disclosure, including provision for private litigation by stockholders and lenders who are adversely affected by deficient financial reporting and disclosure. (p. 128, Text in brackets added)

[2] The rules of different regulatory bodies are interrelated. The exchanges made rules that meet some of the SOX requirements before July 2002; for example, the NYSE requires an audit committee made up wholly of independent outside directors and also requires registrants to have a code of conduct.

We will focus on the Act. Bear in mind that there might be tighter exchange requirements and that companies can signal value to shareholders through their own governance rules.

The Motivation for the Sarbanes-Oxley Act

According to Coffee (2002, 2003b), regulatory reforms take place in the aftermath of meltdown of the capital markets and economic crises because they expose firms that engaged in pernicious earnings management. Becht, Bolton, and Roell (2003, p. 13) state, Many of these cases [corporate failures] concern accounting irregularities that enabled firms to vastly overstate their earnings. Such scandals often emerge during economic downturns: as John Kenneth Galbraith once remarked, recessions catch what the auditors miss. [Text in brackets added]

The recent crisis happened with the burst of the high-tech bubble in the first quarter of 2000, followed by accounting scandals in 2001 and 2002; the most severe scandal involved restatements by WorldCom in 2002 that approximated in total over $10.8 billion. The federal government responded by enacting the Sarbanes-Oxley Act — the SOX. This act combines the initiatives of Representative Michael Oxley, chairman of the House Financial Services Committee, and Senator Paul Sarbanes, chairman of the Senate Banking Committee. Rep. Oxley introduced a bill in the House on February 13, 2002, to strengthen auditor independence and establish a public accounting regulatory board. Senator Sarbanes introduced a similar bill on June 25, 2002. The final legislation, the Sarbanes-Oxley Act of 2002, was passed in the House and Senate on July 25, 2002 and signed by President Bush on July 30, 2002.[3]

The implementation of the Act took time. The earliest implementation was the SEC's imposition of the requirement that management certify financial reports, which has applied since August 29, 2002. One of the last portions to take effect was §404 on internal controls, since it becomes effective for smaller firms only in the year ending after July 15, 2007.

Since the SOX opens up new opportunities for research into earnings management, we next address the existing research on the repercussions of the SOX.

---

[3] For a description of intervening events, consult Li, Pincus, and Rego (2006).

Research on the Sarbanes-Oxley Act

The Sarbanes-Oxley Act has inspired research in the legal, accounting, finance, and economics[4] disciplines.

Legal researchers debate the Act (see, e.g., Backer, 2002, 2004; Chandler and Strine, 2002; Fairfax, 2002a, b, 2005; Ribstein, 2002; 2003, 2005; Brickey, 2003; Cunningham, 2003; Gordon, 2003; Langevoort, 2003; Mitchel, 2003; Paredes, 2003; Bainbridge and Johnson, 2004; Blumberg and Kelleher, 2004; Bratton, 2004; Henning, 2004; Karmel, 2004, 2005; McDonnell, 2004; Marks, 2004; Young, 2004; Ahdieh, 2005; Anand, 2005; Galindo, 2005; Romano, 2005; Bainbridge, 2006; Butler and Ribstein, 2006; Frankel, 2006; Garrie and Armstrong, 2006; Moberly, 2006; Perino, 2006a, b; Cross and Prentice, 2006; Tippett, 2006). The concerns of the legal research can be roughly classified into two categories: the first follows from the view that the act was created in a rush to extinguish the fire of accounting scandals by Republicans mindful of the coming elections. Ribstein (2005), summarizes,

> Congress passed SOX in the summer of 2002. The Act was enacted hurriedly, without significant debate, in a panic atmosphere created by crumbling securities prices and daily revelations of fraud, particularly including the massive accounting fraud at WorldCom. (p. 6)

From this angle, the Act raises the question whether it is effective in preventing accounting scandals and the concern that it might be riddled with inconsistencies. An example of inconsistency is §806, on whistle-blowers and SEC rule 205.[5] Section 806 shifts the burden of responsibility for getting a response to the whistle-blower because it requires him to keep at it "up the ladder" if the authority he approaches does not respond satisfactorily. In contrast, SEC Rule 205 establishes a Qualified Legal Compliance Committee in the board of directors to handle whistle-blowing by attorneys, which thus relieves attorneys of similar responsibility when they possess information that requires them to blow the whistle.

The second category of debate concerns the legal repercussions of the Sarbanes-Oxley Act, such as the extension of federal regulation into the territory of state legislators and courts, which weakens the latter. In their evaluation of the repercussions of the Sarbanes-Oxley Act in effecting changes in state laws, Chandler and Strine (2002, pp. 7–8) observe, "Although it is difficult to predict the full ramifications of the Reforms for state law, what is clear is that the Reforms represent a marked increase in

---

[4] See Holmström and Kaplan (2003), Kirchmaier and Selvaggi (2006), and Wasserman (2005).
[5] SEC is the body that implements the SOX.

federal government and Exchange regulation of the corporate board-room."[6] Another concern is the increased liability of officers of firms, which can be exploited opportunistically. Ribstein (2005), warns,

> The main problems with the internal controls reports are, however, more subtle and may persist even after firms have established report-ing procedures and infrastructures. Most importantly, SOX imposes significant new liability risks, since a clever trial lawyer might be able to trace virtually any business problem, in hindsight, to a failure to im-plement some internal control. Thus, the litigation risks are associated not merely with fraud or mismanagement, but with inherent business uncertainty. (p. 10)

The Economic Costs

The provisions considered most costly are §302 and §404. Section 404 requires public firms to strengthen their internal control systems and to re-port material weaknesses, and §302 requires management to certify the re-ports.[7] Compliance with §302 is not feasible if the internal control system has material weaknesses. The SEC issued a rule, "Management's Reports on Internal Control Over Financial Reporting and Certification of Disclo-sure in Exchange Act Periodic Reports" (Release No. 33-8238), which be-came effective August 14, 2003. This rule defines "internal control over financial reporting" as follows:

---

[6] The policymakers of corporate governance in the United States are the following:
1. the Federal government (by acts and the initiatives of the Securities and Exchange Commission),
2. state governments (through corporate codes and the common law of cor-porations), and
3. the stock exchanges (by making rules and establishing listing require-ments).

Although these bodies may interfere with each other, each still enjoys a great deal of freedom (Chandler and Strine, 2002, footnote 12).

[7] Material weakness in internal control is defined as "a significant deficiency, or combination of significant deficiencies, that results in more than a remote likeli-hood that a material misstatement of the annual or interim financial statements will not be prevented or detected (PCAOB, Auditing Standard #2)."

Auditors are now required to follow the guidelines of Auditing Standard 2 of the Public Company Accounting Oversight Board (PCAOB). The PCAOB was established under the supervision of the SEC by the Sarbanes-Oxley Act to set audit, ethics, and independence standards, and to monitor auditing firms, which must register with the PCAOB in order to conduct audit for public firms.

A process designed by, or under the supervision of, the registrant's principal executive and principal financial officers, or persons performing similar functions, and effected by the registrant's board of directors, management and other personnel, to provide reasonable assurance regarding the reliability of financial reporting and the preparation of financial statements for external purposes in accordance with generally accepted accounting principles and includes those policies and procedures that

1. Pertain to the maintenance of records that in reasonable detail accurately and fairly reflect the transactions and dispositions of the assets of the registrant;
2. Provide reasonable assurance that transactions are recorded as necessary to permit preparation of financial statements in accordance with generally accepted accounting principles, and that receipts and expenditures of the registrant are being made only in accordance with authorizations of management and directors of the registrant; and
3. Provide reasonable assurance regarding prevention or timely detection of unauthorized acquisition, use, or disposition of the registrant's assets that could have a material effect on the financial statements.

Section 302 became effective on August 29, 2002, for all filers, and §404 became effective for fiscal years ending after November 15, 2004, for accelerated filers.[8] For non-accelerated filers, §404 will be effective for years ending after July 15, 2007.

Compliance with §302 and §404 imposes the *direct* costs of an investment in internal control systems and an increase in audit fees caused by the

---

[8] See http://www.sec.gov/answers/form10k.htm

Category of filer	Revised deadlines for filing periodic reports	
	Form 10-K deadline	Form 10-Q deadline
Large accelerated filer ($700MM or more)	75 days for fiscal years ending before December 15, 2006, and 60 days for fiscal years ending on or after December 15, 2006	40 days
Accelerated filer ($75MM or more and less than $700MM)	75 days	40 days
Non-accelerated filer (less than $75MM)	90 days	45 days

requirement that an auditor assess the internal control systems.[9] Regulators, professional organizations, media, and researchers have all examined
the estimated increment in audit fees. Eldridge and Kealey (2005), estimate an average cost of $2.3 million dollars from 2003 to 2004 for 648
Fortune 1000 firms that fully disclose audit fees; Asthana, Balsam, and
Kim (2004), report that in their sample of 5,208 firms with available data
on audit fees in 2003, the average audit fee increased from $748,204 in
2000 to $1,099,581 in 2002, and, as a percentage of total assets, it in-
creased from 0.092 to 0.157%. Raghunandan and Rama (2006), find that
audit fees paid in 2004 by 660 manufacturing firms are higher than the corresponding fees for 2003 (the mean and median fees for 2004 are higher by
86 and 128%, respectively). Audit fees are even higher for the 58 firms
that disclosed material weaknesses in internal controls over financial reporting. Compliance also entails indirect costs, such as a diversion of
management's effort from investment or production decisions to monitoring of internal controls. Block (2003, p. 37), for example, states that in his
sample, time-consuming internal control systems were a driving force in
inducing firms to go private: "While a traditional reason for not enjoying a
public company status is the time required to meet with security analysts
and other interested parties, this was not an issue with the respondents of
this study. Rather, their time was being absorbed in another manner:
overseeing auditors, attending committee meetings of the board to insure
SEC compliance, ..." Bryan and Lilien (2005, p. 3), summarize,

> In a survey of 224 firms conducted by Financial Executives Interna-
> tional (in July 2004), respondents revealed that they will spend in the
> first year of SOX, on average, an extra $3 million in order to comply
> with Section 404. The largest companies (those with over $5,000 mil-
> lion in revenues) will spend an average of $8 million. Respondents
> stated that audit fees are expected to increase, on average, by 53% in
> order to pay for the attestation over internal control.... Additionally,
> the costs associated with these steps include not only "out-of-pocket"
> costs but also the indirect costs of diverting managerial attention from
> the critical decisions that pertain to operating and investing activities of
> the firm.[10]

---

[9] The initial estimates of the costs understate them. In 2003, the SEC expected
the incremental section 404 costs of "compiling documentation, implementing
new processes, and training staff" to amount to $1.24 billion, or $91,000 per
company (Release No. 33-8238).

[10] Over 50% of the respondents were large firms with annual revenues of at least
$1 billion.

Many other provisions of the Sarbanes-Oxley Act are costly, too, such as restrictions on non-audit services (Zhang, 2005), the establishment of whistle-blower protections and the acceleration of the dates at which reports must be filed (Block, 2003), and the funding of the PCAOB, which, because it is proportional to a firm's total market capitalization, can reach $2 million per year for a large company (Branson, 2006). Additional indirect costs include the increase in proprietary disclosures. For example, Barrett (2003), notes that valuable information on what a firm thinks about litigation can be obtained by observing the reserves put aside for that purpose in compliance with §401(a) of the Act. Moreover, SOX has also led to an increase in the cost of incentives for directors (Linck, Netter, and Yang, 2006).

The Sarbanes-Oxley Act has been more costly for smaller firms.[11] For example, 23 of 30 Dow Jones firms experienced an increase of just 40% in audit fees from 2003 to 2004 (Eldridge and Kealey, 2005, citing a *Wall Street Journal* report), the average firm experienced an increase of over 50%. Smaller firms proportionally have borne more of the cost of the new requirements because they were less likely to adopt the SOX provisions voluntarily before 2003 (Aggarwal and Williamson, 2006). They also tend to spend less resources on internal controls, which increases the cost of their audits (Eldridge and Kealey, 2005), and they find it harder to recruit talent and gain the attention of large auditors because they are more risky.

The Accounting and Economic Benefits

The other side of the SOX coin is that internal controls, especially over financial reporting, are important, and they are valued by the market. In 2004, Donald T. Nicolaisen, the Chief Accountant of the SEC, stated,

> [G]iven the massive financial scandals, decline in market capitalization and resulting loss of investor confidence in our markets, I believe that, of all the recent reforms, the internal control requirements have the greatest potential to improve the reliability of financial reporting. Our capital markets run on faith and trust that the vast majority of companies present reliable and complete financial data for investment and policy decision-making. Representing to the world that a company has in place an appropriate control system, free of material weaknesses, that gathers, consolidates, and presents financial information strengthens public confidence in our markets and encourages investment in our nation's industries.

---

[11] The unequal impact of regulatory compliance costs on small and madcap firms is not unique to SOX (see Hsu, 2004).

The evidence seems to confirm the value of §404 of the Sarbanes-Oxley Act since low quality internal controls are associated with more earnings management (Bédard, 2006; Chan, Farrell, and Lee, 2006) and with more restatements (Bryan and Lilien, 2005).

The empirical research in accounting and related disciplines focuses on the consequences of SOX. Broadly speaking, three issues have been investigated:

- *The market reaction*: to the events leading to the Act (Bhattacharya, Groznik, and Haslem, 2004; Chhaochharia and Grinstein, 2005; Zhang, 2005; Jain, Kim, and Rezaee, 2006; Li, Pincus, and Rego, 2006; Rezaee and Jain, 2006); to the impact of the Act on foreign firms listed in the United States (Litvak, 2006; Smith, 2006); to specific provisions, such as the certification requirement (Bhattacharya, Groznik, and Haslem, 2003, 2004; Griffin and Lont, 2005a; Gupta and Nayar, 2006);[12] to the disclosure of material weakness in internal control (De Franco, Guan, and Lu, 2005; Hammersley, Myers, and Shakespeare, 2005; Beneish, Billings, and Hodder, 2006; Chan, Farrell, and Lee, 2006); to the requirement that stock grants be reported within 2 days (Narayanan and Seyhun, 2005[13]); and to improvements in governance (Aggarwal and Williamson, 2006).

If the responses have been favorable, then SOX has accomplished its stated mission of restoring investors' confidence in the integrity of the capital markets.

Overall, it appears that this goal has indeed been achieved. The research on the market response to the events leading to the enactment of the Act indicates that it was successful (Jain, Kim, and Rezaee, 2006; Li, Pincus, and Rego, 2006; Rezaee and Jain, 2006), with a stronger positive reaction to firms that engaged more in earnings management (Li, Pincus, and Rego, 2006).[14] This surge in confidence has proved to be justified, as earnings management has declined. Cohen, Dey, and Lys (2005a), who study 80,963 firm-quarter observations for 5,538 firms in the 1987–2003 period, observe that earnings management increased steadily before SOX and declined thereafter. Furthermore, certification by management of the veracity of the financial reports (see the

---

[12] Vermeer (2005), examines voluntary certification by management. He finds a negative association between earnings management (measured by discretionary accruals) and certification.

[13] See the backdating scandal in Chap. 3.

[14] An exception is Zhang (2005), who finds a loss in total market value of about $1.4 trillion around the most significant rulemaking events. The events chosen by Zhang are not in perfect congruence with the choices made in Li, Pincus, and Rego (2006).

discussion in Chap. 3) has reduced earnings management and increased conservatism (Lobo and Zhou, 2005).[15] Williams, DaDalt, Sun, and Yaari, (2006, 2008), Bartov and Cohen, (2007), and Koh, Matsumoto, and Rajgopal, (2007) also establish that earnings management declined after the enactment of SOX by analyzing the phenomenon of firms meeting/beating analyst expectations (see Chapter 5).

- *Disclosure of material weaknesses in internal control systems, as required by §302 and §404 of the SOX* (Bryan and Lilien, 2005; Ge and McVay, 2005; Hammersley, Myers, and Shakespeare, 2005; Krishnan and Visvanathan, 2005a; Ashbaugh-Skaife, Collins, and Kinney, 2006; Bédard, 2006; Beneish, Billings, and Hodder, 2006, Doyle, Ge, and McVay, 2006; Ettredge, Heintz, Li, and Scholz, 2006; Ghosh and Lubberink, 2006; Ogneva, Subramanyam, and Raghunandan, 2006; Ettredge, Li, and Sun, 2007).

  Such disclosures appear to be value-relevant because the market responds negatively (De Franco, Guan, and Lu, 2005; Hammersley, Myers, and Shakespeare, 2005; Beneish, Billings, and Hodder, 2006), especially when management declares the system to be effective (Hammersley, Myers, and Shakespeare, 2005). De Franco, Guan, and Lu (2005), find that the investors' response is largely caused by small investors' selling of their holdings.

  The picture that emerges is that material weaknesses are more likely in firms that have more complex operations, more accounting risk exposure, and fewer resources to invest in internal control. Furthermore, firms that reported ineffective internal controls experienced higher SOX-related audit costs and higher probability of future restatement than those that reported effective internal controls.

- *The economic repercussions of the SOX, whether or not intended* (Block, 2003; Lai, 2003; Smith, 2006; Asthana, Balsam, and Kim, 2004; Hsu, 2004; Jain and Rezaee, 2004; Bris, Cantale, and Nishiotis, 2005; Bryant-Kutcher, Peng, and Zvinakis, 2005; Cohen, Dey, and Lys, 2005b; Collins, Gong, and Li, 2005; Griffin and Lont, 2005b; Heflin and Hsu, 2005; Kamar, Karaca-Mandic, and Talley, 2005; Krishnan and Visvanathan, 2005a; Markelevich, Hoitash, and Barragato, 2005; Schwarzkopf and Miller, 2005; Stadtmann and Wissmann, 2005; Ahmed, Duellman, and Abdel-Meguid, 2006; Bédard, 2006; Carney, 2006; DiGabriele and Gottesman, 2006; Engel, Hayes, and Wang, 2006; Gordon, Loeb, Lucyshyn, and Sohail, 2006; Leon, 2006; Leuz, Triantis,

---

[15] Bhattacharya, Groznik, and Haslem (2004), who study the market's reaction to certification by 664 of the 688 firms that were required to certify by August 14, 2002, find no evidence that the CEO and CFO certification requirements were significantly priced by investors. Jain and Rezaee (2004), find no change in accounting conservatism.

and Wang, 2006; Linck, Netter, and Yang, 2006; Roberts and Chava, 2006; Schloetzer, 2006; Williams, 2006; Williams, DaDalt, Sun, and Yaari, 2006; Zhang, Zhou, and Zhou, 2006; Brochet, 2007; Williams, Sun, and Yaari, 2007).

The scope of this strand of literature is quite rich. As an example, Lai (2003), finds that the Sarbanes-Oxley Act enhanced auditor's independence, as evidenced in an increase in the likelihood of modified audit opinions and lower discretionary accruals in financial statements. Cohen, Dey, and Lys (2005b), find that management's equity compensation increased and cash compensation decreased with concurrent decrease in R&D. Gordon, Loeb, Lucyshyn, and Sohail (2006), find that voluntary disclosure of the quality of computer security has increased (since compliance with section 404 enhances the importance of tighter computer security).

Several studies examine the effect of the SOX on the decision to become private and the decision to go dark (Block, 2003; Hsu, 2004; Marosi and Massoud, 2004; Subramanian, 2005; Carney, 2006; Engel, Hayes, and Wang, 2006; Leuz, Triantis, and Wang, 2006; and Smith, 2006).[16] The phenomenon of firms going dark, that is, ceasing to be registered with the SEC so that they would no longer need to issue financial reports and thus would be spared the costs of compliance, seemed to gain momentum after SOX was enacted. For example, Leuz, Triantis, and Wang (2006), report that the number of firms going dark (going private) increased substantially: from 28 (23) and 29 (54) in 1998 and 1999, respectively, to 183 (79) and 122 (66) in 2003 and 2004, respectively.[17] Still, it is clear that some firms go private[18] for reasons that have little to do with the regulatory environment: high cash flows and low growth opportunities combined with high insider ownership (Ma-

---

[16] It seems that SOX chased foreign firms away from U.S. markets (Hsu, 2004; Bris, Cantale, and Nishiotis, 2005; Stadtmann and Wissmann, 2005) and led to a negative market response to foreign firms that cross-list in the United States (Litvak, 2006). In December 2006, the SEC issued new rules that facilitate delisting by foreign firms.

[17] Going private in the United States is quite time-consuming, in part because companies beyond certain size can go private only if the number of their shareholders falls below 300 (or fewer than 500 holders of record and less than $10 million of assets in each of the prior 3 years, where shareholders of record are typically "street names"). Firms that chose this path had to take a number of steps, such as reverse stock splits, before they could accomplish the change.

[18] One way to go private is freeze-outs—a controlling shareholder buys out the minority shareholders (Subramanian, 2005). For additional discussion of the different ways to go private, consult Kamar, Karaca-Mandic, and Talley, (2005).

rosi and Massoud, 2004) may leave a company with no real need to raise capital in the market; a firm may experience low liquidity due to lack of interest from institutional investors (see, e.g., Block, 2003; Hsu, 2004); or the company may be acquired by a private firm (Kamar, Karaca-Mandic, and Talley, 2005). Nevertheless, firms that file Form 13E-3 with the SEC (as required when the change in the firm's status requires the consent of shareholders rather than just the board of directors) often do list the cost of SOX as a factor in their decision.[19] For example, Block (2003), who received 110 responses to questionnaires sent to 236 Nasdaq firms that went private between January 2001 and July 2003, finds that the major reason for going private is cost (the average respondent thought that the cost of being public had increased from $900,000 to $1,954,000). The mirror phenomenon of going private is the phenomenon of Initial Public Offering (IPO). Zingales (2006), finds that international firms that seek to raise money seek non U.S. exchanges. One reason is that these other markets are competitive; another reason is the reluctance to bear the SOX compliance costs.

The Plan of Part 2

In Chap. 3, we discuss earnings management stemming from management-related objectives. We identify four such cases:

1. Compensation—management manipulates earnings to increase lifetime compensation.
2. CEO turnover—a departing CEO makes decisions that increase both his bonus in the last year of operations and his chance to

---

[19] The responses reported by Block (p. 43), indicate that the following *direct* costs induce firms to go private:
- audit, legal, and personnel fees and costs
- management and in-house staff time expended in filing disclosures
- printing and mailing costs necessary to satisfy reporting obligations under securities regulations
- filing fees and other direct expenses associated with the required SEC filings, stock market listing fees, and stock transfer expenses
- administrative expenses in servicing record stockholders (who own a small number of shares), dedication of time to stockholders' inquiries and investor and public relations, and
- the cost of corporate governance requirements—for example, compensation of independent directors

obtain a directorship, while an incoming CEO attempts to build reserves of reported income by taking a bath.

3. Insider trading—does management exploit its superior private information to make speculative gains or manage earnings to make such profits?

4. Management buyout—management attempts to reduce the price paid to shareholders when it plans a buyout.

In Chap. 4, we discuss earnings management that relates to users, where our list of users includes distant shareholders, liquidity traders, and market-makers, as well as lenders, competitors, customers, suppliers, employees, and regulators. We identify six such cases:

1. Meeting or beating a benchmark—firms strive to meet or beat a benchmark number, such as zero profit. That is, firms avoid reporting losses. Alternative benchmarks are driven by past performance.

2. Initial public offerings (IPO), seasoned equity offerings (SEO), and new listings—firms manage earnings to increase the price of their stock when issued.

3. Mergers and acquisitions—firms that pursue mergers financed by stock increase their stock price through earnings management, effectively reducing the cost of the merger to their own shareholders.

4. Bond covenants and debt—firms manage earnings to affect the cost of debt before borrowing and to relax bond covenants after the debt is incurred.

5. Negotiations with employees' unions—firms manage earnings to appear less healthy financially than they really are in order to depress wage increases.

6. Regulation and tax considerations—firms manage earnings in response to regulatory constraints, such as taxes.

In Chap. 5, we discuss earnings management that relates to gatekeepers. Gatekeepers are monitors that are supposed to alleviate the information asymmetry between firms and other stakeholders. Notable gatekeepers are analysts, institutional shareholders who are blockholders and activists, boards of directors and their audit committees, auditors, the press, and investment bankers, and credit agencies. We focus on three gatekeepers:

1. Analysts who are associated with meeting or beating analysts' expectations (MBE)—this is similar to meeting a benchmark, but the benchmark is analysts' consensus forecast.
2. Gatekeepers invovled in firms' governance—some characteristics of firms' ownership, boards of directors, and audit committees facilitate or hinder earnings management.
3. Auditors—the quality of auditors affects the probability that firms successfully manage earnings.

Notably, some phenomena involve more than one type of a participant. For example, compensation is designed by the compensation committee of the board of directors, so it involves both managers and gatekeepers.[20] When choosing where to place a category, we use at least one of two criteria. The first focuses on the party that is motivated to manage earnings rather than to suppress earnings management. For example, we believe that managers might prefer to manage earnings to increase compensation, while the board of directors would prefer to suppress it. The second criterion considers the phenomena that are associated with the existence of a given player. For example, in an abstract economy without lenders, firms would not need to manage earnings to avoid violation of debt covenants.

We refer the readers to the summary where we present a table that summarizes the relationship between the decision-makers and the categories of earnings management. In parentheses we specify a representative empirical study that falls in that particular category.

---

[20] Core, Holthausen, and Larcker (1999), for example, find that weaker governance is associated with higher CEO compensation and with poorer performance.

3 The Management

In this chapter, we describe how management's participation in the accounting scene contributes to earnings management. Before we start, however, one comment is in order concerning the officers discussed in this chapter. An earnings management perspective requires a focus on those senior officers who are responsible for reporting the firm's earnings: the chief executive officer (CEO), the controller, and the chief financial officer (CFO). In some studies, however, the samples include additional officers; in others, CFOs and controllers are excluded. For example, research on turnover in senior management tends to examine the CEO, the chairman of the board, and the president. Studies of compensation focus on the five officers with the highest compensation. Research on insider trading lumps senior management with other corporate insiders.[1] The reader should be aware of these differences while considering the discussions below. Whether these differences matter remains to be seen. In some cases, the distinction is important. Aier, Comprix, Gunlock, and Lee (2005), for example, find that the likelihood of a restatement is negatively associated with the financial expertise of the CFO (measured by his experience as a CFO, having an MBA degree, and being a CPA). Another example is provided by Geiger and North (2006). They find that incoming CFOs tend to be associated with a lower level of earnings management. As discussed below, incoming CEOs, in contrast, tend to be associated with a higher level of earnings management. The expertise of the CEO–CFO team thus is more important than the expertise of the CEO alone. In other cases, the distinctions among the different definitions of senior management might be innocuous (see, e.g., Huddart and Lang, 1996, 2003; Kasznik, 2003). In the last backdating scandal, for example, "in the money" option, grants were given not just to the senior executives but to the rank and file employees too, which might induce them to collude in earnings management with the CEO.

---

[1] By Rule 16a-1(f) of the 1934 Securities and Exchange Act, the list of corporate insiders includes the CEO, the CFO, and the controller, as well as the president, vice presidents (in charge of a principal business unit, division or function, such as sales, administration or finance), and any other officer.

3.1 Background

3.1.1 The Role of Management in Reporting Earnings

Senior management has a leadership role in generating and reporting earnings (e.g., Wasserman, Nohria, and Anand, 2001; Desai, Hogan, and Wilkins 2006; Karpoff, Lee, and Martin, 2007b, and the citations therein).[2] Although boards of directors have to approve key managerial decisions, the truth is that management makes operating, investment, and financing decisions, such as the design and execution of a business strategy, capital investment, and budgeting, as well as issuance of dividends and acquisition of debt and securities. In the process of making these decisions, management also acquires superior knowledge of the economics of the firm, as discussed in Chap. 1. Studies on insider trading, for example, show that, on average, insiders sell stock when it is overvalued and buy stock when it is undervalued (Seyhun, 1988; Beneish and Vargus, 2002; Ke, Huddart, and Petroni, 2003). This superior knowledge implies that management can either manage earnings to convey useful, value-relevant information—engage in beneficial earnings management—or try to hide unwelcome truth—engage in pernicious earnings management (see the definitions in Chap. 2).

The Sarbanes-Oxley Act (SOX) has redefined management's fiduciary duty. Specifically, sections 302 and 404 of the Act have increased senior management's responsibility for the financial reports. Backer (2002), notes,

> In a pre-Enron world, a CEO candidate was expected to conduct a certain amount of due diligence about a potential job opportunity—but much of that due diligence was directed at "fit" and corporate performance. In our new post-Sarbanes-Oxley Act world of liability, a CEO candidate must exercise care and judgment, and must conduct her due diligence in some significantly new ways. That care and judgment should be focused on: (1) internal corporate controls; (2) ethical rules in place. (pp. 907–908)

Section 302(a) requires that "principal executive officer or officers and the principal financial officer or officers, or persons performing similar functions, certify in each annual or quarterly report...." The certification is an affirmation of the following:

---

[2] Fama (1980, p. 290), describes top management in this way: "Management is a type of labor with a special role—coordinating the activity of inputs and carrying out the contracts agreed among inputs, all of which can be characterized as 'decision making.'"

(1) the signing officer has reviewed the report;

(2) based on the officer's knowledge, the report does not contain any untrue statement of a material fact or omit to state a material fact necessary in order to make the statements made, in light of the circumstances under which such statements were made, not misleading;

(3) based on such officer's knowledge, the financial statements, and other financial information included in the report, fairly present in all material respects the financial condition and results of operations of the issuer as of, and for, the periods presented in the report....

The latter two requirements have a few implications. First, certification becomes a bottom-up procedure, which effectively makes subordinate managers certify as well.[3] Second, CEOs can no longer feign ignorance when an earnings management attempt is discovered.[4] Third, it affects the relationships between managers and auditors. To illustrate the latter point, consider the termination of the employment of Kirk Gorman, the CFO of the Universal Health Company (as reported by the New York Times on February 15, 2004). Gorman was forced to leave the company after KPMG, the auditor that replaced Andersen, told the firm that it would not attest to the financial statements if Gorman stayed with the company as CFO. KPMG's decision was a response to a letter that Gorman sent on December 12, 2003, stating that he signed the representation letter attesting to the accuracy of the results that the auditing firm had asked him to sign but that he did not know the details of all accounting rules and had relied on KPMG's expertise. "As part of my own due diligence," he wrote, "I have asked KPMG to provide me a representation letter or certificate regarding KPMG's ongoing review of our financial statements and disclosures. KPMG has refused to provide me any such representation letter or

---

[3] For companies with revenues that exceed $1.2 billion, the certification requirement was imposed by the SEC on June 27, 2002, before SOX. Notably, CEOs of firms with higher quality of earnings certified even before the SEC deadline date of August 14, 2002 (Lobo and Zhou, 2005).

[4] As anecdotal evidence, consider the case of Richard Scrushy, the founder and the former CEO of HealthSouth Corp., who claimed ignorance of his firm's practice of inflating earnings by recording revenues at the price it billed health insurance companies instead of the lower price that was actually collected. To collect evidence that Scrushy knew about the questionable revenue recognition practice, his CFO was wired during a supposedly private conversation with him. Eventually, Scrushy was charged with willfully and knowingly certifying a false report in HealthSouth's second quarter filing with the SEC on August 14, 2002 and attempting to force the company's CFO to certify a false report in March 2003. He was acquitted of all charges (see Werhane, Mead, and Collier, 2006).

certificate." Interestingly, the auditors who performed the audit were the same professionals who performed this audit for Andersen.

As this example indicates, the certification requirement is vacuous if the certifier is ignorant. To ensure that the certifier has the necessary knowledge, section 302(a)-4 specifies that the signing officers are responsible for establishing and maintaining internal controls (302(a)-4(A)), with specific requirements for an evaluation (302(a)-4(C)) and for bringing deficiencies in the internal control system, and the measures to correct them, to the attention of the audit committee and to the auditor (302(a)-5 and 302(a)-6). Furthermore, if a firm fails to comply with section 404 on internal control, the manager cannot certify to the financial reports. The penalties for failing to comply with honest reporting and disclosure have become more severe, regarding both incarceration and fines. Hence, the cost of pernicious earnings management has increased.

SOX has additional provisions that affect financial reporting, including the establishment of a code of ethics for senior financial officers (section 406) and a prohibition on managers' taking private loans from the company (section 402), which has induced firms to arrange for third-party loans at lenient terms for their executives (Baker, 2006). See the introduction for additional details on the implementation of section 302 in conjunction with section 404.

3.1.2 The Management's Objective Function

Since management has always been responsible for the financial reports, the new demands made by SOX prompt us to ask why such new tightened rules were needed. Specifically, what drives management to manage earnings in the absence of such regulation? Once we understand the answer to this question, we can debate whether the new regulation will be effective in stopping executives from managing earnings.

In this section, we describe what is known about management's objective function by discussing the difference between it and the shareholders' objective function. The rationale lies in the observation that if the objectives of management were congruent with those of shareholders, or the existing mechanisms were successful in aligning the objectives of the two, no shareholder would have needed the protection of SOX.

Unlike management, shareholders are not a homogenous group. *The Wall Street Journal* (Mandelbrot Benoit B. and Richard L. Hudson. A look at market—moving numbers—literally, July 27, 2004, C1, C6) cites Richard Olsen, a Swiss fund manager and specialist in mathematical finance, who states,

> People aren't rational, and they don't all think alike. Some are quick-trigger speculators who pop in and out of the market hundreds of times a day. Some are corporate treasurers, deliberately buying or selling big contracts to fund a merger or hedge an export risk. Some are central bankers, who trade only occasionally, and at critical moments. Others are long-term investors who buy and hold for months or years.

Some shareholders want the firm to maximize long-term value, while others want the firm to maximize short-term price because they plan on selling in the near future (Hart, 1995a; Ronen and Yaari, 2002).

The evidence suggests that the objective of management differs from those of shareholders for a number of reasons:

- Managers and shareholders have different access to company perks, and at the same time, some of the firm's investment and production decisions inflict personal costs on managers alone;
- The manager's portfolio includes firm-specific human capital that cannot be diversified away;
- The horizon of the manager's decision making is different from the horizon of investors and the firm.

Suppose that you pulled a representative shareholder and made him a CEO. At that moment you gave him the opportunity to enjoy perks that are inaccessible to shareholders, such as the use of the company's airplanes (Yermack, 2006a) and apartments, medical coverage, membership in clubs, and, before SOX, the financing of private consumption at a favorable interest rate.[5] As an anecdotal example, observe the perks of Michael S. Ovitz, who was hired to serve as president of Disney in 1995 and was fired 15 months later with a $140 million severance package:

> According to an internal review sought by Disney in 1997, Mr. Ovitz spent $76,413 of the company's money for limousines and rental cars, $48,305 for a home screening room and $6,500 for Christmas tips. He also charged the company as much as $125 a person for food served at executive meetings at his house, an amount later reduced to $15 as he neared the end of his tenure. The bill for flowers for these breakfasts and dinners for the 14 months tallied $9,535. The company also paid for Mr. Ovitz's subscription to Playboy magazine. (Holson, Laura, M., Investor suit at Disney puts exits in a spotlight. *New York Times*, October 18, 2004, C1)

---

[5] Since December 2006, companies are required to fully disclose perks worth more than $10,000. Commentators expect boards to respond by curbing excessive perks they will be aware of for the first time when the disclosure is made (Nanette Byrnes and Jane Sasseen, Board of hard knocks, *Business Week*, January 22, 2007, pp. 36–39).

Jensen and Meckling (1976), refer to these activities as agency costs. It is easy to see that the manager's consumption of a company's resources is likely to be excessive: the manager enjoys 100% of every dollar of perk, but he bears only a fraction of the cost in proportion to his (much lower) relative equity holding.

Shareholders can increase the cost of such private consumption by designing equity-based compensation (Balsam, 2002): stocks, restricted stocks, and options, and an explicit requirement that managers hold a minimum number of shares. Compensation, however, is not a perfect solution for a number of reasons. One is the presence of contract frictions. For example, limited liability protects managers' compensation from downward risk (Gaver and Gaver, 1998; Leone, Wu, and Zimmerman, 2006; Ronen and Yaari, 2007).[6] That is, the firm may accumulate losses and shareholders may incur losses on their investments, but the manager's compensation may not reflect this. Ronen and Yaari (2007), show that the limited liability of managers may lead shareholders to design contracts that induce pernicious earnings management even when truth-inducing contracts are feasible. Another reason is that shareholders do not design management's compensation directly. The board of directors does. When the board is captured by the manager, he might be paid beyond the optimal

---

[6] Fama (1980), makes two arguments regarding disciplining management to make optimal decisions. The first centers on the labor market, both internal and external. This market puts such a weight on management's reputation that a first-best allocation can be achieved whereby managers receive their due reward. This argument, however, ignores the horizon problem. That is, since the horizon of management's employment within the firm is finite, the marginal value of reputation is likely to decrease with the manager's age. Indeed, the fact that the average top brass is much older than the average entry-level manager has led some scholars to be skeptical regarding the efficiency of reputation as a mechanism to ameliorate the conflict of interests between shareholders and management (Coffee, 2003a). The second argument is that the noise in the outcome of the manager's unobservable effort can be filtered away by reviewing the history of outcomes and resettling the contract in order to pay the manager for his actions or marginal productivity (p. 300). (Resettling is an arrangement whereby at each point the payment is the difference between the total of the optimal wages so far and the total payments actually paid, given the available information. The manager then either pays back excessive wages or gets a higher wage.) As Fama himself notes, there is no guarantee that the statistical properties of the noise that masks the manager's actions allow resettling, so some shirking (and pernicious earnings management) remains possible. Besides, resettling implicitly assumes away limited liability because if the manager has been overpaid, he is supposed to return some of his extra payment. If he has limited liability, such an arrangement is no longer feasible.

level and take unanticipated actions that increase the value of his options by increasing the volatility of the firm's performance (Cohen, Hall, and Viceira, 2000; Huang, 2005; Coles, Daniel, and Naveen, 2006a; Adams, Almeida, and Ferreira, 2005) or reduce his risk by smoothing earnings (Grant, Markarian, and Parbonetti, 2007). Moreover, when compensation is supposed to serve as a commitment mechanism to reconcile the conflicting interests of shareholders and debtholders (John and John, 1993), it will not necessarily maximize expected shareholders' value. Furthermore, since incentives are sensitive to earnings (Bushman and Smith, 2001), compensation motivates the manager to manage earnings, contrary to shareholders' wishes (see the discussion below).[7]

Although Jensen and Meckling (1976), focus on the manager's excessive benefits, another theory of agency costs operates from the perspective that managers bear personal costs in their employment with the firm. We refer here to the principal-agent paradigm, which is discussed in some detail in Part 3 (Harris and Raviv, 1978, 1979; Holmström, 1979; Shavell, 1979; Sappington, 1983, 1991; Grossman and Hart, 1993; Demski, 1994; Christensen and Feltham, 2005; Evans, Kim, and Nagarajan, 2006). The shareholder–manager relationship is characterized by moral hazard. To induce the work-averse, risk-averse manager to exert more effort and not shirk his duty, shareholders must impose risk on him at a higher level than some first-best level. The means is to offer options (Hirshleifer and Suh, 1992; Hemmer, Kim, and Verrecchia, 1999; Feltham and Wu, 2000; Core and Qian, 2001; Jenter, 2001; Lambert and Larcker, 2004). Options impose risk on the manager because they are valuable only if the (volatile) market price of shares has risen when they are exercised (Guay, 1999[8]). Thus, a manager who is reluctant to bear personal cost will still take the right action in order to increase the firm's value and enrich himself in the process.

The research on options revolves around two interrelated questions. The first concerns whether incentives ought to increase or decrease with the riskiness of the outcome. After all, if the outcome is already risky, why would one need more risky incentives to induce the manager to take the desirable actions? On the other hand, the scope for moral hazard is greater for

---

[7] The fact that the market's pressure might have negative consequences for a firm's value has already inspired a strand of literature that examines the effect of the stock market in inducing myopic decision making by managers regarding the firm's long-term investments (see, e.g., Bebchuk and Stole, 1993).

[8] Guay finds that options and not holdings of common stock affect the sensitivity of the manager's wealth to stock price performance. The risk induces managers to make more value-enhancing investments in risky projects.

managers of riskier firms. Hence, as Holmström and Milgrom (1987), and Prendergast (2000), established, it is optimal to reward those managers with greater incentives (see, e.g., the debate between Aggarwal and Samwick, 1999; Core and Guay, 2002a; see also Lambert, 1986; Core and Qian, 2001). Raith (2003), discusses the situation when the volatility of the outcome results from the fierceness of the competition.[9] Raith's result that incentives are positively correlated with the intensity of the competition, however, is controversial, since while some empirical studies find support for such positive correlation (e.g., Cuñat and Guadalupe, 2005), others find either that incentives are negatively related to the number of competitors (Santaló, 2002) or that the support is mixed (e.g., Karuna, 2004).

The second issue concerns the efficiency of options in aligning the manager's incentives with shareholders' objectives (Holmström and Kaplan, 2003, p. 8). Some studies seem to indicate that efficiency is driven by the economic dynamics. Successful firms exhibit a positive association between options and the firm's performance (Agrawal and Mandelker, 1987; Hanlon, Rajgopal, and Shevlin, 2003; Sullivan and Spong, 2004[10]; Aggarwal and Samwick, 2006), but struggling companies exhibit the opposite association (Hall and Leibman, 1998; Core and Guay, 2002b). One reason for the latter finding is that options are a favorite way to provide employees with incentives when firms are already pressed for liquidity (Yermack, 1995; Core and Guay, 2001). Building on the work of Demsetz and Lehn (1985), Himmelberg, Hubbard, and Palia (1999), attempt to pinpoint variables that are related to moral hazard: size, capital intensity, R&D intensity, advertising intensity, cash flow, and investment rate. Further testing leads them to conclude that management ownership and the firm's performance are determined by common firm-specific factors. Hence, an incentive contract can be much simplified without sacrificing efficiency (see the discussion of this work by Zhou, 2001). For further discussion of efficiency of compensation contracts, consult Pavlik, Scott, and Tiessen (1993), Core, Holthausen, and Larcker (1999), Rajgopal and Shevlin

---

[9] See also Hart (1983a), Fershtman and Judd (1987), Scharfstein (1988), and Schmidt (1997).

[10] Sullivan and Spong study 267 banks in the 1990–1994 period, 157 managed by a hired manager and 110 whose top manager is a member of the ownership group with the largest stake in the bank. They find that the banks run by a hired manager have a stronger performance (ROA, return on equity, and ratio of operating income to average assets). The more the wealth of the manager is tied to the bank's performance, the lower the riskiness of the bank as measured by earnings variation, interest rate risk, and bankruptcy.

(2002), Core, Guay, and Larcker (2003), Hanlon, Rajgopal, and Shevlin (2003), Huang (2005), and Grant, Markarian, and Parbonetti (2007).

A related question concerns the effect of SOX on compensation. The answer is not clear. Although Cohen, Dey, and Lys (2005b) and Carter, Lynch, and Zechman (2006), find that the compensation became less risky after SOX (because of an increase in the salary component and a decrease in bonuses), practitioners believe that SOX did not effect much change in compensation. "Executive compensation is perhaps the most significant issue that has shown little change. Despite continued—indeed, mounting—public criticism that executive compensation has been out of line and that the typical board structure for setting executive pay is seldom arm's length and effective, few systemic changes appear to have occurred" (Coglianese and Michael, 2006).

3.1.2.1 Firm-Specific Human Capital in Management's Portfolio

Broadly, management's wealth comprises human capital, the firm's specific financial capital, and other capital that is not related to the firm. Often, the human capital of managers is firm-specific, which implies that managers cannot diversify away risk involved with this portion of capital optimally (e.g., Agrawal and Mandelker, 1987). (In contrast, general human capital can be leveraged in other employment.) This implies that the average manager's tolerance of risk is likely to be lower than that of investors, which results in investment decisions that are too conservative from the shareholders' point of view (Bebchuk and Fershtman, 1994; Nohel and Todd, 2002).[11] Again, the remedy is to design a compensation package that aligns their interests (Balsam, 2002). In the jargon of people in the field, to induce a manager to be more of a risk-taker requires designing compensation with a convex payoff, which is riskier than a linear or concave payoff. The intuition is that a concave compensation formula has a marginally decreasing reward, while a convex schedule has a marginally increasing reward. To ensure the manager the same level of reservation utility, the concave payoff gives him more for low outcomes and less for high outcomes than a convex compensation formula and thus is flatter and less risky (Yaari, 1991, 1993).

Similarly, the manager's total wealth and his attitudes toward risk may also give him preferences regarding risk that are different from those of shareholders (Lambert, Larcker, and Verrecchia, 1991). Core, Guay, and Larcker (2002, p. 39), emphasize the importance of wealth with the

---

[11] For additional decisions wherein managers and shareholders do not see eye to eye, consult Bebchuk and Fershtman (1991, 1993).

following example: "[S]uppose that there are two CEOs who have the same wealth, the same constant relative risk-aversion utility functions, the same marginal product, and the same cost of effort. Each CEO has the same efficient contract. Then one CEO inherits a lot of money, but the second loses all outside wealth in a divorce. ... [B]oth CEOs have incentives to take actions that do not maximize firm's value, the first by working less and the second by taking fewer risks." Options once more can be used to change the manager's risk-taking behavior (e.g., Rajgopal and Shevlin, 2002) and to encourage personally costly investments (Aggarwal and Samwick, 2006).[12] From the earnings management perspective, the important feature of options is that their value depends on the stock price, which implies a motivation to manage earnings to the extent that earnings have an impact on the price.

Another consequence of the extensive use of stock and options is that managers sell their shares. In general, insiders sell more than they buy (Beneish and Vargus, 2002; Hochberg, Newman, and Rierson, 2003).[13] Managers sell most of their exercised options immediately after exercise (Lakonishok and Lee, 2001). Those with large stock holdings sell their stock, obtained either by direct purchase or through the exercise of options (Ofek and Yermack, 2000; Safdar, 2003), and the higher a manager's equity, the higher his volume of sales (Cheng and Warfield, 2005). Ofek and Yermack state,

> Although boards state that they intend stock option and other awards to boost the ownership positions of managers, executives are not likely to have the same goal. Modern portfolio theory predicts that managers receiving additional stock in their firms should sell these shares or equivalently, sell other shares they already own, to diversify

---

[12] Murphy (1999), expresses the concern that options might "overdo" it: "[S]ince the value of options increase[s] with stock-price volatility, executives with options have incentives to engage in riskier investments" (p. 16). Abowd and Kaplan (1999), hold the opposite view. They contend that the riskiness of stock and options induces managers to take fewer risks. For further discussion of the pros and cons of options, consult Hall and Murphy (2002, p. 6), and citations therein.

[13] Hochberg, Newman, and Rierson (2003), comment,

> [O]n average, insiders across all groups sell more than they buy, in terms of unit sales and dollar proceeds, during periods of both aggressive and normal accounting. This is consistent with much of the previous literature on insider trading,.... Firm insiders likely have significant portions of their wealth tied up in the shares of their own firm, and, as a result, are motivated to continually sell their holdings for reasons such as portfolio rebalancing, tax planning, estate planning, and periodic liquidity needs. (p. 16)

away the unsystematic risk associated with concentrating wealth in a single asset. This risk is higher for managers than for ordinary investors because executives already have human capital value correlated with firm performance. (pp. 1367–1368)

We segment our data into subsamples based on whether an executive owns as many shares as those awarded in new grants of stock options or restricted stock.... For higher-ownership executives, we find active selling during years with new option awards,... These sales effectively neutralize much of the incentive impact of high-ownership managers' stock based pay. (p. 1368)[14]

The fact that management sells shares implies that insider trading could be yet another determinant of the demand for earnings management.

3.1.2.2 The Horizon Problem

Another reason for the incongruence in the objective functions of managers and shareholders is their different decision-making horizons. Managers have career concerns that span their entire working career. These concerns imply that managers have to build reputation through the records of their firms' performance, since reputation as a high-quality manager plays a crucial role in drawing lucrative contracts (e.g., Gibbons and Murphy, 1992b; Baber, Kang, and Kumar, 1998; Holmström, 1999) and in the ability to attract directorships in other companies (e.g., Brickley, Coles, and Linck, 1999).

On the one hand, reputation might lead managers to maximize the long-term value of the firm, because if the firm fails they are ousted (see below). On the other hand, reputation might trigger the opposite effect.

---

[14] Safdar (2003), Cheng and Warfield (2005), and others note that the substitution of bonus plans and salaries for stock options in compensation schemes has increased the idiosyncratic exposure of managerial wealth to the firm's stock price.

Kasznik (2003), too, notes the effect of portfolio balancing on sales of stock by corporate insiders:

[M]ore recent studies (e.g., Lakonishok and Lee, 2001; Jeng et al., 2001) find that, while purchases of stock appear to be informative, sales of stock by 16(a) insiders take place primarily for non-informational reasons, and that evidence from the earlier studies are sensitive to the measurement of post-sale abnormal returns, particularly to size, risk, and price momentum factors. Insiders, particularly 16(a) insiders, accumulate large holdings of stock through their compensation plans, and thus, sales of stock are driven mainly by liquidity and portfolio rebalancing needs unrelated to private information. In contrast, purchases of stock are more discretionary and therefore could more likely reflect a desire to exploit private information. (p. 34)

Narayanan (1985), shows that reputation building might induce managers to behave myopically and sacrifice shareholders' value. The dynamic lies in the managers' unknown ability (ability that is crucial to the firm's value). Since managers who are perceived as having higher ability reap higher compensation (see also Malmendier and Tate, 2005), investing in short-term projects that yield higher short-term output thus is preferable in order to generate a signal of greater ability. This argument, however, is likely to apply to managers at the beginning of their tenure. Allgood and Farrell (2003), show that the likelihood that a CEO leaves the firm increases in the first 5 years of his tenure and declines thereafter.

Yet another aspect of the situation is that older managers have shorter expected work horizons, so any impact on their reputation will be smaller. When a manager nears the end of his term, the investment horizon may be longer than his likely remaining tenure with the firm, inducing the manager to take actions that increase short-term earnings at the expense of long-run value.

The horizon issue implies that *turnover* is an important factor in earnings management because an impending departure determines the remaining horizon of the departing CEO and ascending to the CEO's job starts the clock of the incoming CEO. We discuss turnover further below.[15]

Interestingly, the importance of tenure in the conflict of interests between managers and shareholders is corroborated by its effect on the design of the former's incentives. Gibbons and Murphy (1992b), document that on average, an increase of 10 % of shareholder wealth corresponds to a 1.7 % change in cash compensation for CEOs less than 3 years from retirement, but only a 1.3 % change for CEOs more than 3 years from retirement.[16] Clinch and Magliolo (1993), find that the length of their CEOs' tenure influences banks' compensation practices. They divide earnings into three components: earnings from recurrent operating activities, such as earnings from the usual lending function, discretionary non-operating earnings with direct cash flow impact, such as selling the bank's credit card portfolio, and discretionary accounting earnings with no direct cash flow

---

[15] Managers behave myopically for reasons beyond the shorter decision horizon before retirement (Stein, 1988, 1989; Shleifer and Vishney, 1990; Narayanan, 1996; Garvey, Grant, and King, 1997; Bange and De-Bondt, 1998; Bushee, 1998; Behn, Nagy, and Riley, 2002). For the empirical research design, however, turnover provides data where the short-horizon issue is easily detectable.

[16] Although this book is concerned with the U.S. scene, this phenomenon seems to be borderless. For example, Korczak (2004), finds that in the Polish-traded capital market, reputation building is associated with low stock ownership, and entrenchment is associated with higher voting ownership.

impact, such as a settlement of pension plan liabilities through the purchase of annuities. They find that when the tenure is longer, the association between operating earnings and compensation and the association between discretionary accounting earnings with cash flow effect and the compensation are both weaker. Dechow, Huson, and Sloan (1994), examine how restructuring charges affect compensation design because restructuring charges tend to be quite large, and if they affect compensation, management may not carry out the restructuring even when it is value-enhancing. They find that the shorter the CEO's expected horizon, the higher the likelihood that the CEO's compensation will not adjust downward because of the unfavorable effect of restructuring charges on earnings, especially if they are less recurrent. Baber, Kang, and Kumar (1998), study the weight of persistent earnings in management's cash compensation (salary plus bonus). They partition their sample according to whether the CEO is 60 years of age or younger. They find that the coefficient of the product of earnings persistence and the age's binary dummy variable is positive and significant at the 0.05% level. This result indicates that compensation committees assign a greater weight to earnings persistence for CEOs who are closer to retirement age. [Interestingly, the increase in cash compensation for senior CEOs is less than the increase paid to younger ones.]

Another notable source of earnings management behavior is a change in management's stock ownership via a buyout. The arithmetic then is simple. The premium paid to shareholders to induce them to concede to the buyout reduces the wealth of management. Since the price reflects the earnings-generating potential on the basis of the history of earnings, management has incentives to manage earnings downward.

In sum, the conflicting interests of managers and shareholders with respect to the following provide incentives for managing earnings for personal gain:

- Compensation
- Insider trading
- Turnover
- Management buyouts.

3.2 Compensation

In this section, we review the components of a typical compensation package of a CEO and explain how such a package motivates earnings management. The institutional aspect is that the board of directors has the responsibility of designing compensation (see Chap. 5 for further discussion). The board determines six components of compensation: changes in salary, short-term cash and stock bonuses, long-term bonuses, grants of stock options or stock appreciation rights (SAR), grants of performance units, and grants of restricted stock. The CEO can sit in on the deliberations of the compensation committee but cannot be a member if the firm wishes to take advantage of IRS Rule 162(m), which allows the firm to treat the CEO's incentive payments as a deductible expense. De facto, however, management is involved in the design of its compensation package. Murphy (1999), describes the typical process:

> Although all major decisions related to top-level pay are passed through this committee, the committee rarely conducts market studies of competitive pay levels or initiates or proposes new incentive plans, and only seldom retains its own compensation experts. Rather, initial recommendations for pay levels and new incentive plans typically emanate from the company's human resource department, often working in conjunction with outside accountants and compensation consultants. **These recommendations are usually sent to top managers for approval and revision** before being delivered to the compensation committee for consideration.... The committee either accepts the recommendations or sends them back for revision. If accepted, the committee passes its recommendations for the approval of the full board of directors. (p. 2509, emphasis added)[17]

3.2.1 The Compensation Package

The basic package[18] for a CEO contains a formula that relates payment of cash, stock, and options to performance measures, where performance

---

[17] Although Murphy expresses his trust in the good intentions of the compensation committee because his contacts with such directors convey that directors lean toward managers only when they face two options that are equal from the firm's perspective, other researchers believe that executives use their power to influence their own pay to extract rents at the expense of shareholders (see the legal approach in Chap. 1). Bebchuk, Fried, and Walker (2002), for example, claim that rent extraction may lead to the use of inefficient pay arrangements that provide suboptimal incentives, thereby hurting shareholders. Zingales (1998), adopts the perspective that contracting is optimal, but unanticipated shocks give temporary power to the manager at the expense of shareholders, who correct the inefficiency in the long run.

[18] We restrict attention to compensation during the tenure of the manager. We do not consider his severance pay, known as golden parachute (e.g., Yermack, 2006b), and how it affects incentives to manage earnings (Kedia and Philippon, 2005).

measures include stock returns and earnings (Healy, 1985; Jensen and Murphy, 1990a; Gaver, Gaver, and Austin, 1995; Ely, 1991; Dechow, Huson, and Sloan, 1994; Murphy 1999; Jensen, Murphy, and Wruck, 2004). Key performance measures that are directly tied to earnings and earnings components are the following:

- Accounting returns
- Sales revenue
- Net interest income
- A balanced scorecard index of multiple indicators
- Economic Value Added (EVA).

This list is not exhaustive, and companies frequently employ multiple performance standards, either additively or multiplicatively. Ely (1991), states,

> It might seem that the odds are in favor of the accounting variables because there are three of them to one return variable. But that is one of the strengths of the accounting system. There are many accounting variables and each one might convey different information. It should not be surprising that, in some circumstances, a combination of accounting variables can provide more explanatory power than one return measure which aggregates all of this information. (footnote 22, p. 57)

To understand why earnings and stock returns are valuable in the context of the principal-agent relationships between shareholders and managers, denote accounting earnings and price by x and p, respectively; the utility function of shareholders by W; the utility function of the manager over monetary compensation, s, by U; and the manager's disutility over effort, e, by G. Then, if the manager's reservation utility obtained by an alternative job is u_0 and the manager's optimal effort (the level of effort that is chosen in equilibrium) is e^*, the principal solves the following optimization program:

Max EV(.)
s,e
s.t.
$EU(s(p,x)) - G(e) \geq u_0.$ (IR)
$e^* \in$ argmax $EU(s(p,x)) - G(e),$ (IC)
       $e \geq 0.$

Solving this program when the joint distribution of price, p, and earnings, x, is denoted by $f(p,x)$, and the notations λ and μ are assigned to the shadow prices (Lagrange multipliers) of the first and second constraints, respectively, yields the following pointwise equilibrium condition:

$$\text{For each} <p,x>, \quad \frac{W'}{U'} = \lambda + \mu \frac{f_e(p,x|e)}{f(p,x|e)}. \quad {}^{19}$$

$$(3.1)$$

The first-order conditions reveal that the contract depends on the information content of the signals p and x regarding the manager's unobservable effort (as captured by the fraction on the right-hand side). If the information content in either signal is already contained in the other, this signal is not valuable.[20] In other words, the value of each signal depends on how much it reveals about the effort relative to the other available signal. Holmström (1979), dubbed the condition that a signal is included in the contract only if it contains new marginal information the "informativeness condition." For further elaboration on this point, consult Christensen and Feltham (2005).

The application of the theory to the signals of earnings and market price is clear. If each signal conveys new information about the CEO's effort, then both ought to be incorporated into the compensation contract (Lambert and Larcker, 1987; Bushman and Indjejikian, 1993; Holmström and Tirole, 1993; Kim and Suh, 1993; Sloan, 1993; Feltham and Xie, 1994; Feltham and Wu, 2000; Core, Guay, and Verrecchia, 2003; Bolton, Scheinkman, and Xiong, 2006). Furthermore, when the distribution function of stochastic earnings is normal, the relative weight of each signal is proportional to its relative marginal informativeness concerning the unobservable effort (Lambert and Larcker, 1987; Banker and Datar, 1989; Bushman and Indjejikian, 1993; Kim and Suh, 1993; Sloan, 1993; Baiman and Verrecchia, 1995; Core, Guay, and Verrecchia, 2003). This implies that as the sensitivity of a performance measure to the agent's action increases, its weight in the compensation increases as well. When the agent's action space is multidimensional, however, this relationship may

---

[19] Note that the distribution function of price and earnings depends on the manager's effort, as the manager chooses the firm's technology. Since we are interested in giving just a taste of the theoretical arguments, we refer the reader to the analytical literature for finer regularity conditions and technicalities.

[20] Technically, suppose that the information content of earnings is fully contained in the price; i.e., $f(p,x|e) = f(p|e) * f(p,x)$. Then, $f_e(p,x|e) = f_e(p|e) * f(p,x)$, and $\frac{W'}{U'} = \lambda + \mu \frac{f_e(p,x|e)}{f(p,x|e)} = \lambda + \mu \frac{f_e(p|e)}{f(p|e)}$. The first-order conditions reveal that earnings are redundant for contracting.

break down even if the measure under scrutiny is perfectly congruent with the firm's outcome (Datar, Kulp, and Lambert, 2001).[21]

Given the importance of earnings to the topic of this book, it is worthwhile noting that another use of the informativeness argument is made in the study of the usefulness of earnings and the components of earnings: Gaver and Gaver (1993), and Baber, Janakiraman, and Kang (1996), find that the weight assigned to accounting earnings relative to security returns decreases when firms are growth firms that make more investments (Gaver and Gaver) or when investment opportunities are substantial components of firm value (Baber, Janakiraman, and Kang). The Theory is that the price reflects information on future earnings that provide a valuable signal on effort exerted in investment decisions because of the multi-period consequences of the effort. Clinch and Magliolo (1993), analyze the link between earnings and cash compensation of CEOs of bank holding companies. As discussed above, they divide earnings into several categories: earnings from recurrent operating activities, discretionary non-operating earnings that have cash-flow implications, and discretionary accounting earnings that do not have cash-flow consequences. They find a link between cash compensation and the first two types only. Their interpretation is that discretionary transactions that do not involve cash flows provide a less reliable performance measure. Dechow, Huson, and Sloan (1994), find that restructuring charges are excluded from calculating the earnings as a basis for contracting. Natarajan (1996), uses this theory to explain his findings that accruals and cash from operations have different weights in the compensation package. Working capital from operations has incremental explanatory power for cash compensation when added to earnings. Kren and Leauby (2001), explore the effect of reductions in non-cash earnings caused by firms' adopting FAS 106—recognition of postretirement benefits when the liability arises instead of when the cash is actually paid—on the compensation of CEOs. They find that in firms that responded to the newly reported expense by cutting postretirement benefits (which effectively transfer wealth from employees to shareholders) the mangers were rewarded. In other firms, compensation did not reflect the decline in earnings.[22]

---

[21] Empirical support for this theory is readily available (Sloan, 1993; Yermack, 1995; Clinch and Magliolo, 1993; Baber, Janakiraman, and Kang, 1996; Natarajan, 1996; Bryan, Hwang, and Lilien, 2000; Core, Guay, and Verrecchia, 2003; Engel, Hayes, and Wang, 2003; Shin, 2004).

[22] For a study that finds that earnings reported in the wake of a change in accounting method affect compensation, consult Healy, Kang, and Palepu (1987). Their result corroborates our discussion in Chap. 1; they observe that earnings are

There are two main reasons why earnings and stock price provide different signals on management's effort. First, earnings may lag unobservable actions because of the artificial construct of the periodicity principle in accounting, which implies that effort can affect earnings in more than a single accounting period. That is, effort may entail making investment decisions in period 0 that generate economic earnings (and reported earnings) in that period as well as in future periods, period $1,2,..,N$. In contrast, since the stock price equals the total of current and discounted future free cash flows, the price contains expectations of yet unrealized (and certainly unreported) future earnings. For example, Lehn and Zhao (2004), report that the market's response to the announcement of an acquisition predicts whether it will be value-enhancing or value-decreasing. A related issue is that the stock price contains expectations of yet undelivered performance (Barclay, Gode, and Kothari, 2000; Leone, Wu, and Zimmerman, 2006). DeAngelo (1998b), for example, finds that dissident shareholders who blame management for poor performance tend not to cite market price because the market price increases in response to expectations that incumbent management will improve performance or be replaced by more competent leadership.

Second, accounting measurement issues may confound the link between effort and the firm's performance. As an example, consider the conservatism principle's asymmetric recognition of revenues and expenses. (For further discussion of measurement issues, consult Basu, 1997, and Barclay, Gode, and Kothari, 2000).

3.2.2 Cash Compensation: Salary and Bonus

Cash compensation comprises base salary and bonuses. The base salary is a fixed payment that provides management with a certain degree of insurance, since compensation cannot fall below this base. A bonus, on the other hand, is conditional on achieving a performance target. Both elements are sensitive to the firm's size and growth (Ittner, Larcker, and Rajan, 1997; Prendergast, 2002; Indjejikian and Nanda, 2002; Nagar, 2002). In response to public outcry at exorbitant CEO salaries, section 162(m) of the Internal Revenue Code was introduced in 1993. This tax rule specifies that compensation that exceeds one million dollars for each of the highest paid executives is tax deductible for the firm only if it is "performance based,"

---

important because contracts do not perfectly adjust to new earnings numbers even though they measure the same economic performance.

such as bonuses, stock grants and stock options.[23] As a result, salaries declined and bonuses and equity-based compensation increased (Perry and Zenner, 2001), a change that enhances incentives to manage earnings.

The way a bonus is calculated has changed over time, from being a discretionary decision of the board of directors to being set as a "budget-based" target.[24] As an example of the latter, consider a "80/120 plan" (Murphy, 1999, Figure 5). At the beginning of the year, a target is set. At the end of the year, no bonus is paid unless performance exceeds 80% of the performance standard, and the maximum bonus obtains when performance reaches 120% of the performance standard. The lower and upper thresholds can vary by firm and with time. The second popular plan is a hybrid that involves setting a "budget-based" target for each employee in the bonus pool (a higher rank gives the employee a higher bonus percentage) and adding it up to form a "bonus pool." At the end of the year, the board uses discretion to adjust the actual size of the bonus pool, which cascades to all parties covered by the plan.

---

[23] To enjoy the tax deduction, firms are required to qualify their bonus plan. Incentives must satisfy the following conditions:

1. The performance goals are determined by a compensation committee comprising solely two or more outside directors.
2. The performance goals under which the remuneration is to be paid are disclosed to the shareholders and approved by a majority vote.
3. Before any payment of such remuneration, the compensation committee certifies that the performance goals and other material terms were satisfied.

Reitenga, Buchheit, Yin, and Baker (2002), and Balsam and Yin (2005), note that some firms elect not to qualify the bonus plan, forgoing the tax benefit. Balsam and Yin blame the reluctance to fully save taxes on contracting costs:

> [T]he firm, or more importantly, the decision makers in the firm, trade off the benefits of preserving deductions against the costs of doing so. The benefits of preserving deductions include the tax savings, ..., as well as a reduction in the political costs of the executive and firm. The costs include the costs of rewriting executive compensation contracts, costs of seeking shareholder approval of performance-based compensation plans, the adverse effect on firm value of the changed incentives of the executives involved, and paying additional compensation to compensate those executives for additional risk. (p. 305)

[24] Murphy (1999), describes executive bonus plans based on a proprietary survey of 177 plans collected by a large compensation consulting firm. Most companies choose performance standards based on the business plan or budget, or on prior-year performance; only 11% of the surveyed companies report that they rely heavily on standards that are determined by industry performance or other external determinants.

3.2.3 Managing Salary

Although salary does not change within a given year, it changes between years in response to the level of satisfaction with the manager's performance. The relative weight of salary in the compensation package has declined over the years,[25] but it is still important. The main reason is that salary affects other payments, such as the bonus (Holthausen, Larcker, and Sloan, 1995; Murphy, 1999) and pension. Murphy (1999), gives the following account:

> Executives devote substantial attention to the salary-determination process, … First, base salaries are a key component of executive employment contracts (which typically guarantee minimum increases in base salaries for the subsequent five years). Second, since base salaries represent "fixed component" in executive contracts, risk-averse executives will naturally prefer a dollar increase in base salary to a dollar increase in "target" bonus or variable compensation. Finally, most components of compensation are measured relative to base salary levels. Target bonuses, for example, are typically expressed as a percentage of base salary, while option grants are expressed as a multiple base salary. Defined pension benefits and severance arrangements also depend on salary levels. Consequently, each dollar increase in base salary has positive repercussions on many other compensation components. (p. 2494)

One possible approach for managers who seek to increase their salaries is to influence the board to lower the benchmark. The intertemporal relationship between current performance and future benchmarks has long been recognized as the "ratchet effect": a good performance in a given year is "punished" in the following year because it raises the expected benchmark performance, which makes it harder to achieve a target in the future (Milgrom and Roberts, 1992). We have not encountered a study that analyzes the ratchet effect on salary per se, but Sheikh (2001), finds evidence that is consistent with it. His study, however, does not focus on salary. Shih studies bonuses because they allow him to construct a sample that distinguishes between ratchet- and non-ratchet firms.[26] We speculate that

---

[25] This statement is qualified, as the data used in empirical research on this phenomenon predates the bursting of the Internet bubble in 2000.

[26] The sample is constructed as follows: Ratchet firms are firms who base bonus awards on year-to-year growth, or on an increase in sales or EPS, or on an improvement in operating profits. Non-ratchet firms are firms who base bonus awards on the performance of the industry or market peer firms, or on fixed standards, such as a prespecified return on assets. Using the findings of Indjejikian and Nanda (1999), who establish that the pay under an optimal principal-agent contract in the presence of ratcheting exhibits higher sensitivity to

an incoming CEO has incentives to lower the benchmark by decreasing income in the first year of his tenure (see the discussion on turnover below). Thereafter, however, the situation is murky: The performance of a given year, say year t, earns an increase if it is better than the previous year, year $t-1$, at the sacrifice of making the bar of the following year, $t+1$, higher.

Gao and Shrieves (2002), examine the association of the components of the compensation package with the intensity of earnings management (measured by the absolute value of current discretionary accruals scaled by size of assets; see the discussion in Chap. 10 for the derivation of discretionary accruals). They find that the intensity of earnings management is negatively associated with salary and positively associated with stock options and bonuses. As their table 4 indicates, the negative effect of salary is about eight (four) times larger in absolute value than the effect of bonuses when controls for capital structure and size are excluded from (included in) the regression. Erickson, Hanlon, and Maydew (2004), study 50 firms that were accused of accounting fraud by the SEC during the period from January 1996 to November 2003. They find that salary is negatively associated with the likelihood of being accused of fraud.

So far, then, it seems that salary takes the edge from the motivation to engage in pernicious earnings management. At the same time, one wonders whether salary also mitigates income-increasing earnings management. That is, salary may induce hoarding of accruals that will enable managers to present better performance in the future, an effect that is exacerbated by the ratchet effect.

3.2.4 Managing Bonuses[27]

Healy (1985), was among the first to link earnings management to bonuses. He attributed to managers lexicographic preferences, wherein

---

performance, Sheikh provides evidence that is consistent with ratcheting. The pay-performance sensitivity is higher in ratcheting firms when the performance measure is stock return.

There is no difference, however, when the performance measure is return on assets. A possible explanation for the conflicting results is that the performance of the ratchet firms is higher. The median ROA for ratchet firms is 7.10 % compared to a median ROA of 3.91 % for non-ratchet firms.

[27] We discuss annual bonuses. However, companies also give their managers long-term incentive plans that are based on rolling average multi-year cumulative performance (3–5 years), which are constructed like the annual bonus plan. For data on establishing a long-term incentive plan in 1996, consult Murphy (1999).

maximization of the current bonus takes priority over maximization of future compensation. Fig.3.1 depicts a standard bonus schedule.

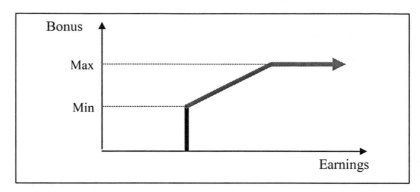

Fig. 3.1 A bonus plan

When the economic earnings yield a bonus that falls between the minimum and the maximum (the "incentive zone"), the manager can increase his current payoff by inflating the accounting earnings. When economic earnings either already yield the maximum bonus or are so low that the manager cannot earn a bonus by inflating earnings, the manager has incentives to hoard reported income for future use by taking measures to deflate the report (i.e., to report less than the economic or objective earnings).[28]

Subsequent researchers do not find that managers "take a bath" when performance is too low (Gaver, Gaver, and Austin, 1995; Holthausen, Larcker, and Sloan, 1995; Reitenga, Buchheit, Yin, and Baker, 2002). On the contrary, they find smoothing. That is, when earnings are low, managers prefer income-increasing behavior. Before concluding that Healy's result may be a consequence of the way Healy measures earnings management (see Chap. 9), note that these studies examine different sample periods and that this difference matters because of the shift in the design of bonuses, as discussed above. Yet some do, however, find that managers "hoard" reported outcome when their performance exceeds the maximum performance measure that still pays a bonus (Gaver, Gaver, and Austin,

---

[28] In Chap. 5, we make the link between governance and earnings management. Governance includes the design of compensation by the board of directors, which is the organ that governs the firm on behalf of shareholders. It is little wonder, then, that many studies find a positive association between the quality of the governance and the level of compensation. Healy's findings can also be an example of the link between poor governance and compensation-related earnings management (see DeAngelo, 1988b).

1995; Holthausen, Larcker, and Sloan, 1995; Guidry, Leone, and Rock, 1999).[29]

It is notable that some studies provide evidence on earnings management induced by bonus considerations when the bonus is a control variable in a regression that studies a related phenomenon. Barton (2001), for example, analyzes the trade-off between derivatives and discretionary accruals as means to smooth out the volatility of earnings. He uses bonuses, stock, and options as control variables proxying the manager's attitude toward risk, which affects his taste for reducing the firm's riskiness by hedging derivatives. Barton is not concerned with the behavior at the extremes (maximum and minimum bonuses). He shows that the coefficient in a regression where the discretionary accruals are the dependent variables and the bonus is one of the independent variables is positive and significant at the 0.01 level (tables 5 and 6).

Indirect support for Healy's bonus hypothesis is provided by Lin and Shih (2002), who study discretionary accruals in the quarterly earnings of 513 Compustat firms for the 1989–1993 period. They find that the time-series behavior of the average discretionary accruals over all firms along their 20 quarters has a U shape: When economic conditions are either poor or strong (mild), the average accruals are negative (positive). They note, "There is evidence that earnings reserves accumulated by firms during the recession were released later strategically, in a pattern consistent with bonus maximization in the long run" (p. 3).

Managers can also manipulate earnings by other means, such as by restructuring transactions (see Chap. 2). Marquardt and Wiedman (2005), find a positive association between a cash bonus (measured as the ratio of the cash bonus to the total cash payment) and the likelihood that a firm issues *contingent* convertible bonds. This decision affects the performance measure of diluted earnings per share (EPS), since by SFAS 128 contingent convertible bonds do not enter into the calculation of diluted EPS.

Also of interest is whether long-term bonus plans exacerbate or alleviate earnings management. Richardson and Waegelein (2002), analyze the earnings management activity of firms that adopt such a long-term plan in addition to a short-term bonus plan. Their findings indicate that the long-term plan both mitigates earnings management and leads to higher annual returns.

---

[29] The connection between non-linear pay-for-performance incentive systems and misrepresentation and manipulation is also noted by Jensen (2001), in his criticism of the traditional budgeting process.

An interesting question is what effect SOX has on bonuses and on earnings management induced by bonuses. Carter, Lynch, and Zechman (2006), examine the association between bonus and earnings management between 1996 and 2004. They show that before SOX, aggressive earnings management increased bonuses disproportionately, while conservative earnings management was not penalized. After SOX, however, they find the reverse pattern: the premium for income-increasing accruals has been eliminated, and a penalty has been imposed on income-decreasing discretionary accruals.

3.2.5 More on Managing Cash Compensation

Several empirical studies analyze cash compensation without distinguishing between components of cash compensation. Balsam (1998) studies 3,439 firm/year observations of Compustat firms that appear in Forbes Compensation Survey during 1980–1993. He finds that although firms use discretionary accruals to achieve earnings goals, only positive discretionary accruals are significantly associated with CEO cash compensation. He, Srinidhi, Su, and Gul (2003), analyze a sample of 7,246 firm-year observations of U.S. corporations during 1992–2001 and find that CEOs are more likely to cut R&D expenditures to avoid decreases in reported earnings when the cash portion of their compensation is greater than the stock portion and when the proportion of cash has increased over time.

3.2.6 Stock and Options

Stock and options have formed a major component of compensation packages in recent years (Hall and Liebman, 1998; Murphy, 1999; Bushman and Smith, 2001; Hall and Murphy, 2002; Gao and Shrieves, 2002; Holmström and Kaplan, 2003;[30] Jensen, Murphy, and Wruck, 2004; and others).

---

[30] In contrast to the view that criticizes the exorbitant payments to executives, Holmström and Kaplan, 2003 observe,

> [I]t would be a mistake to condemn the entire system based on a few cases. That such cases are far from representative can be seen from the pronounced skew[ness] in the distribution of CEO incomes. In 2001, for example, the same year the top ten U.S. CEOs received average option grants of $170 million, the median value of total compensation for CEOs of S&P 500 companies was about $7 million. Thus, U.S. executive pay may not be quite the runaway train that has been portrayed in the press. (p. 14)

Stock-based compensation comes in a variety of forms: stock grants; restricted stock grants, which are shares that cannot be sold before a minimum time with the firm elapses or the firm reaches a performance goal; phantom stocks and stock appreciation rights (SAR), which mimic stock (and option) grants by tying compensation to share prices without actually issuing share certificates; and performance units, which offer the right to receive shares of common stock (or cash, or a combination of shares and cash) when the manager reaches specified performance goals.

An option is different from a share because the employee must pay an up-front fee in order to exercise it,[31] and there is no guarantee that an option will be exercised because the exercise is profitable only when the share price exceeds the exercise price.[32]

Grants have to be approved by the board of directors. It seems that there are two common ways to arrive at the number of options (Hall, 1999; Walker, 2006). One allocates a fixed amount of options over several years. In the other, the compensation committee determines the number of options by dividing optimal incentives by the value of a single option (that is, if optimal incentives are $100,000 and the value of an option is 25 cents, 400,000 grants are awarded). The value is usually calculated by the Black-Scholes formula, which depends on the strike price, the share price at the grant date, the implied volatility of the stock price (which may differ from the actual volatility), the option's time to maturity (adapted to mean the time when the option can be exercised), the dividend yield, and the risk-free rate.

Fig. 3.2 depicts the main events in the life cycle of an option with four vesting periods and the events at each stage in the cycle that might prompt earnings management and other manipulation phenomena.

---

[31] Feltham and Wu (2001), observe that stock is equivalent to exercisable options with a zero exercise price (in a setting where time does not factor into the utility function of managers and shareholders). They model the trade-off between options and stock in a principal-agent game between shareholders and managers. They show that stock is preferable to options because the higher the exercise price, the greater the number of options that must be granted to achieve a desirable level of incentive.

[32] Stock appreciation rights (SAR) are similar to option grants, because the award is earned only if the stock price appreciates. The date that the SAR is earned is fixed, however, while an option's exercise date is at the discretion of the option holder subject to the terms of the grant (see Feltham and Wu, 2000).

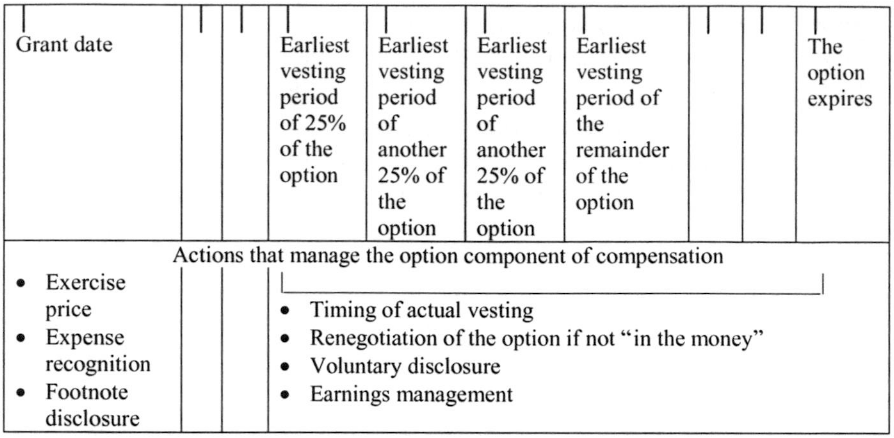

Grant date			Earliest vesting period of 25% of the option	Earliest vesting period of another 25% of the option	Earliest vesting period of another 25% of the option	Earliest vesting period of the remainder of the option			The option expires
Actions that manage the option component of compensation									
• Exercise price • Expense recognition • Footnote disclosure			• Timing of actual vesting • Renegotiation of the option if not "in the money" • Voluntary disclosure • Earnings management						

Fig. 3.2 Manipulation activities during the life- cycle of an option

An option grant specifies the exercise price to be paid when the option is converted into shares, the earliest exercise dates, which mark the vesting period, and an expiration date. In response to tax rules, the exercise price equals the share price at the grant date; i.e., the grant is "at the money." The reason is that if the option were exercised at the grant date, its value to the grantholder is zero. Option grants are intended to induce managers to make value-increasing decisions, as the manager will then make a gain that equals the difference between the share price and the exercise price times the number of shares. The accounting treatment of options has shifted from the concept of zero intrinsic value of at-the-money grants to recognizing that from the firm's perspective the option represents compensation expense. Even if the grant is at the money, the firm could sell the option to outside investors for cash (Jensen, Murphy, and Wruck, 2004). As noted above, the Black-Scholes formula is now used to calculate the compensation expense.

In general, employees' options are neither immediately exercisable nor tradable (short-selling is also forbidden). Murphy (1999), reports that the usual time span between grant and exercise is at least 3 years and hardly ever more than 5 years.[33] In addition, leaving the firm usually results in forfeiture of the options. Given our interest in management alone, it is worth noting that more often than not, top management gets similar grants

---

[33] Tax law sets a minimum period between the grant date and vesting period in order for the grant to qualify for the favorable tax treatment of an incentives plan. Since the purpose of grants is to retain talent, firms prefer to extend the time to vest beyond the minimum period specified in tax rules.

to those awarded to all employees but their awards are much larger. For example, Narayanan and Seyhun (2005) (table 2B) report that about 22% of the grants in their sample of 605 grants awarded between 1992 and 2002 were awarded to the five executives with the highest pay.

In our diagram, options are exercisable in predetermined portions over the first 4 years of the vesting period. Although a vesting date allows exercise of the options, the actual timing and financing of the exercise are at the discretion of the owner of the options (in general, he obtains financing by selling the new shares). In reality, options often are exercised on the day the vesting period starts. Hall and Murphy (2002), explain this phenomenon by the fact that the value of an option with restrictions on its tradability to risk-averse employees is lower than the value of a tradable, unrestricted option.

Clearly, if the market price is lower than the exercise price—the option is not "in the money," so the option will not be exercised. This poses an interesting dilemma, because on the one hand, if the market price has not increased beyond the grant date, the employee did not make the "right" decisions, and he should be penalized by having worthless options. On the other hand, when the stock market is bullish on the grant date and bearish during the vesting period, the exercise price is higher than the share price for reasons beyond the employee's control, which calls for fine-tuning the exercise price. The empirical evidence suggests that repricing is both a political decision and an accounting decision. It is a political decision because it is more likely to take place when the CEO is a member of the compensation committee and when the firm is doing poorly (Brenner, Sundaram, and Yermack, 2000; Carter and Lynch, 2001), and when governance is poor (Ferri, 2004, 2005). In a later study, Chidambaran and Prabhala (2003), find support for the theory that the economic motivation to use options to retain employees mitigates the political motivation because 40% of rapidly growing firms that repriced options after a sudden shock to growth and profitability did not reprice the CEO's compensation. (For further discussion, consult Core, Guay, and Larcker, 2003; Ferri, 2004, 2005.) Since March 2000, repricing is also an accounting decision. Before 2005, companies did not record a compensation expense for options that were either "at the money" or "out of the money" if the grants had fixed terms. Since March 2000, the FASB has required companies that reprice to recognize a compensation expense, since the grant no longer complies with the condition of fixed grant terms. This charge can be avoided by retiring old options and issuing new ones after 6 months and a day. We draw attention to the fact that repricing is economically (if not accounting-wise) costly to the firm, because the unknown exercise price (which is usually the stock price at closing on the grant date) imposes risk on the risk-averse employees. (For a further discussion, consult Jensen, Murphy, and Wruck, 2004, pp. 41-42.) Coles, Hertzel, and Kalpathy (2006), show that firms manage earnings downward before new issues of options and that the market anticipates it.

3.2.7 Equity Holdings and Earnings Management

Research on equity-based compensation focuses on the total wealth generated by stock and option grants.[34] The underlying assumption is that managers' utility increases in the value of their equity holdings, which is equivalent to the price per share times the number of shares and options expressed as shares equivalent.

Given our discussion of the ratchet effect above, it is easy to see that equity-based compensation provides conflicting incentives to manage earnings. On the one hand, the higher the market price, the higher the value of one's holdings. Hence, short-horizon earnings management aimed at inflating earnings is optimal. On the other hand, the higher the market price, the more difficult it is to earn a raise in the future (the ratchet effect). Hence, long-horizon earnings management ought to aim at deflating earnings. The consensus seems to be that equity-based compensation has a short-term perspective. O'Connell (2004), states,

> [T]hese remuneration systems are so imperfect that they do not manage to align the interests of management with shareholders… Rather, in a corporate environment whereby CEOs have average tenure of around 4 years, managers seek to appease the market through various devices that ensure rising short-term stock prices. These devices include aggressive earnings management practices to ensure steadily rising reported earnings that appease stock analysts' forecasts…. (p. 736)

Overall, the research supports the existence of earnings management that is intended to inflate earnings.[35] Gao and Shrieves (2002), find that, in

---

[34] Murphy (1999), reports that approximately 28% of the S&P 500 firms granted restricted stock to their CEOs in 1996; these grants accounted for an average of 6.1% of total compensation (and 22% of the compensation for CEOs receiving grants). Like options, restricted shares are not traded right away and can be forfeited under certain conditions.

[35] It seems that a meaningful discussion of these opposing incentives requires an examination of the patterns of insider trading. Cheng and Warfield (2005), for example, find that managers with higher equity (in their 1993–2000 sample) have higher net sales in subsequent periods, where equity is defined as the total of option grants, unexercisable options, exercisable options, restricted stock grants, and stock ownership. Because higher share prices make for more profit-

contrast to salary, the size of stock options and bonuses is positively related to the intensity of earnings management, as measured by the absolute
value of current discretionary accruals scaled by size of assets. Burns and
Kedia (2006), examine 215 firms that restated earnings between 1994 and
2001 because their financial statements were inconsistent with GAAP.
They find a positive association between restatement and stock option
compensation. (The association is mitigated by offering the manager long-
term incentive plans that promote increasing long-term shareholders'
value.) On average, a CEO of a company that restated earnings held options whose value changed by $567,802 for 1% change in stock price as
compared to $263,595 for a CEO of a non-restating firm. Cohen, Dey, and
Lys (2005a), reveal a positive association between earnings management
and options, where they measure earnings management as a score of a few
variables (see Part 4).

Denis, Hanouna, and Sarin (2006), and Erickson, Hanlon, and Maydew
(2006) find that the likelihood of being accused of fraud increases in the
amount of stock-based compensation, in the percentage of total executive
compensation that is stock-based (in contrast to salary), and in the sensitivity
of executives' stock-based wealth to changes in the stock price.

Bauman, Braswell, and Shaw (2006), offer an exception to these findings. They conjecture that stock options increase the pressure on managers
to meet the market's expectations. Studying a sample of S&P 1,500 firms
between 1992 and 2002, they find that firms whose managers are rewarded
with more stock options meet expectations by guiding expectations down
rather than by inflating reported earnings. In contrast, Bauman and Shaw
(2006), show that a greater volume of stock options in compensation plans
increases the chance that firms meet analysts' forecasts by a small amount
(between zero and one penny per share). See Chap. 5 for a discussion of
the Meeting or Beating Expectations phenomenon.

A related question concerns whether this earnings management is beneficial or pernicious. It seems that the answer to this question is case-
specific. Warfield, Wild, Wild (1995), note a positive association between
stock ownership and the earnings content of stock returns. Behn, Nagy,
and Riley (2002), find that a higher level of stock ownership is associated
with improvements in the usefulness of earnings and with reductions in the
magnitude of discretionary accrual adjustments, manipulation of advertising expenditures, and, to a lesser extent, research and development investments. Bizjak, Brickley, and Coles (1993), investigate how concern for
the current stock price may motivate managers to use investments to signal

---

able sales, managers might take actions to manage the share price through earnings management.

firm's value. They show that firms with high information asymmetries favor contracts that focus on long-run stock returns (current and future) over contracts that focus on near-term stock returns alone.

In contrast, there is evidence of pernicious earnings management in firms that committed fraud. Johnson, Ryan, and Tian (2003), and Erickson, Hanlon, and Maydew (2006), collect a sample of firms that were accused of fraud from the Accounting and Auditing Enforcement Releases (AAER) of the SEC. Johnson, Ryan, and Tian find that executives at fraud firms face significantly greater stock and option payoffs from share price increases than executives at matched "innocent" firms. The median executive at a fraud firm has financial incentives that are 51% greater than those of the median executive at an innocent firm. In dollar terms, a 1% increase in firm value increases executive compensation at fraud firms by approximately $58,844 more than at control firms. Erickson, Hanlon, and Maydew observe that an increase of one standard deviation in the proportion of compensation that is stock-based increases the probability of an accounting fraud by about 68%.

3.2.8 Options and Earnings Management

De facto, options are a substantial part of equity-based compensation. Figure 3 in Jensen, Murphy, and Wruck (2004), shows the increase in the weight of options in the average CEO's pay from 1992 to 2002 when pay is measured in inflation-adjusted 2002 dollars (the grant-date value of the options is determined by the Black-Scholes formula). The weight increased from 24% in 1992's $2.7 million average pay package to almost half of the average pay package in the 1999–2002 period (1999: 47% of $10 million; 2000: 49% of $14 million; 2001: 54% of $12.9 million; 2002: 47% of $9.4 million). Safdar (2003), who examines 4,273 option exercise events in 2,116 firms between 1991 and 1998, comments, "A stylized fact from the ExecuComp database is that option ownership comprises the majority of equity exposure of a firm's CEO in firms with stock option plans. The average number of options owned by a CEO in such firms outnumbers the ownership of common stock by nine to one… "(p. 2).

We restrict our attention to the link between options and earnings management. The fact that options induce earnings management has not escaped the attention of regulators. Arthur Levitt, the former SEC chairman, claims in his 2002 book:

> The use of stock options soon mushroomed,… the options craze created an environment that rewarded executives for managing the share price, not for managing the business. Options gave executives

strong incentives to use accounting tricks to boost the share price on which their compensation depended. (p. 111)

Several studies suggest a connection (e.g., Elitzur and Yaari, 1995; Burns and Kedia, 2006; Efendi, Srivastava, and Swanson, 2006; Kadan and Yang, 2006; McAnally, Srivastava, and Weaver, 2006; Peng and Roell, 2006). Others make this link directly. We here follow those studies in a discussion of the life cycle of an option.

3.2.9 Grant Date

Because the commonly official exercise price equals the share price on the grant date, managers have incentives to take actions that reduce the stock price. Depressing the market price on the grant date increases the difference between the value of the stock when the option is exercised and the cost to exercise. Prior research has uncovered a few means to achieve this goal, including the following: timing grants (Yermack, 1997); repricing the options before a quarter with favorable news and after a quarter with unfavorable news (Callaghan, Saly, and Subramaniam, 2004; Ferri, 2004, 2005); leaking price-decreasing disclosures before the grant date (Chauvin and Shenoy, 2001); deferring the release of good news and bringing forward the release of bad news (Aboody and Kasznik, 2000); managing accruals and preannouncements (Baker, Collins, and Reitenga, 2003[36]); managing accruals (Balsam, Chen, and Sankaraguruswamy, 2003); and specifying an official grant date that is before the true grant date (backdating) or after the true grant date (forward-dating) in order to lower the exercise price and effectively have the option "in the money" (Lie, 2005; Narayanan and Seyhun, 2005; Fleischer, 2006; Heron and Lie, 2006, 2007; Narayanan, Schipani, and Seyhun, 2006; Walker, 2006).[37] As an anecdote, Micrel, Inc., sued its auditor, Deloitte & Touche, for signing off on their scheme of setting strike prices at the lowest closing price during the 30 days following the approval of the grant.[38]

---

[36] Their analysis of 168 firms during the period 1992–1998 shows that managers who anticipate large option awards appear to make income-decreasing accrual choices as a means of decreasing the exercise price of their awards. Furthermore, the negative relation between options and accruals is stronger when the firm makes a public earnings announcement in advance of the award date.

[37] The legal date is the date when the board approved the grant with all its details.

[38] For studies that link the backdating scandal to the quality of governance and the interlocking of boards (i.e., executives of two firms sit on each other's boards), consult Bebchuk, Grinstein, and Peyer (2006), Bizjak, Lemmon, and Whitby (2006), and Collins, Gong, and Li (2006). We discuss governance in Chap. 5.

Unlike *spring loading* (the firm schedules an option grant ahead of the announcement of good news that will boost the stock price) and *bullet dodging* (setting the grant date just after a bad news announcement that will be followed by a rebound in the stock price), backdating has been prosecuted by the SEC and the Department of Justice. At the time this material is written, over 120 firms are under investigation. The loss to investors exceeds $100 billion in those 115 firms investigated by November 15, 2006, as measured by the market's reaction to the announcement that the firm might have backdated its option grants (Bernile, Jarrell, and Mulcahey, 2006).

This backdating scandal has several aspects: Backdating might be illegal because shareholders were not notified of grants issued at the money; this creates stealth compensation, since a lower exercise price reduces shareholders' equity without their knowledge. Second, by the accounting rules *before* SFAS 123R required firms to expense stock options compensation starting June 2005, companies had been required to record a compensation expense for the difference between the exercise price and the grant-date price. By tax rules, this difference is taxable as ordinary income to the employee (and since January 1, 2005, there is a tax liability in the vesting, instead of the exercise, period). In addition, the $1 million limit on non-incentive payment imposed by section 162(m) of the tax code is reduced by the difference between the exercise price and the backdating.

In the twenty-first century, regulatory changes narrow the scope of backdating. Beginning August 29, 2002, SEC release 34-46421 implemented section 403 of SOX by requiring firms to disclose grants within 2 days. Previously, the disclosure was required to occur no later than 45 days after the fiscal year in which the grants were received. Furthermore, the major stock exchanges have mandated that shareholders must approve all stock option plans (NYSE Listed Company Manual sec 303A.08; Nasdaq manual, section 4350(i)). If shareholders are unaware that the strike price is different from the price of the stock on the grant date, then the firm did not comply with the disclosure rules (Campos, 2005; Narayanan, Schipani, and Seyhun, 2006). In July 2006, the SEC issued tightened disclosure rules, which require firms to disclose both the grant date and the date when the board, or the compensation committee, finalized the details of the grant. If the exercise price of an option is different from the stock price at closing on the grant date, the firm should describe the methodology for determining the exercise price (17 C.F.R. 239, 249).[39] Heron and

---

[39] The rules have since been further revised regarding presentation of management's Summary Compensation Table and Director Summary Table, the calculation of the stock option expense in order for it to be consistent with SFAS

Lie, (2006, 2007), and Narayanan and Seyhun (2005, 2006), find that the V-shape figure of stock returns that typifies the backdating of option grants has been partially smoothed out by the SOX requirement of reporting the grant to the SEC within 2 days, but not totally eliminated.[40]

3.2.10 Accounting Recognition

After many years in which firms did not record options "at-the-money" as an expense (APB 25), SFAS 123R now requires them to recognize options as an expense over the vesting period. (See the discussion in Ronen, 2005.) SFAS 123R updates SFAS 123, which allowed firms to choose between expensing options and disclosing them in a footnote, and supersedes SFAS 148, which increased the disclosure requirement of SFAS 123 by specifying a tabular form and by specifying that this disclosure be made in the "Summary of Significant Accounting Policies" footnote.

Most of the research on managing the recognition of stock options deals with the issue as it existed when management had discretion over the expense. The literature on options-related manipulation indicates that managers with large holdings prefer not to advertise them. Dechow, Hutton, and Sloan (1996), for example, find that firms whose managers owned large options holdings led the opposition to expensing stock options before SFAS 123 was issued. In the first year that SFAS 123 was implemented (1996), firms for whose managers stock options were a large portion of compensation, as well as IPO firms, opted to allocate a smaller portion of the value of the options to their disclosures (Balsam, Mozes, and Newman, 2003). Furthermore, most firms chose not to report an expense, although the capital market took it into consideration (Aboody, Barth, and Kasznik, 2004a); the latest estimate is that only about 400 firms voluntarily reported stock options as an expense before it became mandatory in FAR 123R (see also Aboody, Barth, and Kasznik, 2004b).[41]

Managing the recognition of stock options as an expense is feasible because this expense is based on estimates of the parameters that are plugged into the Black-Scholes formula. Given the criticism of too generous incentive pay, managers may prefer to apply a "conservative" estimate and take actions to manage the calculated value of the option expense. Luckily for academic investigators, these estimates must be disclosed, so we can com-

---

123R, and increased transparency of the components of managers' compensation. See Rule 34-55009 (http://www.sec.gov/rules/final/2006/33-8765fr.pdf).

[40] Since the grant date is chosen when the stock price is lowest, returns before the grant date are negative and returns after the grant dates are positive.

[41] This data is based on private communication with Ron Kasznik in 2004.

pare what firms do with the guidance provided by SFAS 123. Researchers detected management of the following assumptions on the parameters that underlie the formula of the stock option expense: the expected life of the option from grant to exercise (Yermack, 1998; Aboody, Barth, and Kasznik, 2004b); future stock price volatility (Coller and Higgs, 1997; Davis-Hodder, Mayew, McAnally, and Weaver, 2004[42]; Johnston, 2006[43]); future dividend yield; and future risk-free interest rates (Aboody, Barth, and Kasznik, 2004b[44]). Other ways to manage the expense involve considerations of how closely to adhere to the formula (e.g., Yermack, 1998, who finds that 40% of the firms in his sample "adjust" the formula to reduce the expense) and the accompanying explanations of the numbers (see Blacconiere, Frederickson, Johnson, and Lewis, 2003,[45] who study disavowals).[46]

---

[42] Davis-Hodder, Mayew, McAnally, and Weaver (2004), compare the model's inputs disclosed in the annual reports to three reference points that are suggested by SFAS 123, and in the March 2004 FASB exposure draft: historical experience, market-implied inputs (i.e., the implied volatility of traded options), and industry benchmarks. They find that the average firm reports a value of $9.98 per share (total fair value of $29 million), which is lower than the fair value of $11.43 per share (total fair value of $36 million) that would have been reported if the firm had not deviated from benchmarks. Yet we cannot jump to the conclusion that all firms understate the stock option expense. Some 25% of the firms in their sample overstated the future value of the stock options. From the perspective of good versus bad earnings management, it is notable that 30% of the firms generated more accurate estimates of the parameters. They thus conveyed changes in future operating risk. The rest seemed to participate in bad earnings management, with the intent to obscure compensation.

[43] Johnston (2006), finds that managers use both historical and forward-looking information in determining the expected volatility parameter in the calculation of the option expense, but the reliance on forward-looking information is limited to situations in which it results in reduced expected volatility and thus a smaller option expense, because the compensation is either excessive or largely stock-based.

[44] Aboody, Barth, and Kasznik (2004b), find that firms that grant more options, and thus have a higher stock-based compensation expense, and firms with CEOs whose compensation could be perceived as excessive assume shorter option lives. However, there is no evidence consistent with the manipulation predictions for expected volatility, dividend yield, and risk-free interest rate when each is considered separately.

[45] Blacconiere, Frederickson, Johnson, and Lewis show that excessive compensation is associated with the use of disavowals.

[46] For additional studies that examine how managers attempt to minimize investors' perception of the magnitude of the stock option expense, consult Lewellen,

3.2.11 Timing of the Exercise

Before 1991, stock obtained from the exercise of an option had to be held for a 6-month period; it was considered another case of insider trading subject to the prohibition on "short-swing" profits (see the section on insider trading below). Hence, the act of exercising options was a signal that insiders expected the market price to increase within 6 months. The empirical research corroborated this explanation, as evidenced by positive abnormal returns (Carpenter and Remmers, 2001). Since 1991, however, the stock can be sold immediately, so the forward-looking information content of the exercise is bad news because it is believed that senior officers may have private information that the share price at present is high and it is optimal to exercise immediately before the share price falls (Beneish, 1999b; Huddart and Lang, 2003; Johnson, Ryan, and Tian, 2003). In a recent study, Cai (2007), refines the argument. He classifies exercise of options by the financing method of the exercise: the executive pays cash (negative returns before the exercise and positive returns thereafter in a 15-day window)[47]; the executive sells a shareholding in the firm to pay in cash for the exercise of the options to get new shares (positive returns before the exercise and negative returns thereafter in a 15-day window); and the executive instructs a broker to sell old shares to finance the exercise of new ones without any actual cash involved (a swap deal; positive returns before the exercise date and negative thereafter in a 15-day window).

The fact that exercise reveals private information may imply active management of earnings for the purpose of making speculative gains. Bartov and Mohanram (2004), examine the earnings management *cum* decision to exercise large stock option awards by top-level executives of nearly 1,200 public corporations over the period 1992–2000. They find that the stock price changes are abnormally positive (negative) in each of the 2 years leading up to (following) the exercise year. Furthermore, the disappointing earnings in the post-exercise period represent a reversal of inflated earnings in the pre-exercise period. Safdar (2003); Bergstresser and

---

Park, and Ro (1995), Murphy (1996, 1998), Baker (1999), and Bartov, Mohanram, and Nissim (2003). In contrast, Balsam, Mozes, and Newman (2003), find little evidence that is consistent with firms' managing the fair values of executive stock options by varying the input parameters.

[47] Cai (2007), studies a sample of exercises in the 1997–2005 period. He compares pre- to post-SOX patterns. The pattern for cash exercise disappears after SOX. Cai provides results for shorter windows as well.

Philippon (2003), and Kedia and Philippon (2005), find similar patterns of exercise and change in stock price.[48]

3.2.12 Related Operating, Investment, and Financing Decisions

Options explain other decisions as well. As Murphy (1999), points out, just before the grant, options provide perverse incentives to distribute dividends because dividends depress the market price. By contrast, once the options have been granted, he claims, "[E]xecutives holding options have incentives to avoid dividends and to favor share repurchases" (p. 2501).[49] This claim is supported by Lambert, Lanen, and Larcker (1989), who find that after adopting executive stock option plans, dividend payment levels are lower than expected. May (1995), Jolls (1998), and Fenn and Liang (2001), likewise show that stock repurchases tend to replace cash dividends with an increase in executive holdings of options. Weisbenner (2000), provides evidence that supports the dividend premise (the grant of stock options to senior officers induces firms to curtail cash dividends), but stock repurchasing is more closely related to whether large stock options are awarded to all employees. Bens, Nagar, and Wong (2002), find that stock repurchases reduce firm's value because they consume cash that is diverted from research and development (for a discussion of this paper, consult Guay, 2002). Gong, Louis, and Sun (2007), analyze earnings management that deflates earnings before stock repurchase. They find that earnings management is associated with CEO holdings. Since firms experience post-repurchase abnormal returns, they conclude that managing earnings downward, before the repurchase, is successful in lowering market expectations of growth in earnings.

---

[48] Safdar (2003), conducts the analysis for a shorter window. His evidence suggests that on average the magnitude of earnings management related to stock options is small. During the quarter immediately preceding exercise, discretionary accruals range from 0.35 to 0.62% of total assets; these are followed by negative abnormal returns of less than 3% (in magnitude) over the two quarters following exercise.

Bergstresser and Philippon (2006), show that CEOs exercise unusually large numbers of options during years of high absolute accruals, followed by negative abnormal returns to shareholders (measured using a three-factor risk model).

[49] This view has gained momentum in recent years (e.g., Gumport, 2006) and replaced the earlier view that repurchases signal good news that the stock price is too low (Bartov, 1991; Hertzel and Jain, 1991) or that the firm's common stock is less risky (Bartov, 1991).

3.3 CEO Turnover

If compensation is the carrot in managers' incentives, then firing is the stick.[50] CEO turnover has two phases because it is essentially a case of "the king is dead, long live the king." That is, turnover involves two distinct decision makers, the departing CEO—the predecessor—and the incoming CEO—the successor. Turnover then raises two independent earnings management issues: how the predecessor manages accounting earnings and how the successor manages them.[51] We find that the answer to both questions is as expected. The departing CEO may try to inflate earnings to mask poor performance to avoid forced separation (*the* "cover-up"), or to obtain a higher bonus in his last years on the job (*the horizon problem*) or to obtain directorships or better employment after retirement (*the post-horizon problem*). The incoming CEO deflates earnings—*the big bath*—in order to report favorable performance in the following year, while blaming his predecessor for the poor performance in the first year, unless the departing CEO becomes a director and can put a stop to such gaming.

3.3.1 Departure

Studies find that the turnover rate averages between 5 and 15%, depending on the period and the sample (see the literature review in McNeil, Niehaus, and Powers, 2004, p. 79). There are two types of departures: routine departures, which are peaceful and orderly, and non-routine departures, which cover all the remaining cases (Pourciau, 1993). In most cases, the incoming CEO is an insider.[52]

---

[50] Empirically, most CEOs leave the firm because they retire. For example, in the 1330-observation sample of Engel, Hayes, and Wang (2003), 851 CEOs retired; another 27 left because of health problems, and 37 died.

[51] One of the challenges of the empirical research is to separate the departure from the advent. Murphy and Zimmerman (1993), state,
[U]ltimate inferences often depend on whether the variable in question is controlled by the outgoing or incoming CEO, and there has been inconsistent treatment of the "transition year" in the literature. We …control for the relative influence of outgoing and incoming CEOs by segmenting the sample by CEOs leaving early and late in the fiscal year. (p. 276)

[52] Agrawal, Knoeber, and Tsoulouhas (2006), who study over 1,000 separations in the 1974–1995 period, report that in over 80% of the cases, the successor was an insider.

A peaceful departure may be the last step of a process that has paved the way for a designated successor, who is an insider. Vancil (1987), describes this "relay process": The successor is selected a few years before the incumbent CEO tenure reaches term (about 65 years old), and during this time, they work together; decision rights are gradually transferred from the departing to the potentially incoming CEO. The departing CEO stays with the company for a few more years on the board of directors, thus maintaining some measure of control over the incoming CEO's choices. An alternative "peaceful" process is a "horse race," in which a few candidates compete for the desirable job shortly before the incumbent CEO's departure.

Non-routine departures are largely associated with poor performance (Weisbach, 1988; Puffer and Weintrop, 1991; Murphy and Zimmerman, 1993; Huson, Malatesta, and Parrino, 1997; Lehn and Makhija, 1997; DeFond and Park, 1999; Huson, Parrino, and Starks, 2001; Farrell and Whidbee, 2003; Fee and Hadlock, 2004; Berry, Bizjak, Lemmon, and Naveen, 2006[53]) and income-decreasing restatements (Collins, Reitenga, and Sanchez, 2005). Brickley (2003), observes,

> CEO turnover is inversely related to firm performance. CEOs are more likely to separate from the firm when stock-price and accounting performance is bad than when it is good. While most of the research focuses on publicly traded firms similar relations have been found within nonprofit hospitals and at the divisional level of the firm. (p. 228)

Because sudden departure is not linked to performance by a precise formula, researchers have employed several metrics. Coles, Lemmon, and Naveen (2003), for example, use the *Forbes*-defined operating profit (income before interest, depreciation, amortization and income taxes), net profit (which excludes extraordinary items), and the ratio of number of

---

To tie turnover to Chap. 5, on governance, note that the likelihood of nominating an outsider to the CEO's post increases with the independence of the board (Borokhovich, Parrino, and Trapani, 1996). The turnover is also associated with governance characteristics. Separation is more likely to follow a class action suit, which is positively associated with the severity of agency conflicts between investors and the firm, as measured by the firm's risk, large size, young age, low market-to-book ratio, and no dividend payments (Strahan, 1998); with a more independent board with higher equity compensation (Perry, 2000) and with the presence of a blockholder (Denis, Denis, and Sarin, 1997), but it is less likely with large management ownership (Denis, Denis, and Sarin, 1997).

[53] Berry, Bizjak, Lemmon, and Naveen (2006), show that the link between poor performance and turnover depends on the firm's type. Diversified firms do not exhibit this relationship in contrast to focused firms.

employees to sales (an indicator of labor efficiency). Puffer and Weintrop (1991), examine earnings that failed to meet analysts' forecasts. Yet other studies link performance to competition in the industry by adjusting earnings to median industry performance (DeFond and Park, 1999). DeFond and Park also show that industry-adjusted earnings have a stronger effect on turnover decisions in less concentrated industries; Engel, Hayes, and Wang (2003), confirm these results. Some studies use market-based measures. Warner, Watts, and Wruck (1988), examine a random sample of 269 firms. They show that the turnover rate of firms in the bottom decile of performance (mean annual return of –51.6%) is 13.9%, while the turnover rate of firms in the top decile (mean annual return of –127%) is only 8.3%.[54] Some link turnover to events that are traumatic for the firm. Gilson (1989), examines changes in senior management at financially distressed firms (the events are bankruptcy, default, or privately restructuring debt to avoid bankruptcy). He finds that in any given year, 52% of such firms experience turnover in senior management, compared to a 19% turnover rate for firms that are extremely unprofitable, but not in financial distress. DeFond and Jiambalvo (1994), find that 29% of their sample of firms that default on debt covenants change their management in the year of the default. Gilson and Vetsuypens (1993), report a change in the CEO turnover rate from 8.5 to 30.7% in the period from 1 year before to 1 year after a bankruptcy filing or a restructuring of debt.

Other researchers examine observable actions of management. Lehn and Zhao (2004), for example, note that although mergers and acquisitions are approved by the entire board of directors, they are usually initiated by the CEO and often considered to be one of his major responsibilities. They analyze the probability that a CEO who made an acquisition that destroys value will be replaced (such as the forced departure of Quaker's chairman and CEO, William Smithburg, after the firm sold Snapple for $300 million just 3 years after acquiring it for $1.7 billion). In their sample of 395 firms that completed acquisitions between 1990 and 1998, they

---

[54] Interestingly, DeAngelo (1988b), finds that stock price is *not* used in her sample of firms going through proxy contests, wherein unhappy shareholders wage a campaign to elect directors to the firm's board in order to replace the incumbent manager. She finds that poor earnings, rather than the share price, are used to support the dissidents' drive to gain the support of other shareholders to take control of the board of directors. As a matter of fact, the share price tends to increase when the market expects that the firm would improve its performance even if the incumbent manager stays. In response, the incumbent manages accruals upward, and the incoming manager takes a bath. We describe this study in more detail in Part 4.

find that the probability of replacement is higher when a value-reducing acquisition was completed. They use buy-and-hold returns measured as the 3-year and 1-year market-adjusted buy-and-hold returns of the acquisition after the completion date and cumulative abnormal returns (CAR) for the same windows.[55]

Unlike compensation, which ties reward to performance by a precise formula, sudden departures seem to be based on a downward trend. Hence, earnings changes are likely more important than the level of earnings. For example, consider the ousting of the CEO of Charles Schwab Corporation. The *New York Times* stated on July 21, 2004[56]:

> The Charles Schwab Corporation ousted its chief executive yesterday ... At the height of the bull market, Schwab was briefly worth more than Merrill Lynch, with a market value of $25.5 billion compared with $25.4 billion for Merrill. Now Merrill's worth, at more than $47 billion, is about four times that of Schwab, with a market value of $12 billion.
>
> Mr. Pottruck said Mr. Schwab informed him yesterday of the board's decision and that it came as a surprise. But he said that he accepted it.
>
> "Our performance since 2001 has been pretty lackluster," he said yesterday.

3.3.2 CEO Departure and Earnings Management

Managers may manage earnings to avoid separation (e.g., Fudenberg and Tirole, 1995; DeFond and Park, 1999; Ahmed, Lobo, and Zhou, 2006). That is, managers present steady performance shifting reported earnings from high- to low-performance years. This strategy results in smoother series of reported earnings (see the discussion in Chap. 7). In what follows, we restrict attention to earnings management associated with observable separation. As described above, there are two types of predecessor CEOs: those who left peacefully and those who were forced to quit.

3.3.2.1 Peaceful Separation

Ceasing to be a CEO does not necessarily put an end to a person's involvement with the firm or with the business world. Brickley, Coles, and Linck (1999), find that past CEOs often become present directors. In

---

[55] Surprisingly, the probability that "bad bidders" are replaced is not significantly related to governance parameters such as the size or structure of the boards, the CEO's holding the position of chairman of the board, and the ownership structure.

[56] Atlas, Rivas. Schwab Ousts Chief and Founder Steps In. C1.

particular, stock price movements correlate more with a person becoming a director with the same firm than accounting earnings do. Hence, managers who retire have incentives to manage earnings in their final years in order to increase the probability of being hired as directors. Reitenga and Tearney ney (2003), find that earnings management in the last year of office is mitigated by the presence of independent directors and by large stock options holdings by the manager, but exacerbated when the departing CEO obtains directorship in the firm after his retirement and when there are institutional shareholders. That is, governance matters. We discuss governance separately in Chap. 5.

Dechow and Sloan (1991), analyze the spending on research and development (R&D) in the last year of a CEO's tenure, finding evidence of managing earnings upward to increase the bonus. This evidence is not as strong in the cases of amicable turnovers and is decreasing in firm's share ownership of the incumbent manager (since the value of shares is reduced when R&D is cut unnecessarily).[57] Conyon and Florou (2004), extend the results to U.K. firms. They find demand by the CEO for opportunistic cuts in capital expenditures in the year of the CEO's departure, but this demand is mitigated by a board of directors with opposing incentives due to allegiance to the firm, and by equity compensation.

3.3.2.2 Forced Departure

The process that starts with poor performance and ends with forced departure usually takes 2–3 years (see Warner, Watts, and Wruck, 1988; Mikkerson and Partch, 1997; Denis and Kruse, 2000; McNeil, Niehaus, and Powers, 2004). Thus, there is an ample opportunity for CEOs to manage earnings in an attempt to slow down the leak of unfavorable information.[58]

---

[57] Murphy and Zimmerman (1993), attempt to reconcile this finding with prior research (Butler and Mewman, 1989; Gibbons and Murphy, 1992a) and their own finding that departing CEOs do not reduce R&D. This is indeed a challenge in the research design. They state,

> [U]ltimate inferences often depend on whether the variable in question is controlled by the outgoing or incoming CEO, and there has been inconsistent treatment of the "transition year" in the literature. We discuss alternative interpretations and control for the relative influence of outgoing and incoming CEOs by segmenting the sample by CEOs leaving early and late in the fiscal year.

[58] The fact that there is no formula that links turnover to performance might explain the weak empirical relationship between the two. Brickley (2003, p. 228), states. "While the relation between CEO turnover and firm performance is statistically significant, its economic significance is arguably quite small.

This point is made more acute because dismissal requires a stand by the board of directors. Pourciau (1993), contends,

> When an executive is performing poorly, it is not easy to ask him or her to leave, as pointed out by Vancil (1987). The manager is given some time to prove himself or herself. Further, information must be gathered, feedback obtained, coalitions formed, and so on, until a majority of the directors request a resignation. (p. 321)

Murphy and Zimmerman (1993), estimate the extent to which managerial discretion explains changes in potentially discretionary variables in a sample of over 1,063 departures in 599 firms in the years 1971–1989. They note, "The inextricable links between performance and discretionary behavior make it difficult to disentangle the effects of poor performance from the effects of managerial discretion" (p. 275). They conclude that the overall economic performance of the firm, rather than the outgoing CEO's decision making, better explains their findings.

Pourciau (1993), finds income-decreasing accruals in her 73 cases of non-routine departures in the 1985–1988 period. Examining earnings, accruals, and cash flows, as well as special items and write-offs in the year preceding through the year succeeding the transition year, she shows that departing executives record accruals and write-offs that decrease earnings during their last year; a result that is consistent with a reversal of previously inflated accruals.[59]

To the extent that management attempts to cover up poor performance, a related question concerns whether earnings management then is a case of jumping out of the frying pan and into the fire. That is, on the one hand, earnings management puts off the release of bad news about performance, which has the benefit of delaying forced departure. On the other hand, when fraud is discovered, the consequences may be more costly than an earlier forced departure because now the manager faces the possibility of fines and incarceration.

Beneish (1999a), and Agrawal, Jaffe, and Karpoff (1999), do not find that fraud increases turnover. Desai, Hogan, and Wilkins (2006), observe that a restatement does. In their sample of 146 firms that restated earnings in the 1997–1998 period, 59.6% of the restating firms experience turnover in at least one top managerial position (Chairman, CEO, or president)

The typical study finds that moving from the top to bottom decile of performance increases the probability of CEO turnover in publicly traded firms by about 4%."

[59] Pourciau offers alternative explanations: the endogeneity of the firm's performance (i.e., performance is not properly controlled in the research design) and an increase in monitoring activities when the firm has poor performance.

within 24 months of the restatement, compared to only 34.9% among age-, size,- and industry-matched firms. Moreover, only 17 of 112 (15%) displaced managers of the sample firms were able to secure a comparable position at another firm, compared to 21 of 63 (21%) displaced managers at the control firms. They state, "Given that the mean age of managers in our sample is less than 50, these results suggest that, on average, managers of restatement firms suffer significant losses in reputation and very likely personal wealth" (p. 86). Other studies corroborate the impact of accounting fraud on turnover. Feroz, Park, and Pastena (1991) find that firms investigated by the SEC for accounting irregularities tend to fire the managers. Jayaraman, Mulford, and Wedge (2005), who compare firms pursued by the SEC to a control group, find that the CEO left in a majority of the cases, and that an accounting fraud increases the likelihood of upper management turnover in the 5-year event window (2 years before and after the event year) surrounding the inclusion of their firms in the SEC Accounting and Auditing Enforcement Release (AAER) database. In a recent paper, Karpoff, Lee, and Martin (2007b), examine the fate of 2,206 individuals identified (by public releases and court filings) as responsible for the misrepresentation in all 788 SEC and Department of Justice enforcement actions for financial misrepresentation that took place between January 1, 1978, and September 30, 2006. They find that the perpetrators (1) lose their jobs (93.4%), (2) are barred from similar employment with other companies (31%), (3) lose wealth in their stockholdings ($15.6 million on average), (4) are assessed fines by the SEC (an additional $5.7 million on average), and (5) are subject to criminal charges filed by the Department of Justice (28%) that may result in jail time.[60]

Finally, when the research does not distinguish between amicable turnover and separation that is driven by poor performance, the pattern that seems to emerge is that earnings are lower in the year the CEO departs, with some evidence of managing earnings upward and higher earnings in the following year (see, e.g., Godfrey, Mather, and Ramsay, 2003).

3.3.3 The Incoming CEO

A CEO change is a big change, since it may be followed by divestiture of poorly performing assets (Weisbach, 1995), restructuring that affects the

---

[60] Karpoff, Lee, and Martin (2007b), criticize the results of prior research (Feroz, Park, and Pastena, 1991; Agrawal, Jaffe, and Karpoff, 1999; Beneish 1999a; Desai, Hogan, and Wilkins, 2006) for limiting the search for turnover to an arbitrary time interval surrounding the fraud event (type I error) and failing to identify the propagators (type II error).

level and composition of assets (Denis and Denis, 1995; Denis and Serrano, 1996; Nam and Ronen, 2007), the departure of other key officials in the management team (Hayes, Oyer, and Schaefer, 2002), and a shift in business strategy to foreign operations (Blonigen and Wooster, 2003). Thus, it comes as no surprise that the incoming CEO is pressured to show results, and the earlier the better. He is also responsible for establishing the benchmark of his performance because he has control over the reported earnings in the first term (a quarter or a year, or both) of his tenure.

Many studies find that the incoming manager takes a bath in his first year by recording big charges, and that the following year shows an increase in earnings, so long as the departing CEO does not remain in the firm as a director.[61, 62] Indeed, the research community shows uncommon unanimity on this point. Indeed, the research community shows uncommon unanimity on this point. Turner (2001b), states,

> there are a number of areas where significant improvements can still be made in the quality of accounting standards

> - A rigorous, practical impairment test that results in declines in value being reported to investors during the periods the declines actually occur; as opposed to the current standards that yield nothing more than one time overnight "Big Bath" charges ... when the CEO changes.

In a recent study, Nam and Ronen (2007), question whether write-offs indicate pernicious earnings management or efficiency-enhancing actions by a manager who is an outsider and is thus less reluctant to undertake corrective measures. An examination of the market response to the incom-

---

[61] Koch and Wall (2006), provide anecdotal evidence:
After being named CEO of Sunbeam Corporation in June 1996, Al Dunlap brought about dramatic change in the firm's reported financial performance. In 1996, Sunbeam reported a loss in excess of $200 million—followed the next year by net income of almost $110 million. When he accepted the CEO position, Dunlap negotiated a compensation package that included substantial stock grants, stock options, and a large salary and benefits. With the improved performance, Dunlap's salary and benefits package was increased further in 1998. In 1998 and 1999 Sunbeam reported losses and Dunlap was no longer CEO. ... [M]uch of the variation in Sunbeam's financials reflected a discretionary use of accruals and other accounting ploys to move expenses to 1996 and increase reported net income in 1997. (p. 1)

[62] Large discretionary write-offs as a measure of earnings management are the focus of research by Elliott and Shaw (1988), Strong and Meyer (1987); and Francis, Hanna, and Vincent (1996). We discuss DeAngelo's (1988b), contribution in Chap. 9. The methodologies of Pourciau (1993), Murphy and Zimmerman (1993), and Godfrey, Mather, and Ramsay (2003), are cited above.

ing CEO and to the announcement of the write-off by the firm from which the CEO departed indicates that the market attempts to distinguish between the two dynamics. Specifically, the market's reaction is sensitive to performance in pervious engagements (reputation of the manager), the expertise of the incoming CEO in the industry in which the firm he just joined operates (which indicates his capability to take value-enhancing actions), and whether the write-off is part of restructuring.

We conclude our discussion with the following comment. Although there has been extensive research on turnover of CEOs, CFOs have received scant attention. Turner (2001b), cites a report in the April 2000 edition of *CFO* magazine that makes the connection between announced earnings and the CFO's being asked to leave the firm:

> As noted in the April 2000 edition of CFO magazine, ten years ago, CFO turnover in the Fortune 500 was about 12 % per year, with retirement the major reason why someone left a company. In 1998, the figure was up to 26 %, and research cited missing an earnings estimate for a quarter as a frequent cause. I find it interesting when it is noted that the "CFO" missed on expectations. What about the CEO, the COO, and the vice presidents of manufacturing, sales, marketing and product developments? Wasn't it really the business that *all* of these executives are responsible for managing that failed to achieve the necessary sales, cost levels and new product introductions and accordingly missed expectations?

Similar sentiments regarding the connection between the CFO's job security and the pressure to manage earnings are expressed in surveys gathered by Graham, Campbell, and Rajgopal (2005).

3.4 Insider Trading

Insider trading, like compensation, is a topic of interest in economics, finance, accounting, and law.[63] Although parties liable for insider trading include corporate insiders and employees,[64] "constructive insiders" such as

---

[63] Insider trading is also related to disclosure. See Bushman and Indjejikian (1995), Noe (1999), Niehaus and Roth (1999), Boyer, Ciccone, and Zhang (2004), Gregoire, 2004; Richardson, Teoh, and Wysocki (2004), and Cheng and Lo (2006).

[64] Employees are not included in the formal definition of corporate insiders, but by agency law, employees are agents of the corporate principal. Hence, the prohibition of insider trading covers employees as well.

In response to the *Chiarella* decision, the Securities and Exchange Commission promulgated Rule 14e-3 under Section 14(e) of the 1934 Exchange Act, making it illegal for persons to trade on the basis of material non-public information

lawyers and accountants who acquire firm-specific information during their contact with the firms, and "tippees" (such as family members of the above), we restrict our attention to the link between earnings management and insider trading by managers.

We begin by outlining the legal aspects of insider trading:

- Section 16(a) of the 1934 Securities and Exchange Act defines "corporate insider" to include not only the CEO and CFO but other officers, directors, and beneficial owners—i.e., owners that either directly or indirectly own more than 10% of any class of the firm's equity.

- All corporate insiders must file their transactions with the SEC to be entered into a public registry. Section 403 of the Sarbanes-Oxley Act of July 2002, requires those insiders to report a change in ownership within two days, effective August 29, 2002. Before August 2002, insiders had a window of nearly 40 days to make the report, because the report had to be filed no later than the 10th of the month following the transaction.

- Section 16(b) of the 1934 Securities and Exchange Act prohibits short-swing abnormal profits within six months (by common law, six months less an evening) between a buy and a sell trans-action (known as a "round trip transaction"). This prohibition also covers short sales.

- The case law of *SEC vs. Texas Gulf Sulphur Co.* (1968-1969)[65] established the illegality of a trade that is based on material

regarding tender offers if they know that the information emanated from an insider. In *Chiarella*, a printer gleaned non-public information regarding tender offers and a merger from documents he was hired to print and bought stock in the target of the companies that hired him. The Supreme Court held that trading on material non-public information in itself was not enough to trigger liability under the anti-fraud provisions, and because the printer owed target shareholders no duty, he did not defraud them.

[65] Texas Gulf Sulphur Co. was a mining company whose key insiders purchased shares in the company at the time that they alone knew of a the presence of rich deposits of zinc and copper on a new tract of land in Ontario. The main reason for remaining quiet was that the company had to acquire the rights to drill, and if the truth about the richness of the deposits became known, the price of these rights might be higher. Insiders took advantage of the secrecy and purchased shares and got grants from ignorant directors in the months preceding the public announcement of the finds in April 1964; an announcement that led to a sharp price increase in the stock price. The case law dealt with insider trading in the 4-month period before the public announcement. There is evidence that the practice started much earlier (Bainbridge, 2001).

nonpublic information, where the criterion for materiality is the effect on the share price.[66] Since then possession of such information presents two mutually exclusive choices: disclose before trading or refrain from trading.

- Rules 10b5-1 and 10b5-2 further elaborate. Rule 10b5-1 deals with the intent to defraud ("scienter"), which is essential for proving a violation of Rule 10b-5. Specifically, a violation of insider trading rules occurs if a trader is "aware" of the material nonpublic information when making the purchase or sale. The rule offers some affirmative defenses, such as the trader's committing to a trading plan before learning of the information. Rule 10b5-2 deals with trades by people who were tipped. This rule covers a lacuna regarding trade by a person who receives confidential information but who has no fiduciary duty to the firm that has a proprietary claim to this information.

- Some companies have bylaws that set out when trading is permissible and when it is not (known as "blackout periods").[67] In every large company, trade in the company's shares must be approved by a designated officer. A typical trading window is about three days following an earnings announcement, and it ends no longer than twelve days after the earnings announcement (Bettis, Coles, and Lemmon, 2000). Trading restrictions are also adopted by smaller firms that attempt thus to attract investors' interest (Jagolinzer and Roulstone, 2004).

---

[66] The ruling was based on Rule 10b-5, which provides, in relevant part:
It shall be unlawful for any person, directly or indirectly

  (a) to employ any device, scheme, or artifice to defraud,
  (b) to make any untrue statement of a material fact or omit to state a material fact necessary in order to make the statements made, in light of the circumstances under which they were made, not misleading, or
  (c) to engage in any act, practice, or course of business which operates or would operate as a fraud or deceit upon any person, in connection with the purchase or sale of a security.

Although Rule 10b-5 does not expressly speak to insider trading, the courts have relied on this rule in cases involving insider trading.

[67] Roulstone (2003), finds that blackout periods are costly to companies, measuring the cost as the increment in the cost of the manager's incentives and establishing the level of incentives by bonuses and stock and option grants. He concludes that the trading restrictions induce managers to favor higher stock prices and higher volatility. Bettis, Coles and Lemmon (2000), however, find that trading restrictions have a favorable effect on market liquidity.

The empirical research offers the following insights:
1. Insider trading is based on private information.

Insider trading is based on private information (Jaffe, 1974; Jenter 2005; Huddart, Ke, and Shi, 2007), which is even superior to that of analysts who base their recommendation on research of the firm and its industry (see, e.g., Hsieh, Ng, and Wang, 2005[68]). Managers exploit trading opportunity that arise from the stock price being mispriced (see, e.g., Lakonishok and Lee, 2001; Jenter, Lewellen, and Warner, 2006, and citations therein). Managers anticipate price movements: they buy in advance of stock price increases and sell in advance of stock price decreases (Seyhun, 2000; Lakonishok and Lee, 2001; Jenter, 2005; Piotroski and Roulstone, 2005). They sell *glamour* stocks—popular stock characterized by recent high earnings growth rate and a price that rises faster than the market average, which are thus likely to be overpriced—and purchase *value* stock—stocks that recently traded at a lower price relative to their fundamentals (i.e., dividends, earnings, sales),[69] which are thus likely to be underpriced (Seyhun, 2000; Sawicki, 2005). There is a link between managers' trades and present and future earnings (Piotroski and Roulstone, 2005). They sell shares with contemporaneous good news and future bad news (Brochet, 2007), and they purchase shares with contemporaneous bad news and future good news. Ke, Huddart, and Petroni (2003), examine earnings management as a function of the string of quarterly earnings, where a string is a sequence of consecutive quarters in which quarterly earnings are increasing (measured relative to the same quarter of the previous year). Denoting by "break" the quarter in which a string ends (when, for the first time, earnings in the current quarter are less than earnings for the same quarter of the previous year), they examine insider trading before a break, given that previous research by Barth, Elliott, and Finn (1999), and DeAngelo, DeAngelo, and Skinner (1996), shows that breaks are associated with economically and statistically significant stock price drops. They find an increase in the frequency of net insider sales in the ninth through third quarters before the break. This selling pattern is stronger for firm quarters that are

---

[68] Hsieh, Ng, and Wang (2005), study the pattern of corporate insiders' trading vis-à-vis analysts' recommendations and find that insiders trade in the opposite direction, but consistently with future stock returns. That is, insiders buy more of their own firms' stock after unfavorable recommendations, and the future returns are consistent with the insiders' trading strategies.

[69] Value stocks are characterized by a high dividend yield, low price-to-book ratio, or a low price-to-earnings ratio.

drawn from growth firms, are part of longer strings, and precede a longer break.

In a recent study, Brochet (2007), provides evidence that informativeness of insiders' transactions has increased, with the SOX mandating prompt disclosure of insider trades.

2. Insider trading is a valuable signal on the quality of earnings.

A few studies make a link between insider trading and quality of earnings. Beneish and Vargus (2002), show that the combination of high levels of insider sales and high levels of positive discretionary accruals are indicative of "low-quality" earnings, where quality is measured in their *persistence* (we discuss persistence of earnings further in Chap. 9). Hochberg, Newman, and Rierson (2003), conjecture that the fact that accruals are expected to reverse (which introduces a negative serial autocorrelation in accruals and in discretionary accruals) implies that the longer the series of positive discretionary accruals, the less informative the firm's reported earnings. To test this hypothesis, they describe a firm as "aggressive" in a particular quarter if that firm's discretionary accruals are ranked in that quarter in the top quintile for all firms. Firms are classified by the number of consecutive quarters in which they are aggressive. Firms that remain aggressive for only one quarter are classified as Group I, while firms that are aggressive for consecutive periods are classified as Group II. To support the hypothesis that the earnings reported by Group II firms convey less information about the true state of the firm than those reported by Group I, Hochberg, Newman, and Rierson examine the pattern of insider trading. They find that the rate of portfolio sales differs dramatically for insiders in each group. In particular, during the aggressive period, insiders in Group I decrease their sales of shares relative to the most recent normal accounting period (selling $3.0 million of shares in the aggressive period relative to $3.6 million in the previous period, a reduction of 13%). In contrast, Group II insiders increase their net dollar sales by as much as 47% during their aggressive periods.

3. Insider trading before takeovers and earnings announcements seems to be controlled.

In 1984 and 1988, Congress passed acts that increased the penalties on insider trading. The Insider Trading Sanctions Act of 1984 (Public Law 98-376 [H.R.559], August 10, 1984) created a treble civil monetary penalty on gains from insider trading, and such penalties do not preclude other actions within the power of the SEC and the Department of Justice. Bainbridge (2001, p. 56), notes, "Because the SEC thus may seek both disgorgement and treble damages, an insider trader faces potential civil liability up to four times the profits gained." The

Insider Trading and Securities Enforcement Act of 1988 (Public Law 100-704 [H.R.5133] November 19, 1988) increased penalties even further. For example 5-year incarceration provided by the 1984 Act was replaced by 10-year incarceration in the 1988 Act. To the extent that crime is an economic decision that weighs benefits against cost, it is not surprising, then, that the combined efforts of the SEC and Congress appear to have eliminated insider trading before earnings announcements and before mergers.[70] Seyhun (1992), observes that the courts played a role in eliminating the phenomenon as well:

> [C]ase law in the 1980s had an important effect on insider trading. Case law in effect defined illegal trading as trading immediately prior to takeovers and earnings announcements and other important corporate announcements. Evidence shows that insiders were less likely to trade immediately before earnings announcements and corporate takeovers in the 1980s. (p. 151)

4. In general, net selling is more common than net buying and less informative.

   Greater selling is explained by incentive programs that reward management with shares and options (see, e.g., Hochberg, Newman, and Rierson, 2003, p. 17, and citations therein). Lower informativeness is attributable to SEC Rule 10b5-1 because managers defend their trading by committing to a trading plan.

---

[70] In response to the *Chiarella v. United States* decision (445 U.S. 222 (1980)), the Securities and Exchange Commission promulgated Rule 14e-3 under Section 14(e) of the 1934 Exchange Act, making it illegal for persons to trade on the basis of material non-public information regarding tender offers if they know that the information emanated from an insider. (In *Chiarella*, a printer gleaned non-public information regarding tender offers and a merger from documents he was hired to print and bought stock in the target of the companies that hired him. The Supreme Court held that trading on material non-public information in itself was not enough to trigger liability under the antifraud provisions, and because the printer owed target shareholders no duty, he did not defraud them.
Other case laws that affect the legal status of insider trading are the following:
In *Dirks v. SEC*, 463 U.S. 646 (1983), the Supreme Court decided that the insider breaches his fiduciary duty if he acts not in the corporate interest. As to the recipient of the information he has an obligation to refrain from trading only if he knows the guilty circumstances under which the information was passed along to him.
In *United States v. O'Hagan*, 521 U.S. 642 (1997), the Supreme Court made clear that the breach of duty by which the information is obtained and its illegal use could involve a duty of trust and confidence other than between a corporate insider and the shareholders of the corporation whose securities are traded.

5. The analytical insight.

The theoretical analysis is divided between market-based research and agency-related research. In the former, insider trading is committed by anonymous traders. This line of research focuses on the characterization of the price in a noisy rational expectations equilibrium (see, e.g., Ausubel, 1990; Laffont and Maskin, 1990; Bhattacharya and Spiegel, 1991; Leland, 1992; Baiman and Verrecchia, 1995; Jain and Mirman, 1999). That is, in expectation, the market price is correct because it is equal to the firm's economic fundamental. Yet it may deviate from the fundamental; a market maker cannot distinguish between the trades of noise traders and those of informed traders, so noise traders can affect the market price. These studies find that insider trading increases the informativeness of the price, but it is costly because the market maker has to set a bid-ask spread that covers expected losses from transacting with insiders with superior information. The existence of anonymous insiders drives away liquidity traders, who are aware that they are at a disadvantage.

The agency-oriented literature is concerned with the effect of the manager's insider trading on the conflicting interests of the owners of the firm (the principal) and the manager (the agent). Following Manne (1966), Easterbrook (1985), argues that insider trading by managers is beneficial because it lessens the conflict of interest between owners and managers. Dye (1984a), proves that insider trading by the manager is beneficial because it is informative about the manager's unobserved effort, so it can lower the cost of the manager's contract. Bebchuk and Fershtman (1991, 1993, 1994), show that the value of insider trading depends on the trade-off between the manager's riskaversion and his speculative gains in trading. Elitzur and Yaari (1995) and Elitzur (2007), find that insider trading by the manager affects the timing of the manipulation of the reported earnings over the manager's tenure. Baiman and Verrecchia (1995), analyze the case in which the market price contains non-contractible perfect information about the manager's unobservable effort. Hence, the optimal incentives contract is based on the stock price alone. They find that although the manager's insider trading affects the formula of the contract, it has no qualitative effect on the market price. Noe (1997), observes that prohibiting insider trading by managers could be superior to mechanisms that restrict their activity since control of the manager's activity weakens the owners' incentives to induce the manager to exert effort. Bolton, Scheinkman, and Xiong (2006), extend Holmström and Tirole (1993), to show that owners convey their expected preferences to the manager by incorporating insider trading into the design of the optimal contract.

3.4.1 Insider Trading and Earnings Management

The fact that insider trading is based on private information suggests that insider trading motivates pernicious earnings management. The clearest evidence of this is provided in studies on the link between such trading and impending fraud or bankruptcy (Seyhun and Bradley, 1997; Summers and Sweeney, 1998; Beneish, 1999a; Agrawal and Cooper, 2007). Beneish finds that managers of firms with overstatements that violate GAAP are more likely to sell their holdings during the period when earnings are overstated than managers in a control group. Earnings management is then pernicious, in the sense that "managers' stock transactions during the period of earnings overstatement occur at inflated prices that reflect the effect of the earnings overstatement" (Beneish, 1999a, p. 426).

Yet such findings need not imply that insider trading is always pernicious. Boyer, Ciccone, and Zhang (2004), examine whether discretionary accruals are consistent with pernicious earnings management, beneficial signaling earnings management, or smoothing. They rank stocks each year into deciles based on discretionary accruals (where the lowest [highest] decile represents firms with the greatest income-decreasing [increasing] discretionary accruals). They then examine the direction of insider trading across the deciles. Their evidence is consistent with the opportunism hypothesis, which predicts that insiders are more likely to sell (buy) stocks if they manipulate earnings upward (downward), in contrast with the predicted pattern under signaling.[71]

McVay, Nagar, and Tang (2006), find that managers who attempt to beat analysts forecast (see Chap. 5 for a discussion of the phenomenon of meeting/beating analysts' expectations) through earnings management sell their shares. Since the market rewards firms that meet or beat analysts' forecasts, such earnings management leads to an inflated price. Insiders' sale then are consistent with the inability of the market to see through the earnings management.

The connection between earnings management and insider trading raises the following question: Do insiders manage earnings to make speculative gains, or does earnings management induce insider trading?

---

[71] Downward earnings management could be a sign of deteriorating future performance; the notion here is that current period earnings are being saved for future periods when performance is expected to decline relative to the current period's unmanaged earnings. Setting aside reserves as a way to maintain future performance is also recognized in Beneish, 2001. On the flip side, upward earnings management could be a signal of expected improvement in performance. Accordingly, the signaling hypothesis predicts managers will buy more (less) if earnings are managed upward (downward).

Analytical papers by Elitzur and Yaari (1995), and Bebchuk and Bar-Gill (2003), prove that in equilibrium insider trading motivates managers to manipulate earnings because the opportunity to make profitable trades increases the benefit of managing earnings without affecting its cost. Thus, cost–benefit considerations tilt in favor of earnings management before trading.[72] The empirical research offers mixed results. Beneish (1999a), for example, studies 64 cases of fraudulent financial reporting over the period 1982–1993 and shows that managers sell *after* overstating earnings. In contrast, Beneish and Vargus (2002), provide evidence that managers sell *before* managing earnings upward. Similarly, Beneish, Press, and Vargus (2005), find that managing earnings follows insider trading, as a defense against potential class action suits alleging that insiders sold their shares for inflated prices at the expense of other investors. They find that insider selling in advance of periods of poor corporate performance generates incentives for income-increasing earnings management.[73] Moreover, they find no evidence of earnings management *before* managers engage in abnormal selling, suggesting that selling stock at inflated prices after artificially increasing earnings (a "pump and dump scheme") is unlikely to describe the insider trading-earnings management association. A difficulty in finding the answer is that both are decisions of management, so some endogeneity cannot be avoided in standard analysis. Park and Park (2004), consider insider trading after announcements in a two-stage least squares analysis. They find support for the notion that increasing discretionary accruals are followed by the selling of shares as part of managers' portfolio decisions. Sawicki (2005), examines earnings management both before and after insider trading. Similar to Beneish and Vargus (2002), she shows that the firm inflates earnings in the year following the one in which insiders purchase shares. Similar to Park and Park (2004), she also finds weak evidence that the firm deflates earnings in the year before insiders sell shares.

---

[72] The only paper that predicts that the effect of earnings management on price and on the wealth transfer from insiders to uninformed investors who trade with them is mitigated by insider trading is that of Ronen, Tzur, and Yaari, (2007). This study dwells on corporate insiders other than management. They show that insider trading by management reveals information that is incorporated into the price and thus reduces the speculative gains of non-management insiders.

[73] They analyze 462 firms that experienced technical defaults on their debt in the period 1983–1997. After testing for discretionary accruals, they support their findings by showing that default firms with abnormal insider selling are more aggressive in their accounting choices: They also tend to report lower depreciation and lower bad-debt expenses than their performance-matched controls.

For additional evidence, consult Bartov and Mohanram (2004), Kedia and Philippon (2005); and others cited in, Sect. 8.2.

3.5 Management Buyouts

A management buyout is "a leveraged buyout in which managers of the firm to be taken private are also equity investors" (Depamphilis, 2003, p. 5). The arithmetic is simple: the managers who purchase the firm would like to pay as low a price as possible, while shareholders who sell them their shares would like to get as high a price as possible. The two parties have bargaining room because the firm's performance tends to improve significantly after a management buyout. Kaplan (1989, 1991), for example, finds that operating income in his 76 management buyout firms in the 1980–1986 period increased by more than 20% by the third post-buyout year, and that cash flows increased by 80%. (See also Muscarella and Vetsuypens, 1990, and Smith, 1990, as well as Holthausen and Larcker, 1996, on reverse leveraged buyouts.)[74]

Improved performance after a buyout has a few possible explanations. Murphy (1993), attributes the increase in value to improved incentives since "the same managers are managing the same assets and employees before and after the restructuring, ..." (p. 2542). Depamphilis (2003), attributes the improvement to better governance and to changes in the economics of business. He states,

> The best candidates for management buyouts are often underperforming divisions of larger companies in which the division is not longer considered critical to the parent's firm's overarching strategy. Frequently, such divisions are saddled with excessive administrative

---

[74] These statistics are quite impressive when one bears in mind that the wave of leveraged buyouts in the 1980s dwindled in the 1990s, principally because of the failure rate of highly leveraged buyouts (Depamphilis, 2003, pp. 560–561), and that the largest and most successful private firms are less profitable than similar public firms by about 50%, as measured by operating profit scaled by sales and net profit to sales (Coles, Lemmon, and Naveen, 2003). Hence, the price of the firm should be somewhere between the value of the firm if its historical performance persists (the minimum to current stockholders) and the value of the firm when managers take over and improve performance (the maximum payment by management). Indeed, DeAngelo, DeAngelo, and Rice (1984), in their study of 72 management buyouts in the 1973–1983 period find that the premium paid upon purchase amounts to 56%, and when there are more than two bids, the premium increases to 76% (see also Muscarella and Vetsuypens, 1990, and citations therein).

overhead, often required by the parent, and expenses are allocated to the division by the parent for services such as legal, auditing, and treasury functions that could be purchased less expensively from sources outside the parent firm. These often represent excellent cost-reduction opportunities once the division becomes independent of the parent. Moreover, lack of attention by the parent often results in missed opportunities for the division because the parent is unlikely to fully fund investment opportunities for the division because the parent is unlikely to fully fund investment opportunities that it does not consider critical to its overall business strategy. (p. 573)

Unsurprisingly, we maintain that it may well be the case that before the buyout, managers manage earnings downward in order to reduce the purchase price. The buyout process is lengthy, especially because it involves debt financing, so managers have a long window in which to manage earnings.

The empirical literature either confirms this hypothesis or at least does not reject it. Perry and Williams (1994), find downward earnings management in the year before a management buyout in their sample of 175 buyouts in 1981–1988. Wu (1997), estimates that on average, earnings management reduces the cost of an average deal by approximately $50 million. Marquardt and Wiedman (2004a), study 100 buyouts in the 1995–1999 period. Their two-stage method first detects earnings management by total discretionary accruals and then identifies the individual accruals that managers might use in reaching their earnings goals: accounts receivable, inventory, accounts payable, accrued liabilities, depreciation expense, and special items. They argue that decreasing revenues (captured by unexpected accounting receivables, UAR) provide a stronger signal on the deteriorating value of the firm. They find that the UAR for the MBO firms are marginally significantly more negative than for the matched control firms (Mean (median) is −1.299% (−0.440) versus 0.376% (−0.226%) for the control sample). Notably, only 38% of the UARs for the management buyouts are positive, compared with 45% for the control sample.

There may, however, be countervailing factors affecting the scope and direction of earnings management. First, because the buyout is leveraged, and the debt financing includes secured debt that uses receivables and inventory as collateral, there are incentives to manage these items upward. Second, distant shareholders require opinions of investment bankers (when the buyout involves a subsidiary, the parent company is expected to know a great deal about its unobservable value). Another factor is the competition of bids by parties other than management. DeAngelo (1986, p. 402), argues, "[I]n some cases, competition from other potential purchasers helps ensure outside stockholders a fair price.... Such competition, however, is of limited effectiveness when managers hold pre-offer majority control (as they do in over one-third of sample firms), since these managers can effectively block another bid."

In Chap. 4, we turn to earnings management incidences that are associated with users of financial reports.

4 Users

In Chap. 3, we focused on management's incentives to manage earnings. As an insider, management represents the supplier of earnings information. In this chapter, we focus on plain-vanilla users: those stakeholders who demand the earnings information so that they can evaluate the firm to conduct their business. In Chap. 5, we focus on a special group of users, monitors, or gatekeepers, who provide valuable signals to other users regarding the credibility and the informational value of the reported earnings.

In this chapter, we discuss the following categories of users:

- Retail shareholders, who have no power over a firm's operating decisions. They need information on earnings to evaluate investment in the firm's shares.
- Bondholders and other creditors. They need information on earnings and cash flows to assess the risk of lending money to the firm and to monitor the firm after the debt has been issued.[1]
- Regulators. Regulators wear two hats: regular stakeholders, studied in this chapter, and monitors, which are studied in Chap. 5. The former need information on earnings in regulated industries, such as the banking and the insurance industries, and for assessing tax liabilities.
- Employees. They need information on earnings to assess the firm's viability and to determine the firm's ability to grant wage increases.[2]

---

[1] One classification would lump bondholders and shareholders together into one category: investors. Since most studies of earnings management distinguish between equity and debt transactions, we separate these groups for the purpose of our discussion. Exceptions to the separation of financing through equity and debt can be found in the following: Dechow, Sloan, and Sweeney (1996), Richardson, Tuna, and Wu (2002), and Erickson, Hanlon, and Maydew (2004b). These studies find that demand for external financing motivates earnings management.

[2] In France, for example, to preserve employees' right, firms beyond a certain size are required to issue 1-year-ahead pro forma earnings to ensure that the firms do not go bankrupt and fire employees. At the time this chapter is written, Delphi, a large supplier of GM, has announced a major wage cut in order to survive. Losses are a warning sign for incumbent employees.

Figures 1a and 1b, reprinted, with permission, from Elsevier. "Earnings management and accounting income," Journal of Accounting and Economics, Volume 43, Number 2/3, 2007, pp. 369–390.

- Competitors, suppliers, and customers. Competitors need information on earnings in order to make numerous business decisions. Suppliers and customers need information on earnings to ascertain the solvency of the firm.

In each section below, we first present the user. We explain why earnings are important to the transactions between this stakeholder and the firm and then discuss the earnings management events that are associated with this particular stakeholder.

4.1 Shareholders

To finance growth, firms raise capital either internally or externally by issuing stock or incurring debt. The U.S. stock markets are notable for their high level of development (Levitt, 1998; Dechow and Schrand, 2004; Yaari, 2005). Hence, the pressure of the stock markets on firms to communicate information through earnings plays a crucial role in the earnings management phenomenon.

In what follows, we restrict attention to a selected group of shareholders: retail, transient institutional investors (e.g., banks, insurance funds, and open-end mutual funds), potential shareholders, and market makers and dealers. Chapter 5 discusses shareholders that intervene in corporate governance and thus play a monitoring role, such as blockholders and non-transient institutional investors.

The role of shareholders in earnings management is derived from the fact that the shareholders' demand for information creates a link between earnings and the stock price. The share price is important to firms for three major reasons. First, it affects the cost of capital. Firms that cannot satisfy their capital needs internally, through retained earnings, do it externally through debt and equity (Myers and Majluf, 1984). The higher the price per share, the lower the cost of capital, since fewer shares need to be issued to raise a given level of capital. Second, shares serve as cash. They form the substance of incentives to employees, especially for young firms facing liquidity problems (e.g., Core and Guay, 2001). Shares are also exchanged in stock-for-stock mergers and acquisitions. Third, shares are also used as collateral. In Enron, for example, its Special Purpose Entities (SPE) raised capital by using Enron stock as collateral under the provision that if the price fell below a given level, Enron would deliver cash. Enron collapsed because it did not have sufficient cash to cover its debt when its shares fell after the market learned how risky Enron really was. In many cases, firms that cannot meet debt obligations renegotiate their debt contracts and persuade lenders to convert debt claims into shares.

4.1.1 The Price-Setting Process

To understand how earnings affect the stock price, we provide the high lights of the price-setting process, modeled after that of the National Association of Securities Dealers Automated Quotations (NASDAQ). A key feature of the process is that the stock price is set in a noisy rational expectations equilibrium (Christensen and Feltham, 2002). The stock prices are rational, in that, in expectation, they equal the expected net present value of future dividends. We will refer to the net present value of future dividends as the fundamental, or the economic value, interchangeably. At any given moment, however, the price might be different from the fundamental value. One plausible reason is that firms manage earnings and the market does not see through the managed earnings (Baber, Chen, and Kang, 2006).

Stock prices are established by market makers (dealers). The market maker possesses stocks and cash. He sets two prices: a "bid" for buyers and an "ask" price for sellers. The maintained assumption in the microstructure literature is that the market maker's goal is to set a price that reflects the firm's expected economic value.

The economic value of the firm is unknown. Some investors spend resources to acquire private information on the firm's value and thus become "informed investors." Since the market maker cannot distinguish between the trades of informed and uninformed traders, he attempts to deduce the information possessed by informed traders from the observable total demand. For example, when demand is high, the market maker weighs interpreting it as a signal that informed traders believe that the price understates the economic value of the firm against the possibility that the high demand reflects a high volume of uninformed trades. The distinction between the two explanations is important for the price. If the value of the firm upon good news (known to informed traders alone) is $10 a share when the current price is $5, then the revised price is going to increase to some point between $5 and $10, depending on the beliefs of the market maker regarding the reason for the high demand. For example, if the rational market maker attaches a probability of 80% that the high demand is triggered by informed traders reacting to good news, the revised price is 80%*$10+20%*$5=$9. In general, the market price tends to fall (rise) when the total volume of asks (bids) is high.[3]

---

[3] Since the study of Glosten and Milgrom (1985), one of the measures for information asymmetry in the capital market is the gap between the "bid" and the "ask" quotes. This gap insures the market maker against losses from transacting with unidentifiable traders with superior information.

4.1.2 The Impact of Earnings on the Share Price

Earnings provide information to investors. Some information is already known before the firm publicizes its results. In this case, the announcement confirms the market's (and market maker's) beliefs. Some information is a surprise. Once investors revise their beliefs about the firm's value, they adjust their investment decisions, which, in turn, affect the market price. The street wisdom is that "better earnings equal a higher stock price" (Anderson and Thomas, Picking up the pieces, The Fall of Refco is Providing a Test for Wall Street, New York Times, October 15, 2005).

The accounting research supports the street wisdom by providing extensive empirical evidence of the positive link between earnings and the market price and between the market price and future earnings (see, e.g., Latane and Jones, 1979; Belkaoui, 1983; Rayburn, 1986; Asquith, Healy, and Palepu, 1989; Easton and Harris, 1991; Swaminathan and Weintrop, 1991; Ball and Bartov, 1996; La Porta, Lakonishok, Shleifer, and Vishny, 1997; Lamont, 1998; Shroff, 1999; Billings and Morton, 2001; Affleck-Graves, Callahan, and Chipalkatti, 2002; Choi, Lee, and Press, 2002; Gelb and Zarowin, 2002; Kinney, Burgstahler, and Martin, 2002; Chambers, Jennings, and Thompson, 2003; Monahan, 2005; Callen, Livnat, and Segal, 2006; Butler, Kraft, and Weiss, 2007; see also the surveys of Lev, 1989; Barth, Beaver, and Landsman, 2001; Holthausen and Watts, 2001; Kothari, 2001; Stolowy and Breton, 2000).

4.1.3 The Effect of Earnings Management on Shareholders' Information

The importance of earnings to the market price prompts two questions:

1. What is the market response to earnings management?
2. Which cases of earnings management are mainly induced by the importance of earnings to the stock price?

4.1.3.1 The Reaction of the Market Response to Earnings Management

The reaction of the market price to earnings management depends on the following joint events: the type of earnings management (beneficial, pernicious, or neutral, as defined in Chap. 2); the economic, unmanaged earnings; and the market's ability to see through the manipulation. Table 4.1 summarizes the possible cases.

Table 4.1 The response of the market price to earnings Management

	Earnings management		
	Beneficial (the market learns the long-term truth)	**Neutral** (the market knows the short-term truth)	**Pernicious** (the report mis leads the market)
The market sees through the manipulation	- The market recognizes the informational content of the managed report - The price changes accordingly	- The market filters the truth from the report - The price changes accordingly	Can earnings management be pernicious?
The market does not see through the manipulation	- Not an equilibrium.	Can earnings management be neutral?	- The market discounts the managed report - The price change is stronger than when the market recognizes the truth

To clarify this table, we offer the following examples. Let the short-term true economic earnings be 100; the long-run true economic earnings can be either 120 or 60, with probabilities of 60 and 40%, respectively. The firm alone knows the long-run true economic earnings.

Beneficial earnings management. When Nature chooses the long-run true economic earnings to be 120 (60), the firm signals its private information by reporting more (less) than 100. If the market understands the implications of the signal, the price increases to 220 with good news and to 160 with bad news.

Beneficial earnings management is inconsistent with the market not understanding the implication of the signal.

Neutral earnings management. Suppose that accounting conservatism requires firms with earnings of 100 to report 80, and the firm succeeds in managing earnings to 95. If the market understands the report, the value of a firm that reports 95 is the value of a firm that reports the truth, $100 + 0.6 \times 120 + 0.4 \times 60 = 196$. If the market does not understand the signal, earnings management cannot be neutral. By definition, neutral earnings management yields the same equilibrium payoffs as a truth-telling report (Stein, 1989; Elitzur, 1995; Ronen, Tzur, and Yaari, 2006).

Pernicious earnings management. It is well known that there is 20% chance that firms with bad news (60) will mimic firms with good news (120). Firms with good news prefer truthful disclosure.

By definition, pernicious earnings management conceals the truth. If the market does not see through the earnings management attempt, it discounts the report. The value of a firm that reports good news is $0.88 \times 220 + 0.12 \times 160 = 212.80 < 220$.[4] The value of firms that report the true bad news is 160. Good-news firms are punished because the price, 212.80, is lower than the one assigned when the long-term value is 220. Yet bad-news firms are "rewarded," as the market puts some weight on the chance that the report is truthful and so their valuation is higher than it ought to be, $212.80 > 160$.

How can we know the type of earnings management and what the market knows about earnings management? One approach is to link earnings management directly to the market's reaction, where earnings management is measured by discretionary accruals[5] (Subramanyam, 1996; Guay, Kothari, and Watts, 1996) and smoothing (Hand, 1989; Chaney, Jeter, and Lewis, 1998; Zarowin, 2002). Another research strategy is based on tests of the earnings response coefficient (ERC). These tests run a linear OLS[6] regression of returns (a dependent variable) on earnings surprise (an independent variable), as follows[7]:

---

[4] By Bayes' rule, the proportion of genuine good-news firms is $(0.6 \times 1/(0.6 \times 1 + 0.4 \times 20\%) = 0.88$. The proportion of bad-news firms pretending to have good news is $0.4 \times 20\%/(0.6 \times 1 + 0.4 \times 20\%) = 0.12$.

[5] See Part 4.

[6] The econometric assumptions behind this model have been challenged. The major concern seems to be the linearity of the returns/earnings surprise connection (Cheng, Hopewood, and McKewon, 1992; Freeman and Tse, 1992; Ali, 1994). In addition, note that one extension is to add the additional regressor of unexpected cash flows and unexpected accruals (see, e.g., Ali, 1994; Pfeiffer, Elgers, Lo, and Rees, 1998). For a recent critical review of the ERC literature, consult Kothari (2001).

[7] The research on accounting conservatism—early recognition of losses and deferral of the recognition of gains to when they materialize (Watts, 2003a, b)—also examines the association between earnings and returns (see Basu, 1997; Ball, Kothari, and Robin, 2000; Gigler and Hemmer, 2001; Basu, Hwang, and Jan, 2002; Givoly and Hayn, 2000, 2002; Penman and Zhang, 2002; Beaver and Ryan, 2005, 2005; Jain and Rezaee, 2004; Pae, Thornton, and Welker, 2005; Balachandran and Mohanram, 2006; Bushman and Piotroski, 2006; Givoly, Hayn, and Natarajan, 2007; Roychowdhury and Watts, 2007). The typical test runs a reverse regression, with earnings as the dependent variable and returns as the independent variable. One advantage of such a design is that it resolves the problematic serial correlations in earnings.

$$R = a + \text{ERC} \times \Delta X + \varepsilon, \qquad (4.1)$$

where

R	=	market price return
ERC	=	earnings response coefficient
ΔX	=	earnings surprise
A	=	an intercept
ε	=	noise.

The commonly used metric of the surprise takes the difference between the firm's performance and the analysts' consensus forecast, taking into account the fact that analysts do not forecast GAAP earnings (see, e.g., Abarbanell and Lehavy, 2002; Digabriele and Eisner, 2005).[8] Other measures for earnings surprise are based on the firm's history of accounting earnings.

The ERC captures the marginal effect of a dollar of earnings on the price. In general, the expectation is that the ERC will be positive (although Antle, Demski, and Ryan, 1994, and Teets, 1994, show that restricted accounting recognition might yield a negative ERC when the market has alternative information resources). Since the price attempts to capture the economic value of the firm, the ERC is sensitive to the persistence of earnings (e.g., Ramakrishnan, 1998; Easton, Shroff, and Taylor, 2000) and any factor that affects the persistence and credibility of earnings, such as a firm's size (e.g., Chaney and Jeter, 1992; Collins, Maydew, and Weiss, 1997), risk (e.g., Willett, Kim, and Jang, 2002; Chambers, Freeman, and Koch. 2005), or growth (Shroff, 1995), as well as environ-

---

[8] Baber and Kang (2002a), show that stock splits can contaminate the data because historically restated data are rounded. Baber and Kang illustrate the issue:

> For example, assume that the consensus analysts' forecast EPS is $0.10 and the actual EPS is $0.09, and that the firm subsequently executes a 2-for-l stock split. Both the forecast and the actual EPS are reported as $0.05 after rounding to the nearest cent. Thus, data from the forecast files erroneously indicate that earnings "meet" the consensus forecast, even though actual earnings reported at the disclosure date differed from the consensus expectation. (p. 278)

Baber and Kang show that split-adjusters are firms with specific characteristics: They have greater accounting performance, pre- and post-announcement period stock price performance, sales growth, and systematic risk, but lower book-to-market and debt-to-asset ratios. For a further discussion of the measurement error involved in taking consensus forecasts as a measure of market's expectations, consult Kim, Lim, and Shaw (2001); and Cohen, Hann, and Ogneva (2007).

mental liabilities (Bae and Sami, 2005) and firm-specific events such as a change of auditors (e.g., Hackenbrack and Hogan, 2002). The ERC is likewise sensitive to the length of the window of measurement of stock returns, which allows the market to gain additional information to evaluate earnings (e.g., Chaney and Jeter, 1992; Shroff, 2002), and the quality of supplemental disclosures (e.g., Lundholm and Myers, 2002, who measure the quality of disclosures by the AIMR ratings of corporate disclosures; and Lennox and Park, 2006, who find that the ERC is positively correlated with firms' earnings forecasts).[9],[10]

How does earnings management affect the ERC? Pernicious earnings management obscures value. If the market suspects earnings management, the ERC should be lower (see the analytical argument in Sankar, 1999; Feltham and Pae, 2000; Ronen, Ronen, and Yaari, 2003; Liang, 2004; Crocker and Huddart, 2006). Empirical support of the negative association between earnings management and the response of the market to earnings is provided by several studies (Christensen, Hoyt, and Paterson 1999; De-Fond and Park, 2001; Choi, 2004; Baber and Kang, 2001, 2002b, 2003; Marquardt and Wiedman, 2004b; Cohen, Dey, and Lys, 2005a; Baber, Chen, and Kang, 2006; Ghosh and Lubberink, 2006; Lin and Shih, 2006). Lin and Shih (2006), for example, examine the ERC of firms that report earnings that meet or just beat analysts' earnings forecasts. As discussed in Sect. 5.2, this phenomenon is suspected to reflect earnings management. If the market does not believe their reported earnings, then the ERC of such firms should be lower since their earnings would be discounted. Lin and Shih show that indeed the ERC for such firms is significantly lower than the ERC of a control group.

The research based on the ERC might convey the impression that all earnings management is pernicious. There is indirect evidence of beneficial earnings management, however, in studies that are concerned with the effect of information asymmetry on the ERC (e.g., Balsam, Bartov, and Marquardt, 2002; Jacob and Jorgensen, 2007. See the survey in Kothari, 2001).

---

[9] See the discussion of the information content of earnings and stock price in Chap. 3.

[10] As discussed in Chap. 1, one of the debates in accounting literature is whether the ERC has declined over time (e.g., Buchheit and Kohlbeck, 2002), and if it has, whether this signals a reduction in the value of earnings, an increase in alternative sources of information (Francis, Schipper, and Vincent, 2003), an increase in the noise of the price (Dontoh, Radhakrishnan, and Ronen, 2004), or an increase in the value of alternative accounting measures. Collins, Maydew, and Weiss (1997), find that an increase in book value, especially for firms with losses, compensates for a decrease in the ERC.

The market's inability perfectly to detect pernicious earnings management implies that earnings management may be associated with an increase in the heterogeneity of the market's beliefs. Cohen, Dey, and Lys (2005a), and Li, Xie, and Xu (2005), for example, find that trading volume is positively associated with the size of earnings management, where trading volume is a signal of heterogeneous beliefs in the market (Dontoh and Ronen, 1993; Kim and Verrecchia, 2001).

4.1.4 When Does the Market Learn About Non-neutral Earnings Management?

Consider the following timeline (Table 4.2), which distinguishes among the following possibilities:

4.1.4.1. Earnings management is anticipated before earnings are managed.

4.1.4.2. Earnings management is suspected after earnings management but before earnings are announced.

4.1.4.3. Earnings management is suspected when earnings are announced.

4.1.4.4. Earnings management is detected in a 12-month window after earnings are announced.

4.1.4.5. The market learns about earnings management when it is exposed.

4.1.4.6. The market never learns about earnings management.

4.1.4.1. Earnings Management Is Anticipated Before Earnings Are Managed

Since the market price contains a discount for information asymmetry (e.g., Easley, Hvidkjaer, and O'Hara, 2002; Easley and O'Hara, 2004), the market probably discounts pernicious managed earnings before it occurs. (Alternatively, the discount reflects the "signal jamming" dynamic of neutral earnings management that is described in Chap. 1 and in Part 3.)

Burgstahler and Eames (2003), and Lin and Shih (2006), provide examples of the anticipation of earnings management by analysts. The former show that analysts anticipate earnings management to avoid small losses and small earnings decreases, and the latter find that the earnings surprises of firms that meet or just beat expectations are discounted in forecasts. Burgstahler and Eames indicate that analysts are unable to pinpoint those specific firms that beat market expectations by managing earnings, so their forecasts exhibit pessimism for firms with zero reported earnings. Lin and Shih show that analysts learn from past observations.

Table 4.2 Time table of detection of earnings management by the market

Date 1	Date 2	Date 3	Date 4	Date 5	Date 6
Before earnings management takes place	After earnings management but before earnings are announced	At the time of earnings announcement or shortly after earnings are announced	Earnings management is detected in a 12-month window after earnings are announced	Long afer earnings are announced or when earnings management is exposed	Never
Chai and Tung (2002), Burgstahler and Eames, (2003), Ghosh and Lubbernik, (2006), Lin and Shih, (2006), and DaDalt and Margetis (2007)	Coles, Hertzel, and, Kalpathy (2006), Desai, Krishnamurthy, and Venkataraman (2005)	Bishop and Eccher (2000), Shivakumar (2000), Balsam, Bartov, and Marquardt, (2002), Baber and Kang (2003), Baber, Chen, and Kang (2006), Hribar, Jenkins, and Johnson (2006), the literature on ERC	Subramanyam (1996), Guay, Kothari, and Watts (1996), Black, Carnes, and Richardson (2000), Francis, LaFond, Olsson, and Schipper (2005), and the mispricing literature	Restatements: Anderson and Yohn (2002), Richardson, Tuna, and Wu (2002), Wu (2002), Palmrose, Richardson, and Scholz (2004), Kedia and Philippon (2005), Efendi, Srivastava, and Swanson (2006), Karpoff, Lee, and Martin (2007). The literature on class action suits and AAERs	Chambers (1999), Daneshfar and Zeghal (2001), Das and Zhang (2003), Beneish and Nichols (2005), Michaely and Roberts (2006)

Ghosh and Lubberink (2006), examine firms that disclosed material weaknesses in their internal control systems after November 2004. They examine the market's response to these firms' earnings in 2001 and 2002, before the material weakness exposure. They find evidence that the capital market perceived these firms as having lower quality financial reporting. During the period before their revelations, these firms had lower ERCs, less favorable common stock rankings and debt ratings, a higher cost of debt, larger errors in analysts' earnings forecasts, and higher audit fees. To the extent that weak control facilitates earnings management, this study provides indirect evidence that the market can be aware of the potential for earnings management.

DaDalt and Margetis (2007), examine the valuation impact of earnings restatements on same-industry competitors by matching firms with GAO restatements during the 1996–2002 period to non-restating firms in the same four-digit SIC. They find that competitors experience significant negative abnormal returns around restatement announcements. A similar result is obtained in Han and Wild (1990). We note, however, that our interpretation that the market's response indicates anticipation of earnings management may require further testing. Regulators forced Fannie Mae, the home-mortgage giant, to employ more conservative accounting and financing methods following an investigation that was triggered by findings about its competitor, Freddie Mac. Thus, in some cases, a response to a competitor's revelation may be concurrent with earnings management.

The market's suspicion of earnings management results in its discounting of the firm's earnings. For instance, rich anecdotal evidence and empirical research note unfavorable reaction by the market to delays in earnings announcements (see Begley and Fischer, 1998, the citations therein). To the extent that this delay indicates earnings management (Trueman, 1990), the market's reaction seems to anticipate such behavior. Yet if a firm delays a report for reasons that are unrelated to earnings management, what is its best response to the ensuing price decline? Chai and Tung (2002), study 2,045 late reporters between 1991 and 1994.[11] They show that late reporters employ income-decreasing discretionary accruals and that the magnitude of these accruals is proportional to the reporting lag. That is, since the market discounts the firm's earnings, the firm opts to build a reserve of reported earnings for future use. Hence, the anticipation of earnings management is a self-fulfilling prophecy. It will happen when the firm delves into the reserves of reported earnings to boost earnings.

---

[11] Firms that reported between 5 and 90 days after their reporting date in the previous year.

4.1.4.2 Earnings Management Is Suspected After Earnings Management but Before Earnings Are Announced

Suspecting earnings management after it took place but before earnings are announced requires some measure of sophistication. Short-sellers, for example, are notable for the link between their position and negative returns on the stock (e.g., Dechow, Hutton, Meulbroek, and Sloan, 2001; Desai, Ramesh, Thiagarajan, and Balachandran, 2002; Desai, Krishnamurthy, and Venkataraman, 2006[12]). The short-sellers interviewed by Desai, Krishnamurthy, and Venkataraman indicate that they target firms with a low quality of earnings, which is synonymous with a suspicion of earnings management, and that are overvalued by the market. Their examination of 412 firms that restated their earnings reveals that short-sellers took their position as early as 18 months before the restatement of earnings. By that time, earnings management had already been committed, but because no restatement had been made, only a few market participants knew about it.

Coles, Hertzel, and Kalpathy (2006), show that the market anticipates earnings management when there is sufficient disclosure before its occurrence. Before firms were required to expense stock options, the firm did not have to record it as a compensation expense if (1) the grant day price was set equal to the exercise price (see the discussion of the backdating scandal in Chap. 3) and (2) the terms of the plan were not variable. The second condition ruled out the repricing of stock options. Hence, if they were out of the money, firms had to cancel the (old) outstanding options and wait 6 months and a day to issue new options, and the SEC's disclosure requirements made this event public knowledge. In a typical case, the firm announces the plan to reissue and then allows a month or so for employees to decide how many options to tender. "Since managers of such '6-and-1' firms benefit from a lower strike price for the reissued options, investors and analysts should be able to anticipate managerial attempts to manage accruals downward prior to the reissue date" (Coles, Hertzel, and Kalpathy, 2006, p. 175). Their evidence supports this observation: they find that the market and analysts see through the earnings management attempt to reduce earnings when the firm announces the reissuance plan.

There are, however, examples that suggest that the market does not understand earnings management even when disclosures are made. Hand (1989), reports that swaps are used to smooth earnings. In his 1990 study, Hand examines how the market responds to the announcement of earnings

---

[12] In contrast, Richardson (2003), does not find that short-sellers trade on accruals.

in the quarter in which the swap was made. If the market sees through earnings management, no reaction to the gains on the swap should take place because of the prior announcement of the swap. Hand shows that the market does not absorb all the implications of swaps since there is a favorable reaction to increases in earnings that result from swaps.

4.1.4.3 Earnings Management Is Suspected When Earnings Are Announced

Some earnings management is detected in the short term, around the announcement date of earnings or (at most) a few weeks later, when detailed reports are available to the public at the time of the filing of financial reports on form 10-Q with the SEC. The difference between the two events is that information available on the 10-Q form is more detailed.[13] If the market fails to identify an earnings management attempt on the announcement date, it has an opportunity to learn of it on the subsequent filing date. We noted above the ERC literature. Since the ERC measures the response of the market to an earnings surprise, this strand of research seems to support the notion that the market discounts earnings suspected of being managed. (The caveat of this research from the perspective of managing GAAP earnings is that it largely uses the analysts' earnings numbers which differ from GAAP earnings (Abarbanell and Lehavy, 2002; Digabriele and Eisner, 2005)).

Bishop and Eccher (2000), examine firms that make a change to the useful life of assets. This action is observable because firms have to report it in their income statements, but a change in estimated useful life may not necessarily be a case of pernicious earnings management. A comparison to a control sample reveals that increasing the estimated useful life of assets represents earnings management, but decreasing their useful life does not. Bishop and Eccher show that the market price undoes the effect of the revised assumption on earnings in the year of the change and in the subsequent 2 years. It discounts an increase and grants a premium for a decrease.

Shivakumar (2000), builds on prior research that found that firms inflate earnings before seasoned equity offerings. He investigates whether the market's response discounts the managed earnings. Shivakumar finds that there is no correlation between discretionary accruals and stock performance in the long run. This leads him to conclude that the market learns

---

[13] In some cases, there may also be a difference between announced and filed earnings (Hollie, Livnat, and Segal, 2004).

about the earnings management attempt at the time of the issuance and un-does its effect perfectly then. In contrast, Louis (2005), in a study of the market's reaction to stock-for-stock mergers, finds that although there is some discounting in the period leading to the merger, there is further correction in the long run. The difference between these results suggests that the market discerns earnings management only imperfectly. That is, the market is aware of earnings management but apparently cannot fathom its exact size; fully grasping the magnitude of a firm's earnings management requires learning over time.

Balsam, Bartov, and Marquardt (2002), examine the effect of earnings management[14] on market returns for two classes of firms that manage earnings: firms with a high level of institutional ownership, which is a proxy for investors' sophistication, and other firms. Their finding of a negative association between unexpected discretionary accruals and cumulative abnormal returns (CAR) over a 17-day window around the filing date indicates that the market discounts pernicious earnings management immediately. To the extent that the market responds immediately to new information, their findings are consistent with the differential response of sophisticated and non-sophisticated investors. Sophisticated investors incorporate the valuation implications of earnings management (through unexpected discretionary accruals) before the formal release of the 10-Q, but not as early as the earnings announcement date. Unsophisticated investors recognize earnings management only when "it hits them in the face" after the 10-Q becomes available.

Baber and Kang (2003), study 42,000 quarterly announcements in the 1993–1999 period. They find that security returns during earnings announcement periods are reliably and negatively related to measures of components of managed earnings. Baber and Kang also conduct tests of the 19% of all quarterly earnings announcements that are "on-target" announcements, defined as earnings per share (EPS) exactly equaling the analysts' consensus forecast. For this sample, the 3-day excess security returns are reliably lower when earnings appear to be overstated than when earnings appear to be understated. Furthermore, the negative association between the components of managed earnings and excess returns is stronger. Baber, Chen, and Kang (2006), examine the effect of supplemental disclosures on the market's suspicion of earnings management at the time the firm announces its earnings in a sample of 10,248 firm/quarters. Denoting earnings management by EM, they conclude,

---

[14] They capture earnings management in two ways: firms that meet analysts' consensus forecasts and firms whose discretionary accruals are at least 1% of total assets.

"This evidence ... suggests that investors attempt to price protect themselves against EM, and that their ability to do so is enhanced when firms disclose information that can be used to disentangle the consequences of EM" (p. 6).

Hribar, Jenkins, and Johnson (2006), consider the effect of stock repurchases as a means to affect the earnings per share and meet the consensus analyst forecast. They observe that the market discounts this earnings management attempt. Such firms have a premium for beating expectations that is about 60% lower than the one for firms that do not use stock repurchase to "make the numbers."

These findings raise the question of why earnings are managed when managers are aware that the market discounts the earnings management effects. We address this question in Part 3, but to briefly review the answer, note that if a firm misses its target by just one penny, the market reaction is negative and strong (see, e.g., Levitt, 1998) because the market suspects that any firm that misses the target is having difficulties that prevent it from reaching it. That is, it is not a matter of "I don't want to," but rather of "I can't." The market thus forces firms to "play the game" or be punished (Nofsinger and Kim, 2003).

4.1.4.4 Earnings Management Is Detected in a 12-Month Window After Earnings Are Announced

Given that earnings are but one signal for market participants, it may well be the case that the market learns of earnings management only over time. Indeed, some earnings management is detected by the market after time has passed, where the evidence is usually collected for a 1-year window (Subramanyam, 1996, table 3, Model 6; Guay, Kothari, and Watts, 1996, table 2, Panels D and E).

Black, Carnes, and Richardson (2000), compare the market's reaction to firms that publicize multiple non-recurrent items and its reaction to firms that report such an item just once (referring to income-statement items such as discontinued operations, special items, and extraordinary items). On the one hand, these non-recurrent items are supposed to have little impact on the firm's valuation, as they are transitory in nature. On the other hand, firms with multiple items tend to declare bankruptcy within 5 years. Examining firms over a rolling 6-year period between 1977 and 1996, Black, Carnes, and Richardson find that the market reacts negatively to firms with multiple items and positively to firms with a single item. The link to earnings management is given by their finding that the patterns of discretionary accruals are consistent with managers' engaging in upward earnings management prior to multiple write-downs.

Francis, LaFond, Olsson, and Schipper (2005), relate the cost of capital to earnings management. They are concerned with a one-quarter-ahead relationship. That is, a cost-of-capital variable in quarter t is measured relative to managed earnings in quarter $t-1$. They find that firms with lower quality earnings have higher costs of capital, as evidenced by lower debt ratings, larger realized costs of debt, larger industry-adjusted earnings-price ratios, larger equity betas, and positive loadings on an earnings quality factor added to the one- and three-factor asset pricing regressions. Several other studies note that earnings management increases the cost of capital (Blackwell, Noland, and Winters, 1998; Anderson, Mansi, and Reeb, 2004; Hribar and Jenkins, 2004; Mansi, Maxwell, and Miller, 2004; Ashbaugh-Skaife, Collins, and LaFond, 2006; Karpoff, Lee, and Martin, 2007a).[15]

For additional discussion of the market's ability to see through earnings within this time frame, consult the accruals mispricing literature (e.g., Xie, 2001). This strand of literature started with Sloan (1996), who showed that the market does not distinguish between accruals and cash flows when it prices earnings, although the persistence of accruals and cash flows is different (see Dechow and Schrand, 2004, for a valuable tutorial, and see also Chap. 9).

4.1.4.5 The Market Learns About Earnings Management When It Is Exposed

Some pernicious earnings management is detected only when it is exposed, long after the managed earnings are announced. The following diagram, which is adapted from figure 1 in Karpoff, Lee, and Martin (2007a), summarizes the time line of exposure of the earnings management event.

The process described in Fig. 4.1 might last years. For example, Cendant Corp. managed earnings for at least 12 years before it was sued. The enforcement period can take years, and in many cases, firms delist before reaching date 8 (see, e.g., Karpoff, Lee, and Martin, 2007a, who report that only 194 firms in their sample of 585 firms that cooked their books survived this process).

---

[15] An indirect evidence is given by studies that find a lower cost of debt with higher quality of governance (e.g., Klock, Mansi, and Maxwell, 2005), since better governance curbs pernicious earnings management. See Chap. 5.

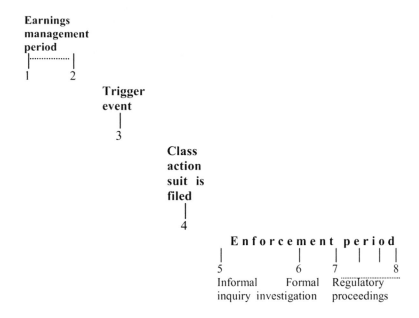

Fig. 4.1 The enforcement process

In this subsection, we focus mainly on the trigger event (date 3) because in most cases, this is the first time the public learns about a firm's earnings management. The most likely trigger event is the announcement of a forthcoming restatement of earnings. Karpoff, Lee, and Martin observe, however, that although every firm that went through the enforcement period restated earnings at least once, restatement is not necessarily the trigger event. That is, some restatements are made in response to the departure of auditors or management, routine review by the SEC, or charges by a whistleblower.[16]

A triggering event is usually followed by a class action suit (date 4). Karpoff, Lee, and Martin observe that in their sample, class action suits were filed any time before or after regulatory proceedings concluded. To illustrate that a class action suit may be prompt, consider Refco, which used to be one of the largest commodities and futures trading firms. It allegedly had $430 million uncollectible accounts receivable when it went public in August 2005. The truth was kept from the public at that time, however, because these accounts were parked at another company, Lib-

---

[16] Note that a trigger event could also be the firm's disclosure of unusual trading. That is, there are some cases in which some market participants know about the accounting fraud before the public at large learns about it.

erty, controlled by Refco's CEO, Phillip Bennet. On Monday, October 10, 2005, the board announced that the accounting reports given in conjunction with the IPO were not accurate, that it had suspended Bennet, and that Refco had collected the balances of $430 million of accounts receivable from Bennet. The share price fell. The next day, Bennet was put under house arrest by Elliott Spitzer. On Wednesday, the first class action suit was filed. Refco had to shut down business lines that required credit, and on Friday, it announced bankruptcy, filed with the court on the following Monday.[17]

The enforcement period starts on Date 5. It is divided into two subperiods. The first is the investigation period, which might start as an informal investigation and proceed to a formal investigation (dates 5–6). The SEC then might drop the case. If it does not, the SEC initiates legal proceedings, which sometimes involve transferring the case to the Department of Justice to make criminal charges against the firm or key personnel (whereas the SEC either begins administrative proceedings or files civil charges). The regulatory period can involve multiple events (between dates 7 and 8). Karpoff, Lee, and Martin, who examine 585 firms that cooked the books between 1978 and 2002, report that the average enforcement action involves 1.70 administrative releases, 2.06 filings of civil actions, and 0.56 filings of criminal charges. The total number of enforcement actions amounts to 2,532; they involved an additional 199 affiliated companies, such as accounting firms and investment banks, and 2,381 individuals.

As readers who follow news of specific cases know, the negative market response is not restricted to the trigger event. Karpoff, Lee, and Martin (2007a), observe that the mean return of 328 firms (with available CRSP data out of 371 firms) with an identifiable trigger event (date 4) is –25.24%; for the 230 cases (with available data out of 278) that disclosed an investigation (dates 5–6), the mean return is –14.41%, and for the 586 regulatory events (with available data out of 1,953) the mean return is –6.56%. (dates 7–8) They interpret the negative impact (which is actually

---

[17] The *New York Times* on October 15, 2005, laments:

The rapid downward spiral of Refco is an illustration that on Wall Street what often matters most is not so much the size of the balance sheet that keeps a firm solvent as it is the character of the person at the top.

Indeed, firms that once dominated the financial landscape, like Drexel Burnham, E. F. Hutton, Salomon Brothers and Kidder Peabody, have all disappeared, done in largely by scandals involving individuals who undermined trust in the firms. (Jenny Anderson and Landon Thomas, The Fall of Refco Is Providing a Test for Wall Street)

larger because some of the firms are delisted) as follows: "The investigation announcement generally confirms suspicions and frequently reveals additional information about the firm's past and future earnings, assets values, and management" (p. 13).

It is notable that a decomposition of the total legal costs indicates that only 47 (or 8%) of the 585 firms faced monetary penalties (the mean is $106.98 million, which drops to $59.8 million upon excluding the $2.28 billion penalty on WorldCom, Inc., which was later reduced to $750 million). Class action suits against 231 firms (or 39.3%) of the 585 firms cost these firms five times as much as the legal penalties (an average of $37.3 million, which drops to $25.55 million upon excluding the outlier case of $2.83 billion class action settlement against Cendant Corp). Legal costs amount to 8.5% of the total losses associated with enforcement actions. The remaining loss is a correction for inflated earnings and loss of reputation—that is, "reputation costs" that cloud the business relationships of the firm with suppliers, creditors, and customers. Karpoff, Lee, and Martin estimate that for every dollar of overstating earnings, a firm loses $4.08.

The research for which this sequence of events is relevant has focused on three events: the restatement, the class actions suit, and the SEC's Accounting and Auditing Enforcement Release (AAER).

- Restatements[18]

See, e.g., Wu (2002), Richardson, Tuna, and Wu (2002), Palmrose, Richardson, and Scholz (2004), and Palmrose and Scholz (2004). The research confirms the market's negative response to restatements. Wu (2002), who identified 1,068 restatements between 1997 and 2000, and Richardson, Tuna, and Wu (2002), who identified 440 restatement firms between 1995 and 2000, find abnormal returns of –11% over a 3-day window surrounding a restatement event; Anderson and Yohn (2002), who identified 161 restatement firms between 1997 and 1999 find abnormal returns of –3.49% over a 6-day

---

[18] For a valuable review of the literature on restatements, consult Eilifsen and Messier (2000). Some of the research is concerned with the incentives to manage earnings that led to restatements. See, e.g., DeFond and Jiambalvo (1991), who are concerned with firms managing earnings to mask poor performance, Burns and Kedia (2003); Collins, Reitenga, and Sanchez (2005), and Efendi, Srivastava, and Swanson (2006), who are concerned with firms managing earnings to maximize management's incentives, and Richardson, Tuna, and Wu (2002), Kedia (2003), Kedia and Philippon (2005), and Efendi, Srivastava, and Swanson (2006), who are concerned with the importance of debt. Agrawal and Chadha (2005), link governance characteristics of the firm to restatements (see Chap. 5).

window surrounding the first time the restatement became public, and Palmrose, Richardson, and Scholz (2004), who identified 403 restatements between 1971 and 1999, find abnormal returns of 9% over a 2-day window of such an event. Richardson, Tuna, and Wu (2002), who identified 440 restatement firms between 1995 and 2000, and Wu (2002), who identified 1,068 restatements between 1997 and 2000, find abnormal returns of –11% over a 3-day window surrounding a restatement event. Wu (2002), notes that when restatement involves revenues, the abnormal return is even lower, –14.4% or less. Kedia and Philippon (2005), find 10% price decrease in the sample of 226 firms that restated earnings between 1995 and 2002. Richardson, Tuna, and Wu find that restatement firms also tend to beat benchmarks (see below and Chap. 5) of positive quarterly earnings growth and positive earnings surprises, and Ryan, Lev, and Wu (2006), find that investors take into account the adverse effect of restatements on earnings reported in previous years.

Restatements also reduce the credibility of the firm's accounting earnings (Wu, 2002; Anderson and Yohn, 2002). Anderson and Yohn show that ERC declines. Hribar and Jenkins (2004), show that a firm's cost of capital increases immediately after restatement.

- Class action suit[19]

Several studies have examined such suits (Kellog, 1984; Francis, Philbrick, and Schipper, 1994; Griffin, 1996; Bhagat, Bizjack, and Coles, 1998; Niehaus and Roth, 1999; Ferris and Pritchard, 2001; DuCharme, Malatesta, and Sefcik, 2004; Griffin, Grundfest, and Perino, 2004; Peng and Roell, 2006). The legal discipline offers a rich literature on the topic (see, e.g., Bauman, 1979; Alexander, 1991; Romano, 1991; Johnson, Nelson, and Pritchard, 2007).

Research in this area is often linked to the trigger event. Ferris and Pritchard (2001), for example, distinguish three dates: the date the alleged fraud is discovered publicly, the date a class action suit is filed, and the date a judge decides whether to dismiss the charge as having no merit. They find abnormal returns of –25% around the date the alleged fraud is

---

[19] A class action suit as an independent event is tricky. In many cases, especially before the Private Securities Litigation Reform Act of 2002, a drop in share price triggered a class action suit, based on a claim that shareholders overpaid for their shares because the firm hid bad news from them. Niehaus and Roth (1999), report that on the average these class actions had merit, as evidenced by abnormal insider selling and abnormal CEO turnover, as well as an abnormal incidence of capital raising activities. In all of these events, management had incentives to withhold bad news.

revealed and additional abnormal returns of −3% when the lawsuit is filed.[20] Unlike some prior work, however, they find no response when the issuer's motion to dismiss the complaint is resolved, even if the motion is dismissed.

- AAER

The research on AAERs is not independent from the research on restatements and class action suits. Palmrose and Scholz (2004), for example, find that 52 firms that restated earnings (11% of their sample) were investigated by the SEC, and 186 firms (38% of their sample) were sued. Wu (2002), finds that 232 firms that restated earnings (41% of her sample) were sued. See also Choi (2005), and Johnson, Nelson, and Pritchard (2007), on the link between class action suits and restatements and Bonner, Palmrose, and Young (1998), on the probability of litigation.[21] Researches employ the existence of an AAER as a simple way to identify a sample of firms known to engage in pernicious earnings management. (See, e.g., Feroz, Park, and Pastena, 1991; Dechow, Sloan, and Sweeney, 1995, 1996; Beneish, 1997, 1999b; Bonner, Palmrose, and Young, 1998).

The research on AAERs is not independent from the research on restatements and class action suits. Palmrose and Scholz (2002), for example, find that 52 firms that restated earnings (11% of their sample) were investigated by the SEC, and 186 firms (38% of their sample) were sued. Wu (2002), for example, finds that 232 firms that restated earnings (41% of her sample) were sued. See also Choi (2005); and Johnson, Nelson, and Pritchard (2007), on the link between class action suits and restatements.

The market responds unfavorably to enforcement action. For example, Feroz, Park, and Pastena (1991), who study 188 firms mentioned in the AAERs between April 1982 and April 1989, find negative abnormal returns in the 2-day window announcement around the reporting violation event. Dechow, Sloan, and Sweeney (1996), who study 92 firms mentioned in AAERs between 1982 and 1992 (see Table 1), find an average price drop of 9%. In addition, there is an increase in the bid-ask spread and a decline in the number of analysts following the firm.

---

[20] Richardson, Tuna, and Wu (2002), report similar findings.

[21] As a signal of earnings management, being included in the AAER is not a sure signal that the firm engaged is fraudulent earnings management. For example, Bonner, Palmrose, and Young (1998), identify 390 companies subject to AAER in the 1982–1995 period. Only 261 companies were subject to enforcement actions. Of the remaining firms, 100 (42%) had no litigation, 98 (38%) had auditor litigation, and 53 (20%) had other litigation.

4.1.4.6 The Market Never Learns About Earnings Management

Discussing the case in which the market never learns about earnings management is difficult, as the market may not detect earnings management because a firm did not manage earnings. We thus at best can offer indirect evidence. For example, earnings management in the pernicious sense cannot survive unless there is some information asymmetry. Michaely and Roberts (2006), in their study of dividends payments, provide an example that shows that information asymmetry is not resolved perfectly. They observe that public firms smooth dividends over time through a policy of gradual increases in dividends, infrequent decreases in dividends, and relative insensitivity of dividends to transitory earnings shocks. In contrast, the dividend policy of private firms is more sensitive to transitory earnings shocks—both positive and negative. As discussed in Chap. 5, a smooth dividend stream is a signal that inventors need not worry about transitory earnings.

Managers indulging in pernicious earnings management do not wish the market to know because such knowledge might defeat their purpose. It stands to reason, then, that some pernicious earnings management is never detected. Chambers (1999), conjectures that firms that use income-decreasing (increasing) earnings management tactics that are not detected by the market will be overpriced (underpriced). He tests his hypotheses by constructing hedge portfolios whose shares are selected by the magnitude of earnings management. He shows that significant abnormal trading returns can be earned in 12- and 24-month windows following an earnings release.

Earnings management also may not be detected because investors do not want to learn unpleasant truths in times of euphoria (Coffee, 2003a). Daneshfar and Zeghal (2001), provide empirical evidence in their study of the discretionary accruals of 1510 firms[22] between the first quarter of 1999 and the end of the first quarter of 2000. In this period, the stock price indices rose: the Dow Jones Industrial Index by 20%, the S&P 500 index by 22%, and the price index of NASDAQ by 108%. Consistent with their conjecture that when the environment is optimistic, investors are more willing to accept good-news earnings, they find that discretionary accruals in each quarter were significantly positive.

Das and Zhang (2003), observe that firms inflate earnings in order to round their reported earnings per share up. It seems that such an attempt

---

[22] The industries and the corresponding SIC codes are Basic Industries, 115; Capital Goods, 385; Construction, 44; Consumer Goods, 813; Energy, 110; Finance, 42.

would be obvious, but the market underreacts. They leave open the question whether the market ever finds out about the earnings management.

For additional studies, consult the mispricing literature (Chap. 9). We conclude this sub section with the observation that some of the findings in the studies we have discussed are consistent with the post-announcement drift phenomenon to the extent that this phenomenon indicates that the market waits for additional information before fully reacting to the informational content of announced earnings.

For a valuable discussion of the post-announcement drift phenomenon, consult Bartov (1992), Bernard and Seyhun (1997), Kothari (2001), Livnat (2003), Jegadeesh and Livnat (2006), and Livnat and Mendenhall (2006). Dontoh, Ronen, and Sarath (2003), show that the phenomenon is consistent with market rationality.

4.2 Earnings Management Events

Researchers have identified three settings in which firms have incentives to manage earnings in order to affect the market price:

4.2.1   Meeting or beating a benchmark.
4.2.2   Issuing shares: initial public offerings (IPO), seasoned equity offerings (SEO), or new listings.
4.2.3   Mergers and stock-for-stock acquisitions.

4.2.1 Benchmark Beating

At the risk of repeating a cliché, accounting numbers have no meaning without being compared to some benchmark. Firms therefore have incentives to manage earnings to beat such benchmarks as zero earnings, expected changes in earnings between parallel periods, and analysts' consensus forecasts.

4.2.1.1. Zero Earnings Level

The understanding is that firms prefer to avoid reporting losses. Why should zero earnings be a desirable benchmark? Burgstahler and Dichev (1997a), and DeGeorge, Patel, and Zeckhauser (1999), offer psychological explanations, such as the notion that investors would like to observe positive earnings. Hayn (1995), Burgstahler and Dichev (1997b), Durtschi and Easton (2005), and Lee, Li, and Yue (2006), base the answer on the fact that the valuation models for losses and profits are different (Hayn, 1995;

Burgstahler and Dichev, 1997b; Durtschi and Easton, 2005; Lee, Li, and Yue, 2006). Durtschi and Easton, for example, report that the median price of a firm that reports a one-cent loss is 0.25, as compared to 1.31 for a one-cent profit. Hence, the earnings game to some extent is binary. Either the firm reports losses and thus belongs to one set or it makes a profit, which puts it in a different valuation model.

An alternative explanation is offered by Xue (2003). Xue argues that beating a threshold[23] is costly because it is achieved by boosting current accruals, which sacrifices flexibility in meeting thresholds in the future. Thus, when the information asymmetry between the firm and the market is large regarding the firm's true value, the firm and the market "communicate" through a tacit agreement on a focal threshold. Strong performers beat the threshold, and poor performers miss it. Xue shows that the market understands this signaling game and rewards firms that slightly beat the target while punishing firms that slightly miss it. A crucial feature of a benchmark is that poor firms cannot beat it. Hayn (1995), finds that losses were frequent for her sample of 9,572 firms in the 1962–1990 period:

> The earnings variable is defined as income (loss) from continuing operations, before extraordinary items, discontinued operations, and the cumulative effect of accounting changes. ... Losses are fairly common, appearing in 19.6% of all firm-years. There is a dramatic increase in the frequency of losses over time, from about 3% in the early 1960's to over 30% in the late 1980's. ...The incidence of losses is shared by almost all firms. ...the majority of firms with at least eight years of data (2,547 out of 4,148, or 61.4%) report at least one loss and one-fifth of them have two to three losses during the 29-year sample period. (p. 129)

For additional studies that find an increase in reported losses over time, consult Burgstahler and Dichev (1997a), DeAngelo, DeAngelo, and Skinner (2004), and Durtschi and Easton (2005).

We observe that according to Xue, the threshold in itself is not important, but rather it is crucial that the market and the firm implicitly agree on it. Indeed, Brown (2001), and others find that the distribution of earnings has shifted over time from small losses to zero profits and lately to small profits. It seems that the focal performance level has shifted over time.

4.2.1.2. Earnings Changes Between Parallel Periods

The understanding is that firms prefer to avoid reporting decreases in earnings relative to the earnings announced in the same quarter in the previous

---

[23] Given the vocabulary of DeGeorge, Patel, and Zeckhauser (1999), we refer to benchmarks as thresholds, interchangeably.

year (Burgstahler and Dichev, 1997a; DeGeorge, Patel, and Zeckhauser, 1999; Matsunaga and Park, 2001; Marquardt and Wiedman, 2004a; Graham, Harvey, and Rajgopal, 2005; Barua, Legoria, and Moffitt, 2006). The preferable strategy is to report a string of earnings increases (DeAngelo, DeAngelo, and Skinner, 1996; Barth, Elliot, and Finn, 1999; Brown, 2001; Richardson, Tuna, and Wu, 2002[24]; Suk, 2005; Myers, Myers, and Skinner, 2006), and the pressure is thus stronger for firms that have profits than for firms with losses (Barua, Legoria, and Moffitt, 2006).

Why should avoiding a decrease be a desirable benchmark? The answer is likely to overlap the explanation for the first benchmark: The market "appreciates" firms that meet this threshold. Rees (2005), shows that a trading strategy that is based on predicting the probability that the firm will report a positive earnings change and meet or beat analysts' consensus earnings forecasts yields abnormal positive returns.

Avoiding a decrease is a desirable benchmark when the increase is persistent. The higher the perceived growth in earnings, the higher the net present value of the firm's future stream of earnings and, hence, dividends payments. Based on interviews and questionnaires received from CFOs, Graham, Harvey, and Rajgopal (2005), state that the benchmark is quarterly earnings of the same quarter in the previous year.

Analysts' consensus earnings forecasts

The understanding is that the firms are under pressure to meet or beat (MBE) analysts' consensus forecasts.

Why should the consensus forecast be a desirable benchmark? The answer is that they represent the market's expectations. And, as Parfet (2000), and other practitioners observe, the first rule for a public firm is not to disappoint the market. We discuss this benchmark at some length in Chap.5.

Graham, Harvey, and Rajgopal (2005), summarize their findings:

> CFOs believe that earnings, not cash flows, are the key metric considered by outsiders. ... two most important earnings benchmarks are quarterly earnings for the same quarter last year and the analyst consensus estimate. Meeting or exceeding benchmarks is very important. Managers describe a trade-off between the short-term need to "deliver earnings" and the long-term objective of making value-maximizing investment decisions. Executives believe that hitting earnings benchmarks builds credibility with the market and helps to maintain or increase their firm's stock price. (p. 5)

---

[24] Richardson, Tuna, and Wu (2002), investigate 440 restatements by 225 firms from 1971 to 2000, finding that restatement firms have longer strings of positive quarterly earnings growth and longer strings of positive quarterly earnings surprises than non-restatement firms.

From an earnings management perspective, the issue is how to interpret the situation when firms meet or beat thresholds. Since the empirical research cannot compare the unobservable truth with reported earnings in order to identify earnings management, researchers adopt one of three approaches. The first is based on the assumption that unmanaged earnings are a draw from the normal distribution. Hence, earnings management is established if the distribution of earnings of all firms deviates from the normal distribution (Hayn, 1995; Burgstahler and Dichev, 1997a; Kang, 2005, and other studies that are cited below). In what follows, we refer to this as the *distributional approach* (McNichols, 2000). See Chap. 11.

The other strategy compares firms in the same industry with dissimilar incentives to manage earnings. Beatty, Ke, and Petroni (2002), examine whether public banks manage earning by comparing the frequency of their earnings changes and their choice of accounting treatment with those of private banks. Clearly, private firms are under no pressure to beat thresholds to please shareholders. Furthermore, private banks are characterized by having fewer owners (Nagar, Petroni, and Wolfenzon, 2002, report that the majority of private banks in their sample had less than five owners), and owners are managers, too. Hence, earnings in private banks are not an important statistic for alleviating the conflict of interests between owners and managers. Earnings in private banks are, however, important for tax assessment. Beatty, Ke, and Petroni find that the frequency of earnings decreases is lower for public banks. The accounting choices of public firms for major line items in their income statements are consistent with earnings management to avoid small earnings decreases. Furthermore, the string of reported earnings increases is longer for public banks.

When a comparable sample is not available, another approach attempts to identify earnings management through comparison of book income to tax income, because tax income is based on fewer estimates (Desai, 2003).

4.2.1.3. The Distributional Test

Studies that employ this approach show that there is a kink in the distribution function of the earnings management object around the benchmark. Figures 4.2 and 4.3 compare the distribution of changes in net income scaled by market value of equity at the beginning of the year for four quarters.

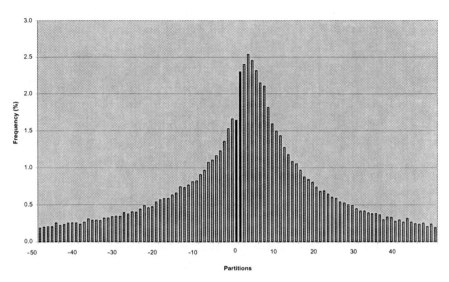

Partitions

Fig. 4.2 Scaled changes in fiscal year net income. This figure is copied, by permission, from the 2005 working paper version of Jacob and Jorgensen (2007) (figure 2A), for a sample of all firms on the quarterly Compustat database between 1981 and 2001 (The sample contains 920,926 quarterly observations for 22,015 distinct firms from 1981 to 2001.)

Figure 4.2 is typical in the literature. It shows an abnormally low number of companies that miss the benchmark (located to the left of the benchmark) and abnormally high number of companies that beat the benchmark (located to the right of the benchmark). Graphically, the graph has a kink. Burgstahler and Dichev (1997a), and others interpret the kink as indicating the migration of firms with small losses to small profits by means of earnings management. Burgstahler and Dichev offer corroborating evidence by examining the cash flows from operation component of earnings.

If the kink is a product of earnings management, it stands to reason that further tests of discretionary accruals (see part 4) should corroborate this hypothesis. Here the evidence is mixed. Kang (2005), finds earnings management using both the Jones model and the IV approach of Kang and Sivaramakrishnan (see Part 4, Chaps. 10 and 11). Marquardt and Wiedman (2004a), examine accruals of firms that are averse to earnings decreases, finding that they do indeed seem to manage earnings when compared to a control sample. Their mean unexpected accruals scaled by lagged assets are 0.745, as compared to 0.039 for the control sample. According to Marquardt and Wiedman (2004a), managers seem to use positive special items (see their *H3*) to adjust earnings, since the mean of special items is –0.59 as compared to a mean –1.591 for their control sample.

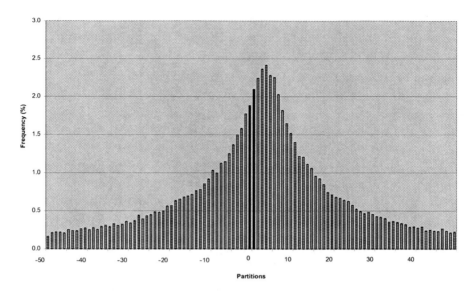

Fig. 4.3 Scaled changes in net income for an annual period ending in quarter one. This figure is copied, by permission, from the 2005 working paper version of Jacob and Jorgenson (2007) (figure 2B), for a sample of all firms on the quarterly compustat database between 1981 and 2001 (The sample contains 920, 926 quarterly observations for 22,015 distinct firms from 1981 to 2001.)

Dechow, Richardson, and Tuna (2003), consider discretionary accruals of firms near zero earnings (small losses or profits). They find that although small-profit firms have significantly high accruals, as expected, firms that report small losses also have high accruals. They attempt to reconcile their findings with the kink by examining alternative explanations:

1.   The distribution is not an indication of earnings management: "The first-order effect of setting a target is that people work harder to achieve the target. The second-order effect is earnings management" (p. 374).
2.   The distribution of public firms is skewed to the right because of the stock exchanges' listing requirements for profits. They find that the kink is more pronounced for young firms listed less than 2 years in the exchanges, but it does not disappear for older firms.
3.   Given that the valuation of loss firms is different from the valuation of profitable firms (Hayn, 1995; Burgstahler and Dichev, 1997b), it might be the case that scaling the results by market value explains the kink. Dechow, Richardson, and Tuna find support for

this explanation. Durtschi and Easton (2005), examine the distribution of earnings per share. They find a concentration around zero, but "there are more observations with a one-cent per share loss than a one-cent per share profit with a peak in the frequency distribution at zero cents per share" (p. 558).[25]

4.   Accounting conservatism pushes firms with small losses to show larger losses and high-profit firms to show smaller profits.
5.   Financial assets induce positive dividend and interest incomes that cannot be negative, which reduces the proportion of firms with small losses in the population.

Interestingly, the same phenomenon of high accruals with no difference between small loss and small profit firms was also detected for Australian firms by Coulton, Taylor, and Taylor (2005).

Hansen (2004), claims that firms use a portfolio of benchmarks so that the findings of Dechow, Richardson, and Tuna do not preclude earnings management by firms with small losses striving to meet alternative benchmarks. For additional evidence that firms use multiple benchmarks, consult Graham, Harvey, and Rajgopal (2005), Rees (2005), Suk (2005).

Another criticism concerns the technique of examining small deviations from the benchmark. The problem is, again, the unobservability of the truth. Several authors (Basu, 1995; Givoly and Hayn, 2002; Jacob and Jorgensen, 2007) report that a scaled earnings distribution is negatively skewed. Is this skewness a result of earnings management, or is it due to the effect of accounting conservatism on the measurement of earnings and the market's tolerance of losses? Jacob and Jorgensen find that skewness is related to earnings management by firms' "taking a bath" when they realize that they will not be able to beat the benchmark.

The findings of Dechow, Richardson, and Tuna (2003), raise the question whether a kink may develop for other reasons besides firms with small losses migrating to the small-profit region (Beaver, McNichols, and Nelson, 2004; Kerstein and Rai, 2005). Beaver, McNichols, and Nelson claim that firms with positive earnings and firms with negative earnings are not drawn from the same distribution because of the asymmetric effect of taxes and special items. They state,

> We argue that under the null hypothesis of no earnings management, the cross-sectional distribution of earnings will nevertheless

---

[25] Durtschi and Easton note a sample selection problem that arises because of the criterion that prices at the beginning of the year be available. The proportion of small-loss firms that are deleted is greater than the proportion of small-profit firms.

exhibit a discontinuity at zero due to the asymmetric effects of certain earnings components for profit and loss firms. First, we expect an increased frequency and magnitude of negative special items for firms incurring losses relative to firms generating profits...[because] evidence suggests that impairment   is associated with poor firm performance. The second earnings component ...is income taxes.... [The] features of the tax environment suggest that a greater proportion of loss firms experience a low or zero effective tax rate....If one or both of these earnings components are asymmetric around zero, there is a violation of the assumption that the distribution of earnings absent discretion is continuous in this region. (pp. 8–9)

Taxes reduce the earnings of profitable firms and fatten thus the density of firms with small profits. There is no mirror effect for small-loss firms because of the asymmetric tax treatment. The effective tax rate of firms with losses is lower than that of profit firms because SFAS 109 requires recognition of benefits from carry-forwards of losses (which would save on future tax expenses) only when this dubious asset is "more likely than not" to be realized. Negative restructuring charges and accounting conservatism that require firms to recognize losses immediately cause firms with small losses to migrate to the region of firms with larger losses, which make the density of firms with small losses thinner.

The formal argument is as follows: denoting earnings by x, an unmanaged profitability parameter by ρ, noise terms drawn from the normal distribution,[26] ε and η, $E(\eta)<0$, and the asset base by A, earnings are

$$\frac{x}{A} = \rho + \varepsilon + \eta \mathrm{I},$$ (4.2)

where I is an indicator function ($\mathrm{I} = 0$ for a profitable firm, $\rho + \varepsilon > 0$, $\mathrm{I} = 1$ for a loss firm, $\rho + \varepsilon < 0$). The difference in effective tax rate, τ, yields a different pattern of reported earnings, NI,

$$NI = (1-\tau_t)x, \quad t = \mathrm{L, P},$$ (4.3)

where t denotes the firm's type (L for loss and P for profit), and, the tax rate on L is lower than the tax rate of P, $\tau_L < \tau_p$. Equations. (4.2) and (4.3) imply that graphically, there would be a local peak to the left of zero, followed by a valley and then another peak. Simulation[27] and empirical test-

---

[26] The normal distribution assumption supports the argument that a kink in the distribution of profits indicates earnings management.

[27] Operating income deflated by market value is assumed to be a normal distribution with mean of 0.10 and variance of 0.0256. Loss firms are assumed to have a 50% probability of write-down with a mean of −0.05 and a variance of 0.0169. The tax rate is 8% for loss firms and 33% for profitable firms.

ing of this model by Beaver, McNichols, and Nelson support the prediction of a kink. However, since the empirical results explain only two-thirds of the discontinuity, regarding the kink as evidence that some firms manage earnings cannot be ruled out.

Kerstein and Rai (2005), test earnings management in annual earnings under the assumption that firms do not manage earnings in the first three quarters.[28] Hence, a comparison of the distribution of firms after the third quarter and after annual reports supports earnings management if a prior (third-quarter) normal distribution develops the kink. Interestingly, they find that a kink does develop between the third and the fourth quarters, but due to a migration to the left. Specifically, firms with small losses migrate to the region of bigger losses, and firms with large profits migrate to the region of small profits. It seems that conservatism and auditors' prudence reign.

As discussed above, Jacob and Jorgensen (2007), contend that the pressure to manage fiscal-year earnings is stronger. This is the time, for example, that bonuses are decided upon for management. Given that managed accruals later reverse, the total of managed earnings in the yearly report and the following quarter's accruals is lower. To illustrate, suppose firms engage in channel stuffing. That is, in December, the firm sells to customers at a reduced price, for, say, 100, which increases accounts receivables and earnings (assuming zero cost) by the full amount of 100. The terms of trade require payment of 60 in January, 20 in February, and 20 in June. Table 4.3 details the example.

Table 4.3 Example

Date	December	January	February	March	April	May	June
Quarter	4	1	1	1	2	2	2
Abnormal accruals	100	−60	−20				−20
Cumulative abnormal accruals (after reversal)	100	40	20	20	20	20	0

---

[28] At first glance, this assumption seems too strong, as some firms might manage earnings in each quarter. The evidence in Dhaliwal, Gleason, and Mills (2004), however, suggests that firms are concerned with annual earnings.

It also seems possible that firms inflate fourth-quarter earnings when the previous three quarters' performance was poor, and deflate the earnings to hoard reserves if the performance was good (e.g., Das and Shroff, 2002). Kerstein and Rai get the same distribution even when testing for each quarter.

The arithmetic shows abnormal accruals of 100 in December. If we examine abnormal accruals for a 12-month period that starts on Q2, i.e., from April 1 to March 31 the following year, the abnormal accruals are just 20, because 80 have reversed. If we shift the four-quarter period to start on Q3, i.e., from July 1 to June 30 the following year, the abnormal accruals are zero. Jacob and Jorgensen thus look at the earnings distribution of any four quarters (Q2-Q1;Q3-Q2;Q4-Q3) and compare the properties of the distribution of any four-quarter earnings with those for the fiscal year's earnings (Q1-Q4). They find that when the earnings management object is the level of earnings, the kink disappears when the last quarter is different from Q4. When it is earnings changes, the kink remains. The latter finding is puzzling in light of the finding of Beaver, McNichols, and Nelson (2004), of a positive correlation between levels of earnings and changes in earnings. If the kink disappears for the level of earnings, it is expected to be weaker for earnings changes as well.

An additional study that criticizes the conclusion that the kink results from earnings management is Durtschi and Easton (2005). They argue that it results from measurement and sample selection procedures. They support their argument by showing that the distribution of earnings per share (EPS) does not have the kink. In the EPS distribution, there is higher mass of firms with a one-cent loss than a one-cent profit, and a peak at zero.

Another question on benchmarks regards their ranking in importance. In their 1974–1996 sample, DeGeorge, Patel, and Zeckhauser (1999), find that avoiding a loss is more important than increasing earnings, and meeting the analysts' forecast comes last. As several researchers note (Brown, 2001; Dechow, Richardson, and Tuna, 2003; Brown and Caylor (2005), however, the relative importance of these benchmarks has changed over time, and the analysts' forecast now takes precedence. Brown (2001), finds that firms have moved from small negative surprises to no surprises, and recently to small positive surprises. Brown and Caylor (2005), who analyze quarterly data from 1985 to 2002, find that early in their study period (1985–1993), managers tried to avoid losses and earnings decreases more than to avoid negative earnings surprises. In the later span, managers exhibited a greater inclination to avoid negative earnings surprises than to avoid losses. In the last 7 years of the study (1996–2002), they preferred to avoid negative earnings surprises rather than to avoid earnings decreases. They conclude that managers took their cues from capital markets and propose that increased media coverage may be responsible for the shift in benchmarks.

Furthermore, Hansen (2004), and Beaver, McNichols, and Nelson (2004), provide evidence that benchmarks are not independent. The latter show that the earnings-changes benchmark is correlated with the level-of-earnings benchmark, which makes earnings changes noisy signals of the earnings-level benchmark.

We end this section with the following comment. Beating benchmarks ties in with Chap. 3 because doing so affects the wealth of managers.[29] Matsunaga and Park (2001), find that failure to avoid a decrease in earnings relative to the same quarter in the previous year for at least two quarters has an adverse effect on CEOs' cash bonuses (regardless of the actual number of disappointing quarters). Furthermore, the common wisdom is that if the CEO is unhappy, so is the CFO (see also Graham, Harvey, and Rajgopal, 2005, for a discussion of the job insecurity of the CFO of a firm that has failed to meet a benchmark). Hence, CFOs are under pressure to beat benchmarks.

4.2.2 Equity Issues and New Listings

We now describe the research on earnings management that revolves around issuance of equity and new listings. We divide the discussion into three subsections: initial public offerings (IPO); seasoned equity offerings (SEO), and new listings.

---

[29] To some extent, the firm's benchmarks determine management's performance benchmarks. Murphy (1999), provides the following classes of benchmarks for internal use:

- "budget" standards, which compare performance against the company's annual budget;
- "prior-year" standards, which compare performance to prior performance after adjustment for growth of EPS or operating profits;
- "peer group" standards, which compare performance to other companies in the industry or market;
- "timeless" standards, which compare performance against some fixed standard, such as a prespecified percentage of return on assets;
- "cost of capital" standards, which compare performance against standards based on the company's cost of capital (such as a plan based on economic value added, EVA);
- "discretionary" standards, which are a combination of the above. Murphy characterizes as discretionary the case in which a company uses "balanced scorecards."

The performance targets are set by the board of directors following a review of the company's business plan, prior performance, budgeted performance, and an evaluation of the difficulty in achieving budgeted performance.

4.2.2.1 Initial Public Offerings

Background: An IPO occurs when the firm goes public. The firm obtains an infusion of capital and changes its ownership structure. Anecdotal evidence shows that firms prepare for an IPO by reorganizing, making changes in ownership, and improving financial reporting systems. When a firm goes public, it goes through a "due diligence" process, and then it publicizes its financial statements for the first time.[30] Insiders and managers already possess private, value-relevant information (e.g., Cheung and Krinsky, 1994; Rao, 1993; Balatbat, 2006; Barzel, Habib, and Johnsen, 2006, and citations therein). Roosenboom, van der Goot, and Mertens (2002), note,

> When a company decides to go public, little is known about the firm. Inside information concerning future cash flows, investment opportunities, managerial skills, and the ability to control future agency costs, among other things, are privy to management. Consequently, an information asymmetry manifests itself *a fortiori*. (p. 2)

The information asymmetry between firms and the market implies that the price of high-quality firms is understated. Hence, high-quality firms have incentives to signal their value in order to separate themselves from low-quality firms. Researchers have considered a few such signals: owners' retention of shares (Leland and Pyle, 1977; Fan, 2007); earnings forecasts (Firth and Smith, 1992); both retention of shares and earnings forecasts (Li and McConomy, 2004); the length of the book-building period (Welch, 1992)[31]; and both retention and publicly observable earnings management (Fan, 2007).

From the perspective of the firm's life cycle, two opposing views of IPOs have emerged in the literature. One view is that an IPO is the end of a process. It allows the initial investors (e.g., venture capitalists) to "cash in" their stock (see, e.g., Ritter, 1998; Elitzur and Gavious, 2003). The other view is that an IPO is just an action undertaken to raise capital needed to finance growth. The firm expects to raise more capital in the future (e.g., Chaney and Lewis, 1998; Ritter, 1998; Roosenboom, van der Goot, and Mertens, 2002; Ritter and Welch, 2002; Block, 2003). The different views affect the desirable earnings management strategy.

The value of earnings: We begin the discussion of the relationship between an IPO and earnings management by addressing the question

---

[30] Oesterle (2006) describes the institutional aspect of IPOs in the United States.

[31] The book-building period starts from the date of filing a registration with the SEC. During this period, underwriters organize "road shows" and contact potential investors. ·

whether earnings are valuable. The IPO event presents the market with the challenge of pricing the new stock. Hence, earnings are valuable if they affect the stock price. If earnings are not valuable, then earnings management is futile.

The anecdotal evidence and the literature doubt that reported earnings are valuable (see Cheng and Firth, 2000). The argument here is that an IPO firm's historical earnings are inadequate to formulate expectations about the future earnings of the still-changing firm. Another reason for skepticism is that IPO firms tend to be young firms that have not yet shown a profit. How can one price losses? The empirical evidence on Internet firms and other start-ups that report negative cash flows and losses suggests that they are not evaluated on the basis of earnings (Bartov, Mohanram, and Seethamraju, 2002; Rajgopal, Venkatachalam, and Koth, 2002; Singer, 2007).

We argue, however, that earnings are valuable on a few counts. First, they pass the "market test." Savvy investors demand to know earnings when they consider buying the IPO's stock, and earnings figure in the formula for evaluating the price of the stock when the firm earns net income.

Second, earnings are valuable as a baseline for future assessments. Later reports are compared to the IPO's earnings to judge the firm's growth. We illustrate this point in a simple example that demonstrates that losses might be also valuable. Consider two firms. In the IPO quarter, one firm reports a profit of $1 and the other a loss of $1. After the IPO quarter, both firms report $1 per share profits. The price of the second firm is likely to be higher because its growth is $2, while the growth rate of the first firm is zero.

Third, earnings are important because disappointed investors can sue the firm if they believe that the firm misled them during the IPO. This is because "information about the firm is revealed over time by the media, analysts' reports, and subsequent financial statements" (Teoh, Welch, and Wong, 1998b, p. 1936). See also the valuable discussion in Ball and Shivakumar (2006). They show that firms' reporting strategies are more conservative before IPOs because of these concerns.

An example that illustrates the value of earnings at the IPO stage is the recent demise of Refco. The press reports:

> On Oct. 10, Refco announced that its chief executive, Phillip R. Bennett, was put on indefinite leave. It said Mr. Bennett had hidden a $430 million debt owed to Refco by a company that he controlled. That debt, which was shifted to a hedge fund called Liberty Corner Capital, was not disclosed or associated with Mr. Bennett in the company's initial public offering in August. Refco also said its financial statements as far back as 2002 could not be relied upon. (Anderson

Jenny, Refco Sells Futures Unit and Seeks Bankruptcy Protection, New York Times, October 18, 2005, Section C, Page 3, Column 1)

According to the company, it now appears that the $430 million "consisted in major part of uncollectible historical obligations owed by unrelated third parties to the company" that arose as far back as 1998.... If the debts were uncollectible, that normally would have led Refco to write off some or all of them, causing its reported profits to fall and conceivably endangering the capital levels that commodities and securities regulators require it to maintain. (Norris, Floyd, and Jenny Anderson, Questions Over Deals at Refco Dating to '98, New York Times, October 12, 2005, Section C, Page 3, Column 1)

The same day that Refco disclosed the hidden receivables and let Phillip Bennet (its CEO, chairman, and president) go on an indefinite leave, the firm reported that Bennet paid the $430 million accounts receivable. Hence, from a cash-flow point of view, the receivables seem innocuous: Liberty paid interest to Refco when they were outstanding, and then they were paid off. But because the firm misreported its IPO earnings (and violated SEC regulations about disclosures during an IPO), these revelations led to bankruptcy less than a week later.[32]

A different view is provided by Singer (2007). Motivated by the findings of Demers and Joos (2006), that IPO firms differ from others regarding dimensions such as profitability, investment in tangible and intangible assets, and growth opportunities, Singer argues that the manipulation of information provided to the market depends on the variable important to investors, given the firm's type, not necessarily earnings. Singer classifies his sample (2,975 firms that went public in the 1988–2000 period) into four groups: the *science-based* group, which comprises firms in biotechnology and pharmaceutical industries; the *assets-in-place* group, which includes firms in more traditional assets; the *technology-based* group, which is made up of firms mostly in the high-tech industry; and, as a separate category, *Internet* firms, which generate most of their revenues from online sales. He shows that the science-based firms and the Internet firms seem to prefer managing R&D rather than earnings, probably because they are not profitable (which is further supported by the manipulation of revenues by Internet firms). The assets-based group manages earnings and sales, and the technology-based group manages sales, earnings, and the R&D expense.

---

[32] The reaction of customers was a "run on the bank." The reaction of shareholders was to file lawsuits. The first was filed 2 days after the disclosures. The reaction of the credit agencies was to downgrade Refco. This response was particularly detrimental since Refco had loan contracts that specified that if its credit rating fell, its creditors could call the loan. Refco could not afford to pay the $1.4 billion outstanding debt.

Earnings management and IPOs: The two views of the role of an IPO in the life of the firm have different implications for the desirable earnings management strategy. If one views the IPO as a vehicle for "cashing in," then the firm's strategy is to inflate earnings to maximize the price of the stock. Consistent with this view is the finding by Li, Zhang, and Zhou (2005), of a positive association between the size of managed earnings and the likelihood that the firm will delist in the future.[33] Singer shows that earnings management is negatively associated with long-run stock returns.

If one views the IPO just as a first step in raising capital externally, then prudence and conservatism are preferable in order to allow the firm to meet future expectations. Teoh, Welch, and Wong (1998b, p. 1939), explain the pressures to manage earnings *after* the IPO, in accordance with the second view:

> [T]he firm also has an incentive to boost earnings soon *after* the IPO to maintain a high market price. The original entrepreneurs may wish to sell some of their personal holdings in the secondary market at the end of the lockup period. (Entrepreneurs commit not to sell their personal holdings during a lockup period commonly lasting 180 days or longer immediately after the IPO.) ... To keep the aftermarket price from dropping below the initial offer price, ... the issuing firm is under pressure to meet those projections in the aftermarket to safeguard its reputations for reliability; to maintain the goodwill of investors, investment bankers, and analysts who made the initial earnings projections; and to avoid lawsuits by disgruntled shareholders after a shortfall in post-IPO earnings.

Most of the empirical research supports the first view, providing evidence that firms manage accruals aggressively to increase the share price of the IPO (Aharony, Lin, and Loeb, 1993; Friedlan, 1994; Teoh, Wong, and Rao, 1998; Teoh, Welch, and Wong, 1998b; Roosenboom, van der Goot, and Mertens, 2003; DuCharme, Malatesta, and Sefcik, 2004; Marquardt and Wiedman, 2004a; Singer, 2007). This aggressive earnings management explains negative abnormal returns in the short- and long-run windows after the IPO.

A further analysis of what accruals are managed reveals that IPO firms use depreciation policies that are income-increasing (Teoh, Welch, and Rao, 1998; Marquardt and Wiedman, 2004a). They also have higher accounts receivable, which indicates that they accelerate sales (Marquardt and Wiedman, 2004a).

---

[33] By the signaling argument above, aggressive earnings management is more costly for low-quality firms than for high-quality firms. The latter can afford to borrow from their future earnings because their earnings will be sufficiently high. The costliness of earnings management renders it a credible signal.

The aggressive behavior might be manifested in real production and investment decisions as well. Darrough and Rangan (2005), find that IPO firms reduce the annual research and development expenses (R&D) when they have an IPO and that the expense resumes its high pre-IPO level after the insiders have sold their shares. Since U.S. GAAP requires firms to expense R&D costs, the reduction in this expense could be attributed either to earnings management or to a liquidity problem solved by raising capital in the IPO. The finding that the R&D level resumes its high level after insiders' sales seems to lend support to the pernicious earnings management hypothesis.

Some interpret high accruals as aggressive, pernicious earnings management. A different perspective is given in Fan (2007). Fan examines two signals. One is earnings and the other is owners' retention of shares (see Leland and Pyle, 1977, for the signaling value of this variable). Fan argues that income-increasing earnings management is the equilibrium strategy of an IPO issuer wanting to signal good-quality prospect in a market that consists of both high- and low-quality firms. Similar to other studies, Fan finds that discretionary accruals are the highest in the IPO year. His finding that discretionary accruals in the IPO year are positively correlated with future earnings leads him to conclude that accruals are a credible signal by high-quality IPO firms. Further support is provided by his finding that earnings (and owners' retention of shares) are strongly positively priced in valuing an IPO firm. Fan also postulates that riskier firms resort to income-increasing earnings management and retain less ownership because the latter is a more expensive signal on value to the risk-averse shareholders. His empirical testing shows that riskier firms indeed substitute the ownership retention signal for more earnings management, which establishes that signaling through earnings management is costly, and hence credible.

If the IPO is the first step in raising capital from the public, aggressive reporting at the IPO stage is undesirable because it robs the firm of future earnings (because accruals have to reverse). It is prudent to hoard reserved income in order to report a smooth series of earnings before subsequent equity offerings (Chaney and Lewis, 1998; Roosenboom, van der Goot, and Mertens, 2002; Ball and Shivakumar, 2006). Teoh, Welch, and Wong (1998b), note that aggressive firms issue 20% fewer seasoned equity offerings than conservative firms.

Hochberg (2005), and Morsfield and Tan (2006), examine the effect of participation by venture capitalists on earnings management by IPO firms. Hochberg in her sample of 1041 venture-capitalist-backed firms in the 1983–1994 period and Morsfield and Tan in their sample of 2630 IPO firms during 1983–2001 find that firms that are backed by venture capitalists mange earnings less than other IPO firms.   Hochberg, for example, finds that the discretionary accruals (deflated by assets) of IPO firms that are backed by venture capitalists is 0.0324, as compared to 0.0949 for her control group of IPO firms. Either venture capitalists can induce firms to manage earnings by reporting conservatively or they curb earnings management. We maintain that since venture capitalists maintain long-term ownership relationships with IPO firms, it stands to reason that they induce conservative earnings management. Both views are consistent with the importance of earnings to venture capitalists in the long run, as was expressed in the comment of Mark G. Heesen, the president of National Venture Capital Association, to the SEC regarding section 407 of SOX (File No. S7-40-02) in 2002[34]:

> Venture capitalists have a special interest in audit committees. Many serve on the audit committees of pre-initial public offering (IPO) companies and continue to serve on audit committees once a venture-backed company becomes publicly traded. Venture capital professionals, representing venture capital funds on public company boards, view the audit committee as the best position from which to protect the large investments that funds have in newly public companies.

In summary, some IPO firms seem to manage earnings to inflate them, but others appear to hoard income in order to have a smooth series of growth in the long run. These conflicting incentives might explain studies that do not find earnings management by IPO firms (e.g., Beaver, McNichols, and Nelson, 2000).

4.2.2.2 Seasoned Equity Offerings

In a seasoned equity offering (SEO), a firm seeks to recruit a new group of investors, unless the firm raises capital through a rights offering: an arrangement whereby the firm makes an offer to its current shareholders to purchase additional shares. The incumbent owners naturally prefer as high a stock price as possible. Hence, it comes as no surprise that firms manage earnings before SEOs (Teoh, Welch, and Wong, 1998a; Rangan, 1998; Kinnunen, Keloharju, Kasanen, and Niskanen, 1999; Shivakumar, 2000; Kim, 2002; Chin, Firth, and Rui, 2002; Ho, 2003; Marquardt and Wiedman, 2004a, b; Zhou and Elder, 2004; Pastor and Poveda, 2005; Baryeh, DaDalt, and Yaari, 2007). Collecting an unjustifiably high market price, however, is problematic because it invites lawsuits that reduce the equity of the existing stockholders (see Beneish, 1998b, p. 210, and the citations above).

---

[34] http://www.sec.gov/rules/proposed/s74002/mghessen1.htm.

The early studies blame the well-documented phenomena of poor performance after an SEO (see, e.g., Loughran and Ritter, 1997, and citations therein) on pernicious earnings management. Shivakumar (2000), and Ho (2003), argue that the market anticipates earnings management and discounts it so that earnings management at SEO is neutral. Baryeh, DaDalt, and Yaari (2007), argue that neutral earnings management at SEO is inconsistent with the information asymmetry that characterizes such an event (see, e.g., Altinkilic and Hansen, 2003) and that the discount may be correct for the average firm but not for each firm individually. They support this argument by examining insider trading before, during, and after the SEO year.

We end this sub section with the following comment. SEO ties in with Chap. 3 because it affects the wealth of managers. Brazel and Webb (2006), argue that a manager with a large proportion of equity would only issue stock if absolutely necessary, since stock prices tend to decline on the announcement of an equity offering both in the short run and in the long run. They find stronger reaction to SEO when the manager's wealth is sensitive to stock price. Marquardt and Wiedman (2004b), show that when management sells shares either at a primary offering or at a secondary offering, the market discounts earnings more. SEO ties in also with Chap. 5, because the market's reaction is affected by the quality of the gatekeepers involved in the SEO such as auditors and underwriters (e.g., Santos, 1998; Slovin, Sushka, and Hudson, 1990; Zhou and Elder, 2004).

4.2.2.3 New Listings

New listings occur when public firms list in a new stock exchange, as when foreign firms list in the United States or U.S. firms move between exchanges. In the former case, the incentives are countervailing. On the one hand, firms have incentives to inflate earnings in order to obtain a higher market price. On the other hand, since the U.S. reporting system has more restrictive requirements, the pursuit of a new listing might induce firms to improve the quality of their earnings and even lead to beneficial earnings management to signal quality.

The research on the link between new listings and earnings management supports the proposition that firms manage earnings if their economic earnings are not strong enough. None detects beneficial earnings management. Charitou and Louca (2003), study 145 Canadian firms that listed on U.S. stock exchanges during 1981–1999. They find that the firms tended to inflate earnings before their entry. The cross-listed firms that managed earnings had negative cumulative abnormal returns over the 3-year period after their listing, in comparison to firms that abstained from earnings management. Additional evidence that the firms engaged in pernicious earnings management is that firms that did not manage earnings outperformed the NYSE and NASDAQ composite indices. Similarly, Lin (2003), looks at 584 firms that migrated from NASDAQ to NYSE and AMEX and from AMEX to NYSE in the 1990–1997 period. He shows that managers manipulated earnings during the year before switching. Lang, Raedy, and Wilson (2006), find that foreign firms that go through cross-listing use smoothing less aggressively. The new cross-listers also exhibit stronger economic performance and lower risk.[35] For recent studies that establish earnings management by cross-listing firms, consult Lang, Ready, and Wilson (2006), Ndubizu (2007), and Ndubizu and Hong (2007). The latter study finds that earnings management is informative (as measured by the correlation of abnormal accruals and future cash flows), especially for firms conducting IPOs who are subject to increased regulators' scrutiny.

4.2.3 Mergers and Stock-for-Stock Acquisitions

Mergers and acquisitions (M&A) are other instances in which the firm's stock is a coin in a transaction (see, e.g., Heron and Lie, 2002, and citations therein). Thus, the price of the acquiring company's stock is important. Common sense dictates that acquiring firms have incentives to inflate earnings in order to transfer as little stock as possible to finance the transaction. Since the shareholders of the acquirer have to ratify the deal, such an earnings management strategy is consistent with their preference against diluting their ownership.

As with the management buyouts studied in Chap. 3, a factor mitigating earnings management is the involvement of investment bankers. Investment bankers provide professional advice on the fair terms of transactions. In addition, repeated aggressive management may not be feasible for acquirers with a business model that is based on growth through acquisitions when such a strategy is pursued through issuance of stock. Inflating earnings in one period makes it harder to inflate them in future periods due to the reversal of accruals. Moreover, transactions typically require lengthy negotiations (normally, they last more than a year). The proximity between the acquirer and the target due to negotiations may render earnings management futile. Erickson and Wang (1999), state,

> [A]cquiring firms, for good reason, may choose not to manipulate earnings. ... In the case of stock for stock mergers, the user of the accounting information is not [uninformed]. On the contrary, the target firm's management and board of directors have the resources and expertise to hire and effectively use expert accountants, auditors, and investment bankers to evaluate the acquirer's financial statements. Target firm managers and the target firm's board of directors are subject

---

[35] An exception is Huijgen and Lubberink (2005), who find that U.K. firms cross-listed in the U.S. report more conservatively than U.K. firms that did not crosslist.

to shareholder litigation if they do not perform their fiduciary duties on behalf of target shareholders. Hence, they have strong incentives to assure that the financial statements of the acquirer, including earnings, are free of material accounting manipulation.

Given ...strong disincentives to manage earnings, the acquirer may choose not to manipulate earnings upward prior to a stock for stock merger. (pp. 153–154)

An opposing view is that the acquirer will try to manage earnings even if the bankers can perfectly see through the attempt. This would be an instance of the "signal jamming" mechanism discussed in Chap. 1 and Part 3. If the firm does not manage earnings, the bankers' discount reduces the price and hence increases the cost of the transaction. Since earnings management does not affect the informational content of earnings, earnings management is neutral.

To the best of our knowledge, only three studies have investigated earnings management by acquirers. Erickson and Wang (1999), study 55 acquiring firms that conducted stock-for-stock mergers in the 1985–1990 period (with an average deal size of $270.4 million, ranging from a minimum of $0.9 million to a maximum of $3.8 billion). They find earnings management preceding the agreement to merge. It seems that manufacturing firms favor increasing inventories in order to inflate earnings, while service firms prefer deferring expenses. Furthermore, Erickson and Wang show that the incentives to manage earnings are positively affected by the size of the deal and by management ownership. The larger the deal, the greater the benefit of artificially reducing the purchase price through earnings management. The larger the management's ownership, the stronger the alignment of management's goals with the objectives of current stockholders.

Efendi, Srivastava, and Swanson (2006), compare 95 firms from the GAO restatement sample (GAO, 2003) with an announcement date in 2000 or 2001 to a control sample of firms matched on size and industry. They find that the likelihood of a restatement also increases significantly for firms that make an acquisition.

Louis (2004), also contributes to understanding earnings management induced by mergers and acquisitions. Louis considers 373 mergers, 236 pure stock swaps, and, as a control sample, 137 pure cash swaps in the 1992–2000 period. He finds that acquiring firms inflate earnings in the quarter preceding the stock swap announcement. As in Erickson and Wang's study, the CEO's holdings are greater in stock-for-stock mergers than in cash mergers.

What is the strategy of the target? Here, the value of earnings is murky. On the one hand, earnings signal potential for future profits, which sets the price of the deal. On the other hand, the fact that the target's value is derived from the synergy of the two firms might imply that earnings per se are of secondary importance. All in all, then, it is not clear whether target firms manage earnings.

Erickson and Wang (1999), find insignificant (positive) earnings management by target firms. Their finding, however, ought to be interpreted with some measure of caution. They measure earnings management in the quarter when announcements of both negotiations and the merger agreement are concluded. Target firms may not manage earnings this late in the process. This finding highlights one of the difficulties in detecting earnings management. When the event lasts for more than one accounting period, when should one measure earnings management?

Easterwood (1998), studies the earnings management strategy of 110 firms that were the targets of tender offers during the 1985–1989 period. He observes that firms subject to hostile takeover attempts manage earnings upward. They inflate earnings in order to thwart the attempt.

As an example of the demand for earnings management in a merger, consider Halliburton. An article by Floyd Norris in The New York Times of August 4, 2004, reported that Halliburton had settled SEC accusations by paying a fine of $7.5 million. The allegation was that Halliburton failed to inform investors that it had made a change in its accounting method for recording cost overruns on projects. In 1998, Halliburton was having large cost overruns on projects in the Middle East operated by its Brown & Root Energy Services business. The old method recognized the cost overruns as losses, but the new method also recorded the revenues Halliburton thought the customer would eventually agree to pay. The change boosted earnings: The 1998 pretax profit of $278.8 million was increased by 46% under the new accounting method.[36] According to Norris,

> At the time the accounting was changed, Halliburton was preparing to merge with Dresser Industries and was dealing with a decline in the company's share price partly caused by slumping oil prices. It reported a 34 % gain in profit for the quarter, far better than other oil services companies were reporting, and Mr. Cheney said then that "Halliburton continues to make good financial progress despite uncertainties over future oil demand."

Finally, to the extent that mergers and acquisitions are a matter of business strategy, diversified firms may be more or less inclined to manage earnings than undiversified firms. Jiraporn, Kim, and Mathur (2004), note

---

[36] The first three quarters of 1999 also had earnings that were about $40 million higher than they would have been, although the percentage increases were smaller.

the existence of two conflicting forces. On the one hand, diversification creates additional organizational complexity, which leads to a higher level of information asymmetry between managers and outsiders. Hence, the firm can exploit this situation and engage in pernicious earnings management, or attempt to alleviate the asymmetry through beneficial earnings management. On the other hand, diversified firms derive their cash flows from diverse sources. The accruals associated with these cash flows are less than perfectly correlated and tend to cancel each other out. Consequently, tests of earnings management through levels of accruals would show a lower level of earnings management. Empirical testing by Jiraporn, Kim, and Mathur indicates that earnings management is lower by 1.8% in industrially diversified firms. Furthermore, a combination of industrial and global diversification reduces the incidence of earnings management by 2.5%.

4.3 Bondholders and Other Creditors

4.3.1 Background

There are numerous debt contractual terms that firms may accept, encompassing security, seniority of the claim, and covenants that limit the firm's freedom to take certain investment and financing actions. In the following, we distinguish between public debt and private debt. Firms incur public debt by issuing bonds. These obligations tend to be long-term, with relatively loose covenants. A trustee monitors them, and there is limited flexibility in renegotiating the contract. Private loans are obtained mostly from banks. They tend to be shorter term, with extensive covenants, and are renegotiable. Syndicated loans are underwritten and financed by a consortium of banks, insurance companies, and other financing entities. They are hybrids since they are private but involve multiple lenders (Zhang, 2003). They usually comprise a portfolio of short-term and long-term loans.[37]

All debt contracts involve a constituency of management, creditors, and shareholders. Admitting creditors into the accounting scene (see the Introduction to Part 2) triples the conflicting interest, as there are conflicts be-

---

[37] Syndicated loans involve information asymmetry and moral hazard among the lenders. Usually, such a loan has a lead bank that has a business relationship with the borrower, and the other members of the syndicate do not. Hence, the lead bank has superior information and may shirk on monitoring activities as a representative of the syndicate (Gorton and Pennacchi, 1995; Dennis and Mullineaux, 2000; Zhou, 2003).

tween creditors and shareholders, and between creditors and management.

The conflicting interests of shareholders and debtors are better known (e.g., Kalay, 1982). Shareholders are aware that creditors have a senior claim on the firm's assets in case of liquidation; part of the security for the debt is the owners' equity in the firm. Shareholders therefore prefer to collect dividends before the debt matures. In return, creditors are concerned that shareholders' withdrawals might jeopardize the firm's ability to pay them back.

To see this conflict, observe the firm at the point when the debt matures and the firm has to pay back the principal plus the last interest installment. Figure 4.4 shows the three possible configurations of cash receipts by lenders and by shareholders.

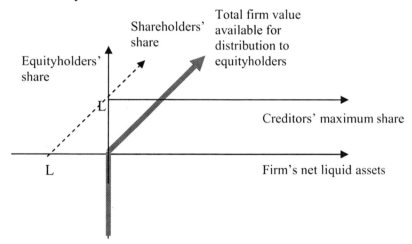

Fig. 4.4 The conflict between shareholders and creditors

If the firm does not have the necessary funds to pay its creditors, they receive nothing, and so do shareholders (the firm's equity value is zero or less). If the firm has some assets that are valued at less than creditors' claims, the creditors receive everything, and the shareholders receive nothing (between zero and point L). If the firm's assets exceed L, the creditors receive just what was agreed upon, L, and the remainder accrues to share holders. This figure reveals one of the consequences of this conflict, the *underinvestment* problem. Projects that have a positive net present value (a value to the right of the origin of the axes) may not be pursued because the shareholders' payoff is reduced by the lenders' fixed claim (see the theoretical study of Moyen, 2000, and the empirical study of Elyasiani, Guo, and Tang, 2002, and the citations therein).

Debtors also have interests in conflict with those of management. Like shareholders, debtors supply the firm with funds. Neither shareholders nor creditors can observe what the management does with the funds. Therefore, they are concerned that management may make choices that jeopardize the firm's ability to repay.

Although shareholders may consider management to be too risk-averse, creditors may regard management as too aggressive. Creditors prefer low-risk projects that increase the probability of being repaid. Share-price maximization dictates otherwise. Shareholders (who design management contracts) are protected from downward risk by having limited liability. Thus, a riskier project increases their expected payoff.

Although we emphasize the conflicting interests of shareholders and debtors, some researchers contend that the latter provide a management monitoring service to shareholders (Jensen and Meckling, 1976; Jensen, 1986). Empirical evidence of this hypothesis is given in several studies (Jaggi and Gul, 1999; Gilson and Warner, 1998; Krishnaswami, Spindt, and Subramaniam, 1999; Hubbard, Kuttner, and Palia, 2002).[38]

There is a difference in the monitoring value of public and private loans. Private debt has more restrictive covenants than public debt (see, e.g., Smith and Warner, 1979; El-Gazzar and Pastena, 1991; Beneish and Press, 1993; DeAngelo, DeAngelo, and Skinner, 1994; Gopalakrishnan and Parkash, 1995; Dichev and Skinner, 2002), but at the same time, renegotiation of contracts is easier with private debt. In a public debt, a trustee is nominated as part of the public debt arrangement with little flexibility (see Smith, 1993).[39]

Harris and Raviv (1990), contend that debtors also provide information about the value of the firm. They point to the following events that speak to the firm's financial health: the payment of liabilities, the renegotiation

---

[38] Jaggi and Gul (1999), find a positive association between debt and free cash flows for low growth firms. Krishnaswami, Spindt, and Subramaniam (1998), observe that firms with more "moral hazard" use more private debt. Gilson and Warner (1998), examine firms that switch from private bank debt to public junk bond financing. The motivation is not deteriorating operating performance, but the wish to free themselves from the tight debt constraints and lender monitoring provided by the bank. Krishnaswami, Spindt, and Subramaniam (1999), observe that firms with more "moral hazard" use more private debt. Hubbard, Kuttner, and Palia (2002), show that banks have advantage in monitoring borrowers because of their relational transactions. HassabElnaby (2006), uses the observable incidences of covenant waiver to show that lending banks possess private information on the borrower, which is used to reduce the agency cost involved in such relationships.

[39] Black, Carnes, Mosebach, and Moyer (2004), show that increased regulatory monitoring of bank reduced the use of covenants in the new debt issuances.

of the debt upon a default, and investigation by accountants and lawyers in the wake of a bankruptcy.[40]

For other benefits of debt, consult the review of the literature on the structure of capital by Harris and Raviv (1991).

4.3.2 The Importance of Earnings to Debt Contracts

Creditors secure their interests by designing contracts that limit firms' ability to make decisions that are contrary to their interests. Broadly, these restrictions are affirmative or negative covenants. Affirmative covenants require firms to maintain predetermined ratios based on accounting numbers. Examples include the current ratio, interest coverage, net worth of tangible assets, and minimum earnings. Negative covenants prohibit certain future investment or financing activities, such as future capital expenditures, acquisitions, dividend payments, and new debt (Smith and Warner, 1979; Begley, 1990; Duke and Hunt, 1990; Press and Weintrop, 1990; El-Gazzar and Pastena, 1990; Smith, 1993; Beneish and Press, 1993, 1995a, 1995b; Chen and Wei, 1993; Sweeney, 1994; Mohrman, 1996; Dichev and Skinner, 2002; Beatty and Weber, 2003).

To illustrate, consider the large sample study of Dichev and Skinner (2002). Using DealScan, they identify the following 12 covenants in the order of their relative frequency with which the same covenant appears in different loans:

Debt to cash flow	3,016
Interest coverage	2,941
Fixed charge coverage	2,720
Tangible net worth	2,446
Net worth	1,945
Debt to tangible net worth	1,735
Debt service coverage	1,480
Leverage ratio	1,400
Current ratio	1,374
Senior debt to cash flow	566
Cash interest coverage	163
Debt to equity	144

---

[40] A similar argument is made by Strobl (2004), who proposes that it is in the best interest of shareholders, who wish to monitor managers, that firms overinvest. Overinvestment increases the uncertainty of the firm's cash flows because the firm pursues both positive and negative NPV projects. This induces outsiders to collect information, which thus increases the informativeness of the price and improves the monitoring of the firm's managers.

Some covenants are calculated differently in different debt contracts. "Debt" can mean total debt, funded debt, or funded debt less cash, and "cash flow" can be cash from operations, EBIT, EBITDA, and soon. (Dichev and Skinner, 2002). Furthermore, tailoring the GAAP is quite prevalent in private debt contracts (Lefwich, 1983; El-Gazzar and Pastena, 1990).

Firms can change their earnings when there are changes in GAAP, but debt covenants may include clauses that limit how the firm reports earnings (Smith, 1993). Some contracts require the borrower to use the same GAAP that prevails on the contract date or furnish the details to reconcile the accounting numbers under a new GAAP (frozen GAAP). Other contracts allow changes in GAAP that were unanticipated when the contract was made (rolling GAAP). Beatty, Ramesh, and Weber (2002), find that lenders require higher interest rates to consent to rolling GAAP and that borrowers are willing to pay in order to avoid having two sets of books, as frozen GAAP require. They also note that although earlier contracts allowed firms to change their accounting treatments within specified GAAP, more recent contracts seem to eliminate this option (see also Mohrman, 1996).

Private debt contracts may also have performance pricing provisions. These provisions adapt the terms of the loan to anticipated changes in the creditworthiness of the borrower, as measured by accounting indicators. From a contract design perspective, it seems that lenders cope with increased riskiness mainly through design of the covenant and with improved risk through performance pricing, although performance pricing may address both (Beatty and Weber, 2000; Dichev, Beatty, and Weber, 2002). Asquith, Beatty, and Weber (2005), state,

> Performance pricing is a relatively new provision in bank debt contracts.... Performance pricing explicitly makes the interest charged on a bank loan a function of the borrower's current credit rating or of their financial ratios such as debt-to-EBITDA, leverage, or interest coverage by having the interest rate in the contract vary directly with changes in measures of financial performance. In so doing, performance pricing expands the importance of accounting information in debt contracts and potentially reduces the contracting costs of private debt. (p.102)

Asquith, Beatty, and Weber (2005), show that performance pricing reflects information asymmetry regarding future creditworthiness, so that it is less likely when multiple performance measures can provide a true picture of the borrower's riskiness. Similarly, Roberts and Panyagometh (2003), observe that performance pricing mitigates information asymmetry between lead bankers and other members of a syndicated loan, since in such settings these members have little contact with the borrower.[41]

Another evidence for the importance of earnings is that having it as a control in the empirical research design may yield a significant result. (The empirical design is discussed in Chapts. 10 and 11.) Burns and Kedia (2006), for example, show that firms that restate earnings due to accounting irregularities have higher leverage than matched control firms.

4.3.3 Earnings Management and Debt Contracts[42]

Since debt is a multi-date phenomenon, discussion of earnings management in this context requires familiarity with these dates. Figure 4.5 below summarizes the potential dates of a breached loan. They do not present the normal sequential developments in the life cycle of a representative breached debt agreement; rather, the events are ordered by their severity as measured by the implication for the firm's cost of capital. For example, Beneish and Press (1995b), find that firms that did not have any (observable) Date 2 event may still go bankrupt (Date 3) and that in some cases debt service violations coincide with bankruptcy proceedings. We depict technical default of a covenant before a debt service default, in which the firm fails to make an interest or principal payment, and then bankruptcy and liquidation. Beneish and Press (1995b), report on average a negative stock price effect from day −1 to +1 of the announcement of the following events: technical default (of a covenant): −3.53%, service default (of failing to submit a payment to the lender)—10.52%, and bankruptcy −29.74%. Multiplying these numbers by the Date 2 market value of equity yields a shareholders' loss effect of $2.5 million, $6.8 million and $20.2 million, respectively. Given firms that default are smaller, these numbers are quite sizable.

---

[41] As an educational exposé that digresses from earnings management per se but is pertinent to researchers, note that the dependence of debt on accounting information has inspired research that examines the effect of new accounting standards on debt, e.g., Frost and Bernard, 1989; Mohrman, 1993, on the SFAS 19 exposure draft that implies the elimination of the full cost method for firms in the oil and gas exploration industry; El-Gazzar, 1993, on SFAS 13 that requires firms to capitalize some leases; Amir and Gordon, 1996; Amir and Livnat, 1997; and D'Souza, Jacob, and Ramesh, 2000, on SFAS 106 that addresses postretirement benefits other than pensions.

[42] Bryan, Nash, and Patel (2006), show that the monitoring role of debt declined in the 1990s with the rise of earnings management.

Date 1: Inception	Date 2: Technical violation that is cured	Date 2: Technical violation that is waived but not cured	Date 2: Technical violation that is NOT waived	Date 3: Debt service violation (DSV)	Date 4: Bankruptcy	Date 5: Liquidation

Fig. 4.5 Possible events in the life cycle of a debt covenant violation

Date 1:

Common sense dictates that before taking a loan, a firm faces two opposing pressures. On the one hand, because creditors, who want to assess the riskiness of the firm in order to evaluate its capacity to pay back loans, analyze financial ratios such as debt/equity, firms have incentives to inflate earnings. On the other hand, since a loan is a long-term commitment, firms are under pressure to report conservatively in order to build reserves. Firms thus also have incentives to deflate earnings.

Studies that use leverage to control for incentives to manage earnings find that firms inflate earnings (e.g., Das and Shroff, 2002; Gul, Tsui, Su, and Min, 2002). Yet DeAngelo, DeAngelo, and Skinner (1994), who study troubled companies that suffered consecutive losses and stopped paying dividends, find no income-increasing accruals in the 10-year period before the event year in their study. We have to be careful in interpreting these results, however, because they do not control for the inception of debt.

Ahmed, Billings, Morton, and Stanford-Harris (2002), provide evidence that firms are rewarded for conservative earnings management. Bharath, Sunder, and Sunder (2004), and Francis, LaFond, Olsson, and Schipper (2005), find that firms manage earnings in both directions, but not necessarily with an eye toward debt negotiations. However, these studies note that earnings management is penalized regardless of its direction. Bharath, Sunder, and Sunder (2004), examine the cost of debt of firms that took syndicated loans, as a function of their quality of earnings, measured by their abnormal accruals (a surrogate for discretionary accruals; see Sect. 4). Collecting a sample of 7,334 private bank loans of 3,082 firms over the 1988–2001 period from the DealScan database, they find a U-shaped relationship. They consider their measure as an indication of pernicious earnings management, which creates more risk for lenders. Regardless of whether abnormal accruals are positive or negative, the cost of a loan in terms of interest, maturity, and collateral is higher for a high absolute level of discretionary accruals. The incremental interest cost is 17–23% higher than the average interest in their sample, maturity is about one month earlier, and the probability of securing the loan by collateral is 11% higher. In addition, since lenders spend costly resources on monitoring loans, the ostensibly poorer earnings quality leads to up-front fees that are 16–37% higher and annual fees that are 50% higher for borrowers with the poorest accounting quality. Francis, LaFond, Olsson, and Schipper (2005), observe that firms with lower quality earnings have lower debt ratings and larger realized costs of debt. Firms with the best earnings quality enjoy discounts of 126 basis points in their cost of debt relative to firms with the worst earnings quality.

The findings of Bharath, Sunder, and Sunder (2004), and Francis, LaFond, Olsson, and Schipper (2005), suggest that lenders pierce the veil of managed earnings, but Janes (2003), finds evidence to the contrary. He investigates the relationship between accruals and tightness in commercial loans in a sample of all Compustat firms with available data (7,007 firms, 36,652 firm-year observations) in the 1990–2000 period. After showing that the level of accruals is a lead indicator of financial distress (367 firms which are 5.2% of the sample), Janes finds that covenants are not set tightly when accruals are high, but only when accruals are low. Janes favors the interpretation that commercial lenders fail to fully process the information content of accruals. An alternative explanation is that they are aware that high accruals increase the likelihood of covenants' violation, and relaxing the covenants saves on costly renegotiations.

We note that some studies examine whether leverage is a proxy for the tightness of debt covenants, which we identify as a Date 2 event. See, e.g., Duke and Hunt (1990), and Press and Weintrop (1990). The evidence is consistent, with leverage being, at best, a noisy signal of tightness (see the discussion in Dichev and Skinner, 2002). Hence, it seems more likely that if leverage motivates healthy firms to manage earnings upward, the explanation may be that they wish to maintain rapport with lenders in anticipation of repeat transactions rather than a wish to avoid covenant violation.

How reliable is leverage as a variable that explains earnings management? Beneish (1997), examines the propensity of firms to violate GAAP as a function of leverage (and other variables that are described in Chap. 10) and finds that the coefficient on the leverage variable conditional on firms being classified as being aggressive accruers with increasing sales is positive (0.587) and significant. He interprets this result as indicating that incentives to violate GAAP increase with the need to comply with covenants or to raise capital on favorable terms. When he estimates his model using random samples, however, he finds that the leverage variable only attains significance in 20 out of 100 random sample estimating aggressive accruers with sales increases (p. 290).

Date 2:

After taking a loan, a firm may experience technical default, failing to comply with one or a few debt covenants. Note that the firm might experience a slight deterioration in its creditworthiness while covenants are still slack. In performance-pricing contracts, the lender might have the flexibility to increase the interest expense as a precaution for a bumpy road ahead.

There are three main cases of technical default:

1.   A technical violation that is forgiven by the lender before the balance sheet date. The covenant violation is *cured* through renegotiation of the original debt contract.

Fortunately for firms but unfortunately for research, such an event may fall "below the radar" unless firms make voluntary disclosure or the lender does not pursue the violation explicitly and the firm has to disclose it. Under Regulation S-X, section 210, Rule 4-08, paragraph (c) and EITF 86-30, firms do not have to disclose violations in the footnotes to the financial statements; under FAS 78, firms do not have to reclassify the debt from long- to short-term debt; under SAS 59, auditors do not have to issue a "going concern" qualification.

Dichev and Skinner (2002), who used DealScan, find that 30% of their sample firms experience a debt violation at least once and that most violations are committed by financially healthy firms.[43] They do not separate cured violations from other waivers because of lack of data on what happened after the violation. They explain the prevalence of violations by observing that covenants are set tightly in private debt contracts. The fact that renegotiation can cure the violation implies that the borrower will not fight it, and at the same time, the lender gets the opportunity to monitor the loan more efficiently by requesting explanations and earnings forecasts from the firm. Thus, the costs of tighter covenants are offset by their value in providing early warning signals.

If it is so easy to waive covenants when the firm is financially sound, will the firm manage earnings to relax the covenants? We are unaware of a study that analyzes cured covenants, but studies that examine accounting choices vis-à-vis the probability of a waiver find evidence that is consistent with common sense. HassabElnaby Mosebach, and Whisenant (2005), show that earnings management is negatively correlated with the probability of a waiver but positively correlated with the probability of costly rene-

---

[43] DeFond and Jiambalvo (1994), also report that violation is a high-frequency event since they find that 345 of the approximately 4,100 firms in the NAARS database had an initial-year violation between 1985 and 1988.

gotiation and the chance that the waiver will be temporary. Beatty and Weber (2003), find that an income-increasing accounting choice is less likely when the debt is raised from a single lender, a setting in which the borrower's bargaining power is greater.

The other two cases of technical default (besides a cured violation) are the following[44]:

2.   The technical violation is waived but not cured, or
3.   The technical violation is not waived.[45]

When a firm violates a technical covenant, it usually violates more than one (Beneish and Press, 1993; Dichev and Skinner, 2002). Also, some covenants are breached more often than others. Beneish and Press (1993), find that the following covenants are violated most often: net worth or tangible net worth (see Sweeney, 1994; Jaggi and Lee, 2000; HassabElnaby Mosebach, and Whisenant, 2005), working capital or current ratio, and leverage. Minimum earnings, minimum interest coverage, and cash flow indicators (such as cash flows from operations or the ratio of cash flow to total debt) are violated less frequently.

Broadly, there are two reasons for such a violation: either the firm is financially healthy and the technical violation occurred because the covenant was set too tightly or the firm is financially distressed.

The lender's response varies according to the reason for the violation.[46]

---

[44] In HassabElnaby, Mosebach, and Whisenant (2005), 263 (58%) firms violated only one covenant, and 194 (42%) violated more than one covenant.

[45] We combine cases 2 and 3 because most samples do not distinguish between them, largely because a firm might get a temporary waiver first.

[46] HassabElnaby (2006), finds "that, before lenders make a waiver decision, they accurately interpret signals provided by accruals before they make a waiver decision ... [and] that accounting procedures and accruals are partial substitutes for low-cost debt covenant violations" (p. 3).

Notably, firms that have to disclose covenant violation may also experience financial difficulties. In Beneish and Press (1993), the percentage of firms that reported losses in the year of violation and disclosed covenant violation is 85.4%, as compared to 24.5% of non-violators, which are matched to violators by industry. DeFond and Jiambalvo (1994), report a median annual earnings decline for their violator firms of 6% of assets, as well as a loss frequency of 80%. Even the sample of Dichev and Skinner, which contains relatively financially healthy firms, has loss proportions that range between 35 and 51% in initial violation quarters and between 33 and 26% in all violation quarters.

As a matter of fact, one criticism of the research in this field is that not all studies distinguish between healthy and troubled firms (Peltier-Rivest, 1999, 2002; Peltier-Rivest and Swirsky, 2000).

Smith (1993), p. 294), observes that "a lender's reactions to default fall along a continuum: at one extreme, the lender grants a permanent waiver without renegotiation; next, a temporary without renegotiation; then, no waiver, but no renegotiation; then, a waiver following renegotiation; finally, renegotiation fails, no waiver is granted, and the firm obtains financing from another lender." If a financially healthy firm violates a covenant, a permanent waiver is a solution. If, however, the lender suspects imminent financial distress, renegotiation takes place, and the borrower must convince the lender that it will return to health. If the firm succeeds, a temporary waiver becomes permanent. If the firm fails, either the contract is renegotiated and the debt is restructured (Beneish and Press, 1993, 1995a, b; Chen and Wei, 1993; DeFond and Jiambalvo, 1994; Sweeney, 1994) or the firm is denied a waiver and it must try to refinance the loan.[47]

Violation can be quite costly to the borrower. Beneish and Press (1993), study 91 violators between 1983 and 1987; they estimate that the costs to a lender due to violations increased the range of interest to a level between 84 and 193% of the market value of equity (MV), and restructuring costs due to asset sales and refinancing were on the average 37% of MV.[48] As discussed above, there are additional costs, since covenants are tightened and operations are constrained. Although these costs are lower for firms that get a waiver, the lender can extract fees and concessions such as accelerated principal repayments in exchange for granting the waiver.

To emphasize, although a waiver lets the firm "off the hook," in truth this escape can come at some cost, which is one reason why firms that are close to violating debt covenants experience a negative market price reac-

---

[47] Chen and Wei (1993, Table 5, p.229), examine a sample of 52 firms (between 1985 and 1988) that got a waiver and provided information in the reports; the waiver is either permanent (P) or temporary (T). The distribution of the developments after the covenant violations shows that permanent and temporary waiver for the case of "Payment demanded by creditor" are four (P) and four (T), respectively; "Debt restructured, or debt becomes demand loan" are one (P) and two (T) respectively; "Terms of debt tightened" are two (P) and two (T), respectively, and "No changes in the terms of the debt" are twenty-one (P) and ten (T), respectively. So the total permanent waivers are twenty nine to twenty three temporary waivers.

[48] DeFond and Jiambalvo (1994), report that firms incur costs due to the following: debt classified to current (21 firms); lending limits reduced (7 firms); additional assets pledged or increases in compensating balances required (6 firms); cash receipts controlled or deposits seized by bank (5 firms); interest rate increased (3 firms); partial payoff forced (2 firms); other unique costs (9 firms).

tion (Beneish and Press, 1995a, b), a greater negative stock price reaction to bad news (Core and Schrand, 1999), and a negative market price reaction to the announcement of new accounting policies that may reduce the slack of covenants (El-Gazzar, 1993).

We summarize this discussion with the following conjecture:

> The debt-covenant hypothesis: Firms that are concerned that the violation of a covenant will not be cured manage earnings upward in order to relax the covenant.[49]

This hypothesis has been tested by Healy and Palepu (1990), Beneish and Press (1993), Beatty and Weber (2003); DeFond and Jiambalvo (1994), DeAngelo, DeAngelo, and Skinner (1994), Sweeney (1994), Jaggi and Lee (2002), Dichev and Skinner (2002), and Beatty and Weber (2003).

Table 4.4 summarizes the research and findings. First, almost all studies[50] show that firms manage earnings upward *before* the violation takes place. Second, the findings depend on the level of the sample firms' financial distress. Healthy firms that expect a permanent waiver do not manage earnings. Healthy firms that are concerned that a permanent waiver may not be obtained manage earnings upward to relax debt covenants, and firms in financial distress manage earnings downward, probably in order to affect new negotiations with lenders and employees.

Additional evidence that debt covenants might explain the demand for earnings management is provided in studies on firms that make restatements (e.g., Dechow, Sloan and Sweeney, 1996, on firms subject to enforcement of the SEC). Richardson, Tuna, and Wu (2002), find that restatement firms (in their sample of 225 firms that restated annual earnings between 1971 and 2000) have higher industry-year-adjusted leverage than non-restatement firms: 0.069 vs. 0.028, t-statistic 4.76. Efendi, Srivastava, and Swanson, 2006, show that the likelihood of a restatement (in their sample of 100 firms from the GAO restatement sample with an announcement date in 2000 or 2001) increases significantly for firms that are constrained by a debt covenant.

---

[49] For a discussion of this hypothesis, consult Watts and Zimmerman (1986, pp. 215–217).

[50] Sweeney (1994), is the lone exception.

Table 4.4 Studies that examine the debt-covenant hypothesis

Study[a]	Earnings management tool	Financially distressed[b]	Support of the debt-covenant hypothesis
Healy and Palepu (1990)	Accounting choices (depreciation methods, inventory pricing, extent of LIFO use, investment tax credit method, amortization period for intangibles, amortization period for prior service pension costs, and pension rate of return assumptions	Yes	No significant accounting changes surrounding the dividend-covenant event. Firms prefer to cut dividends There are income-increasing choices in year –2 Only income-increasing, cash-conserving pension accounting decisions in years –1 and 0
Beneish and Press (1993)	Depreciation, LIFO, amortization of past pension service costs (changed by SFAS 87 in 1986), deferral of investment tax credit (abolished in 1985)	Yes	Firms adopt new standards that increase reported earnings in the year of violation
DeAngelo, DeAngelo, and Skinner (1994)	Abnormal operating accruals (income minus cash flows from operations) after controlling for sales and cash flows; Changes in accruals, components of working capital, accounting choices such as write-offs and provisions for losses (Tables 5, 6)	Yes	In year –3, income-increasing accruals. In years –1 to –10, there is no difference between the troubled firms (29) and the matched sample (47). Year 0 is the first year in which dividends are cut In general, the evidence supports income-decreasing choices such as large inventory write-offs
DeFond and Jiambalvo (1994)	Abnormal accruals in time-series and cross-sectional analysis	Yes	Income increasing discretionary accruals 1 year before the violation. Although no earnings management is detected in the year of the violation, there is possibly

Study[a]	Earnings management tool	Financially distressed[b]	Support of the debt-covenant hypothesis
			some management in this year, after controlling for management changes and auditor's going concern qualifications
Sweeney (1994)	Accounting methods (inventory, depreciation, investment tax credit, and amortization of pension costs), voluntary accounting change (e.g., pension accounting assumptions or cost method, LIFO and FIFO adoptions or extensions, depreciation method depreciable lives, investment tax credit treatment), changes in estimate and the timing of the adoption of mandatory accounting changes	Mixed	Firms having accounting flexibility and bearing technical default costs are more likely to make income-increasing accounting choices Violators make more income-increasing changes in the default year than in the surrounding years and more income increasing changes than the control group (matched by industry) Default firms accelerate (delay) adoption of income-increasing (decreasing) mandatory methods
Peltier (1999)	Discretionary accruals	Yes	Firms adopt income decreasing accruals
Jaggi and Lee (2000)	Discretionary accruals	Mixed	Firms manage earnings upward to relax a waiver and manage earnings downward before restructuring debt
Peltier-Rivest and Swirsky (2000)	Discretionary accruals	No	Firms relax debt covenants through income-increasing accruals
Dichev and Skinner (2002)	Distribution of differences between firms' reported accounting measures and the relevant	No	An unusually small (large) number of loan-quarters with financial measures that are just below (above) covenant

Study[a]	Earnings management tool	Financially distressed[b]	Support of the debt-covenant hypothesis
	covenant thresholds (i.e., "covenant slack")		thresholds. These patterns are more pronounced before initial violations of the debt covenants
Beatty and Weber (2003)	Voluntary changes in accounting choices	Probably not	Performance pricing motivates income-increasing choices Managers who pay higher interest to keep their accounting flexibility manipulate earnings upwards
HassabEl-naby, Mose-bach, and Whisenant (2005)	Accounting treatment choices and discretionary accruals	Yes	Firms are less likely to manage earnings if the expected cost of technical violation is low because, for example, a permanent waiver is likely

[a] See Appendix for the samples of studies
[b] Consecutive losses, dividend cuts, or negative cash flows

Date 3

A Date 3 event involves a *debt service* violation, in which the debtor does not pay an interest payment or a portion of the principal. Such an event could take place in conjunction with a bankruptcy, but need not.

From an earnings management perspective, a firm may default as a strategic move. Since the payment is costly, the firm may consider skipping a payment in order to keep the cash or to avoid seeking costly alternative funding of the payment. Francis (1990), examines defaults in a randomly selected sample of 150 firms (75 of which are troubled, as per the Altman Z-score) in the 1982–1984 period. She finds that when the coupon rate exceeds current interest rates, firms are more likely to default, even when they plan to continue payments in the future. Although she does not restrict her attention to private debt a priori, her sample includes mainly private debt. It seems that lenders are willing to overlook an isolated episode of non-payment in anticipation of future payments and more business.

Date 4

Bankruptcy changes the relationship between creditors and the firm. Since the lenders now become the residual claimants to the firm's assets, they have more say in the firm's operating and investment decisions. For example, within 120 days of a bankruptcy declaration, a company must prepare a reorganization program that puts it back in health. Approval of this program by a court requires the consent of the majority of each class of creditor. Filing bankruptcy under Chap. 11 allows a firm some relief from immediate payment of its debts.

Given our extensive discussion of debt covenants, it is notable that loosening covenants does not prevent bankruptcy. For example, Asquith, Gertner, and Scharfstein (1994), show that 59% of the firms in their sample with loosened covenants nevertheless filed for bankruptcy, as compared to 68% of the firms with tightened covenants.

As bankruptcy has been given a good deal of attention in the accounting, finance, and legal disciplines, we pursue it no further. From an earnings management perspective, the bankruptcy phase is uninteresting because this is the time when the truth is exposed and there is no more room for pernicious earnings management.

Date 5

Liquidation (bankruptcy under Chap. 7) marks the end of the firm. Its assets are sold when possible, and the proceeds are used to pay debtors in order of seniority of claims. As with bankruptcy, there seems to be little advantage in earnings management.

4.4 Regulators

Researchers have had great success in detecting earnings management driven by regulation, the political environment, and taxation. The current approach to research on management of discretionary accruals (see Sect. 4) started with Jones's, (1991), study on earnings management by firms that are subject to import relief investigations. These firms have incentives to appear in need of protection from competing imports. Consequently, they manage earnings downward. Similarly, Cahan (1992), shows that firms under investigation for anti trust violations report income-decreasing abnormal accruals while under investigation. Cahan, Chavis, and Elmendorf (1997), find that chemical firms that anticipated financing a Superfund cleanup of environmental waste significantly deflated earnings in 1997, while legislation governing such activity was pending. Key (1997), examines unexpected accruals for firms in the cable television industry at the time of Congressional hearings on whether to deregulate the industry. Her evidence indicates that the industry deferred earnings while under scrutiny. Han and Wang (1998), show that petroleum-refining firms delayed reporting earnings and selected income-decreasing accruals during the 1990 Gulf Crisis, when they made extraordinarily large profits. Several additional studies highlight the importance of political costs and regulation in motivating firms to manage earnings (see Hall and Stammerjohan, 1997, on the oil industry; Makar and Alam, 1998, on antitrust investigations; Lim and Matolscy, 1999, on firms subject to produce price controls; and Navissi, 1999, and Bowman and Navissi, 2003, on managing earnings downward to induce regulators to increase the price in price-controlled Industries).

China has been an interesting case for the study of earnings management induced by regulation because the Chinese economy is centralized, and numerous decisions are subject to examination and approval by the regulator.[51] Below, we discuss two studies that illustrate how earnings management is used to gain a favorable outcome with the Chinese regulator; for more studies on China, consult Zou and Chen (2002).

Aharony, Lee, and Wong (2000), examine the motivation to manage earnings in order to acquire a license for an IPO. They distinguish between two types of industries: protected industries, wherein firms can relatively easily obtain the required approval to issue stock, and unprotected industries, wherein the competition for the privilege to issue stock is fierce. They find that firms in the latter group manage revenues, as evidenced by comparing pre- and post-issue earnings, but to a lesser degree when the shares are issued in Hong Kong, indicating that the Hong Kong exchange provides valuable monitoring.

Chen and Yuan (2004), examine rights issues, whereby firms issue additional shares that are offered to the shareholders in place. They explain that the state controls the growth of the market by setting an annual quota of IPOs, which is allocated through provincial and municipal governments (as well as the ministries in charge of industries). Because of the high demand for the limited quota, local governments dole out their shares to as many firms as possible, leaving the capital needs of each successful applicant unsatisfied. These firms therefore turn to share rights, which also require a license that is awarded based on the history of the accounting rate of return. Chen and Yuan find that Chinese firms manage their income through non-operating items to achieve the desired number, which was 10% in 1996, and when that number decreased in 1999 to 6%, it seems that firms moved their target number toward this lower figure.

---

[51] China is different from market economies such as the United States, in that it has an informal, "black economy" local stock market (Liu and Green, 2004).

4.4.1 Tax Expense and Deferred Taxes

Another vein of research motivated by regulation is the research on tax expenses, deferred taxes, and the deferred tax asset allowance. From an earnings management perspective, two research questions arise. First, do firms manage their valuation allowance in order to achieve a given target? In what follows, we refer to research that pursues this question as employing the earnings-target approach (Gramlich, 1991; Boyton, Dobbins, and Plesko, 1992; Dhaliwal and Wang, 1992; Manzon, 1992; Sweeney, 1994; Burilovich and Kattelus, 1997; Miller and Skinner, 1998; Visvanathan, 1998; Lu, 2000; Bauman, Bauman, and Halsey, 2001; Kumar and Visvanathan, 2003; Schrand and Wong, 2003; Phillips, Pincus, and Rego, 2003; Dhaliwal, Gleason, and Mills, 2004; Gleason and Mills, 2004; Holland and Jackson, 2004; Krull, 2004; Phillips, Pincus, Rego, and Wan, 2004; Cook, Huston, and Omer, 2006; Frank and Rego, 2006).

By SFAS 109 (effective December 15, 1992), firms are required to recognize a deferred tax asset that meets certain requirements. This is a dubious asset, however, because the firm can enjoy the future benefit only when it has taxable income, so firms are required to provide for a valuation allowance to be offset against the deferred tax asset. The allowance requires management to exercise judgment, since it is created if the evidence on hand implies that there is a likelihood of more than 50% that the deferred tax asset will not be realized.

Deferred taxes are among the last accounts that are closed before the earnings are publicized. By the time these accounts are prepared, firms fully know whether they have reached their target earnings. They therefore have incentives to flex the accounts to achieve the desired level of earnings management. Further support for the fact that firms use tax expenses and deferred taxes to manage earnings is provided by the negative correlation between earnings management and tax compliance internationally, since both are affected by the laws that protect investors and by accounting standards (Wysocki, 2004).

The literature on deferred tax accounts examines circumstances known to induce firms to manage earnings, such as meeting a benchmark (Bauman, Bauman, and Halsey, 2001; Phillips, Pincus, and Rego, 2003; Phillips, Pincus, Rego, and Wan, 2004; Frank and Rego, 2006), issuing or repurchasing stock (Bauman, Bauman, and Halsey, 2001), meeting analysts' forecasts (Bauman, Bauman, and Halsey, 2001; Phillips, Pincus, and Rego, 2003; Dhaliwal, Gleason, and Mills, 2004; Lu, 2000; Schrand and Wong, 2003; Gleason and Mills, 2004; Frank and Rego, 2006), taking a bath (Visvanathan, 1998; Lu, 2000; Bauman, Bauman, and Halsey, 2001), smoothing (Miller and Skinner, 1998; Visvanathan, 1998; Schrand and Wong, 2003;

Holland and Jackson, 2004), debt-related motivations as proxied by leverage (Miller and Skinner, 1998; Visvanathan, 1998; Lu, 2000; Bauman, Bauman, and Hasley, 2001), bonuses (Visvanathan, 1998), and conveying information to investors (Kumar and Visvanathan, 2003). In general, prior research has found that firms do manage the deferred tax allowance in order to meet their target earnings.

The second question concerns whether firms manage earnings in order to minimize the present value of their tax expenses. Research on this subject treats a firm's tax expense as the object of management, with managed earnings as the derived outcome of such management—the tax-target approach (Boynton, Dobbins, and Plesko, 1992; Dhaliwal and Wang, 1992; Scholes, Wilson, and Wolfson, 1992; Warfield and Linsmeier, 1992; Dhaliwal, Frankel, and Trezevant, 1994; Guenther, 1994; Hunt, Moyer, and Shevlin, 1996[52]; Maydew, 1997; Collins, Kemsley, and Lang, 1998[53]; Jenkins and Pincus, 1998; Beatty and Harris, 1999; Mikhail, 1999; Calegari, 2000; Seida and Wempe, 2004; Badertscher, Phillips, Pincus, and Rego, 2006b).

The theory (John, John, and Ronen, 1996) and empirics support income-decreasing earnings management and an intertemporal shift of reported earnings in order to minimize the tax expense. The Tax Reform Act of 1986 has received special attention from researchers in this regard. One of the provisions of the Act establishes book income as a part of the basis for calculating the minimum tax for firms that did not pay significant taxes before the act. Specifically, the Act specifies an alternative-minimum-tax-book-income adjustment (henceforth, "adjustment") to be added to taxable income. Several studies (Gramlich, 1991; Boynton, Dobbins, and Plesko, 1992; Dhaliwal and Wang, 1992; Manzon, 1992) have found that firms used discretionary accruals to reduce income in 1987, the first year the Act applied. The Act also reduced the maximum statutory tax rates from 46 to 34% over a 2-year period, giving firms incentives to shift net income forward. Maydew (1997), estimates that by pushing gross margin forward and selling and administrative expenses backward, firms

---

[52] In some cases, managing tax expense does not compromise reported earnings. For example, Dhaliwal, Frankel, and Trezevant (1994), and Hunt, Moyer, and Shevlin (1996), show that firms manage inventories to reduce taxable income without compromising reported earnings in the financial reports. They find that LIFO firms manage tax expense by accelerated purchases to inventory when the tax rate is high and delayed purchases when the rate is low.

[53] This study is different from the others, in that it shows that firms with foreign units shift income from countries with high tax rates to countries with lower tax rates.

with net operating loss carrybacks shifted income to quarters with lower tax rates, which yielded an aggregate savings of $2.3 billion. Similarly, Scholes, Wilson, and Wolfson (1992), and Guenther (1994), document the shifting of income from years with high rates to years with lower tax rates.[54]

Warfield and Linsmeier (1992), consider the sale of investment securities by banks in order to manage their "Securities Transactions gains and losses" account, which is a component of their ordinary income. The banks record investments at cost so that gains and losses are recognized when a sale takes place. They note that the tax-expense-minimizing strategy of profitable banks is to sell losing investment securities and withhold the rest, while the strategy of banks that have accumulated losses is the opposite. From the earnings management perspective, the strategy creates a smoother earnings series. Even if the firm did not mean to do so, an external observer might suspect that the firm managed earnings by timing the sale of investment securities.

Since we expect firms to minimize their taxes, it is noteworthy that income-increasing earnings management increases the tax expense. This leads Eilifsen, Knivsfla, and Saettem (1999), to theorize that, at least in the short run, taxation has a favorable effect on the occurrence of pernicious earnings management because it renders the behavior costly. Klassen (1997), provides support for this theory by showing that firms with a lower level of pressure from the capital market (proxied by insiders' ownership, where higher ownership indicates lower pressure from the capital market) indeed manage their tax outlays by engaging in divestiture of assets with lower gains and higher losses. At the same time, some firms are willing to manage earnings and pay taxes on non-existent income. Erickson, Hanlon, and Maydew (2004a), study the excess tax paid by 27 firms under enforcement actions by the SEC between 1996 and 2002, finding that in total they paid $320 million in taxes on non-existent profits.[55] See also Matsunaga, Shevlin, and Shores (1992).

---

[54] Marsden and Wong (1998), report that New Zealand electric power boards, which were tax exempt before 1987, decreased their earnings through accruals management in 1987, the first year they paid taxes.

[55] The fact that taxable income does not coincide with financial-reporting income does not alter the reality that taxation increases the cost of managing earnings to inflate income. Agreement between book income and taxable income tends to reduce Internal Revenue Service scrutiny and thus the consequent costs of tax examinations (Cloyd, 1995; Cloyd, Pratt, and Stock, 1996; Mills and Sansing, 2000; Mills and Newberry, 2001).

How do firms balance incentives to manage earnings upward with incentives to minimize taxes by reducing taxable income? The answer is mixed. Frank, Lunch, and Rego (2004), who observe that in the 1990s, there is was a trend of avoiding taxes and engaging in aggressive earnings management, study a sample of 5,641 firms (28,076 firm-years) from 1991 to 2003. They find that firms with more aggressive financial reporting also have more aggressive tax reporting. In contrast, Badertscher, Phillips, Pincus, and Rego (2006a), argue that there is a trade-off between managing earnings upward and managing taxable income downward because aggressive earnings management increases the gap between book and tax income, which, in turn, leads to increased scrutiny by the Internal Revenues Service (Mills, 1998) and the SEC (Jenkins and Pincus, 1998). They examine the mix of earnings management tactics that increases current tax expenses and earnings management with no effect on taxable income in a sample of 159 firms that are identified by the GAO as restating earnings downward due to accounting irregularities. They find that firms use earnings management with tax consequences when their tax position reduces the cost of such a strategy: having net operating loss carryovers, having sufficiently high free cash flow, having a Big 4/5/6 auditor.[56] They also show that in general, firms prefer to manage earnings without paying more taxes.

Of course, the association between taxation and earnings management can be more complicated. Aharoni and Ronen (1989), investigate a manager's response to changes in tax rates, when the manager's compensation comprises a bonus (a function of accounting earnings before taxes) and options (a function of the market price). They show that the manager responds to an increase in the tax rate by increasing reported income in order to undo the harmful effect of the tax on his wealth. We illustrate this in a highly simplified version of their model.

Let the firm be a two-period contract between risk-neutral shareholders and a risk-neutral manager with limited wealth, whose shares' price is determined by the market. Each period, the firm generates earnings, X_t, $t = 1$, 2. The shareholders design the manager's contract to include a net bonus, B[57], as a function of reported earnings, R_t (i.e., $B_t = \beta R_t$, $t = 1, 2$), and shares that award the manager a fraction γ of the firm's end-of-the-first-period market capitalization, V_1. Assuming a rational expectations equilibrium, the price equals the total expected earnings conditional on the first-period report, $V_1 = E(X_1 + X_2 | X^R_1)$. The market designs a stochastic monitoring technology that determines at the end of the second period whether the

---

[56] They also find that firms that manage earnings fraudulently tend to use tax-saving tactics more.

[57] B is given net of personal income tax of the manager.

firm reported the truth in the first period. This technology detects misrepresentation with probability p^* and penalizes the management for a "biased" report by P. If this technology successfully induces the manager to report the truth at the end of the first period, the manager reports $R_1 = X_1$.

Since the market knows that earnings follow a random walk—i.e., $X_2 = X_1 + \varepsilon$, where ε is white noise, $E(\varepsilon) = 0$—the firm's expected value net of tax when the tax rate is τ, $0 < \tau < 1$, is given as $V_1 = E(X_1 + X_2 | R_t) = 2(1-\tau)E(X_1| R_1)$. When the manager tells the truth, his expected wealth at the end of the first period is

$$B_1 + E(B_2) + \gamma V_1 = 2\beta X_1 + 2\gamma(1-\tau)X_1 = 2[\beta + \gamma(1-\tau)]X_1. \tag{4.4}$$

Suppose that the manager inflates the first-period reported earnings by ρ and that no accruals reverse in the following period. The manager's expected wealth at the end of the first period, under the assumption that no accruals reverse in the following period, given that the market believes the report, is[58]:

$$\begin{aligned} B_1 + E(B_2) + \gamma V_1 - p^*P = \\ \beta X_1(1 + \rho) + \beta E(X_2) + 2\gamma(1-\tau)X_1(1 + \rho) - p^*P = \\ 2[\beta + \gamma(1-\tau)]X_1 + \rho[\beta + 2\gamma(1-\tau)]X_1 - p^*P. \end{aligned} \tag{4.5}$$

It is clear that $d\rho/d\tau = 2\gamma[1 + \rho]/[\beta + 2\gamma(1-\tau)] > 0$ when p is set optimally. That is, the manager is indifferent to telling the truth only if $\rho(\beta + 2\gamma(1-\tau))X_1 - p^*P = 0$. Suppose that, ex ante, p^* is set as a function of earnings, the variables of the manager's compensation, possible penalties, and the tax rate, so that the manager is indifferent to telling the truth as follows, $p^* = [2\rho(\beta + \gamma(1-\tau))X_1/P]$. If the tax rate unexpectedly goes up, the manager has incentives to compensate for his loss of wealth by overstating earnings, $\rho > 0$. In equilibrium, as the tax rate goes up, income-increasing earnings management takes place.

Keating and Zimmerman (1999), examine the effect of changes in taxation on accruals (depreciation) in the aftermath of the 1981 change in depreciation for tax purposes, which mandated fixed depreciation schedules for taxes. "Prior to 1981, if a firm estimated longer lives and higher salvage values (i.e. income-increasing estimates) for financial reporting than for taxes, the IRS could challenge the company's estimates for tax purposes and, if successful, increase the firm's tax liability. The 1981 tax law removed this indirect link between financial and tax reporting by mandating fixed depreciation schedules for taxes" (p. 360). They find that when

---

[58] The argument is that if a truth-telling is the Nash equilibrium, we ought to check that the manager does not wish to deviate unilaterally.

managers were no longer concerned with being challenged by the IRS (and having the firm's tax liability increase unexpectedly), the likelihood of an estimate revision increases and the likelihood of a depreciation method revision decreases.

For further discussion of the research on taxation, consult Shackelford and Shevlin (2001), and their discussant, Maydew (2001).

4.4.2 Regulated Industries: Insurance Companies and Banks

Two regulated industries that received a great deal of attention are banking and insurance.[59]

The importance of accounting reports for regulating explains insurance companies' incentives to manage their financial numbers. The Insurance Regulatory Information System (IRIS) has been the principal analytical tool for identifying troubled insurance companies (Petroni, 1992, provides a detailed description of IRIS). An IRIS analysis has two parts. First, 11 financial ratios are computed based on the accounting data available from insurers' annual statutory statements. Each of these 11 ratios is defined as either "usual" or "unusual," where the usual ranges are predetermined by the National Association of Insurance Commissioners (NAIC). Firms are classified as "failing" this statistical stage when more than three ratios are outside the usual ranges. These firms enter the analytical stage of the system, in which a team of examiners and senior financial analysts review their statutory statements. The team designates some of the firms as re-

---

[59] Although we focus on the effect of regulation on the incentives to manage earnings, there is research on the insurance industry that parallels cases that are discussed in other sections of this book. Browne, Ma, and Wang (2004), for example, study whether stock options to management create incentives to be more accurate in the estimation of loss reserves. On the one hand, inflating earnings seems logical, but since the market sees through the errors and penalizes the firm, they expect to find, and indeed their evidence shows, that stock options are associated with increased accuracy. These findings are consistent with the result in Anthony and Petroni (1997), that earnings response coefficients are smaller for insurers with more variable reserve estimation errors. Beaver, McNichols, and Nelson (2000), examine whether property-casualty insurance companies manage earnings before equity issuances: 80 initial public offerings and 116 seasoned equity offerings. Petroni and Beasley (1996), and Gaver and Paterson (2001), explore whether the quality of external monitors such as auditors or actuaries mitigates the incentives of financially weak insurers to deflate loss reserves. Ke, Petroni, and Safieddine (1999), discuss the relation between CEO compensation and accounting performance measures in the property-liability insurance industry.

quiring "immediate regulatory attention" or "targeted regulatory attention" by state regulators.

Banks, too, are regulated based on their accounting capital ratios because the government wishes to prevent bank failures, as it is the ultimate insurer of deposits. In 1991, Congress passed the FDIC Improvement Act. The act provides a classification system with five tiers based primarily on capital ratios, with the lowest tier having a capital-to-assets ratio of less than 2%. Regulators are strongly encouraged to close any bank falling into the lowest tier if the bank is unable to raise the ratio within 90 days of falling below 2% (see Wall and Peterson, 1996, and citations therein). A variant of a capital-to-assets ratio is the ratio of primary capital (which is roughly equal to stockholders' equity plus loss loan reserves) to adjusted gross assets (assets plus loss loan reserves). Clearly, an increase in earnings increases this ratio.

4.4.2.1 Earnings Management in the Insurance Industry

Firms that are close to having alarming statistics may use upward earnings management. Insurance firms manage earnings by reinsuring (Adiel, 1996; Mikhail, 1999),[60] adjusting the level of loss reserves (Grace, 1990; Petroni, 1992; Collins, Shackelford, and Wahlen, 1995; Chen and Daley, 1996; Mikhail, 1999; Gaver and Paterson, 2000, 2001; Beaver, McNichols, and Nelson, 2000, 2003), revising their (estimated) losses (Collins, Shackelford, and Wahlen, 1995; Petroni, Ryan, and Wahlen, 2000), and entering into interest swaps, which affect the largest operating component of net interest income (Song, 2004).[61] .

Grace (1990), finds that insurers use their loss reserves to smooth earnings (which reduces their perceived riskiness) and to reduce their tax burden. Grace's sample includes property-liability insurers from 1966 to 1979, before the Tax Reform Act of 1986, which increased the minimum tax rate and decreased the maximum tax rate, effectively changing the incentives to manage earnings to reduce the tax burden (Adiel, 1996). Petroni (1992), and Gaver and Paterson (2000), find evidence that insurers

---

[60] SFAS 113 describes reinsurance as follows:

An insurance enterprise may purchase reinsurance to reduce exposure to losses from events it has agreed to insure, similar to a direct insurance contract purchased by an individual or noninsurance enterprise. The insurance enterprise may also contract with a reinsurer to facilitate the writing of contracts larger than those normally accepted, to obtain or provide assistance in entering new types of business, or to accomplish tax or regulatory objectives.

[61] Other tools were examined as well with lesser measure of success, for example, capital gains and losses; dividends, common stock, and preferred stock.

"close" to undergoing regulatory review manage their losses, where Petroni defines the proximity of regulatory review as the level of posted reserves, and Gaver and Paterson measure it as the extent of potential violation of the ratios (IRIS ratios), since reducing the number of violations to less than four avoids triggering regulatory scrutiny. Gaver and Paterson (2000), observe that the NAIC's accreditation program indeed has been successful, as weak insurance companies do increase their loss reserves, although they have incentives to boost performance by decreasing these reserves.

As a side issue, insurance companies tend to have large holdings of liquid assets, such as debt securities and stocks. Under SFAS 115, there are three categories of investments:

- Held-to-maturity—This category includes debt securities that management has the intent and ability to hold to maturity. The accounting treatment is to report these at amortized costs; unrealized holding gains and losses are not recognized.
- Trading—Debt and equity securities that the firm expects to sell in the near future (for short-term profit). The accounting treatment is to report them at fair value. The difference between the cost of purchase and the market value is defined as a holding gain or loss and is included in income.
- Available-for-sale—All other debt securities and stock. The accounting treatment is to record them at fair value, but the holding gains and losses are reported as a separate component of owners' equity.

Clearly, SFAS 115 creates an opportunity for firms to manage earnings by selling shares from the available-for-sale category that have gains—a practice nicknamed "cherry picking" (Beatty, Chamberlain, and Magliolo, 1995; Jordan, Clark, and Smith, 1997–1998; Lee, Petroni, and Shen, 2006; Hirst, 2006).

4.4.2.2 Earnings Management in Banks

Minimum capital requirements induce banks to manage earnings (Ma, 1988; Beaver, Eger, Ryan, and Wolfson, 1989; Barth, Beaver, and Wolfson, 1990; Moyer, 1990; Scholes, Wilson, and Wolfson, 1992; Ahmed and Takeda, 1995; Beatty, Chamberlain, and Magliolo, 1995; Collins, Shackelford, and Wahlen, 1995; Beaver and Engel, 1996; Ahmed, Takeda, and Thomas, 1999; Gray, 2004; Gray and Clarke, 2004). There is considerable evidence that banks that are close to their minimum capital requirements understate loan loss provisions, understate loan write-offs,[62] and recognize abnormal realized gains on securities portfolios. Strong governance, however, as measured by more active audit committees, audit committees with greater governance expertise and more active boards, is associated with less earnings management (Zhou and Chen, 2004). For governance as a separate topic in earnings management, consult Chap. 5.

There are other reasons for banks to manage earnings, such as taxation and a demand for stability (e.g., Greenawalt and Sinkey, 1988; Moyer, 1990; Bhat, 1996) and smoothed performance (Liu and Ryan, 2006). Beatty and Harris (1999), find evidence that public banks manage earnings more than private banks, partly to reduce information asymmetry. Other studies indicate management of loss provisions has a signaling value for banks (e.g., Beaver, Eger, Ryan, and Wolfson, 1989; Wahlen, 1994).

4.5 Employees

As this is being written, Delta Airlines has negotiated wage cuts with key employees that exceed $1 billion under the threat of bankruptcy. Clearly, firms that negotiate labor contracts have incentives to use income-decreasing accruals. Liberty and Zimmerman (1986), investigate earnings management during negotiation of wage contracts (242 contracts from 105 firms in the annual sample and 134 contracts from 85 firms in the quarterly sample of contract negotiations in the 1965–1981 period). They do not find earnings management, however, and their result calls for explanation. We suggest either that the negotiating firms were already experiencing poor performance, so incentives to mask good performance were nonexistent, or that earnings management in the short run does not draw the wool over employees' eyes. If employees can be fooled by managed earnings, perhaps the firms have incentives to use income-increasing earnings management to lull employees into believing their jobs to be secure.

Later studies either detect earnings management or are able to provide explanations why firms may not manage earnings (DeAngelo, 1990; Bowen, DuCharme, and Shores, 1995; Peltier-Rivest, 1999; D'Souza, Jacob, and Ramesh, 2000; Peltier-Rivest and Swirsky, 2000). Empirical findings suggest that firms have incentives to make income-decreasing choices when the firms believe that unions will be affected by lower earnings and be more accommodating partners to negotiations of the compensation terms (Bowen, DuCharme, and Shores, 1995; D'Souza, Jacob, and

---

[62] As Moyer (1990), notes, the evidence regarding loss charge-offs is mixed.

Ramesh, 2000; Peltier-Rivest and Swirsky, 2000). On the other hand, however, when firms are already suffering financial stress, the pressure to manage earnings lessens because the gloomy truth achieves the goal. The observable behavior is that these firms either do not manage earnings (Peltier-Rivest, 1999) or take additional measures such as massive layoffs and sacrifices by white-collar employees to support low earnings (DeAngelo and DeAngelo, 1991).

4.6 Competitors, Suppliers, and Customers

Competitors are important factors in the earnings management phenomenon. First, increased competition may cut into a firm's profits and induce it to manage earnings in order to hide the downturn from other stakeholders. Second, competitors convey useful information about the firm (consider the importance of bellwether firms that publicize their financial reports first). Dadalt and Margetis (2007), for example, show that restatement by competitors might lead to significant negative abnormal returns around a firm's announcement date. Third, financial reports contain information that is useful for rivals' decision making. As a matter of fact, some disclosures, such as the formula for calculating management's incentives, are not required because they would involve the release of proprietary information.

Competition plays a role in inducing firms to manage earnings. Dharan (2003), comments, "Companies in highly competitive industries may want to maintain an edge in revenues or market share." Notable examples of firms that managed earnings in response to competitive pressure include the following: Xerox, which resorted to earnings management when it realized that its profits were slipping because Asian companies produced similar products at lower prices; WorldCom, which pursued a strategy of acquisitions to drive away competition and thus acquired excessive capacity (Sidak, 2003); Shell, which found itself facing stronger competition after the merger of Exxon and Mobil and resorted to overstatement of its oil reserves by nearly 20%, and so on.

Competitors can also take actions that induce firms to manage earnings. Fudenberg and Tirole (1986), and Bolton and Scharfstein (1990), argue that competitors may threaten a borrowing firm's survival. Short-term liquidity needs make a firm susceptible to approval by creditors. This motivates rival firms to try to make the borrower appear unprofitable, driving away potential lenders and investors.

Although competition drives earnings management, competitors are also an audience for managed reports. Krishnan (2005), shows that hospitals' competition on price creates a demand for cost-cutting, which in turn creates a demand for accounting information among a hospital's competitors; competition on quality does not result in the same demand.

Finally, competition also explains firms' reluctance to reveal proprietary information; it thus has an effect on the quality of earnings in general, and not just on earnings management (e.g., Ettredge, Kwon, and Smith, 2002).

The empirical research on this constituency is scant. This is puzzling, because as the relationships between these stakeholders and the firm have acquired a longer horizon, such as just-in-time dealings with suppliers, there is more demand for managing the relationships through accounting-based contracts. To the best of our knowledge, only two studies have examined earnings management behavior in response to the demands of suppliers and customers (Bowen, DuCharme, and Shores, 1995; Peltier-Rivest, 2002), although Matsumoto (2002), discussed in Chap. 5, gives the matter some attention when she seeks to find characteristics of firms that meet or beat analysts' expectations.

Bowen, DuCharme, and Shores (1995), advance the hypothesis that firms have reputational capital in their long-term relationships with suppliers and customers, which provides them with incentives to use income-increasing accruals in the long run:

> Although firms often enter into explicit contracts with their stake-holders, many ongoing relations remain implicit (e.g., implied promises of continuing availability of parts and service to customers who purchase durable goods). Since implied commitments generally have no legal standing, they have been viewed as self-enforcing. The terms of trade (e.g., price, payment terms, quantity) that a firm is able to negotiate with its stakeholders depend in part on the firm's reputation for fulfilling its implied commitments. (p. 256)

They hypothesize that firms build their reputation by making income-increasing accounting choices. Specifically, using a composite score that aggregates the chosen assumptions on inventory flow with depreciation methods, they find evidence in support of their conjecture. In contrast, Peltier-Rivest (2002), observes that troubled manufacturing firms have incentives to adopt income-increasing accounting choices only when they are highly dependent on suppliers, and implicit claims with customers do not appear to provide incentives to manage earnings.

Appendix

Table 4.5 The sample of the studies that examine the debt-covenant hypothesis

Study	Sample
Healy and Palepu (1990)	26 firms close to violating no-dividend-payments covenants in the 1981–1985 period but not in 1980
Beneish and Press (1993)	91 firms that had a technical violation for the first time between 1983 and 1987
DeAngelo, DeAngelo, and Skinner (1994)	76 NYSE firms that reported at least 3 years of losses in the 1980–1985 period, but before that were healthy, as measured by positive income and payment of dividends
DeFond and Jiambalvo (1994)	94 firms in the National Automated Accounting Research System (NAARS) database that disclosed a violation in the 1985–1988 period, with a violation only in the initial year
Sweeney (1994)	130 first-time violators in manufacturing (SIC industries 20–39) that did not violate covenants between 1977 and 1979
Peltier-Rivest (1999)	127 firms with at least 3 years of consecutive losses in the 1985–1995 period that reduced dividends either in the year prior to the first reported loss or during the loss period, which had positive income and paid dividends in the year before the first loss
Jaggi and Lee (2000)	135 Firms with a technical default,[63] 81 firms that restructure debt (80 without technical default), 21 firms that restructure debt after technical default (1989–1996)
Peltier-Rivest and Swirsky (2000)	161 firms with 5-year non-negative income (3 years before the event period through 1 year afterward) in the 1986–1994 period
Dichev and Skinner (2002)	8,004 loans of 2,810 firms in the period from January 1989 to December 1999, 1313 loans of 971 firms with current ratio covenants, and 288 loans of 236 firms with net worth covenants

---

[63] Permanent waiver.......37
    Temporary waiver.......51
    No waiver................ 47
    Total....................135

Study	Sample
Beatty and Weber (2003)	125 firms with material bank debt between January 1995 and June 2000 (as detected by the "preferability letter" filed by the auditors regarding whether they preferred the new accounting choice to the old one — Exhibit 18 in the 10K)
HassabElnaby, Mosebach, and Whisenant (2005)	457 firms that violated debt covenant restrictions during the period 1982–2000[64]

---

[64] Number of firms that violated:
One covenant 263
Two covenants 115
Three covenants 36
Four covenants 18
Five covenants 11
Unspecified .... <u>14</u>
    Total.......................457

5 Gatekeepers

Gatekeepers are monitors who participate in the capital market. Coffee (2001, 2003a), defines gatekeepers as reputational intermediaries who provide verification services to investors:

> Corporate governance depends upon "gatekeepers" to protect the interests of investors and shareholders by monitoring the behavior of corporate "insiders" and by reporting the financial results of corporate performance in an accurate and unbiased fashion that permits objective valuation of the firm.... "gatekeepers" [are] independent professionals who are interposed between investors and managers in order to play a watchdog role that reduces the agency costs of corporate governance. (Coffee, 2001, p. 2.)

5.1 The Demand for Gatekeepers

The demand for gatekeepers arises from the asymmetry of information between firms and investors. Information asymmetry might provide the better-informed parties (firms) the opportunity to take advantage of those less well informed (potential investors). This, in turn, could cause *market failure*. In such a situation, despite the firms' wish to raise much-needed capital and the presence of investors looking to invest in these firms, actual capital transfers will not take place, as rational investors will not trust that firms will not attempt to sell securities at an inflated price.[1]

Akerlof (1970), produced the first study of the connection between information asymmetry and market failure, in the context of the used car market. The market contains two types of car—speaches and lemons, where the value of a lemon is lower than the value of a peach. There is information asymmetry between sellers and buyers because the sellers alone know the truth about their cars. A buyer's maximum bid price is the expected value of the car, which is a weighted average of the values of

---

[1] Dye's (1988), overlapping generation model avoids the issue of market failure since each generation must purchase the stakeholdings of the previous one.

lemons and peaches.[2] Because the bid is lower than the value of a peach, no peach owner will be willing to sell his car. Owners of peaches thus are driven out of the market, leaving only lemons. Rethinking the situation, potential buyers will bid the value of a lemon. The inability of buyers to distinguish between peaches and lemons results in a market failure: Although there are buyers and sellers willing to trade peaches, such trade will not take place.

In the accounting arena, the goods are firms' securities—shares, bonds, and commercial papers. The buyers are investors, the firms are sellers, and the information asymmetry concerns the true value of the securities. Some firms are a good investment prospect (peaches), while others are a poor prospect (lemons). Although earnings provide a signal on a firm's true value, they may be too noisy to fully eliminate information asymmetry regarding the firm's value.[3]

One means to overcome the information-asymmetry problem is to let sellers (buyers) employ signaling (screening) mechanisms that *separate* the good investment prospects from the poor ones. The mechanisms range from signaling future earnings by smoothing current income (see Chap. 7) and choosing the quality of the auditor (Bachar, 1989; Datar, Feltham, and Hughes, 1991; Feltham, Hughes, and Simunic, 1991; Bewley, Chung, McCracken, and Ng, 2006), to financial decisions such as a dividend policy (Bhattacharya, 1979; Eades, 1982; Miller and Rock, 1985; Ramasastry, John, and Williams, 1987; Ofer and Siegel, 1987; Michaely and Roberts, 2006), capital structure (Leland and Pyle, 1977; Myers and Majluf, 1984; Maksimovic and Titman, 1991), and stock splits (Ikenberry, Rankine, and Stice, 1996; Louis and Robinson, 2005). Additional cases of signaling through earnings management are presented in Part 3.

Signaling mechanisms have several caveats. First, they are costly. To have a *separating equilibrium*, these mechanisms must entail costs that only the good investment prospects are willing to bear. Second, sometimes the cost is not steep enough to force the poor prospects from making choices that reveal their type. In a *pooling equilibrium* where lemons

---

[2] To illustrate, suppose the value of a peach and lemon is 10 and 0, respectively. Ninety-five percent of the used cars are peaches. Hence, the maximum price the seller is willing to pay is $0.95 \times 10 + 0.05 \times 0 = 9.5 < 10$.

[3] This observation is supported empirically. For example, based on the theoretical papers of Glosten and Milgrom (1985), who found that information asymmetry increases the bid-ask spread, Affleck-Graves, Callahan, and Chipalkatti (2002), show that the bid-ask spread is larger for firms with less predictable earnings. To the extent that information asymmetry thus increases the firms' cost of capital, these firms have incentives to manage earnings to signal value.

mimic the peaches, the situation is characterized by a loss of social welfare, since both types spend costly resources without eliminating the information asymmetry.

Another problem with signaling mechanisms is that in a sense they are mute; investors may need interpreters with sufficient financial and governance expertise to evaluate the signal. An additional mechanism must be added to enhance the efficiency of the signaling: gatekeepers.[4] As an example of this interpretative role, consider Gretchen Morgenson, a journalist of the New York Times, who wrote a report "Why Buybacks aren't Always Good News." This piece, published on November 12, 2006, provides investors with a better understanding of the buyback signal.

Gatekeepers breach the information asymmetry between firms and investors because they either interpret firms' reports, as when analysts revise their forecasts after firms publicize financial reports, or provide additional, independent, information to investors, as when auditors issue opinions that accompany financial reports or when credit-rating agencies assign such ratings.[5]

We identify the following gatekeepers:

- *Analysts.* Analysts follow firms and issue forecasts of earnings and recommendations on whether to buy or sell shares.
- *Auditors.* Auditors attest to whether firms' financial reports fairly present their financial positions according to Generally Accepted Accounting Principles (GAAP).
- *Boards of directors and audit committees.* Directors supervise management under a mandate to maximize shareholders' wealth.
- *The press.* The media disseminates information to the public and thus affects other users' decision making.
- *Others: corporate lawyers* advise on earnings management; *credit-rating agencies* examine firms' riskiness and liquidity and grade the quality of their debt; and *investment bankers* conduct a "due diligence" process to confirm the disclosures of firms that seek to raise capital.

---

[4] Besides complying with mandatory earnings reporting requirements, firms can make voluntary disclosures. Given that voluntary disclosure is made by self-serving management, its credibility is suspect. There thus is demand for interpreters with financial acumen, such as analysts, to digest the information content of these disclosures.

[5] As an example of this interpretative role, consider Gretchen Morgensen, a journalist of the New York Times, who wrote a report "Why Buybacks Aren't Always Good News." This piece, published on November 12, 2006, provides investors with a better understanding of the buyback signal.

We devote separate discussions to the gatekeepers in the first four categories in Sects. 5.2–5.5. We know little about the role of other gatekeepers in earnings management. Investment bankers (credit agencies) are addressed in Section 705 (702) of the Sarbanes-Oxley Act (SOX), which calls for a study of their involvement in the recent accounting scandals. Investment bankers make extensive use of accounting information when, for example, they are called to issue opinion on firm's value in management buyouts (DeAngelo, 1990). In the recent accounting scandals, bankers allegedly designed transactions that facilitate pernicious earnings management, such as derivatives swaps for Global Crossing and the Italian conglomerate Parmalat's banks pending litigation.[6] A step toward understanding the role of credit ratings agencies in earnings management is made by Jorion, Shi, and Zhang (2005), and Ashbaugh, Collins, and La-Fond (2006). Jorion, the former study, finds that one reason for a decline in average rating over time is the increase in pernicious earnings management, which by virtue of being pernicious, decreases the quality of earnings.[7] The latter study finds that firm's credit ratings are positively correlated with good governance (blockholders who own at least a 5% in the firm, shareholder rights, financial transparency, board independence, board stock ownership, and board expertise) and negatively related to CEO power on the board. In addition, CEOs of firms with speculative grade credit ratings are overcompensated relative to firms with investment grade ratings, and that the overcompensation exceeds the CEO's share of additional debt costs related to lower credit ratings.

---

[6] A notable example for such allegations is the SEC's complaints against Frank P. Quattrone, a former highflying technology banker at Credit Suisse First Boston, for putting pressure on analysts and passing hot offerings to clients in return for banking business.

[7] Anecdotal evidence points to credit-rating agencies playing a major role in toppling companies that restate earnings because it allowed their debtors to call for payment prematurely. For example, after Refco's disclosure in October, 2005 that the accounting reports during its IPO in August, 2005 were inaccurate (see Chap. 4), New York Times reported on October 11, 2005:

> Standard & Poor's lowered its credit rating to B+ from BB—and placed it on credit watch with negative implications, indicating a further downgrade was possible.

Tom Foley, an analyst with the credit-rating agency, said bondholders and banks that had lent Refco money could use the latest disclosure to force it to repay the debt sooner than scheduled, putting Refco under financial pressure. Also, he said, "this indicates a possibility that there could be other accounting control issues."

The egregious earnings management by giants such as WorldCom and others raises the question whether the failure of their gatekeepers to deter earnings management was the norm or the exception. The answer seemed to be the former. SEC commissioner Cynthia Glassman (2002), observed that "nearly all of the market institutions that provide protection against large-scale fraud—including investment bankers, buy- and-sell-side analysts, lawyers, rating agencies, auditors, officers and directors—failed to varying degrees."

Richard Breeden, a former SEC Chair, similarly commented in his 2003 report, entitled Restoring Trust:[8]

> [B]oards of directors, outside auditors and outside counsel are the gatekeepers of behavior standards who are able to prevent damage before it occurs, if they are alert, and above all if they are willing to act when necessary.
>
> A common denominator in many of the major frauds has been the failure of these gatekeepers to stop improper practices at the outset. Sometimes the gatekeepers were unaware of the details of what management was doing. Other times the gatekeepers were too trusting in accepting management rationalizations for practices that proved far more risky than the board might appreciate. Still other times, typically in the compensation area, boards simply went along with unnecessarily large programs that created powerful incentives for managing or inflating reported earnings. Finally, all too often the judgment and actions of outside accountants and counsel were tempered due to the magnitude of fees generated by powerful clients. (p. 39)

The failure of gatekeepers to prevent pernicious earnings management has been attributed mainly to the conflicts between their own interests and their monitoring responsibilities. We elaborate on these conflicts in the following sections.

5.2 Analysts

Analysts are intermediaries who research a firm and prepare recommendations and forecasts of future earnings and other financials, such as revenues and cash flows. There are two categories of analysts. Buy-side

---

[8] See also Coffee (2002, 2003a, 2005), Ribstein (2005), and Goldman and Slezak (2006, footnote 3). Cohen, Dey, and Lys (2005a), compare earnings management before (Q1, 1987 through Q2, 2002) and after the passage of SOX (Q3, 2002 through Q4, 2003). They show a rapid increase in earnings management before the enactment of SOX. They conclude, "our evidence indicates that the problem was much more endemic, and not due to 'a few bad apples' " (p. 2).

analysts are employed by institutional investors, such as mutual funds, who require the analysts' expertise in order to balance their portfolios. Sell-side analysts are employed by brokerage firms that earn commissions on trade in securities. Some brokerage firms are quite small, employing no more than several analysts. Others also offer investment banking services (Agrawal and Chen, 2006), including underwriting of new issues of stock and consultation on mergers and acquisitions. The largest are the following: Citigroup/Salomon Smith Barney, Merril Lynch, Credit Suisse First Boston, Morgan Stanley, Goldman Sachs, JP Morgan/Chase, and Lehman Brothers.

The sell-side analysts are gatekeepers because they make public forecasts of earnings per share and publicize recommendations and other information, such as descriptions of firms' characteristics. Recommendation terminology may vary by firm and analyst. Common recommendations range from "strong buy" and "buy" through "hold" to "sell" and "strong sell," but other analysts use different terms such as "overweight" versus "equal weight," "positive" versus "neutral," and "market (sector) perform" versus "market (sector) outperform."

At first sight, it seems that analysts may use differing terminology to obscure the implications of their recommendations. Not so. The meaning behind the terms usually is well understood. As anecdotal evidence, consider the pressure exerted by Sanford Weill, the former chairman of Citigroup, on "Jack B. Grubman, his star telecommunications analyst, to change his rating on AT&T stock from neutral to positive. Mr. Grubman had a neutral rating—Wall Street code for negative..." (New York Times, April 29, 2003, emphasis added).

5.2.1 Background

There are a number of reasons for the demand for analysts' forecasts and recommendations. First, as discussed above, analysts reduce information asymmetry between investors and management (e.g., Brennan and Hughes, 1991). Although one could argue that firms already report information that can mitigate this asymmetry, this information tends to be quite complex, and not every user is sufficiently sophisticated to grasp its implications. Additional complexity issue arises for high-tech firms and firms with complex operations. Second, firms report quarterly, while investors make decisions continuously,[9] so investors demand interim information,

---

[9] A firm's interim disclosures are of no help either because these disclosures revolve around single events or firm's value depends on numerous other factors

which analysts can provide. Third, earnings mainly report past transactions; investors wish to predict future cash flows,[10] which render analysts' forecasts valuable.

The importance of these gatekeepers is evident in the response of security prices to revisions of analysts' forecasts (see, e.g., the theoretical studies of Barry and Jennings, 1992; Teo, 2000; Abarbanell, Lanen, and Verrecchia, 1995; Barron, Kim, Lim, and Stevens, 1998; Mittendorf and Zhang, 2005; Wang, 2006; Arya and Mittendorf, 2007; and the empirical studies and surveys of Francis and Soffer, 1997; Healy and Palepu, 2001; Kothari, 2001; Francis, Chen, Philbrick, and Willis, 2004; Shroff, Venkataraman, and Xin, 2004; Bagnoli, Levine, and Watts, 2005b; Barron, Stanford, and Yu, 2006).[11] Francis and Soffer (1997), for example, find that forecasts and recommendations together account for 5% of the variation in excess returns over a 3-day window surrounding the earnings announcement event, and Shroff, Venkataraman, and Xin (2004), show that even the marginal forecast—that is, the last one made after other analysts have issued a forecast—affects a firm's market price.

Greater coverage by analysts is associated with a higher level in efficiency of the stock price with respect to the publicly available financial information (e.g., Barth and Hutton, 2000; Elgers, Lo, and Pfeiffer, 2001) and with improved liquidity (see Brennan and Tamarowski, 2000, and the citations therein). The number of analysts following a given firm, which varies between one and a few dozens, is negatively related to the information asymmetry between firms and investors (e.g., Brennan and Subrahmanyam, 1995; Easley, O'Hara, and Paperman, 1998; Houston, Lev, and Tucker, 2006). Hence, analyst coverage has been used as a proxy for the richness of a firm's information environment and the extent of the information asymmetry between investors and the firm (see, e.g., Xue, 2003; Louis and Robinson, 2005).

---

and transactions. Again, it is left to the analysts to provide an interpretation of the firm's disclosure and impact on the firm's value as an investment prospect.

[10] At first glance, it might appear that pro forma earnings (see Chap. 2) mitigate the complexity issue since some items are left out. Firms have flexibility, however, in their choice of which items to exclude, which makes inter-period and intercompany comparisons difficult. Furthermore, as Frankel, McVay, and Soliman (2006), and others have shown, firms may abuse this discretion and sacrifice transparency.

[11] There is also some evidence that the market fails to immediately recognize the information content of analysts' forecasts (e.g., Zhang, 2000).

Barron, Byard, and Kim (2002), Byard and Shaw (2003a, b), [12] Asquith, Mikhail, and Au (2005); Bagnoli, Levine, and Watts (2005b), Chen, Cheng, and Lo (2006), and others confirm the interpretive role of analysts' disclosures. Barron, Byard, and Kim (2002), make the argument that if analysts were just conduits to firm's management, they ought to agree after the release of earnings because they share the same information. [13] The evidence is that the consensus among analysts declines steadily after the release of earnings, which they interpret as indicating that analysts contribute their own interpretations. Bagnoli, Levine, and Watts (2005b), show that investors' response to firms' disclosures uses forecast revisions of analysts as an input for evaluating the disclosures. In particular, when a disclosure focuses on financial statement information, the stock price reacts strongly and quickly to a cluster of revisions. When the disclosure involves strategic information about the firm's business, the reaction is slower and weaker since this kind of event has relatively more uncertain implications for the firm's value. [14] A different research approach is to

---

[12] Byard and Shaw (2003)a, study a sample of the survey data of AIMR that rank large public firms in the years 1985–1995 on the quality of their private and public disclosure. Private (public) disclosure is scored based on investor relations activities (by the financial disclosure). If analysts were just conduits to a firm's disclosures, their private (public) information ought to be correlated with the score of investor relations activities (the score of public disclosures). Byard and Shaw find that both types of analyst information are significantly correlated with the quality of the firm's public disclosures.

[13] They use the measure of Barron, Kim, Lim, and Stevens (1998), for consensus of analysts forecasts (ρ),

$$\rho = \frac{SE - \dfrac{D}{N}}{SE - \dfrac{D}{N} + D},$$

where SE=the expectation of the squared error of mean analysts' forecast where the error is measured as the difference between actual earnings and the mean forecast; D=forecast dispersion which is measured as the unconditional expectation of the cross-sectional variance of the forecasts; and N=the number of analysts. Their sample comprises 990 firm/year observations in the 1986–1997 period, with a window that starts 14 months before the earnings announcement date.

[14] There is also evidence that a greater number of analysts follow high-technology firms (Barth, Kasznik, and McNichols, 2001) and that the level of analysts' consensus for these firms is also lower (Barron, Byard, Kile, and Riedl, 2002). To the extent that the quality of the financial disclosures of high-tech firms is compromised because their accounting reports do not reflect their intangible assets,

check whether analysts' research complements or substitutes for a firm's disclosures. Chen, Cheng, and Lo (2006), find complementarity in the week following the announcement of earnings, in terms of a positive association between the market response to earnings and the market response to analysts' research and a negative association otherwise, when the window of the test is measured in weeks surrounding the announcement. The complementary role of analysts' research is more pronounced for firms with complex information.

A different angle on the role of analysts as informational intermediaries is provided by the fact that institutional investors, who prefer transparency over secrecy (see the discussion below) tend to avoid investing in firms that analysts do not cover (see, e.g., O'Brien and Bhushan, 1990).

Analysts also serve as a communication channel that conveys market expectations to firms. Puffer and Weintrop (1991), and Farrell and Whidbee (2003), for example, find that management's turnover is influenced by its expected performance, proxied by analysts' forecasts. Furthermore, Farrell and Whidbee (2003), show that when the forecast of the long-term EPS growth is low, the new CEO is more likely to be an outsider, who is expected to change the firm's policies and strategies. Bolliger and Kast (2004), find that meeting analysts' expectations has a favorable effect on a CEO's bonus.

As anecdotal evidence that analysts convey market expectations to firms, consider the following example:

> Costco's average pay, for example, is $17 an hour, 42 % higher than its fiercest rival, Sam's Club. And Costco's health plan makes those at many other retailers look Scroogish. ...Emme Kozloff, an analyst at Sanford C. Bernstein & Company, faulted Mr. Sinegal as being too generous to employees, noting that when analysts complained that Costco's workers were paying just 4 % toward their health costs, he raised that percentage only to 8 %, when the retail average is 25 %. ...Mr. Sinegal [the CEO of Costco Wholesale] says he pays attention to analysts' advice because it enforces a healthy discipline, but he has largely shunned Wall Street pressure to be less generous to his workers. (New York Times, July 17, 2005, bracketed text is added)

Finally, we note that analysts follow larger firms. Block (2003), cites a 2003 report by Talley in the Wall Street Journal with the following statistics on the relationship between size and analysts: firms with market caps

---

analysts are financial intermediaries who reduce information asymmetry. Alternatively, high growth requires more capital and hence more attention from investment bankers, who "purchase" research in order to promote the shares they were underwriting.

of $20 billion to $99 billion ($500 million to $1 billion) are followed, on average, by 18 (6) analysts, while firm below $50 million or less are not covered at all.

5.2.2 Decision Making and Incentives

Given the richness of the literature on analysts, we narrow our discussion to the role of analysts in earnings management.[15] We focus on two issues:

- Do analysts take into account the financial information released by firms, and if they do, do they discount reports that are suspected of being inflated by earnings management?
- Do analysts have incentives to collude with management in an attempt to manage earnings rather than to issue unbiased report "[to] offer investors independent, fair-minded opinions on the health of American companies" (New York Times, February 27, 2003), or, do they curb earnings management?

5.2.2.1 The Importance of Earnings to Analysts

In their testimony to the 1994 Jenkins Committee (AICPA 1994), analysts testified to being users of the financial disclosures. Indeed, quarterly and annual earnings announcements and public earnings guidance (from management) trigger a great deal of revision (e.g., Bagnoli, Levine, and Watts, 2005a; Stuerke, 2005; Cotter, Tuna, and Wysocki, 2006). As users, analysts seem to satisfy the Jenkins Committee's recommendation that the users, not firms, forecast future performance. The more experienced they are, the more efficient is their use of historical earnings and accuracy (Mikhail, Walther, and Willis, 2003)

How, then, do analysts use the information in earnings? The answer is not unambiguous. On the one hand, there is evidence that analysts do not fully extract the information in the accounting reports (e.g., Abarbanell and Bernard, 1992; Easterbrook and Nutt, 1999; Ali, Klein, and Rosenfeld, 1992; Cheng, 2005, and the citations therein). Hopkins, Houston, and Peters (2000), conducted an experiment with 113 buy-side equity analysts. The subjects were asked to evaluate firms that amortized goodwill because in their accounting they applied the *purchase* method rather than the *pooling of interests* method, and thus had lower earnings. Hopkins, Houston, and Peters (2000) find that analysts valued lower earnings less, although

---

[15] We are indebted to Donald Byard for his invaluable input to this part of the book.

economically the underlying transaction was the same, and that this effect was more pronounced when the valuation took place 3 years after the purchase than when the valuation took place 1 year afterward. Bradshaw, Richardson, and Sloan (2001), provide evidence on analysts' *accruals' mispricing* (see Chap. 9 for a survey of this topic). Analysts attach the same persistence to accruals and cash flows, although accruals are less persistent because they reverse.

On the other hand, analysts seem to have financial expertise,[16] in that their earnings are more informative than street earnings (Gu and Chen, 2004), and they consider additional signals beyond earnings. Drawing on their experience (e.g., Brown and Mohd, 2003; Mikhail, Walther, and Willis, 2003), analysts consider a firm's history, the industry to which it belongs (since analysts are usually assigned to cover industries or a few firms within the same industry), macroeconomic variables (e.g., Byard and Shaw, 2003a), and recent forecasts by other analysts (which creates a herding of forecasts; see Graham, 1999; Hong, Kubik, and Solomon, 2000; Welch, 2000).[17] As an example that analysts use additional signals to interpret the accounting information, consider Barton and Mercer (2004). They conducted an experiment in which 124 analysts were required to evaluate firms' explanations for weak performance; these explanations were meant to convey the impression that the poor performance should be attributed to transient shocks and thus should have no significant impact on valuation. The findings are consistent with the analysts' interpretative role in that the credibility attached to the explanations affected their valuation.

To the extent that analysts consider earnings in their decision making, an obvious question is whether they discount earnings management. The evidence at hand is mixed. Abarbanell and Lehavy (2003b), link two types of earnings management to the distribution of bias in forecasts. "Taking a bath" (which is evidenced by high negative discretionary accruals) leads to an average positive forecast bias. This strategy could explain the fat lower tail in the distribution of forecast errors.[18] Inflating earnings (by a smaller magnitude) to beat forecasts implies that analysts are pessimistic in the

---

[16] Breton and Taffler (1995), for example, find that experienced analysts pay more attention to earnings during boom years.

[17] Our order of citing bibliography by publication dates obscures the fact that the literature seems to spring from a book by Welch published in 1996.

[18] Abarbanell and Lehavy (2002) observe that although the number of observations that create asymmetry in the tails of the distribution of forecast errors is relatively small (5% in the negative lower tail, and 2.5% in the positive, upper tail), the magnitude of these extreme errors has a disproportional impact on the mean forecast error.

neighborhood of zero forecast errors. In a sequel to Bradshaw, Richardson, and Sloan (2001) and Ahmed, Nainar, and Zhou (2005), show that analysts do not generally distinguish between discretionary and non-discretionary accruals.

Opposing evidence that indicates that analysts discount aggressive earnings management is provided by Brown (2004), and Lin and Shih (2006). Brown examines the association between disclosed financial accounting data and firm value, while incorporating the effect of managerial discretion in reporting those data. He finds evidence that is consistent with analysts' being aware of managers' reporting incentives. When analysts inferred that such incentives had induced managers to choose assumptions that reduced obligations, the analysts treated $1 of reported obligation as if it were an obligation of more than $1. Lin and Shih (2006), find evidence that analysts take into account the history of a firm regarding its meeting analysts' forecast or beating it slightly when they revise their next-quarter earnings forecasts. We discuss meeting or beating expectations (MBE) below.

We end with the following warning. Some of the evidence ought to be interpreted with a measure of caution. Basu and Markov (2004), show that the evidence of the analysts' consensus forecast, being a biased measure, might be attributed largely to testing their prediction error by OLS regression. They recommend instead the Least Absolute Deviation regression, which accounts for the fact that the analysts' loss function is a linear, rather than a quadratic, function of the forecast error.

5.2.2.2 The Incentives of the Analysts

Francis, Chen, Philbrick, and Willis (2004, p.48) note that between 1980 and 1996, the number of analysts increased at a rate of 10.2% annually, far above the 3.2% annual growth in the number of firms. The percentage of companies followed by at least one analyst increased from 26% in 1980 to 66% in 1996. These statistics indicate that analysts have assumed a greater role in the capital market.

Securities firms, the analysts' employers, generally, do not charge their clients for research. Nonetheless, analysts are paid because their research and recommendations generate commissions for the brokerage and investment banking components of their employers.

Brokerage

Since satisfied customers generate commissions, recommending stocks to clients induces analysts to make accurate forecasts. Mohd's (2005), analysis of the turnover of financial analysts indicates a link between switching and performance.[19] Analysts with superior performance relative to their peers switch to a new brokerage house where they continue to follow a subset of the same firms as before, or switch to a larger firm and continue to perform better, which is now attributed also to their having a lighter work load. Those who quit and seem to disappear from the industry performed poorly before leaving (see also, Mikhail, Walther, and Willis, 1999). Furthermore, sell-side analysts are graded by scores prepared monthly by passing questionnaires to the largest clients—institutional traders (Reingold and Reingold, 2006). Hence, to the extent that the buy-side analysts prefer accurate and timely information, analysts are pressured to issue accurate forecasts.

The demand for objective evaluation, however, is hindered by the fact that the analysts' major source of information is management.[20] Firms have sanctioned analysts who criticized them (see the discussion below),[21] by barring access to firm-specific information. Furthermore, each brokerage house has its own list of stocks from which it wishes to generate a large volume of trade. There is thus additional pressure on analysts from their employers to issue recommendations that shed favorable light on these preferred stocks. For studies that examine the pressure to issue favorable reports, consult Francis and Philbrick (1993), Dugar and Nathan (1995, 1996); Lin and McNichols (1998), Francis and Soffer (1997), Michaely and Womack (1999), Dechow, Hutton, and Sloan (2000), Lim (2001), Chan, Karceski, and Lakonishok (2003), O'Brien, McNichols, Lin (2005),[22] and Agrawal and Chen (2006).

---

[19] Since the I/B/E/S data set lets analysts keep their code even when they change employers, Mohd could trace the relationships between pre-turnover performance and the turnover event. Apparently, turnover is substantial for analysts. About 71% of the analysts in their sample leave the profession. Nine thousand six hundred and thirty-eight analysts left I/B/E/S in 2002 versus 339 in 1984.

[20] As an extreme anecdotal case of analysts rowing the boat with management, consider the relationships between Jack B. Grubman, the telecommunications stock analyst at Smith Barney, and Bernard J. Ebbers, the founder of World-Com. Grubman has revealed that he attended board meetings at WorldCom, and when rumors of pending financial crisis at WorldCom began to circulate, he coached Ebbers on how to handle a forthcoming conference call with analysts (New York Times, February 27, 2003), in addition to recommending the stock after the price started to decline.

[21] This dynamic is responsible for Regulation FD, effective in October 2000, which does not allow private communication of firms' financial results to analysts.

[22] Most of the cited studies focus on the pressure from investment bankers by examining analysts' forecasts and recommendations around equity offerings. All

Investment Banking

In the late twentieth century, trading commissions decreased, but analysts could still generate income by serving investment bankers.[23] When a corporation raises capital, investment bankers make money as underwriters, and the warm recommendation of in-house analysts promotes a higher stock price. A 2001 investigation by New York Attorney General, Eliot Spitzer, unearthed some cases in which the investment banker paid analysts employed by competitors for independent research to ensure that the consensus forecast was favorable. In the bull market of the 1990s, investment banking activity blossomed, and so did the usefulness of the analysts' forecasts. Moreover, until this practice was abandoned in 2003, analysts' compensation often was directly related to bringing in investment banking business.[24]

The demand to bring in business puts analysts under pressure to maintain rapport with a firm's top brass, who decide where to direct its investment banking business. O'Brien, McNichols, and Lin (2005), examine the recommendations of analysts following 4,640 firms that issued new equity in the 1994–2001 period. They find that affiliated analysts treat good and bad news asymmetrically: They respond promptly to good news but prefer not to issue bad news. An examination of the revision of recommendations during the 2 years, following the equity offering, reveals that affiliated analysts are slower to downgrade from "Buy" and "Hold" recommendations and faster to upgrade from "Hold."

Indirect evidence of the pressure to be optimistic is provided by Clarke, Ferris, Jayaraman, and Lee (2006), who examine a sample of 384 firms that filed for bankruptcy in the 1995–2001 period. They detect no optimistic bias in recommendations of analysts as such firms are not likely to supply lucrative business to investment bankers. They find a monotonic reduction in analysts' recommendations in the eight quarter-period before

---

find that the analysts associated with investment bankers are more optimistic in their forecasts and recommendations.

[23] We do not use the term serving cynically. Gasparino (2005, p. 10), reports an interview with an analyst, Gerry Rothenstein, who warned his son in 1997, at a time that Wall Street research seemed like the place to be, not to follow in his footsteps, "unless you want to be a servant for investment banking."

[24] Formally, there was supposed to be a "Chinese wall" between investment banking and research. De facto, however, with the implicit cooperation of the SEC, this separation was not maintained (see Reingold and Reingold, 2006).

the filing and less favorable recommendations as compared to a control group that did not file for bankruptcy.[25]

How do analysts balance the opposing pressures?[26] The literature debates three views. First is that analysts are gatekeepers, so they curb earnings management. Second is that analysts balance the different pressures, and the third is that cooperation with management compromises analysts' objectivity.

Some studies, especially studies in the international arena, corroborate the role of analysts as gatekeepers by finding that analysts enhance transparency and reduce the scope of discretionary accruals. Ke (2001), discovers a negative relationship between the number of analysts who follow a given company and the likelihood of reporting small increases in earnings or of having a long string of consecutive earnings increases. Since a high concentration of firms reporting small increases (in the distribution of all firms' earnings increases) is largely construed as a reflection of pernicious earnings management (see Chap. 4), Ke's findings are consistent with analysts' deterring earnings management. DeGeorge, Ding, Jeanjean, and Stolowy (2004), investigate a sample of 53,656 observations for 11,085 non-financial firms in 26 countries from 1994 to 2002. They find that the greater the number of analysts that follow a firm, the lower the likelihood of earnings management. Because, however, this relationship is stronger in transparent environments than in opaque ones, the presence of analysts does not, by itself, remove the incentives to manage earnings. Rather their effectiveness as gatekeepers depends on whether the environment provides them with the necessary support. Frankel and Li (2004), provide indirect evidence. They show that an increase in the number of

---

[25] Enron is a counter example whose bankruptcy occurred so fast that analysts did not have a chance to revise their beliefs on this darling of Wall Street. Clarke, Ferris, Jayaraman, and Lee (2006), observe the following:

> A triggering event that resulted in the call for new legislation and prompted extensive criticism of analysts by the press, investors, politicians, and regulators was the meltdown of Enron in late 2001. Although Enron filed for bankruptcy in December 2001, analysts continued to be optimistic about the stock as late as October 2001. Indeed, of the 17 analysts then following the company, 10 had a strong buy rating on the stock and five others had a buy rating, despite massive reported accounting losses and a 50% loss in Enron's market value during the quarter preceding bankruptcy. (p. 170)

[26] A different picture is portrayed by Cowen, Groysberg, and Healy (2006), who find evidence that analysts employed by firms that provide both trading and underwriting services seem less optimistic than analysts who are employed by brokerage firms that do not provide underwriting.

analysts following a firm is associated with reduced profitability for insiders' trades and a lower level of purchases by insiders. This finding indicates that analysts reduce the information asymmetry between insiders and outsiders (see Chap. 3 for the link between insider trading and earnings management). Lang, Lins, and Miller (2004), investigate the relation between the firm's ownership structure, the number of analysts following, investor protection, and valuation in a sample of 2,500 firms from 27 countries. They find that analysts are less likely to follow firms with a poor governance structure since such firms have stronger incentives to withhold or manipulate information. There is a positive valuation effect when analysts cover firms that have both the potential for poor internal governance and weak country-level external governance, indicating their value as gatekeepers.[27]

One way for analysts to curb earnings management is to issue supplemental information that enables the market to see through earnings management, such as cash-flow forecasts[28] (McInnis and Collins, 2006) and revenue forecasts (Rees and Sivaramakrishnan, 2006). McInnis and Collins (2006), compare 5,237 firm/years with both an EPS forecast and a cash flow per share forecast with 32,308 firm/years with only an EPS forecast in the period 1993–2004. By definition, if the market has both cash flows and earnings forecasts, it also knows the accruals forecast, and thus managing accruals to beat the market's expectations is more difficult. McInnis and Collins find that firms with cash-flow forecasts manage earnings less. Rees and Sivaramakrishnan (2006) provide evidence that the market discriminates between firms that did not perform up to the expected forecasts of revenues and firm that did, even when both successfully beat earnings targets.

There is also evidence for the alternative view that analysts are not pure gatekeepers, but that they walk a fine line between finding favor with firms' management and their employers and maintaining a reputation as responsible forecasters (Easterbrook and Nutt (1999); Mest and Plummer (2003); Agrawal and Chen, 2006). Easterbrook and Nutt, 1999, provide evidence that is consistent with analysts' "shaving" their reaction to

---

[27] In some cases, the correlation between a company's performance and the number of analysts following is spurious. Analysts are likely to be silent and later stop following a company for which they do not wish to issue a favorable recommendation (see Francis, Chen, Philbrick, and Willis, 2004, and the citations therein).

[28] DeFond and Hung (2003), show that firms that issue cash-flow forecasts are induced to do so by a combination of poor quality earnings, poor financial health, and high capital intensity relative to firms that do not issue cash-flow forecasts.

accounting earnings in the direction that is preferred by management. Analysts overreact (underreact) to earnings with positive (negative) information. This asymmetry in the reaction explains their observable overoptimistic forecasts. Mest and Plummer (2003), compare the forecast error for earnings with the forecast error for sales. Consistent with their argument that earnings are more important to management than sales, they find that the forecast error in the prediction of sales is smaller. Although one can argue that earnings are more difficult to predict because they are made up of a number of items, including sales, still, a systematic difference in the forecast error is likely to reflect the balance between accurate prediction (no prediction error) and positive treatment of the firm (forecast error is consistent with optimism). Agrawal and Chen (2006), compile a unique dataset[29] that contains the revenue breakdown of analysts' employers (most of which are private firms not subject to the usual disclosure requirements for publicly traded companies) into revenues from investment banking, brokerage, and other businesses. They find that the conflict of interest that arises from investment banking or brokerage activity has no effect on the accuracy and bias of the analysts' quarterly earnings forecasts. It does, however, have an effect on the frequency of revisions of quarterly earnings forecasts and on optimism in long-term forecasts of growth. They contend that their findings seem to support the evidence of pressure to issue a favorable opinion since "[a]nalysts' forecast revisions have been, shown to increase share trading volume (see, e.g., Ajinkya, Atiase, and Gift (1991)) and to significantly affect stock prices apart from earnings news, dividends, or other corporate announcements (see, e.g., Stickel (1991))" (p. 9).

A third alternative is that analysts collude with management. In the next section, we discuss how firms manipulate the market's expectations and manage earnings in order to meet or beat analysts' forecasts (MBE). At the beginning of the quarter, analysts' forecasts tend to be more optimistic than the (downward) revised forecasts made closer to the earnings announcement date. Lowering the forecast makes it easier for the firm to announce earnings that meet or beat expectations. Bartov, Givoly, and Hayn (2002, p. 203), wonder "why analysts do not correct their forecasts for what appears to be a systematic downward bias in their late-in-the-period forecasts. Or, to put it in more concrete terms, how could analysts continue to underestimate Microsoft's quarterly earnings 41 times in a row? " Apparently, analysts have incentives to play along (see Lim, 2001;

---

[29] The dataset covers over 170,000 quarterly earnings forecasts and over 38,000 forecasts of long-term growth made by over 3,000 analysts employed by 39 publicly traded securities firms and 124 private securities firms for about 7,400 U.S. public companies in the period January 1994 to March 2003.

Abarbanell and Lehavy, 2003a; Chan, Karceski, and Lakonishok, 2003; Dopuch, Seethamraju, and Xu, 2003; Durtchi and Easton, 2005; Burgstahler and Eames, 2006).

The view that analysts succumb to pressure from management suggests that, overall, analysts are a weak gatekeeper. For example, analysts almost never warn the public of impending revelations of pernicious earnings management attempts, and on numerous occasions, they did not revise their recommendation even when it was evident that a company was in poor financial health. Griffin (2003), analyzes a sample of 847 companies that were sued in a federal securities class action from 1994 through 2001. He found that analysts responded to the suit by either dropping coverage or downgrading their recommendation *after* the public disclosure of the earnings management events (i.e., after the restatements). Cotter and Young (2004), report similar results. They examine whether sell-side analysts anticipated restatement due to accounting fraud by analyzing a sample of firms that were subject to SEC investigation (publicized by the Accounting and Auditing Enforcement Release) between 1995 and 2002. They find that about 60% of the analysts did not drop coverage, and more than 50% of the analysts did not lower their recommendations before the first public disclosure of fraud.

Which of these three views is a better representation of reality? In particular, the last view might raise the suspicion that *all* analysts publicize biased reports *all* the time. We do not know how to attach weights to the different views. In his speech before the U.S. Senate Committee of Banking, Housing, and Urban Affairs on July 26, 2005, an SEC Commissioner, Roel Campos, stated,

> In the three years of my service, the Commission has fulfilled Congress' mandate, met the deadlines, and implemented through often complicated rulemakings, the requirements of Sarbanes-Oxley. Unfortunately, in those three years, many other threats to investor confidence and the stability of the markets have erupted. Securities analysts were discovered to be recommending companies they believed were "dogs," in their own words, to promote bank business…
>
> I continue to believe that in America, the vast majority of businesspersons, broker dealers, investment advisers, and professionals are honest and scrupulous.

Unfortunately, honest recommendations are not a foolproof defense against earnings management. Abarbanell and Lehavy (2003a), for example, find that firms that receive "sell" recommendations manage earnings by taking a bath to build a reserve for future reported earnings.

5.2.3 Analysts in the TWENTY-FIRST Century

So far, we focused mostly on findings in the twentieth century. The reality is that the industry has gone through a dramatic change in recent years (Williams, 2006). In March 2000, the Internet bubble burst, and with it came a recession. Effective October 2000, Regulation FD bars analysts from privately learning a firm's true earnings from its management before the market. On the one hand, Regulation FD reduces the private information available to analysts (Francis, Chen, Philbrick, and Willis, 2004; Francis, Nanda, and Wang, 2006; Williams, 2006) with the consequent decrease in the accuracy of forecasts following earnings announcements (Agrawal, Chadha, and Chen, 2006; Shane, Soderstrom, and Yoon, 2001) and increases in information asymmetry in the market (Sidhu, Smith, and Whaley, 2006). Regulation FD slowed analysts' response to earnings (Janakiraman, Radhakrishnan, and Szwejkowski, 2006) and shifted their attention from firms that are already followed by several analysts because the marginal benefit from following such firms does not justify the added cost of unaided post-Regulation FD research (Mohanram and Sunder, 2004). On the other hand, Regulation FD has led to more public announcements by firms and to an increase in the richness of the disclosures (Bailey, Li, Mao, and Zhong, 2003; Heflin, Subramanyam, and Zhang, 2003; Wasley and Wu, 2005), to an increase in the weight of alternative sources of information in analysts' forecasts (Shane, Soderstrom, and Yoon, 2001), such as credit ratings (Jung, Sivaramakrishnan, and Soderstrom, 2006), and to leveling the field for analysts, in that the dispersion of analysts' forecasts after earnings announcements is lower (Shane, Soderstrom, and Yoon, 2001).

Another change started in 2001, when the New York Attorney General, Eliot Spitzer, started his investigation into in-house e-mails at Merril Lynch, which unearthed a conflict of interest induced by the proximity of investment banking and research. The investigation culminated in a settlement with state regulators and the SEC, in which the ten largest investment banks agreed to pay nearly $1.4 billion (without admitting to wrongdoing)[30] and two analysts were barred from the industry. Besides the money, the settlement included structural changes, such as an agreement that analysts would no longer be rewarded financially for brining in in-

---

[30] Salomon Smith Barney ($400 million), Merril Lynch ($200 million), Credit Suisse First Boston ($200 million), Morgan Stanley ($125 million), Goldman Sachs ($110 million), JP Morgan Chase ($80 million), Lehman Brothers ($80 million), Bear Steams ($80 million), UBS Paine Weber ($80 million), and U.S. Bank Corp Piper Jaffray ($32.5 million).

vestment banking business.   The settlement was reached in December 2002 and signed in April 2003.

The settlement was reached a few months after the enactment of the Sarbanes-Oxley Act in July 2002.   Section 501 of this act imposes on the SEC the task of making rules that isolate analysts from the influence of investment banking.   In 2003, Congress passed the Analyst Certification Regulation effective April 2003, which requires analysts to certify that their report reflects their true beliefs.

The industry that grew so rapidly in the later part of the twentieth century subsequently shrank.   The New York Times on July 29, 2005 cited a finding by the Securities Industry Association that the financial industry had shed some 55,000 jobs, mostly in equity research (see also Mohd, 2005)   To the extent that the regulators were successful in mitigating analysts' conflict of interests, it seems that the marginal benefit of research has declined, and with it, the compensation of analysts.   "The broad appeal for college hires has diminished, especially in terms of compensation" (New York Times, July 29, 2005).[31]

When Eliot Spitzer was interviewed by J. Cremer on the TV show "Mad Money" on July 28, 2005, he said that he believed that a great deal of corruption was eliminated but not all problems were completely dealt with.[32] Yet there is no doubt that things are in the process of change.   For example, on July 26, 2005, Tad LaFountain, a semiconductor stock analyst with Well Fargo Securities, announced that he was dropping coverage of the Altera Corporation.   What happened before this "highly unusual move"[33] was not unusual at all.   Altera blacklisted the analyst by refusing to communicate with him or answer his questions during conference calls, after the analyst criticized their share buyback to offset the company's stock price as a poor use of shareholders' cash (see Chap. 3).   The move was unusual because LaFountain "went public" and put the company in the wrong.   The shift in power from management to analysts was manifest in

---

[31] Regulation FD affected the industry by leveling the field between lead analysts with close ties to the firm and other analysts.   Janakiraman, Radhakrishnan, and Szwejkowski (2006), find that the first-forecast horizon (computed as the number of calendar days between the issue of the analysts' first earnings forecast for a quarter and the fiscal quarter-end date) decreased by about 12 days after RFD, and the decline was stronger for leading analysts, as measured by their average first-forecast horizon over each year.

[32] In an investors' conference in New York City in February 2005, one of the presenters commented that "the analysts are located on a different floor, but you can take the elevator."

[33] Quoted from Morgenson, Gretchen, "You'll Never Do Research in This Town Again," New York Times, July 31, 2005, section 3, page 1, column 2).

the fact that Natahn M. Sarkisian, Altera's CFO, apologized, and the company promised full communication access to all analysts.[34]

These were not sweeping changes. Mayew (2006), for example, shows that during conference calls with analysts, firms favor analysts with more favorable recommendations in deciding whom to give the opportunity to ask a question (see a further discussion on the firm's control over information given to analysts below). Chen and Matsumoto (2006), conjecture that there is relationship between analysts' accuracy and the information given to them by the firm. They find that before Regulation FD, there was an increase in the relative accuracy of forecasts of analysts who made more favorable recommendations; but this association disappeared after Regulation FD. Hence, Regulation FD mitigated the asymmetry of information caused by firms' control over selective disclosure, but not perfectly.

5.2.4 Meeting or Beating Expectations—MBE

> In an earnings season preceded by a flood of warnings, everything seems to be coming up roses.
> More than half of the Standard & Poor's 500 companies reporting earnings in the last two weeks topped Wall Street's expectations—most by just a penny or so. (New York Times, February 2, 2003)
> Boeing reported a 6.8 % decline in second-quarter profit yesterday, but the company still beat Wall Street's expectations and raised its earnings outlook for the year. (New York Times, July 28, 2005)
> Sprint, the telecommunications provider, said yesterday that its profits more than doubled in the second quarter, with growth being driven by adding and retaining more wireless customers. The earnings report surpassed Wall Street analysts' expectations, though some analysts said they had hoped to see Sprint do even better in the competitive mobile phone sector. (New York Times, July 28, 2005)
> Alcoa reported an 86% jump in net income for the third quarter, but the company sharply missed analysts' expectations amid lower metals prices. Its shares slid in after-hours trading. The report started the quarter's earnings season off on a sour note. (Wall Street Journal, October 10, 2006)

MBE is the phenomenon of firms announcing earnings that either meet or beat the consensus analysts' forecasts of earnings. The importance of MBE follows from the fact that earnings are the statistic most predicted by

---

[34] The same New York Times story discloses, "What Altera did not say was that it had also blacklisted Chris Danely of J. P. Morgan Securities. A seven-page letter dated April 22, from Mr. Sarkisian began succinctly: 'Be advised that we do not intend further interaction or communication with you or your staff.' Mr. Danely's transgression? Bias against the company, according to the letter."

analysts (e.g., DeFond and Hung, 2003). Hence, successfully meeting expectations or failing to beat them earns a great deal of attention in the press and from investors.

Research indicates that the phenomenon increased in the later years of the twentieth century. Bartov, Givoly, and Hayn (2002), who studied 64,872 firm-quarters between January 1983 and December 1997, noted that "[t]he number of firm-quarters increases steadily from an average of about 400 per fiscal quarter in the first five years of the sample period to over 1,500 per fiscal quarter in the last five years of the period" (p. 180). A similar trend is reported in the 1985–1997 sample of Matsumoto (2002) (41% of firm/quarters in 1985 to 70% in 1997 in the Zacks Surprise Files database)[35] and Brown (2001) (the median earnings surprise is slightly negative in the years 1984–1990, zero in 1991–1993, and slightly positive in 1994–1999).

MBE remains prevalent today.[36] Reuter reported that more than half of the Standard & Poor's 500 companies that reported earnings in the second half of January 2003, met or beat expectations by just a penny. A study by Thompson Financial of the 30 companies in the Dow Jones in the 1999–2004 period found that 46.1% met consensus estimates or beat them by a penny during each quarter over the 1999–2004 period. For the first three quarters of 2004, 10.9% missed their expected results, down from 11.7% in 2003 and 25% in 2002 (as reported by the New York Times, November 7, 2004). MBE is also quite widespread across industries. Williams (2006), examines the phenomenon from 1999 to 2003 in a sample of 11,503 firm/quarters in 59 two-digit SIC codes (after deleting observations with missing data, financial institutions, and industries with less than ten firms). She finds some concentration in industries with intangible assets: Business Services (17.06%), Electrical and Electronic Equipment (10.07%), Chemical and Allied Products (9.98%), and Instruments and Related Products (7.87%). The rest (55.02%) are evenly distributed over the remaining 55 industries.

---

[35] Matsumoto notes that

> The increase is unlikely to be due to analysts underestimating the effect of positive macroeconomic events on firm profits... there is no significant trend over time in the percent of quarters with increases in earnings per share before extraordinary items (quarterly Compustat data item no. 8) from the same quarter in the previous year (i.e., the seasonal change in earnings).... From 1991, onward, however, the percent of quarters that meet or exceed analysts' expectations has increased steadily, whereas the percent of quarters with increases in earnings has not (p. 489).

[36] MBE declined with SOX (Williams, DaDalt, Sun, and Yaari, 2006, 2008; Bartov and Cohen, 2007; and Koh, Matsumoto, and Rajgopal, 2007).

There has, however, been a change in the pattern of MBE in the twenty-first century in that earnings surprises are larger than one penny, with accompanying increases in price changes. "Due to Regulation FD (Fair Disclosure),… CEOs and chief financial officers have to keep their lips sealed regarding their firms' performance until official announcements. The result? Earnings surprises have become more literally a surprise. That's why a growth stock can move 10%, 20% or even more in just one day" (David Saito-Chung, "Even Leaders Get Burned by Dismal Profit Outlooks," Investor's Business Daily, July 25, 2005).[37] Furthermore, the Thompson Financial study cited above also finds that the market price is less responsive to beating the target by a penny and that fewer firms beat the consensus by a penny.[38]

Why do firms meet or beat expectations? The answer is that the market rewards this behavior. Barth, Elliott, and Finn (1999), Bartov, Givoly, and Hayn (2002), Kasznik and McNichols (2002), Lopez and Rees (2002), Bhojraj, Hribar, and Picconi (2003), Chen (2003), Das and Zhang (2003), Brown, Hillegeist, and Lo (2006), and others find a significant stock price premium (penalty) for meeting or beating (missing) analysts' earnings forecasts, after controlling for the magnitude of the forecast error.[39] The range of earnings surprise over which the market's reaction is the strongest lies in the vicinity of one penny (+1 penny of MBE firms and—1 penny for firms that missed the forecast). The window over which the market reaction is measured also matters.[40] As the return window expands, the absolute

---

[37] For a review of extensive research of the effect of Regulation FD on the quality of analysts' forecasts, consult Francis, Chen, Philbrick, and Willis (2004).

[38] Firms in the Dow Jones composite that beat expectations by a cent experienced a stock rise of 0.78% at the date of announcement in 1998 but just 0.15% in 2004, and the percentage of MBE companies declined from 60% in 1998 to 35% in 2004. The number of Dow component companies that beat expectations by more than a penny rose from 27.2% in 2002 to 54.3% percent in 2004.

[39] The Thompson Financial study reports that companies whose results came in below analysts' estimates lost 1.08% of their value, on average, the day of the announcement. The loss averaged 1.59% over 5 days.

[40] The interpretation of these studies warrants some caution because of stock splits. After stock splits, databases offer restated historical data which are rounded to the nearest cent. The combination of stock splits and measuring surprises by analysts' forecasts rounded to the nearest cent biases the data. Baber and Kang (2002a), observe,

> For example, assume that the consensus analysts' forecast EPS is $0.10 and the actual EPS is $0.09, and that the firm subsequently executes a 2-for-1 stock split. Both the forecast and the actual EPS are reported as $0.05 after rounding to the nearest cent. Thus, data from the forecast files

value of the stock price premium or penalty increases, since additional earnings pre-announcements and other signals are likely.

A special class of MBE firms includes firms that do it habitually. Once a firm starts the expectations game, it cannot back out without risking severe repercussions from the reaction of disappointed investors (Barth, Elliott, and Finn, 1999; Kim, 2002; Skinner and Sloan, 2002; Graham, Harvey, and Rajgopal, 2005; Myers, Myers, and Skinner, 2006). We discuss this class below.[41]

5.2.2.3 MBE as an Earnings Management Strategy

MBE is considered to be another case of managing earnings in order to beat a threshold (see Chap. 4); the threshold is the consensus analysts' forecast. The benchmarks of zero earnings and the-same-quarter-last-year earnings (discussed in Chap. 4) are ostensibly objective and unchangeable. The same cannot be said about consensus forecasts. First, analysts follow only those firms they consider large enough to generate sufficient trade. Many public firms thus are not followed. Durtschi and Easton (2005), compare the Institutional Brokers Estimate System (I/B/E/S), with the database of firms' GAAP earnings (Compustat).[42] They report that in the 1983–2002 period, I/B/E/S followed 4.4% (11.6%) of the COMPUSTAT firms that reported a one-cent loss (profit). "This difference alone could cause an almost threefold difference between the number of I/B/E/S firms reporting a one-cent loss and the number of firms that report a one-cent profit" (p. 582). Second, management information is a valuable input to analysts' research. Firms thus can influence analysts' expectations, especially if the disclosure is given in terms of estimated future earnings, that is, guidance and preannouncements.

---

erroneously indicate that earnings "meet" the consensus forecast, even though actual earnings reported at the disclosure date differed from the consensus expectation. (p. 278)

Baber and Kang show that splitters (non-splitters) who meet their target enjoy positive (negative) 3-day abnormal returns. See also Kim, Lim, and Shaw (2001), who observe that a consensus analysts' expectations is a biased measure because it overweights the public information available to all analysts.

[41] See also the discussion in Matsumoto (2002), and Williams (2006), on the capital-market pressure to meet or beat expectations in order to sustain the firm's market price.

[42] I/B/E/S earnings are different from GAAP (e.g., Abarbanell and Lehavy, 2002; Bhattacharya, Black, Christensen, and Larson, 2003; Durtschi and Easton, 2005; Frankel and Roychowdhury, 2005).

The timeline of the game between the firm and analysts is as follows (based on figure 1 in Cotter, Tuna, and Wysocki, 2006).

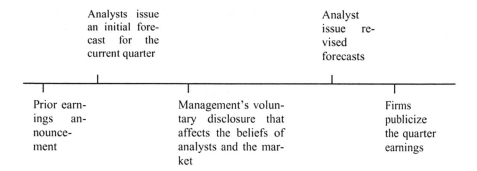

Fig. 5.1 The MBE game

Fig. 5.1 illustrates that firms can meet or beat expectations by managing expectations and managing earnings.[43] A former MCI employee, Dan Reingold, describes the games played by firms to manage expectations before Regulation FD:

> I quickly learned that investor relations was more of an art than a science–especially when it came to managing analysts' earnings expectations. (p. 19)
> ...If it had been a bad quarter, we needed to leak that information slowly and quietly, so that the stock would drop during the week or two before the earnings announcement, but without generating any media attention. That was a lot better than the stock plummeting at the earnings day, when the world was focused on it. Positive news also would be leaked out but downplayed a bit, so that the stock would still see a decent bounce when the better-than-expected news hit. It was common practice, so common that I didn't even take note of it at the time. (Reingold and Reingold, p. 20)

The literature provides evidence that firms manage earnings in order to beat expectations. Bannister and Newman (1996), find that firms that may fail to beat the forecasts engage in income-increasing earnings management more than firms whose earnings exceed the expectations. Abarbanell and Lehavy (2003a), find that firms that received "buy" recommendations

---

[43] Ke and Yu (2006), show that analysts had incentives to play along the expectations game before Regulation FD. Analysts who played the expectations game issued on the average more accurate forecasts and enjoyed a higher job security. This result supports the quotation that indicates that firms are sophisticated players in channeling value-relevant information to the market.

were more likely to manage their earnings to meet analysts' expectations. Kasznik (1999), shows that firms manage earnings in order not to disappoint the market given expectations formed in response to earlier voluntary disclosures.   Moehrle (2002), examines 121 reversals of restructuring charges that were recorded between 1990 and 1999, finding that they were used as a means to achieve the desired earnings forecast (and other benchmarks).   Bange and De-Bondt (1998), examine whether executives manage research and development budgets in order to manage earnings, since the U.S. GAAP require firms to fully expense these costs in the period they are made.   Their study of 100 U.S. companies between 1977 and 1986 indicates that R&D budget adjustments reduce the anticipated gap between analysts' earnings forecasts and reported income.   Das and Zhang (2003), found that firms report the digit immediately to the right of the decimal in the earnings per share number (expressed in cents) such as to round the EPS up.   For example, if EPS is 10.435, the firm can report 10.44.   Further examination shows that the rounding is more pronounced for firms that meet or beat expectations by one penny![44]   McVay (2006), shows that firms meet analysts' expectations by expense shifting, that is, they move items between cost of goods sold and selling, general, and administrative expenses—core earnings—to special items.

Empirical research has established that both strategies (managing expectations and managing earnings) have been employed.[45]   Kinney, Burgstahler, and Martin (2002), provide evidence that between 1992 and 1997, the characteristics of forecasts changed in a manner that is consistent with increases of both earnings management and expectations management.   As an example, the average age of revised forecasts (relative to the annual earnings release date) decreased by 52%, and the proportion of firms with zero earnings surprise increased by 41%, with positive surprises increasing 14% and negative surprises decreasing 29%.   Since analysts revise their forecasts after firms' disclosures, the lower forecast age indicates

---

[44] For example, when the object of rounding is net income, 56.1% (60.1%) of all firms that meet expectations (beat expectations by one penny) use a rounding scheme to do so.

[45] The earnings management tactics of guiding analysts has been the subject of separate research.   Cotter, Tuna, and Wysocki (2006), obtain data on guidance events between 1995 and 2001 from the First Call "company issued guidelines" database.   They find that managers are selective about which quarters to issue public guidance.   Public management guidance occurs in 2,382 of the total 8,198 guidance instances.   The mean days prior to earnings announcements of publicizing guidance is 29 days.   Firms "talk analysts down" in that a 100% increase in analyst optimism (measured relative to actual earnings) leads to a 5% increase in the likelihood of public management guidance to lower the expectations.

greater use of expectations management, since the closer the revision of earnings, the more accurate it is likely to be. Louis (2004), documents aggressive earnings management by acquiring firms in the quarter that preceded the stock swap in stock-for-stock mergers. The effect of this earnings management strategy is to create reversals of accruals that reduce post-merger earnings (see Chap. 4). Louis finds that analysts who do not fully revise their forecasts to account for the reversal of the managed accruals in the month following the merger announcement fully account for the reversal by the time the acquiring firm makes the subsequent quarterly earnings announcement. He concludes that the firms apparently "walk down" the analysts. Comprix, Mills, and Schmidt (2004), uncover a clever ploy that kills two birds with one stone. The joint management of expectations and earnings is achieved by quarterly estimates of the effective tax rate. By announcing a higher rate in earlier quarters, the firm builds slack that allows it to beat the target annually. At the same time, it lowers analysts' forecasts because they fail to take into account the fact that the year-end tax rate is likely to be lower than the one in the quarterly reports.

More empirical evidence on the use of both tactics to meet or beat expectations is provided by Bartov, Givoly, and Hayn (2002), Matsumoto (2002), Bernhardt and Campello (2003), Burgstahler and Eames (2003), Chen (2003), Ayers, Jiang, and Yeung (2006), Bauman, Braswell, and Shaw (2006), Brown, Hillegeist, and Lo (2006), and Williams (2006). Specifically, when earnings management is pernicious, firms manage expectations to lower analysts' expectations and inflate earnings to meet or beat expectations.

Firms vary in their approach to MBE. Some firms prefer to manage expectations only, others prefer to manage earnings only, some do neither, and some employ both.[46] A clue to the considerations behind employing these strategies is given in Matsumoto (2002). Table 5.1 summarizes her findings.

Firms that prefer to meet or beat expectations through earnings management are of two types. One is concerned with earnings because its shareholders are mainly institutional owners who make decisions based on the firm's observable ability to meet earnings expectations. The other is high-growth firms whose growth rates determine their valuation.

---

[46] Lin, Radhakrishnan, and Su (2006) examine earnings management tools, in addition to discretionary accruals to meet or beat expectations: classification shifting (similar to McVay, 2006) negative abnormal selling, general and administrative expenses (similar to Gunny 2005) and positive abnormal production and negative abnormal cash flow from operations (similar to Roychowdhury, 2005). They find that the increase in the probability of meeting or beating analysts' earnings forecasts ranges from 5 to 10%, depending on the tool.

Table 5.1 The strategies used for MBE

	Manage earnings	**Do not manage earnings**
Manage expectations	Firms with high level of institutional ownerships, especially transient ownerships	1. Firms that rely on implicit claims with stakeholders 2. Earnings are more value-relevant
Do not manage expectations	High-growth firms	Firms with history of losses

F that are likely to meet or beat expectations by managing expectations are firms that are concerned with the integrity of their earnings numbers, or those that prefer to filter the information to the capital market as soon as possible in order to avoid lawsuits.

Baik and Jiang (2006), examine incentives to manage expectations only (i.e, they do not address earnings management). They show firms with transient institutional ownership and firms with a long string of meeting or beating expectation are more likely to forecast with a negative bias. Companies that incur losses are less likely to issue forecasts with a negative bias because they have incentives to dampen the bad-news content of their losses. Complementing this study is that of Barua, Legoria, and Moffitt (2006), who show that the pressure to manage earnings to meet or beat expectations is stronger for firms with profits than for firms with losses.

When the market sees through earnings management and hence does not reward MBE (Bolliger and Kast, 2004; Lin, Radhakrishnan, and Su, 2006), the incentives to meet or beat expectations are unclear. Most research finds, however, that the MBE firms are rewarded by the market. This raises the apprehension that the market might be rewarding pernicious earnings management. The consensus that it is pernicious is manifested in the 1998 "The Numbers Game" speech of the then chief commissioner of the SEC, Arthur Levitt:

> Increasingly, I have become concerned that the motivation to meet Wall Street earnings expectations may be overriding common sense business practices.... In the zeal to satisfy consensus earnings estimates and project a smooth earnings path, wishful thinking may be winning the day over faithful representation.

Gretchen Morgenson of the New York Times writes (Pennies That Aren't From Heaven, Nov. 7, 2004):

> Ask any chief executive officer if he or she practices the art of earnings management and you will undoubtedly hear an emphatic "Of course not!" But ask those same executives about their company's recent results, and you may very well hear a proud "we beat the analysts' estimate by a penny."

Pulling off such a feat in an uncertain world smacks of earnings management. "It is not possible for this percentage of reporting companies to hit the bull's-eye," said Bill Fleckenstein, principal at Fleckenstein Capital in Seattle. "Business is too complicated; there are too many moving parts."

Williams, DaDalt, Sun, and Yaari (2006), hypothesize that MBE signals strong performance by firms that commit to reported performance repeatedly. That is, if a strong firm inflates its report, it can afford to do so. Overstatement of earnings today leads to a reversal of earnings in the future that jeopardizes the firm's ability to beat and meet future expectations. Hence, firms that undertake this risk signal future value. Some empirical evidence indicates that on average MBE firms have superior performance over time (e.g., Chevis, Das, and Sivaramakrishnan, 2001; Bartov, Givoly, and Hayn, 2002; Dopuch, Seethamraju, and Xu, 2003).[47] Chevis, Das, and Sivaramakrishnan (2001), for example, analyze MBE in the period 1988–1998 and find that firms that habitually meet or beat expectations are likely to have higher growth and a higher pattern of increasing earnings, as well as more stable earnings. As a result, they attract a larger analyst following whose forecast dispersion is lower. Taking this further, Brown, Hillegeist, and Lo (2006), argue that the reward to meet or beat expectations is justified because MBE has a real cash-flow effect by reducing the firm's cost of capital. MBE changes the dynamics of the market response to the firm, with increased trading, attracting informed traders, and better liquidity. This in turn, reduces the information asymmetry between the firm and its investors, which has a favorable effect on the firm's cost of capital.

The reward for MBE explains the incentives of poor performers to pool with strong performers. If the market cannot distinguish between weak and strong MBE firms, it rewards the average firm. To illustrate, suppose that 40% of firms are strong, with an economic value of 1, and the remaining 60% are weak, with an economic value of 0.2. If only strong firms meet or beat expectations, the market price of an MBE firm is 1 and that of a non-MBE firm is 0.2. Yet what if the weak firms attempt to meet or beat expectations as well? Since the market cannot distinguish between the two types, the price would average over both. The price then will be 60% x 1 + 40% x 0.2 = 0.68. Since this price is higher than 0.2, weak performers have incentives to meet or beat. If they are found out, their price drops to

---

[47] An exception is Bhojraj, Hribar, and Picconi (2003). They find that firms that did not manage earnings and thus failed to meet or beat expectations outdid firms that did.

0.2, but no lower. Clearly, they are worse off if they do not meet or beat expectations.[48]

Evidence that the market cannot distinguish between weak and strong MBE firms is provided in Bhojraj, Hribar, and Picconi (2003). They compare two types of firms: firms that miss the target without making an overt attempt to manage earnings and those that meet or beat expectations but seem to do so by aggressively managing earnings. They find that the market rewards the latter. In windows of 2 and 3 years, however, the firms that manage earnings are outperformed by those that did not, in terms of both returns and earnings changes.

Williams, DaDalt, Sun, and Yaari (2006), study the market's ability to distinguish between strong and poor performers in the wake of Regulation FD and SOX. This study offers a richer model than our simple example by admitting financial analysts. Because financial analysts face "prisoners' dilemma" incentives, they recommend both strong and weak firms.[49] That is, analysts do not make discriminating recommendations that allow the market to distinguish between the two types, which incentivizes the weak type to MBE by managing expectations downward and earnings upward. These strategies are determined by cost–benefit considerations. Hence, this model also implies that the regulatory shocks of Regulation FD and SOX will affect how the weak firms meet or beat expectations. This prediction was tested using a sample of habitual MBE firms that are more likely to be strong firms. The market response to MBE indicates that Regulation FD (SOX) improved (had no effect on) the market's ability to discern a firm's type when MBE is accomplished through guiding the analysts' expectations (earnings management).

Assuming that MBE entails some costs, when is the pressure to perniciously meet or beat the strongest? Payne and Robb (2000), who study a sample of 13,532 I/B/E/S firms between 1986 and 1997, test the association between aggressive earnings management and the dispersion in the analysts' forecasts. Since dispersion measures the agreement among ana-

---

[48] To continue with this example, suppose that because of investors' lawsuits (see Chap. 8), the post-revelation price falls to zero. Then if the chance of being found out is less that 70%, MBE is still preferable. The bad firm is indifferent to MBE if $0.68 \times (1-x) + 0 \times x = 0.2$. Hence, $x = 0.48 / 0.68 = 0.7$

[49] Consider a game with two analysts following the same weak firm. The payoffs of the analysts are such that if only one issues an honest opinion that the firm is weak, he is penalized and the analyst that pays accolade to the firm is rewarded. Only if both analysts condemn the firm, their payoff is higher than when they both hide the truth. A numerical illustration of such a setting shows that if both analysts misrepresent, each gets utility of 5 and if both are truthful, each gets 7. If only one is truthful, he gets 4 and the other analyst gets 9.

lysts and analysts affect the market's expectations, the lower the dispersion, the more solid the market's expectations of a certain performance. Payne and Robb find that managers are more likely to meet or beat expectations through income-increasing strategies when the dispersion of analysts' forecasts is lower. Richardson, Teoh, and Wysocki (2004), who study 53,653 firm-quarter observations between 1984 and 2001, show that managers who plan to engage in insider trading have stronger incentives to surprise the market favorably. McVay, Nagar, and Tang (2006), test a sample of 21,952 firm quarters from 1990–1999, for firms that just met (by zero or one cent) or just missed (by one or two cents) the quarterly consensus forecast. They too find that the likelihood of just meeting versus just missing the consensus forecast is strongly associated with subsequent managerial stock sales. Sales by managers of the "just met" firms (scaled by shares owned) were about 56% higher than those of the "just missed" firms. Cheng and Warfield (2005), obtain similar results for their sample of non-financial and unregulated ExecuComp firms between 1993 and 2000. They show that stock options induce managers to act strategically in their earnings management and insider trading. They avoid reporting large earnings surprises and are more likely to meet the market's expectations. Bolliger and Kast (2004), find in their sample of 8,714 firm/year observations between 1993 and 2001 that stock options explain the capital market pressure on management to meet or beat expectations by guiding analysts down. In contrast, Bauman, Braswell, and Shaw (2006), who examine MBE accomplished by both opportunistic accounting choices and expectations guidance, claim that stock-based compensation induces expectations management rather than earnings management. If the market is unsure whether the numbers are good or a product of pernicious earnings and expectations management, it is likely to

(a) discount the MBE and

(b) search for additional clues.

If firms meet or beat expectations in order to obscure their financial health, then the rational market will discount MBE. That is, the premium for MBE is lower when the market suspects earnings management or guidance (Baber and Kang, 2001, 2002b, 2003; Bartov, Givoly, and Hayn, 2002; Das and Zhang, 2003; Bolliger and Kast, 2004; Choi, 2004; Lin and Shih, 2006; Williams, 2006). Williams, for example, finds that the reward for meeting or beating by expectations management is lower than the than the reward for earnings management because it is easier for the market to detect management of expectations. In some cases, the market seems to penalize firms that meet or beat expectations by aggressively managing earnings, in that the return around the earnings announcement date is negative (e.g., Baber and Kang, 2003; Dopuch, Seethamraju, and Xu, 2003; Williams, 2006).[50]

If the market discounts MBE, then why doesn't it ignore the MBE event?[51] Our answer is that the MBE game acquires credibility from the firms that missed the target by as little as one cent. To expand the above example, suppose now that 50% of the weak performer that attempt to meet or beat expectations might miss the target by one penny but every strong firm is going to beat the target. If a firm misses the target, its price will be 0.20 because a failure to meet or beat expectations reveals the firm's type. By Bayes' rule, since 80% of the firms do meet or beat expectations (60% + 50% × (100%—60%)), the market price of MBE firms is $\dfrac{60\% \times 1}{80\%} + \dfrac{40\% \times 50\% \times 0.20}{80\%} = 0.80 > 0.68$. MBE has some credibility, then, because not every firm can do it successfully.[52] Note that now "good" firms also have incentives to meet or beat expectations, because if they do not try to signal their worth, no firm will and the market price will be just 0.68.

Another way to deal with MBE is to find more evidence of the credibility of the MBE firms. Dopuch, Seethamraju, and Xu (2003), examine the credibility of MBE by examining whether firms also meet expectations

---

[50] Dechow, Richardson, and Tuna (2000), report that firms that meet or beat expectations tend to have fewer negative special and extraordinary items relative to other firms, although in general, they are characterized by a high level of working capital accruals and a high level of special items.

[51] In some cases, the market ignores MBE. DeFond and Hung (2003), show that analysts forecast cash flows in addition to earnings when institutional factors cast doubt on the quality of earnings as a signal on firm's value, because, for example, the firm is characterized by a weaker protection of shareholders' rights. Ertimur and Stubben (2005), also find demand for sales and cash forecasts when earnings cannot be trusted because they are too volatile or negative, or contain large accruals.

[52] This argument makes sense only if there are firms that do miss the forecast. The fact is that although more firms beat the forecast than miss it (see e.g., Durtschi and Easton, 2005, figure 10), there are many firms that miss expectations by one cent. Hence, a few questions arise: Who is to blame? The firms that were not adroit in playing the expectations game? The firms that were reluctant to manage earnings to beat the target? The analysts that did not play along? Chen (2003), hypothesizes that the fault lies with managers and that they are more likely to miss their own forecasts when the costs of meeting their predictions exceed the benefits. Chen finds that firms whose managers miss have less accounting flexibility and less experience at forecasting and whose earnings are more difficult to predict because they are more risky (as evidenced in more negative abnormal return days during the quarter).

when one considers the time-series behavior of their earnings. In their sample of 33,575 firm-quarters between 1993 and 2000, they observe that the market premium to firms that successfully beat both thresholds was 4.5%, which was higher than the premium for beating just one threshold. Further testing reveals that the CAR (cumulative abnormal return) was significantly negative (—0.009) for the set of firms that met or beat only analysts' forecasts, compared to the CAR of 0.045 for firms that met or beat both benchmarks. They conclude that "investors did not blindly reward firms that merely beat the analysts' forecasts; rather they also incorporated incremental information from the time-series forecasts" (p. 11).

Dopuch, Seethamraju, and Xu (2003), also shed light on the relationships between MBE and the other thresholds that were discussed in Chap. 4. In particular, are the different targets complements or substitutes? Hansen (2004), Graham, Harvey, and Rajgopal (2005), and Rees (2005), find that firms try to beat multiple thresholds. Hence, they suggest there may be some substitution among different thresholds. Brown and Caylor's (2005), finding that the market reward for MBE is greater than that for meeting other earnings thresholds seems to imply that even if some targets are substitutes, MBE is likely to carry a greater weight because the market's reaction to MBE is stronger.

Another signal is revenues. Rees and Sivaramakrishnan (2006), show that when an MBE firm fails to fulfill analysts' sales forecasts, the premium for meeting earnings forecasts is completely eliminated. Stubben (2006), however, observes that firms whose revenues are highly valued by the market inflate revenues to meet revenue targets.

Yet another signal is a firm's reputation for habitually meeting or beating expectations. Barth, Elliott, and Finn (1999), Kim (2002), Skinner and Sloan (2002), and others observe that the market rewards firms with a longer history of MBE. (Lopez and Rees, 2002, and Choi, 2004, show that their ERC (see Chap. 4) is higher.) Once a firm fails to achieve this target, however, its market price plummets, a phenomenon known as the torpedo effect. Clearly, each quarter that the firm succeeds increases the market's confidence in its long-term value. Once the firm fails to meet expectations, the market punishes the firm because it revises its opinion downward. Since research has found that firms that miss targets do not do well in the future (Dechow, Richardson, and Tuna, 2003; Chen, 2003), this response is rational. The anecdotal evidence indicates that one reason for the torpedo effect lies in the reaction of money managers. They tend to discard all the firm's shares. Also, to the extent that the firm's stock price affects its production and investment decisions, the negative shock to the price generates a self-fulfilling prophecy that the firm will likely not do well in the future.

In sum, analysts' presence in the accounting scene induces earnings management by firms to meet or beat analysts' expectations. It is not known yet why some firms meet the target, and some beat it by just one penny.

5.3 Governance—Ownership

5.3.1 A Definition and the Framework of U.S. Corporate Governance

We employ the definition of governance in the 2004 "Principles of Corporate Governance" of the Organization of Cooperation and Development (OECD): "Corporate governance deals with the rights and responsibilities of a company's management, its board, shareholders, and various stakeholders."[53] We focus on the U.S. system.[54] The United States regards the objective of the governance system as the creation of long-term shareholder value (Gertner and Kaplan, 1998; Dallas, 2002; Jensen, 2005a, b; Niskanen, 2005; Skousen, Glover, and Prawitt, 2005). Contrast this, for example, with the views of the customers of the IT sector in India. Agrawal and Fuloria (2004), find that the objective that ranks the highest is the maximization of stakeholders' value. The U.S. perspective is that maximization of stakeholders' value might sacrifice shareholders' value. Niskanen (2005), states,

> [Regarding the] view that corporate managers should also be accountable to other "stakeholders" affected by their decisions–such as employees, creditors, the local community, the environment, etc.... I am wholly unsympathetic with this view... Although I recognize that a corporation's contracts with these other constituencies are not complete, they are *far* more complete than the open-ended contract with shareholders. Good managers will pay attention to the interests of the several types of stakeholders to the extent that this attention is consis-

[53] Some researchers prefer to emphasize the legal aspects of governance (e.g., Garrod, 2002; Gillan and Starks, 1998). Governance is the system of laws, rules, and factors that control operations at a company. The inclusion of factors recognizes the pressure from markets such as the labor and financial markets.
For a discussion of the different definitions of corporate governance, consult Gillan and Starks (1998); and Farinha (2003).
[54] For example, contrast the two-tier governance system of Germany and Netherlands with the board of directors of United Kingdom and United States.

tent with the interests of the general shareholders. But making corporate managers accountable to multiple constituencies would substantially increase managerial discretion, increasing the prospect that they
would not serve any constituency very well. (pp. 337–338)

Maximization of shareholders' value poses a challenge because of the
myriad principal–agent relationships that characterize U.S. public firms.
In general, the firm is a hierarchy of principal–agent relationships, between
shareholders (institutional and retail) and directors, and between directors
and senior management. The shareholders act as a principal to the directors. The directors are an agent of the shareholders and a principal of the
senior management, and senior management is an agent of the board.

There are also principal–agent relationships between senior management and its subordinates, and between institutional shareholders and their
beneficiaries, since, by definition, institutional owners manage assets for
others.[55] In a September 2005 conference of the Investor Responsibility
Research Center (IRRC) in Beverly Hills, Rich Koppes, the former general
counsel of CalPERS (California Pension Employees' Retirement System),
remarked that institutional investors are also fiduciaries and should "examine their own governance house." He recommended that institutional
shareholders focus solely on what is best for their beneficiaries.[56] A concern that institutional investors might compromise their fiduciary duty has
motivated the SEC to require institutional owners to disclose how they
vote (see the discussion in Latham, 2005). For a recent study that shows
that they fulfill their fiduciary duty, consult Adams and Santos (2006).

Figure 5.2 depicts the principal–agent relationships.

---

[55] Coffee (1991), observes,

The problem of who will guard the guardian is a timeless one, but it is particularly complicated when the proposed guardian is the institutional investor. Not
only do the same problems of agency cost arise at the institutional investor
level, but there are persuasive reasons for believing that some institutional investors are less accountable to their "owners than are corporate managements to
their shareholders. Put simply, the usual mechanisms of corporate accountability are either unavailable or largely compromised at the institutional level. (p.
1283)

[56] http://www.irrc.com/company/news_fulltext.htm#CII

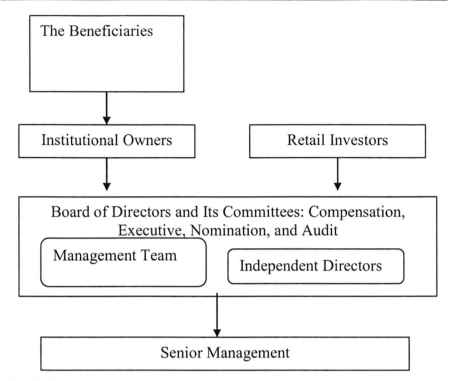

Fig. 5.2 The principal–agent relationships in the governance structure

In contrast to Chap. 3, where we portrayed the CEO as an agent of shareholders, in this chapter the CEO participates in governance as a principal to management. CEOs and top officers serve as a communication channel between insider management and the shareholders. The insider management is concerned with strategy and day-to-day operations, while shareholders are concerned with balancing an efficient portfolio (Jensen, 2005a). Booth (2005), claims that the role of CEOs as a principal explains why they deserve high compensation as partners to shareholders.

Section 5.3 proceeds as follows: shareholders are discussed first and the board of directors thereafter. For each group, we ask whether earnings are important to it and what its incentives to encourage or deter earnings management are. We conclude by presenting the studies that have examined earnings management.

5.3.2 Shareholders

5.3.2.1 The Role of Shareholders in Governance in the United States[57]

There are two classes of shareholders: institutional and retail. The former includes banks, insurance companies, mutual funds, pension funds, and university endowments, while the latter refers to individual investors. The discussion to follow will focus on institutional shareholders. In some instances, shareholders hold at least 5% of outstanding shares; they are known as blockholders. They often can elect members to the board to monitor management closely. See Shleifer and Vishny (1986), Admati, Pfleiderer, and Zechner (1994), Winton (1993), Huddart (1993), Chidambaran and John (1999, 2003), Kahn and Winton (1998), Maug (1998), Noe (2002), Aghion, Bolton and Tirole (2004); Faure-Grimaud and Gromb (2004); and Oded and Wang (2005). For example, Warren Buffet serves as a director on the board of the Washington Post. Buffet is the chairman, president, and CEO of Berkshire Hathaway, Inc., which holds a block of 17% of the Washington Post's shares.[58] Another example of blockholders is the family-controlled firms, such as Wal-mart, which is controlled by the Walton family.[59]

---

[57] The metrics of the quality of governance from the point of view of owners is largely either the shareholders' rights score of the Investor Responsibility Research Center (IRRC), which focuses on the antitakeover provisions, or the governance score of Institutional Shareholder Services (ISS), which provides additional governance attributes, such as audit, board of directors characteristics, the compensation of directors and executives, and so on. The former metric is associated with Gompers, Ishi, and Metrick (GIM) (2003), who found that weak governance is associated with poor performance and corresponding low returns. The efficiency of this governance score was later challenged by Brown and Caylor (2005) and Core, Guay, and Rusticus (2006). Brown and Caylor find that it is the charter/by-laws category in their governance score (which is closely related to the GIM score) that is associated with *poor* performance. For a further evaluation of the GIM score, consult Bebchuk, Cohen, and Ferrell (2004).

[58] http://archives.cjr.org/year/98/6/buffett.asp

[59] U.S. public firms are characterized by a wide variety in the concentration of ownership. Demsetz and Lehn (1985), for example, find that when concentration is measured by common stock equity holdings by the five largest shareholders, this variable takes value that range from 1.27 to 87.14 around a mean value of 24.81, and when the measure is the percentage of shares owned by the largest shareholders, this variables ranges from 1.27 to 91.54 around a mean value of 37.66. For recent data, consult Dlugosz, Fahlenbrach, Gompers, and Metrick (2006).

Institutional shareholders who manage at least one hundred million dollars are required to file with the SEC, which implies that the samples in empirical research tend to be comprised of large institutions.[60] The Federal Reserve regularly publishes the report on the Flow of Funds Accounts of the United States,[61] which provides the following breakdown of equity holdings (in billions of dollars):

	The first quarter of 2005	The first quarter of 2006
Market value of equity held by U.S. households and institutions [a]	14840.2 ======	16425.8 ======
Household sector	(39.9%) 5774.3	(34.6%) 5684.5
Commercial banking	19.4	28.0
Savings institutions	27.1	26.2
Property-casualty insurance companies	196.0	214.9
Life insurance companies	1037.5	1214.7
Private pension funds	1995.7	2220.6
State and local government retirement funds	1581.0	1811.8
Federal government retirement funds	99.5	122.5
Mutual funds	3669.9	4529.2
Closed-end funds	87.8	109.1
Exchange-traded funds	217.4	305.8
Brokers and dealers	134.6	158.5
Total holding of institutional owners	(61.1%) 9065.9	(65.4%) 10741.3

[a] The total equity holdings in the first quarter in 2005 (2006) are $16998.10 ($19025.3) billion, which includes foreign holders of $2067.9 ($2506.2) billion and holdings by state and local governments of $90.0 ($93.3) billion

As the table indicates, institutional shareholders hold about 50% more equity than households. Are they sufficiently large to affect a firm's decisions? On the one hand, the answer is no because institutional shareholders prefer large companies (Gompers and Metrick, 2001). Even blocks of millions of shares make their holdings small relative to outstanding shares. Furthermore, there is evidence that they avoid holding a share of 10% or more, in order not to be classified as insiders who must comply with the SEC's insider-trading reporting requirements. On the other hand, the

---

[60] For the list of requirements to file, consult http://www.sec.gov/about/forms/form13f.pdf.

[61] http://www.federalreserve.gov/releases/z1/Current/z1.pdf.   The data are extracted from Table L.213.

answer is yes because as a group, they cannot be ignored, and they might have the power to affect management's decisions.

To tie this to Chap. 1, we note that a meaningful discussion of shareholders' power ought to consider the legal limitations. Since shareholders can veto, but not initiate, major decisions that affect their wealth, such as mergers, law scholars conclude that shareholders are in essence weak owners. Bebchuk (2003, p.1) states, "[M]anagement power and shareholder weakness... [are] not largely an inevitable product of the dispersion of ownership, but are partly due to the legal rules that insulate management from shareholder intervention."

So what can shareholders do? In principle, they have four mutually exclusive alternatives: cooperating with management by voting with it; leaving the game by selling their shares—a strategy that is known as "voting with the feet," inducing changes by purchasing a block of shares that gives them a seat on the board and the ability to monitor management directly, or by becoming "activists."

5.3.2.2 Shareholders' Activism

We devote a separate discussion to shareholder activism because of the recent rise of shareholders' activism, not so much in volume of activity as in the way their opinion is heard in the boardroom. There is still some distance to go before the grim picture that presented shareholders as weak in Chap. 1 will be redrawn, but the fact that the SEC has considered giving shareholders power over the nomination of directors is but one signal of the changes toward increasing their power, and thus the importance of activism (see Coglianese and Michael, 2006, who summarize a roundtable on the changing relationships in corporate governance in the twenty-first century held at Harvard university).[62]

Activists are defined as shareholders who take measures to effect changes without a change in control (Gillan and Starks, 1998, 2007; Black, 2002). This definition covers shareholders' proposals and shareholders' negotiations with management. It rules out takeovers and a purchase of a minority control in a firm with the intent of influencing decision making.

---

[62] "[P]ressure to move to majority voting for directors clearly has been mounting steadily in recent years, with hundreds of shareholder proposals on the subject introduced in recent proxy seasons. Although many of these proposals have been rejected, there have been some notable cases where they have been approved. Attempts to pass proposals increasing shareholder influence over the selection of directors are likely to continue in the future" (p 12).

An activist can prepare a *shareholder resolution* for a vote in the company's annual meeting.[63] The SEC has specified rules on the following:

- procedure (the proposal is first submitted to the executive office of the company with a copy to the SEC)
- content (SEC rule 14a-8 of the 1934 Securities and Exchange Act specifies the 13 types of resolutions that are barred, such as any resolution that requires the corporation to break the law)
- length (no more than 500 words)
- timetable (proposals for a regularly scheduled annual meeting must be received at the company's principal executive offices not less than 120 calendar days before the release date of the previous year's annual meeting proxy statement)
- eligibility of the sponsor of a resolution ($2,000 worth of stock or 1% of equity, whichever is lower, held at least 1 year before the resolution, and when the sponsor is a beneficial owner (a brokerage holds his shares), he has to include a letter certifying his holdings)
- resubmission of a previously rejected proposal (a resolution that was not accepted in the shareholders' meeting can be resubmitted, but if it receives less than 3% of the votes, or less than 6% in its second year, or less than 10% during the previous 5-year period, the resolution is barred from future annual meetings for 3 years.

The topics of most proposals are governance and environmental issues. For example, in 2005, CalPERS announced the five U.S. companies in its "Focus List" of poor financial and poor corporate governance performers: American International Group (AIG), AT&T, Delphi, Novell, and Weyerhaeuser.[64] This list includes firms that are CalPERS' target for activism: "The CalPERS Corporate Governance Program annually identifies long-term poor performing companies within the System's domestic equity portfolio. Companies identified as among the relative poorest long-term performers in CalPERS domestic stock portfolio serve as the focus of the

---

[63] Besides the institutions, individual activists, known as gadflies (Gillan and Starks, 1998), and, since 1995, the Investors' Rights Association of America (IRRA) also submit resolutions.

[64] CalPERS has a "Monitoring List" and a "Focus List." For example, CalPERS elevated Novell from its 2004 Monitoring List to its Focus List in 2005, after the company continued to perform poorly, and "Novell failed to design a true performance-based executive compensation plan tied to operational performance following months of negotiations with the pension fund" (press release, April 20, 2005).

System's corporate governance activism" (http://www.calpers.ca.gov/eip-docs/about/facts/corpgov.pdf, p. 2).[65]

It might appear that the ability to make resolutions empowers shareholders. Resolution, however, are limited in scope and costly. The limits on their scope has led to the criticism that "[t]he SEC's Rule 14a-8 appears to do more to protect corporations from shareholders, than to protect shareholders, employees, human rights, or the environment from corporations" (http://www.scn.org/earth/wum/2Whatsr.htm).[66] Activism is costly because, besides the direct costs involved, it "requires knowledge of the firm and of the environment in which it operates" (Oded and Wang, 2005, p. 1). The direct costs are the result of the bureaucratic process of a proposal: After it is submitted to the corporation, management may opt to "omit" the resolution. It has 14 days to notify the sponsor of the resolution, who can take corrective actions to correct faults identified by the firm. The SEC is also involved, since the corporation must file a "no-action request" with the SEC no later than 80 days before the proxy statement is issued. A copy is sent to the sponsor. Although legally the SEC is not supposed to act as a mediator between the sponsor and the firm, in fact it does, because it listens to both sides.[67] If the SEC does not agree to

---

[65] In Chap. 3, we described backdating. It is interesting to note that by September 30, 2006, CalPERS announced that it also pursues major pay-for-performance initiatives, including the following:

- Engagement of the executive compensation consulting industry in the practice of employee stock option backdating and spring-loading, which is causing dozens of companies to come under investigation by the Securities and Exchange Commission (SEC);
- Direct engagement of dozens of companies to request responses to published media allegations of stock option backdating practices for top executives;
- Sole lead plaintiff in a federal court lawsuit against UnitedHealth Group over its stock-option grant practices (http://www.calpers.ca.gov/eip-docs/about/fa cts/corpgov.pdf, p. 1).

[66] Recently shareholders have made resolutions to impose a majority voting for electing directors (before that only one vote in the shareholders' annual meeting was required to elect a director) and recognition of stock options expense (Glassman, 2006a, b).

[67] To illustrate, consider activism concerning equity compensation. The SEC (14A) reports:

In the 2001–2002 proxy season, shareholders submitted proposals to several companies relating to equity compensation plans. Some of these proposals requested that the companies submit for shareholder approval all equity compensation plans that potentially would result in material dilution to existing shareholders. We received four

a "no-action" request, the resolution is attached to the proxy statements, and it is discussed in the corporation's annual shareholders' meetings.

Even if a resolution is presented in the annual meeting, there is no guarantee that it will obtain the necessary majority vote. The incumbent board has the right to explain why it opposes the proposal, and to attempt to convince shareholders to vote against it. Furthermore, when some shareholders also do business with the corporations, as is the case with insurance companies and banks, they are likely to cooperate with management by giving it their vote (see, e.g., Brickley, Lease, and Smith, 1988,[68] Fields and Keys, 2003; Monks and Minow, 2004; Borokhovich, Brunarski, Harman, and Parrino, 2006).[69] As discussed above regarding the response of shareholders to the firm, Coffee (1991), footnote 29 reports the Wall Street Rule:[70] The basic notion underlying the 'Wall Street Rule' was that institu-

---

no-action requests from companies seeking to exclude these proposals from their proxy materials in reliance on rule 14a-8(i)(7). In each instance, we took the view that the proposal could be excluded in reliance on rule 14a-8(i)(7) because the proposal related to general employee compensation, an ordinary business matter.

The Commission has stated that proposals involving "the management of the workforce, such as the hiring, promotion, and termination of employees," relate to ordinary business matters. Our position to date with respect to equity compensation proposals is consistent with this guidance and the Division's historical approach to compensation proposals. Since 1992, we have applied a bright-line analysis to proposals concerning equity or cash compensation:

- We agree with the view of companies that they may exclude proposals that relate to general employee compensation matters in reliance on rule 14a-8(i)(7); and
- We do not agree with the view of companies that they may exclude proposals that concern *only* senior executive and director compensation in reliance on rule 14a-8(i)(7) ."

[68] Brickley, Lease, and Smith find that unaffiliated blockholders are (no) more likely to oppose antitakeover amendments that deter hostile takeovers than affiliated blockholders when the stock price reaction to the proposal is positive (negative).

[69] For the SEC's clarifications, see http://www.sec.gov/interps/legal/cfslb14.htm.

[70] This goes beyond the border of the United States. Amzaleg, Ben-Zion, and Rosenfeld (2002), analyze the actual votes of mutual fund managers on 792 management-sponsored proposals in Israel. They find that they vote against only 30% of the "bad" (i.e., harmful to shareholders) proposals. The odds of voting against "bad" proposals are negatively associated with the holdings and the size of funds as well as with firm size. There is also indirect evidence that voting with management is influenced by business relationship between the mutual fund and the firm.

tions should support and vote with management—or sell their shares. Some trace the origins of this informal rule of behavior to guidelines developed in the 1940s by the American Bankers Association....[71]

Although shareholder resolutions are usually defeated (e.g., Maug and Rydqvist, 2006), activism may still be valuable. The immediate consequence is that a proposal opens a communication channel with senior management and directors. The benefit is that after negotiations, either the sponsor achieves what he wanted in the proposal or a compromise is reached (Gillan and Starks, 1998; Black, 2002). The common wisdom is that when the activist expects a positive response from the corporation, negotiations are less costly than sponsoring a shareholder resolution. When the activist anticipates opposition, the proposal serves as a threat to encourage cooperation.

Activism may fall below its socially optimal level, since it is undertaken when the institutional shareholder believes that it yields benefits that justify the cost. The benefit is twofold: an increase in the firm's value after intervention (since the market discounts the firm before activism) and acquisition of private information. Because the activist holds just a fraction of the firm's ownership, the benefit from an increase in value also accrues to other shareholders that do not engage in the costly activism. That is, activism suffers from a free-rider problem that may reduce its benefit to the institutional investor. The free-rider problem explains the tendency of activists to increase their shareholding. Bethel, Liebeskind, and Opler (1998), find that activists tend to purchase shares in diversified firms with poor performance and stay away from firms with "shark repellent"[72]

---

[71] We are aware that an exception to the this rule was a 1988 ruling by the Department of Labor that determined that voting rights are subject to the same fiduciary standards as other plan assets, since proxy voting can add value. This rule applied only to institutional owners that had to comply with ERISA. We are unaware of any new developments regarding this rule in the twenty-first century, except that on January 23, 2003, the SEC ruled that proxy votes made by mutual funds must be disclosed. This rule enables their shareholders to monitor that the votes are congruent with their own interests.

[72] Shark repellent amendments are changes to the firm's charter that weaken shareholders rights in order to allow incumbent management team to deter hostile takeover that will throw them out. Agrawal and Mandelker (1990), list five such provisions:
1. A "supermajority voting" provision. This increases the majority vote needed to approve a merger to between 66 and 95%.
2. A "supermajority with board-out" clause. Similar to (1), but it allows the board of directors to waive this requirement. Still, the power of shareholders is diminished as in (1).

amendments and large stock options plans. This effect is mitigated if the institutional activist acquires private information that allows it to trade at the expense of ignorant, non-activist shareholders. This private benefit requires sufficient liquidity of the stock, as well as ignorance on the part of other traders regarding the institutional investor's private knowledge (Maug, 1998).[73] Liquidity may have an undesirable effect on activism, however, because it makes it easier to "vote with the feet." In sum, the benefit is diluted due to the free-rider problem and institutions' preference for diversification and liquidity (Coffee, 1991; Roe, 1991; Admati, Pfleiderer, and Zechner, 1994; Maug, 1998; Parrino, Sias, and Starks, 2003).

The argument for activism is that it increases value. The evidence is mixed. On one hand, Karpoff (1998), who surveys the literature, concludes that activism improves governance somewhat but has a negligible effect on earnings and returns. A subsequent study by Bhagat, Black, and Blair (2004), using a 1983–1995 sample, confirm no effect on value. On the other hand, Bethel, Liebeskind, and Opler (1998), who examine changes at firms following the acquisition of blocks by investors, find that acquisitions by activist investors are followed by increases in value. There is an increase in divestitures of asset and industry-adjusted operating profitability, as well as a decrease in mergers and acquisitions, and abnormal stock price appreciation. Interestingly, CalPERS also found that shareholder value increased in commissioned studies that examined the corporations wherein CalPERS was an activist.[74]

---

3. A "fair price" provision. This requires a bidder to offer a "fair price," defined either as the highest price paid by the bidder for any target shares it has acquired or as a price approved by the target board. Failure to meet this requirement triggers a supermajority voting provision. Consequently, the bidder cannot acquire the firm by "divide and conquer."
4. A "staggered board" provision. See the discussion in Sect. 5.4. If not all board members are nominated in the same year, taking over the firm is a lengthy process.
5. Poison pills, through the provision of an "authorization to issue preferred stock" that allows the board to increase the voting rights disproportionably to its stock ownership.

[73] Trading boards show the selling and buying activities of traders by code. After a while, one learns the identity of the trader behind the code especially since it is close to the initials. But traders can also obscure their identities by trading through intermediaries.

[74] For details, consult the CalPERS website.

5.3.3 The Importance of Earnings

The following discussion distinguishes between institutional shareholders with short horizons and those with long horizons. We argue that the importance of earnings and the demand for earnings management are sensitive to differences in investment horizons.[75]

5.3.3.1 Short-term Shareholders

Some institutional shareholders are transient, with a short horizon (e.g., Lang and McNichols, 1997; Parrino, Sias, and Starks, 2003; Bhagat, Black, and Blair, 2004; and the citations therein). Lang and McNichols (1997), note that, on average, institutions trade more frequently than individuals, partly because their transaction costs are lower.[76] Bhagat, Black, and Blair (2004), find that although the number of blockholders in their 1983–1995 sample more than doubled in some categories (employee benefit and pension plans, holding companies, investment advisers, investment companies, and partnerships), most holdings by institutional investors were sold quickly. The finance literature in fact blames stock price volatility in part on their active trading (Lakonishok, Shleifer, and Vishny, 1992; Potter, 1992; Sias, 1996; Nofsinger and Sias, 1999; Bushee and Noe, 2000; Dennis and Strickland, 2002; Hotchkiss and Strickland, 2003).

Earnings factor into investment decisions, as discussed in Chap. 4. Hotchkiss and Strickland (2003), use a unique data set to classify the investment strategies of institutional shareholders into growth, aggressive growth, value, income, and momentum.[77] The momentum strategy is based on identifying the market trend in order to buy or sell the shares be-

---

[75] Another classification is offered by Brickley, Lease, and Smith (1988). They separate institutional investors into three groups based on their willingness to challenge management: pressure-resistant institutions (public pension funds, mutual funds, endowments, and foundations), pressure-indeterminate institutions (corporate pension funds, brokerage houses, investment counsel firms, and miscellaneous others), and pressure-sensitive institutions (banks, insurance companies and non-bank trusts), which have current or potential business relationships with the firm. They examine voting on antitakeover amendments and find that pressure-sensitive institutions are less likely to challenge management.

[76] They find that even if institutions sell their shares, they do not necessarily liquidate all of their holdings.

[77] The database was purchased from Gerogreson and Co. It included data on 203 institutional investors in the period between the fourth quarter of 1992 and the fourth quarter of 1997.

fore the price increases or decreases, all other strategies depend on earnings.[78]

Even though earnings seem important to institutional shareholders (see e.g., Lang and McNichols, 1997, that is detailed below), it is not clear how important they are. Institutional investors also use non-earnings information, which reduces the relative weight of earnings in their decision making, and hence, reduces the benefit from managing earnings. Jiambalvo, Rajgopal, and Venkatachalam (2002), report, for example, that a firm's *order backlog* is given more weight in its valuation by institutional owners than by other owners. Institutional shareholders also have buy-side analysts who trace the investments they make. As a matter of fact, institutional owners are used as a proxy for sophisticated investors, who have superior ability to acquire and process value-relevant information (e.g., Hand, 1990; Walther, 1997; Bartov, Radhakrishnan, and Krinsky, 2000; Jiambalvo, Rajgopal, and Venkatachalam 2002).

It may well be the case that institutional investors have less need for information about earnings than individual investors do, because earnings are a summary statistic and sophisticated institutional shareholders have access to detailed information by virtue of sitting on boards and engaging buy-side analysts. Still, earnings are useful because performance of institutional shareholders is judged by their beneficiaries according to their own earnings and returns, which in turn are determined by the earnings of their holdings. In addition, as explained in Chap. 1, earnings are valuable in the design of management's compensation. The compensation of management is more sensitive to the price of the firm's shares and imposes more risk on management, the higher the concentration of institutional holding in the ownership of the firm (Hartzell and Starks, 2003) and the higher the institutional shareholders' turnover (Kim, 2005). Since earnings and earnings surprises are an input to the market price, earnings are important.[79]

---

[78] Growth investment strategies target firms with growth in earnings above average.

[79] As discussed above, restructuring compensation has long been a subject of shareholder resolutions. Gillan and Starks (2000), find that 233 out of 2,042 proposals in the proxies were concerned with executive compensation. As an anecdote, consider the focus list of CalPERS in 2005. One of the five companies is AT&T.

"These severance payouts are obscene," said Valdes (CalPERS Investment Committee Chair). "AT&T's leaders ran this company into the ground, sold it, and were the architects of compensation plans that will pay many of them millions. CalPERS will strongly consider withholding support for these AT&T directors should they land on the SBC Board or other corporate boards to prevent

Lang and McNichols (1997), provide evidence on the importance of earnings to institutional investors. They classify institutions by their turnover, which is measured as the ratio of shares sold during a quarter to average quarterly holdings. Low-turnover institutions are long-term owners, which include colleges and universities (turnover of 5.6% per quarter), private foundations (turnover of 3.1% per quarter), and public pension funds (turnover of 4.7% per quarter). High-turnover institutions are short-term owners, which include banks (turnover of 8.1% per quarter), insurance companies (turnover of 11.7% per quarter), investment advisers (turnover of 14.5% per quarter), and investment companies (turnover of 11.5% per quarter). Lang and McNichols (1997) find that the correlation between return and trading is negative for low-turnover institutions and positive for high-turnover institutions. The association between trading and earnings, however, is positive for both types (tables 7 and 8).

5.3.3.2 Long-Term Owners

For the sake of discussion, we equate the long-term perspective with activism because activism requires holding shares for more than a year. Activists are unlikely to have the resources or the expertise to manage companies. Still, they have a fiduciary duty[80] to their own shareholders that requires them to monitor the firm's performance. Proposals such as requiring a firm's board to have a majority of independent directors fulfill this monitoring goal.

Earnings are useful in monitoring performance. Consider CalPERS.[81] It targets corporations for governance overhaul if their performance, as

---

a repeat of the egregious AT&T severance payouts." (Press release, April 20, 2005. The text in brackets is added.)

[80] The duty is loyalty and due care (see Monks and Minow, 2004).

[81] The role of CalPERS in the history of institutional owners' activism is quite known. Gillan and Starks (1998), report,

> [I]nstitutional activism began in January 1985, when Jesse Unruh, California state treasurer formed the Council of Institutional Investors. The formation of this group was a response to the greenmailing of Texaco by the Bass Brothers. As state treasurer, Unruh had ultimate responsibility for both the California Public Employees Retirement System (CalPERS) and the California State Teachers Retirement System (CalSTRS). On discovering that the Bass Brothers received a $137 million premium that was not accorded to other investors, including CalPERS and CalSTRS, Unruh decided to take action by establishing the Council of Institutional investors to lobby for shareholder

measured by economic value added (operating earnings net of tax minus a charge for the cost of capital), and governance are both poor. Hence, earnings are important as a performance measure.

Interestingly, in 2005, before it was mandated by the FASB, shareholders made proposals to expense stock options that would reduce reported earnings. The list of firms with such shareholder resolutions includes Dell, Adobe Systems, Inc., Hewlett-Packard Co., Intel Corp., International Business Machines Corp., PeopleSoft, Inc., and Texas Instruments, Inc. (The resolution was not adopted by Dell because it got only 44% of the vote. In all other companies the resolution received a majority.)

A special category of long-term owners is made of *relational investors*. They hold blocks of shares that allow them a say in the management of the firm, and they are committed to staying for an extended period. Bhagat, Black, and Blair (2004), define relational investing as holding at least 10% equity for at least 4 years. This class is important because it can monitor management more effectively than regular activists can. Earnings are important to these investors to the extent that the corporation is judged on the basis of its earnings by other stakeholders. At the same time, it seems that they want to prevent earnings management because the market discounts the value of firms suspected of earnings management. Healy and Palepu (1993, p. 6), comment, "Financial communication problems are also mitigated if the firm's ownership is concentrated, and these large-block shareholders actively participate in the corporate governance process."

5.3.4 Earnings Management

The discussion so far indicates that the role of institutional shareholders in earnings management is not *a priori* clear. It stands to reason that their role in earnings management depends on their investment horizon. Transient institutional shareholders are not harmed by earnings management if they sell their shares before the discovery of pernicious earnings management: If they sell shares at an inflated price or buy shares at a deflated price, they are not likely to complain. If, however, they sell at a deflated price or buy at an inflated price, they have the recourse of filing a class action suit against the firm and its management (and the auditor) and get reimbursement at the expense of the incumbent shareholders (see Ronen and Yaari, 2002).

---

rights. The group has evolved to become a focal point for institutional shareholder activists. (pp. 13–14)

Transient institutional owners may even exert pressure on firms to inflate earnings because of the pressure to manage their own earnings. Lakonishok, Shleifer, and Vishny (1991), observe "window dressing," whereby institutions purchase winners and sell losers at the end of a quarter to appear less risky or to have higher returns. Clearly, there are pressures to be classified as a winner that might induce earnings management.

Long-term institutional owners do not lose because of the price decline following the allegation of earnings management even if the price decline is substantial (CalPERS, e.g., reports that in 2005, it lost about $240 million in its investment in AIG) as long as they do not sell the shares. But because they stayed behind, they do lose equity due to the ensuing litigation and reputation costs as discussed in Chap. 4. That is, when short-term shareholders file a class action suit, it is the long-term owners who bear the brunt of the cost of such a lawsuit.

The empirical research supports the role of institutional shareholders as gatekeepers who prevent earnings management (DeFond and Jiambalvo, 1991; Rajgopal and Venkatachalam, 1997, Bange and De-Bondt, 1998; Bushee, 1998; Shang, 2003; Cheng and Reitenga, 2006). Overall, there is a negative association between institutional holdings and earnings management.[82] For example, Rajgopal and Venkatachalam find that the mean value of institutional ownership in the highest quintile of managed accruals is 4.5%, as compared to a mean value of 69.5% in the lowest quintile. The mean of the absolute values of discretionary accruals decreases from the lowest quintile (0.060) to the highest quintile (0.037) (see their Table 2). Furthermore, when researchers distinguish between long-term and short-term owners, the relationship is as expected: Short-term institutional holders are associated with inflating earnings and long-term owners are associated with curbing earnings management. Bushee, for example, finds that when the institutional ownership is transient (permanent), managing earnings by reducing R&D tends to be higher (lower).

The finding of a negative association between institutional shareholding and earnings management is explained by a sampling design that aggregates both types. That is, the non-transient shareholders dominate the sample when all institutional shareholders are examined together. For example, Shang (2003), provides evidence that institutions see through earnings management (e.g., they sell shares following management of earnings

---

[82] Some of this effect is attributable to the fact that the higher the level of institutional ownership, the better the firm's performance (e.g., McConnell and Servaes, 1990), so that there is less pressure to engage in pernicious earnings management to mask poor performance.

to inflate the price). He concludes that this ability to see through earnings management explains why institutions outperform individual investors.

5.4 Governance—the Board of Directors

5.4.1 Introduction

As the body that governs the firm, the board of directors' fiduciary duty is "to ensure that a company is run in the long-term interests of the owners, the shareholders" (Monks and Minow, 2004, p. 195). The board's responsibilities include attending meetings several times a year and voting on key decisions. The agendas of these meetings include reviews of management's reports on the financial health and performance of the firm and votes on proposals regarding financing matters, such as dividends, business strategies, such as mergers and acquisitions, and operating issues, such as firing a CEO and selecting a new one or designing management's compensation.

The typical board of a large public firm has committees with specific charters: the compensation committee, which is responsible for management's compensation; the audit committee, which is responsible for issues pertaining to accounting reports and internal control; the nomination committee, which is responsible for nominating directors; and the executive committee, which has the power to decide routine matters on behalf of the entire board (Blair, 1995).[83] The executive committee allows the firm to act quickly without waiting for the board's regular meeting (Vance, 1983). All committees are expected to report to the board.

The board fulfills two functions: monitoring management and providing useful connections and expert advice. The first role implies that the board plays a part in corporate governance (e.g., MacAvoy and Millstein, 1999; Melis, 2004; Adams, 2005). Becht, Bolton, and Roell (2003), summarize, "[An a]lternative for solving the collective action problem among dispersed shareholders is monitoring of the CEO by a board of

---

[83] The charter of Continental's executive committee, for example, specifies that the executive committee has "and may exercise all the powers and authority of the Board of Directors in the management of the business and affairs of the Company" (http://www.continental.com/company/investor/docs/continental_charterexeccte_2003_02_26_01.pdf).

directors."[84]   The second role renders the board a factor-of-production in the firm's performance (Dalton, Daily, Johnson, and Ellstrand, 1999; Johnson, Daily, and Ellstrand, 1996; Agrawal and Knoeber, 2001; Carpenter and Westphal, 2001; Adams, 2005; Adams and Ferreira, 2007).   Klein (1998), and Agrawal and Knoeber (2001), for example, observe that a substantial number of outside directors have experience in government, politics, or law, but scant business acumen.   Their skills may be useful because the government is an important buyer, or because the firm's profits are vulnerable to the decision of regulatory bodies, such as the Food and Drug Administration, the Environmental Protection Agency, and the Equal Employment Opportunity Commission.

Both functions imply demand for information.   The board requires information to evaluate management's performance and to make decisions that promote shareholders' interests.   Directors also need information in order to make the best use of their expertise and connections.   The necessary information is supplied by management.   That is, although "[a] central and well-settled principle of U.S. corporate law is that all major corporate decisions must be made, or at least initiated, by the board (Bebchuk, 2005, p. 836)," most of the proposals on board agendas require background work that is prepared by management, even when management does not initiate them.   The informational requirements of the two roles may be different, as the expertise role requires cooperation between management and the board, but monitoring may put the two parties at odds.

As an anecdotal example of the antagonism that results from monitoring, consider Richard Breeden, a former chief commissioner of the SEC, who was appointed by the court as a "corporate monitor" to oversee MCI's (previously WorldCom) emergence from bankruptcy.   The antagonistic nature of monitoring is captured by the following quotation.

> In taking the unprecedented step of appointing a corporate monitor, the judge initially told Mr. Breeden to "look into any nook and cranny" to make sure MCI runs fraud-free.   The monitor's close scrutiny of most issues means Mr. Capellas [the CEO] "has sort of been playing with one hand tied behind his back," says board colleague Dennis Beresford.   "At times, the people at WorldCom have found [Mr. Breeden] to be a pain...," says Nicholas Katzenbach, another director of the telecom giant. (Wall Street Journal, April 20, 2004)

---

[84] The other alternatives are hostile takeovers, which discipline managers by the threat of being removed if the takeover is successful, and ownership by a large blockholder, who makes the effort to monitor management and has the power "to implement management changes" (Becht, Bolton, and Roell, 2003, p. 31).

We note that Richard Breeden could be an effective monitor because by his appointment by the court, he had access to every document and to every employee. His monitoring saved shareholders thousands of dollars, but in the process, he antagonized management, by refusing, for example, to consent to a hefty compensation packages. According to the press, Breeden is unlikely to be nominated to serve as the chairman of the board after the appointment ends.

The importance of information for effective directing puts pressure on directors not to antagonize management because if they do, then management may neither share information nor seek advice. Consider for example, the criticism of Fisch and Jentile (2003), of SEC's Rule 205 that requires firms to establish a legal committee (QLCC) that is effectively the police of the firm and its management:

> Management…, is thus likely to resist the creation of a QLCC. If the issuer decides, nonetheless, to establish a QLCC, management is likely to mistrust its activities and fail to support investigations in which it is engaged, particularly because management will not be fully informed of the subject of the investigations. Similarly, a concern about the QLCC's investigative role and potentially antagonistic relationship with corporate executives may lead those executives to share less information with the board of directors as a whole. For example, the chief executive officer may become reluctant to seek the advice of members of the board of directors, particularly those serving on the QLCC, regarding concerns related to the accounting methods used to record the revenues of a new business. (pp. 140-141)

This discussion raises the issue of the balance of power between the board and management and its effect on the balance between the board's two roles. The literature offers two views. The first is that directors are nominated so that the mix between monitoring and expertise is optimal given the specific needs of the firm (e.g., Gillan, Hartzell, and Starks, 2003[85]; Chidambaran and Brick, 2005[86]; Lehn, Patro, and Zhao, 2005[87]).

---

[85] Gillan, Hartzell, and Starks (2003), find that the governance structure is determined by the industry's investment opportunities vis-à-vis leverage and strategic business variables such as competition and product uniqueness, as well as the information and regulatory environments. These findings suggest that the monitoring level depends on firm-specific characteristics.

[86] Chidambaran and Brick (2005), find a negative association between riskiness (measured by stock price volatility) and board independence and monitoring (proxied by the number of independent directors, the percentage of independent directors on the board, and the product of the number of independent directors and the number of board meetings). Since riskier companies are more difficult to monitor, this finding suggests that the composition of boards is efficient.

The other is that the board is just a rubber stamp of the CEO's decisions (e.g., Jensen, 2000; Baker and Gompers, 2003;[88] Becht, Bolton, and Roell, 2003; Hermalin and Weisbach, 2003; Boone, Field, Karpoff, and Raheja, 2004[89]). The CEO can control the board in a number of ways. For example, "managers inherently dominate the board by choosing outside directors and providing the information they analyze" (Farinha, 2003, p. 34). Alternatively, Branson (2006), observes that an executive committee that is made up of insiders "easily could usurp the prerogatives and powers of the full board" (p. 29) because of the full board's power delegated to it to make decisions (with some exceptions that are specified by statute) between meetings.

Under the latter view, the board is a façade. That is, nominees to the board are selected for their fame, and the committees, such as the audit committee, are ceremonial (Menon and Williams, 1994; Wolnizer, 1995; Spira, 1999; Cohen, Krishnamoorthy, and Wright, 2002; Vafeas, 2005). Directors agree to serve on boards because it is considered to be a perquisite (e.g., Ferris, Jagannathan, and Pritchard, 2003).[90] If the board is just a front, then the meetings are a formality that requires minimal effort. For example, the audit committee of Enron had the following agenda on February 12, 2001, as cited in Allaire and Firsirotu (2005):

1. Receive and discuss the auditors' report on their audit;
2. Discuss with the auditors Enron's internal controls, accounting procedures, and financial reporting;

They also find support for the second view, however, as firms in which the CEO exerts more power on the board (proxied by his tenure and equity ownership) have less monitoring activity.

[87] Lehn, Patro, and Zhao (2005), study 81 public firms that survived in the 1935–2000 period. They find that the size of the board (insider representation) is increasing (decreasing) in firm's size and decreasing (increasing) in growth. Higher growth increases the riskiness and complexity of operations which decreases the effectiveness of monitoring and the consequent demand for outside directors. Larger size may increase the demand for a variety of directors' skills. Hence, these results are consistent with the optimality of the board.

[88] Baker and Gompers (2003), show that IPO firms with the backing of venture capitalists have more outsiders, which is consistent with the ability of venture capitalists to twist the arms of reluctant insiders to have more monitoring.

[89] Boone, Field, Karpoff, and Raheja (2004), show that IPO tend to have a higher percentage of independent directors.

[90] Throughout the discussion, we assume that the supply of directors is infinitely elastic so that the composition of the board is the firm's decision choice. In reality, however, it is not clear that this is the case. This issue has been exacerbated since SOX.

3. Review the significant reserves included in Enron's 2000 financial statements;
4. Review all transactions with LMJ during 2000 as well as the special procedure for approval of such transactions;
5. Review the report on legal matters.
6. Review the 2000 financial statements and recommend to the Board that they be included in Enron's annual report and Form 10-K;
7. Review and approve the Audit and Compliance Committee charter;
8. Review the internal control audit plan for 2001;
9. Review the company's policies and practices for management's communications with analysts.

What's remarkable here is not the agenda but that all the above subjects were dealt with in **1 hour and 35 minutes**. (pp. 7–8)[91]

This picture raises the concern that directors might have incentives to collude in pernicious earnings management. Yet how can the board serve as a façade unless the directors have sterling reputation? The importance of the directors' reputation to the firm is pointed out, for example, by Fich and Shivdasani (2006), who report that if directors are interlocked (i.e., directors sit on mutual boards), the stock price of the interlocked firm declines with a class action event against a firm that is accused of security fraud, and increases when the sued director quits (see also Borden, 2007).

Reputation is valuable not only to firms on whose boards the director sits but to the director personally as well. Poor reputation is costly on two counts: first, companies that experience poor performance or that are sued by shareholders overhaul their boards (Gilson, 1989; Kaplan and Reishus, 1990; Hermalin and Weisbach, 1998; Agrawal, Jaffee, and Karpoff, 1999; Ferris, Lawless, and Makhija, 2001; Bhagat and Black, 2002; Farber, 2005; Fich and Shivdasani, 2005; Srinivasan, 2005). For example, MCI, the new entity that replaced the bankrupt WorldCom, overhauled its board with directors known for their integrity. Dennis Beresford, the former chairman of the Financial Accounting Standards Board (FASB) became

---

[91] It comes as no surprise that a great deal of criticism was directed at Enron's board. The 2002 senate hearing found:

"**Fiduciary Failure.** The Enron Board of Directors failed to safeguard Enron shareholders and contributed to the collapse of the seventh largest public company in the United States, by allowing Enron to engage in high risk accounting, inappropriate conflict of interest transactions, extensive undisclosed off-the-books activities, and excessive executive compensation. The Board witnessed numerous indications of questionable practices by Enron management over several years, but chose to ignore them to the detriment of Enron shareholders, employees and business associates." (U.S. Senate's Committee of Governmental Affairs, 2002)

the chairman of the new audit committee. Agrawal, Jaffee, and Karpoff (1999), report that turnover of inside directors is positively correlated with fraud, where fraud is not restricted to financial accounting fraud. In support of the façade view of the board, they find that firms with relatively high proportions of outside board members are more likely to add new inside members, and less likely to add new outside members, than other firms. Srinivasan (2005), studies a sample of 409 companies that restated their earnings from 1997 to 2001, finding that outside directors, especially audit committee members, bear reputational costs for financial reporting failures in the labor market for directors. For example, in the 3 years after the restatement, director turnover is 48% for firms that restate earnings downward as compared to 33% for a performance-matched sample. Directors of firms that overstate earnings lose about 25% of their positions on other boards; the loss is greater for audit committee members. Second, directors lose directorships in other firms as well. Gilson (1989), and Kaplan and Reishus (1990), show that directors associated with poorly performing firms hold substantially fewer directorships thereafter. Gilson (Kaplan and Rieshus) finds (find) a reduction in board seats of executives that resigned from firms in financial distress (firms that cut dividends). Fich and Shivdasani (2005), report that the decline in other directorships of directors in firms accused of securities fraud is proportional to the severity of the fraud and the outside director's responsibility to monitor fraud.

In Ronen, Tzur, and Yaari (2006), we did not consider the cost of lost reputation as a deterrent to pernicious earnings management because we question the importance of the economic benefits from reputation. With the minor exceptions (such as WorldCom), directors do not pay damages in successful class action suits. Indeed, Chalmers, Dann, and Harford (2002), show that directors of poorly performing IPO purchase more insurance; and Kim (2006), shows that excessive insurance coverage to officers and directors induce earnings management. Furthermore, most of them have already amassed wealth in previous jobs and thus are not really desperate to earn a director's salary. This is especially true for pensioned directors who are former CEOs and former partners in audit firms. We show that directors have incentives to induce managers to engage in earnings management because this creates information asymmetry between them and other investors, which can be exploited to make trading gains.

In recent years, directors get "more attention" in cases involving accounting irregularities. In a testimony to the Senate Committee of Banking, Housing, and Urban Affairs on September 9, 2003, William H. Donaldson, on the implementation of SOX, stated,

> For the fiscal year through August 20, 2003, the Commission has filed
> 543 enforcement actions, 147 of which involve financial fraud or report-
> ing violations. ...the Commission has sought to bar 144 offending corpo-
> rate executives and directors from holding such positions with publicly
> traded companies. (pp. 2–3)

We are aware of the shift in the role of directors toward better monitoring. The change is induced both by new rules, such as those that require
the board to fully disclose the details of management's compensation
package, "And investors and regulators are subjecting their actions to
higher scrutiny. Long gone are the days when a director could get away
with a quick rubber-stamp of a CEO's plans" (Nanette Byrnes and Jane Sas-
seen, "Board of hard knocks," Business Week, January 22, 2007, p. 36).

In the remainder of this section, we discuss key observable characteristics of boards of directors and the findings in the research on the association between earnings management and these characteristics. The opposing views on the value of the board are useful for explaining the findings.
We conclude with a separate discussion of the audit committee because of
its prominent role in financial reporting and earnings management.

5.4.2 Board Characteristics

The observable characteristics of boards, as examined in the literature, include their size and composition, the number of meetings, equity holding
by directors, and directors' ages and tenure. In addition, boards can be
classified according to whether the directors hold multiple directorships
and whether the CEO is also the chairman of the board.

5.4.2.1 Size

Background
The size of the board is simply the number of directors. A few factors that
determine the optimal size have been identified in the literature: the firm's
size, the complexity of operations, and its ownership profile.

From an economic angle, since a larger board enhances the expertise
and knowledge brought to the table by directors, the firm's size is crucial
in determining the board size (Yermack, 1996; Denis and Sarin, 1999; Gillan and Starks, 2003; Belkhir, 2004; Boone, Field, Karpoff, and Raheja,
2004; Coles, Daniel, and Naveen, 2006b). Belkhir (2004), studies a sample of 174 banks and savings-and-loan holding companies between 1995
and 2002. He finds that on average two directors are added to the board
when the size is doubled. Boone, Field, Karpoff, and Raheja (2004),
report an average of 6.2 directors in a sample of IPO firms with a mean

equity value of $150.2 million. In comparison, Denis and Sarin (1999), observe an average of 9.35 directors in a sample of seasoned firms with mean equity value of $434.6 million.

The firm's size in itself does not explain all variation in board size. The complexity of the firm's operations matters because increased complexity requires more diverse expertise which can be acquired by enlarging the board. Complexity is measured by such factors as diversification (Ferris, Jagannathan, and Pritchard, 2003; Coles, Daniel, and Naveen, 2006b); the riskiness of the firm's operations, as evidenced in its growth opportunities (Lehn, Patro, and Zhao, 2005); the intensity of R&D (Coles, Daniel, and Naveen, 2006b); the demands for coordination of subunits in a decentralized organization (Adams and Mehran, 2005); leverage (Coles, Daniel, and Naveen, 2006b); and so on. The distribution of owners matters too, since the board is expected to reflect their wishes (Bennedsen and Wolfenzon, 2000; Bennedsen, Kongsted, and Nielsen, 2004). The more diverse the owners, the greater the number of representatives required to represent their interests on the board.

In the second half of the twentieth century, concurrent with the trend of downsizing in order to pursue a business strategy of focusing on core operations, the average board size was on the decline as well (Blair, 1995; Vafeas, 2005). The decrease was also attributed to pressure from activists, such as CalPERS (Wu, 2000, as cited in Hermalin and Weisbach, 2003) because it was believed that large boards allow management to control them. In the wake of the Sarbanes-Oxley Act and the ensuing reforms by the stock exchanges, boards of large public firms grew by adding independent directors (Linck, Netter, and Yang, 2006). The anecdotal evidence suggests that the opposite happened for small firms, which find it harder to hire talent that both fulfills the new SOX requirements and stock exchanges' demands and is willing to bear the additional risk imposed on directors.[92]

---

[92] From the testimony of William H. Donaldson to the Senate Committee of Banking, Housing, and Urban Affairs on September 9, 2003, on the implementation of SOX:

> For the fiscal year through August 20, 2003, the Commission has filed 543 enforcement actions, 147 of which involve financial fraud or reporting violations.... the Commission has sought to bar 144 offending corporate executives and directors from holding such positions with publicly traded companies. Further, we are holding accountable not just the companies who engage in fraud, but also the other participants. For example, recent actions signify the Commission's willingness to pursue directors who are reckless in their oversight of management. And we have in-

The relationship between size and earnings management is better understood through the effect of the board size on performance. The common wisdom is that smaller boards are more effective (Lipton and Lorsch, 1992; Blair, 1995; Jensen, 2000) and less likely to be controlled by management (Dechow, Sloan, and Sweeney, 1996; Jensen, 2000). Effectiveness requires a costly flow of information from the company to the directors and among the directors, and smaller boards reduce these costs. Blair (1995), for example, claims that a board that is larger than 15 people is likely to waste time because a single meeting of such a board typically lasts more than 4 hours. Lipton and Lorsch (1992), and Jensen (2000), recommend an optimal board size that does not exceed seven or eight directors. A free-rider problem occurs, too when directors must make decisions. To illustrate, consider anecdotal evidence (taken from an anonymous source) of decisions that require legal expertise. Suppose that the board has ten members, with only one lawyer. When a decision involving legal matters is to be made, everyone in the room waits to get the lawyer's input first. What happens if the lawyer makes a mistake? The free-rider problem seems to be mitigated in smaller boards, where the burden of responsibility per director is more strongly felt.

The empirical evidence supports the negative association between board size and performance, where performance is measured by Tobin Q, ROA, the sales-to-assets ratio, or other accounting measures. Yermack (1996), was the first to examine this issue. Studying 452 large U.S. industrial corporations between 1984 and 1991, whose boards ranged in size between 10 and 30 members, Yermack shows that smaller boards are more effective. Gertner and Kaplan (1998), study reverse leveraged-buyout (LBO) firms controlled by LBO specialists. These specialists have incentives to take actions that maximize shareholders' value. They show that these firms have smaller boards. International evidence also supports this connection: see Eisenberg, Sundgren, and Wells (1998), who study small and medium-size Finnish firms; Odegaard and Bøhren (2003), for Finnish firms; and Mak and Kusnadi (2002), for Singaporean and Malaysian firms.

Paul (2001), examines firms that initiated value-destroying mergers and acquisition bids. He shows that firms with smaller boards are less likely to complete value-destroying transactions.[93] Bennedsen, Kongsted, and Niel-

---

creasingly designed strategies that take advantage of the creative provisions of the Act to return funds to investors who have suffered losses rather than merely collect those funds for the government. (pp. 2–3)

[93] As is common in empirical research, there are some conflicting results, too. Dalton, Daily, Johnson, and Ellstrand (1999), conduct a meta-analysis of 20,620 observations from different studies. They conclude that the relationship be-

sen (2004), refine the argument on the connection between the size of the board and performance by arguing that the relationship is not linear. Conducting empirical investigation of 5,000 small and medium-sized closely held corporations in Denmark, they show that a negative association between performance and board size holds only when size exceeds seven. (No such relationship exists for smaller boards.)

The negative association between board size and performance makes sense if the board acts more as a façade and the CEO shirks his duty to maximize shareholders' value, because larger boards enable him to capture the board (Hermalin and Weisbach, 2003).

Earnings Management and Board Size
The connection between earnings management and board size is not straightforward. On the one hand, if a smaller board is more efficient, we expect to see a positive relationship between size and pernicious earnings management, least of all reasons is that poor performance induces earnings management. On the other hand, since larger boards also include more independent directors, who have incentives to monitor earnings management, we expect to see a negative association between size and earnings management. Finally, if a board is just a façade, then there ought to be no relationship between size and earnings management.

The only theory that hints at the effect of size on earnings management is given in Aggarwal and Nanda (2004). Their starting point is that the principal–agent relationship between the board and the manager are characterized by the board's undertaking the task of setting the firm's objectives and communicating them to management. A larger board is likely to require management to meet more diverse objectives. The manager then faces a multitasking situation. If required to allocate effort to more objectives, the manager may reduce the effort spent on profit-maximization ac-

---

tween board size and financial performance is significantly positive. Beiner, Drobertz, Schmid, and Zimmerman (2003), find no relationship between size and performance in their sample of Swiss firms. Since further tests indicate that size is important, they conclude that the board size is in equilibrium, that is, it is optimal (see Hermalin and Weisbach, 2003). Belkhir (2004), also finds that there is no relationship between size and performance in his sample of banks and savings-and-loans holding companies. Adams and Mehran (2005), find a positive relationship between size and performance due to the complex organizational structure of bank holding companies. They postulate that the establishment of subsidiaries in different states is likely to require a larger board. Core, Holthausen, and Larcker (1999), find a positive relationship between board size and the CEO's compensation, which is consistent with the view that a larger board is a poorer monitor, but no association between board size and company performance.

tivities. Because the manager is expected to spend less effort on profit-increasing activities, both his incentives and the firm's performance are weaker. The authors do not consider earnings management specifically. Their analysis implies that if earnings management consumes manager's precious time, the manager might manage earnings *less* when the board is larger.[94] Alternatively, if diverse objectives impose conflicting demands on the manager's scarce time, the manager might manage earnings *more* as the least time-consuming venue to meet these demands.

The empirical evidence on the relationship between size and earnings management is indeed mixed.

	The association between size and earnings management		
	Positive	Negative	Insignificant
Study	Dechow, Sloan, and Sweeney (1996), Abbott, Parker, and Peters (2004), Larcker, Richardson, and Tuna (2005)	Chtourou, Bédard, and Courteau (2001), Xie, Davidson, and DaDalt (2003), Anderson, Mansi, and Reeb (2003), Larcker and Richardson (2004), Larcker, Richardson, and Tuna (2005)	Ferris, Jagannathan, and Pritchard (2003), Bradbury, Mak, and Tan (2004), Uzun, Szewczyk, and Varma (2004), Baber, Kang, and Liang (2005), and Farber (2005), and Vafeas (2005)

Abbott, Parker, and Peters (2004), find a positive relationship between restatements and size (the coefficient is 0.093, with a t-statistic of 2.566). Studying a sample of firms with either large income-increasing accruals or large income-decreasing accruals, Chtourou, Bédard, and Courteau (2001), find a negative relationship between discretionary accruals and size in their 1996 sample that is significant when the discretionary accruals are income-decreasing. Xie, Davidson, and DaDalt (2003), find a negative relationship between the level of abnormal working-capital accruals and size (for a discussion of measuring earnings management by abnormal accruals, consult Part 4). Larcker and Richardson (2004), find that firms characterized by a positive association between non-audit fees and discretionary accruals have smaller boards. Larcker, Richardson, and Tuna (2005), find a positive relationship between discretionary accruals and size but a negative association between the absolute value of accruals and size (see Chap. 10 for a discussion of the methodologies for measuring earnings management). Anderson, Mansi, and Reeb (2003), provide indirect evidence on a negative association between size and the cost of debt. In particular, one addi-

---

[94] Aggarwal and Nanda (2004), test and confirm their theory in a sample of 2,148 firm/years of 842 firms between 1998 and 2001 from the S&P 500, S&P Mid-Cap 400, and S&P SmallCap 600.

tional director is associated with a ten-point decrease in the cost of debt. Helland and Sykuta (2005), examine the firms that are defendants in securities litigation. Although this study does not distinguish between lawsuits due to fraudulent earnings management and other incidences of securities litigation (e.g., omission of correcting disclosures), it is interesting to note that they find that the average board size in a matched-firm control sample is lower by 1.5 directors.

The literature also articulates a weak or no association. Bradbury, Mak, and Tan (2004), find a negative but insignificant association between discretionary accruals and size. Ferris, Jagannathan, and Pritchard (2003), find insignificant relation for firms facing fraud litigation. Uzun, Szewczyk, and Varma (2004), and Farber (2005), find that size is insignificant when fraud firms are matched with a control group. The average of the two groups approximates eleven in Uzun, Szewczyk, and Varma's study and six in Farber's study. Baber, Kang, and Liang (2005), find no association between the probability of restatements and size. Vafeas (2005), finds that there is a positive but insignificant relationship between size and firms' managing earnings either by avoiding negative earnings surprises or reporting small earnings increases (see Chap. 4 for a discussion of managing earnings to meet benchmarks).

What is the meaning of these conflicting findings? Some are consistent with the opposing views of the board. If the board is a façade, elected for the sole purpose of impressing investors, observations ought to cluster around the size that investors believe to be efficient. A larger size may suggest that the CEO attempts to control the board or that the firm's operations are risky and complex. A smaller board may indicate that potential directors are reluctant to lend their prestige to the firm. In this case, we are unlikely to find a relationship between board size and earnings management. If, however, the board is a monitor and a smaller board is more effective monitor, then we would expect a positive relationship between board size and earnings management. Neither view, however, explains the negative association between board size and earnings management. Xie, Davidson, and DaDalt comment on their finding: "[T]his result is counterintuitive.... One argument for larger boards is that they may bring a greater number of experienced directors to a board. Perhaps our findings reflect this, since experienced directors seem to play a role in limiting earnings management" (p. 305).

Another explanation is that size is correlated with other variables (Harris and Raviv, 2005), so that the interpretation of the connection between size and earnings management is confounded by these other variables.

5.4.2.2 Composition and Independence

Broadly, boards are composed of three types of directors: insiders, outsiders, and affiliated directors. Inside directors are employees, such as the CEO and other officers, that is, they are both management and directors. Outside directors, who are also known as independent directors, have no affiliation with the firm apart from being a director. Affiliated directors are connected through business dealings, such as suppliers, consumers, employees of affiliated companies and the audit firm, consultants, lawyers, investment bankers, executives of advertising agencies, former employees, and directors with ties to charitable organizations to which the firm makes contributions.[95]

Each type assumes a different role. Outsiders are associated with monitoring. The SEC comments, "Effective boards of directors exercise independent judgment in carrying out their responsibilities" (Release 34-50298, August 31, 2004). Insiders are considered an obstacle to efficient monitoring. As an anecdotal example, consider Blair (1995), who complains that in one directorship, monitoring performance was made impossible because the inclusion of the head of division, an insider, in the committee on which Blair served, hampered free communication among other independent committee members (see also Salmon, 1993).

Insiders are better informed on the firm's operations. They already have firm-specific information, unlike outside directors, who "...arrive at their firms with... little direct knowledge of the company's operations,..." (Yermack, 2004, p. 2282), and spend a few days per year in meetings (before SOX, the average was about eight days).[96] Insiders thus are better equipped to predict the repercussions of a decision on the firm given its unique business arena. Klein (1998), for example, finds that firms that increase the percentage of inside directors on the finance and the investment committees earn a higher rate of return on their investments than firms that

---

[95] Applying this classification to interlocked directors is not trivial. Interlocked directors sit on each other's board, that is, a director of company A is employed by company B and a director of company B is employed by company A. Rule 34-50298 of the SEC considers interlocked directors dependent if they sat on each other's compensation committee in the previous 3 years.

[96] Gillan, Hartzell, and Starks (2003), state,

There are, however, costs of having too high a proportion of outsiders on the board. Outside directors do not have the detailed information that inside directors possess from their involvement in firms. In addition, outside directors may not have the same time and commitment as insiders due to their other responsibilities. (p. 8)

decrease this percentage. Similarly, Bathala and Rao (1995), find a negative relationship between independence and growth opportunities. Boumosleh and Reeb (2005), who study S&P-500 firms in the 1997–1999 period (a sample of 814 firm/years), find that firms with more insiders on the board pay their CEOs less. Also, consistent with the proposition that accounting-based performance measures (ABPM) are more valuable than market-based measures (MBPM) when they are less noisy, they find that ABPM are used more than MBPM when the number of insiders is larger.

A crucial issue with regard to the value of insiders concerns their allegiance. If they are brought to the board to be groomed as future CEOs (Vancil, 1987), there is a high likelihood that they will associate with the outside directors in order to increase their chance of being selected as the next CEO. If not, they have incentives to collude with management because CEOs control their careers. (In contrast, such career concerns do not affect outside directors, especially if they are assured of their ability to attract alternative directorships (Beatty and Zajac, 1994; Boumosleh and Reeb, 2005).) For example, before 2003, the compensation committee might be pressured to award management options with the same vesting dates for all managers. This would create incentives to collude to manage earnings so as to reduce the strike price and increase the price on the exercise date (see Chap. 3). Boumosleh and Reeb (2005), provide evidence in support of the latter view. They find that the gap between CEOs' pay and other executives' pay is lower in firm with a high presence of insiders. This finding can indicate collusion between the insiders and the CEO to jointly earn more.

Affiliated directors are a hybrid. These directors are less likely to monitor managers than independent directors in order not to damage their rapport with management. Shivdasani and Yermack (1999), for example, provide evidence that when the CEO has more legal power over the nomination of directors, the board has fewer outside monitors and more such "gray" directors. Still, in some studies, researchers aggregate them with independent directors (see, e.g., the literature review of Gillan and Starks, 1998).

We note that this classification does not reveal how directors behave behind closed doors. Are outside directors more independent than affiliated directors? The answer is not straightforward. For example, there is some evidence that independent directors who are managers in other companies are more sympathetic to management (Chtourou, Bédard, and Courteau, 2001; DeZoort and Salterio, 2001; Vafeas, 2005).

Another classification of directors focuses on the experience and the monitoring power they bring to the board (e.g., Rosenstein and Wyatt, 1990a, 1990b; Baker and Gompers, 2003; Xie, Davidson, and DaDalt, 2003;

Vafeas, 2005). For example, Xie, Davidson, and DaDalt (2003), categorize affiliated and outside directors according to their background: corporate directors (74%), finance directors (16.3%), and legal directors (10.8%).[97] Corporate directors are current or former executives in public corporations; they are expected to have business acumen. Finance directors are current or former executives in financial institutions,[98] they are expected to have knowledge pertinent to leverage and connections with financial institutions. Legal directors are lawyers. Besides having knowledge of the law, they are valuable in the firm's dealings with regulators. (See also, Block, 1999.) As discussed below, directors' experience can shed some light on the mixed results regarding the relationship between performance and the percentage of outside directors.

Composition and Performance

The literature on composition focuses mainly on the contribution of independent directors to performance. The measures of independence are the proportion of independent directors to total board size and the number of independent directors.

Some studies support the regulators' view that independent directors improve the alignment of management's and shareholders' objectives (e.g., Weisbach, 1988; Byrd and Hickman, 1992; Lee, Rosenstein, Rangan, and Davidson, 1992; Brickley, Coles, and Terry, 1994; Borokhovich, Parrino, and Trapani, 1996; Cotter, Shivdasani and Zenner, 1997; Mayers, Sivdasani, and Smith, 1997; Hermalin and Weisbach, 1998; Huson, Parrino, and Starks, 2001; Bhagat and Black, 2002; Perry and Peyer, 2005; Perry and Shivdasani, 2005; Aggarwal and Williamson, 2006; Borokhovich, Brunarski, Donahue, and Harman, 2006).

Weisbach (1988), and Huson, Parrino, and Starks (2001), report that poorly performing managers are more likely to be removed if the board has a majority of outside directors. Borokhovich, Parrino, and Trapani (1996), examine the succession decisions in 969 cases in 855 large firms between 1970 and 1988. They show that the price response to succession by outsiders is favorable. In particular, if a new CEO is an insider who replaces a CEO who was fired, the reaction to this insider is negative. Otherwise, the market response is more strongly positive to an outsider. The relationship with independence follows from the finding that boards with a

---

[97] They also consider blockholders representing 8.8% of all independent and affiliated directors.

[98] Xie, Davidson, and DaDalt also categorize this group according to whether the finance directors are current or past employees of commercial banks (4.2% in their sample) or investment banks (3.5% in their sample).

higher percentage of outside directors are more likely to nominate outsiders to be CEO.

Byrd and Hickman (1992), and Cotter, Shivdasani, and Zenner (1997), show that the premium to shareholders when the board is more independent is higher when a hostile takeover is successful, and the former also report positive returns to the adoption of *poison pills* to deter takeover when the board is independent, since such a board is seen as likely to take these measures to prevent the destruction of shareholders' value. Brickley, Coles, and Terry (1994), provide further support to this finding by showing that the stock-price reaction to an announcement of a poison pill, is positive (negative) when the majority of the directors are (not) outsiders.

Lee, Rosenstein, Rangan, and Davidson (1992), study management buyouts. This setting is interesting because the CEO is likely to have double loyalty. As a buyer, he prefers a low price and quick deal. As a member of the board, he owes allegiance to the shareholders, who prefer a high price. Lee, Rosenstein, Rangan, and Davidson show that when the management aims to purchase 100% of the firm, the independence of the board increases the premium to shareholders. Otherwise, the results are inconclusive. Mayers, Shivdasani, and Smith (1997), find that outside directors increase shareholders' value because they are associated with lower expenditures on salaries, wages, and rent. Perry and Peyer (2005), find a favorable price response to adding an outside director even when he is a full-time employee with directorships in other companies. The returns are higher when the board does not have a majority of independent directors before the addition of this director or when the firm performs poorly. Perry and Shivdasani (2005), show that boards with a majority of outside directors are less afraid to make painful decisions on restructuring, layoffs, and asset sales. The fact that outsiders are better monitors is evidenced by the subsequent improvement in the performance of the restructuring firms. This effect is consistent with the finding of Borokhovich, Brunarski, Donahue, and Harman (2006), that the positive market reaction to the event of CEO's death without a successor is higher the more independent the board, especially when the firm performed poorly. Additional evidence is given by the findings that independence decreases the cost of debt (Bhojraj and Sengupta, 2003; Anderson, Mansi, and Reeb, 2004; Ashbaugh-Skaife, Collins, and LaFond, 2006). Aggarwal and Williamson (2006), study independence in conjunction with other governance attributes[99] in a sample of 5,200 firms between 2001 and 2005. They find a

---

[99] Aggarwal and Williamson (2006), study the effect of the following guidelines on value (controlling for firm and size):
1.   The board must consist of a majority independent directors.

premium for good governance, especially when governance provisions were adopted voluntarily.

Some studies detect no association between composition and performance (e.g., Klein, 1998; Bhagat and Black, 2002; Singh and Davidson, 2003; Dionne and Triki, 2004; Lehn and Zhao, 2004; Adams and Mehran, 2005; the meta-analyses of Dalton, Daily, Johnson, and Ellstrand, 1999; and Deutsch, 2005). Other studies find a negative association between performance and independence (e.g., Agrawal and Knoeber, 1996, 2001).

Several explanations are possible for these mixed results. One views governance as a portfolio: ownership profile, debt financing, and so on. (e.g., Bathala and Rao, 1995; Agrawal and Knoeber, 1996; Bhagat and Jefferies, 2005; Hermalin and Weisbach, 2003; Singh and Davidson, 2003; Harris and Raviv, 2005; Larcker, Richardson, and Tuna, 2005; Vafeas, 2005; Berry, Fields, and Wilkins, 2006).[100] firms choose this portfolio optimally, balancing both advantages (e.g., tighter monitoring) and disadvantages (e.g., higher information costs).[101] for example, biotechnology companies may prefer less board independence because the cost of conveying technical information to independent directors is very high, whereas food processing firms may prefer greater board independence because information costs in this industry are fairly low. The implication is that in equilibrium, no significant relationships can be expected. If the system is not in equilibrium, however, as in the case, for example, when performance deteriorates, a positive association is likely to be detected because a drastic action is required.

---

2.   Non-management directors must have executive sessions without management.

3.   The nominating committee must have only independent directors.

4.   The compensation committee must have only independent directors.

5.   The audit committee must have only independent directors and a minimum of three members.

6.   The firm must adopt corporate governance guidelines.

[100] For an analytical investigation of the optimal board's composition, consult Warther (1998), Kumar and Sivaramakrishnan (2002), Raheja (2005), and Adams and Ferreira (2007).

[101] This view is important to empirical research because it implies that the optimal governance structure is sensitive to industry affiliation. This has led some researchers to focus on a single industry: the U.S. airline industry (Kole and Lehn, 1999); the banking industry (Adams and Mehran, 2005); banking and savings-and-loans holding companies (Belkhir, 2004); closed-end investment companies (Dann, Del Guercio, and Partch, 2003); hospitals (Eldenburg, Hermalin, Weisbach, and Wosinka, 2004); the insurance industry (Mayers, Shivdasani, and Smith, 1997); and the U.S. mutual fund industry (Tufano and Sevick, 1997).

An alternative explanation views the board as controlled by management. CEOs have power over the nomination of directors even when they do not sit on the nomination committee. Monks and Minow (2004), report that their interviews with directors on nomination committees that exclude CEOs revealed that the directors consult management about nominees. In that case, does the committee's composition matter? Monks states, "Independent directors are an oxymoron because they are a group of self-selecting people. Having the status of a director is important to people. They are loyal to the rules of the club rather than to shareholders. If an independent director is bumptious or truly independent then they won't get work" (from an interview with Crainer, 2004, p. 36). According to this view, if there is a positive association between composition and performance, a successful façade pays off because outside stakeholders treat the firm more favorably when the board conforms to their expectations of what a good board ought to be.[102]

Another explanation is that the relationship between performance and composition might be non-linear. Block (1999), who studies 1,026 announcements of appointment of independent directors between 1990 and 1994, finds that although the stock price responds favorably to the appointment of an outside director, this effect disappears beyond a critical mass of outside directors (over 60%). Anderson and Reeb (2004), construct a sample of 141 of the Standard Poor's 500 whose founding families are still large shareholders. These shareholders tend to have high stakes in the firm. In some cases, a family member is also the CEO (e.g., Ford); in other cases, they have non-management representatives on the board (e.g., Disney and HP). Such firms are characterized by a conflict of interests between the founding family shareholders and other shareholders, as the former can appropriate perks that are not given to other shareholders even if their representative is not the CEO. In their earlier work, Anderson and Reeb (2003a, b), established that founding family shareholders have a favorable effect on performance, which indicates that they monitor management effectively. But who monitors them? A natural candidate is the group of outside directors. Anderson and Reeb (2004), provide indirect evidence that the outsiders might check the power of the founding family members by finding that the boards have fewer outside directors when the family members sit on the nomination committee (apparently, outside di-

---

[102] The argument here is subtle. The market includes strong firms with certain characteristics and firms that pool with them. Unable to distinguish between the two types, stakeholders reward firms with what they consider optimal board composition. We expect that this dynamic is exacerbated by multiple director ships.

rectors are not favored by the founding family members). They, however, detect a U-shaped relationship between independence and performance. Specifically, when the family representation on the board is either low or high (neither low nor high), the higher the ratio of family directors to independent directors, the better (worse) the firm's performance.

This non-linearity is important to future research because the exchanges have imposed restrictions regarding independence. The NYSE, for example, requires that all registrants have fully independent nomination and compensation committees and that the boards have a majority of independent directors.[103] Furthermore, independent directors are expected to meet without management directors (Securities and Exchange Commission, Release No. 34-50298; File No. SR-NYSE-2004-41). Companies that did not have a majority of independent directors before compliance may move to an inefficient board profile that induces a negative relationship between performance and independence. The response of firms to the new requirements provide a glimpse into whether boards are an efficient mechanism to represent shareholders' interests or just a façade. On the one hand, if governance were optimal before the new regulation, companies might be averse to make more changes than those prescribed by law. If their governance was a sham, however, the new regulation would induce firms that wish to signal value to adopt further improvements. For example, since SOX, more companies have separated the post of the chairman of the board from the post of CEO (e.g., Dell) and restricted directors from trading in the firm's equity during their tenure, in order to promote long-term value maximization (e.g., Disney).

For a further discussion of the effect of recent regulations on governance, consult Hertig (2005), Lavelle (2002), Hartman (2005), and Broshko and Li (2006).

Earnings Management

Directors cannot manage earnings by themselves, but they can collude with management. Better monitoring checks pernicious earnings management, giving rise to a negative association between independence and earnings management (Beasley, 1996; Dechow, Sloan, and Sweeney, 1996; Xie, Davidson, and DaDalt, 2003; Bowen, Rajgopal, and Venkatachalam, 2004; Kelly, Koh, and Tong, 2004; Uzun, Szewczyk, and Varma, 2004; Farber, 2005; Helland and Sykuta, 2005; Hochberg, 2005; Vafeas, 2005). Beasley (1996), for example, compares a sample of 75 firms accused of financial fraud to a 75-firm control group in the 1982–1990 period. He finds that higher proportions of independent and gray di-

---

[103] For a discussion on the gap between rules and compliance prior to SOX, consult Klein (2003).

rectors reduce the probability of accounting fraud. Dechow, Sloan, and Sweeney (1996), examine 82 firms accused of financial fraud in the 1982–1992 period. They show that fraud firms are more likely to engage in fraud when the board lacks a simple majority of outsiders and no owner is a blockholder. Vafeas (2005), finds that avoidance of negative earnings surprises is negatively correlated with independence.

Yet directors might not see any harm in earnings management, regardless of their independence. Jensen (2005b), states,

> I have observed (perfectly honest upstanding) people in their roles as board members condone manipulation of financial reports because it never occurs to them it is lying–its just part of what it means to manage.

Hence, it stands to reason that there is no connection between independence and earnings management (Wright, 1999;[104] Chtourou, Bédard, and Courteau, 2001; Abbott, Parker, and Peters, 2004; Zhou and Chen, 2004; Agrawal and Chadha, 2005; Baber, Kang, and Liang, 2005).

Other studies examine the related issues of timeliness and transparency of earnings (e.g., Vafeas, 1999a; Bushman, Chen, Engel, and Smith, 2004; Dey, 2005; Larcker, Richardson, and Tuna, 2005). With the exception of Vafeas (1999a), who does not find that independence has an effect on the earnings–returns relationship, researchers find that better governance leads to higher quality earnings. Frankel, McVay, and Soliman (2006), who examine the association between the characteristics of expense items excluded from street earnings and the independence of the board, find that fewer independent directors are associated with less informative street earnings.

For further discussion of governance and the quality of earnings, consult Cohen, Krishnamoorthy, and Wright (2004).[105]

5.4.2.3 Other Board's Characteristics

Besides composition and size, research examined the following characteristics of the board:

---

[104] Wright (1999), finds a higher quality of financial reporting, as rated by analysts, with a lower percentage of gray directors, but no association between quality and the percentage of insiders.

[105] We draw attention to the fact that we separate the discussion of management's compensation (see Chap. 3) and governance, but these mechanisms might be interrelated (e.g., Core, Holthausen, and Larcker, 1999; Vafeas, 1999b; Chidambaran and John, 2003; Kim, 2005; Larcker, Richardson, Seary, and Tuna, 2005).

- Multiple directorships—the number of directorships held by a director (Gilson, 1990; Kaplan and Reishus, 1990; Beasley, 1996; Booth and Deli, 1996; Bhagat and Black, 1999; Carpenter and Westphal, 2001; Ferris, Jagannathan, and Pritchard, 2003; Harford, 2003; Adams, 2005; Fairchild and Li, 2005; Fich, 2005; Keys and Li, 2005; Perry and Peyer, 2005; Vafeas, 2005; Conyon and Muldoon, 2006) (see also the literature review in Conyon and Read, 2006).
- Duality—whether the chairman of the board is also the CEO (Dechow, Sloan, and Sweeney, 1996; Brickley, Coles, and Jarrel, 1997; Agrawal, Jaffee, and Karpoff, 1999; Goyal and Park, 2002; Gul and Lai, 2002; Chtourou, Bédard, and Courteau, 2001; Xie, and DaDalt, Davidson, 2003; Bowen, Rajgopal, and Venkatachalam, 2004).
- The number of meetings (Gertner and Kaplan, 1998; Vafeas, 1999a; Anderson, Mansi, and Reeb, 2003; Xie, Davidson, and DaDalt, 2003; Bowen, Rajgopal, and Venkatachalam, 2004; Zhou and Chen, 2004; Weber, 2004; Krishnan and Visvanathan, 2005a; Anderson, Deli, and Gillan, 2006; Jiraporn, Davidson, DaDalt, and Ning, 2007).
- Equity holding by directors (Beasley, 1996; Yermack, 1996; Denis, Denis, and Sarin, 1997; Bhagat, Carey, and Elson, 1998; Wright, 1999; Perry, 2000; Chtourou, Bédard, and Courteau, 2001; Paul, 2001; Cyert, Kang, and Kumar, 2002; Abbott, Parker, and Peters, 2004; Lehn, Patro, and Zhao, 2005; Bushman, Chen, Engel, and Smith; 2004; Collins, Reitenga, and Sanchez, 2005; Cremers, Driessen, Maenhout, and Weinbaum, 2005; Dey, 2005; Vafeas, 2005).
- Age (Larcker, Richardson, and Tuna, 2005) and tenure (e.g., Vafeas, 2003, 2005; Adams and Mehran, 2005).[106]

When multiple directorships involve an outside director who serves as an officer in another firm, the phenomenon has two aspects. First, the sender firm has an executive who commits some of his time to a service in another company, which could either decrease the time he dedicates to his own firm or help his firm acquire valuable networking. Second, the receiving firm benefits from an outside director with corporate expertise and connections (Rosenstein and Wyatt, 1990a; Perry and Peyer, 2005; Conyon and Read, 2006). Most of the research focuses on the receiving firm's perspective.

The scope of this phenomenon is limited. In their sample of 4190 public firms that held at least $100 million in assets at the beginning of 1995, Fer-

---

[106] Expertise is another characteristic that has been examined extensively in the research on audit committees. We discuss audit committees below.

ris, Jagannathan, and Pritchard (2003), find that only 16% of 23,673 directors held two or more directorships, and only 6% held three or more. Perry and Peyer (2005), collected 349 announcements of new director appointments in the years 1994 through 1996, finding that in only 20% of the events, the directors already held two or more outside directorships in publicly traded firms. The distribution of multiple directorships is skewed toward larger, more successful firms, with larger boards (Gilson, 1990; Kaplan and Reishus, 1990; Bhagat and Black,1999; Ferris, Jagannathan, and Pritchard, 2003; Harford, 2003; Fich, 2005; Keys and Li, 2005; Perry and Peyer, 2005). Ferris, Jagannathan, and Prtichard (2003), for example, find that directors with three or more directorships hold approximately half of their directorships in Forbes 500 firms. They conclude that "multiple directorships are primarily a large-firm phenomenon" (p. 1091). The prevalence of the phenomenon in larger firms implies that there is high probability that a director with multiple directorships will sit on boards with other directors with multiple directorships (Ferris, Jagannathan, and Pritchard, 2003; Conyon and Muldoon, 2006). This feature enhances the clubby portrayal of boards. Holding multiple directorships signals a director's value (Fairchild and Li, 2005). It is difficult, for example, to acquire additional directorships after sitting on the board of a firm that performed poorly unless the director can prove that he fulfilled his monitoring role by, for example, not fighting a hostile takeover (Harford, 2003). Brickley, Coles, and Linck (1999), find that CEOs are more likely to attract directorships after retirement if their firm was successful in the last 4 years the CEO was in office. Yermack (2004), who examines the incentives of 734 directors elected to the boards of Fortune 500 firms between 1994 and 1996, shows that an increase of one standard deviation in the firm's median performance increases the wealth of directors who serve a fifth year by $285,000. He also finds that a director can expect a $0.043 increase in wealth from acquiring new board seats for each $1,000 increase in the firm's market cap. Even the payment per meeting, which seems like an insignificant prize, may be important. Adams (2005), who examines proxies that reported on directors with "attendance problem," finds a positive correlation between attendance and the amount paid per meeting.

Duality is an indicator of the CEO's power and his ability to control the board. He, Srinidhi, Su, and Gul (2003), for example, find that the probability of CEO quitting the firm is negatively associated with the event that the CEO is also chairman of the board. Although rare in Canada and the United Kingdom, this situation is quite prevalent in the United States; in the late twentieth century, the CEO is also the chairman of the board in more than 80% of large public firms.[107]

The number of meetings is an indicator of the effort put in by the directors. To the extent that the board is an agent of the manager, it is unknown what directors do behind closed door and how much effort they put into doing a good job. The following conveys the impression that the twentieth century regime did not require much effort, which is consistent with the façade view of the board: "Boards meet quarterly, often with one board meeting held as a 'fly away' meeting at a resort or in a more distant city. The corporation may have invited spouses. The meeting was often held as a planning meeting or strategic retreat.... Meetings lasted 3–4 hours, often a morning or a morning and into the early afternoon" (Branson, p. 27). It stands to reason that governing a multibillion firm requires more meetings in a work environment.

Equity holdings indicate the extent to which the directors' incentives are aligned with the maximization of shareholders' value. Bhagat, Carey, and Elson (1998), and Perry (2000), find that outside directors who hold more equity are more likely to replace the CEO of a poorly performing company. On the other hand, short-term holdings may lead to collusion with management to manage earnings to increase the price (Chtourou, Bédard, and Courteau, 2001, Table 3). Anecdotal evidence comes from Cynthia Coopers, the heroine of the WorldCom accounting scandal, who told the audience at the AAA meeting in San Francisco in 2005 that the chair of the audit committee did not cooperate with her effort to set up a meeting to communicate her suspicions, because, allegedly, he was apprehensive that if the street learned about such an investigation, the price of WorldCom stock would decline, and the directors of WorldCom would lose wealth. The fact that equity compensation can be harmful is seen in the work of Collins, Gong, and Li (2006), who examined the backdating of options (see Chap. 3). They find that firms whose directors receive more stock options collude more with management in backdating the option grants to the date that the stock price was the lowest, which ensures that the options are "in the money" (because the strike price is typically set to the grant-date stock price).

Age and tenure are similarly contentious variables. On the one hand, age indicates valuable experience and tenure allows directors more familiarity with the firm's normal business and resources, which facilitates their

---

[107] Xie, Davidson, and DaDalt (2003), for example, report that in 85% of their sample, the firm/years had the same person chairing the board and serving as CEO. (Their sample comprises 282 firms/years of the first 100 S&P firms in 1992, 1994, and 1996.)

monitoring. On the other hand, these variables may indicate stronger bonds with management. For example, their long tenure has been offered as an explanation of the failure of Enron's directors to act (Niskanen, 2005).

Recent regulations have induced a number of changes in governance. The most obvious is the requirement for increased independence, a trend that started late in the twentieth century (e.g., Vafeas, 2005). Companies have responded to the requirement of increased independence by increasing the size of their boards. Composition changed too: Independence has reduced the weight of executive directors in favor of lawyers, consultants, and former executives (Linck, Netter, and Yang, 2006).

Directors work more, especially those on the audit committee. The risk of litigation and the greater responsibility imposed on directors is seen in the fact that almost 91% of companies give their boards the authority to hire their own advisers. The number of meetings has increased, especially those held by the audit committee, which has more than doubled its number of meetings (Linck, Netter, and Yang, 2006). Moreover, the incidence of multiple directorships has declined, concurrent with growth in directors' equity and total payments (Coglianese and Michael, 2006; Linck, Netter, and Yang, 2006).

Boards of directors are now more costly, especially for smaller firms. Linck, Netter, and Yang (2006), report that small (large) firms paid $3.19 ($0.32) in director fees per $1,000 of net sales in 2004, which is $0.84 ($0.07) more than they paid in 2001 and $1.21 ($0.10) more than in 1998.

Additional changes include a decline in duality and an increase in the number of "lead directors"—independent directors in charge of executive sessions of non-management directors (Coglianese and Michael, 2006.)

Aggarwal and Williamson (2006), report that the following governance characteristics, some of which hardly existed in 2001, characterize more than 90% of firms in 2005:

- All directors attended 75% of board meetings or had a valid excuse.
- The CEO serves on the board of two or fewer companies.
- Consulting fees paid to auditors are less than audit fees paid to auditors.
- There is a single class of stock (no dual class).
- The board has express authority to hire its own advisers.
- Shareholder proposals are not ignored.[108]

---

[108] For additional provisions, consult Aggarwal and Williamson (2006).

They note that because regulations have improved governance by all complying firms, they eliminated the premium for good governance. However, firms seem to improve governance in areas not mandated by recent regulations.

5.4.2.4 Audit Committees

At the forefront in the board's role as a gatekeeper defending against pernicious earnings management stands the audit committee. In a letter sent by Arthur Levitt to the chairs of audit committees of over 5,000 public firms on January 5, 2001, he comments,

> When auditors and the board engage in frank and meaningful discussions about the significant, but sometimes gray areas of accounting, both the company's and its shareholders' interests are served. In this way, the board, including the audit committee, management, and outside auditors form a "three-legged stool" of responsible disclosure and active oversight.

In the late twentieth century, regulators concerned with earnings management designed mechanisms to enhance the accountability of the audit committee, the outside auditors, and management. The new measures were meant to strengthen the independence of audit committees to ensure they were effective gatekeepers. In September 1998, the SEC, NYSE, and NASD announced a Blue Ribbon Committee chaired by John C. Whitehead and Ira M. Millstein, which in February 1999, announced a ten-point plan to improve the effectiveness of audit committees. Implementation took place during December 1999 and January 2000. Companies listed with NASD, AMEX, and NYSE were required to make changes in the structure and membership of their audit committees and in the charters of these committees, such as adding a requirement that all members of the audit committee be financially literate and at least one have financial expertise[109] (SEC release numbers, 34-42231,[110] 34-42232, and

---

[109] For a study that illustrates the difference between literacy and expertise, consult the experimental study of McDaniel, Martin, and Maines (2002). They designate audit managers as financial experts and executive MBA graduates as financially literate. They detect different patterns in their evaluation of which issues are important in determining the quality of earnings.

[110] The charter of the audit committee must specify the following:

> "(i) the scope of the audit committee's responsibilities, and how it carries out those responsibilities, including structure, processes, and membership requirements;

34-42233).[111] They also mandated changes in their disclosures to include discussions with auditors regarding financial statements and the considerations behind hiring the auditor to perform non-audit services (34-42266).[112]

The Sarbanes-Oxley Act (SOX) of July 2002 reinforces the requirements that every publicly traded company must have an audit committee. Under SOX, each member of the audit committee must be independent, and at least one must have financial expertise. To be independent, a person must not be an executive officer of the company or a shareholder holding over 10% of the firm's equity (section 301). SOX delegates to the SEC the responsibility of defining a financial expert. The SEC defines a financial expert as one who has

- understanding of GAAP and financial statements;
- uhe ability to assess the application of accounting principles for estimates, accruals, and reserves;
- understanding of audit committee functions and internal control for financial reporting;
- experience in auditing, preparing, analyzing, or evaluating financial statements with the appropriate level of complexity of accounting issues in comparison to the complexity of the company's expected financial statements.

Section 407 of SOX demands disclosure of whether the audit committee has a member with the required financial expertise and the knowledge to understand the report at a level of complexity as that of the firm (who must be ethical, with no past of any disciplinary action), and whether this expert is independent.

(ii) the audit committee's responsibility for ensuring its receipt from the outside auditors of a formal written statement delineating all relationships between the auditor and the company, consistent with Independence Standards Board Standard 1, and the audit committee's responsibility for actively engaging in a dialogue with the auditor with respect to any disclosed relationships or services that may impact the objectivity and independence of the auditor and for taking, or recommending that the full board take, appropriate action to [ensure] oversee the independence of the outside auditor; and

(iii) the outside auditor's ultimate accountability to the board of directors and the audit committee, as representatives of shareholders, and these shareholder representatives' ultimate authority and responsibility to select, evaluate, and, where appropriate, replace the outside auditor (or to nominate the outside auditor to be proposed for shareholder approval in any proxy statement).

[111] A summary of the requirements of the exchanges in comparison with the requirements of SOX is provided in a document prepared by KPMG, available at http://www.kpmg.com/aci/docs/Final_comparison.pdf.

[112] See http://www.sec.gov/news/headlines/audind.htm.

As discussed in the next section, SOX granted the audit committee more responsibility in areas involving the auditor. The audit committee also has the responsibility for ensuring compliance by senior financial officers and CEO with the code of ethics.[113] Section 301 gives the committee the authority to hire consultants (reimbursed by the company).

Research has examined the association between audit committee disclosures (Liu, 2004) and earnings management (see Beasley, 1996; Gerety and Lehn, 1997; Parker, 1997; Klein, 1998, 2002b; Beasley, Carcello, Hermanson, and Lapides, 2000; Carcello and Neale, 2000; Chtourou, Bédard, and Courteau, 2001; Abbott, Parker, Peters, and Raghunandan, 2003; Felo, Krishnamurthy, and Solieri, 2003; Xie, Davidson, and DaDalt, 2003; Abbott, Parker, and Peters 2004; Bédard, Chtourou, and Courteau, 2004; Bradbury, Mak, and Tan, 2004; Bryan, Liu, and, Tiras, 2004; Uzun, Szewczyk, and Varma, 2004; Zhou and Chen, 2004; Agrawal and Chadha, 2005; DeFond, Hann, and Hu, 2005; Zhang, Zhou, and Zhou, 2006). (For valuable reviews of the literature, see DeZoort, Hermanson, Archambeault, and Reed (2002); and DeFond and Francis (2005.))

Academic work on audit committees focuses on two main characteristics: the independence of its members, and their financial expertise (see the valuable discussion in Krishnan and Visvanathan, 2005b, of the different definitions of expertise). To a lesser extent, other variable may be considered too: tenure, which allows the directors to acquire firm-specific experience but might compromise objectivity; the size of the audit committee, which determines its resources; the frequency of its meetings, which indicates its activity,[114] members' stock option holdings, which determine their incentives to collude with management or align their interests with shareholders; and governance expertise, which determines the committee members' power in dealing with management and the board.

Earnings management and the quality of earnings are tested by different measures: directly by conservatism, restatements, fraud, discretionary accruals, and indirectly, by, for example, auditors' resignations (Archambeault and DeZoort, 2001; Carcello and Neale, 2003; Lee, Mande, and Ortman, 2004), which are likely to be induced by a conflict with manage-

---

[113] SOX had a material effect on small businesses because since 1999 and before SOX, small businesses were exempted from the requirement of having a fully independent audit committee. This exemption was repealed by SOX.

Another difference effected by SOX is that boards no longer can choose to appoint non-independent directors to the audit committee.

[114] Bédard, Chtourou, and Courteau (2004), also use the audit committee's charter as a measure of its activity because the charter provides the committee with power to make decisions.

ment over compromising reporting requirements, and the purchase of non-audit services (e.g., Abbott, Parker, Peters, and Raghunandan, 2003), which might compromise the independence of the audit process. The overall picture that arises from the findings is as expected. A stronger audit committee is associated with higher quality earnings.

The evidence on the response of the market is mixed. Anderson, Deli, and Gillan (2006), find that the response to earnings surprises in their sample of firms with a fiscal year in 2001 is stronger with an independent board but the audit committee's independence has no incremental significance. Two other studies—Davidson, Xie, and Xu (2004),[115] and DeFond, Hann, and Hu (2005)—find that the market rewards firms that appoint financial experts to their audit committees.

5.5 Auditors

> While the beginning of the 21 century has been marked by accounting scandals, a major stock market crash, and the most sweeping securities market reforms since the 1930s, one unexpected consequence of these events is an increased awareness that auditing matters. In particular, regulators, market participants, and the public all seem to have a greater appreciation for the crucial role auditing plays in the successful functioning of the U.S. financial markets. (DeFond and Francis, 2005, p. 5)

Because auditors attest to financial reports, auditors are probably the most important gatekeeper for blocking pernicious earnings management. Historically,

> [i]nvestors in the U.S. capital markets have depended for over a hundred years on an independent third party, an external auditor to examine the books and financial reports prepared by management. Investors and the New York Stock Exchange demanded independent audits first in the 1890's after confidence in the markets had ebbed due to fictitious financial reporting. They demanded it again in the 1930's after a bull market in the "new" technologies of radio and automobiles crashed. And they still demand it today, perhaps more than ever, after

---

[115] Davidson, Xie, and Xu (2004), investigate stock returns surrounding the appointment of directors to audit committees as per 136 voluntary appointment announcements over 1990–2001, concentrated mostly in 1999 for mostly small NASDAQ firms. DeFond, Hann, and Hu (2005), examine 3- day cumulative abnormal returns (CAR) of 850 announcements of appointments of directors to the audit committee in 1993–2002 period (broken into 126 accounting financial experts, 489 non-accounting financial experts, and 235 who do not qualify for either definition of financial expert).

the Asian market crisis and demise of the dot.coms in this "new" age of technology and information. (Turner, 2001c)

In this section, we address two issues. We first consider the structure of the relationships between auditors and management in the past (before SOX), at present (after SOX), with recommendations for the future (the Financial Statements Insurance). This allows us to understand the conflict of interests that characterize this gatekeeper, since one of the alleged causes of pernicious earnings management has been the auditing profession's failure to fulfill its role as an independent gatekeeper. We then turn to the role of auditors in earnings management.

5.5.1 The Institutional Setting of the Relationships Between Auditors and Management Before SOX[116]

Figure 5.3 depicts the relationships between auditors and management before SOX. Formally, the appointment for the following year is ratified by the shareholders in the annual meeting. Yet shareholders do not pay auditors. Rather auditors are paid by the companies they audit. Before SOX, auditors depended on CEOs and CFOs, who de facto decided on their employment and compensation (see e.g., Abdel-khalik, 2002).

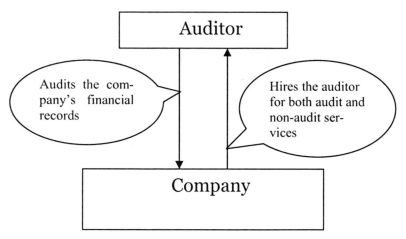

Fig. 5.3 Relationship between the auditor and company before the Sarbanes-Oxley Act[117]

---

[116] Some features of the audit scene are true after SOX as well.

[117] Source of diagram: Rona Barton's Report on Financial Statement Insurance (FSI), University of Maryland, 2005.

The audit process validates data (GAAS) and measures of financial statement items (GAAP). Data validation purports to verify the appropriateness, completeness, accuracy, and timelines of the accounting data. Validation of financial statement items involves judgment of the reasonableness of the values presented in the financial statements, for example, the quantification of inventory at cost or market, whichever is lower, or the impairment of goodwill.

Audit failure occurs when the audit does not discover improprieties in data or in presentation in the financial reports. For example, the auditors at the Italian concern Parmalat noticed that the document that confirmed that Parmalat had a $4.9 billion in an account at its Cayman Islands affiliate at the Bank of America, Bonlat, was blurry but attributed it to its being faxed when in fact the document was a forgery.

Audit failures might be attributed to various factors, such as weak controls, since the audit relies on inputs of the firm, or the complexity of business contracts and transactions (e.g., one of the explanations for the failure of the audit at Enron was auditor's inability to understand that Enron had transformed itself into a hedge fund with excessive financial risks). Ronen and Berman (2004), provide additional explanations. The foremost is the change from an industrial economy to an information economy. In an industrial economy, the audit verified tangible assets as inventory and property, plant, and equipment. Furthermore, by the time the auditor had completed the audit, the operating cycle was likely to be complete: most of the inventory turned over, most of receivables collected, and most of the payables settled. This facilitated the validation process.

The information economy involves a change in the nature of assets and liabilities. Specifically, the volume of intangible assets, which are harder to quantify, has increased, and liabilities have become opaque, with principal and terms that depends on yet unrealized conditions, such as derivatives. As an example, consider the move to mark-to-market accounting, which allowed companies to capitalize long-term contracts and record profits on losing contracts by basing the present value of the contracts on optimistic assumptions. Ronen and Berman observe,

> Such largely unverifiable intangibles make financial statements difficult to audit. They constitute private information that cannot be perfectly verified ex post. We can only observe whether a manager's forecasts were accurate; we cannot know that he did not truly believe that the forecasts were accurate when made. (p. 338)

5.5.1.1 The Auditor's Incentives

The auditor's incentives determine his ability to be independent, which is vital for his gatekeeping role of preventing pernicious earnings management. Turner (2001a), states, "While high quality auditing standards are an important component of a reporting infrastructure, auditor independence is paramount." This explains, for example, why auditors' fees are independent of their findings, although principal–agent theory recommends otherwise.

Concurrent with the change in the economic conditions, a number of additional changes took place in the second half of the twentieth century that reduced auditor's independence. The first was increased competition, with a consequent struggle to acquire clients by offering them large discounts at the beginning of the engagement-low-balling (DeAngelo, 1981a; Francis and Simon, 1987; Nofsinger and Kim, 2003). Second, the liability of auditors in class actions suits declined (Coffee, 2003a), which reduced their conservatism.[118] Third, the consulting business flourished. Since the hiring of both audit and consultation services were management's responsibility, the auditor's loyalty shifted to management. Cohen, Krishnamoorthy, and Wright (2002), for example, show that auditors equated governance with management, ignoring boards of directors.[119] Coffee (2002), summarizes,

> Today, the client cannot easily fire the auditor. Firing the auditor is a costly step, inviting potential public embarrassment, public disclosure of the reasons for the auditor's dismissal or resignation, and potential SEC intervention. However, if the auditor also becomes a consultant to the client, the client can then easily terminate the auditor as a consultant (or reduce its use of the firm's consulting services) in retaliation for the auditor's intransigence. This low visibility response requires no disclosure, invites no SEC oversight, and yet disciplines the audit firm so that it would possibly be motivated to replace the intransigent audit partner. In effect, the client can both bribe (or coerce) the auditor in its core professional role by raising (or reducing) its use of consulting of services. (p. 16)[120]

---

[118] Seetharaman, Gul, and Lynn (2002), provide evidence that is consistent with the liability cost of auditors in the United States being larger than that in other countries. We discuss liability below.

[119] Mayhew and Pike (2004), provide experimental evidence that shifting the power to hire the auditor from management to investors reduces violations of independence.

[120] The SEC and the AICPA have mandated three reporting requirements. First, the registrant must submit a Form 8-K to the SEC within 5 business days of the change in auditor. Second, the AICPA requires the auditor to independently no-

An egregious example of an auditor's lack of independence is the allegation that[121] Andersen's handing over its audit plan to its client, WorldCom, for fear of being replaced by a rival since WorldCom was located in a Mississippi area where no other such large client could be found. Since the audit planned to examine capital expenditures, at the time the audit took place, capital expenditures were properly accounted for. Later, WorldCom restated earnings because it capitalized excess capacity instead of writing it off.

Researchers have examined whether non-audit services compromise auditor's independence and whether the consequence is that the auditor allows pernicious earnings management[122] (Magee and Tseng, 1990; Gigler and Penno, 1995; Reynolds and Francis, 2000; Coffee, 2001, 2002, 2003a; Chaney and Philipich, 2002; Craswell, Stokes, and Laughton, 2002; DeFond, Raghunandan, and Subramanyam, 2002; Frankel, Johnson, and Nelson, 2002; O'Connor, 2002; Abbott, Parker, Peters, and Raghunandan, 2003; Ashbaugh, LaFond, and Mayhew, 2003; Healy and Palepu, 2003, Demski, 2003, Chung and Kallapur, 2003; Coffee 2003a, 2003b; Hyeesoo and Kallapur, 2003; Abbott, Parker, Peters, and Rama, 2004; Kinney, Palmrose, and Scholz, 2004; Larcker and Richardson, 2004; Mayhew and Pike, 2004; Meuwissen, Moers, Peek, and Vanstraelen, 2004,[123] Reynolds, Deis, and Francis, 2004; Abbott, Parker, Peters, and Rama, 2005; Agrawal and Chadha, 2005; DeFond and Francis, 2005; Louis, 2005; Ahmed, Duellman, and Abdel-Meguid, 2006; Antle, Gordon, Narayanamoorthy, and Zhou 2006; Beaulieu and Reinstein, 2006; Francis, 2006; Francis and Ke, 2006; Krishnan, Sami, and Zhang, 2005; Ghosh, Kallapur, and Moon, 2006; Gleason and Mills, 2006; Lu, 2006; Moore, Tetlock, Tanlu, and Bazerman, 2006; Nelson, 2006; Ruddock and Taylor, 2006).[124]

---

tify the SEC of the event. Third, the registrant must file an "auditor's exhibit letter" from the former auditor to the SEC within 10 business days of the filing of Form 8-K, in which the auditor either agrees with the statements in the Form 8-K, or explain why he disagrees.

[121] Based on the presentation of Cynthia Cooper, the former vice president of Intenal Audit at WorldCom, at the AAA meeting in San Francisco in 2005.

[122] Coffee (2002, p. 32) cites a survey by the Chicago Tribune on February 24, 2002 that found that the 100 largest corporations in the Chicago area (determined on the basis of market capitalization) paid consulting fees to their auditors that were on average over three times the audit fees paid to the same auditors.

[123] This study is less concerned with the consultation carrot than with the regulation of independence.

[124] DeFond and Francis (2005), raise another independence issue: the ability of accounting research to be objective:

Empirical findings largely support the complaints of observers. Krishnan and Gul (2002), for example, find that in the 1995–2000 period, the quality of the earnings of the clients of the Big 5 audit firms declined in terms of abnormal accruals, qualified opinions, and pricing of discretionary accruals.

Turner (2001c), summarizes the changes in the audit industry in the late twentieth century:

> The major accounting firms have undergone tremendous changes in the last decades due to globalization, consolidation of the profession and the rapid growth of consulting services. According to information publicly reported by the largest firms, auditing now accounts for 30 % of total revenues—down from 70 % in 1977. Consulting and other management advisory services now represent more than half—up from 12 % in 1977. Since 1993, auditing revenues have been growing by 9 % per year on average—while consulting and similar services have been growing at a rate of 27 % each year. These services include corporate finance, large-scale IT planning and installation, in addition to traditional accounting, audit, and tax work.[125]

The Street and regulators have become aware that auditors might not be as independent as is desirable for an effective monitor. In his 1998 speech on the "numbers game", Arthur Levitt laid out a plan that included measures to enhance auditors' independence. In 2000, after much debate and pressure from audit firms, the SEC revised regulation S-X (rule 33-7919, effective February 5, 2001) regarding the conditions for auditor's independence.[126] These meausres led to the reorganization of audit firms. They divested signifincat portion of their consulitng businesses through

> In calling on academics to "fix" the auditing profession we feel it is important to recognize that here is an inherent threat to our won independence when we investigate the auditing profession. This threat arises because the auditing industry hires our students, makes donations to our departments and schools, funds professorships and chairs, gives us subjects for experiments and proprietary data, and hires us as expert witnesses. All of these factors create a cozy relationship and a temptation for auditing researchers, referees, and journal editors to adopt a sympathetic view to the profession, and while such sympathy might be driven by a rational fear of "biting the hand that feeds us" succumbing to this sympathy would seriously erode our intellectual integrity. If auditing researchers become apologists for the auditing profession then we are doing the profession, our students, society and ourselves, a huge disservice. (p. 10)

[125] http://www.sec.gov/news/headlines/audind.htm.
[126] http://www.sec.gov/rules/final/33-7919.htm.

sales to third parties or public offerings. Still, these changes did not prevent the accounting scandals that led to the enactment of SOX and additional provisions to enhance auditors' independence in 2003.

5.5.1.2 The Audit Committee After the Sarbanes-Oxley Act of 2002

The most pronounced change effected by SOX was the addition of another rule-making body with enforcement abilities to a previously self-regulated industry. SOX established the semi-governmental Public Company Accounting Oversight Board (PCAOB). The PCAOB is empowered by SOX to "protect the interests of investors and further the public interest in the preparation of informative, accurate and independent audit reports" (section 101(a)). PCAOB's responsibilities include establishing or adopting by rule "auditing, quality control, ethics, independence, and other standards relating to the preparation of audit reports for issuers"(section 103). Figure 5.4 shows the new structure of the auditing industry. The company and the auditor still interact directly, since the company (albeit now through the audit committee) hires the auditor, and the auditor audits the company. The PCAOB oversees the auditor.

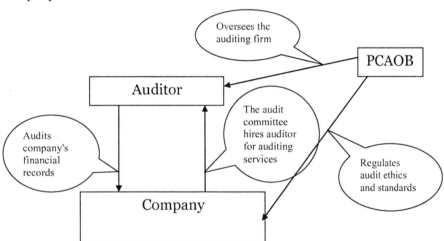

Fig. 5.4 Relationship among the auditor, the company, and the PCAOB after the Sarbanes-Oxley Act

The power to engage an audior shifted from management to the audit committee. SOX requires the audit committee to exert oversight of both financial reporting and the audit process. The audit committee now hires, pays, and retains the company's independent auditor. It is given the authority to settle disputes between management and the auditor, and to hire the services of the auditor to carry out non-audit services. SOX specifies the communications between the audit committee and the auditor.[127]   The auditor needs to furnish the committee with (1) the details of the accounting policies used in the preparation of the financial reports, (2) the ramifications of choosing an accounting treatment from a set of GAAP alternatives, and (3) disclosure of other material written communications between the auditor and the firm's management.

Another provision that is supposed to enhance auditor's independence is section 201, which narrows the scope of consulting services. Auditors are no longer allowed to provide the following:

- Bookkeeping or other services related to the accounting records or financial statements of the company being audited;
- Design and implementation of financial information systems;
- Appraisal or valuation services, fairness opinions, or contribution-in-kind reports;
- Statistical services;
- Internal audit outsourcing services;
- Management functions or human resources;
- Broker or dealer, investment adviser, or investment banking services.
- Legal services and expert services unrelated to the audit.

In addition, although tax services are not barred, auditors are prohibited from representing audit clients on tax issues in court proceedings (Beale, 2004). Other non-audit services have to be pre-approved in advance by at least one member of the audit committee.

In a number of alleged accounting scandals, the auditor faced his previous colleagues (i.e., the CFO and other personnel in the controller department had been previously employed as auditors in the same firm as the current auditor). Research confirms regulators' concerns by showing that such relationships increase the likelihood of earnings management indicators, such as abnormal accruals and qualified opinions (Dowdell and Krishnan, 2004; Menon and Williams, 2004; DeFond and Francis, 2005; Geiger, Marshall, and O'Connell, 2005; Lennox, 2005). For example, Dowdell and Krishnan (2004), find that earnings management is more prevalent when the CFO is a former employee of the audit firm than when the CFO is nominated from outside. SOX dealt with this aspect of auditor–auditee relationships by specifying a "cooling-off" period for CEOs, CFOs, controllers, and Chief Accounting Officers (CAOs). These officers cannot have been employed at the accounting firm conducting the audit for

---

[127] Before SOX, the SEC required audit committees to disclose only some details of their communications with the auditors.

at least a year before the audit (section 206). There are additional provisions that deal with retention of documents (section 802), to guarantee that document shredding is illegal, and with preventing officers from improperly influencing the auditing process (section 303).[128]

Sections 203 and 207 are concerned with the tenure of auditors. Section 203 requires the rotation of the partner that conducts the audit every 5 years. Section 207 calls for more study on audit firm rotation. The empirical evidence on audit tenure is mixed. Johnson, Khurana, and Reynolds (2002), find low-quality earnings for Big 6 clients less than 3 years tenure. Myers, Myers, and Omer (2003), find that such a rotation has an unfavorable effect on the quality of reported earnings. Hatfield, Jackson, and Vandervelde (2006), establish that there is little difference between rotation of partners and rotation of audit firms. Davis, Soo, and Trompeter (2006), study 27,377 I/B/E/S firm/years encompassing 1988–2001 and observe non-linear relationships between tenure and meeting or beating analysts expectations. They find a general decrease in the absolute earnings forecast error and, more important, an increase in the use of discretionary accruals to meet or beat earnings forecasts when the auditor's tenure is 3 years or less *and* when tenure is 15 years or longer.

The overhaul of the audit industry also affects the FASB, since the FASB is no longer funded by its constituency. It is now funded in the same way as the PCAOB (section 109). Moreover, the SEC is studying whether to replace rules-based accounting with principles-based accounting (section 108(d)).[129]

Some provisions were already in effect. For example, the SEC had mandated that auditors belong to the AICPA body, the SEC Practice Section, which already required rotation of partners. Large companies already had an audit committee whose members were independent, and most firms with audit committees delegated the duty to select and retain the auditor to the audit committee (Parker, 1997; Urbanic, 1997, cited in Abbott and

---

[128] **SEC.303. IMPROPER INFLUENCE ON CONDUCT OF AUDITS.**
(a)RULES TO PROHIBIT—It shall be unlawful, in contravention of such rules or regulations as the Commission shall prescribe as necessary and appropriate in the public interest or for the protection of investors, for any officer or director of an issuer, or any other person acting under the direction thereof, to take any action to fraudulently influence, coerce, manipulate, or mislead any independent public or certified accountant engaged in the performance of an audit of the financial statements of that issuer for the purpose of rendering such financial statements materially misleading.

[129] The motivation is that rules-based GAAP encourages corporate officers to view accounting rules as analogous to the tax code (Benston and Hartgraves, 2002).

Parker, 2001). Hence, the harshest blow to the audit industry was its loss of autonomy. Revsine (2002), expresses the industry's feelings:

> Auditing standards are currently set by the American Institute of Certified Public Accountants. I see no immediate need to change this. Auditors themselves possess the expertise necessary to develop appropriate guidelines. Surely, the AICPA now understands that tougher rules and stringent procedures are in the long-run interests of its membership. (p. 139)

Yet auditors have lost more ground because of their perceived failure to police themselves adequately. In January 2003, for example, California passed laws that required that state boards that license auditors include public members besides accountants and that restatements are to be reported to such boards so that they could decide whether the accountant responsible for the restated reports acted ethically.

To give a balanced view of recent changes, we note other developments more to the liking of the audit industry. As noted in the Introduction to Part 2, fees since SOX have increased by about 50% to compensate accountants for the additional work. At the same time, SOX has turned the perception of auditors around (see the citation at the beginning of this section). Branson (2006, p. 15), comments, "The accounting profession—reviled as the moral equivalent of porn merchants just two years ago—has been lofted to unexpected new heights of power and prosperity."

Some of the additional fees compensate for increased liability. These costs can be avoided by reorganizing the industry, as explained in the next subsection.

5.5.1.3 Financial Statements Insurance (FSI)

One proposal to change incentives and reduce the chance of misleading financial reports is the FSI scheme pioneered by Ronen in 2002 (see Ronen, 2002a, b, c). Under FSI, companies would insure their financial statements against audit failure and the audit would be carried out by an auditor hired by the insurer.[130] See the Introduction to Part 3 and the discussion below for the details of the FSI mechanism.

Without FSI, the auditor may or may not cooperate in earnings management. Evidence of cooperation is provided, for example, by Petroni and Beasley (1996), and Bradshaw, Richardson, and Sloan (2001). The former find that claim loss estimation errors in the insurance casualty industry were material in their 1979–1983 sample, regardless of the auditor's

---

[130] Insuring bodies could also include the audit firm that would integrate the insurance function in one form or another.

type. The latter find that before SOX, auditors did not issue more qualified opinions when accruals were abnormal, although abnormal accruals are associated with enforcement actions by the SEC.

Of course, auditors also have incentives not to collude, including the threat of costly litigation and the taint of lost reputation. At present, they can deal with the risk of unwelcome earnings management in the following ways:

(1) Screening out high-risk clients. For evidence before SOX, consult Krishnan and Krishnan (1997), and Shu (2000). For evidence on resignations of the Big 4 after the enactment of SOX, see Hertz (2006), and Rama and Read (2006). Landsman, Nelson, and Rountree (2006), also find that turnover at the biggest firms changed after SOX, but they doubt whether the riskiness of clients' portfolios indeed has decreased.

(2) Charging riskier clients a premium. See the evidence in Gul and Tsui (2001), Gul, Chen, and Tsui (2003), Schelleman and Knechel (2005), and Abbott, Parker, and Peters (2006) (who establish a link between audit fees and the intensity of earnings management).

(3) Increasing their effort. See the theoretical paper of De and Sen (2002).

(4) Negotiating adjustments to the financial statements. Heninger (2001), finds that the litigation risk increases in the clients' discretionary accruals, where discretionary accruals are a measure of the intensity of earnings management. Hence, auditors prefer more conservative reports. See, e.g., DeFond and Jiambalvo (1993), Kinney and Martin (1994), Cahan and Zhang (2006) and Libby, Nelson, and Hunton (2006).[131]

(5) Reducing the threshold for issuing a modified report, despite pressure from management. See Francis and Krishnan (1999); Carcello and Neale (2000, 2003); and Willekens (2003).[132]

Clearly, none of these measures insures auditors against their clients' earnings management because after all is said and done, earnings management is a decision of a firm's insiders. Furthermore, some measures might even reduce investors' welfare. For example, Kothari, Lys, Smith, and Watts (1988), observe that increased litigation, which is expected to protect investors, also has an unfavorable effect on management's incentives to disclose value-relevant information because of the premium charged by the auditor to cover expected litigation costs. Ronen and Yaari

---

[131] Libby, Nelson, and Hunton (2006), show that auditors are more adamant on recognition than on disclosure in footnotes.

[132] Willekens (2003), finds that the Big 4 became more conservative after Enron and issued more qualified opinions than other accounting firms did. She attributes this behavior to the threat of litigation.

(2002), show that increased litigation may suppress disclosure and thus reduce the transparency of the financial reports.

FSI benefits auditors by eliminating the need to use these imperfect mechanisms to address the risk of costly litigation by investors who are disappointed in the performance of a firm's stock price (see, e.g., Lys and Watts, 1994; Bonner, Palmrose, and Young, 1998).[133] FSI aligns auditors' and managers' incentives with those of shareholders, ensuring better quality audits, better quality financial statements, and fewer omissions and misrepresentations (O&M) in the financial statements, and in return smaller shareholder losses resulting from O&M. At the same time, securities prices would reflect the quality of firm's financial statement more accurately, contributing toward a more complete market and enhancing allocative efficiency. Moreover, audit firms would compete along the dimension of quality rather than price, thus enhancing the profession's reputation for independence and competence.

The FSI process begins with companies soliciting offers from insurance carriers of insurance coverage for their shareholders against losses caused by O&M in financial statements during the year. The carriers would engage an underwriting reviewer (that could be either an independent organization or the external auditor) to assess the risk of O&M by examining firm-specific internal controls, management incentive structures, the competitive environment, the history of past O&M, past earnings surprises and the market's responses to such surprises, and so on. Detailed underwriting review reports would be the basis for the carriers' decisions on whether to offer coverage, the maximum amount of such coverage, and the associated required premium (they might also offer a schedule of coverage amounts and premia). Based on the offer, managers would put forth their own recommendation for buying FSI coverage in their proxies for shareholders' voting (including zero coverage—no insurance). After the vote, the shareholders' approved coverage and premium would be publicized, becoming common knowledge. Companies that opted for zero coverage and companies that chose not to solicit FSI coverage would stay with the existing regime, under which they would hire external auditors to issue opinions on their statements. Companies whose shareholders approved insurance coverage would then select an external auditor from a list of audit firms approved by their chosen insurance carrier. This auditor would be hired and paid by the carrier. Audit firms would also be rated by an independent organization (likely the same as the one that conducted the underwriting re-

---

[133] From the perspective of auditors, the U.S. system is extremely litigious as compared to common-law countries, such as Australia, Canada, and the United Kingdom (Khurana and Raman, 2004).

view). The auditor would coordinate the audit plan with the underwriting reviewer to adapt it to the findings of the review. Eventually, the insurance coverage would become effective only if the auditor issued an unqualified opinion on year t's financial statements (sometime in year t+1). If the opinion were not unqualified, there would be no coverage, or the policy terms would be renegotiated. In either case (no coverage or renegotiated coverage and premium), the new terms would be publicized.

The essence of FSI is that it deters O&M. If, however, shareholders have grounds to sue the company, losses caused by O&M within the limits of the policy would be settled through an expedited process. A judiciary body, agreed upon in advance by both the insured and the insurer, would receive the claims upon the detection of O&M, hire the necessary experts to estimate the damages, and establish a settlement within the policy limits; the carrier could hire its own experts to analyze the damages (Fig 5.5).

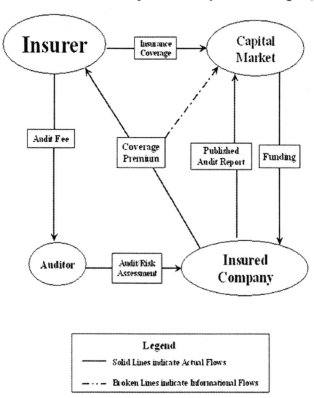

Fig. 5.5 The relationships among the auditor, the company and the insurance company according to FSI

To see how this mechanism confers the benefits listed above, consider the incentives of each of the parties.

Insurers: Once it had underwritten an FSI policy, the insurer's objective would be to minimize the cost of claims against the policy. This is tantamount to minimizing shareholder losses that could be claimed. Hence, the insurer's incentives would be aligned with those of shareholders. To minimize losses, the insurer would use a combination of rewards to give its hired auditor incentives to perform an audit that would ensure zero or minimal O&M. That is, audit quality would be optimized for any given coverage and premium. It can be shown that audit quality (effort) would be higher than in the existing regime. The fee paid by the insurer would be reimbursed by the insured and separately publicized. The premium charged would be tailored to the risk assessed by the underwriting reviewer and would credibly and accurately signal the quality of the financial statements. The insurer would charge neither too high a premium (lest it lose market share in a competitive insurance industry) nor too low (lest it bankruptcy itself).

The market: Because the publicized coverage and premium would become credible signals on the quality of financial statements, being based on a detailed assessment of the risk of O&M, investors would pay a higher (lower) price for the securities associated with a lower (higher) premium for a given coverage. As a result, prices, in addition to reflecting expected cash flows, would impound the information on the quality of financial statements embedded in the publicized coverage and premium. The markets would become more complete, and security prices would become better signals for resource allocation.

The insureds: Anticipating the effect of publicized coverage and premium on the price of their issued securities, and hence on their cost of capital, managers of companies with high-quality financial statements would voluntarily buy insurance to credibly signal their higher quality. Managers of firms with poorer-quality financial statements would understand that their only option is to improve the quality of their statements so as to obtain a smaller premium. Thus, the FSI arrangement would drive companies to a race to the top regarding the quality of their financial statements. Moreover, with more transparent and truthful financial reports, investors would be able better to distinguish between companies with low potential returns and those with high potential returns, resulting in improved resource allocation.

Auditors: Because they would be hired by the insurers, they would no longer be subject to the conflict of interest that afflicts their relations with clients under the existing arrangement. Their independence, both real and perceived, would be assured. They would be freed from client pressure to go along with dubious accounting or disclosures; they would be rewarded for better quality rather than for being willing to "fail to detect" material O&M. Because they would be rewarded for better quality, they would compete on that dimension rather than on price or willingness to acquiesce to clients' wishes. This competition would reshape the profession, making it possible for smaller firms to compete effectively, as they would not need to have deep pockets to be hired by the insurers. Moreover, auditors' legal liability would decrease on the average since plaintiffs would encounter difficulty proving scienter (motive and opportunity) in 10B-5 cases.

Furthermore, the debate now raging over principles versus rules would have a more clear-cut resolution. When the incentives of auditors and managers are not aligned with those of shareholders, principles can be abused, as clients can use the absence of rules to pressure auditors into accounting treatments or disclosures that the managers prefer. With FSI, and the aligned incentives that FSI engenders, a regime of "principles" would become feasible, and indeed desirable: no constraining bright-line rules would impede the reflection in the financial reports of a "fair view" of the company.[134]

In a recent article, Ronen and Sagat (2007), propose a different version of insurance. Specifically, under their proposal, auditors would voluntarily insure their clients' financial statements against restatements, and would be granted immunity from legal liability arising from restatements and charge a premium for the degree of assumed audit risk. In the event of a restatement, the auditor/insurer would pay a calculated amount of investor losses directly into an SEC Fair Fund, no proof of fault is required, which would then be paid to investors. The significance of the modified FSI is that immunity from litigation arising from restatements is a strong incentive for both auditors and companies. Other benefits of the FSI are unaffected by this modification.

5.5.2 Earnings Management

Usually, when audit failure takes place, the auditor blames management for hiding information from him.[135] Anecdotal evidence, however, indi-

---

[134] For additional information on the weaknesses of recent regulations that can be addressed by FSI, consult Ronen and Berman (2004).

[135] In an interview in the wake of the Refco scandal, Lynn Turner recalled, "I remember working on an audit once where the prior auditors had sent out confirmation to outside third parties that these were good receivables and good accounts... The third-party companies confirmed the receivables, but it turned out that managers at the audit client had bribed them,... I think that anyone would've missed it." (Glater, Jonathan D., "A Smaller

cates that before SOX auditors were aware of what was going on because they were called to advise on how to pursue earnings management within the boundaries of GAAP. The Washington Post asks "Remember 'earnings management,' which used to be the subject of how-to seminars offered by accounting firms?" (Pearlstein Steven, More Middleman Feel Belt Tighten around Them, October 20, 2004, E1) Turner (2001b), expresses skepticism regarding auditors' innocence even when earnings management constitutes fraud:

> Often in these press reports the auditors say management fraud is the reason the errors were not detected during the audit or, in some cases, during a number of audits. But I ask you, "How can an auditor miss a billion dollars?" This is not pocket change! And keep in mind it is not just one auditor who missed the problem, but rather an entire experienced team that includes an engagement partner and a second experienced reviewing partner; both of whom probably have 12 to 30 years of experience, as well as, a manager with 6 to 12 years of experience. Quite often there also is a third SEC reviewing partner involved if the company is registering securities.

De facto, the final report is the product of the negotiations between management and the auditor (see, e.g., Antle and Nalebuff, 1991; Dye, 1991; Zhang, 1999; Beattie, Fearnley, and Brandt, 2004; Gibbins, McCracken and Salterio, 2005). Direct evidence of the pressure exerted on auditors by registrants and the items that are likely to be managed is provided in Nelson, Elliott, and Tarpley (2002, 2003).[136] They survey 253 audit partners and managers of one of the Big 5, who describe 515 specific instances of potential earnings management detected during the course of their audits. Fourty-four percent of these resulted in adjustments; the rest did not. Only seven led to modification of the opinion.[137] This pressure provides a rationale for auditors' demand for conservatism, as auditors are aware that their clients are looking to increase their reported earnings (Antle and Nalebuff, 1991).

Broadly, the research addresses the following issues:

Auditor, Entangled Just the Same," New York Times, October 19, 2005, Section C, Page 4, Column 4).

[136] Libby and Kinney (2000), provide experimental evidence to that effect. They show that auditors are more likely to waive a justified adjustment to the report "to help" the client meet analysts forecasts.

[137] "Moreover, these seven modifications could be due to disagreements between management and the auditor about the application of GAAP rather than earnings management" (Butler, Leone, and Willenborg, 2004, p. 143).

- Does a qualified opinion from the auditor signal earnings management?
  See Francis and Krishnan (1999), Bartov, Gul, and Tsui (2000) Butler, Leone, and Willenborg (2004). Schelleman, Caren and Knechel (2005).
- Is there an association between the auditor's quality and earnings management?
  See Petroni and Beasley (1996); Becker, DeFond, Jiambalvo, and Subramanyam (1998), Francis, Maydew, and Sparks (1999), Basu, Hwang, and Jan (2002), Brown (2003), Kim, Chung, and Firth (2003), Krishnan (2003a, b, 2005b), Butler, Leone, and Willenborg (2004), and Zhou and Elder (2004).

The answer to the first question is that at best a qualified opinion (in contrast to unqualified, which is a clean opinion) is a negative but noisy signal. Lennox (2005), for example, finds that an unfavorable audit report causes a significant fall in executive compensation, especially if the report is newly modified or unrelated to going concern uncertainties. The noise in this signal stems from the fact that the auditor may issue a qualified opinion to protect its interests.

The answer to the second question is mostly in the expected direction. A higher quality of the auditor results in more conservative earnings. One interpretation is that the quality of earnings is indeed higher. Another is offered by Kim, Chung, and Firth (2003). They show that managing earnings downward is more likely to be unnoticed by the Big 6 firms. See also Balsam, Krishnan, and Yang (2003).

One measure of quality is whether the auditor belongs to the Big 6 (until 1998, when Price Waterhouse merged with Coopers and Lybrand to form PricewaterhouseCoopers) or the Big 5 (until 2002, when documents' shredding of Enron's audit working papers caused Andersen to dissolve[138]),

---

[138] Chaney and Philipich (2002), and Krishnan (2005a), provide evidence that indicates that Andersen's permitting of earnings management has to do more with lax treatment of its office in Houston than with the audit firm as a whole. Still, the negative price response for Andersen's other clients indicates that it had lost its reputation as a credible assurance mechanism, which led to its being dissolved. (Interestingly, Eisenberg and Macey, 2004, who examine over 1,000 large public firms from 1997 through 2001 find no evidence that Andersen's performance, as measured by restatements, was significantly different from that of the other large accounting firms, after controlling for client size, region, time, and industry.) Some contend that this was for the best because if it had not dissolved quickly, it would have dissolved anyway through a "death of a thousand cuts" brought about by lawsuits by disgruntled investors. Interestingly, al-

or the Big 4 and whether it is a national audit firm or a local one. The motivation for this measure is that larger auditors have more resources and
can benefit from economies of scale (Danos and Eichenseher, 1981).[139]
They are also more concerned with their reputation because they stand to
lose more clients upon an audit failure (DeAngelo, 1981b). Coffee (2002,
p. 6) explains,

> To be sure, the gatekeeper as watchdog is typically paid by the party
> that it is to watch, but its relative credibility stems from the fact that it
> is in effect pledging a reputational capital that it has built up over many
> years of performing similar services for numerous clients.
>
> In theory, a gatekeeper has many clients, each of whom pay it a fee
> that is modest in proportion to the firm's overall revenues. Arthur An-
> dersen had, for example, 2,300 audit clients. On this basis, the firm
> seemingly had little incentive to risk its considerable reputational capi-
> tal for any one client.

Clearly, the biggest firms have managed to acquire a brand name (see,
e.g., Francis and Wilson, 1988). Furthermore, their response to the litigious U.S. environment is to be more conservative—their clients have
lower levels of accruals (Basu, 1997; Francis and Wang, 2004).

Direct measures of quality include reduced litigation activity (Palmrose,
1988), a higher reaction to earnings surprises (Teoh and Wong, 1993), perceptions of preparers and users (Carcello, Hermanson, and McGrath,
1992), and higher engagement costs (Craswell, Francis, and Taylor, 1995).
A further measure is industry expertise, measured, for example, by an industry's share in the auditor's portfolio of client industries or market's
share of the auditor (Carcello and Nagy, 2002; Balsam, Krishnan, and
Yang, 2003; Krishnan, 2003b); and years of experience (e.g., Brown, 2003).

An issue that is related to the signaling value of auditors is auditors' resignations. Auditors' resignations result from disagreements with their clients. In some case, dissatisfaction arises because the auditor issues qualified opinions, where the dissatisfaction is magnified if shareholders were

---

though in many instances the same personnel that did the audits under the Andersen name do the audit within a new affiliation, the conservatism in their reports has increased on average (Cahan and Zhang, 2006), possibly reflecting
concerns about litigation.

For alternative explanations for Andersen's demise, see Jensen (2006).

[139] Doogar and Easely (1998), present an opposing view, claiming that the size of
the clients and the effort required of the auditor better explain the structure of
the audit industry than economy of scale.

unhappy (Nichols and Smith, 1983; Sainty, Taylor, and Williams, 2002).[140] Before such a resignation, firms typically exhibit income-increasing discretionary accruals (DeFond and Subramanyam, 1998). After the resignation, the client firm shops for an auditor that is willing to issue an unqualified opinion, and may change from a high- to a low-quality auditor (Bryan, Tiras, and Wheatley, 2005; Amoah, 2006; Davidson, Jiraporn, and DaDalt, 2006). Some studies thus examine the link between a change of auditor and earnings management (DeFond and Subramanyam, 1998; Bradshaw, Richardson, and Sloan, 2001; Davidson, Jiraporn, and DaDalt, 2006). An indirect evidence on resignations signaling problematic earnings management is the negative stock price reaction to the resignation (see Choi and Jeter, 1992; DeFond, Ettredge, and Smith, 1997). Beneish, Hopkins, and Jansen (2001), find a negative reaction for the dropped client and a positive reaction for continuing clients, and Hackenbrack and Hogan (2002), show that the market response to an earnings surprise is sensitive to the reason for the separation mentioned in the filing of Form 8-K.

5.6 The Press

In Chap. 1, we noted that before the accounting scandals, many households had their savings invested in stocks. There thus was a great deal of public interest in news on public companies, interest that could be satisfied by reading the press. As Borden (2006), observes, journalists serve two main roles: informing the public and the regulators of accounting improprieties and fraud, and informing the public of recent changes in regulation.

As a gatekeeper, journalists have been praised where other gatekeepers have been chastised. Branson (2006), compares lawyers to journalists:

> As law morphed from a profession to a business, the attorney's role lessened from that of a deal guru and wise counselor to that of a technician that could be replaced by any of several others, many of whom might perform the task more cheaply. Public accounting, once universally regarded as a repository of integrity and probity, had become a commodity offered at prices which met or undercut those of competitors. By contrast, the financial press, arguably more a monitor than a gatekeeper, gathered strength and prospered. Seemingly, each corpo-

---

[140] Johnson and Lys (1990), and Shu (2000), draw attention to the fact that changing clients can be a result of mismatch between the auditor and the client. DeAngelo (1982), however, notes that new accounting rules can cause disagreement between auditor and firm that worked in harmony before. She finds disagreements and resignations in the wake of FASB's promulgation of the Successful Effort method for the oil and gas Industry.

rate earnings report has become the source of a news story while 20 or 30 years ago earnings were simply numbers the press reported in the back pages (p. 5).

The press does not manage a firm's earnings, but throughout Part 2, it has played a crucial role in the earnings management scene by collecting facts and disseminating them; its actions affect the decision making of other stakeholders.[141] As a matter of fact, public firms publicize earnings information in press releases soon after the end of a fiscal quarter and a few weeks before the full financial reports are filed with the SEC. These disclosures are important to draw attention to the company's performance and they can affect its market price. When a firm possesses bad news, it wishes to evade the radar of the press. For example, the former MCI employee, Dan Reingold, reports,

> If it had been a bad quarter, we needed to leak that information slowly and quietly, so that the stock would drop during the week or two before the earnings announcement, but without generating any media attention. That was a lot better than the stock plummeting at the earnings day, when the world was focused on it. (Reingold and Reingold, 2006, p. 20)

A media revelation of an accounting scandal triggers a decline in the firm's stock price. As a matter of fact, a whiff of such a scandal is enough. Abraham Briloff of Baruch College used to publish critical analyses of firms' financial statements. Foster (1979, 1987), reports that such disclosures triggered price declines that approximated 20%.

---

[141] Academics also rely on the press to tell us what is what. For example, Romano (2005), criticizes the Sarbanes-Oxley Act, stating:
[I]t was widely perceived in the media that members of Congress were motivated by reelection concerns when a statute was hurriedly enacted in the summer prior to the mid-term elections, after months of languishing in committee, following heightened attention on corporate malfeasance when the WorldCom scandal erupted (p. 3).
The media is also important for designing event studies. Zhang (2005), who investigates the market's reaction to the Sarbanes- Oxley Act writes,
I identify the legislative events leading to the passage of SOX by a keyword search of "accounting" through the *Wall Street Journal* (*WSJ* hereafter) and the *Washington Post* (*WP* hereafter) via *Factiva*, from November 2001 to July 2002. To identify related rulemaking events post-SOX, I search the *WSJ* and *WP* for "Sarbanes-Oxley" from August 2002 to December 2003 and also check press releases of the SEC and the PCAOB during this period. The *WSJ* is widely considered the most influential and timely business journal and its news filtering system is likely to extract the legislative activities that are most relevant to the business community (pp. 4–5).

Although the media itself cannot take disciplinary action against companies, members of its audience, such as the SEC, can. In many cases, the SEC learns about accounting scandals by reading the press. Feroz, Park, and Pastena (1991), and Beneish (1997) note that the troubles of about one third of their sample of firms under enforcement actions by the SEC were first mentioned in the press. Turner (2001b), admits,

> Restatements have been increasing in the past few years, topping 230 in 2000,... and while some in the profession argue that 150 or 230 restatements in one year and $100 billion in losses over the last several years are not significant in relation to 10,000 to 12,000 actively traded public companies and a total U.S. market capitalization of $16 trillion, I don't think the average U.S. investor is going to buy it.... **And unfortunately, we at the SEC find out about the vast majority of these restatements the same way the investors do, we pick up the morning paper and read about the latest "surprise." In fact, the FEI survey noted only 21 of the 156 restatements were due to an inquiry by the SEC.** [Emphasis added]

This picture raises the question whether the press is an objective, reliable monitor. Miller (2005), provides an answer. He examines the trade-off between the benefit to the press from increasing circulation through providing interesting stories and the costs of identifying such cases and alienating business partners and advertisers. Miller does not find that the severity of the violation, based on the length and number of violations noted, influences the likelihood of press coverage. On the other hand, the press does a professional job by relying on credible sources, notably analysts, lawsuits, and auditor changes.

Dyck, Morse, and Zingales (2007), also show that the press is a valuable gatekeeper. They examine which party revealed alleged earnings management in 243 firms with a least $750 million in assets (and satisfying additional criteria) in the 1996–2004 period (found in the Stanford database of security class actions). In 25% of the cases, the firm itself made the revelation. But in 10% of the cases, the media discovered the alleged impropriety. (Other whistleblowers are stakeholders (17%), regulators (mostly industry regulators other than the SEC) (15%), and analysts (11%).)[142]

---

[142] Finally, readers who are interested in the role of the press in the case of Enron are referred to Smith and Emshwiller (2003), and Niskanen (2005).

Part 3

In this part, we discuss the analytical studies that have examined the empirical data. As we shall see below, most studies are done at the single-firm level. They examine the external demand for earnings management, which emanates from the stock market, and the internal demand for earnings management, which emanates from the contracting value of earnings management in the principal–agent relationships between shareholders and managers (Dye, 1988). Despite the importance of economic forces to induce earnings management, very little has been accomplished on this front at the time this book is written.

The Demand for Theory

Earnings management has been covered extensively both empirically and theoretically. Although both strands of research recognize that earnings management is important, each has a different outlook. The empiricist is likely to adopt a case-specific approach (see Part 2), while theoreticians look for generalizations. Contrast, for example, Xie, Davidson, and DaDalt (2003), with Arya, Glover, and Sunder (2003). The literature review in the former provides a list of different instances of earnings management. The latter organize the material around the three main conditions that violate the Revelation Principle in any setting: Communication, Commitment, Contract.

Each type of research stands to gain from the insights provided by the other. The empiricist can benefit from theory for a number of reasons: First, it is much easier to conduct empirical research when the null hypothesis, H_0, is specified by theory.[1]

---

[1] For example, the Nobel Prize winner in Economics, Dan Kahnman, is a cognitive psychologist, who started his enquiry into realistic decision making under uncertainty by constructing experiments based on the mathematical models of expected utility maximization by Savage, von Neumann and Morgenstern, and their colleagues.

Second, the interpretation of results is easier. Regressions show correlations among variables, but what are the conclusions to be drawn from such findings? More often than not, the researcher states that the findings *"are consistent with* hypothesis X," but since we cannot be sure that this is the only explanation, the interpretation of the results is vague. Kothari (2001, p. 106), states, "I review almost exclusively empirical capital markets research. However, empirical research is (or should be) informed by theory, since interpretation of empirical analysis is impossible without theoretical guidance."

This issue is exacerbated with mixed results, which demand good theory to settle the differences. For example, Baber and Kang (2003), indicate that the average CAR (cumulative abnormal returns) of firms that just meet the expectations of analysts' forecasts (UE = 0) is weakly negative (– 0.140%, $Z = -1.61$); Bartov, Givoly, and Hayn (2002), and Dopuch, Seethamraju, and Xu (2003), however, detect a positive premium for meeting and beating expectations (MBE). No existing theoretical work can explain this seeming contradiction.

Third, consider the endogeneity in earnings management studies. For example, we noted in Parts 1 and 2 that poor governance might lead to earnings management (EM); that is, the causality is poor governance → EM. Poor governance might result, for example, in inflated compensation packages that induce CEOs to manage earnings more aggressively. Yet firms that deliberately manage earnings will not look forward to having high-quality governance that might expose earnings management; that is, the causality is EM → poor governance. This confounds the empirics: The empirical work may not detect an association between EM and governance if the system is in equilibrium, If it does detect such an association, in the absence of theory, it is hard to distinguish between a case where the sys is not in equilibrium, and there is a causal relationship between earnings management and governance and a case where the system is in equilibrium, and the correlation between the two variables is spurious (for more on this point, consult Hermalin and Weisbach, 2003).

Fourth, theory enhances the contribution of empirical findings. To illustrate, Johnson, Kasznik, and Nelson (2000), find that the Private Securities Litigation Reform Act of 1995 (PSLRA), which limits frivolous class-action suits based on violation of Rule 10b-5, had a favorable effect on shareholders' wealth, as measured by the response of the price. As authors of papers on the effect of Rule 10b-5 on the stock price (Ronen and Yaari, 2002; Ronen, Ronen, and Yaari, 2003), we consider this result exciting. Our analysis shows that before the PSLRA, the stock price could be biased (either upward or downward). The empirical findings are consistent with our prediction that the effect of the PSLRA would be to lower the negative bias.

Theoretical work likewise benefits from empirical research. An analysis is conducted through modeling, which by definition admits only a few features of reality. The quality of the model depends on whether it captures key features. Empirical research provides information on these features. Moreover, if the empirical findings of different studies agree with each other, then the empirical research enhances the intuition of the theorist, if not, even better, because the theorist now faces the challenge of reconciling conflicting findings.

The Plan of Part 3

The next three chapters follow different strategies, truth-telling, smoothing, and maximization/minimization/taking a bath.

We organize each chapter around four major themes:

- capital markets
- governance
- product and factor markets
- the legal/political/regulatory system.

Capital markets encompass investors and gatekeepers, as discussed in Part 2. Governance relates to the principal–agent relationship between management, boards of directors, and shareholders. Product and factor markets determine economic earnings and the firm's ability to sustain relationships with suppliers, customers, and employees in the long run. The legal/political/regulatory system determines "the rules of the game."

Capital Markets

Studies on earnings management that admit capital markets into the analysis are mostly concerned with the effect of managed earnings and disclosure on the stock price. Such an approach requires modeling the stock price and making assumptions about how earnings are incorporated into it. Clearly, if the stock price were fully revealing with respect to a firm's true economic value, earnings management would be a moot issue. In such a regime, the audience would neither require good earnings management nor be misled by pernicious earnings management. The consensus today is that prices are set in a noisy rational expectations equilibrium. The basic premise is that firms' values are random variables. Some investors spend costly resources to acquire private information on value, and they buy (sell) when the stock price understates (overstates) the value of the firm according to their signal. Other investors are liquidity investors who buy and sell for non-informational reasons. A market-maker, who has the role of setting the price, cannot distinguish between the two types of traders. Hence the stock price is a noisy signal of the informed traders' private information. The equilibrium is rational because, in expectation, the price equals the true value of the firm.

Governance

In formal analysis, governance is captured by modeling the firm as a hierarchy of principal–agent relationships, between shareholders and directors, and between directors and managers. The shareholders act as principal to the directors. The directors are an agent of the shareholders and a principal of management, and management is an agent of the directors. Most studies concentrate on the shareholders–management interaction, applying the framework of Holmström (1979), Demski (1994), and Christensen and Feltham (2005). The situation involves a conflict of interests. Management is work averse because effort exerted in making production and investment decisions is costly. Shareholders prefer management to exert as much effort as possible because it increases the expected value of the firm. They do not observe the effort of the risk-averse, work-averse management. Since effort and nature jointly determine the economic earnings of the firm, shareholders cannot tell whether earnings are low (high) because the manager worked little (hard).

The unobservability of effort combined with conflicting interests implies a demand for a mechanism that aligns the interests of management with those of shareholders. The mechanism is an incentives contract. The contract is based on a mutually observable performance measure, such as reported earnings.[2] Earnings management enters the equation when the audit technology allows management to report earnings that are different from the true, unobservable, economic earnings.

---

[2] The commonly made assumption is that the principal has all the bargaining power, so he can design a contract that guarantees the agent his reservation utility level, that is, the utility the agent could have obtained had he worked somewhere else.

Product and Factor Markets

The product and factor markets determine revenues and costs, which net the cash from operations and the resulting earnings. Hence, as a matter of good management and vision, companies design and implement strategies to manage revenues, growth, and costs. In other words, managing assets to generate earnings is a responsible and rational decision of management in response to the conditions in its markets.

The markets create demand for accounting reports and disclosure. Employees, customers, and suppliers use accounting information in their dealings with the firm. Consider the recent requirement in the Sarbanes-Oxley Act that companies disclose immediately the loss of a major customer. In order to maintain value for its shareholders when it loses such a customer, a firm must find an alternative. If the potential customer is aware that the firm is desperate, the firm's bargaining power is diminished, so that it may not be able to obtain a true replacement for the lost customer.

As you read on, you will find that this aspect of earnings management has been neglected. Yet it is crucial for understanding earnings management. For example, Xerox, which had the largest restatement of earnings as of 2000, did not respond quickly enough to competition from Far East suppliers who manufactured the same good at a lower price. Sidak (2003), blames the bankruptcy of WorldCom on its strategy to deter entry by investing in excess capacity. Niskanen (2005), contends:

> Almost all of the attention of the public, the press, and politicians has focused on changes in accounting and auditing in an attempt to restore investor trust in corporate accounts. Enron's collapse, however, was a result of a series of bad business decisions, *not* because it manipulated its accounts, and almost all of the costs to Enron's investors, creditors, employees, and local communities were a consequence of the bankruptcy, *not* because of the accounting scandal. (pp: viii–ix)

The Legal/Political/Regulatory System

As discussed in the Introduction to Part 2, the regulatory system sets the rules that determine the scope of earnings management. For example, Generally Accepted Accounting Principles (GAAP) determine the degree of flexibility in the choice of accounting treatments. In this book, we focus mainly on a proposal to revise the audit industry in order to improve the efficiency of audits in preventing pernicious earnings management. The basic proposal has two elements. One is that financial reports be insured. Investors thus would benefit from a reduction in the risk currently imposed by imperfect audit technology. Furthermore, making the insurance policy public would convey the private information of management, the procurer of the policy, to less-informed investors. The other element is that auditors would be employed by the insurance companies. This would ensure that the auditors' loyalty would be directed toward the users of the accounting information. See Ronen (2002a, b, c), Ronen and Berman (2004), Shapiro (2005), Cunningham (2006), Dontoh, Ronen, and Sarath (2007), and Ronen and Sagat (2007).

As a final comment, note that these four factors are overlapping. For example, regulation determines the scope of the financial market's development. Regulation also determines the scope of moral hazard and the asymmetry of information in the capital markets, because, for example, it restricts insider trading based on private information and defines what type of information the firm has an affirmative duty to disclose (see, e.g., Daouk, Lee, and Ng, 2006). Governance and capital markets also overlap. Liang (2004), and Crocker and Huddart (2006), for example, show that when the principal designs a contract that allows the agent to bias the report by shifting reported earnings intertemporally, the valuation of the firm is an S-shape curve because valuation takes into account the manager's reporting incentives (for additional studies that link governance to the stock market, consult Bushman and Indjejikian, 1993; Kim and Suh, 1993; Ronen and Yaari, 1993; Sloan, 1993; Goldman and Slezak, 2006 (Fig. 1).

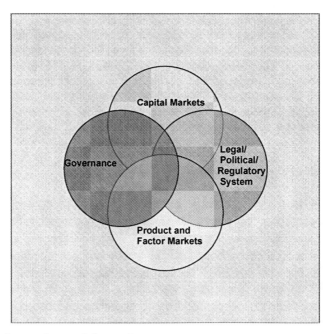

Fig. 1 The forces that explain earnings management

6 Truth-Telling

> Managers' manipulation incentive is only one aspect that affects the preparation and use of accounting information. After all, accounting is a language used to describe the firm's business activities in a reliable way and, as such, it is a very important instrument for the management, both internally and externally. If users perceive that the accounting has been manipulated, they might start relying on some other information system. In turn, this might cause problems for the managers in terms of decreased trust and less overview and control. *Therefore, I believe managers also have an incentive to avoid manipulation of the accounting.* (Hellman, 1999, p. 496, emphasis added)

Truth-telling and pernicious earnings management are antithetical. Yet there are cases in which a firm's earnings management strategy is to report the truth. What are its incentives to do so?

Consider the reporting game to be a sender–receiver games. The sender—the firm—possesses private information, which can be either good or bad news. The receiver responds to a message from the sender by making decisions that determine the payoffs of both. The sender will choose a truthful message only if this strategy maximizes his own payoff given his expectations regarding the receiver's response.

We proceed along the four dimensions that are discussed in the introduction to Part 3: capital markets, governance, product/factor markets, and regulatory system.

6.1 Capital Markets

Some public firms do indeed report the truth. People who are close to the street, such as Levitt (1998), and Parfet (2000), as well as Warren Buffett (2003)[1] agree that many firms are telling the truth within the framework of Generally Accepted Accounting Principles (GAAP):

---

[1] In his 2003 letter to shareholders, Buffett writes,

Well, today, I'd like to talk to you about another widespread, but too little-challenged custom: earnings management.... Many in corporate America are just as frustrated and concerned about this trend as we, at the SEC, are. They know how difficult it is to hold the line on good practices when their competitors operate in the gray area between legitimacy and outright fraud. (Levitt, 1998, pp. 1–2)

In the capital markets, the following scenarios induce truth-telling:

- Disclosure principle games.

  The disclosure principle states that, under certain conditions, when the truth is ex post verifiable and the disclosure strategy involves a choice between full disclosure and non-disclosure, the preferable choice is to fully reveal the truth. We explain this principle in the Appendix to this chapter.

- Signaling games.

  In signaling games, the senders take actions with regard to such items as leverage, dividends, and capital expenditures in order to signal their private information. In a *separating equilibrium*, all senders reveal their private information. That is, all firms report the truth and strive to convince the investors that they do. In a *pooling* or *semi-pooling equilibrium,* some are honest, but others try to *pool* with them and pretend to have good news even when they do not.

- Fully revealing signal-jamming games.

  In some situations the report is biased, but because the magnitude of the bias is well understood, the non-truthful disclosure is de facto fully revealing (see Chap. 1 for examples). Hence, in what follows, we treat situations with neutral earnings management that reveals the truth as truth-telling.

- Games with a randomized strategy equilibrium.

  The players—the sender and the receiver—mix their choices among the pure strategies that are available to them. In our context, the sender randomizes between truth-telling and misrepresentation (see, e.g., Ronen and Yaari, 2002).

Charlie and I... enjoy a rare sort of managerial freedom. Most companies are saddled with institutional constraints. A company's history, for example, may commit it to an industry that now offers limited opportunity. A more common problem is a shareholder constituency that pressures its manager to dance to Wall Street's tune. Many CEOs resist, but others give in and adopt operating and capital allocation policies far different from those they would choose if left to themselves (p. 2).

6.1.1 The Disclosure Principle

In the capital markets, the sender is the firm, and the receiver is investors. At a glance, it is unclear why the disclosure principle applies to earnings management, because financial reporting is mandatory, and disclosure is voluntary. Yet even within GAAP, firms have discretion over the transparency of reported earnings.[2] Moreover, when firms publicize earnings, they accompany them with additional disclosures that affect the informational content of the reported earnings, such as the pro forma earnings discussed in Chap. 2.

In its original formulation, the disclosure principle applies to situations wherein disclosure is certifiable ex post, so that the only alternative to full revelation is omission, that is, keeping the truth a secret. For example, Shell made a restatement on January 9, 2004, regarding a previous overstatement of its oil and gas reserves. Later publications revealed that the company's top executives had known of this overstatement for some time.

The disclosure principle applies in sender–receiver games because the receiver interprets non-disclosure as a signal that the firm possesses the worst possible news. In some circumstances, this grim conjecture is unjustified. Verrecchia (1983), proves that if disclosure entails costs, then non-disclosure is rational when the benefit is lower than these costs. Dye (1986a), extends this result when the cost is that the information is proprietary—that is, its disclosure reduces the value of the firm. Dye (1985a), proves that if some firms are ignorant and investors cannot spot them (because e.g., the ignorant firms cannot signal that they do not have the information), then some firms with bad news will pool successfully with the ignorant ones and not disclose. Suijs (2005), establishes that proprietary costs may induce disclosure of bad news and the suppression of good news.

Dye (1985a, p. 127), summarizes the general conditions under which full disclosure occurs:

---

[2] Consider the following excerpt from Enron's financial report in the quarter preceding the October 2001 report with its huge restatement:
> Enron has entered into agreements with entities formed in 2000, which included the obligation to deliver 12 million shares of Enron common stock in March 2005 and entered into derivative instruments which eliminated the contingent nature of existing restricted forward contracts executed in 2000.... In exchange, Enron received notes receivable from the Entities totaling approximately $827.6 million. (Smith and Emshwiller, 2003, p. 45)

Neither Wall Street journalists nor sophisticated users, such as analysts, understood these reports.

If investors know a manager is endowed with one particular bit of nonproprietary, relevant, effable information, the release of which does not alter the manager's compensation, and investors can take positions on markets prior to this information's release, then this information will be disclosed.

In some cases, disclosure may reduce the welfare of risk-averse persons because it adds uncertainty, so they would prefer suppression (see, e.g., Verrecchia, 1982). Hence, another requirement for the disclosure principle to hold is that investors can protect themselves against the additional riskiness of disclosure.

This list of conditions is not exhaustive. Consider, for example, the case when the firm is in possession of an imperfect signal. That is, suppose that the firm learns that its value is either α_1 or α_2, with corresponding probabilities of 1/3 and 2/3, respectively. The firm can make full disclosure, reveal just one signal, or reveal neither. What will the equilibrium be? Even if the firm discloses both signals, it still can "play" with the probabilities and never be proved wrong.

Finally, we make the following note. So far we have identified non-truth-telling with omission. Another non-truth-telling strategy is garbling, whereby the sender adds pure noise to the truthful message. Crawford and Sobel (1982), prove that when there is a conflict of interests between the sender and receiver, the sender garbles the message to reduce the receiver's ability to decipher it.

6.1.2 Signaling Equilibria

When the market cannot know firms' true value, the stock price discounts high-quality firms and overstates the value of low-quality firms. To illustrate, suppose that the market contains only two types, B (bad) and G (good), with a proportion of $1 - \gamma$ and γ, respectively. G has a higher value than B; $B<G$. If both types report the truth, type-B firms report r^B, and type-G firms report r^G, where $r^B < r^G$. Accounting flexibility, however, allows type-B firms to attempt a report of r^G. The success of thus managing earnings depends on the imperfect audit technology. This technology has a one-sided error (see, e.g., Schwartz, 1997); it confirms truthful reports with certainty, and it discovers the truth when the firm misrepresents with some positive probability π, $1/2 < \pi < 1$. What will the stock price, $P(r^t)$, $t = B,G$, be when a given report is observed and firms have incentives to inflate the price?

If a firm reports r^B, investors reason that the audit discovered the truth. Hence, the report is credible.

$$P(r^B) = B. \tag{6.1}$$

If, however, the firm reports r^G, two scenarios are reasonable. Either the report is truthful, because a proportion of γ firms are indeed type G or the audit failed to discover the truth. Hence, by Bayes' rule, the stock price is a linear combination of the values of the two types:

$$P(r^G) = \delta G + (1 - \delta)B, \tag{6.2}$$

where

$$\delta = \frac{\gamma}{\gamma + (1 - \gamma)(1 - \pi)}; \quad 1 - \delta = \frac{(1 - \gamma)(1 - \pi)}{\gamma + (1 - \gamma)(1 - \pi)}. \tag{6.3}$$

The problem now is that the stock price discounts type-G firms because it puts weight of $1-\delta$ on the event that the reporting firm is B, and at the same time, it overstates the value of some type-B firms because it puts weight of δ on the event that the reporting firm is type-G.

Type-G firms now have incentives to take actions that separate them from type-B firms. The actions must be costly, so that only type-G firms will profitably choose them. Consider, for example, cash dividends. Dividends are costly because they deplete the funds available for investment; creditors may regard the firm as less profitable and more risky and therefore increase its cost of debt. Suppose that dividends reduce value by λ; that is, a firm's value after paying dividends is $\alpha - \lambda$, $\alpha = G,B$.

In a separating equilibrium in which type-G firms pay dividends and type-B firms do not, two conditions must be met:

First, type-G firms pay dividends because

$$G - \lambda \geq P(r^G). \tag{6.4}$$

A type-G firm pays dividends because the price when the market believes a report of G net of the cost of dividends (weakly) exceeds the price when the market cannot distinguish between types of firms.

Second, type-B firms do not pay dividends because

$$B \geq \pi B + (1 - \pi)P(r^G) - \lambda. \tag{6.5}$$

The price of a type-B firm that reports the truth and does not pay dividends (weakly) exceeds the expected price conditional on reporting as type-G net of the cost of the dividend payment. The expected price is a weighted average of its true value (when the auditor detects the truth) and the price when the market cannot distinguish between type-G firms and type-B firms that misrepresent.

Adding Eqs. 6.4 and 6.5 yields

$$G{+}B \geq \pi B + (2{-}\pi)P(r^G). \tag{6.6}$$

Rearranging indicates that a *separating equilibrium* is feasible only if $\gamma \leq \frac{1}{2}$. That is, if the proportion of type-G firms is low, a separating equilibrium with dividend payments is feasible. The higher the proportion of good firms, γ, the higher the price for a report of r^G when the market cannot distinguish between the two types. This increases the appeal of earnings management with costly dividend payments to type-B firms. Note that the probability that the truth is discovered, π, has offsetting effects on payoffs upon misrepresentation by type-B firms. On the one hand, a high-detection probability increases the chance of the discovery of the truth, which reduces the benefit from false signaling. On the other hand, a high-detection probability increases the price achieved by successful misrepresentation when the market cannot distinguish between the two types, which increases the benefit from false signaling.

As simple as this example is, it illustrates that when the report is imperfectly audited, a reporting requirement in itself may not be sufficient to ensure a truth-telling equilibrium.

6.1.3 Signal Jamming

To the best of our knowledge, Stein (1989), was the first to establish that although firms manage earnings in order to affect the stock price, the market is not fooled, and it interprets the message correctly. In this case, truth revelation replaces truth-telling. Consider the case when the firm's earnings are a random variable that might take any non-negative real value. That is, denoting earnings by x, $x \in [0,\infty)$. Furthermore, assume that a firm's value is a multiple of accounting earnings; that is, $V = k \times x$, where k is known to all, $k > 0$. Hence, when the firm reports r, the stock price $P = k \times E(x|r)$. The dynamics are those of a Stackelberg game. After nature chooses the earnings, x, the firm renders a report, r (the firm is the Stackelberg leader), and the market responds by setting the price, P (the market is the Stackelberg follower).

We start to unravel the equilibrium by analyzing the market's response first. As Elitzur (1995), and others note, GAAP afford firms well-understood flexibility in making their accounting reports. For the purposes of this example, assume that the firm can inflate earnings at most by 10% within GAAP, and that this is common knowledge. Consequently, when the market believes that firms wish to maximize the price by inflating reported earnings, the market discounts the report by 10%, $P(r) = k\,(r|1.10)$. A firm that wishes to maximize its stock price solves the following program:

Max $P(r) = k(\,r|1.1)$
r

s.t. $r \leq 1.10x$.

The firm inflates the report by 10%.[3] Yet this inflation does not mislead the market because it discounts the report by the correct amount of bias. This is a "signal-jamming" equilibrium (see Narayanan, 1985; Fudenberg and Tirole, 1986; Stein, 1989; Elitzur, 1995; Holmström, 1999; Bagnoli and Watts, 2005).

6.1.4 Randomized Strategies

John Nash, the 1994 Nobel Prize winner, proved that every game has at least one equilibrium in mixed strategies.[4] In our context of truthful reporting of earnings, firms may sometimes report the truth as part of their overall reporting strategy.

We illustrate truth-telling in a mixed-strategy equilibrium with the following example. Suppose that there are only two types of firms, G and B, as discussed above, with an imperfect audit technology that allows some firms to manage earnings successfully. Now assume that a firm that first reports itself a type-G firm and later is discovered to be B bears additional costs, such as an SEC investigation and the associated penalties and class action suits by investors. Denote this expected incremental cost by λ. Fur-

---

[3] The Lagrangian of this program is $L = k(\,r|1.10) + \rho(1.10x - r)$, where ρ is a Lagrange multiplier, $\rho \geq 0$. Taking a derivative with respect to r yields the following Kuhn–Tucker conditions:

$k|1.10 - \rho \leq 0$ and   (1)
$r[k|1.10 - \rho] = 0$.   (2)

Equation (1) holds only if $\rho > 0$, that is, only if the reporting constraint is binding, $r = 1.10x$.

[4] Game theorists are divided in their willingness to accept mixed strategies. Some argue that an intelligent player does not choose an action based on a throw of a die. Others argue that a mixed strategy makes perfect sense when a player wants to prevent the opponent from taking advantage of his predictability. After all, who wants to play the same strategy all the time in a poker game? Harsanyi (1973), offers a "purification theorem," under which what seems a mixed strategy to a external observer is in fact a pure strategy by the player in response to small random variations in the parameters of the game that are observed by the player alone.

thermore, suppose that λ is sufficiently large to make misrepresentation that is discounted by the market too costly, but not large enough to deter misrepresentation believed by the market. That is,

$$\text{if } G > P(r^G), \ G - B > \lambda > P(r^G) - B. \tag{6.7}$$

Consider now the strategies of the type-B firm and the market when the audit detects the truth with probability π (Table 6.1).

Table 6.1 The expected price of a type-B firm's shares

The firm		The market	
		Believes a report of r^G	Discounts a report of r^G
	Truth-telling	B	B
	Misrepresentation	$\pi B + (1-\pi)G - \lambda$	$\pi B + (1-\pi)P(r^G) - \lambda$

By Eq. 6.7, if the market believes the report, misrepresentation is superior to truth-telling, and if the market discounts the report, truth-telling is superior to misrepresentation. Since the market's best response to truth-telling is to believe the report, this game does not have a pure-strategy equilibrium. It does, however, have a mixed-strategy equilibrium in which the firm randomizes between truth-telling and misrepresentation, and the market randomizes between discounting and believing the report (for another such result, consult Ronen, Tzur, and Yaari 2006).[5]

Guttman, Kadan, and Kendal (2006), also find an equilibrium with partial truth-telling but in pure strategies. They show that a reporting game might have an equilibrium with truth revelation when outcomes are extreme (either very high or very low). If the outcome lies in the intermediate range, the manager reports the same amount regardless of the truth. This semi-pooling behavior creates an endogenous discontinuity in the distribution of the reports.

---

[5] Denote the probability that the market believes the report by θ and the probability of truth-telling by τ. Then, if the market's loss equals the difference between the firm's true value and the price, the payoffs of the type-B firm and the market are as follows:

The firm:

$\theta\{\tau B + (1-\tau)[\pi B + (1-\pi)G]\} + (1-\theta)\{\tau B + (1-\tau)[\pi B + (1-\pi)P(r^G)]\} - \lambda$.

The market:

$\gamma[(1-\theta)(P(r^G) - G)] + (1-\gamma)(1-\pi)(1-\tau)[\theta(B-G) + (1-\theta)(B - P(r^G))] - \lambda$,

where γ is the prior probability that the firm is type G.

Differentiating the objective function of the market with respect to θ and that of the firm with respect to τ solves for the equilibrium strategies.

6.2 Governance

The main model used to analyze governance issues has been the principal–agent game between management (the agent) and shareholders (the principal). On one hand, this game depicts management in an unfavorable light since it assumes that managers are averse to exerting effort. (The agent's disutility over effort explains the conflicting interests of the principal and the agent. The agent prefers to exert less effort, while the principal prefers more because higher effort increases expected profits.) On the other hand, the game captures the reality that a firm's shareholders neither observe nor can infer management's unobservable actions from the financial reports and other observable variables.

Since enforceable contracts must be based on observable variables, accounting earnings have been used as a basis for the contract between shareholders and management. As discussed in Chap. 3, possession of private information gives managers an opportunity to manage earnings. When earnings management is pernicious, managers earn "information rent" at the expense of shareholders. Why, then, would managers report the truth?

The answer is given by the Revelation Principle (RP).[6] The RP is a tool for solving games with information asymmetry. There may be too many ways to design the *rules of the game* in a given situation, some of which may yield non-truthful reporting strategies. This creates a multiplicity problem, which the RP addresses. The RP states that there is no loss of generality in restricting attention to a truth-telling equilibrium, in the sense that the players achieve the same payoff under a prespecified sequence of actions. Specifically, when the game involves a principal and an agent who alone observes economic earnings (and the contract thus is based on the reported earnings), the sequence of actions proceeds as follows:

1. The principal designs a truth-inducing contract.
2. The agent exerts unobservable effort.
3. Nature chooses the economic profits given the agent's efforts.
4. The agent alone observes the economic profits. He submits a report.
5. After the report is received, the agent is paid in accordance with his contract. Later, the principal collects his residual share of the economic earnings.

---

[6] We restrict our attention to a single-agent setting. The Revelation Principle is problematic in multi-agent settings (Demski and Sappington, 1984; Mookherjee, 1984; Ma, 1988; Ronen and Yaari, 2002).

The rationale of the Revelation Principle is that being truthful is beneficial to privately informed players in general, and to the agent in particular, simply because no one can achieve a higher utility by being dishonest. That is, a truth-inducing contract solves the following program[7]:

$$\text{Max } EW[x-s(r)) \mid e]$$
$$s,e$$

s.t.

$$EU[s(r) \mid e] - V(e) \geq U, \tag{IR}$$

$$(e=e^*, r^*=x) \in \arg\max_{\substack{e \geq 0 \\ r \in X}} EU[s(r) \mid e] - V(e), \tag{IC}$$

where

W	=	the principal's utility function;
U	=	the agent's von Neumann–Morgenstern utility function;
V	=	the agent's utility over effort;
U	=	the agent's reservation utility, obtained in an alternative job;
x	=	unobservable economic earnings, $x \in X$;
s	=	the agent's compensation[8];
r	=	reported earnings;
e	=	the agent's effort.

The principal designs a contract, $s(r)$, based on the report, r, that maximizes his expected utility over his share of the economic earnings, $x-s(r)$, subject to the contract's guaranteeing the agent his reservation utility, U (the individual rationality (IR) constraint) and the agent's choosing effort and a report that maximize his utility (the incentive-compatibility (IC) constraints).[9]

---

[7] Throughout this part, we assume that the players are rational in a Savage and von Neumann and Morgenstern sense. For a study that links earnings management to the psychological variables of managers, consult Subrahmanyam (2003), and Yaari (2005).

[8] Compensation comprises base salary, a bonus based on earnings, and stock and options, whose value depends on market price. In general, because we solve for the contract in terms of the agent's utility, there are many contracts with different portfolios that yield the agent the same payoff. If researchers are interested in exploring this dimension of the contract, they will incorporate it into their assumptions (see, e.g., Elitzur and Yaari, 1995).

[9] The RP requires a communication channel between the principal and the agent. When the report is submitted publicly, as in the financial reporting game, and shareholders' activism is costly, the RP fails. Still, the literature comes up with three different outcomes of the principal's program: (1) It does not have a solution because the contract pays the agent more for higher outcomes, which, in

To illustrate the RP, we present an example of a renegotiation-proof contract in a setting that simplifies our analysis (Ronen and Yaari, 2001) and then show how the RP is applied to yield the same payoffs to both the principal and the agent.

The firm is managed by a risk-averse manager who alone observes the true performance, which is realized from a binary set, $\{G, B\}$, where G stands for good performance and B for poor performance. The greater the effort exerted by the manager in his production and investment decisions, the higher the probability of G, and hence the better the expected performance.

At the beginning of the period, the compensation committee of the board of directors designs a contract that maximizes shareholders' expected wealth. Since the true outcome is unobservable, the contract is based on the firm's imperfectly audited report, r. As before, we assume one-sided audit technology: A truthful report is perfectly verified, and an attempt to misrepresent is detected with some positive probability, π, $1/2 < \pi < 1$.

The literature on incentives has established that an equilibrium contract awards the manager more for a report that indicates that the outcome is G, r_G, than for a report that indicates that the outcome is B, r_B. Imposing risk on the agent in that way induces him to expend more effort, which increases the expected outcome (Holmström, 1979; Grossman and Hart, 1983; Harris, 1987; Milgrom and Roberts, 1992, Chapter 7; Demski, 1994; Christensen and Feltham, 2005).

The contract can be renegotiated after the outcome is realized but before the auditor examines the books and issues a report.[10] Given that the man-

---

turn, induces the agent to misreport (Hart, 1983b). (2) The contract is a piecewise contract. It first increases, awarding 100% of outcomes to the agent, then it levels off, awarding the agent a fixed payment regardless of the report (Gjesdal, 1989). The increasing part provides incentives. The agent does not have incentives to bluff because either he gets everything or the payment is not affected by the report. (3) The contract coincides with the contract based on a mutually observable outcome; it is a strictly increasing schedule. The agent, however, pays the principal first and then himself. If there is a surplus when the outcome is realized and publicly observed, the principal receives it (Ronen and Yaari, 2002). The increasing schedule provides incentives to exert effort. Truth-telling obtains, because if the report were inflated, the principal would get some of the agent's share, and if the report were deflated, the agent would be paid less than for reporting the truth.

[10] Renegotiation before the outcome is realized has a destructive effect on effort because the renegotiation leads to imposing all the risk on the risk-neutral investors. Anticipation that the risky incentive contract will be replaced by a fixed

ager at this point knows whether the outcome is G or B, the committee prefers to screen the true outcome by offering him a choice between two options, O_G and O_B, designed so that the manager will choose O_G when he knows that performance is G and O_B when the performance is B. Since O_G is likely to be more lucrative than O_B, the committee also uses the audited report to either corroborate or refute the manager's choice. That is, renegotiation replaces the original contract with four payments that are based on the possible combinations of the manager's choice of an option and the audited report:

S_{GG} = the payment for choosing the good-performance option when the financial reports corroborate it.

S_{BB} = the payment for choosing the bad-performance option when the financial reports corroborate it.

S_{GB} = the payment for choosing the good-performance option when the financial reports refute it.

S_{BG} = the payment for choosing the bad-performance option when the financial reports refute it.

The equilibrium subset is $\{S_{GG}, S_{BB}\}$, where the audited report corroborates the manager's disclosure. Since the incentive contract pays the manager more for G than for B, it is clear that the manager will not misrepresent G. If, however, the outcome is B, the manager will be deterred from choose O_G, because the audited report, r^B, might reveal the "wrong" choice, with probability of π, which triggers a penalty for misrepresentation. Specifically, when the outcome is B, the manager chooses O_B if

$$U(S_{BB}) \geq \pi U(S_{BG}) + (1-\pi)U(S_{GG}). \tag{6.8}$$

The utility over the payment received with option O_B when the outcome is B exceeds what the manager expects to obtain by choosing O_G. With a probability of π, the audited report reveals the truth, and the manager is penalized by obtaining (or paying) S_{BG}, and with a probability of $1-\pi$, the manager succeeds and obtains the higher reward associated with earnings of G.

Equation (6.8) dictates the penalty for misrepresentation:

---

salary provides the agent with disincentives to exert effort. In some instances, the principal avoids such a scenario by committing not to renegotiate (Aghion, Dewatripont, and Rey, 1994). Both are better off renegotiating, however, when unverifiable, non-contractible, information that can lead to a first-best allocation is available after contracting (Hermalin and Katz, 1991).

$$S_{GB} \leq U^{-1}\left(\frac{U(S_{BB}) - (1-\pi)U(S_{GG})}{\pi}\right). \tag{6.9}$$

To see the RP in action, think carefully. Is there another way to achieve these same payoffs? The answer is affirmative. You can ask the manager to report the outcome before the report is audited. The truth can then be discovered by comparing the unaudited report to the audited report (Ronen and Yaari, 2006). Alternatively, you can ask the manager to report only one of the two possible outcomes. The absence of a report indicates the other outcome. You might consider writing the renegotiation contracts into the original contract—that is, designing a renegotiation-proof contract, so that no renegotiation takes place at a later date. In short, there are many ways to obtain the same payoffs in this setting. The RP solves this dilemma by stating that there is no loss of generality in solving the game with the manager fully disclosing what he knows privately to the board, before the audit and the reimbursement take place. We leave it as an exercise to the reader to establish that the program for the design of the incentive contract under the RP is identical to that for designing a renegotiation-proof contract.[11]

6.3 Product/Factor Markets

As Verrecchia (1990a), notes, private information in product markets is proprietary. That is, reporting the truth might lead to reactions from competitors and other stakeholders that destroy the discloser's value. For example, revealing that production costs are low (or that demand is high) might prompt competitors to enter the market. The phenomenon most studied in this context is the transmission of information in oligopolies when firms possess private information on their private unit cost, the unknown market demand, or both (e.g., Fried, 1984; Gal-Or, 1985; Wagenhofer, 1990; Darrough and Stoughton, 1990; Darrough, 1993; Ziv, 1993; Sankar, 1995; Raith, 1996; Fischer and Verrecchia, 2004; Suijs, 2005). Most studies analyze the choice between truthful disclosure and withholding disclosure. An exception is Ziv (1993), who observes that because proprietary information is an asset, a firm has incentives to manipulate its revelation. Hence, an equilibrium with a truthful disclosure will also include mechanisms to enforce truthful revelation.

The effect of product/factor markets has not been much investigated beyond firms competing with regard to quantities or prices. We make tentative steps toward filling this *lacuna* by identifying the following three factors that might explain why firms nevertheless report the truth:

---

[11] For further discussion of the RP, consult Ronen and Yaari (2002).

- The firm regards its credibility as an asset, and the cost of damaging this asset by not adhering to a truth-telling strategy overwhelms any benefit from misrepresentation.
- Earnings management may require cooperation from other firms.
- The firm has multiple audiences, and their interests are in conflict with respect to managing earnings.

6.3.1 Credibility as a Valuable Asset

Credibility is important when losing it is costly. Truth-telling then might be preferable even if undiscovered misrepresentation is more profitable otherwise.

Consider the following example. Two firms operate in the market. Their unit costs are random variables taking values on the interval $[0,1]$ according to a mutually known distribution with mean c_0 and variance σ^2. Each firm knows its own unit cost, and it announces this cost at the beginning of the period, before the production of q units starts. The firm's financial report at the end of the period must corroborate the disclosure lest the firm lose credibility. The firms compete with regard to quantities (Cournot competition; see Christensen and Feltham, 2002). The inverse demand function is given by the relationship $P=a-Q$, $a>2$, where Q is the total quantity produced by the two firms, $Q=q_1+q_2$.

Under truth revelation, firm i chooses quantity q_{it} after observing the disclosure of its competitor, by maximizing its expected profits, $E[R_i]$, where $R_i = (P-c_i)q_i=(a-q_i-q_j-c_i)q_i$, $i,j=1,2$, $i\neq j$. We assume that the threat of litigation deters the firms from forming a cartel.

The profits of the truth-telling firms are $R_i= \left[\dfrac{a+c_j-2c_i}{3} \right]^2$, $i,j=1,2$,

$i\neq j$.[12] Suppose that a firm deviates from truth-telling and misrepresents its

---

[12] Taking the first-order condition with respect to q_{it} yields the response function of each firm:

$$q_i = \frac{a-q_j-c_i}{2}, \quad i,j=1,2, i\neq j.$$

Solving a system of two equations in two unknowns, q_1 and q_2, yields the equilibrium quantities:

$$q_i^* = \frac{a+c_j-2c_i}{3}, \quad i,j=1,2, i\neq j.$$

cost by ε, where the magnitude of ε is a decision variable. That is, the firm reports $c_i - \varepsilon$. In order not to lose credibility, it must now produce as if this is indeed its cost; that is, $q_i = \dfrac{a - 2(c_j - \varepsilon) + c_i}{3} = q_i^T + \dfrac{2\varepsilon}{3}$, where q_i^T is the production level under truth-telling reporting. The trusting competitor's quantity is $q_j = \dfrac{a - 2c_j + c_i - \varepsilon}{3} = q_j^T - \dfrac{\varepsilon}{3}$, and the profits under optimal mis-representation, $\varepsilon = \dfrac{3}{4} q_i^{T}$,[13] are $R_i = R_i^T + q_i^T \varepsilon / 3 - 2\varepsilon^2/9 = R_i^T + (q_i^T)^2/8 > R_i^T$, where q_i^T and R_i^T would be the quantity and profits under truth-telling. That is, if the firm has perfect flexibility,[14] then the optimal misrepresenta-tion is equal to half the truth-telling quantity, and the firm increases its profits by inducing its competitor to lower production.

If the audited report reveals the true cost with probability π, $\frac{1}{2} < \pi < 1$, misrepresenting is equivalent to gambling. With probability $1 - \pi$, the de-viator will succeed, and the competitor will not find out. With probability π, however, the auditor uncovers the truth, and the firm loses credibility. Assume that the competitor's retaliation reduces the misrepresenting firm's expected profits by C. If $C \geq (a-2)^2/8\pi$, truth-telling is preferable.[15]

The resulting price is $P = \dfrac{a + c_j + c_i}{3}$, and the contribution margin $P - c_i = \dfrac{a + c_j - 2c_i}{3}$, which yields profits of $R_i = \left[\dfrac{a + c_j - 2c_i}{3}\right]^2$.

[13] $P = a - q_i - q_j = a - \dfrac{a + c_j - 2c_i + 2\varepsilon}{3} - \dfrac{a - 2c_j + c_i - \varepsilon}{3} = \dfrac{a + c_i + c_j - \varepsilon}{3}$, with a corresponding contribution margin of $P - c_i = \dfrac{a + c_j - 2c_i - \varepsilon}{3}$. Profits are

$$R_i = \left[\dfrac{a + c_j - 2c_i - \varepsilon}{3}\right]\left[\dfrac{a + c_j - 2c_i + 2\varepsilon}{3}\right] = R_i^T + \left[\dfrac{a + c_j - 2c_i}{9}\right]\varepsilon - \dfrac{2\varepsilon^2}{9}.$$

Taking a derivative with respect to ε yields $\varepsilon = \dfrac{3}{4} q_i^T$.

[14] See Elitzur (1995), for a valuable discussion of the plausibility of such flexibility.

[15] The upper limit on C is derived from the condition that C be sufficiently large to deter deviation from truth-telling, $R_i^T \geq \pi[R_i^T + (q_i^T)^2/8 - C] + (1-\pi)[R_i^T +$

Although this example is simple, it illustrates that the concern about credibility may deter misrepresentation even though the proprietary value of private information calls for it.

6.3.2 Tacit Cooperation Among Firms

Some earnings management practices involve decisions that do not affect other firms' profits, such as estimating a bad-debt expense (McNichols and Wilson, 1988) or the yield on the assets of pension funds (Bergstresser, Desai, and Rauh, 2005). Earnings management through revenues, however, may require cooperation between buyer and supplier, as illustrated by the following example.[16]

Consider a vertical industry with two monopolies, Upstream, U, and Downstream, D. U sells an intermediate product to D, which transforms it into a final product that is sold to consumers. The consumers' inverse demand function is $P = \tilde{a} - Q$, where P and Q are the price and quantity of units sold, respectively, and $\tilde{a}$ is a random variable that takes values on the interval $[\underline{a}, \overline{a}]$, with known moments: mean, μ, and variance, σ^2, $\tilde{a} \sim (\mu, \sigma^2)$. The cost structure assigns a unit cost of c to the production of the intermediate good by U, $c < \underline{a}/3$, and D incurs the cost of purchasing the intermediate product. The following table summarizes the key features of the interaction between U and D (Table 6.2).

Table 6.2 Key features of the model

	Upstream (U) (supplier)	Downstream (D) (buyer)
Decisions	The price of the intermediate good, P_w	The volume of purchases and sales, Q
Private information	The realized demand parameter, $\tilde{a} = a$	
Profits	$R_{\underline{U}} = (P_w - c)Q$	$R_{\underline{D}} = (P - P_w)Q$

P = price of the finished good to consumers
P_w = price of the intermediate good
C = unit cost of the intermediate good

$(q_i^T)^2/8]$. Rearranging, $C \geq \dfrac{\left(q_i^T\right)^2}{8\pi} = \dfrac{\left(a + c_j - 2c_i\right)^2}{8\pi}$. Since, by assumption, $0 \leq c \leq$ 1, the lower limit is obtained.

[16] We are grateful to Joseph Kerstein for pointing out this observation.

We assume that D observes the demand, $\tilde{a} = a$, before choosing Q. This assumption reflects the close relationships between suppliers and consumers, whereby consumers submit forecasts of orders to their suppliers. In other circumstances, D observes key leading indicators that allow it to make an accurate forecast of sales.

D chooses Q by maximizing its profits, R_D, which (upon substituting the price $[R_D = (a - Q - P_w)Q]$ and deriving with respect to Q) yields the following quantity, price, and profits:

$$P = \frac{a + P_w}{2}, Q = P - P_w = \frac{a - P_w}{2} \text{ and } R_D = \left[\frac{a - P_w}{2}\right]^2. \tag{6.10}$$

Since U chooses the price that maximizes its profits, $(P_w - c)Q = (P_w - c)\left(\frac{a - P_w}{2}\right)$, the price it charges, P_w, and the equilibrium are

$$P_w = \frac{a + c}{2}, \quad Q = \frac{a - c}{4}, \quad R_D = \left[\frac{a - c}{4}\right]^2, \quad R_U = 2\left[\frac{a - c}{4}\right]^2. \tag{6.11}$$

Suppose that U applies for a private loan to finance expansion and that D is a public firm that is scrutinized by analysts and institutional investors and thus is concerned with not lowering its rate of return on its assets, A (ROA). If sales contracts have already been signed, purchasing additional units increases D's inventory and reduces its ROA. It therefore will consider purchasing more units only if offered a discount. Denote the discount by d and the additional purchases by I. D is willing to "help" U if $(a - Q - P_w)Q/A \leq (a - Q - P_w + d)Q/(A + I)$, where Q and P_w are determined as above. Rearranging shows that the minimum ratio of discount to additional purchases is $d/I \geq (a - c)/4A$. U is willing to sell more at a discount if $(P_w - c)Q \leq (P_w - c - d)(Q + I)$. Rearranging shows that the maximum ratio of discount to additional purchases is $d/I \leq (a - c)/2(Q + I)$. D therefore will "cooperate" with U only if $2A > Q$. Otherwise, U will not be able to manage earnings by this means.

6.3.3 Multiple Audiences Exert Conflicting Pressures

In some cases, a firm's constituency imposes conflicting pressures to manage earnings, so that the firm's best strategy is to report the truth and take actions that are consistent with its truthful report.

Consider the case of a firm that is a monopoly with unknown unit costs. The cost can be either high, H, or low, L, $H > L$. The firm knows that after the release of its financial reports, it faces negotiations with the employees' union and the threat of an entry of a competitor into its market. We refer to the monopoly as the incumbent and the competitor as the entrant. The payoffs of both are summarized in Table 6.3.

Table 6.3 The payoffs of the incumbent and the entrant

	The incumbent's type	
	L	**H**
The entrant enters the market	$-1, 2\pi$	$2, \pi$
The entrant does not enter	$0, 3\pi$	$0, (\pi+0.5)$
The first term is the payoff to the entrant; the second term is the payoff to the incumbent.		
π is characterized in Table 6.4.		

Clearly, the entrant prefers not to enter the market if the incumbent has low costs because it then incurs losses ($-1 < 0$), and it prefers to enter the market if the incumbent has high costs because it then makes profits ($2 > 0$). If the entrant were its only audience, the incumbent would have incentives to take steps, including managing earnings, to appear to have low costs in order to deter entry.

Before the competitor's entry, the incumbent negotiates salaries with the union that represents its employees. The payoffs of the employees and the incumbent are given in Table 6.4.

Table 6.4 The payoffs of the incumbent and the employees

	The incumbent's type	
	L	**H**
The employees make high demands	$\beta, \pi = 1 - \beta$	$-c, \pi = -c$
The employees do not make demands	$0, \pi = 1$	$0, \pi = 1$
The first term is the payoff to the employees; the second term is the incumbent's profit, π, $\beta > 0$.		

Clearly, the employees make high demands if the incumbent's type is low ($\beta > 0$) and make no demand if the incumbent's type is high ($-c < 0$). Consequently, if the union were the only audience, the firm would have incentives to pass as a type H in order to discourage a large salary increase.

Next, let us combine the two tables and focus on the incumbent's payoff for a given profile of reactions of the two audiences (Table 6.5).

Table 6.5 The payoffs of the incumbent given the actions of the employees and the entrant

	The incumbent's type	
	L	**H**
The entrant enters, and the employees make high demands	$2(1-\beta)$	$-c$
The entrant enters, and the employees make low demands	2	1
The entrant does not enter, and the employees make high demands	$3(1-\beta)$	$-c+0.5$
The entrant does not enter, and the employees make low demands	3	1.50

As per Table 6.5, the second and third rows cannot occur in equilibrium since the employees make demands only when the firm reports L, and the entrant enters only when the firm reports H. A comparison of the first and fourth rows indicates that the incumbent's best response is to report the truth: if it is type-L, it obtains 3 $(3>2(1-\beta))$, and if it is type-H, it obtains 1.50 $(1.50>-c)$.

For additional studies in the accounting discipline that involve multiple audiences, consult Darrough and Stoughton (1990), Wagenhofer (1990), and Hayes and Lundholm (1996).

6.4 Regulation

One of the institutions designed to curb earnings management is the mandatory audit. There is a rich body of literature on stochastic monitoring (e.g., Townsend, 1979; Evans, 1980; Gale and Hellwig, 1985; Baiman, Evans, and Noel, 1987; Border and Sobel, 1987). This literature assumes a perfect, costly stochastic monitor. Because it is costly, the monitor is used sporadically. The mandatory audit, in contrast, is always used, but it is imperfect. The analysis of the equilibrium is invariant with respect to whether a perfect audit is used stochastically, with probability π, or an audit that detects the truth with probability π is always used.[17]

In Introduction to Part 3, we presented a proposal to revise the audit market by letting auditors work for insurance companies that insure firms' financial reports. In this section, we illustrate that such a scheme can re-

---

[17] The only difference is that π is determined endogenously when the monitor is costly.

duce the intensity of earnings management when the quality of the accounting report is uncertain.

6.4.1 The Financial Reports Insurance Setting

A basic model in the auditing literature considers a project whose value is random: profitable, G, with probability γ, or unprofitable, B, with probability $1-\gamma$. An audit verifies G perfectly and B with probability π, $\frac{1}{2}<\pi_A<1$. The quality of the audited report is measured by the detection rate, π_A, which could be high, h, or low, ℓ, where $\pi_{Ah}> \pi_{A\ell}$. The quality of the audit is a decision of the auditor. The auditor must have incentives to choose π_{Ah} since it is more costly than $\pi_{A\ell}$. We denote his differential cost by C_A.

In the current state of affairs, the payment to an auditor is not contingent on the auditor's opinion (report). Hence, auditors are likely to expend just enough effort to secure the low detection probability of $\pi_{A\ell}$. At first glance, it seems that the new monitoring mechanism, the Public Company Accounting Oversight Board (PCAOB), which audits the auditors and has enforcement abilities, might ensure a higher probability, π_{Ah}. Since it can test whether procedures conformed to some minimum standard, however, it cannot induce higher π_A when the interim findings call for the kind of initiatives not covered by the PCAOB's checklist. Furthermore, after the Sarbanes-Oxley Act, clients are reluctant to share information about earnings management attempts to their auditors in light of the requirement that auditors report their findings to the audit committee in great detail.

When the firm has incentives to appear to have a good project, a B report is credible. The stock price then is B, $P(B)=B$, justified by the belief that the audit was successful. A report of G triggers a price $P(G(\pi_{A\ell}))$, which is

$$P(G(\pi_{A\ell})) = \delta_\ell G+(1-\delta_\ell)B, \qquad (6.12)$$

where

$$\delta_\ell = \frac{\gamma}{\gamma + (1-\pi_{A\ell})(1-\gamma)}.$$

When auditors are employed by insurance companies, their allegiance shifts to the insurance company. Clearly, any benefit from collusion with one client at the expense of the insurance company is outweighed by the loss of business once the insurance company severs its ties to the auditor. Thus, if the net present value of future profits exceeds C, auditors exert more effort. The audit detection probability then is π_{Ah}. This in itself improves the situation because more cases are reported as B, the increase in frequency of such reports is $(1-\gamma)(\pi_{Ah} - \pi_{A\ell})$, and the type-G firms' price better approximates their true value:

$$P(G(\pi_{Ah})) = \delta_h G + (1-\delta_h)B, \tag{6.13}$$

where

$$\delta_h = \frac{\gamma}{\gamma + (1 - \pi_{Ah})(1 - \gamma)}.$$

The managers: Consider the incentives of management. If the project's value is G, management prefers to disclose the truth to reduce the cost of capital and increases bonuses. On the other hand, if the project is B, earnings management yields a payoff of $\pi_{Ai}B + (1-\pi_{Ai})P(G(\pi_{Ai})) - C_M$, where C_M is the expected cost if the firm will not have future profitable projects to mask the poor one. When there is no insurance, the cost results from the fact that discovery of the truth triggers investors' lawsuits. With insurance, the cost is designed by the insurance company as part of the policy. The market learns the quality of the financial statements (such as the incidence of earnings management) from the disclosed premium, which serves as a credible signal. Thus, the cost imposed on management as a result of potential misrepresentation is both the premium and a lower expected stock price upon disclosure of a higher premium, if the insurer determines that there is a high probability of pernicious earnings management.

The decision to manage earnings depends on whether the payoff from managing earnings, $\pi_{Ai}B + (1-\pi_{Ai})P(G(\pi_{Ai})) - C_M$, is larger than the payoff upon truth-telling, B. Since we made scant assumptions on the model's parameters, there are three possible cases:

(1) $\pi_{Ai}B + (1-\pi_{Ai})P(G(\pi_{Ai})) - C_M > B$, $i=h,\ell$.

(2) $\pi_{A\ell}B + (1-\pi_{A\ell})P(G(\pi_{A\ell})) - C_M > B > \pi_{Ah}B + (1-\pi_{Ah})P(G(\pi_{Ah})) - C_M$.

(3) $B > \pi_{Ai}B + (1-\pi_{Ai})P(G(\pi_{Ai})) - C_M$, $i=h,\ell$.

Note that the comparison can be streamlined into whether $(1-\pi_{Ai})[P(G(\pi_{Ai}))- B] - C_M$ is negative or positive.

Case (1) occurs when earnings management dominates truth-telling regardless of the audit's accuracy. This case, however, cannot be an equilibrium since the insurance company can increase the cost of the policy to such a level that the firm does not purchase a policy at all and chases investors away or it takes additional steps to reduce its perceived audit risks. Case (2) occurs when the improvement in detecting the truth by having auditors be hired by insurance companies deters earnings management that takes place under the existing regime. This case is the most interesting, as it shows how the insurance scheme eliminates earnings management. Case (3) occurs when truth-telling dominates earnings management. Although we cannot rule out that this is true for some managers, the avalanche of restatements and blatant earnings management fraud indicate that this case is not realistic.

Appendix: The Disclosure Principle

The dynamic that drives the disclosure principle is that when the receiver is aware that the sender is in possession of relevant information, he expects a message from the sender. Non-disclosure is construed as bad news (Grossman, 1981; Milgrom and Roberts, 1986; Darrough and Stoughton, 1990; Wagenhofer, 1990; Ronen and Yaari, 2002; Shin, 2006).

To see the receiver's expectations, consider the following example. The firm's value is a random variable. That is, firm i's value is V_i, $V_i = \alpha$, where α is distributed uniformly on the interval $[0,1]$. The higher the value of α, the better the firm's news. The firm makes a disclosure if the stock price upon disclosure exceeds its price upon omission. Thus, if there is a cutoff value, say α^C, at which the firm is indifferent between disclosure and omission, then all firms whose value exceeds α^C will certainly prefer disclosure, and all firms whose value is lower than α^C will strictly prefer omission. Under full disclosure, α^C is set to the minimum α, $\alpha^C = 0$. That is, there is no positive cutoff α^C.

Suppose, by contradiction, that some positive α is the cutoff equilibrium, $\alpha^C > 0$. The market then assumes that non-disclosing firms' values lie in the $[0, \alpha^C]$ range. The average value of a non-discloser is $(\alpha^C + 0)/2 = \alpha^C/2$.[18] This creates incentives for firms whose value exceeds $\alpha^C/2$, $\alpha^C \geq V_i > \alpha^C/2$, to separate themselves from non-disclosers. Hence, the interval $[0, \alpha^C]$ of non-disclosure shrinks to $[0, \alpha^C/2]$. If the market now figures that all firms with news in this interval do not make a disclosure, it assumes that the expected value of a non-discloser is $\alpha^C/4$, so that

---

[18] Since α is distributed uniformly, the density function of α conditional on non-discloser is $\dfrac{1}{\displaystyle\int_{0 \leq \alpha \leq \alpha^C} 1\, dx} = \dfrac{1}{\alpha^C}$. Hence, $\mathrm{E}(\alpha \,|\mathrm{ommission}) = \displaystyle\int_{0 \leq \alpha \leq \alpha^C} x\, \dfrac{1}{\alpha^C}\, dx$.

all firms with news higher than $\alpha^C/4$ will have incentives to disclose, and so on. This dynamic ends when $\alpha^C=0$, that is, all firms prefer disclosure.[19]

To see Dye's (1985a) result that firms with bad news pool with firms without news,[20] suppose that β firms are ignorant. The critical α^C is determined at the level where a firm that is type α^C is indifferent between revealing its type and being evaluated as α^C and withholding information and pooling with ignorant firms. Denoting non-disclosure as $\varnothing$,

$$E[V_i \,|\, \varnothing] = \frac{\beta}{\beta + (1-\beta)\alpha^C} \times \frac{1}{2} + \frac{(1-\beta)\alpha^C}{\beta + (1-\beta)\alpha^C} \times \frac{\alpha^C}{2} = \alpha^C. \qquad (6.14)$$

Rearranging yields a quadratic equation in α^C: $(1-\beta)(\alpha^C)^2 + 2\beta\alpha^C - \beta = 0$. Solve for α^C, noting that the solution must be nonnegative because α^C is nonnegative:

$$\alpha^C = \frac{-\beta + \sqrt{\beta^2 + \beta(1-\beta)}}{1-\beta} = \frac{-\beta + \sqrt{\beta}}{1-\beta} = \sqrt{\beta}\,\frac{1-\sqrt{\beta}}{(1+\sqrt{\beta})(1-\sqrt{\beta})} =$$
$$\frac{\sqrt{\beta}}{(1+\sqrt{\beta})}. \qquad (6.15)$$

---

[19] We are grateful to Amir Ziv for valuable discussions of this sender–receiver game.

[20] Dye's argument is based on the assumption that ignorant firms cannot separate themselves from firms with bad news. When firms reveal their ignorance, the full-disclosure equilibrium is restored (Feng, 2004).

7 Smoothing

Earlier in the decade and during prior decades, earnings management was more a game of "smoothing out" the peaks and valleys in a corporation's income flow in order to reduce the apparent volatility in the corporation's returns. Thus, managements characteristically attempted to hide "excess earnings" in "rainy day reserves" in order to use such funds later to smooth out undesired declines in the firm's earnings. (Coffee, 2003a, pp. 22–23)

An earnings management strategy that has survived the test of time is smoothing (Buckmaster, 2001).[1] Smoothing is the dampening of fluctuations in the series of reported earnings. There are two types of smoothing: real and artificial. Real smoothing involves making production and investment decisions that reduce the variability of earnings. Artificial or cosmetic smoothing is achieved through accounting choices (see Chap. 2).

---

[1] Smoothing has been studied extensively. For a survey of research before 1980, consult Ronen, Sadan, and Snow (1977); Ronen and Sadan (1981). An incomplete list of later studies includes the following: Belkaoui and Picur (1984), Moses (1987), Greenawalt and Sinkey (1988), Brayshaw and Eldin (1989); Craig and Walsh (1989), Hand (1989), Albrecht and Richardson (1990), Bartov (1993), Ashari, Koh, Tan, and Wong (1994), Beattie, Brown, Ewers, John, Manson, Thomas, and Turner (1994), Fern, Brown, and Dickey (1994), Sheikholeslami (1994), Wang and Williams (1994), Michelson, Jordan-Wagner, and Wootton (1995), Bhat (1996), Bitner and Dolan (1996), Booth, Kallunki, and Martikainen (1996), Hunt, Moyer, and Shevlin (1996), Saudagaran and Sepe (1996), Subramanyam (1996), Carlson and Bathala (1997), DeFond and Park (1997), Chaney and Lewis (1998), Chaney, Coleman, and Lewis (1998), Oyer (1998), Barth, Elliott and Finn (1999), Godfrey and Jones (1999), Barth, Elliott, and Finn (1999), Hallock and Oyer (1999), Hwang and Ryan (2000), Payne and Robb (2000), Barton (2001), Gul, Leung, and Srinidhi (2002), Zarowin (2002), Elgers, Pfeiffer, and Porter (2003), Wan-Hussin Nordin and Ripain (2003), Kanagaretnam, Lobo, and Yang (2004), Cheng and Warfield (2005), Abdel-Khalik (2006), Myers, Myers, and Skinner (2006), Tan and Jamal (2006), Tucker and Zarowin (2006), and Grant, Markarian, and Parbonetti (2007). See Buckmaster (2001).

There are a number of differences between the two types. First, because earnings are a random variable that depends on past production and investment decisions, real smoothing is likely to precede artificial smoothing. Second, real smoothing involves decisions that reduce the volatility of economic earnings. In contrast, artificial smoothing involves both overstatement and understatement of economic earnings: It overstates low earnings and understates high earnings. In that way, the series of reported earnings has the same average as the series of economic incomes, but with lower variability. Figure 1 depicts artificial smoothing.

The reported earnings (M_t) are closer to the long-term average earnings line than the unmanaged earnings (X_t)—earnings that would have been publicized had the reporting strategy been neutral.

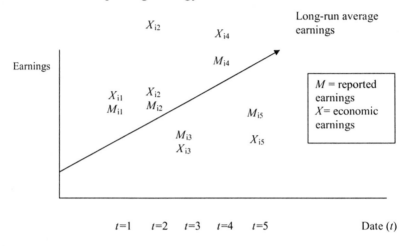

Fig. 7.1 Artificial smoothing

Smoothing can also be pernicious, in that reported earnings are made to be close to an earnings trend line that differs from what management truly believes it to be. To the extent that smoothing is pernicious, the Sarbanes-Oxley Act (SOX) is likely to affect the relative occurrence of real and artificial smoothing. Intuitively, accruals management seems more appealing than real smoothing because it does not reduce the firm's value as much. On the other hand, real smoothing has the added benefit that it is less *transparent* and thus much harder to detect and deter (Ewert and Wagenhofer, 2005).

In this chapter, we describe the motivation to smooth along the four dimensions of capital markets, governance, competition, and regulations. The capital-market-oriented motivation centers on the informational value of smoothing and the demand for consumption smoothing. The governance motivation centers on the smoothing incentives of an agent in multi-period principal–agent relationships. Competition has received no attention in the literature, so we develop a signaling example. The regulation-based motivation centers on taxation. Finally, we explain how reform in the market for auditors can enhance beneficial smoothing and deter pernicious smoothing.

7.1 Capital Markets

The capital-market incentives for smoothing can be divided into two categories. The first concerns the stock market; the second concerns the banking system, which allows individuals to borrow and save funds in order to finance private consumption.

7.1.1 The Stock Market

The first question to be addressed is whether smoothing affects valuation. Practitioners seem to think that it does. Graham, Harvey, and Rajgopal (2005), surveyed chief financial officers (and officers with similar financial reporting tasks but different titles, such as controllers, vice presidents, etc.). They report that 96.9% of their respondents preferred a smooth earnings path. When asked to explain why smoothing is preferable, the respondents gave the following explanations (see their table 8, panel A). Some support beneficial smoothing, and others support pernicious smoothing (Table 7.1).

Table 7.1 The response to the question on preference for smoothing

	Question: A smooth earnings path is preferred because it ...	Agree or strongly agree%
(1)	is perceived as less risky by investors	88.7
(2)	makes it easier for analysts and investors to predict future earnings	79.7
(3)	assures customers and suppliers that business is stable	66.2
(4)	reduces the return that investors demand	57.1
(5)	promotes a reputation for transparent and accurate reporting	46.5
(6)	conveys higher future growth prospects	46.3
(7)	achieves or preserves a desired credit rating	42.2
(8)	clarifies true economic performance	24.3
(9)	increases bonus payments	15.6

7.1.1.1 *Beneficial Smoothing*

By our definition of earnings management in Chap. 2, smoothing is beneficial when it conveys valuable information on future results. As Ronen and Sadan (1981) Chapter 3, Suh (1990); Sankar and Subramanyam (2001) have noted, smoothing can be beneficial by reducing distortions in market prices. To illustrate, suppose that the firm lasts two more periods. At the beginning of the first period, its books value is $10,000. By the end of the first period, it generates profits of $50,000. It is known that the second-period earnings are either $140,000 or zero with equal probabilities. The firm alone learns the true second-period earnings before it reports the first-period financials. Suppose that the second-period earnings are $140,000. The valuation of a firm that reports the truth is $130,000, which is the total of its first-period book value, $10,000, the first-period reported earnings of $50,000, and the expected second-period report (=½ x 140,000 + ½ x 0). Since the second-period outcome is $140,000, this firm's value is $200,000, so its value is underestimated by $70,000. In contrast, a firm which smooths the first-period report by reporting half of its total reported earnings at the end of the first period, $95,000 (=½ x ($50,000 + $140,000)), is correctly valued at $200,000 (=10,000 + 95,000 x 2). Smoothing, then, improves the information content of its reports.[2]

In our example, smoothing is accomplished by reporting the average earnings, which reduces the variability of reported earnings to zero. Yet any first-period report between $50,000 and $95,000 dollars would reduce the variability of earnings! This raises a question regarding the optimal degree of smoothing.

Chaney and Lewis (1995), and John, John, and Ronen (1996), provide answers that rely on the costliness of signaling value through smoothing. Chaney and Lewis analyze a two-period reporting model with two types of firms: high value, h, and low value, ℓ, $h > \ell$, where the market cannot distinguish between the two. Since the first-period managed earnings must reverse in the second period, the reports of the two types in each period are as follows:

---

[2] Under uncertainty, beneficial smoothing can backfire when management's expectations are not realistic. In that case, smoothing increases the prediction error of the value of the firm (Hoogendoorn, 1985). To illustrate, suppose that the managers of both firms in our example erroneously assume that the second-period cash flows will be zero. Hence, to smooth, the firm reports $25,000 ((50,000+0)/2). The market's valuation now is $60,000, which underestimates the firm by $140,000, in contrast to the valuation of the truth-telling firm, $130,000, which is only $70,000 short.

$$\tilde{R}_{j1} = \tilde{X}_{j1} + \gamma_j (\mu_j - \tilde{X}_{j1}) + \delta_j, \qquad j = h, \ell. \qquad (7.1)$$

$$\tilde{R}_{j2} = \tilde{X}_{21} - \gamma_j (\mu_j - \tilde{X}_{j1}) - \delta_j, \qquad j = h, \ell.$$

$\tilde{R}_{jt}$ is the report of a type j, $j = h$, ℓ, in period t, $t = 1, 2$; $\tilde{X}_{jt}$ is the economic earnings, generated by a mean-reverting process, $\tilde{X}_{jt} = \mu_j + \varepsilon_j$, μ_j are the means, and ε_j are white noise terms with known variance. The reporting strategy is made up of two variables, the first-period smoothing variable, $\gamma_j, 0 < \gamma_j < 1$, and the first-period bias variable, δ_j.

Clearly, if the market cannot distinguish between the two types, it understates the value of a type-h firm and overestimates the value of a type-ℓ firm. The type-h firm therefore has incentives to choose a report that separates it from the type-ℓ. Chaney and Lewis prove that in a separating equilibrium, type-ℓ firms report the truth, and the type-h firms combine smoothing with a positive bias that is costly because it increases taxes. Although this study calculates the optimal bias in the first period, clearly, there are many profiles of γ and δ that yield the same report. The equilibrium therefore is not unique.

In John, John, and Ronen (1996), smoothing results from signaling value to investors because of the tax implication of reporting profits earlier. The point is that a signal is valuable only if it is costly enough to deter low-value firms from mimicking high-value firms. Taxation provides such a signal, where shifting taxable income to an earlier period causes the series of reported numbers to exhibit a smoother path than the series of economic earnings. To illustrate, consider a market with two types of firms, high value, which gross $450,000 during their life, and low value, which gross zero. The tax rate is 30%, and the marginal borrowing rate (which affects the cost of cash paid as taxes) is 10%. In the absence of incentives to use tax payments to signal, deferring tax payments is preferable. Suppose that both types accumulated losses of $100,000 and in this year earn $100,000. The high-value firm anticipates earning another $200,000 next year and $250,000 in the following year. The low-value firm anticipates zero earnings in the next 2 years. In a signaling equilibrium, the low-value firm nets the accumulated losses against the net gain and pays nothing, saving $3,000,[3] while a high-value firm reports $150,000 each year and pays the tax. That is, instead of reporting earnings of $100,000 in year 1, $200,000 in year 2, and $250,000 in year 3, the high-value firm reports $150,000 in each year, producing a smoother series

---

[3] 10% of $30,000 avoidable taxes.

of reported earnings. It is, however, highly likely that the firm shies away from perfect smoothing because it wishes to minimize the signaling costs, which in turn dictate the reported earnings. The exact earnings reported in the first period are set at a level that deters low-value firms from pooling with high-value firms. The difference between this study and that of Chaney and Lewis is that the equilibrium here is unique because the reporting strategy comprises one variable only.

As a final comment, note that when we calculated the smoothed reported earnings, we aggregated the earnings of three periods and divided by three. That is, smoothing requires an intertemporal aggregation. The importance of aggregation in accounting has long been noted (Sunder, 1997). Hence, our discussion indirectly also touches on the issue of when aggregation provides more information and when it obscures the truth (see Indjejikian and Nanda, 1999; Christensen, Demski, and Frimor, 2002; Arya, Glover, and Liang, 2004; and Feltham, Indjejikian, and Nanda, 2006).

7.1.1.2 Neutral Smoothing

Earnings management is neutral when it has no effect on cash flows. In this section, we explore settings in which firms smooth but the market sees through the smoothing.

Goel and Thakor (2003), describe neutral smoothing. They analyze a stylized rational expectations equilibrium. The firm's shareholders are principally uninformed traders, who, for liquidity reasons, must sell their shares after the publication of the accounting reports. They sell to informed traders, who acquire costly value-relevant information that can neither be communicated by the firm nor publicly observed without cost. The informed traders recoup the cost of the signal by trading with the uninformed traders, and the higher the variance of the firm's income, the greater the informed traders' profits and the higher the incumbent shareholders' losses. Hence, a firm's stock price is negatively correlated with its volatility. This provides the firm with incentives to smooth to reduce volatility. There are four possibilities along two dimensions: the firm smooths or does not smooth, and the market expects or does not expect smoothing. Clearly, in equilibrium, either the firm smooths and the market correctly expects it to smooth, or the firm does not smooth and the market does not expect it to do so. The latter profile cannot be an equilibrium because if the market does not expect the smoothing, the firm can increase its price by reducing the volatility of the series of reported earnings. Hence, the only equilibrium profile is the former: (a) the firm smooths and (b) the market expects it to smooth.

Smoothing is neutral because the market undoes the smoothed report to learn the truth. In other words, the payoffs to all players is the same as the payoffs had the firm reported the truth and the market believed the report. The reason that truth-telling equilibrium is not feasible is that the dynamics are those of the "signal-jamming" equilibrium in sender–receiver games: If a deviant firm (the signal's sender) does not smooth, it is punished because the ignorant market (the receiver) evaluates its income stream at a lower price to "correct" for smoothing. (These dynamics also drive Dye, 1988, discussed in Chap. 8; Stein, 1988; and Elitzur, 1995, discussed in Chap. 2).

Another study with neutral smoothing is Elitzur and Yaari (1995). The authors analyze multi-period decision making by a manager who times accounting accruals and his trading strategy in the firm's shares during his tenure with the firm (his compensation package comprises a base salary, a bonus based on accounting earnings, and stock). Lifetime consumption considerations yield a smoothed series of reports. Smoothing is neutral if the market is perfectly rational with sufficient information to know the truth.[4]

7.1.1.3 Pernicious Smoothing

Firms may have incentives to smooth without signaling management's true expectations of future earnings[5] because they perceive that a lower variance in the series of reported earnings affects valuation favorably. (For an empirical documentation of the link between variance and the valuations based on reported accounting earnings, see, e.g., Bitner and Dolan, 1996; Hunt, Moyer, and Shevlin, 1996; Subramanyam, 1996; Hann, Lu, and Subramanyam, 2007.) The question is under what circumstances a firm can perniciously smooth in a rational market.

Pernicious smoothing can occur if the market lacks sufficient information (see the discussion in Elitzur and Yaari, 1995). It involves pooling equilibria in signaling games, where pernicious smoothers mimic firms with a genuinely smoother earnings series. Trueman and Titman (1988), analyze the case in which firms take a loan. Because of the risk of bankruptcy, debt-holders require a higher rate of return for firms with more variable income. The fact that some firms cannot smooth gives sufficient

---

[4] Smoothing is not innocuous when the market is unable to filter the noise in the report to learn the truth.

[5] For empirical investigations that show that when opportunities for earnings management present themselves, earnings management is more likely to take place, see Part 2.

credibility to the smoothed reports of firms that can to make it worthwhile to smooth. As Newman (1988), and others argue, it is not clear why firms with stable earnings will not take measures to distinguish themselves from those that try to pool with them to reduce their cost of capital.

Pernicious smoothing can survive in a rational market in part because firms may smooth only conditionally upon good news. Kirschenheiter and Melumad (2000), and Yaari (2005), provide a rationale for inconsistent smoothing. To see the logic, consider the following simple example. The value of the firm is a random variable, V; that is,

$$V= \mu + \varepsilon_v, \tag{7.2}$$

where ε is white noise, $E(\varepsilon_v) = 0$, and $\mathrm{Var}(\varepsilon_v) =1/h$.

The firm's long-run economic value is μ. Investors learn the reported earnings y, which are a noisy and unbiased signal on V, $y=V+\varepsilon_y$, $E(\varepsilon_y) =0$ and $\mathrm{Var}(\varepsilon_y) =1/g$. The reported earnings, y, are an unbiased estimate of the economic earnings.

Suppose that V and y belong to conjugate family distribution functions where the posterior mean is a linear function of the prior mean and the signal (as is the case when all variables are normal). Then,

$$E\left(V|y\right) = \frac{h}{h+g}\mu + \frac{g}{h+g} y = \mu + \frac{g}{h+g}(y-\mu). \tag{7.3}$$

Management's objective function is to increase the valuation of the firm, $E(V|y)$, given that investors do not know g. Since it has discretion over the precision of reported earnings, g, its strategy is to set g is as high as possible (i.e., $g/(h+g)\rightarrow 1$, and overstate the report when the accounting earnings covey good news, $y > \mu$). This strategy smooths out the variability of the report relative to the true earnings. When the news is bad, $y > \mu$, Kirschenheiter and Melumad, show that, under certain conditions, the firm prefers "taking a bath." This strategy takes the edge off from setting the precision g to be very high and is inconsistent with smoothing out the reported earnings.

Yaari (2005), shows that when firms wish to beat a target in future periods, the firm hoards reserves of reported earnings to beat the target. When current earnings are high, the firm understates earnings, which is consistent with smoothing. However, when, earnings are low, the understatement of earnings increases earnings variability (the opposite of smoothing).

7.1.2 The Banking System

Consumption smoothing can motivate smoothing of reports[6] (e.g., Monsen and Downs, 1965; Dye, 1988; Suh, 1990; Christensen and Feltham, 1993;[7] Sivaramakrishnan, 1994; Boylan and Villadsen, 1998; Haas, 2000; Sankar and Subramanyam, 2001; Srinidhi, Ronen, and Maindiratta, 2001). See the Appendix for a rigorous presentation of this type of smoothing.

To illustrate the argument, assume that the firm lasts two periods, stochastically generating earnings of x_t, $t=1,2$, in each period.[8] Because economic earnings are unobservable, the manager's compensation in period t, S_t, is based on the accounting report, m_t:

$$S_1 = S(m_1), \quad S_2 = S(m_2). \tag{7.4}$$

The only restriction on reported earnings, m, is that in the long run they equal the truth; that is, given the firm's internal rate of discount, r,

$$(1+r)m_1 + m_2 = y, \tag{7.5}$$

where

$$y = (1+r)x_1 + x_2. \tag{7.6}$$

Suppose that the manager alone has perfect knowledge of the second-period earnings, x_2, when the firm issues the first-period report, m_1. The decision on m_1 affects the timing of the recognition of the firm's value, y, between the two periods, because once m_1 is disclosed, m_2 is determined: $m_2 = y - (1+r)m_1$.

If the manager's goal is to obtain a perfect consumption-smoothing path, $c_1 = c_2$, then if $S_1 = S_2$, perfect smoothing of the reports ensues, $(1+r)m_1 = m_2 = y/2$.

The argument that consumption smoothing yields smoothed reports is based on two assumptions: First, it is presumed that the capital market is imperfect, so smoothing the reports is the only vehicle to achieve consumption smoothing. If the capital market were perfect, the reporting strategy would maximize total compensation, and the manager would

---

[6] A different way to express the consumption-smoothing explanation is to model the agent's preferences as an indirect utility over the periodic income and then show that smoothing spreads risk across periods. These explanations are equivalent because of the duality between direct utility over consumption and indirect utility over income for a given vector of consumption good prices.

[7] Christensen and Feltham (1993), are concerned with the value of communication, not with earnings management per se.

[8] For studies that derive smoothing in an infinite horizon model, consult Boylan and Villadsen (1998), and Srinidhi, Ronen, and Maindiratta (2001).

achieve his optimal consumption path through transactions in the capital market.

Second, the argument assumes away the hoarding of compensation, which might affect the reporting strategy (Yaari, 1991). In other words, what prevents the manager from reporting y and earning $S(y)$ in the first period and zero in the second period, and dividing consumption between the two periods by hoarding a portion of $S(y)$ in the first period? Hoarding is optimal if the compensation is a sufficiently convex function of the report.

To see this point, suppose the manager can save unconsumed compensation. The manager has a constant relative risk-aversion utility function, $U(z) = Z^{1/2}$, and his compensation contract is a piecewise schedule, if $x_t > \mu$, $S_t = (x_t - \mu)^2$, and , if $x_t \leq \mu$, $S_t = 0$, $t = 1,2$, where μ is mean earnings.[9] Let $\mu = 100$, $r = 0$, $x_1 = 200$, and $x_2 = 400$. If the manager smooths by reporting 300 in each period, he enjoys utility over consumption of 200 in each period. If he reports 600 in the first period and zero in the second, he can obtain total compensation of 250,000; dividing consumption between the periods yields him utility of 353.55 in each.

This argument illustrates that smoothing can occur in perfect markets as well if the compensation is sufficiently concave (Dye, 1988; Yaari, 1993; Sivaramakrishnan, 1994; Demski, 1998) because in such cases the marginal dollar compensation decreases in the reported earnings. Total compensation is maximized by shifting reported outcome from the period with the low marginal compensation to the period with the high marginal compensation, until $S_1'(m_1) = S_2'(m_2)$. This yields a smoothed series of accounting reports, $m_1 = m_2$. In contrast, if the compensation is a linear function with the same marginal rewards in each period, earnings management does not take place in a perfect capital market regime (Liang, 2004).

Realistically, capital markets are not perfect. As Stiglitz (1969), and others notice, the capital market allows access to individuals, but it discriminates between individuals and firms, because the latter are considered to be more profitable clients. Yaari (1993), explores this fact in a study in which a firm's owners design the contract and the reporting strategy. The owners solve the following program:

$$\max \ EV\left(m_1 - S_1\left(m_1\right)\right) + \left(1 + \rho^O\right)^{-1} EV\left(m_2 - S_2\left(m_2\right)\right)$$

s.t.

$$EU\left(c_1\right) + (1 + \rho^M)^{-1} EU\left(S_2\left(m_2\right) + (1+i)^{-1}\left(S_1\left(m_1\right) - c_1\right)\right) \geq U_0, \quad \text{(IR)}$$

---

[9] For a derivation of such a contract in a one-shot game, consult Christensen and Feltham (2005, chapter. 16).

where $m_2 = y - (1 + r)m_1$, ρ^O and ρ^M are the discount factors of the owners and the manager, respectively, and i is the manager's cost of capital.

The owners maximize expected utility (V) over the stream of reported earnings $m_t - S_t(m_t)$, subject to the constraint that the contract guarantees the manager his reservation utility level, U_0. The second-period consumption is determined by the budget constraint, $c_2 = S_2(m_2) + (1+i)^{-1}(S_1(m_1) - c_1)$. The manager's cost of capital, i, is different from the firm's cost of capital, r. When the manager borrows, his interest payment is higher, $r < i$, and when the manager saves, his interest is lower, $r > i$.

Denote the Lagrange multiplier of (IR) by λ. The equilibrium contract satisfies the pointwise optimality condition:

$$S_1: \quad \frac{V'}{U'} = \hat{\lambda},$$

$$S_2: \quad \frac{V'}{U'} = \hat{\lambda}(1+\rho^O)^{-1}(1+i),$$

where $\hat{\lambda} = \lambda(1+\rho^M)^{-1}(1+i)^{-1}$.

The contract has two components: an optimal risk-sharing element, captured by $\frac{V'}{U'} = \lambda$, and a financial component that reflects the term rates and the discount factors of the two players, captured by $(1+\rho^M)^{-1}(1+i)^{-1}(1+\rho^O)^{-1}(1+i)$. Yaari shows that smoothing is no longer uniform across firms. Compared to the perfect smoothing that produces a series of reported earnings with zero variability, some firms smooth with an upward bias, while others smooth with a downward bias. These results settle the issue of the multiplicity of possible smoothed reports discussed above. That is, smoothing is a family of reporting strategies. Firm-specific characteristics determine the particular smoothing path chosen by a firm.

Yaari (1993), does not capture the reality before the Sarbanes-Oxley Act of 2002 (SOX) because some managers then borrowed funds from the firm that they managed at rates that were even superior to the borrowing rates of the firm from which they took the loan (Nofsinger and Kim, 2003). For example, Mattel Corp. gave a loan of $7.2 million to the CEO, Jill Barad; when she was ousted, the loan was absolved, and the company agreed to pay an addition $3.3 million to cover the cost of incremental taxes that arose from absolving the loan. Section 402(a) of SOX prohibits such personal loans. Public companies are not permitted "directly or indirectly,...

to extend or maintain credit, to arrange for an extension of credit, or renew an extension of credit, in the form of personal loan to or for any director or executive officer (or equivalent thereof) of that issuer." We conjecture that section 402(a) would increase the motivation to manage earnings to achieve consumption smoothing.

7.2 Governance

The relationships between smoothing and governance are captured by the principal–agent relationships between owners and managers. Owners face the challenge of designing a mechanism—a compensation contract—that induces the manager to make the "right decisions."

A clue regarding the effect of moral hazard on smoothing is provided by the finite-horizon principal–agent literature, which documents that the current-period compensation must be conditioned on the history of outcomes (Lambert, 1983; Rogerson, 1985a; Christensen and Feltham, 1993, 2005). If the agent has the option to choose the timing of the report that is the basis of the contract, he is likely to smooth the stream of reports when the total of the reported numbers and the sum of the outcomes are equal. The question is whether the owners allow it. Allen (1985b), proves that a long-term contract dominates a series of short-term contracts because it allows intertemporal risk-sharing and provides additional information. This result suggests that smoothing is likely to be desirable to the principal. On the other extreme, in the perfect capital market framework of Holmström and Milgrom (1987), for example, there is no difference between a contract that pays the manager periodically and a contract that pays the agent just once at the end of the contract's period; in such a framework, artificial smoothing is valueless, since the timing of reported earnings is unimportant.[10]

Admitting the manager's actions into the analysis leads to dividing our discussion between real smoothing—actions that produce smoother accounting reports—and artificial smoothing—smoothing merely the series of reported outcomes.

---

[10] Additional studies that have dealt with a multi-period contract versus a series of short-term contracts include Townsend (1982), Fellingham, Newman, and Suh (1985), Fudenberg, Holmström, and Milgrom (1990), and Spear and Srivastava (1987), Malcomson and Spinnewyn (1988).

7.2.1 Real Smoothing

Real smoothing involves production and investment decisions. Oyer (1998), who studies smoothing by salespeople, explains how it is done:

> Consider a company that sells parts to car manufacturers. Car manufacturers are concerned with inventory costs and want to avoid buying materials they never use. Also, they are likely to purchase parts at a contracted price, so threats of future price increases are not an effective way to rush orders. Now consider a company selling complex and expensive computer systems to corporations. The salesperson may be in a position to share or hide information about price and technology changes. Similarly, the executives of the computer company can share or hide information from the public and sometimes even from the salesperson. In this way, unlike agents at the parts company, the computer salesperson and the executives for whom he works can influence the date a computer is purchased and shipped. The computer salesperson has more opportunity to attain quota in current and future years, while computer executives can move sales to the year where they have the most impact on their own compensation.
>
> This timing influence, which I will call "timing gaming," can take two forms. The salesperson can "pull in" potential business from the next fiscal year to make quota this year, or the salesperson, knowing he has achieved quota or giving up for the current year, can "push out" business to the next year. Without knowing salesperson turnover rates and the form of the sales distribution, it is not possible to determine for sure whether the pull-in or push-out effect dominates. (p. 156)

Although the literature on the finite-horizon repeated principal–agent game had detected intertemporal links in the choice of actions (Lambert, 1983; Rogerson, 1985a), the first study that analyzes the connection between moral hazard and real smoothing is that of Lambert (1984).

To illustrate, consider a two-period principal–agent game in which the manager takes unobservable actions at the beginning of each period that, together with nature, determine the economic earnings. The utility function of the risk-averse, work-averse manager is separable in monetary reward, S, and effort, e; that is, $U(S,e)=U(S)-W(e)$, where U is a Von Neumann–Morgenstern (VNM) utility function with risk aversion, $U'> 0$, $U''<0$, and W is a strictly increasing, strictly convex function of effort, e, $W'> 0$, $W''>0$. The outcomes in each period, x_i, are independent variables drawn from continuous distribution functions, with certain characteristics, $f(x \mid e)$. The manager's expected payoff in period 2 is

$$\int U\big(S(x_1,x_2)\big)f\big(x_2 \mid e_2\big)\,\mathrm{d}x_2 - W\big(e_2\big).$$

The manager's actions at the beginning of the second period satisfy

$$\int U(S(x_1,x_2))f_{e_2}(x_2|e_2)\mathrm{d}x_2 - W'(e_2) = 0. \qquad (7.7)$$

$f_{e_2}(x_2|e_2)$ is the derivative of the distribution function of outcome, x_2, with respect to the second-period effort.

Note that the compensation, S, depends on the history of outcomes, x_1 and x_2. The manager exerts effort at a level that equates the expected marginal utility over compensation to the marginal cost of expending effort.

From Eq. 7.7, we obtain

$$\frac{\mathrm{d}e_2}{\mathrm{d}x_1} < 0. \qquad (7.8)$$

The higher the first-period outcome, the smaller the effort expended by the manager in the second period. The intuition: a higher first-period outcome gets the agent a higher monetary reward. Since the marginal utility decreases with monetary compensation, the marginal benefit from expending more effort decreases. At the same time, because the marginal cost of effort increases with effort, the marginal cost of effort decreases as less effort is expended.

This dynamic introduces a negative correlation between the first- and second-period outcomes, even though the underlying stochastic variables are independent. Consequently, the variability of the total outcome is reduced. That is,

$$\mathrm{var}(y)=(1+r)^2\mathrm{var}(x_1)+\mathrm{var}(x_2)+2(1+r)\mathrm{cov}(x_1,x_2) \qquad (7.9)$$

$$< (1+r)^2\mathrm{var}(x_1)+\mathrm{var}(x_2).$$

The question that is yet to be answered is whether real smoothing and artificial smoothing are complements or substitutes.

Effort is shorthand for the unobservable actions of the manager. To the best of our knowledge, Gavious, Ronen, and Yaari (2002), are the first to link effort to investment and hence to the firm's valuation.[11] We analyze a model in which effort affects the growth rate of economic earnings, which

---

[11] Narayanan (1996), examines the optimal compensation of a manager with unknown ability who has the discretion of choosing between a long-term and a short-term investment. He shows that a combination of cash flows and restricted stock is required to ensure that the choice maximizes shareholders' value, given that the manager is compensated on perceived ability alone (based on the cash-flow signal), while the market price depends on both the investment and the manager's actual ability.

in turn affects valuation, since growth rate is a parameter in the firm's valuation model.[12]

Our model builds on the standard valuation model. The firm generates periodic earnings, x_t, as a function of the permanent earnings generated in that period, x_t^P,

$$x_t = x_t^P + \varepsilon_t, \tag{7.10}$$

where ε_t is white noise. The growth in permanent earnings is determined by the investment in excess of replacement capital, I_t, which, in turn, is determined by the manager's choice of effort, e_t, and nature, $I_t \sim N(n_t e_t, \sigma_g^2)$, where n_t is a firm- or industry-specific parameter.[13] The uncertainty in net investment captures the potential divergence between planned investment—the effort expending stage—and the ex post actual investment, which depends on factors beyond the manager's control. Denote the rate of return on an incremental investment by r, $0 < r < 1$. The net investment in the $(t\text{-}1)$th period, I_{t-1}, increases future permanent earnings, x_t^P, by rI_{t-1}. The manager's choice of effort thus affects the growth rate in permanent earnings, g_t, defined as

$$g_t = \frac{x_t^P - x_{t-1}^P}{x_{t-1}^P} = \frac{r\, I_{t-1}}{x_{t-1}^P}. \tag{7.11}$$

If owners are decision makers who make the investment decision (a first-best scenario), they prefer the early investment to be as high as possible to accumulate its benefits. If the manager makes the decision as a steward of owners (a second-best scenario), he might postpone the investment decision to defer the utility sacrificed in making the investment. The consequence is that the path of the expected growth rate is strictly concave in the first-best and strictly convex in the second-best scenario.

---

[12] An empirical investigation into the link between investment and earnings management is given by McNichols and Stubben (2005). They find overinvestment with earnings management and underinvestment following the period in which misreporting occurred.

[13] Effort affects the mean, and not the variance, in order to ensure that smoothing is not driven trivially by the risk-averse manager's reluctance to bear risk, as measured by variance. For analytical one-shot studies that allow effort to affect the variance of a performance measure, see Meth (1996), and Demski and Dye (1999).

An additional study that links earnings management to growth is Jevons Lee, Li, and Yue (2006). They show that when the firm manages earnings to affect valuation, the intensity of earnings management increases in earnings and decreases in growth.

7.2.2 Artificial Smoothing

The analytical literature offers insights into the incidence of artificial smoothing in principal–agent relationships. The mechanics are similar to those presented in our discussion of smoothing under limited borrowing conditions (Penno, 1987; Sivaramakrishnan, 1994). When the agent knows current earnings and has an imperfect signal on future earnings, the agent smooths the first-period report around the future signal when he is restricted to communicating only the current period's outcome. Hence, although the current report is not truthful, it is forward-looking.

Fudenberg and Tirole (1995), examine the reporting strategy of an incumbent manager who is anxious to keep his job. The manager has to cope with the reality of information decay, which implies that being successful one period ago is less meaningful than being successful today. They prove that the agent smooths the report: If it is very good news, deflating it by deferring reporting to the future "saves" it from the information decay. If the information is bad news, inflating the report ensures continuous employment.[14]

One question that has plagued the principal–agent works on smoothing is whether it is beneficial or pernicious to the principal. Demski (1998), formulates conditions for each case. The harmful case is obvious, in that artificial smoothing reduces the quality of the accounting message in its role as a monitor of the agent's effort because it garbles the message. Even here, however, there are different shades of gray, as, in some instances, the principal (weakly) tolerates smoothing. The beneficial case obtains when the opportunity for smoothing arises only if the agent exerts the high, desired level of effort.[15] Arya, Glover, and Sunder (1998), prove

---

[14] The importance of future earnings, emphasized by this model, motivates the empirical tests in DeFond and Park (1997), Elgers, Pfeiffer, and Porter (2000), and Payne and Robb (2000). For recent corroboration of the theory, consult Ahmed, Lobo, and Zhou (2006).

[15] This issue applies to the single-period case as well. Verrecchia (1986), analyzes the one-shot principal-agent game in which the principal does not observe economic earnings but knows that the agent can acquire at a cost a signal that improves the financial reporting so that it coincides with the economic earnings. Verrecchia shows that the principal may prefer to allow the manager to manipu-

that smoothing can improve the welfare of a principal who cannot commit not to fire his manager in response to poor short-run performance. The threat of early termination of employment is costly because the requirement that the contract guarantee the agent his reservation utility level can only be met with a higher compensation cost. (This result depends on the parameters of the problem because earnings management is also costly; inflating the first-period report to cover up for poor performance delays the principal's ability to infer that the incumbent manager is inefficient and should have been replaced by a more efficient manager sooner.) Similar to Ronen and Sadan (1981), Suh (1990), and Sankar and Subramanyam (2001), show that the informativeness of smoothing is valuable, albeit costly, too. The former notes that the cost of smoothing is that earnings are a less informative signal on the agent's effort, and the latter observe that the cost arises from providing the privately informed, utility maximizing manager with more discretion over the choice of accounting treatment. Srinidhi, Ronen, and Maindiratta (2001), study the optimal reporting strategy of a manager who cannot access the capital market, but who can use his private knowledge of future outcomes to smooth his consumption stream in an infinite horizon model, through the smoothed stream of reports. They show that the manager smooths and that smoothing is a policy that satisfies the GAAP requirements of consistency, unbiasedness, and cash-flow convergence.

7.3 Product Market Competition

We are unaware of any published analytical study that explains the demand for smoothing in the context of the economics of the business and the product markets in which the firm operates, but the evidence is there. For example, smoothing is valuable to reassure suppliers and customers (Graham, Harvey, and Rajgopal, 2005, as cited above). Smoothing is also useful as part of a firm's business strategy to reduce risk. Barton (2001), who examines whether firms smooth earnings through accruals or through their financial derivatives, uses diversification as a control because "less diversified firms are more likely to use derivatives and manage accruals because they lack naturally smooth earnings and cash flows" (p. 13).

   To get a taste of the usefulness of smoothing for profit maximization, consider a vertical industry that includes two monopolies, an upstream, U, and a downstream, D. D purchases an intermediate product from U at a

---

late the report in order to obtain a better signal to monitor the agent's unobservable effort.

price $\tilde{P}_w$ and sells a finished good to customers for a price, $\tilde{P}$ (like the situation in Sect. 6.3). Each unit of the intermediate good is used to produce one unit of the finished good.

It is common knowledge that the inverse demand function is $\tilde{P} = \tilde{a} - Q$, where Q is the quantity sold. The price is a random variable because $\tilde{a} = \mu + \eta\varepsilon$, where μ is the mean demand, η is determined by D's sales effort, $\eta \in [\underline{\eta}, \overline{\eta}]$, $\eta > 0$, and ε is white noise with zero mean and a known variance, σ^2. The greater the effort D invests in creating clientele, the lower the riskiness of the demand.

U and D first negotiate the price of the intermediate good. D then observes the demand and chooses the quantity of purchases (and sales).

We assume that D is risk-neutral. Hence, it can be shown that after demand is realized, the price of the good to the final consumers and the quantity, given the price of the intermediate good, are determined by an equation similar to Eq. 6.10:

$$P = \frac{\tilde{a} + P_w}{2} \text{ and } Q = P - P_w = \frac{\tilde{a} - P_w}{2}. \tag{7.12}$$

We assume U is risk-averse with strictly increasing, strictly concave von Neumann–Morgenstern utility function over profits, henceforth denoted by V; that is, $V' > 0$, $V'' < 0$. U agrees to an intermediate price that maximizes its expected utility over its profits, $\tilde{R}^U$:

$$EV(\tilde{R}^U) = EV(P_w - c)\tilde{Q} = EV\left[(P_w - c)\left(\frac{\tilde{a} - P_w}{2}\right)\right], \tag{7.13}$$

which, upon denoting the absolute risk-aversion coefficient of U by r^U yields the following price:[16]

---

[16] $EV\left[(P_w - c)\left(\frac{\tilde{a} - P_w}{2}\right)\right] = EV\left[(P_w - c)\left(\frac{\mu - P_w}{2}\right) + (P_w - c)\left(\frac{\eta\varepsilon}{2}\right)\right].$

The first-order-condition with respect to P_w yields
$(\mu - 2P_w + c)EV' + \eta E(V'\varepsilon) = 0$.

By Taylor's expansion around the mean profits,
$$V'(R^U) \cong V'(ER^U) + V''(ER^U) \times (P_w - c)\left(\frac{\eta\varepsilon}{2}\right),$$

$$V'(R^U)\varepsilon \cong V'(ER^U)\varepsilon + V''(E\pi^U) \times (P_w - c)\left(\frac{\eta\varepsilon^2}{2}\right).$$

Taking expectations,

$$P_w = \frac{\mu + c(1 + \eta^2 r^U \sigma^2 / 2)}{2 + \eta^2 r^U \sigma^2 / 2}. \tag{7.14}$$

The profits of D, are

$$R^D = \left[\frac{\tilde{a} - \mu + (\tilde{a} - c)(1 + \eta^2 r^U \sigma^2 / 2)}{2 + \eta^2 r^U \sigma^2 / 2} \right]^2. \tag{7.15}$$

Taking a derivative with respect to η shows that

$$\text{Sign} \left[\frac{\partial R^D}{\partial \eta} \right] = \text{Sign} \left[\tilde{a} + \mu - 2c \right]. \tag{7.16}$$

If $\tilde{a} + \mu - 2c > 0$, D can increase profits by taking actions to smooth the variability of the demand, which in turn reduces the variability of both firms' reported earnings.

7.4 Regulation

Liang (2004), studies a two-period model wherein regulators design and enforce the accounting standard to be applied to reporting economic earnings. Some measure of smoothing is desirable to reduce agency costs because it allows the risk-averse manager to spread intertemporal risk optimally. In this case, a regulatory attempt to eliminate earnings management can reduce the firm's value.

Regulation has attracted more interest since the enactment of the Sarbanes-Oxley Act, and we refer the readers to the Introduction to Part 2 for more discussion of this legislation.

$$EV'\left(R^U\right) \cong V'\left(ER^U\right), \text{ and } EV'\left(R^U\right)\varepsilon \cong V''\left(ER^U\right) \times \left(P_w - c\right)\left(\frac{\eta\sigma^2}{2}\right).$$

Denoting the absolute risk-aversion coefficient of U by r^U, $r^U = -V''/V'$, and rearranging yields, $P_w = \dfrac{\mu + c(1 + \eta^2 r^U \sigma^2 / 2)}{2 + \eta^2 r^U \sigma^2 / 2}.$

Appendix: Artificial Smoothing Motivated by Consumption Smoothing

7.5.1 The Game

Observe the contract between risk-averse owners and a risk-averse manager in a two-period model. The former are assumed to be able to diversify their risk, and their objective is to maximize their expected total wealth. The latter's consumption stream depends on the temporal compensation. Hence, his objective is to maximize his expected income.

The owners design a two-period contract, in which the first-period payment is based on the manager's message, m_1, because the manager alone observes the realized first-period economic earnings, x_1, $x_1 \in X_1$. In addition to observing x_1, the manager alone learns the second-period outcome, x_2, $x_2 \in X_2$, at the end of period 1. Since total economic and reported earnings must coincide (see, e.g., Sunder, 1997), the owners know the total actual earnings, y, $y = x_1 + x_2$, at the end of the second period. For each first-period report, m_1, the firm must report $m_2 = y - m_1$ at the end of the second period (Fig. 7.2).

The time-line of main events is as given in Fig. 7.2.

Period 1		Period 2	
Date 1	**Date 2**	**Date 3**	**Date 4**
The owners and manager contract	- Nature chooses x_1 - The manager observes x_1 and a perfect signal on x_2 - The firm publicizes a message m_1 - The manager is paid and consumes what he earns	- Nature chooses x_2 - The firm reports m_2 - The manager is paid	... The owners collect liquidating dividends

Fig. 7.2 The main events

The question is twofold. What is the optimal contract, given the manager's reporting strategy? What is the manager's optimal reporting strategy in response to the contract?

The fact that the owners are expected-wealth maximizers provides a clue to the first question, because it implies that the owners are interested only in the total net earnings, $y - [s_1(m_1) + s_2(m_2)]$. That is, for a given total compensation of s_y, $s_y=s_1+s_2$, dependent on a given level of total earnings, y, the owners are indifferent to how it is divided between the two periods.

In contrast, because the manager derives utility over periodic income, the division of the compensation between the two periods matters to him. For any given total payment, s_y, he prefers a smooth payment schedule wherein the total compensation is divided equally, $s_1=s_2=\frac{1}{2}s_y$. Moreover, the information available to the manager guarantees that the first-period message, m_1, ensures an equal division of total payments between the two periods.

One possible scenario that makes both the owners and the manager happy is having the owners design only one schedule by finding the optimal total payments, $S(y)$. Then the manager is paid at the end of the first and second periods accordingly, $s_1=S(m_1)$ and $s_2=S(m_2)$. In the off-equilibrium event that $s_1 \neq s_2$, the manager is penalized.

The manager achieves his desired compensation stream by smoothing the report:

$$m_1 = \tfrac{1}{2}y \quad \text{and} \quad m_2 = y-m_1 = \tfrac{1}{2}y. \tag{7.17}$$

Characterizing the contract requires additional notation. We denote the utility functions of the risk-averse owners and the manager by V and U, respectively, and the reservation utility level of the manager that can be obtained in an alternative employment by $\hat{u}$.

The owners design a contract by solving the following program:

$$\max_{S} EV[y - S(y)]$$

s.t.

$$EU=2EU\left[\frac{S(y)}{2}\right] \geq \hat{u}. \qquad \text{(PC)}$$

The owners maximize their expected utility over the residual value, $y-S(y)$, subject to the contract's inducing the manager to participate (PC)because the contract guarantees that the manager's expected utility, EU, does not fall below the manager's reservation utility level.

The Euler equation of this program yields a pointwise equilibrium condition:[17]

---

[17] Denote the density function of y by f. The Lagrangian is

$$L = \int\left[V(y-S(y)) + \lambda\left(2U\left(\frac{S(y)}{2}\right)-\hat{u}\right)\right] f(y)dy,$$

and the accompanying Euler equation is

$$\forall\, y,\quad \frac{V'(y-S(y))}{U'\!\left(\dfrac{S(y)}{2}\right)}=\lambda, \tag{7.18}$$

where λ is the Lagrange multiplier of (PC). This equilibrium condition is also known as the Borch condition because Borch (1962), was the first to analyze the division of an uncertain outcome between risk-averse players.

To find the slope of the contract, we totally differentiate the Borch condition, denoting the absolute risk-aversion measures of the owners and the manager by R^O and R^M, respectively:

$$S'=\frac{4R^O}{4R^O+R^M}. \tag{7.19}$$ [18]

If, for example, both players have utility functions with constant risk-aversion measures, β^O and β^M, respectively, the contract is a linear function of the total outcome, y. For other utility functions, the relative change in the absolute risk-aversion measures determines the convexity of the contract.

This example illustrates that smoothing is valuable on three accounts. First, the manager achieves his desired consumption smoothing. Second, the first-period report contains full information about the second-period report. If we regress m_2 on m_1,

---

$$L=\int\left[-V'(y-S(y))+\lambda U'\!\left(\frac{S(y)}{2}\right)\right]f(y)\mathrm{d}y=0.$$

The Euler equation obtains only if the argument in brackets is zero pointwise.

[18] Take a total derivative of the Borch condition with respect to y:

$$\frac{V''(y-S(y))}{U'\!\left(\dfrac{S(y)}{2}\right)}(1-S'(y))\mathrm{d}y-\frac{U''\!\left(\dfrac{S(y)}{2}\right)V'(y-S(y))S'(y)}{4U'\!\left(\dfrac{S(y)}{2}\right)}\mathrm{d}y=0.$$

Since the absolute risk-aversion measure is

$$R^O=-\frac{V''(y-S(y))}{V'(y-S(y))},\ R^M=-\frac{U''\!\left(\dfrac{S(y)}{2}\right)}{U'\!\left(\dfrac{S(y)}{2}\right)},$$

multiplying and dividing by the ratio of marginal utilities yields

$$\frac{V'(1-S)}{U'\!\left(\dfrac{S}{2}\right)}\left\{-R^O[1-S']+\frac{1}{4}R^M S'\right\}\mathrm{d}y=0.$$

$$m_2 = \alpha + \gamma m_1 + \varepsilon. \tag{7.20}$$

We obtain $\alpha = 0$, $\gamma = 1$, and $R^2 = 1$. Since γ is the persistence parameter of earnings, the results of the regression indicate that current earnings have high quality with an ability to predict future earnings in full.

Third, smoothing reduces the observable variability of reported earnings, which has a favorable effect on valuation (e.g., Bitner and Dolan, 1996). The variance of the series of economic earnings is

$$\frac{\left[x_1 - \dfrac{x_1 + x_2}{2}\right]^2 + \left[x_2 - \dfrac{x_1 + x_2}{2}\right]^2}{2} = \frac{[x_1 - x_2]^2}{4} \geq 0. \tag{7.21}$$

Ordinarily, the variability is zero only in the highly unlikely event that $x_1 = x_2$, but under smoothing, the variability is zero for any realization of x_1 and x_2. To the extent that perceived variability affects the market's evaluation of the riskiness of the firm, the firm enjoys a higher price. This point, however, contains a sour note because although achieving optimal consumption smoothing and informativeness through smoothing serves the manager's greater good, the owners and investors in general are misled by the reduction in perceived variability, unless the earnings generation process is mean reverting.

7.5.2 Issues

This example raises a number of issues. The first concerns the validity of the smoothing phenomenon. Smoothing is not the only option to obtain the optimal payoffs. If the manager reveals x_1 and x_2 at the end of the first period, the owners can do the arithmetic themselves, $y = x_1 + x_2$, find s_y, and pay the manager half of s_y. That is, full revelation of the truth yields the same payoffs. Note that the informativeness goal is served as well, without embellishing the role of perceived riskiness.[19]

This point has been recognized by several researchers (Dye, 1988; Evans and Sridhar, 1996; Lambert, 2001; Crocker and Slemrod, 2006; Ronen

---

[19] This insight is universal. For example, Suh (1990, p. 705), states, "Delegation of accounting method choice to the agent is shown to be an alternative Pareto-equivalent mechanism to direct communication...." Arya, Glover, and Sunder (1998), and Ziv (1998), note that a contract with a high severance payment can achieve the same outcome as earnings management.

and Yaari, 2007).[20] The first four handle the issue by assuming that a truth-telling equilibrium does not exist (e.g., the manager cannot communicate all dimensions of his private information to the owners). Our study employs a one-period model, but it is relevant to smoothing because it shows that limited liability renders truth-telling too costly to the principal. A truth-telling contract must be a penalty contract, but if liability is limited, penalties lose their effectiveness.

Another answer that focuses on the principal–agent relationship between the owners and the manager is given by Ronen and Yaari (1993). Since the second-period earnings depend on actions that the manager has yet to take, paying him for x_2 at the end of the first period provides him with disincentives to exert the costly second-period effort to achieve this outcome *after* being paid.

Paying the agent an advance raises additional concerns, especially because the information on the second-period outcome may be uncertain. If the manager is dishonest, he will report high m_1 so that $s_1(m_1) > y$, take the first-period compensation, and divide it for consumption between the two periods himself. Alternatively, suppose the manager is honest, but he has limited liability. Although he exerts effort, nature nullifies his actions, resulting in lower earnings than expected in the second period. Although both principal and agent agree that the agent was overpaid and ought to return some of his first-period payment to the principal, the agent's limited liability prevents the principal from recouping the advance.

---

[20] See also Natarajan (2004), who studies reporting discretion from the perspective of the reporting set, which constrains the manager's ability to manage earnings (at one extreme, the manager must report the truth only, and at the other, he can report any outcome). Natarajan points out that reducing the agent's discretion does not always increase the principal's welfare.

8 Maximization and Minimization

> Despite this earlier preference for income-smoothing, by the end of the 1990s, these same firms were robbing future periods for earnings that could be recognized immediately. In short, "income smoothing" gave way to more predatory behavior. Interestingly, restatements involving revenue recognition produced disproportionately large losses. (Coffee, 2003a, p. 23)

In this chapter, we review studies on earnings-management strategies other than smoothing: maximization, minimization, and an extreme case of minimization—"taking a bath" (Scott, 2003). In one-shot games, this list of strategies is exhaustive; in repeated relationships, it might not be. Yaari (2005), for example, discusses "conservative smoothing," which combines smoothing with "taking a bath." Others (Yaari, 1991; Demski and Frimor, 1999; Koch and Wall, 2006) present a "maximizing variability" strategy in which the manager intends to dump all reported earnings in a single period. Demski and Frimor prove its optimality when the compensation contract can be renegotiated after the release of the accounting report. The other two link this strategy to the convexity of the contract.

> *Definition:* The earnings-management strategy is **maximization** (**minimization**) if the report inflates (deflates) earnings.[1] Let a firm that earns x, $x \in X$, adopt a reporting strategy, M, $M: X \to \hat{M}$. Then, given a report m, $m \in \hat{M}$, the report resulting from maximization (minimization) exceeds (is lower than) earnings, $m > (<) x$.

This definition assumes that truth-telling is unique and thus serves as a cutoff: higher (lower) reported earnings constitute maximization (minimization). The well-known strategy of "taking a bath" is minimization that sets the report to a very low level, by recording, for example, unusually large write-offs.

Although we lump maximization and minimization together, two characteristics separate them. First, minimization transfers the reported out-

---

[1] Our terminology draws on Scott (2003, pp. 383–384). That is, maximization is a strategy of inflating reported earnings and minimization is the strategy of deflating reported earnings.

come to future reports, while maximization either depletes past reserves of reported outcome or borrows from future reports. Hence, previous aggressive behavior might lead to accounting scandals when economic conditions deteriorate. Becht, Bolton, and Roell (2003), state,

> As we are writing, a series of scandals and corporate failures is surfacing in the United States.... Many of these cases concern accounting irregularities that enabled firms to vastly overstate their earnings. Such scandals often emerge during economic downturns: as John Kenneth Galbraith once remarked, recessions catch what the auditors miss.
> (p. 13)

The dynamics of this reporting strategy have been used to link fraud and fraud detection to the conditions of the economy (see Kedia and Philippon, 2005; Povel, Singh, and Winton, 2005; Goldman and Slezak, 2006).

Second, there is evidence that firms prefer to maximize rather than minimize. For example, Kinney and Martin (1994), who analyze nine sets of audit-related adjustments from more than 1,500 audits across 15 years, conclude that such adjustments are overwhelmingly negative. In other words, audits correct a positive bias in pre-audit earnings and assets. (See also Nelson, Elliott, and Tarpley, 2003.) In this chapter, we largely focus on maximization. Minimization has been studied not as a local reporting strategy that specifies a report after the true earnings are realized but rather as the product of choosing accounting conservatism. That is, conservatism specifies an accounting system that produces lower signals with a higher probability than high signals (Gigler and Hemmer, 2001; Venugopalan, 2004; Bagnoli and Watts, 2005).[2]

As a general comment, note that the distinction between maximization and minimization in repeated relationships is problematic. Because the total reported earnings and total cash flows are equal, present minimization will lead to future maximization, and vice versa.[3] Consequently, the research into maximization and minimization deals mostly with one-shot games, restricting attention to deliberate interference in reporting current earnings.

---

[2] For additional studies on conservatism, consult Kwon, Newman, and Suh (2001), and Kwon (2005), who study conservatism from the perspective of a principal who has to design the accounting information system and the contract of an agent with limited liability. Bagnoli and Watts (2005), look at conservatism when the firm wishes to meet expectations. For valuable discussions of conservatism in general, see Watts (2003a, b).

[3] Lin and Shih (2002), address the effect of the intertemporal aspect of earnings management on the timing of maximization and minimization. Following Hayn's (1995) finding of a smaller market response to loss than to profit, they

We divide the discussion in accordance with the following considerations: the capital market, governance, competition, and regulation.

8.1 Capital Market

As discussed in Part 2, firms have numerous reasons to maximize their share price in the short run.[4] For example, the share price determines the cost of financing a new project (Bebchuk and Bar-Gill, 2003) and the profitability of insider trading by management that holds shares (Benabou and Laroque, 1992; Bebchuk and Bar-Gill, 2003; Kadan and Yang, 2006). In short, the motivation for inflating prices exists. Yet motivation is not enough; vehicle and opportunity are important, too. As several researchers (Elitzur and Yaari, 1995; Dye, 1988; Fischer and Verrecchia, 2000; Fischer and Stocken, 2004; Crocker and Slemrod, 2006; Goldman and Slezak, 2006; Kadan and Yang, 2006; Elitzur, 2007) have noted, earnings management is such a vehicle. A firm can maximize its share price because the firm's valuation by the market increases in reported earnings. The opportunity is provided by imperfect audit technology because audits cannot with certainty detect an earnings-management attempt.

In Chap. 6, we presented a simple example of maximization, which we consider again here. Our binary example includes high- and low-quality firms. The low-quality firms attempt to pool with the high-quality firms by publicizing the same report, and some may succeed. Since audits lend a measure of credibility to the reports, inflating the report successfully rewards the low-quality firm with a stock price that is higher than the price under truth-telling.[5] As the capital-market facet of earnings management is

---

suggest that "shifting income from a loss quarter during a recession to a profit quarter in the future may boost the share price in the profit quarter more than it depresses the share price in the loss quarter, thus giving an overall positive boost to the share price in the long run" (p. 6).

[4] Our presentation is based on the assumption that firms wish to maximize share price. Some studies have analyzed earnings management when firms wish to meet or beat the market's expectations (e.g., Dutta and Gigler, 2002; Bagnoli and Watts, 2005; Yaari, 2005; Guttman, Kadan, and Kandel, 2006). The interesting facet of such an objective function is that it might induce firms to engage in minimization.

[5] This basic dynamic is used in Tzur and Yaari (1999); Ronen and Yaari (2002, 2007), Ronen, Ronen, and Yaari (2003), Kedia and Philippon (2005), and Bergstresser and Philippon (2006).

well understood, in this chapter we take the analysis one step further by examining the repercussions of earnings management on the response of the stock price to an earnings surprise.

The basic framework postulates that the price is set in Noisy Rational Expectations Equilibrium (NREE). That is, the market includes a market maker and the following three types of participants: firms, informed traders, and liquidity traders (Bhattacharya and Krishnan, 1999).

Firms: Each firm generates unobservable earnings, x, $x \in \{x_1, x_2\}$, $x_1 < x_2$. The prior probability that earnings are high, θ, $\theta = \Pr(x_2)$, is common knowledge. Firms decide whether to manage reported earnings, r, $r \in \{r_1, r_2\} = \{x_1, x_2\}$,[6] when they give a rough draft of the financial reports to the auditor. The audit technology is imperfect; the audit verifies a truthful draft perfectly and detects the truth with some positive probability, π, $0.5 < \pi < 1$, when the draft misrepresents it (see, e.g., Schwartz, 1997). Denote the firm's reporting strategy by R, $R: \{x_1, x_2\} \rightarrow \{x_1, x_2\}$. The audit technology implies that $\Pr[r_i | x_i, R(x_i) = x_i] = 1$; $\Pr[r_j | x_i, R(x_i) = x_i, j \neq i] = 0$, $\Pr[r_i | x_i, R(x_i) = x_j, j \neq i] = \pi$, and $\Pr[r_j | x_i, R(x_i) = x_j, j \neq i] = 1 - \pi$, $i, j, = 1, 2$.

Informed traders: Informed traders receive a perfect signal on economic earnings, x. Because the stock price does not fully reflect the information they possess, they maximize profits by choosing low demand, ℓ^t, when their information indicates x_1 and high demand, h^t, when their information indicates x_2.

Liquidity traders: Some investors buy and sell shares for liquidity reasons. Their trading introduces noise into the market-making price because the observable market demand aggregates the demand of informed and liquidity traders. Denote the market demand by w, which can be low, ℓ, or high, h, $w \in \{\ell, h\}$, $\ell < h$. The market demand is a noisy signal of the informed's demand; that is, $\Pr[\ell | \ell^t] = \Pr[h | h^t] = \rho$; $\Pr[\ell | h^t] = \Pr[h | \ell^t] = 1 - \rho$; $0.5 < \rho < 1$.

The noise in the price implies that the price is not transparent with respect to the informed traders' private information. Specifically, the market demand is a noisy signal of the outcome; $\Pr[x_1 | \ell] = \Pr[x_2 | h] = \rho$ and $\Pr[x_1 | h] = \Pr[x_2 | \ell] = 1 - \rho$, $\rho > 0.5$.

The market maker: The price is set by a market maker who owns shares and cash. The assumption in the literature is that the market maker's objective is to make normal profits, which are assumed to be zero. Hence, he

---

[6] Note that we constrain r to coincide with x, but this restriction is innocuous if a report r_i is associated with x_i.

sets the price to the firm's expected value, where expectations are based on all available information: the firm's financial reports and market demand.

We assume that the relationship between earnings and the firm's value is captured by a multiplicative firm-specific scalar, η. That is, the firm's value equals ηx, $\eta = (1 + g)/(k_s - g)$, $\eta > 0$, where k_s is the risk-adjusted equity cost of capital and g is the earnings growth rate.[7] Henceforth, η is referred to as *the multiplier*. Bartov, Lynn, and Ronen (1999), and Kothari (2001), calculate that a typical η approximates 11 and that it might range from 8 to 20.

The summary of the notation is as follows:

x = economic earnings, $x \in \{x_1, x_2\}$, $x_1 < x_2$.

r = the firm's financial reports, $r \in \{x_1, x_2\}$.

η = a multiplier that translates short-term earnings to long-run value. The firm's value equals ηx.

θ = the prior probability of high earnings, $\theta = \Pr(x_2)$.

w = the market demand, $w \in \{\ell, h\}, \ell < h$.

P = the stock price, $P = \eta E(x|r,w)$.

ρ = the probability that the market demand correctly reflects earnings, $\rho = \Pr[x_1 | \ell] = \Pr[x_2 | h]$; $1 - \rho = \Pr[x_1 | h] = \Pr[x_2 | \ell]$, $0.5 < \rho < 1$.

r = the firm's reporting strategy, $R: \{x_1, x_2\} \rightarrow \{r_1, r_2\}$.

π = the probability that an audit detects misrepresentation,
$\pi = \Pr[r_i | x_i, R(x_i) = x_j, j \neq i]$, $i,j = 1,2$, $0.5 < \pi < 1$.

Figure 8.1 summarizes the four stages of the model:

Date 1	Date 2	Date 3	Date 4
- Nature chooses the firm's earnings - Informed traders receive privately a signal on the earnings	The share price, P_2, is set by a market maker	The firm observes its economic earnings and submits a draft of its financial report to the auditor	- The firm publicizes the audited report. - A price, P_4, is set

Fig. 8.1 The main events

8.1.1 The Equilibrium

Our assumption that the market maker is rational implies that he updates his beliefs about the firm's value after observing market demand and the

---

[7] The economic earnings, then, are *permanent* earnings. For a derivation of the multiplier in the general case, consult, e.g., Gavious, Ronen, and Yaari (2002).

firm's report. In what follows, we denote his prior belief that the firm's value is ηx_2 by α_{wt}, $w = \ell, h$, $t = 2, 4$. If firms with low earnings, x_1, attempt to pool with firms that have high earnings by reporting r_2, the price system is as follows[8]:

$$P_2(w) = \alpha_{w2}\eta(x_2 - x_1) + \eta x_1 > \eta x_1; \tag{8.1a}$$

$$P_4(r_1, w) = \eta r_1 = \eta x_1, \quad w = \ell, h; \tag{8.1b}$$

$$P_4(r_2, w) = \alpha_{w4}\eta(r_2 - x_1) + \eta x_1 > \eta x_1, \tag{8.1c}$$

where

$$\alpha_{\ell 2} = \frac{(1-\rho)\theta}{(1-\rho)\theta + \rho(1-\theta)}; \quad \alpha_{h2} = \frac{\rho\theta}{\rho\theta + (1-\rho)(1-\theta)},$$

$$\alpha_{\ell 4} = \frac{(1-\rho)\theta}{\theta(1-\rho) + (1-\pi)(1-\theta)\rho} \quad \text{and} \quad \alpha_{h4} = \frac{\rho\theta}{\theta\rho + (1-\pi)(1-\theta)(1-\rho)} > \alpha_\ell.$$

On Date 2, the price equals the firm's expected value, given the market demand. The report on Date 4 allows the market maker to better estimate the firm's value relative to Date 2. The Date 4 price system supports the motivation for the maximization strategy because the price for r_2 is higher than the price for r_1. The price for r_2 is discounted because of the uncertainty regarding whether the report of r_2 is truthful. Since the optimal reporting strategy is maximization, a report of low earnings, r_1, reveals the truth because the only plausible explanation for such a report is that the audit detected an attempt to manage earnings.

Earnings management is clearly pernicious. It introduces distortion into the price system because the price of firms that truly earn x_2 is discounted, and the price of firms that earn x_1 and successfully misrepresent is inflated.

A numerical example illustrates our arguments.

EXAMPLE 1:   Suppose that x_1=10,000, x_2=20,000, θ=0.5, π=0.75, ρ=0.8, and η = 10. Then, $P_2(\ell)$ = 120,000, $P_2(h)$ = 180,000, $P_4(r_1,\ell)$ = $P_4(r_1,h)$ = 100,000, $P_4(r_2,\ell)$=150,000, and $P_4(r_2,h)$ = 194,118. The Date 4 prices associated with reporting r_2 are lower than 200,000 and exceed 100,000. Note that a report of low (high) earnings on Date 4 triggers a price decline (increase), which shows that the earnings-management strategy of maximization is optimal. Consequently, the Date 4 price for a high earnings report understates the value of firms with x_2.

---

[8] To simplify the presentation, note that instead of writing the price as $(1-\alpha)x_1 + \alpha x_2$, we can present it as $\alpha(x_2 - x_1) + x_1$.

8.1.2 The Earnings Response Coefficient

The earnings response coefficient, ERC, is the coefficient of the earnings surprise in the regression of returns on the earnings surprise:

$$\frac{P_4 - P_2}{P_2} = A + \text{ERC} * \frac{r - Er}{P_2} + \text{noise}, \tag{8.2}$$

where A is the intercept and $(r - Er)$ is the earnings surprise. The expected earnings, Er, are the expected Date 4 report, given the information available at Date 2.[9] If the firm reports low (high) earnings, r_1 (r_2), the earnings surprise is negative (positive).

Note that the earnings surprise is deflated by the price at the beginning of the period, P_2, a practice that originated with Christie (1987). This deflator has the added advantage of always being positive. We note that some research overcomes the problem of measurement error in earnings by using an inverse equation, in which returns are the independent variables and earnings are the dependent variables. The R^2 of the inverse regression measures the *timeliness of earnings* (see, e.g., Basu, 1997; Engel, Hayes, and Wang, 2003).

Mathematically, Eq. 8.2 indicates that the ERC is also the derivative of the Date 4 price with respect to the report, r, $\text{ERC} = \dfrac{\partial P_4}{\partial r}$. Hence, the following ERCs obtain:

$$\text{ERC}(r_1, \ell) = \eta; \tag{8.3a}$$

$$\text{ERC}(r_1, h) = \eta; \tag{8.3b}$$

---

[9] Once again, the analytical research does not suffer from the problems that plague the empirical research: unobservable variables. Consider the measurement of an earnings surprise. If the stochastic process is a random walk, last year's earnings are the basis to calculate the earnings surprise, but if earnings develop by a mean-reverting process, then some cross-sectional constant is a proxy for expected earnings (see the discussion in Easton and Harris, 1991). Some studies use analysts' forecasts (e.g., Brown and Kim, 1993; Baber and Kang, 2001, 2002a, b; Abarbanell and Lehavy, 2002; Baber, Chen, Kang, 2006; Williams, 2006). The fact that results are sensitive to how one measures expected earnings is indisputable. Abarbanell and Lehavy (2002), for example, show that the market's response to a non-GAAP earnings surprise is higher than its response to a GAAP earnings surprise.

$$\mathrm{ERC}(r_2, \ell) = \alpha_{\ell 4}\eta < \alpha_{h 4}\eta < \eta; \qquad (8.3\mathrm{c})$$

$$\mathrm{ERC}(r_4, h) = \alpha_{h 4}\eta. \qquad (8.3\mathrm{d})$$

Note that when the report is unmanaged, the ERC that measures the valuation effect of a dollar report, r, coincides with the valuation effect of one dollar of earnings, x; that is, ERC=η (as in Eqs. 8.3a and 8.3b). Earnings management reduces the ERC because a report of r_2 is suspected of being managed. Consequently, the ERC for reporting high earnings is lower than the ERC for reporting low earnings.

Because a report of r_1 is truth revealing, the market-demand signal is redundant. Hence, the ERC is unaffected by this additional signal. In contrast, since the market compensates for the earnings management in the high reported earnings by considering the market's demand signal, the ERC for high reported earnings is sensitive to the market's demand. In particular, high demand that supports high earnings generates a higher ERC. Hence, For each level of market demand, the ERC for high earnings exceeds the ERC for low earnings.

The effect of earnings management on the ERC has been the object of several studies (Sankar, 1999; Gigler and Hemmer, 2001; Fischer and Stocken, 2004; Bagnoli and Watts, 2005; Crocker and Huddart, 2006). Most note that earnings management might reduce ERC (and explains non-linear relationship between earnings and market's response). An exception is Fischer and Stocken (2004), who study the effect of a speculative trader's private information on the intensity of earnings management and its impact on price. Like us, they show that earnings management decreases the quality of earnings; for some parameters, however, earnings management increases the *ERC* because it generates a greater earnings surprise.

A numerical example illustrates our arguments.

EXAMPLE 2: Proceeding with the same parameters as in Example 1, ERC(r_1,ℓ)= ERC(r_1,h) =10; ERC(r_2,ℓ)=5.0; ERC(r_2,h)=9.41. Had the firm reported the truth, ERC(r,w) would be 10 for each combination of market demand and report.

Empirical evidence of the discount of the ERC due to earnings management is provided in, for example, DeFond and Park (2001), and Cohen, Dey, and Lys (2005a). Indirect evidence for the effect of this discount is provided by Lougee and Marquardt, 2004, and Marquardt and Wiedman (2004b). They find that pro forma earnings figures have significantly greater information content when earnings surprises are positive.

If r_2 is profit and r_1 is loss, our insight seems inconsistent with Hayn (1995). She finds that the response to positive earnings is larger than the response to losses. Hayn explains her finding in this way:

> Losses are likely to be considered temporary since shareholders can always liquidate the firm rather than suffer from indefinite losses. In other words, equity holders have a put option on the future cash flows of the firm whereby they can sell their shares at a price commensurate with the market value of the net assets of the firm. (p. 126)

The abandonment option is corroborated by Subramanyam and Wild (1996), who show that the informativeness of earnings is inversely related to various characteristics that proxy for the likelihood that the firm will be terminated. Our result differs because we do not vary the valuation multiplier η with the reported earnings, which is apparently an unrealistic assumption.

One of the alarming puzzling phenomena in recent years has been the decline of the ERC over time (see, e.g., Lang, 1991; Sinha and Watts, 2001; Kothari, 2001; Ryan and Zarowin, 2003; Dontoh, Radhkrishnan, and Ronen, 2004). This finding has been interpreted as indicating a decline in the value relevance of accounting, but other explanations have been offered. One is that earnings management is recognized by the market and discounted. This argument implies that the level of earnings management has increased over time. Empirically, however, the evidence is conflicting. Cohen, Dey, and Lys (2005a), find that earnings management was on the rise between 1987 and 2001, but other studies show that discretionary expenditures have declined (see Lang, 1991, and citations therein).

Additional explanations are that the noise of the price (e.g., Dontoh, Radhakrishnan, and Ronen, 2004) or the richness of alternative sources of value-relevant information has increased over time (e.g., Lang and Lundholm, 1993; Ryan and Zarowin, 2003). The increase in the noise of the price is explained by the reduction in the transaction costs of trading by small investors and other traders whose trading decisions may not be driven by information about a firm's fundamental value.[10]

---

[10] A variation of this explanation is based on the relationship between size and the ERC. If the benefits associated with information collection are increasing in a firm's size, then the fact that the size of sample firms tends to increase over time implies that the amount of information collected about firms from non-accounting sources (see, e.g., the speculative trader in Fischer and Stocken,

So far, we have dwelt on maximization. Sometimes, however, capital markets induce "taking a bath"—an extreme case of minimization—or prompt a conservative reporting strategy (only bad news are fully recognized). In a one-shot game or myopic relationship, there is no room for this. In repeated relationships, though, such minimization might be optimal, since earnings not reported today can be added to reported earnings tomorrow (Benabou and Laroque, 1992; Kirschenheiter and Melumad, 2000; Yaari, 2005; Ewert and Wagenhofer, 2005).

Benabou and Laroque (1992), argue that the release of information to the market when the manager wishes to engage in profitable insider trading induces him to increase the market's misperception of the firm's true value. If the market overestimates the firm's value, the manager is better off inflating the report and selling shares at the inflated price, and if the market underestimates the value, the manager is better off minimizing and buying shares at a deflated price.

The fact that repeated relationships are important for a minimization strategy is evident in Ewert and Wagenhofer (2005), which extends the one-shot game of Fischer and Verrecchia (2000), to a two-period model. (In Fischer and Verrecchia's paper, minimization is determined arbitrarily by nature.) The model features firms whose shares are traded in a market with risk-neutral investors. The terminal value of the firm, $\tilde{x}$, is a normally distributed random variable with mean $\overline{x}$, $\overline{x} > 0$, and known variance, σ_x^2. The price at the beginning of the game, P_0, equals the expected value, $\overline{x}$. The accounting system provides a noisy signal, y_t, of the firm's value, $\tilde{x}$; that is, $y_t = \tilde{x} + \tilde{\varepsilon}_t$, where $\tilde{\varepsilon}_t$ are independent white noise variables. The firm's manager alone observes the realized accounting signals, and the firm issues reports m_t. If the manager engages in cosmetic earnings management, the report deviates from the truth by b_A. If the manager engages in real earnings management, the report deviates from the truth by b_R. The difference between the two types is that although both reverse in the second period, accounting manipulation is costless, but real earnings management is costly. To derive an interior solution, the authors assume that real earnings management reduces the second-period earnings proportionally to the square of the first-period bias, by $c(b_R^2)/2$, where c is a cost parameter. The managed reports are

$$m_1 = x + \tilde{\varepsilon}_1 + b_A + b_R \qquad (8.4a)$$

2004) before their earnings announcements would also be expected to increase, so the information content of earnings is already included in the price.

and

$$m_2 = x + \tilde{\varepsilon}_2 - b_A - b_R - c(b_R^2)/2. \tag{8.4b}$$

The reader might wonder why real earnings management reverses. Ewert and Wagenhofer assume that real smoothing concerns the timing of a transaction, rather than a lost opportunity that cannot be recouped. Because they show that regulation can shift earnings management from one type to the other, this assumption enhances the comparability between the two types.

Similar to Sankar and Subramanyam (2001), the manager's compensation depends on the earnings and stock price of the firm. The precise form is assumed to be a linear function of the reports and the first-period price net of the disutility from engaging in both types of earnings management:

$$U = sm_1 + m_2 + pP_1(m_1) - r(b_A^2)/2 - (b_R^2)/2, \tag{8.4c}$$

where s is the weight of m_1 in the manager's utility function relative to m_2, $s > 0$, p is the weight of the first-period price in the manager's payoff, and r is a parameter that represents the effect of regulation, such as the Sarbanes-Oxley Act, on the relative cost of managing earnings through accounting treatment rather than real transactions. (That is, the last two arguments represent the manager's disutility from engaging in cosmetic and real earnings management, respectively.)

The price at the end of the first period is a linear function of the report,

$$P_1(m_1) = \alpha + \beta m_1.^{[11]} \tag{8.4d}$$

Earnings management is not neutral in this setting because the market does not know the weight, p. The market is aware that p is a draw from a normal distribution with known moments. Different pairs of first-period signal and weight of the price, p, thus could yield the same first-period report.

Since firms release earnings as an input to the stock price, the equilibrium is a Stackelberg equilibrium wherein the leader is the firm and the follower is the market. Given the manager's conjectures about the price,

---

[11] This assumption is justified by the statistical properties of the model. Since uncertain variables are drawn from a normal distribution, the posterior beliefs are a linear combination of the prior estimate and the accounting report. Denote by hats the conjectures of the market regarding earnings management. Then,

$$P_1(m_1|\hat{b}_A, \hat{b}_R) = E\left[\tilde{x}|m_1, \hat{b}_A, \hat{b}_R\right] - \frac{c}{2}\hat{b}_R^2 = \bar{x} + \frac{\text{cov}(\tilde{x}, \tilde{m}_1)}{\text{var}(\tilde{m}_1)}\left(m_1 - \hat{b}_A - \hat{b}_R - \bar{x}\right) - \frac{c}{2}\hat{b}_R^2 \equiv \alpha + \beta m_1.$$

$\hat{P_1} = \hat{\alpha} + \hat{\beta}m_1$, the first-order conditions of the manager's objective function with respect to the earnings management variables are as follows:

$$\frac{\partial U}{\partial b_A} = s - 1 + p\hat{\beta} - rb_A = 0; \tag{8.4e}$$

$$\frac{\partial U}{\partial b_A} = s - 1 - cb_R + p\hat{\beta} - b_R = 0. $$

Hence,

$$b_A = \frac{s - 1 + p\hat{\beta}}{r}; \tag{8.4f}$$

$$b_R = \frac{s - 1 + p\hat{\beta}}{c + 1}. \tag{8.4g}$$

Note that if $r = 1$, cosmetic smoothing is preferable to the costly real earnings management. Hence, owners can induce a lower level of real earnings management by designing a compensation function that decreases s. Thus, if $s + p\hat{\beta} < 1$, the firm might deflate the report in the first period.[12]

Kirschenheiter and Melumad (2000), find that "taking a bath" when economic earnings are low is preferable to smoothing because it is a means of hoarding accounting earnings for future reports (see Chap. 7 for details).

In general, the capital market is the villain because it induces earnings management rather than disciplining it. Fischer and Stocken (2004), acknowledge the role played by informed traders who wish to make speculative gains (although they too portray the capital market as a motivating force in earnings management). In particular, if these traders obtain private information about a firm's earnings management, the firm responds by managing earnings more. If, however, these speculators have superior information on a firm's economic value, they reduce the scope of earnings management because their trades affect the stock price set by a market maker. The better the price as a signal of value, the less beneficial earnings management is to the firm.

---

[12] For a study that models trade-off between real and cosmetic earnings maangement in order to analyze the timing of each type, consult Zang (2007).

8.2 Governance

We illustrate the role of governance in earnings management by first extending the model in the previous section by adding a principal–agent relationship between shareholders and senior management.

For the sake of clarity, we continue the scenario studied in the previous section. Figure 8.2 summarizes the five stages of the principal–agent model:

Date 1	Date 2	Date 3	Date 4	Date 5
The owners design the manager's contracts, C.	- The manager chooses unobservable effort, *a.* - The market opens, and the market maker sets the price	The unobservable true earnings, *x*, are realized	- The manager observes the outcome and communicates it to the auditor - The firm publicizes the audited report - **The manager is paid**	- The firm liquidates. - **The owners collect net liquidating dividends**

Fig. 8.2 Timeline of the principal–agent model

The principal–agent relationships are depicted in Fig. 8.2 in boldface. On Date 1, the shareholders contract with the manager and design his contract. On Date 2, the manager exerts unobservable effort in production and investment decisions that will determine the true earnings jointly with nature. The outcome is realized on Date 3. To allow for earnings management, we assume that the manager alone observes the true earnings. The firm reports the outcome on Date 4, and the manager is paid in accordance with the Date 1 contract. On Date 5, the owners collect liquidating dividends.

We inject effort into the model by assuming that the manager chooses between a poor-performance effort, a_p, and a good-performance effort, a_g, $a \in \{a_p, a_g\}$, where $a_p < a_g$.[13] The expected outcome is higher if the manager exerts a_g, since the probability that the outcome is x_2 conditional on effort, *a*, denoted by θ_a, $\theta_a = \Pr[x = x_2|a]$, is higher when the manager exerts the

---

[13] Having a binary choice set entails little loss of generality since "much of the general insights from studying hidden action models can be conveyed in the simplest setting, where the agent has only two actions to choose from" (Hart and Holmström, 1985, p. 79).

good-performance effort, $\theta_g > \theta_p$. The manager is risk-averse and work-averse, with preferences that are separable between compensation and effort: a von Neumann-Morgenstern utility function over compensation, U, and a strictly convex disutility function over effort, V; that is, $U(C,a_g) = U(C) - V(a_g)$. Shareholders are risk-neutral; they prefer to pay more to induce the manager to exert the good-performance effort.

The owners design a contract that solves the following program:

min $E[C(.)]$
C

s.t.

$E[W(C(.))] - V(a_g) \geq W_0.$ (PC)

$a_g \in$ argmax $E[W(C)] - V(a_g).$ (IC)
$a \in \{a_p, a_g\}$

Since the optimal effort is unique, owners maximize value by minimizing the manager's expected share, $E[C]$. The contract must guarantee the manager his reservation utility level, (PC), where if the manager manages earnings,

$$E[W(C(.)) \mid a_g] = [\rho \theta_g + (1-\pi)(1-\rho)(1-\theta_g)]W(C(P(r_2,h,a_g))) + \quad (8.5)$$

$$[(1-\rho)\theta_g + (1-\pi)\rho(1-\theta_g)]W(C(P(r_2,\ell,a_g))) + \pi(1-\theta_g)W(C(P(r_1))).$$

The contract must also provide the manager with incentives to exert the good-performance effort, (IC), by ensuring that the manager's expected utility is at least as high as that obtained by exerting the poor-performance effort, $E[W(C(.)) \mid a_g] - V(a_g) \geq E[W(C(.)) \mid a_p] - V(a_p).$[14]

$$E[W(C(.)) \mid a_g] - E[W(C(.)) \mid a_p] = (\theta_g - \theta_p)\{QW(C(P(r_2,h,a_g))) + \quad (8.6)$$
$$[\pi - Q]W(C(P(r_2,\ell,a_g))) - \pi\, W(C(P(r_1)))\},$$

where $Q = \rho - (1-\pi)(1-\rho)$; $\pi - Q = .1 - \rho - (1-\pi)\rho.$

When the report is r_1, the contract is independent of the price. This is a special case of the informativeness criterion of Holmström (1979). A report of a low outcome fully reveals the actual outcome, $r^{-1}(r = x_1) = x_1$, eliminating the need for additional information that garbles the actual-outcome signal.

To see that this earnings management is also pernicious because it increases the cost of the contract and decreases shareholders' value, contrast the first-order conditions (FOC) for truth-telling with the FOC for earnings

---

[14] The prices corresponding to a_p are the same as for a_g because the Nash equilibrium considers only unilateral deviations.

management. Denote the Lagrange multipliers of (PC) and (IC) by λ and μ respectively. The FOC are as follows:

$$\frac{1}{U'(C(r_1))} = \lambda - \mu \frac{\theta_g - \theta_p}{1 - \theta_g}. \tag{8.7a}$$

$$\frac{1}{U'(C(r_2, \ell))} = \lambda + \mu \frac{(\theta_g - \theta_p)[\pi - Q]}{\theta_g(1 - \rho) + (1 - \pi)(1 - \theta_g)\rho}. \tag{8.7b}$$

$$\frac{1}{U'(C(r_2, h))} = \lambda + \mu \frac{(\theta_g - \theta_p)Q}{\theta_g \rho + (1 - \pi)(1 - \theta_g)(1 - \rho)}. \tag{8.7c}$$

The comparison between the contract under earnings management and the contract under truth-telling is easily made, as a truth-telling equilibrium is mathematically equivalent to a scenario with perfect audit technology, $\pi = 1$. Under truth-telling, the first-order conditions are

$$\frac{1}{U'(C(r_2, \ell))} = \frac{1}{U'(C(r_2, h))} = \lambda + \mu \frac{\theta_g - \theta_p}{\theta_g} > \frac{1}{U'(C(r_1))}. \tag{8.7d}$$

The shareholders do not need the additional signal of market demand to undo the noise in a managed report. Since the payments' schedule dictated by an earnings management contract is feasible with truth-telling, the fact that the earnings management contract is not adopted indicates that it is more costly to the shareholders.

A numerical example illustrates our argument.

EXAMPLE 3: Suppose that the manager has a constant relative risk-aversion coefficient utility function, $U(z) = Z^{1/2}$, and that his disutility over good-performance effort and poor-performance effort is 0.75 and 0, respectively, and also that his reservation utility is 9.25. The probability of x_2 is 0.50 with good-performance effort and 0.25 with poor-performance effort. The remaining parameters are the same as in Examples 1 and 2.

The optimal contract under earnings management is the following: $C(r_1)$ = 62; $C(r_2, \ell)$ = 100; $C(r_2, h)$ = 141, with expected costs of 103; the shareholders' payoff is 149,897.

The optimal contract under truth-telling is $C(r_1)$ = 72; $C(r_2, \ell)$ = $C(r_2, h)$ = 132, with expected costs of 102; the shareholders' payoff is 149,898.

If the contract does not induce the good-performance effort, $C(r_1)$ = $C(r_2, \ell)$ = $C(r_2, h)$ = 100, with expected costs of 100, and the shareholders' payoff is 124,900 < 149,897.

The example indicates that earnings management is costly to the principal, but the cost relative to the expected outcome is almost negligible. Still, earnings management is pernicious because it both distorts the market price and reduces shareholders' value. Why, then, would the principal not take measures to curb it? The literature offers three answers: either the alternative to earnings management is too costly, or earnings management is beneficial, given other frictions in the contracting environment, or the self-interested principal prefers earnings management (Dye, 1988; Evans and Sridhar, 1996; Dutta and Gigler, 2002; Demski, Frimor, and Sappington, 2004; Gao, 2006; Goldman and Slezak, 2006; Ronen, Tzur, and Yaari, 2006; Goel and Thakor, 2007; Hermalin and Weisbach, 2007[15]).

In several studies (Dye, 1988; Evans and Sridhar, 1996; Crocker and Slemrod, 2006; Goldman and Slezak, 2006), the only alternative to designing a contract based on the managed report is offering the agent a flat wage, which creates disincentives to exert effort. Such an alternative is costly to the principal. Since the managed report is informative (on the efforts of the agent) because the reporting technology sets a limit on how large the gap between the truth and the managed report may be, a contract with earnings management is preferable to a contract that induces truth-telling. Preventing earnings management may also be costly because it diverts the effort of either the agent (Demski, Frimor, and Sappington, 2004) or the board of directors (Gao, 2006) from productive activity. Thus, in a world of second best (the outcome is unobservable costlessly), earnings management is optimal. According to Dutta and Gigler (2002), earnings management can be beneficial. This is the case when earnings management reduces the cost of inducing managers to issue forecasts in the face of uncertainty. Managing earnings allows managers to meet the forecasts under adverse conditions. In Ronen, Tzur, and Yaari (2006), we study the firm is a hierarchy of principal–agent relationships between shareholders and the board of directors, and between the board and management. The principal that designs management's incentives is the board. Preventing earnings management is costly to the board because it wishes to avoid conflict with management. Still, neutral earnings management is feasible be-

---

[15] Goel and Thakor (2007), are not concerned with earnings management per se. Yet, because earnings management could be the result of poor internal control and lower information in general (see Part 2), their study contributes to the earnings management literature by showing that an overconfident manager invests less in information production. They show that up to a point, having an overconfident manager rather than a rational one maximizes firm's value. Hence, it is in the self-interests of shareholders to hire overconfident managers and bear the consequences of earnings management.

cause the board can use the manager's compensation to signal when the report is managed. We show that the informed board encourages pernicious earnings management because it thus can make insider trading gains.[16]

We have thus far restricted attention to maximization. Maximization is largely a single-period phenomenon, but managers usually have multiyear incentive contracts. Healy (1985), observes that minimization is also logical for some economic earnings. If an inflated report does not increase the manager's reward, because performance is either above the maximum threshold or below the minimum threshold, then the efficient strategy is to deflate reported earnings in order to hoard them for future use.[17] Demski and Frimor (1999), find that when the contract can be renegotiated, the optimal reporting strategy is to issue a garbled report. An informative report destroys the manager's advantage in renegotiating the contract. In addition, because both parties are interested in the total payoff, any division of the total output between the two periods is innocuous as long as the total remains intact (by the definition of earnings management in Chap. 2, earnings management is neutral. See also the comments of their discussant, Rick Lambert, 1999). Christensen, Demski, and Frimor (2002), study the effect of the accounting system chosen by the principal on the equilibrium effort choices of the agent in a two-period model with renegotiation, under five regimes: truth-telling, aggregate reporting (the agent reports once at the end of the second period), conservative reporting (which allows either the truth or a minimization strategy in the first period with reversal in the second), aggressive reporting (which allows either the truth or maximization in the first period with reversal in the second), and a liberal system that allows both conservative and aggressive strategies. Their results seem to corroborate Demski and Frimor (1999), since the accounting systems that allow the aggregate strategy dominate the others. Gao (2006), derives conditions for maximization and minimization. She studies a two-period model in which the manager has access to a perfect capital market. The two-period contract is not based on the total outcome of both periods because of the correlation between the first- and the second-period outcome. That is, the first-period report contains valuable contracting information for the second-period compensation. Gao shows that there are

---

[16] Sing (2005), examines how the board of directors can design an inefficient compensation scheme to falsely signal to investors that the board has high quality and thus enhance the directors' reputation for running a well-governed firm. (This result is consistent with the scenario of the board as a facade, as discussed in Chap. 5.)

[17] We consider Healy's study at length in Chaps. 3 and 10.

equilibria where the board prefers to divert effort from monitoring to productive activity, which thus allows the manager to manage earnings. The linear contracts in each period have a different slope (Proposition 2), which induces the wealth-maximizing manager to shift reported earnings intertemporally. Minimization occurs when the marginal reward in period 2 is higher than the marginal reward in period 1.

We end this section with the following comments. First, we have so far analyzed earnings management at the level of the individual firm. Murphy (1999), and others report that bonuses are often based on relative performance, where the benchmark is the performance of other firms in the industry. Hence, relative performance evaluation provides new incentives to manage earnings. Bagnoli and Watts (2000), prove that relative performance induces each firm to appear to be outperforming the others. In equilibrium, then, each firm is a maximizer. Nagar and Petacchi (2005), solve for the optimal earnings management at a country level. The greater the number of firms engaging in earnings management, the smaller the benefit to a single firm but the likelihood of enforcement declines as well.

Second, our discussion has revolved around a principal–agent game with a costless, post-outcome, public signal (the market demand). We note that the principal–agent literature examines the optimal contract when the agent also possesses private pre-decision information (see, e.g., Baiman and Evans, 1983; Demski, 1994; Gigler and Hemmer, 2001; Lambert, 2001; Ronen and Yaari, 2001; Christensen and Feltham, 2005).

8.3 The Competitive Environment

Given the proprietary value of information in product markets, firms have many reasons to manage earnings. In Fischer and Verrecchia (2003), for example, disclosing news that is better than the truth in a Cournot competition with unknown demand is preferable to telling the truth when the firm can commit to produce according to what it discloses, not according to the truth. Such a setting is another instance of the well-known game-theoretic phenomenon, the "tyranny of the weak." Pretending to be irrational forces the other rational players to adapt their behavior in such a manner that the payoff of the pretender is larger than it would be if it behaved rationally.

We present another example, which involves a vertical market with two monopolies. The upstream firm produces an intermediate product at a unit cost of $\tilde{c}$ per unit, where $\tilde{c}$ is a random variable with mean $\bar{c}$ and variance s^2, taking values in the interval $[\underline{c}, \bar{c}]$. The upstream firm alone learns its unit cost and communicates this cost (via its financial reports) to the downstream firm before they negotiate the contract between them.

The contract between the firms specifies the quantity, q, and the intermediate product's price per unit, p_w. The downstream firm purchases the intermediate product after observing the final demand and communicating it to the upstream firm in its own financial reports. The inverse final demand is $\tilde{p} = \tilde{a} - q, \tilde{a} \in [\underline{a}, \overline{a}]$, where $\tilde{p}$ is the price to consumers and q is the quantity sold. Without loss of generality, assume that each unit of the intermediate good is transformed into one unit of the final product.

Since each firm can bias its own report, we denote the bias by $b_j, j = $ u, d, where u represents the upstream firm and d represents the downstream firm. The upstream firm's message is $c + b_u$; the downstream firm's message is $a + b_d$. Truth-telling obtains if $b_j = 0$; maximization obtains if $b_j > 0$; minimization obtains if $b_j < 0$.

Figure 8.3 summarizes the four stages of our model:

Date 1	Date 2	Date 3	Date 4
Each firm learns its own uncertain parameter. The upstream firm learns its unit cost, $\tilde{c}$, and the downstream firm learns the demand, $\tilde{a}$	Each firm prepares accounting reports based on its estimate of future performance. The report might include a bias of $b_j, j =$ u,d	The upstream and downstream firms set the price, p_w, and quantity, q, of the intermediate good	The firms realize their profits

Fig. 8.3 The main events

What will each firm's earnings management strategy be? To make this scenario interesting, assume that the two firms have infinite-horizon relationships, so that if a firm reports a certain variable, it is expected to act upon it. If not, the receiver of the report punishes any deviation from a strategy that is consistent with the report by ignoring messages from then on. That is, the Date 1 financial report is a commitment mechanism for a certain activity level.

The downstream firm chooses the quantity by maximizing $\pi_d = (p - p_w)q = (a + b_d - q - p_w)q$. The latter expression derives from substitution of the price of the final product, given its biased report, $p = a + b_d - q$. Taking the first-order condition with respect to q yields $q = \dfrac{a + b_d - p_w}{2}$. The upstream firm maximizes its profits, $\pi_u = (p_w - c - b_u)q =$

$\left[p_w - c - b_u \right] \dfrac{a + b_d - p_w}{2}$.   Taking the first-order condition with respect to p_w yields $p_w = \dfrac{a + c + b_d + b_u}{2}$. [18]

The reported profits of both firms, as a function of their biased reports, are as follows:

$$\pi_d = 2 \left[\frac{a - c}{4} + \frac{b_d - b_u}{4} \right]^2 . \tag{8.8a}$$

$$\pi_u = 2 \left[\frac{a - c}{4} + \frac{b_d - b_u}{4} \right]^2 . \tag{8.8b}$$

The profit functions indicate that if the upstream firm deflates its cost and the downstream firm inflates the demand, the reported profit per unit declines but the quantity sold and profits of each firm increase. The intuition is clear when one considers the equilibrium in the absence of earnings management. As Tirole (1988), and others have shown, the industry output and revenues are lower than the optimal level (for the industry) when each firm is a monopoly that maximizes its own profits. Hence, an expansionary earnings management strategy increases total reported profits. By deflating (inflating) its reported unit cost (demand), the upstream (down stream) firm sells (buys and sells to consumers) more. We leave to the reader the exercise of finding the cash flows effect of managing the reported earnings.

It seems that there are rich opportunities to characterize how competition in product markets induces earnings management. We hope to see more such work in the future.

---

[18] Solving the equilibrium yields the following:

$$q = \frac{a - c}{4} + \frac{b_d - b_u}{4} .$$

The reported contribution margins of the downstream and the upstream firms are

$$p_w - c - b_u = p - p_w + b_d = 2q .$$

8.4 Regulation

8.4.1 The Effect of Voluntary Disclosure on the ERC When the Firm Manages Earnings

In this section, we analyze how earnings management affects the value of regulation. Specifically, we study its effect on Rule 10b-5 of the 1934 Securities and Exchange Act in inducing firms to make honest voluntary disclosure.

Rule 10b-5 of the 1934 Securities Exchange Act states:
> It shall be unlawful for any person, directly or indirectly...
> (a)   [t]o employ any device, scheme, or artifice to defraud,
> (b)   [t]o make any untrue statement of a material fact or to omit to state a material fact necessary in order to make the statements made, in light of the circumstances under which they were made, not misleading, or
> (c)   [t]o engage in any act, practice, or course of business which operates or would operate as a fraud or a deceit upon any person, in connection with the purchase or sale of any security.
> 17 C.F.R 240.10b-5.

This rule has played a major role in investors' class action suits because it allows them to sue for damages caused by a deviation of the price they paid (or sold) from the correct price. The majority of cases involve earnings management by maximization, but, in recent years, suits have alleged other earnings management strategies. Still, common law indicates that failure to correct previous disclosures comes under this rule. Here we will restrict our attention to misrepresentation in a one-shot model. For an analysis that considers both misrepresentation and omission, consult Ronen and Yaari (2002).

8.4.2 The Analytical Model

Consider the principal–agent game studied in the previous section with the following modifications: First, each firm observes a private signal s, $s \in \{u,f\}$, that is indicative of the economic earnings x, $x \in \{x_1,x_2\}$, $x_1 < x_2$. The notation for s is nemophonic: u stands for "unfavorable"—bad news—and f stands for "favorable"—good news. The expected economic earnings when the signal is favorable are higher than when the signal is unfavorable. Denoting by θ^s the probability of x_2 conditional on a signal s, $\theta^s = \Pr[x=x_2|s]$, we assume that $\theta^f > \theta^u$. The prior probability of a favorable signal, γ, is common knowledge, $\gamma = \text{Prob}[s=f]$. Consequently, each firm makes two decisions: whether to make voluntary disclosure on s on Date 2, m, $s \in \{u,f\}$, and whether to manage earnings in the financial report, r, $r \in \{r_1,r_2\} = \{x_1,x_2\}$. None of these disclosures has to be truthful.

Second, there are two types of firms, reflecting their different dominant clientele (e.g., Hart, 1995): a fraction δ of the firms maximize the expected earnings, $E(x)$, and $1-\delta$ maximize the expected price, P. In what follows, we refer to the first type as VM and to the second as PM. We assume that the market cannot distinguish between the two types.

The application of Rule 10b-5 is based on the comparison between the expectations raised by the voluntary disclosure and the subsequent reported earnings and the price. Given that investors' information also includes the market-demand signal, the following cases are plausible:

Table 8.1 Incidence of Rule 10B-5 recoveries under different prices and disclosures[19]

The firm discloses (*m*)	The Price (*P*)	Report of a high outcome ($r=x_2$)	Report of a low outcome ($r=x_1$)
Favorable news	$P_2(f,h)$	0^1	Purchasers claim D^f
Favorable news	$P_2(f,l)$	0^1	0^2
Unfavorable news	$P_2(u,h)$	0^2	0^1
Unfavorable news	$P_2(u,l)$	Sellers claim D^u	0^1
Non-disclosure	$P_2(\varnothing,w)$, $w=l,h$	0^3	0^3

[1] Rule 10b-5 is not invoked because the report is consistent with the disclosure

[2] Rule 10b-5 cannot be invoked because the conflicting market-demand signal implies that there was "information on the market"

[3] Rule 10b-5 cannot be invoked because the information is not subject to an "affirmative duty to disclose"

Table 8.1 makes use of the "information on the market" doctrine. The premise of this doctrine is that the market is rational, in that the price correctly reflects all available information. Specifically, the market price is higher when demand is high than when demand is low because high market demand indicates a high likelihood of reporting $r=x_2$, while low demand is associated with reporting $r=x_1$. If the firm reported favorable (unfavorable) news and the market demand was low (high), the court will take

---

[19] We do not consider partial disclosure (i.e., the firm truthfully discloses only the favorable signal or truthfully discloses only the unfavorable signal). Proposition 3 in our paper addresses this family of strategies.

it for granted that the market knew the truth in advance that the report was going to be low (high). As the only source of information for the market is the firm itself (and its agents), conflicting signals of voluntary disclosure and market demand are treated by the court as indicating that the market receives information that allows it to correct the potential misconception induced by a misleading voluntary disclosure.

8.4.3 The Effect of Earnings Management on the Value of Rule 10b-5

We focus on the verifiability of the disclosure. If a disclosure is verifiable ex post, numerous mechanisms can be employed to induce truthful disclosure, such as enforceability in court. Alternatively, the market can induce truthful disclosure by treating non-disclosure as a cover-up of bad news. Hence, the firm is better off making a disclosure, which is truthful, because it is verifiable. In this case, Rule10b-5 is just one of many feasible mechanisms to elicit the truth and hence has no marginal value.

If disclosure is unverifiable, the equilibrium depends on the incentives of the owners to induce the manager to disclose the truth. If the firm did not manage earnings, the manager's private communication to the owners has no contracting value (Holmström, 1979) because it is a noisy signal of the truthfully reported outcome. Clearly, in this case Rule 10b-5 is redundant. Being indifferent to disclosure, some firms might voluntarily disclose the private signal, s. If they do, they will disclose the truth because they have no incentives to misrepresent.

The math shows that when the firm manages earnings, both a signal on market demand and voluntary disclosure are valuable, since they reduce the expected contracting cost. Hence, VM firms will disclose the truth. In equilibrium, PM firms pool by disclosing good news. This equilibrium involves a distortion in the market price because the good-news firms are underpriced. The question is whether Rule 10b-5 can improve the equilibrium.

Our answer is negative. The improvement requires deterring PM firms from making false disclosures. However, PM shareholders can benefit from pooling with VM firms and from the feasibility of class action suits based on Rule 10b-5. Because they sell their shares, they have a right to sue if the price is deflated. If the price is inflated, they are not required to disgorge their excessive proceeds because the defendants in the lawsuit are the firm and its directors and officers, not the shareholders. The buyers of their shares will not discount the price to account for the possibility that the price is inflated because they too can sue the firm. The only possible change is that the cost to the incumbent shareholders might deter VM firms from making disclosures. In this case, the regulation actually depresses a valuable mechanism that reduces the effect of earnings management on the quality of the financial reports as a signal of a firm's value. (For additional analysis, consult Ronen and Yaari, 2002; Ronen, Ronen, and Yaari, 2003.)

As a final comment, note that the analysis in this section is based on a principal–agent model with voluntary disclosure of private information. As a research topic, voluntary disclosure has attracted a great deal of interest, both theoretical (Verrecchia, 2001; Dye, 2001) and empirical (King, Pownall, and Waymire, 1990; Healy and Palepu, 2001; Core, 2001).[20] The topic of earnings management *cum* disclosure has several aspects.[21] As just discussed, research (Fischer and Verrecchia, 2000; Dutta and Gigler, 2002; Ronen, Ronen, and Yaari, 2003) has shown that disclosure reduces the pernicious scope of earnings management. Indeed, in some cases, it can eliminate it altogether because the market can compare the two signals and penalize the firm or manager if the signals do not agree.

---

[20] The consensus is that disclosure is a strategic decision (Dechow and Schrand, 2004). This does not necessarily imply that the disclosure strategy is consistent over time. For example, Jaggi and Sannella's (1995) sample comprises 274 forecasts from 209 forecasters: 146 firms disclosed forecasts only once during the study period, 1979–1988; 62 firms disclosed twice, and one disclosed four times. Miller and Piotroski (2000), in contrast, find that a prior disclosure choice is a strong predictor of current disclosure decisions, which suggests that a firm's disclosure policy is independent of current economic conditions and that the market disciplines firms to make disclosures. A plausible explanation is that creating expectations for future disclosure might depress current disclosure in order not to create unrealistic expectations; see the survey by Harvey, Graham, and Rajgopal (2005), of CFOs' decisions to provide guidance.

[21] King, Pownall, and Waymire (1990, p. 114) identify three stages in disclosure:
Stage A: The firm deliberates between no disclosure and the **information** to be disclosed: earnings forecasts, sales forecasts, and so forth.
Stage B: The firm chooses the **channel**: public disclosure or private disclosure.
Stage C: Tertiary choices regarding public disclosure. The firm chooses the **quality** of the signal, ranging from a precise point estimate to a vague qualitative forecast.
The second stage has not existed in U.S. markets since the SEC issued Regulation FD (2000), as private communication with select analysts and money managers is now illegal.

8.4.4 The Effect of Regulation on Earnings Management

In several studies, regulation determines the institutional setting for the earnings management phenomenon. In some, regulation is the reason that the revelation principle does not apply (Ronen and Yaari, 1993). For example, the revelation principle requires that the agent sends a message confidentially to the principal (Myerson, 1979, 1991). In some instances, however, this could violate insider trading regulations that bar receipt of private information by the trader at the time of the trade (see Chap. 3).

Other studies make a direct connection between regulation and earnings management. Dye (2002), examines the issue by modeling a firm's type as a continuous random variable, where accounting regulations identify a cutoff point, such that the accounting treatment of all types with a higher value is different from the accounting treatment applied to all types below, and each firm prefers to appear as belonging to the high end. Earnings management enters the picture by the assumption that firms can spend costly resources to appear in a better light. Because these costs are common knowledge, readers of the reports can distinguish between the official regulatory cutoffs and the one actually used (a shadow cutoff), which is much lower. Dye's study explores the relationship between these cutoff points. He shows that because the cost of earnings management is proportional to the gap between the truth and the actual classification, the two cutoffs are not independent. That is, regulators cannot choose both; the choice of one dictates the choice of the other. Moreover, if manipulation cost is low all firms attempt to report as if their type exceeds the regulatory cutoff.

In Ewert and Wagenhofer (2005), regulation determines the cost of managing earnings. If regulators increase the cost of managing earnings through accounting treatments, the firm may substitute the cosmetic earnings management strategy for real smoothing that consumes cash flows.

Nagar and Petacchi (2005), study the link between earnings management and regulation on the economy level, in that the proportion of firms managing earnings, and its effect on the capital market, is different in different economies. They find that the greater the number of firms that manage earnings, the greater the difficulty a regulator faces in punishing them, but their results indicate that the rewards of earnings management decline as well. As a result, the profile of earnings management in different economies varies with the regulatory regime.

Goldman and Slezak (2006), consider regulation as expressed through the penalties imposed on those caught managing earnings. If penalties are sufficiently large, the regulator can induce truthful reports. If not, regulation might instead increase earnings management (or decrease firms' value). The intuition of this result lies in the effects of incentives on the manager's effort and the likelihood of earnings management. Stronger incentives induce the manager to exert more effort but they also induce him to manage earnings more intensely. This creates a trade-off because higher effort increases the expected firm's value and earnings management reduces firm's value because it consumes economic resources.

Recent research has examined the effect of certain provisions of Sarbanes-Oxley Act (SOX) on earnings management. Friebel and Guriev (2005), for example, discuss the effect of whistle-blower regulations on the collusion between middle management with senior management to manage earnings. Since whistle-blowing regulation increases the number of insiders whom upper management has to bribe to overlook its earnings management attempt, the benefit of earnings management declines. The added effect of the SOX of inducing auditors to monitor earnings management more carefully implies that the SOX is effective in reducing earnings management. Goldman and Slezak (2006), delineate the effect of improved monitoring by auditors resulting from the SOX prohibition on audit services, which decreases earnings management but also decreases firms' value.

8.5 Summary

We summarize Part 3 with a numerical example that illustrates how different reporting strategies yield different series of reported earnings. The example features a four-period horizon, and the total economic and accounting earnings must coincide at the end of the horizon. Hence, the average report is the same across categories, but the variability of the reports is zero when the firm smoothes. Since the example features growth in earnings, a minimization strategy yields the highest variability, and this variability exceeds the variability of the series of truthful reports (Table 8.2).

Table 8.2 Summary table

Year	Economic earnings (1)	Truth-telling (2)	Taking a bath (3)	Minimizing (4)	Maximizing (5)	Smoothing (6)
1	$ 1,370	$ 1,370	(200)	$ 1,233	$ 1,507	$ 7,000
2	3,940	3,940	?	3,546	4,334	7,000
3	15,690	15,690	?	16,221[a]	15,159[a]	7,000[a]
Total	$21,000	$21,000	$21,000	$21,000	$21,000	$21,000
Average	$7,000	$7,000	$7,000	$7,000	$7,000	$7,000
(Variance[b])	(2,776)	(2,776)	(?)	(3,100)	(2,473)	(0)

1. Given
2. The report equals (1)
3. The firm reports the minimum Earnings in the first period
4. The report is 90% of the truth
5. The report in 110% of the truth
6. The report is smoothed perfectly, $7,000=$21,000/3

[a] Plugged numbers
[b] Variability deflated by total earnings

Part 4

In this part, we deal with the mechanics of the empirical research on earnings management. As noted below, most of the research has identified earnings management with the detection of discretionary accruals. Hence, we first offer a short discussion of accruals.

Accruals

Accruals arise when there is a discrepancy between the timing of cash flows and the timing of the accounting recognition of the transaction. One notable example involves the recognition of revenues. Revenues may be recognized after customers advance cash and before total collection is assured (Table 1).

Table 1 The accruals process

Period	1	2	3
Event	An advance from a customer	Shipment of the merchandize to the customer	The customer settles his account
Cash flows	Inflow of advance	None	Inflow of the final payment
Accounting recognition of revenue	None	Recording of revenues	None
Accruals	Increase in "unearned revenues"	Decrease in "unearned revenues" and/or increase in "accounts receivable"	Decrease in "accounts receivable"

The advance creates a liability termed "unearned revenues." The final payment decreases the asset termed "accounts receivable."

Over the firm's lifetime, reported revenues must equal total (gross) cash inflows, and total accruals must equal zero; that is, accrued balances of assets and liabilities reverse. In our example, the unearned revenues liability is reduced to zero upon the shipment of the merchandize, and the accounts receivable asset is reduced to zero when the customer pays his debt.

The research on accruals management attempts to distinguish between accruals resulting from managed earnings and normal accruals.

> *Definitions*:   **Non-discretionary accruals** are accruals that arise from transactions made in the current period that are normal for the firm given its performance level and business strategy, industry conventions, macro-economic events, and other economic factors. **Discretionary accruals** are accruals that arise from transactions made or accounting treatments chosen in order to manage earnings.[1] **reversals** are accruals originating from transactions made in previous periods.

Note that this definition is consistent with our definition in Chap. 2 in that we wish to distinguish between normal transactions and accounting treatments and abnormal transactions and accounting treatments aimed at managing earnings, and we allow for beneficial and neutral earnings management.

In some cases, discretionary accruals may be quite large. Beneish (1997), finds that in his sample of 43 firms that were subject to enforcement actions by the SEC between 1987 and 1994, the mean overestimation of earnings was 42.5% of retained earnings and 11.5% of total assets (table 2, panel B). Richardson, Tuna, and Wu (2002), whose accruals encompass both working-capital and asset acquisition accruals, find that total accruals amount to 8.7% of average total assets in their sample of 440 firm-years (of 225 firms) that restated earnings between 1971 and 2000, as compared to 3.9% of the average assets for the control group of non-restatement firms (t-statistic = 4.50).[2]

---

[1] In this definition, *accrued balances* are all non-cash assets and all liabilities that are not borrowings (such as bank debt, bonds, etc.).

[2] Beneish's 64-firm sample contains firms with missing data. Hence, the statistics applies to 43 firms only. Beneish's sample can be criticized on the ground that it is composed of young firms, so perhaps the percentages should be attributed to size. McNichols (2000), reports that the median net income before extraordinary items for Compustat firms for the 1988–1998 period is 3.8% of the beginning of the period total assets. She observes that an average earnings management of even 1% of total assets would be material to most firms' earnings.

Our definition implies that the total accrued balances of firm i in period t break down as follows:

$$EBTA_{it} = DA_{it} + NA_{it} + Reversal_{it} + EBTA_{i,t-1.} \tag{1a}$$

where

$EBTA_{ik}$	$=$	ending accrued balances of firm i in period k, $k=t,t-1$;
DA_{it}	$=$	Discretionary accruals of firm i resulting from transactions and events occurring in period t;
NA_{it}	$=$	non-discretionary accruals of firm i resulting from transactions and events occurring in period t;
$Reversal_{it}$	$=$	reversal in period t of balances accrued by firm i in previous periods.

To illustrate Eq. 1a, consider this example. Suppose that the firm makes a $200 sale. The normal credit period is 30 days. Unable to make the sale without relaxing the credit policy, the firm boosts earnings by agreeing to 50% payment in 30 days, and the remaining 50% in 60 days. The breakdown of account balances and accruals is as follows:

	Month			
	1	**2**	**3**	**Total**
$EBTA_{i,t-1}$	0			
$EBTA_{it}$	+200	100	0	
DA_{it}	+ 100			+100
ND_{it}	+ 100			+100
$Reversal_{it}$		−100	−100	− 200
Total				0

In the first month, the non-discretionary accrued balance increases by 100, and the discretionary accrued balance increases by 100. In the second month, the non-discretionary accrued balance decreases by 100, and in the following month, the discretionary accrued balance decreases by 100. The payments of 100 in months 2 and 3 are the reversals. The reversals ensure that the changes in accrued balances add up to zero.

The reversal of accrued balances limits the ability to manage earnings. To illustrate, consider a case in which revenues are boosted in the current year by shipping unsolicited merchandise to customers. The merchandize is expected to be returned in the next accounting period (see Chap. 2 on

Similarly, Kothari, Leone, and Wasley (2005, table 1) show that the discretionary accruals measured by the Jones model are –0.19 of total assets, as compared to average total accruals of –3.03% of total assets in their 122,798 firm-year sample collected for the 1963–1999 period. The negative value is explained by depreciation.

"channel stuffing"). The revenues of the next period are thus lowered by "sales returns," and the "accounts receivable" accrued balance thus reverses. Suppose, for the purpose of the example, that in the next year unmanaged earnings and the expected reported earnings remain the same. The firm then must double the size of managed earnings to offset the negative impact of the reversal of the previous year's earnings management. In the following year, the firm must triple the managed sales, and so on.

Although reversals are important, it seems that most empirical research ignores them (in Chap. 11, we detail studies that attempt to deal with reversals), largely because they are unobservable. The studies equate total accruals with the difference between the ending and the beginning accrued balances. Unfortunately, this injects a measurement error into the accruals, as in the following example.

The beginning balances (BB) of cash and accounts receivable are 50 and 80, respectively. The firm conducts two sales transactions, a normal sale of $2,000, which increases non-discretionary accruals, NDA, by $200, and an aggressive "channel stuffing" that increase sales and discretionary accruals (DA) by $50. The beginning accrued balance of accounts receivable was paid in the current period.

The change in the balances of accruals is $170 ($250–$80), which also equals the difference between earnings and cash flows ($2050–$1880), but the total of NDA and DA is $250 ($200+$50).

Cash		Accounts receivable		Sales	
BB 50		BB 80			
1,800		(NDA) 200			2,000
		(DA) 50			50
80			80 (Reversal)		
EB 1,930		EB 250			2,050 EB

A reversed BB of $80 created this difference. If, however, the BB was not paid in the current period, the difference between the beginning and ending balances correctly reflects the sum of NDA plus DA, as would the difference between earnings (revenue) and cash flows ($2,050–$1,800).[3]

---

[3] As we shall see, empiricists ignoring reversals implicitly correct for the omission by relating their measured accruals to the difference in sales rather than to sales. However, a measure of accruals that ignores the reversals fails to reflect all what management purposefully accrues during the current period. Consequently, such a procedure fails to calibrate the full magnitude of purposeful discretionary accruals.

The Plan of Part 4

Chapter 9 presents an analytical model of the accruals generation process in the absence of earnings management. We expand on this model and examine the effect of earnings management on the statistical properties of accruals. This framework underlies the research on both earnings management and the relationships between accruals and cash flows.

Chapter 10 describes the evolution of the empirical research in accruals management up through the publication of the Jones model in 1991. The second half of Chap. 10 evaluates the efficiency of the Jones model.

Chapter 11 details the progress since 1991, ending with the synthesis model of Ye (2006). We also discuss alternative methodologies: the accounting choices approach and the distributional approach. The former focuses on certain accruals that are known to have a material impact on earnings. The latter assumes that a deviation of the distribution of earnings from the normal distribution indicates earnings management. A special case is the penny approach, which tests whether firms manage the penny in earnings per share to round the number in the preferred direction.

9 The Accruals Process

In the Introduction to Part 4, we separated accruals into three components: discretionary accruals, non-discretionary accruals, and reversals arising from transactions that took place in previous periods. The unobservability of the composition of accruals poses a challenge to the earnings management research. Elgers, Pfeiffer, and Porter (2003, p. 406), state, "A fundamental issue in assessing earnings management is the unobservability of the managed and un-managed components of reported earnings."

Apart from mistakenly ignoring reversals, a reason for this difficulty is that non-discretionary accruals vary with performance. A change in total accruals is consistent with both a change in non-discretionary accruals that is induced by varying performance and the accumulation of discretionary accruals produced by managing earnings. Hence, researchers need to understand what to expect of normal accruals in order to identify managed accruals and strengthen the power of their empirical tests of earnings management (see, e.g., Guay, Kothari, and Watts, 1996; Jiambalvo, 1996; Dechow, Sabino, and Sloan, 1998; McCulloch, 1998a; Black and McCulloch, 2003). As a discussant of Dechow and Dichev (2002; discussed in Chap. 11), McNichols (2002, p. 67), states, "[T]his paper suggests several future research directions. The first direction is to enrich the modeling by specifying the process generating cash flows, …."

We turn our attention, then, to non-discretionary accruals. In the following section, we explain how earnings management can affect observable accruals by introducing discretion in the firm's report.

9.1 Non-discretionary Accruals

9.1.1 The Non-discretionary Accruals Generation Process

It is customary to start with an assumption about the behavior of sales over time for two good reasons. First, as in budgeting processes, sales determine a firm's production and inventories, which, in turn, determine the cost of sales, other operating costs, and investment decisions. Second, sales have the highest persistence of any component of the income statement, where persistence measures the effect of increasing a certain variable by $1 on the future value of the same variable.[1] Dechow and Schrand (2004, table 2.1, p. 13), summarize 56,940 firm-year observations between 1987 and 2002 and find that sales have the largest persistence, 0.85; operating income (before and after depreciation) comes next, 0.76, then pretax earnings, 0.72, and finally earnings before special items, 0.71 (all variables are deflated by assets). It therefore seems that the sales variable is an efficient statistic for describing the characteristics of a firm.

A characterization of the sales process follows:

$$S_t = (1+\lambda)[\mu + \phi(S_{t-1}-\mu)] + \varepsilon_t, \tag{9.1}$$

where

S_t = sales in period t;
λ = growth;
μ = mean sales;
ϕ = a persistence parameter that measures the effect of the previous period's drift on this period's sales, $0 \leq \phi \leq 1$;
ε = serially independent white noise, $E(\varepsilon)=0$, $E(\varepsilon^2)= \sigma^2 >0$, and $Cov(\varepsilon_t, \varepsilon_{t-1})=0$.

The sales generation process encompasses the most often used stochastic processes in the accounting literature: If $\phi =0$, the process is mean-reverting. If $\phi=1$, the process is a random walk, and if $0 < \phi < 1$, the process is a random walk with a drift.

Mean reversion characterizes mature large firms and firms with extreme performance (Fama and French, 2000). It is a property of performance measures such as the rate of return on assets (Barber and Lyon, 1996; Sloan, 1996) in long windows. Several authors note that the reversion to the mean tends to require more than one fiscal accounting period, and the reversion is faster when a firm's performance is extreme (Finger, 1994; Sloan, 1996; Dechow, Sabino, and Sloan, 1998; Fama and French, 2000; Nissim and Penman, 2001 Feng 2004 Richardson, Sloan, Soliman, and Tuna, 2005).

Other authors have adopted the assumption that $\phi=1$ (and $\lambda =0$), that is, that the process is a random walk (Finger, 1994; Dechow, Kothari, and

---

[1] Mathematically, for a given variable, Z, its persistence is $\dfrac{\partial Z_{t+1}}{\partial Z_t}$. Empirically, Z_{t+1} is regressed on Z_t, $Z_{t+1}=a_0 + a_1 Z_t+$noise, and a_1 is the measure of persistence.

Watts, 1998; Barth, Cram, and Nelson, 2001; Kothari, Leone, and Wasley, 2005). This characterizes the sales generation process of an average firm in a short window. In a test of the validity of the random walk, Dechow, Kothari, and Watts (1998), find that the serial correlation of the white noise in sales, before they make the required adjustment for a small sample, is just 0.17 in their quarterly earnings sample.

Sales determine the change in working-capital accrued balances: accounts receivable on credit sales, and change in inventory and accounts payable on credit purchases. We proceed with the special case in which the inventory is zero (See the Appendix for a model with inventory). If we assume that beginning accrued balances reverse in full in the current period, total accruals in our model are the difference between the change in accounts receivable, ΔAR_t, and the change in accounts payable, ΔAP_t, that is, $TA_t = \Delta AR_t - \Delta AP_t$. We assume that $\alpha\%$ of sales, S, are on credit, $0 < \alpha < 1$. The accrued balance of accounts receivable, AR, at the end of period t is

$$AR_t = \alpha S_t. \tag{9.2}$$

Similarly, $\beta\%$ of purchases, P, are on credit, $0 < \beta < 1$. The accrued balance of accounts payable, AP_t, at the end of period t is

$$AP_t = \beta P_t, \tag{9.3}$$

where

$$P_t = (1-\pi)S_t. \tag{9.4}$$

π is the gross profit as a percentage of sales. Denote by δ the increase in total accruals per dollar of sales, $\delta = \alpha - \beta(1-\pi)$. The total accruals in any given period, TA_t, are the sum of non-discretionary accruals, δS_t, and the reversal of the beginning accrued balance in period t–1, $-\delta S_{t-1}$, and the corresponding ending accrued balance, $EBTA_t$, is

$$TA_t = \delta\Delta S_t, \tag{9.5a}$$

$$EBTA_t = \delta S_t, \tag{9.5b}$$

where $\Delta S_t = S_t - S_{t-1}$. With such a sales generation process, ΔS_t is determined by the growth rate, $\Delta S_t = \lambda S_{t-1}$. The growth rate can differentiate between a growth industry, $\lambda > 0$, and a declining industry, $\lambda < 0$. An example of the latter is the airline industry after 9/11.

9.1.2 The Statistical Properties of Accruals

At the beginning of period t, all sales and expenses, and the gross margin up to period t-1, are known history, H_{t-1}, but the current-period sales innovation, ε_t, and future sales innovations are unknown. In what follows, we restrict attention to conditional moments, expectations, variance, and co variance.

The conditional expectation, variance, and serial covariance of the unmanaged accrual changes are as follows:

$$E[TA_t | H_{t-1}] = \delta E\Delta S_t, \quad \text{where } E\Delta S_t = (1+\lambda)(1-\phi)(\mu - S_{t-1}) + \lambda S_{t-1}. \quad (9.6)$$

$$\text{Var}[TA_t | H_{t-1}] = \delta^2 \sigma^2. \quad (9.7)$$

$$\text{Cov}[TA_t, TA_{t+1} | H_{t-1}] = \delta^2[(1+\lambda)\phi - 1]\sigma^{2}.^2 \quad (9.8)$$

The conditional expected accruals given the history depend on the growth in sales, λ, the type of the sales generation process, ϕ, and the relative size of accruals, δ. If the process is a random walk with zero growth, the expected accruals are zero.

The conditional variance of accruals depends on the variability of the sales innovation, σ^2, and the intensity of accruals, δ. For growth firms with $\lambda > 1/\phi - 1$, accruals are positively correlated despite the negative impact of reversals on intertemporal correlation. For lower growth rates, however, the effect of reversals dominates and accruals are negatively correlated intertemporally.

We next examine whether accruals have predictive power for future earnings, X, and the net cash inflows, CF:

$$\text{Cov}(TA_t, X_{t+1} | H_{t-1}) = \delta\pi(1+\lambda)\phi\sigma^2. \quad (9.9)$$

Since $CF_{t+1} = X_{t+1} - TA_{t+1} = (\pi - \delta)S_{t+1} + \delta S_t$,

$$\text{Cov}(TA_t, CF_{t+1} | H_{t-1}) = \delta(\pi - \delta)(1+\lambda)\phi\sigma^2 + \delta^2\sigma^{2}.^3 \quad (9.10)$$

Accruals are correlated with future earnings when current sales have some persistence, $\phi > 0$, and thus with future cash flows. The correlation of

---

[2] Note that $S_{t+1} - E(S_{t+1}) = (1+\lambda)\phi\varepsilon_t + \varepsilon_{t+1}$. Hence,
$\text{Cov}[TA_t, TA_{t+1}|H_{t-1}] = E[\delta\varepsilon_t(\delta(1+\lambda)\phi\varepsilon_t - \lambda\varepsilon_t)] = \delta^2[(1+\lambda)\phi - 1]\sigma^2$.

[3] $\text{Cov}[TA_t, CF_{t+1}|H_{t-1}] = \delta E[\varepsilon_t((\pi-\delta)(1+\lambda)\phi + \delta)\varepsilon_t] = \delta(\pi-\delta)(1+\lambda)\phi\sigma^2 + \delta^2\sigma^2$.

current accruals with future cash flows reflects the reversal of current accruals. In sum, accruals are value-relevant.

9.2 The Effect of Earnings Management on Accruals

The injection of earnings management into our model is problematic because there are many earnings-management strategies. The common denominator of all of them is that the firm makes a report X^r that is different from the truth, X. It stands to reason that the decision on the gap between the reported and true earnings is made close to the date of the report, depending on its audience and the firm's accounting flexibility (see Chap. 2). Since Part 3 discusses such games, we here just aim to show the impact of DA on the statistical properties of earnings and accruals. We narrow the discussion to two strategies that involve the timing of the recognition of the innovation in sales, ε. One strategy defers recognition (SD), and the other accelerates it (SB). Each strategy intertemporally shifts the innovation in sales, ε.

Deferral is attractive, for example, to a firm that plans an IPO and wishes to show a steep growth in sales in order to generate a higher valuation due to a higher growth rate. In contrast, a firm that plans to raise capital may accelerate recognition because it wishes to show stronger financial health to lower its cost of capital.

Suppose that the firm reports the truth until period t-1 and manages earnings in period t alone (i.e., the firm does not manage earnings in period t+1). Consequently, no reversal of discretionary accruals takes place in period t. SD defers reported earnings by setting $DA_t = -\theta(\pi\varepsilon_t)$, $0 < \theta < 1$. SB accelerates reported earnings by setting $DA_t = \rho(\pi\varepsilon_{t+1})$, $0 < \rho < 1$.

For notational purposes, we combine the two types in the analysis below. The earnings-management strategy produces the following report, X^r, in period t:

$$X_t^r = \pi\{S_t - \theta\mathbf{1}\varepsilon_t + \rho(1-\mathbf{1})\varepsilon_{t+1}\}, \qquad (9.11a)$$

where $\mathbf{1}$ is an indicator function that takes the value of one under SD and zero under SB. Since the firm adopts either strategy, Eq. 9.11a indicates that under SD, $X_t^r = \pi\{S_t - \theta\varepsilon_t\}$ and under SB, $X_t^r = \pi\{S_t + \rho\varepsilon_{t+1}\}$.

Because of the reversal of accruals, the following period's reported earnings are

$$X_{t+1}^r = \pi\{S_{t+1} + \theta\mathbf{1}\varepsilon_t - \rho(1-\mathbf{1})\varepsilon_{t+1}\}. \qquad (9.11b)$$

A comparison of Eqs. 9.11a and 9.11b confirms that earnings management concerns the timing of the recognition of sales. Under our assumption that accruals change by δ per one unit of sales, the corresponding accruals are

$$\text{TA}_t = \delta\left[\Delta S_t - \theta 1 \varepsilon_t + \rho(1-1)\varepsilon_{t+1}\right]; \qquad (9.12a)$$

$$\text{TA}_{t+1} = \delta\left[\Delta S_{t+1} + \theta 1 \varepsilon_t - \rho(1-1)\varepsilon_{t+1}\right]. \qquad (9.12b)$$

9.2.1 The Statistical Properties of Managed Accruals

From Eqs. 9.12a and 9.12b, we derive the following statistical properties of total accruals conditional on history up to period t-1:

$$E[\text{TA}_t \mid H_{t-1}] = \delta E \Delta S_t. \qquad (9.13)$$

$$\text{Var}[\text{TA}_t \mid H_{t-1}] = \delta^2\left[(1-\theta 1)^2 + \rho^2(1-1)\right]\sigma^2. \qquad (9.14)$$

$$\text{Cov}[\text{TA}_t, \text{TA}_{t+1} \mid H_{t-1}] = \delta^2 \sigma^2 M, \qquad (9.15)$$

where $M = (1+\lambda)\phi(1-\theta 1) - (1-\theta 1)^2 + \rho(1-\rho)(1-1)$.[4]

Our assumption that the instrument of earnings management is the sales innovation implies that, in expectation, the expected total accruals are the same as when the firm does not manage earnings (the expected sales innovation is zero). The effect of earnings management on the conditional variance is sensitive to the strategy used. If the firm defers earnings to period t+1, it reduces variability. This strategy smoothes earnings. Backdating sales has the opposite effect. The effect of earnings management on the temporal covariance of accruals is sensitive to the type of earnings management. Under SD, two competing effects take place. On the one hand, deferring reported sales innovation implies obscuring the effect of current sales innovation on future earnings, and hence on future accruals; that is, SD lowers the covariance between successive accruals. On the

---

[4] The deviation of TA_t from their mean is $(1-\theta 1)\varepsilon_t + \rho(1-1)\varepsilon_{t+1}$.

The deviation of TA_{t+1} is $(1+\lambda)\phi\varepsilon_t - (1-\theta 1)\varepsilon_t + (1-\rho(1-1))\varepsilon_{t+1}$.

$\text{Cov}[\text{TA}_t, \text{TA}_{t+1}]$ is the expectations of the product of these deviations. Note that $\rho(1-1)[1-\rho(1-1)] = \rho(1-\rho)(1-1)$.

other hand, a smaller amount reverses in period $t+1$, which mitigates the negative correlation introduced by the reversal and increases the covariance. The net effect depends on $(1+\lambda)\phi-(1-\theta)$. If it is negative (positive), the temporal covariance decreases (increases). Under SB, however, the temporal covariance increases because the current accruals also signal future sales innovation.

By construction, future cash flows are $CF_{t+1} = X^r_{t+1} - TA_{t+1} = (\pi-\delta)(S_{t+1} + \theta 1\varepsilon_t - \rho(1-1)\varepsilon_{t+1}) + \delta S_t$. The cash-flow effect stems from the restructuring of the revenue transaction designed to manage earnings (see Chap. 2). Hence, parallel to Eqs. 9.9 and 9.10, respectively,

$$Cov(TA_t, X^r_{t+1}|H_{t-1}) = \delta\pi\sigma^2 M.^5 \tag{9.16}$$

$$Cov(TA_t, CF_{t+1}|H_{t-1}) = Cov(TA_t, X^r_{t+1}|H_{t-1}) - Cov(TA_t, TA_{t+1}|H_{t-1}). \tag{9.17}$$

Given that the term in brackets in Eq. 9.16 is the same as that in Eq. 9.15, a discussion of the informativeness of the change in current accruals with regard to future reported earnings (Eq. 9.16) and future cash flows (Eq. 9.17) would echo the discussion of the temporal covariance. The signaling strategy, SB, improves informativeness, and smoothing, SD, has an ambiguous effect.

Finally, we examine the relationships between discretionary accruals, DA_t, $DA_t = -\theta 1\varepsilon_t + \rho(1-1)\varepsilon_{t+1}$, and non-discretionary accruals, $NDA_t = \delta\Delta S_t$

$$Cov(DA_t, NDA_t) = -\delta\theta 1\sigma^2. \tag{9.18}$$

As in McCulloch (1998a), and Black and McCulloch (2003), smoothing out sales innovation (SD) introduces a negative correlation between the two types of accruals. The signaling strategy (SB) still maintains no correlation between the two types.

Managing earnings to adjust the timing of the recognition of sales changes the contemporaneous statistical properties of accruals and earn-

---

[5] Since the deviation of TA_t from their mean equals $\delta[(1-\theta 1)\varepsilon_t + \rho(1-1)\varepsilon_{t+1}]$,

$Cov(TA_t, X^r_{t+1}|H_{t-1}) = \delta\pi E[A \times B]$,

where $A = (1-\theta 1)\varepsilon_t + \rho(1-1)\varepsilon_{t+1}$. $B = (1+\lambda)\phi\varepsilon_t - (1-\theta 1)\varepsilon_t + (1-\rho(1-1))\varepsilon_{t+1}$.

Since $\rho(1-1)(1-\rho(1-1)) = \rho(1-\rho)(1-1)$,

$Cov(TA_t, X^r_{t+1}|H_{t-1}) = \delta\pi[(1+\lambda)\phi(1-\theta 1) - (1-\theta 1)^2 + \rho(1-\rho)(1-1)]\sigma^2$.

ings, while leaving expected accruals intact. The qualitative effect depends on the strategy. If earnings management uses forward-looking information, it is beneficial because it increases the predictability of accruals. If, however, earnings management attempts to hide information on current sales innovation by smoothing it out, earnings management might be pernicious, in that it reduces the correlation between changes in accruals and current and future performance. We will use the insights of this chapter in the following one.

We conclude with the following comment. In the Introduction of Part 4, we presented accrued balances, but in the analysis in Chap. 9, we used changes in accrued balances. The difference between the two approaches is not perfunctory. It is easier theoretically to focus on balances because reversal then is salient. As we shall see in Chaps. 10 and 11, however, the empirical research largely employs changes in accrued balances.

9.3 Accruals and Cash Flows

9.3.1 Accruals Mispricing

It is worth noting that the modeling of accruals is relevant to investigations beyond earnings management. For example, research has been concerned with the *persistence* of accruals and cash flows and whether the market correctly evaluates them. Persistence of each variable is defined as the weight of current variable in predicting the same variable one year ahead (see footnote 1) (see Dechow, 1994; Subramanyam, 1996; Guay and Sidhu, 1996; Dechow, Kothari, and Watts, 1998; Dechow and Schrand, 2004).

The perception that accruals reverse and hence are less persistent than cash flows gave rise to a literature dealing with "accruals mispricing" (or accruals anomalies) that started with Sloan (1996). Studies examined whether the stock market can distinguish between accruals and cash flows when valuing earnings and found that it could not (see Pfeiffer, Elgers, Lo, and Rees, 1998; Pfeiffer and Elgers, 1999; Ali, Hwang, and Trombley, 2000; Bradshaw, Richardson, and Sloan, 2001; DeFond and Park, 2001; Xie, 2001; Burgstahler, Jiambalvo, and Shevlin, 2002; Beneish and Vargus, 2002; Fairfield, Whisenant, and Yohn, 2002; Hribar and Collins, 2002; Collins, Gong, and Hribar, 2003; Sun, 2003; Zach, 2003; Ahmed, Billings, and Morton, 2004; Desai, Rajgopal, and Venkatachalam, 2004; Ahmed, Nainar, and Zhou, 2005; Atwood and Xie, 2005; Beneish and

Nichols, 2005, 2006; Dopuch, Seethamraju, and Xu, 2005; Levi, 2005; Melendrez, Schwartz, and Trombley, 2005; Richardson, Sloan, Soliman, and Tuna, 2005; Wei and Xie, 2005; Barone and Magilke, 2006; Chambers, 2005; Core, Guay, Richardson, and Verdi, 2006; Dechow, Richardson, and Sloan, 2006; Cheng and Thomas, 2006; Louis, Robinson, and Sbaraglia, 2006; Mashruwala, Rajgopal, and Shevlin, 2006; Papanastasopoulos, Thomakos, and Wang, 2007).

9.3.2 Highlights of the Research

Sloan (1996), finds in his 40,679 firm-year sample that the market does not distinguish between accruals and cash flows in annual reports even though the accrual component of earnings is less persistent than the cash-flow component. Specifically, he shows that firms with high levels of current accruals experience systematic reductions in future earnings and that stock prices behave "as if" investors do not anticipate the declines. Collins and Hribar (2000), and Core, Guay, Richardson, and Verdi (2006), extend this result to quarterly data, showing that it is distinct from the post-earnings drift phenomenon.

Collins, Gong, and Hribar (2003), observe that large firms with high institutional ownership experience less mispricing of accruals than smaller, less profitable, and less liquid firms.

Bradshaw, Richardson, and Sloan (2001), Ahmed, Nainar, and Zhou (2005), study analysts' forecast errors, finding that analysts do not differentiate correctly between the persistence of accruals and cash flows. Bradshaw, Richardson, and Sloan (2001), show that auditors, who are expected to be sophisticated users of accounting information, also misprice extreme accruals. In contrast, Mashruwala, Rajgopal, and Shevlin (2006), find that the mispricing of accruals is not arbitraged away by sophisticated risk-averse arbitragers because it is too risky for them to do so.

Xie (2001), observes that the abnormal accrual component is less persistent than the normal accrual component, which in turn is less persistent than the cash-flow component. Beneish and Nichols (2005), also show that earnings management can explain mispricing. Since investors cannot pierce the veil of accruals, they perceive the inflated earnings (as reflected in high accruals) as a signal of future high earnings instead of a warning of a reversal that will lead to a decline in reported earnings. Inspired by Fama (1998), Mitchell and Stafford (2000) and Chambers (2005) complements the tests in Sloan, (1996) and Xie, (2001) by formulating new tests and by controlling for risk factors in the test of abnormal returns.

Beneish and Vargus (2002), link accruals and earnings persistence to insider trading. After finding that income-increasing accruals and unexpected accruals have lower (higher) persistence when managers engage in abnormal selling (buying), they show that the mispricing is attributable to the mispricing of *positive* accruals. That is, investors make the mistake of pricing all positive accruals without paying attention to the information. Beneish and Vargus conclude that earnings management to support insider trading may explain mispricing (see the discussion in Chap. 3).

Fairfield, Whisenant, and Yohn (2002), note that earnings performance is typically defined as 1-year-ahead operating income divided by 1-year-ahead average total assets (which transforms operating income into return on assets). They therefore examine the relationships between accruals and cash flows and assets. Their findings that accruals are less persistent than operating cash flows in predicting 1-year-ahead return on assets, while accruals and cash flows have equivalent associations with 1-year-ahead operating income, lead them to question whether mispricing is to be attributed to measurement issues (see also Pfeiffer and Elgers, 1999), or whether there is a broader growth anomaly. Similarly, Desai, Rajgopal, and Venkatachalam (2004), present evidence that is consistent with mispricing disguising the overpricing of glamour stock (stocks that are overvalued in the wake of a history of high growth). Papanastasopoulos, Thomakos, and Wang (2007), find that the accruals anomaly is a special case of the anomaly of the market's mispricing of retained earnings.[6]

Sun, (2003), observes that mispricing occurs only in firms that report profits. Dechow, Richardson, and Sloan (2006), question the existence of the accruals mispricing anomaly. They show that the persistence of cash flows is driven by payments to equity holders, which account for a small portion of cash flows. Otherwise, cash flows are not persistent.

Atwood and Xie (2005), examine the finding of Burgstahler, Jiambalvo, and Shevlin (2002), that the market does not take full account of the negative correlation between special items and (standardized) earnings surprises. They show that this is special case of mispricing. Special items affect the extent to which the market overprices accruals: negative special items aggravate overpricing, and positive special items alleviate it.

Levi (2005), finds that accruals mispricing disappears when assessed within a short window of about 90 days, starting 6 days after the 10-Q filings with SEC. That is, the accruals information of firms that voluntarily disclose such information in a 10-Q filing is fully impounded into stock prices upon the disclosure.

---

[6] For further research on the connection between known anomalies and the mispricing of accruals, consult Zach (2003), and Wei and Xie (2005).

Richardson, Sloan, Soliman, and Tuna (2005), extend Sloan's (1996) results by decomposing accruals into accruals from operating activities, accruals from non-operating activities, and financing accruals. They show that when the reliability of accruals is taken into account, the relationship between the persistence of accruals and their mispricing is aggravated: the market does not distinguish among accruals, although accruals with lower quality have lower persistence (see also Richardson, 2003).[7]

Appendix: Accruals when the Firm Carries Inventories

The Model

We adopt the approach of Dechow, Kothari, and Watts (1998), Barth, Cram, and Nelson (2001), and Kothari, Leone, and Wasley (2005), who apply a random walk model to a framework with a mean-reverting process with zero growth. That is,

$$S_t = \mu + \varepsilon_t. \tag{9.19a}$$

The expected sales in period $t+1$, $ES_{t+1} = \mu$, and the difference between consecutive sales, ΔS_t, $\Delta S_t = S_t - S_{t-1}$, equal the change in consecutive sales innovations, $\Delta S_t = \Delta \varepsilon_t$.

We assume that the firm holds a target ending inventory, where the optimal level, I_t^{T*}, is a percentage γ_1 of the expected cost of goods sold, $COGS_{t+1}$, where $0 < \gamma_1 < 1$. Specifically,

$$I_t^{T*} = \gamma_1 E(COGS_{t+1} | H_{t-1}) = \gamma_1(1 - \pi)\mu. \tag{9.19b}$$

Purchases are either sold, as is manifested in the COGS, $(1-\pi)S_t$, or not, as manifested in a change in inventory, I_t-I_{t-1}. Ending inventory might differ from the target level because of uncertain COGS. For example, a supplier may offer a hefty discount for increasing the volume of purchases, or a supplier may fail to ship the goods because of truck drivers' strike, and so on. We assume that the deviation from the optimal purchase level is a per-

---

[7] This paper is also valuable for a discussion of the realism of assumptions underlying the modeling of the accruals process outlined in the first part of this chapter.

centage γ_2 of the innovation in the COGS in period t, $0 < \gamma_2 < 1$. That is, the actual ending inventory is

$$I_t^T = \gamma_1(1-\pi)[\mu - \gamma_2\varepsilon_t] \text{ and} \qquad (9.20a)$$

$$I_{t-1}^T = \gamma_1(1-\pi)[\mu - \gamma_2\varepsilon_{t-1}]. \qquad (9.20b)$$

Hence, for a given level of inventory, I_{t-1}, purchases, P, are

$$P_t = (1-\pi)S_t + I_t^T - I_{t-1} = (1-\pi)[S_t - \gamma_1\gamma_2\Delta\varepsilon_t]. \qquad (9.21a)$$

The corresponding change in accounts payable, AP, since the firm does not pay $\beta\%$ until the following period, is given by

$$\Delta AP_t = \beta(1-\pi)[\Delta S_t - \gamma_1\gamma_2(\Delta\varepsilon_t - \Delta\varepsilon_{t-1})]. \qquad (9.21b)$$

Accruals

The change in total short-term (working-capital) accruals in period t equals the sum of the changes in ending inventory, ΔI_t, and accounts receivable, ΔAR_t, less the accounts payable, ΔAP_t,

$$TA_t = \Delta I_t + \Delta AR_t - \Delta AP_t. \qquad (9.22)$$

By Eqs. 9.A2a, 9.A2b, 9.A3b, and our assumption on accounts receivable,

$$
\begin{aligned}
TA_t &= -(1-\pi)\gamma_1\gamma_2\Delta\varepsilon_t + \alpha\Delta S_t - \beta(1-\pi)[\Delta S_t - \gamma_1\gamma_2(\Delta\varepsilon_t - \Delta\varepsilon_{t-1})] \\
&= \delta\Delta S_t - (1-\pi)\gamma_1\gamma_2\{(1-\beta)\Delta\varepsilon_t - \beta\Delta\varepsilon_{t-1}\}, \qquad \delta = \alpha - \beta(1-\pi)
\end{aligned}
$$

We see now that inventory creates a dependence on the innovations in sales in periods t-1 and t-2.

10 The Accruals Methodology

In Chap. 9, we laid the foundation for this chapter by presenting a stylized model of the earnings generation process. Here, we introduce the empirical approach that examines earnings management through abnormal accruals.

The milestone in the accruals approach is the study of Jones (1991). Hence, we divide the discussion into two parts. The first details the evolution of research up to and including the Jones model. The second presents an evaluation of the Jones model.

Because of the importance of earnings management to accounting, a few literature reviews have been published in recent years (Beneish, 1999b; Healy and Wahlen, 1999; McNichols, 2000; Stolowy and Breton, 2000; Beneish, 2001; Fields, Lys, and Vincent, 2001; Dechow and Schrand, 2004). The focus of a typical review is the Jones model, and its implementation in event studies, similar to Part 2 of this book. We expand this literature by providing a comprehensive review of the evaluation of the empirical research design and of recent developments.

10.1 The Evolution of Accruals-Based Research[1]

Milestones in research that attempted to model normal accruals before Jones's study include the following:

- Ronen and Sadan (1981);
- Healy (1985);
- DeAngelo (1986, 1988b); and
- Dechow and Sloan (1991).

The merits of presenting these early works are threefold. First, they provide a benchmark against which we can evaluate the Jones model. For

[1] Acknowledgments: We are grateful to Jimmy Ye, Pete DaDalt, and Hila Yaari for their invaluable input to this chapter. In addition, the organization of this section was inspired by presentation by Bill Baber in a seminar at the University of Maryland in 2003.

example, Ronen and Sadan's model considers only the sales regressor for estimating non-discretionary accruals; the Jones model considers sales and PP&E. We elaborate on this difference below. Second, they contain a kernel of thinking about modeling normal accruals that can be incorporated into contemporary research to gain new insights. For example, Ronen and Sadan (1981), focus on classificatory smoothing (in addition to intertemporal smoothing) whereby net income is not affected by earnings management, but items are moved "above the line" and "below the line." Third, these studies offer research opportunities. Readers could redo the earlier studies in "modern" ways. For example, Gaver, Gaver, and Austin, (1995), replicate Healy (1985), for a later sample using Jones's methodology.

10.1.1 Ronen and Sadan (1981)

10.1.1.1 The Research Question

Ronen and Sadan investigate the smoothing of *ordinary income*, as defined in Chap. 7.[2] In this setting, the firm deliberately smoothes out fluctuations in its reported earnings "above the line," which are presumed to carry more weight in valuation. Smoothing can be achieved by any (or any combination) of the following means:

---

[2] Previous researchers had already tested smoothing (e.g., Beidleman, 1973; Ronen and Sadan, 1975; Barnea, Ronen, and Sadan, 1976. See Ronen, Sadan, and Snow, 1977; Ronen and Sadan, 1981), and smoothing has been tested in subsequent studies as well (Belkaoui and Picur, 1984; Moses, 1987; Greenawalt and Sinkey, 1988; Brayshaw and Eldin, 1989; Craig and Walsh, 1989; Hand, 1989; Albrecht and Richardson, 1990; Bartov, 1993; Ashari, Koh, Tan, and Wong, 1994; Beattie, Brown, Ewers, John, Manson, Thomas, and Turner, 1994; Fern, Brown, and Dickey, 1994; Sheikholeslami, 1994; Wang and Williams, 1994; Michelson, Jordan-Wagner, and Wootton, 1995; Bhat, 1996; Bitner and Dolar, 1996; Booth, Kallunki, and Martikainen, 1996; Hunt, Moyer, and Shevlin, 1996; Saudagaran and Sepe, 1996; Subramanyam, 1996; Carlson and Bathala, 1997; DeFond and Park, 1997; Chaney and Lewis, 1998; Chaney, Coleman, and Lewis, 1998; Oyer, 1998; Barth, Elliott and Finn, 1999; Godfrey and Jones, 1999; Hallock and Oyer, 1999; Hwang and Ryan, 2000; Lim and Lusgarten, 2002; Payne and Robb, 2000; Barton, 2001; Buckmaster, 2001; Gul, Leung, and Srinidhi, 2002; Elgers, Pfeiffer, and Porter, 2003; Wan-Hussin, Nordin, and Ripain, 2003; Kanagaretnan, Lobo, and Yang, 2004; Cheng and Warfield, 2005; Abdel-Khalik, 2006; Liu and Ryan, 2006; Tan and Jamal, 2006; Tucker and Zarowin, 2006).

- *Real smoothing*—smoothing through production or investment activities, which affect cash flows;
- *Intertemporal smoothing*—cosmetic smoothing through allocating total accruals strategically among a few accounting periods; and
- *Classificatory smoothing*—cosmetic smoothing through choosing where to place a certain item: above the line (in ordinary outcome) or below the line (as an extraordinary item). For example, at the time their sample was collected, non-recurring revenues and expenses could be *classified* as either ordinary or extraordinary.[3]

Ronen and Sadan estimate the long-run earnings first. Since firms must report, in total, the true earnings, smoothing involves the timing of the recognition of the income-statement items. To decrease the variability of its series of reported earnings, firms report an income figure that is closer to the long-run average income—the "trend income"—than the truth (Fig. 10.1).

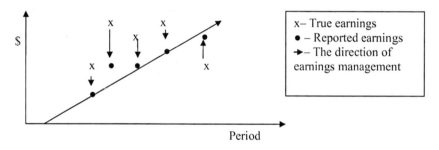

Fig. 10.1 Smoothing around a "Trend Income"

The straight increasing line is the "trend income." The smoothed earnings are closer to this line than the true earnings.

Ronen and Sadan base the modeling of expenses on the following classified income statement:

(1)	Sales	L
(2)	Cost of goods sold and operating expenses	X_0
(3) = (1)–(2)	Operating income	OP
(4)	Non-operating expenses related to continuing operations	X_1
(5) = (3)–(4)	Ordinary income	$OP–X_1=L–XX$
(6)	Extraordinary expenses	X_2
(7) = (5)–(6)	Net income	$L–XX–X_2$

---

[3] In recent years, classificatory smoothing is also reflected in pro forma earnings.

10.1.1.2 The Design of the Empirical Test

Ronen and Sadan estimate the trend of operating income with the following two-stage procedure:

$$L_t = a_{0L} + a_{1L}t + u_t \tag{10.1}$$

and

$$OP_t = a_{0P} + a_{1P}t + a_{2P}u_t + s_t, \tag{10.2}$$

where s is the deviation of reported income from the long-run trend—abnormal income, also referred to as abnormal operating income.

The model relates operating income, OP, linearly to time (i.e., year) and to abnormal sales, u, where normal sales are also estimated as a linear function of time.[4] The main motivation for the two-stage estimation is that the abnormal operating income, s, indicates the demand for smoothing (since OP is the object of the earnings management). If s is positive, the firm is likely to manage income downward, and vice versa. At this point, one wonders how one can be sure that this is the correct dynamic. After all, the unmanaged earnings are unobserved. The answer lies in the reasonable assumption that if economic earnings are below the trend, then the firm increases the reported earnings but never overshoots; if above, the firm decreases its earnings likewise. To illustrate, suppose that the "trend income" is 100 and the firm's pre-management earnings are 90. The firm then attempts to report more than 90, but *no more than 100*. If it reports 95, the gap between the reported earnings and the target is -5, which is smaller than the true gap, -10, but both are negative.

An advantage of the two-stage procedure is that it addresses the relation between performance and accruals. One issue with the standard OLS estimation of accruals is that the relation between normal accruals and performance might be non-linear.[5] By regressing operating income on abnormal sales, u, one controls for the exceptional performance (for a non-linear model, consult Ronen and Sadan, 1975).

Ronen and Sadan run the following regressions:

$$X_{2t} = f_0 + f_{1t}t + f_{2t}u_t + q_t; \tag{10.3}$$

$$X_{0t} = c_0 + c_{1t}t + c_{2t}u_t + c_{3t}q_t + \text{error}; \tag{10.4}$$

---

[4] Both the sales growth model and the operating income growth model are quite simple. Since estimating an exponential model did not change their results qualitatively, Ronen and Sadan keep to this specification.

[5] We consider this issue at some length below, when discussing studies by Dechow, Sloan, and Sweeney (1995), and Kothari, Leone, and Wasley (2005).

$$X_{1t} = b_0 + b_{1t}t + b_{2t}u_t + b_{3t}q_t + b_{4t}s_t + \text{error}; \tag{10.5}$$

$$XX_t = d_0 + d_{1t}t + d_{2t}u_t + d_{3t}q_t + \text{error}, \tag{10.6}$$

where u_t, q_t, s_t, are abnormal sales, abnormal extraordinary expenses, and abnormal ordinary income, respectively.

In the introduction to Part 4, we presented abnormal accruals as discretionary accruals. Ronen and Sadan, too, regard abnormal expenses, q, as an indicator of earnings management. That is, any expense is the sum total of cash flows, discretionary accruals, and non-discretionary accruals. The cash flow component and the non-discretionary accruals of X_{2t} are captured by $f_0 + f_{1t}t + f_{2t}u_t$, and the residual, q_t, is discretionary.

10.1.1.3 The Findings and Alternative Methods to Detect Smoothing

Artificial intertemporal smoothing implies that $b_{4t} > 0$. The higher the abnormal operating income, s, the higher the demand for dampening ordinary income by increasing non-operating expenses. Classificatory smoothing occurs when abnormal extraordinary items are used as substitutes for expenses in other slots on the income statement. Hence, classificatory smoothing implies that b_{3t}, c_{3t}, and d_{3t} are negative.

Ronen and Sadan successfully present evidence of intertemporal and classificatory smoothing. For further discussion of their research methods, consult their work.

Alternative indicators of smoothing have been employed: earnings volatility (e.g., Hunt, Moyer, and Shevlin, 2000; Abdel-Khalik, 2006); the serial correlation of earnings, which is expected to be negative under smoothing (e.g., Guay, Kothari, and Watts, 1996); the ratio of the coefficient of variation of pre-managed earnings to the coefficient of variation of reported earnings, where pre-managed earnings are defined as net income minus discretionary accruals (Barton, 2001, table 7; and Pincus and Rajgopal, 2002); in cross-sectional design, the ratio of the standard deviation of operating earnings to the standard deviation of cash flow from operations (e.g., Leuz, Nanda, and Wysocki, 2003; Zarowin, 2002; Bhattacharya, Daouk, and Welker, 2003; Cohen, Dey, and Lys, 2005a); extreme negative contemporaneous correlation of a change in accruals and a change in cash flows (e.g., Leuz, Nanda, and Wysocki, 2003; Myers, Myers, and Skinner, 2006); the negative correlation of a firm's change in discretionary accruals with the change in its pre-managed earnings (Tucker and Zarowin, 2006); and accounting choices opposite the boom or recession in the industry, such as banks' accelerating provisions for losses (e.g.,

Liu and Ryan, 2006). For a discussion of the methodologies that use target income as a benchmark for testing for smoothing, consult Lim and Lusgarten (2002).

10.1.2 Healy (1985)

10.1.2.1 The Research Question

Healy analyzes the incentives of management to manage earnings downward when its marginal bonus is "out of the money." Graphically, the compensation package of a manager who receives a base salary and a bonus is a piecewise contract as depicted in Fig. 10.2.

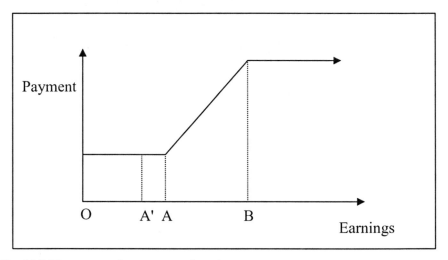

Fig. 10.2 The manager's compensation

The compensation is based on reported earnings, with a bogey at A and a cap at B (Scott, 1997). If accounting flexibility allows the manager to inflate earnings by the difference between A' and A, this compensation schedule can be divided into three zones[6]: to the left of A', between A' and B, and to the right of B. If the true earnings fall in the second zone (A'-B), the manager can increase his current bonus by inflating the report. If the true earnings fall in the interior of the first or in the third zone, inflating the report will not yield higher compensation. The manager can create a "re-

---

[6] We present the argument somewhat differently than Healy, consistent with Gaver, Gaver, and Austin (1995). Healy does not distinguish between A' and A.

serve" of reported earnings that can be used to earn a bonus in the future by deflating the report through such means as recognizing future expenses immediately (i.e., by "taking a bath").

10.1.2.2 Healy's Research Design

Healy defines DA as follows:

$$DA = -DEP - X_2 D_1 + \Delta WORK - (TP + D_1) \times D_2, \tag{10.7}$$

where

DA	=	discretionary accruals, which are equated with Total accruals (denoted by ACC);
DEP	=	depreciation;
X_2	=	extraordinary items (denoted in the paper by XI);
D_1	=	dummy variable; $D_1=1$ (0) if bonus plan earnings are defined after (before) extraordinary items;
$\Delta WORK$	=	the change in select accruals from working capital: the increase in accounts receivable (ΔAR) plus the increase in inventory (ΔINV) plus the decrease in accounts payable (ΔAP);
ΔTP	=	the change in income tax payable;
D_2	=	dummy variable; $D_2=1$ (0) if bonus plan earnings are defined after (before) income tax.

Healy collected data from a population of the 250 largest U.S. industrial corporations listed in the 1980 *Fortune* directory, which yielded 1,527 firm-year observations (from 94 firms with sufficient disclosure of their bonus plan and with no disclosure of their long-term incentive plan) between 1930 and 1980. Healy then categorizes each observation into LOW, MID, and UPP portfolios, depending on whether the income that is defined as the basis for calculating the bonus is below A, between A and B, or above B, respectively. In addition, Healy distinguishes between firms with a formal cap, B, and firms that do not disclose B, classified for lack of better information as firms with no cap. (He and Holthausen, Larcker, and Sloan, 1995, observe that such a threshold exists and that it might not be disclosed or be unofficial.)

Healy compares the frequency of firms with negative discretionary accruals to the frequency of firms with positive discretionary accruals, and his table 2, panel b shows that the evidence supports his hypothesis, since the frequency of firms with negative accruals below A (and to a lesser extent above B) is higher than the frequency of firms with positive accruals.

His test is based on total accruals, TA. One interpretation is that all accruals are discretionary—that is, TA = DA, because NDA = 0. (We discuss studies that employ this assumption below, in Sect. 10.1.2.2.) This holds for zero growth mean-reverting or random-walk processes. Otherwise, this is a questionable interpretation, because normal accruals might have non-zero expectations, say, K, $K \neq 0$. Then, the cutoff point for classifying firms is K, where firms with accruals that exceed K are "positive," and firms with accruals less than K are "negative." Yet K might also vary with performance; that is, there is one K at A' and another, K^0, at B. If both K and K^0 were positive, then Healy's results would be stronger, because they underestimate the true magnitude of the "taking a bath" phenomenon. Critics of Healy's work are willing to concede that K^0 is positive at the cap, B, but not that K at the bogey, A. Negative accruals at A may be attributable not to firms' taking a bath to manage earnings but to low performance; that is, TA=NDA, and DA=0. (See, e.g., Kasznik, 1999, who finds positive [negative] discretionary accruals with high [low] earnings.)[7]

Healy was aware that total accruals aggregate discretionary and non-discretionary accruals. He states, "Total accruals (ACC_t) include both discretionary and non-discretionary components ($ACC_t = NA_t + DA_t$), and are estimated by the difference between reported accounting earnings and cash flows from operations" (p. 94). Hence, another interpretation is that NDA is not zero, but TA =NDA +DA, with positive DA for only the performance subset between A' and B and negative DA in other subsets. Still, the same critique applies, as NDA can be sensitive to performance, so a comparison across performance subsets is tainted by potentially identifying accruals that are normal for an abnormal level of activity as discretionary accruals. We discuss this interpretation further in the next subsection, in our account of Healy's contribution to earnings management studies.

As for the first interpretation, that TA=DA, we note that although using total accruals is not in vogue nowadays, still, some studies use them as a proxy for the quality of earnings and to detect earnings management (see Aharony, Lin, and Loeb, 1993; Chan, Chan, Jegadeesh, and Lakonishok, 2004; Dechow and Dichev, 2002; Richardson, Tuna, and Wu, 2002, table 5; Leuz, Nanda, and Wysocki, 2003; Phillips, Pincus, and Rego, 2003; Ahmed, Billings, and Morton, 2004; Bergstresser and Philippon, 2006; Li, Xie, and Wu, 2005[8]; Yan, 2006).

---

[7] Even with this comment in mind, Healy's study is notable for refuting the hypothesis that managers always inflate earnings in order to collect higher bonuses and for being a seminal paper that identifies compensation as an incentive to manage earnings (Kothari, 2001).

[8] Li, Xie, and Wu test the association between trading volume—a signal of information asymmetry among a market's participants—and the absolute values of

10.1.2.3 The Contribution to Earnings Management Research

The methodology that is associated with Healy defines normal accruals as the deflated long-run accruals:

$$\text{NDA}_{t+1} = \frac{1}{n} \sum_{i=t-n}^{t} \frac{\text{TA}_i}{A_{i-1}}, \tag{10.8}$$

where A_{i-1} are the lagged assets. In most applications, the average is calculated over 5 years, $n=5$ (see, e.g., Dechow, Sloan, and Sweeney, 1995; Dechow, Sabino, and Sloan, 1998; Thomas and Zhang, 2000; Ye, 2006). Equation 10.8 coincides with Healy's 1985 design when the sales generation process is mean reverting with zero growth, since in expectations, $\text{NDA}_{t+1}=0$, and $\text{DA}_{t+1}=\text{TA}_{t+1}$; that is, discretionary accruals in the event year equal total accruals.

Healy's methodology is consistent with the second interpretation of Healy's (1985). Discretionary accruals are those accruals that differ from the long-run average, $\text{DA}=\text{TA}-\text{NDA}$, and NDA may not be zero. Dechow, Sloan, and Sweeney (1995), explain the motivation:

> Healy (1985) tests for earnings management by comparing mean total accruals (scaled by lagged total assets) across the earnings management partitioning variable. Healy's study differs from most other earnings management studies in that he predicts that systematic earnings management occurs in every period. His partitioning variable divides the sample into three groups, with earnings predicted to be managed upwards in one of the groups and downward in the other two groups. Inferences are then made through pairwise comparisons of the mean total accruals in the group where earnings is predicted to be managed upwards to the mean total accruals for each of the groups where earnings is predicted to be managed downwards. This approach is equivalent to treating the set of observations for which earnings are predicted to be managed upwards as the estimation period and the set of observations for which earnings are predicted to be managed downwards as the event period. The mean total accruals from the estimation period then represent the measure of nondiscretionary accruals. (p. 197)

Note that because accrued balances reverse, the average accrued balances over a 5-year period might be zero, and the difference between the two interpretations disappears.

---

accruals around quarterly earnings announcement dates. They argue that trading volume indicates information asymmetry regarding a firm's value (e.g., Dontoh and Ronen, 1993) and that pernicious earnings management increases information asymmetry.

To illustrate Eq. 10.8, we conduct a 1,000-trial simulation, assuming a mean-reverting process with a mean of 10,000. Sales innovations are drawn from the Beta distribution with a minimum of −10,000, a maximum of 10,000, and parameters $\alpha = \beta = 30$. Since earnings are serially correlated (Kothari, 2001), we set each sales innovation to be correlated with the previous year's random component, with the following coefficients (Table 10.1).

Table 10.1 The assumptions on the serial correlation coefficients of earnings

Year	Correlation coefficient	Year	Correlation coefficient
1	0.49	4	−0.34
2	0.44	5	0.72
3	0.67	6	0.27

Changes in accrued balances of working-capital accruals are assumed to be 0.144 of the change in sales in each year. The average accruals in years 1–5 are a measure of year 6's NDA (net of reversals). Figure 10.3 presents the results of our simulation.

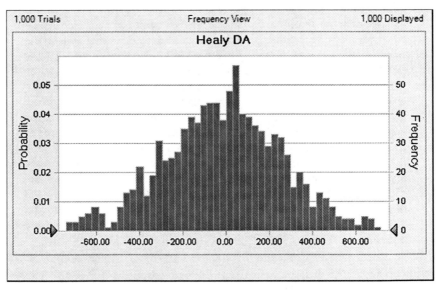

Fig. 10.3 The discretionary accruals under Healy's methodology

Since the symmetric Beta distribution when $\alpha = \beta$ is Gaussian, and since we assume that the minimum equals the negative of the maximum, the mean is zero. The derived simulated curve has a t-student distribution with a mean −14.06; the standard deviation is 268.06. DA range between a minimum of -740.15 and a maximum of 714.02. It is not a priori clear that this result generalizes to smaller and non-homogenous samples. However, it is interesting to note that we do not get zero DA (i.e., the distribution does not collapses to a mass around zero DA) although there is no earnings management in the simulation. That is, this methodology identifies normal accruals for abnormal performance as discretionary.

10.1.3 DeAngelo (1986, 1988a)

10.1.3.1 The Research Questions

DeAngelo sets out her approach in her 1986 and 1988a studies. In the 1986 study, she examines the accounting decisions made by managers of 64 public firms who attempted a management buyout during 1973–1982. In the 1988a study, she considers the earnings behavior of 42 firms engaged in 43 proxy contests during 1971–1982.[9]

In both studies, managers of the sample firms have incentives to manage earnings. In the 1986 study, management and investors have to agree on the transaction price. The price-setting is obscured by uncertainty regarding the firm's value, which is likely to increase after the buyout is completed.[10] The observable, reported earnings are a valuable input into the negotiations process. From the management's perspective, the situation is a zero-sum game wherein they have incentives to manage earnings down ward in the periods preceding the leveraged buyout in order to reduce the price.

In the 1988a study, the dissident shareholders attempt to gain the support of other stockholders by quoting poor earnings as an indicator of poor performance. DeAngelo finds that the market price is unlikely to be cited, or is cited only together with poor earnings, because the price tends to rise before the contest, indicating that the market anticipates that the firm will

---

[9] A proxy contest is a political campaign in which stockholders who disagree with managerial policies (dissident shareholders) seek election to the firm's board of directors, with the intent to replace the incumbent manager.

[10] Even if the market price were a perfect signal of future events, it still would understate the future value. To illustrate, suppose that the firm's value is zero before a buyout and one after the buyout. Then, if there is 25% chance that the buyout will not be completed, the expected value of the firm is $0.75 \times 1 + 0.25 \times 0 = 0.75 < 1$. The market price understates the value, conditional on a buyout. Not surprisingly, buyout prices are known to exceed the market price of the shares prior to the buyout event.

improve its performance regardless of whether the dissident shareholders succeed. Clearly, the incumbent managers have incentives to manage earnings upward, to disprove the allegation of poor performance. (See also DeAngelo, 1988b.)

10.1.3.2 The Contribution to Earnings Management Research

DeAngelo's model calculates normal accruals as the previous period's accruals deflated by lagged assets:

$$NDA_{t+1} = \frac{TA_{t-1}}{A_{t-1}}, \tag{10.9}$$

where A_{t-1} are the lagged assets.[11]

This characterization fits a constant growth mean reverting or random-walk processes. The expected accruals this year are equal to those of last year, and thus all *changes* in accruals are discretionary.[12]

To illustrate DeAngelo's model, we conduct a 1,000-trial simulation, assuming the same parameters as in our simulation of Healy's model. Figure 10.4 presents the distribution of discretionary accruals, $DA = TA - NDA$, after we drop four extreme observations.

---

[11] For a variation on DeAngelo's model, consult Friedlan (1994). He deals with non-stationarity by deflating variables by sales.

[12] Consider the accruals generation process studied in Chap. 9 (Eq. 9.5):

$$CAB_t = \delta[S_t - S_{t-1}] = \delta\{(1+\lambda)[S_{t-1} + \phi(\mu - S_{t-1})] + \varepsilon_t - S_{t-1}\},$$

where

CAB_{t+1}	=	the change in accrued balances in period t;
δ	=	intensity of accruals as a fraction of sales, $0 < \delta < 1$;
ϕ	=	persistence of the drift of sales from the mean;
μ	=	mean sales.

When the sales generation process is a random walk, $\phi=0$, and the growth rate is zero (i.e., $\Delta S_{t+1} = S_t + \varepsilon_{t-1} - S_t$), the expected change in accrued balances is zero, because $E[\varepsilon_t] = 0$. Since research equates accruals with CAB, such a process justifies DeAngelo's definition of DA.

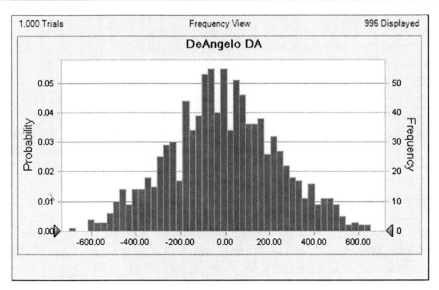

Fig. 10.4 The discretionary accruals by DeAngelo's methodology

We use the same data as in Sect. 10.1.2. Here, too, we get a student t-distribution of DA with mean close to zero (the mean is -7.62 and the standard deviation is 246.92). It seems that although our simulation assumes a mean-reverting process, DeAngelo's model is marginally better than Healy's model. The reason lies in the serial correlation of the sales innovations. NDA in Healy's model contains information in the past accruals that is irrelevant for estimating DA in period $t+1$.

A regression of $DA^{DeAngelo}$ (the difference between the change in accrued balances and (10.9)) on DA^{Healy} (the difference between the change in accrued balances and (10.8)) yields the following:

$$DA^{DeAngelo} = \underset{(0.157)}{0.93} + \underset{(27.75)}{0.61} \, DA^{Healy}. \qquad (10.10)$$

Equation 10.10 has an R^2 of 0.44; the numbers in parentheses are the t-statistics. The intercept is insignificant, but the slope is significant. The relatively high association between the two DA models is not an artifact of our specific simulation. The reason is that accruals are defined as the difference in balances. This cancels out the effect of the long-term mean on accruals. That is, if accrued balances are 0.144 of earnings, which are generated from a mean-reverting process with $\mu=10,000$ (i.e., $X_t=10,000+\varepsilon_t$), then the difference in accrued balances—that is, accruals—is $0.144 \times \Delta\varepsilon_t$. In contrast, if the mean sales were not stationary, the correlation between the two models might have been lower.

10.1.3.3 The Tests

DeAngelo defines total accruals as in Healy (1985), except that in her earlier study DeAngelo adjusts earnings to reflect the impact of the equity method of accounting for intercorporate investment.

In the 1986 study, DeAngelo does not detect earnings management, but in the 1988 study she is more successful. Her test results indicate that earnings increase during a contest by about 1% of total assets, but accruals increase by about 2%, although the change in the mean cash flows is close to zero. Hence, the evidence is consistent with earnings management rather than improved performance in response to the pressures of the contest.

Most studies nowadays do not employ DeAngelo's approach unless they seek to compare the efficiency of different models of discretionary accruals (see, e.g., Dechow, Sloan, and Sweeney, 1995; Guay, Kothari, and Watts, 1996; Young, 1999; Thomas and Zhang, 2000; Bartov, Gul, and Tsui, 2002). Nevertheless, because DeAngelo inspired later research, her work continues to have an impact.

10.1.4 Dechow and Sloan (1991)

10.1.4.1 The Research Question

Dechow and Sloan analyze the spending on research and development (R&D) during the last year of the tenure of an outgoing CEO. They formulate the following hypotheses:

A reduction in expenditures on R&D activities is

H1: more likely during the years immediately before a CEO's departure.

H2: less likely if the CEO's wealth is sensitive to the firm's value, and

H3: less likely if the turnover is peaceful.

The first hypothesis arises from the fact that net income is a basis for the CEO's bonus. Hence, CEOs have incentives to increase earnings by reducing the R&D expenditure. The second hypothesis is based on the observation that a reduction in R&D reduces the firm's expected value, so the CEO's incentives to reduce R&D are weakened when he holds shares of the firm. The third is based on the fact that when a departing CEO passes his authority to his designated successor a few years before his retirement, by the time the CEO quits the post, he has no authority over these decisions (Vancil, 1987).

10.1.4.2 The Contribution to Earnings Management Research

Dechow and Sloan base their research design on **the assumption** that the variation in the determinants of non-discretionary accruals is common across all firms in the same industry. This industry model for normal non-discretionary accruals (e.g., Dechow, Sloan, and Sweeney, 1995; Guay, Kothari, and Watts, 1996) is

$$NDA_{t+1} = \gamma_1 + \gamma_2 \text{ median } (TA_{t+1}), \tag{10.11}$$

where median (TA_{t+1}) is the median value of total accruals, scaled by lagged assets for all non-sample firms in the same industry and year (Dechow, Sloan, and Sweeney, 1995, use the two-digit SIC code).

The advantage of this approach is that the researcher does not have to formulate a model of how the normal item under investigation (in this case, R&D) behaves. Dechow and Sloan state, "We have no explicit theory concerning the expected level of R&D expenditures in the absence of manipulation" (p. 55). The test considers instead the difference in TA between a firm with incentives to manage earnings and its colleagues that lack these incentives.

There are a couple of disadvantages: first, the model applies only to event studies in which not all firms experience the same event. Second, even if not all firms in the industry have the same incentives to manage earnings, if other firms in the industry also manage earnings in the same direction, the test biases against finding earnings management, and if other firms manage earnings in the opposite direction, the test might indicate non-existent earnings management.

10.1.4.3 The Tests

Using a sample of 91 firms with 517 usable firm-years (in order to have an 11-year window), Dechow and Sloan perform the following regression:

$$\Delta R\&D_{it} = \alpha + \beta_1 DUM_{it} + \delta \Delta R\&D_{m(i)t} + \varepsilon_{it}, \tag{10.12}$$

where
$\Delta R\&D_{it}$ = the change in R&D;
DUM_{it} = a dummy variable that takes the value of 1 in the last 2 years of the CEO's tenure and zero otherwise;
$\delta \Delta R\&D_{m(i)t}$ = An index of economy-wide changes in R&D expenditures, calculated for all firms in the three-digit SIC, where the weight of a given firm-year is relative to its market value as a percentage of the value of all firms.

They find lower expenditures in the final year of a CEO's tenure and a large increase in R&D by his successor, but this effect is attenuated if the departing CEO owns a sufficiently large number of shares of the firm.

10.1.5 The Jones Model

10.1.5.1 The Research Question

Jones (1991), examines accruals by U.S. firms during import relief investigations by the U.S. International Trade Commission (ITC). Import relief is meant to protect domestic producers against competition by foreign firms through measures such as tariff increases, quota reductions, market agreements that limit imports, and federal adjustment assistance to relocated employees. The ITC bases its decisions on accounting earnings, inventory levels, and unused capacity. Relief is granted if the competition leads to severe deterioration in these accounting signals.

The optimal earnings management strategy is to reduce earnings to convey the impression that the foreign competition is harmful, especially because the ITC does not adjust the financial data to reflect accounting choices.

10.1.5.2 The Contribution to Earnings Management Research

Jones's work is an event study, so it implicitly assumes that firms do not manage earnings before the event. Hence, the time series of a firm's earnings can be decomposed into two subperiods, an estimation period, in which DA=0, and the event period.

Jones employs the following procedure:

Stage 1: Estimation period

In the estimation period, the normal accruals are

$$NDA_{it}/A_{it-1} = TA_{it}/A_{it-1} = \alpha_i[1/A_{it-1}] + \beta_{1i}[\Delta REV_{it}/A_{it-1}] + \qquad (10.13)$$
$$\beta_{2i}[PPE_{it}/A_{it-1}] + \varepsilon_{it},$$

where

TA	=	total accruals;
A	=	assets;
REV	=	revenues;
PPE	=	gross property, plant, and equipment;
ε	=	error term;
i	=	index for firm, i=1,2,…,N.

T =   index for the period (year) in the estimation period,
$t=1,2,…,T$.

Δ =   change in a given variable.

Equation 10.13 does not have an intercept because the first term is the reciprocal of the asset at the beginning of the period. We obtain this equation by deflating all variables in the model of $NA_t = B_1 + B_2\Delta REV_{it}/A_{it-1} + B_3 [PPE_{it}/A_{it-1}] + \varepsilon_{it}$ by lagged assets, to correct for heteroskedasticity. Equation 10.13 is based on the understanding that working-capital accruals are related to changes in sales, and depreciation is related to assets.

The regression yields estimates of the coefficients $\hat{\alpha}_i, \hat{\beta}_{1i}, \hat{\beta}_{2i}$. What should the signs of these coefficients be? Clearly, the coefficient on property, plant, and equipment is negative because PP&E determines the depreciation expense. The consensus is that the coefficient on change in sales should be positive. The argument is that changes in accounts receivable and accounts payable are related. Since the sales of a profitable firm exceed its expenses, the net working-capital accruals will be positive if the credit policies of the firm and its suppliers are similar. Theoretically, however, working-capital accruals can be negative. To illustrate, let the change in current accruals be made up of the change in accounts receivable less the change in accounts payable.[13] Suppose that all sales are made for cash only but some of the purchases are made on credit. As sales increase, the accounts payable increase as well, so the coefficient on the change in sales is negative.

We conduct the following examination.[14] We ran a cross-sectional regression of current accruals[15] on the reciprocal of lagged assets and change in sales deflated by lagged assets.[16] Our sample comprises all Compustat firms in the 1991–2004 period (1990's data is used to calculate the change in sales regressor in 1991, and so forth). We employ the following filters: We exclude financial institutions (SIC 6000-6999) because their accounting

---

[13] To tie the discussion to the parsimonious model in Chap. 9, the issue arises when δ is positive; $\delta = \alpha - (1-\pi)\beta$, where α is the contribution of accounts receivable and β is the contribution of trade-accounts payable, which are a fraction $1-\pi$ of sales. Then, $\delta < 0$ only if $\alpha < (1-\pi)\beta$.

[14] We are grateful to Hila Yaari for assistance with the simulations and the empirics in this chapter.

[15] Current accruals are defined as the difference between earnings from operations (Compustat #123) and cash flows from operations (Compustat #308) after adding the depreciation expense (Compustat #125) and losses (gains) from asset disposal (Compustat #213), that is, Compustat #123–#308+#125+#213.

[16] A current-accruals version of the Jones model omits the PP&E regressor, since it explains depreciation.

is different from the rest, and we require that each firm have more than $1 million in sales and in assets because the Jones model does not apply to extreme performance (see the discussion below). We exclude firms with missing data and firms whose current accruals exceed lagged assets.

We ran one regression for every year for any industry that contained at least 30 firms. Hence, the assumption of normality of the disturbance terms in the OLS is likely to hold. We grouped firms by three-digit SIC code. Altogether, this resulted in 586 regressions: 359 with a positive coefficient, and 227 with a negative coefficient. That is, 39% of the regressions the coefficients on change in sales are negative.

In general, the negative depreciation accruals dominate the sign of total accruals. For example, Barth, Cram, and Nelson (2001), find that although accounts receivable and accounts payable are 1% of average assets (beginning assets plus ending assets divided by 2), depreciation amounts to five times that much. Hence, in some cases, the empiricist chooses to restrict attention to short-term accruals and omits the long-run accrual of depreciation (see, e.g., Teoh Welch, and Wong, 1998a, b).

Stage 2:

In the test period, the parameters $\hat{\alpha}_i, \hat{\beta}_{1i}, \hat{\beta}_{2i}$ are plugged into Eq. 10.13. The residual accruals (the equation's prediction error) are the abnormal accruals, which are fully equated with discretionary accruals. That is,

Total accruals	Derived from the financial data of firm i, TA_{ip}.
Normal accruals	Estimated from the change in sales and PPE, deflated by the beginning-of-the-period assets, given the coefficients estimated in Eq. 10.13: $$\hat{TA}_{ip}/A_{ip-1}= \hat{\alpha}_i\,[1/A_{ip-1}]+ \hat{\beta}_{1i}\,[\Delta REV_{ip}/A_{ip-1}]+ \hat{\beta}_{2i}\,[PPE_{ip}/A_{ip-1}]$$
Discretionary accruals	Equal to total accruals minus normal accruals: $$u_{ip}= TA_{ip} - \hat{TA}_{ip}.$$

10.1.5.3 The Tests

Total accruals are calculated from the balance sheet: Δcurrent assets (Compustat #4) $-$ Δcash (Compustat #1) $-$ [Δcurrent liabilities (Compustat #5) $-$ Δcurrent maturities of long-term debt (Compustat #44) $-$ Δincome taxes payable (Compustat #71)] $-$ depreciation and amortization expense (Compustat #14). Jones deflates all variables by the beginning-of-the-year assets to overcome heteroskedasticity.[17]

---

[17] Kothari, Leoni, and Wasley (2005), complain that White's (1980), adjusted statistics for the annual cross-sectional industry models show that deflation by

The results of Jones's study reject the null hypothesis that firms do not manage accruals to affect the consequences of the relief investigation. The Z-statistics for the years before the investigation and the investigation period (–1 and 0, respectively) are –0.372 (with a one-tailed significance level of 0.356) and –3.459 (with a one-tailed significance level of 0.0003), respectively.

10.2 An Evaluation of the Jones Model

We divide the discussion into two parts. The first part presents our own questions and illustrates the arguments with simulations. The second summarizes the findings that are already established in the literature.

10.2.1 Unexplored Questions

Jones's coefficients on normal accruals are estimated in a time-series analysis so that the parameters of the regressions are tailored to each firm. The time-series approach, however, has its own caveats. Specifically, it raises the following unrelated questions:
- Do firms abstain from earnings management in the estimation period?
- Are firm-specific fundamentals stable over time?

10.2.1.1 *Assumption: No Earnings Management in the Estimation Period*

The Jones's approach covers two stages: an estimation stage, wherein the coefficients of the normal accruals are determined, and the event period, wherein the abnormal accruals are isolated in order to test for earnings management. But is reality so pristine that no earnings management takes place in the eight to fifteen annual reports in the estimation period?

Consider the following means and medians of statistics taken from table 1 in Ye (2006), for a sample of all Compustat firms between 1987 and 2003.

---

beginning-of-the-period total assets reduces, but does not eliminate, heteroskedasticity. Hence, they add an intercept to the estimation of non-discretionary accruals. See our discussion in Chap. 11.

Table 10.2 The composition of accruals

	Item	Mean (median)[a]	% of total accruals
1	Total accruals	−6.443 (−5.489)	100
2	Current accruals	−0.650 (−0.144)	10.08 (2.62)
3	Depreciation[b]	−0.080 (−0.051)	1.24 (0.93)
4=2+3	Total of current accruals and depreciation	−0.73 (−0.195)	11.33 (3.55)
5=4−1	The difference between total accruals and total current accruals and depreciation	5.713 (5.294)	88.67 (96.44)

[a] All variables are deflated by the beginning balance of total assets.

[b] Ye reports that the average (median) PP&E is 0.666 (0.553) of total assets and that the average (median) depreciation rate—the ratio of depreciation expense to assets—is −0.121 −0.093). Hence, the depreciation expense is calculated as the product of the depreciation rate and PP&E as a fraction of total assets: −0.080 = −0.121 × 0.666 and −0.051= −0.093 × 0.553.

As Table 10.2 indicates, the sum of current accruals and depreciation yields a much lower estimate than the actual total accruals. The difference can be attributed to losses on sales of assets.[18] Obviously, the book value of those assets just before the sale was overstated relative to their economic value. Although it might be the case that firms sell unproductive assets at a loss, the magnitude of this variable is quite large, considering that a reduction in the value of an asset ought to be written off immediately. This implies that the assets may have been overstated due to an overoptimistic depreciation policy.

We conducted simulations of the accruals of the Jones model assuming that firms manage depreciation during the estimation period. The advantage of the simulation is that we know the correct discretionary accruals. The shortcoming is that we impose our own tastes on the accruals generation process. Hence, generalization of our results requires a measure of caution (a reservation that is also applicable to empirical studies in general because different samples can yield different, and possibly inconsistent, insights). The simulation is based on the following parameters:

---

[18] These gains and losses are subtracted from total accruals net of the depreciation expense in order to derive current accruals.

1. Sales follow a random walk, $S_t = S_{t-1} + \varepsilon_t$, where ε_t, the sales innovation, is a draw from the Beta distribution, with $\alpha = \beta = 3$, minimum=100, and maximum 1,000 (i.e., a symmetric distribution with a mean of 450).
2. Depreciable property, plant, and equipment is 0.553 of total assets. The economic useful life is 4 years, with zero salvage value.
3. Earnings are a stochastic percentage of sales; the profit margin is distributed uniformly between 0.08 and 0.25. The firm's earnings augment ending assets.
4. The change in accrued balances of current accruals is 0.144 of the sales innovation. That is, changes in current accruals are 0.144ε, and the long-run accruals are the depreciation expense.
5. The initial parameters are the following: assets = 141.3; sales = 2000.
6. Thereafter, every 4 years the firm makes a capital expenditure that is set at the level of one tenth of the previous year's sales.
7. The firm manages earnings by optimistically depreciating one eighth of depreciable assets for the first 3 years of their life. The remaining depreciable cost is expensed at the end of the fourth year.

We ran the simulation 1,000 times, treating each run as representing a different firm. Each firm has 16 years of data. The first 4 years are used to induce variation in the parameters described above for different firms. The simulation's sample contains the fifth to sixteenth years of each firm, so the 12-year simulation is composed of three cycles of 4 years each (years 5–8, years 9–12, years 13–16).

Our model's simulation of the non-discretionary accruals is

$$\text{NDA}_{it}/A_{it-1} = 0.144[\Delta \text{REV}_{it}/A_{it-1}] - 0.25[\text{PPE}_{it}/A_{it-1}]. \qquad (10.14)$$

The true total accruals and discretionary accruals, given the simulated NDA, are as follows:

In each of the first 3 years in each cycle (years 5–7, 9–11, 13–15),

$$\text{TA}_{it}/A_{it-1} = \text{NDA}_{it}/A_{it-1} + 0.125[\text{PPE}_{it}/A_{it-1}]; \qquad (10.15a)$$

that is

$$\text{DA}_{it}/A_{it-1} = 0.125[\text{PPE}_{it}/A_{it-1}]. \qquad (10.15b)$$

In the last year of each cycle (years 8, 12, 16),

$$\text{TA}_{it}/A_{it-1} = \text{NDA}_{it}/A_{it-1} + \text{Reversal}_{it}/A_{it-1}, \qquad (10.15c)$$

where

$$\text{Reversal}_{it} = -0.375\text{PPE}_{it-1}; \qquad (10.15d)$$

that is,

$$DA_{it}/A_{it-1}=0. \tag{10.15e}$$

Since the Jones model does not distinguish between years 1–3 and 4 in each cycle, it yields biased coefficients. The difference between the coefficient of change in sales and our simulation parameter of 0.144 is distributed as shown in Fig. 10.5.

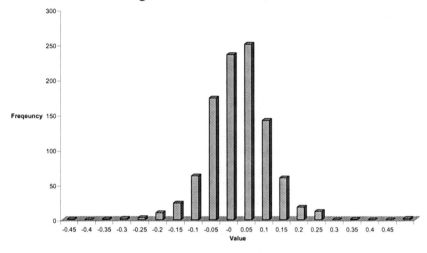

Fig. 10.5 The deviation of the estimated coefficient of change in sales from the assumption of the simulation

Only 23.6% of the observations are correct; 42.5% are within a distance of 0.05 around zero, and the remainder are further away.

We tested the Jones model twice. Test 1 uses data for years 5–14 to estimate DA in year 15, DA_{15}. The true magnitude of earnings management, EM_{15}, equals 50% of the depreciation expense in year 15. Test 2 uses data for years 5–15 to estimate DA in year 16, DA_{16}. In year 16, however, no earnings management takes place. Accruals are abnormal due to the reversals of accruals in the previous 3 years, $Reversal_{16}$.

We ran a cross-sectional regression of Jone's estimated discretionary accruals on the expected discretionary accruals based on the simulation parameter.

Test 1 yields

$$EM_{15} = 1.677 \times JonesDA_{15} \quad (R^2 = 0.44). \tag{10.16}$$
$$(t = 27.89)$$

Here the Jones model does underestimate EM_{15}. As a test of the existence of earnings management, however, the Jones model is efficient, as it captures earnings management significantly in the right direction. See Fig. 10.6.

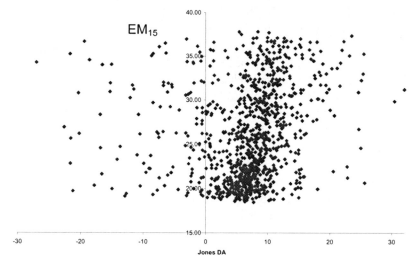

Fig. 10.6 The association between EM in year 15 and Jones DA

Test 2 yields

$$\text{Reversal}_{16} = \underset{(t = -512.58)}{-0.68} \times \text{Jones DA}_{16} \quad (R^2 = 0.995) \qquad (10.17)$$

The Jones model explains the reversal as statistically significant, negative discretionary accruals. This result is misleading because the difference between the economic and the reported depreciation expense in year 16 is the reversal of managed accruals in the previous three periods. The extremely high R^2 results from a spurious correlation between *Reversal* and Jones's DA, since both are associated with sales: *Reversal* because investment is proportional to sales of the fourth period before, and DA because they are calculated by regressing accruals on current sales, which are a noisy measure of sales of the fourth period before.

Overall, our results confirm that earnings management during the estimation period contaminates the tests.

10.2.1.2 Assumption: Stationarity of the Accruals Intensity Coefficients

The basic assumption behind time-series analysis is that the coefficients α_i, β_{1i}, and β_{2i} are time invariant (and orthogonal to the error terms). This assumption is at odds with survival in the long run. That is, a time-series analysis requires a long series of observations. Dechow, Sloan, and Sweeney (1995), report that the average age of a surviving firm exceeds 20 years. It is hard to imagine that the firms do not adapt their business policies and accruals policy over long windows, which affect their NDA.

Furthermore, the Jones model also makes an implicit assumption about the stationarity of expenses because the model has a regressor for sales only. Not considering expenses as an independent regressor might lead to an omitted variables problem, unless there is additional stationarity in the relationships of expenses to sales. In the Jones model, the ratio of accruals from expense transactions to accruals from sales transactions is assumed to be fixed.

Yaari, DaDalt, Ronen, and Yaari (2007), draw attention to the fact that stationarity in revenues and expenses creates an "accrual conundrum." Consider the following covariances of earnings, cash flows and accruals, and their signs, as documented:

$$\text{Cov(TA,}X) > 0. \tag{10.18a}$$

$$\text{Cov(}F,X) = >0. \tag{10.18b}$$

$$\text{Cov(TA,}F) = <0. \tag{10.18c}$$

The empirical research has established that the first two are positive, and the third is negative (see McNichols and Wilson, 1988, table 1; Finger, 1994; Sloan, 1996; Dechow, Kothari, and Watts, 1998; Dechow, Sabino, and Sloan, 1998; McNichols, 2000; Barth, Cram, and Nelson, 2001; Dechow and Dichev, 2002).

To see the "accrual conundrum," denote the ratio of accruals to earnings, which henceforth is referred to as the accruals intensity, by α. $TA \equiv \alpha X$, and $F \equiv (1-\alpha)X$, where X is earnings and F is cash flows, respectively. Then,

$$\text{Cov(TA,}X) = \alpha\text{Var}(X) > 0. \tag{10.19a}$$

$$\text{Cov(}F,X) = (1-\alpha)\text{Var}(X) > 0. \tag{10.19b}$$

$$\text{Cov(TA,}F) = \alpha(1-\alpha)\text{Var}(X) < 0. \tag{10.19c}$$

Positive (10.19a) and (10.19b) imply that both α and $1-\alpha$ are positive, which implies that (2c) must be positive, which, in turn, contradicts the finding that the covariance between cash flows and accruals is negative!

Suppose, for example, that the variance of earnings is 1 and that earnings are decomposed into 10% accruals and 90% cash. The covariances between the components of earnings—accruals and cash flows—and earnings are 0.01 and 0.09, respectively, and the covariance between cash flows and accruals is 0.09 >0.[19]

An alternative assumption is that accruals intensity is a random variable. Let $TA \equiv \alpha X + v$, and $F \equiv (1-\alpha)X - v$, where v is white noise ($E(v)=0$, $E(v^2)=\tau^2$) that is assumed to be uncorrelated with the noise in earnings ($E(X,v)=0$). The revised covariances are as follows:

$$Cov(CF_t, X_t) = \alpha \sigma^2. \tag{10.20a}$$

$$Cov(TA_t, X_t) = (1-\alpha)\sigma^2. \tag{10.20b}$$

$$Cov\ (CF_t, TA_t) = \alpha(1-\alpha)\sigma^2 - \tau^2 < 0. \tag{10.20c}$$

When the absolute value of the second term in (10.20c) is higher than the first term, the correlation between cash flows and accruals is negative.

This problem has been known for sometime (Healy, 1996; Dechow, Sabino, and Sloan, 1998; Kothari, Leone, and Wasley, 2005). Dechow, Sabino, and Sloan, 1998, for example, model the accruals process with a random intensity (i.e., the ratio of accruals to sales is a random variable). The implication is that abnormal accruals might not reflect discretionary accruals but rather changes in the underlying economic model.

To see the impact of combining sales and lagged sales into one regressor in the Jones model, we ran a regression that decomposed the sales regressors into current and past sales. We use all Compustat firms with more than one million in sales and assets and available data that are not financial institutions (SIC 6000-6999) for the period 1991–2004 and group them by three-digit SIC code and year. After deleting observations with missing data and instances of accruals exceeding total assets, we obtain 586 industry-year regressions in industries containing at least 30 firms.

We employ a decomposed version of the current accruals model of Teoh, Welch, and Wong (1998b):

$$NDA_t = \frac{1}{Assets_{t-1}} + \lambda_t S_t + \lambda_{t-1} S_{t-1} + \varepsilon_t. \tag{10.21}$$

Figure 10.7 presents the distribution of the differences in the coefficients on sales and lagged sales in comparison with the normal distribution. In our paper, we explain that the difference between λ_t and λ_t can be addressed in the Jones model by adding a regressor. Figure 10.7 thus

---

[19] For example, $Cov(TA,X) = E[(TA-E(TA))(X-E(X))= E[(0.1X-0.1E(X))(X-E(X))]=0.1Var(X)$.

indicates that this regressor is approximately normally distributed around the positive mean.

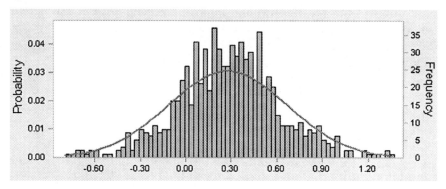

Fig. 10.7 The distribution of the differences in the coefficients of sales and lagged sales

We employ a cross-sectional analysis because it assumes that all firms in the industry have the same operating cycle and that they all are at the same phase of the cycle. The time-series analysis does not make this assumption because its estimated coefficients are firm-specific. Yet, given that time-series analysis requires long periods during which firms manage to survive by adapting business plans and credit policies, the cross-sectional analysis appear to be the more promising route. Furthermore, it is not clear that a firm is at the same phase of the operating cycle at the end of each fiscal year. To illustrate, suppose that customers pay within 2 weeks after their purchase date. In year 2xx1, most sales in December took place in the first 2 weeks. In year 2xx2, most sales in December took place in the third week. Even if there is no change in credit policy, accounts receivable, and hence accruals, as a percentage of sales are still going to be different in the consecutive years.

10.2.2 Evaluations of the Jones Model

The main concerns of the literature that evaluates the Jones model are contaminated data and model misspecification. The papers that are summarized below offer remedies as well. Here, then, we focus not on the problems but on the quality of the solutions.

10.2.2.1 Abnormal Accruals and DA

The first question concerns the validity of equating abnormal accruals with DA. Some variation in accruals results from changing business conditions and the consequent change in strategy and operating decisions rather than from earnings management (Healy, 1996). In other words, is there a type I error when the researcher rejects the null hypothesis of no earnings management?

One solution to this problem is to add regressors that proxy for business strategy factors.

Hansen (1999), regresses the discretionary accrual estimated by the Jones model on the levels and lagged variables of cash flows or funds used for acquisitions, *Acq*, cash flows or funds used for capital expenditures, *Capexp*, discontinued operations, *Disc*, and cash flows from sales of property, plant, and equipment, *PPEsales*:

$$\frac{|DA_t|}{A_{t-2}} = \beta_0 \frac{1}{A_{t-2}} + \beta_1 \frac{|Acq_t|}{A_{t-2}} + \beta_2 \frac{|Acq_{t-1}|}{A_{t-2}} + \beta_3 \frac{|Disc_t|}{A_{t-2}} + \beta_4 \frac{|Disc_{t-1}|}{A_{t-2}} \qquad (10.22)$$

$$+ \beta_5 \frac{|Cap\exp_t|}{A_{t-2}} + \beta_6 \frac{|Cap\exp_{t-1}|}{A_{t-2}} + \beta_7 \frac{|PPEsales_t|}{A_{t-2}} + \beta_8 \frac{|PPEsales_{t-1}|}{A_{t-2}} + \varepsilon_t$$

His motivation is that abnormal accruals might reflect changes in the economic model rather than DA. Hansen's finding that the independent variables are all positive and statistically significant at the 0.01 level leads him to conclude that structural changes produce measurement errors in the discretionary accrual models. Evaluating this study's contribution to earnings management research requires considering it in conjunction with Hribar and Collins (2002), detailed below.

Another approach concerns sample selection. The approach is to delete smaller companies, which are usually high-growth companies that are characterized by an unusually high level of accruals unrelated to DA. McNichols (2000), controls for performance by adding rate of return on assets (ROA). She shows that abnormal accruals are sensitive to growth, where growth is measured by analysts' one-year-ahead forecasts. The results confirm that some abnormal accruals are related to high-growth firms. The current approach to controlling for ROA nowadays is to have lagged ROA as an additional regressor in the first stage of the Jones' procedure (see our discussion of Kothari, Leone, and Wasley, 2005, in Chap. 11).

10.2.2.2 Small Samples

In general, a small sample tends to weaken the power of the tests because it generates large standard errors. A small sample thus increases the chance of type II error (of erroneously accepting the null hypothesis that earnings management does not take place). This is a particular matter of concern because pernicious earnings management aims to avoid being detected. If the sample is sufficiently large, however, the empirical research "can potentially isolate systematic effects that characterize the aggregate, but which are not so evident to outsiders on a case-by-case basis" (DeAngelo, 1986, p. 405). To some extent, small samples are unavoidable because the number of observations tends to be low to begin with in event studies. In Jones's (1991) study, the sample comprises just 23 firms in five industries (Automobiles (4), Carbon Steel (5), Stainless and Alloy Tool Steel (2), Cropper (4), and Footwear (8)).[20]

In response, some studies use cross-sectional analysis, employing a larger sample. Bartov, Gul, and Tsui (2002), for example, report that the median number of observations for estimating normal accruals is 140 in a cross-sectional analysis as compared to only eight observations in a time-series analysis.[21] Some studies resort to using a pooled sample (see, e.g., Erickson and Wang, 1999; Cahan, 1992; Han and Wang, 1998; Hribar and Collins, 2002; Park and Park, 2004).

This methodology, however, poses issues that do not exist in the time-series analysis. First, what is the appropriate benchmark of normal accruals? The literature offers a few approaches: matched firms (e.g., Kang, 2005; Kothari, Leone, and Wasley, 2005); matched-portfolio technique

---

[20] Another reason for small samples is the survival bias mentioned above. This bias arises because firms with less than 9–11 annual observations are dropped from the sample. Jeter and Shivakumar (1999), note,

> Typically, time-series models (such as the Jones model) require at least ten observations in the estimation period to obtain minimally reliable parameter estimates. For studies using annual data, this requirement implies that the sample firms must survive for at least 11 years. Since such firms are more likely to be large, mature firms with greater reputation capital to lose if earnings management is uncovered, this methodology introduces a selection bias. (p. 301)

[21] Additional examples of cross-sectional and pooled studies are Subramanyam (1996) (21,135 firm/years during 1973–1993); DeFond and Subramanyam (1998) (503 firms that changed auditors during 1990–1993); Becker, DeFond, Jiambalvo, and Subramanyam (1998) (10,379 Big-Six and 2,179 non-Big-Six Compustat firm/year observations tested for earnings management in the 1989–1992 period); Francis, Maydew, and Sparks (1999) (sample base is 74,390 of Nasdaq firms between 1974 and 1994); Chambers (1999) (59,016 firm/years during 1976–1995); Klein (2000b) (692 firm/years extracted from S&P 500 in the 1992–1993 period); Xie, Davidson, and DaDalt (2003) (281 firms extracted from S&P 500 firms in 1992, 1994, 1996); Bédard, Chtourou, and Courteau (2004) (3,451 Compustat firms with fiscal year-end at December 1996); Kang (2005) (83,765 firm/years in the 1987–1996 period); and Kothari, Leone, and Wasley (2005) (123,000 Compustat firm between 1962 and 1999).

(Kasznik, 1999; Klein, 2002b)[22]; all firms in the same industry and year (DeFond and Jiambalvo, 1994; Bartov, Gul, and Tsui, 2002); firms in the same industry for the same year, excluding the event firms (Matsumoto, 2002); and the industry's performance in the previous year (Teoh, Welch, and Wong, 1998a, b; Xie, Davidson, and DaDalt, 2003; Williams, 2006). For further discussion of this issue, consult Baber and Lyon (1996).

Second, regardless of the benchmark, a cross-sectional design raises the problem of whether those observations that are used for estimating the coefficients of normal accruals include some managed accruals themselves. Jeter and Shivakumar (1999), illustrate,

> [C]onsider an industry that is enjoying favourable economic conditions. If firms smooth reported earnings, then the "actual" abnormal accruals for the firms in this industry will be negative. Cross-sectional models are unlikely to capture all the negative abnormal accruals, however, since the earnings management is contemporaneously correlated across firms in the sample. Thus only those firms whose accruals are negative relative to the industry benchmark will be identified as earnings managers. This introduces a potential limitation of the cross-sectional approach, or a bias against finding evidence of earnings management in some cases. (p. 301)

Third, cross-sectional analysis within industries discards observations of industries with fewer firms.[23] Furthermore, one may question the validity of the assumption of homogeneity—that is, that all firms in an industry have the same operating technology, which yields the same normal accruals for a given level of performance, and if all firms are at the same stage of the operating cycle. Although a two-digit SIC code provides a larger number of firms in the same industry, it may aggregate firms that have little in common (Bernard and Skinner, 1996).

Researchers nonetheless agree that a cross-sectional design dominates a time series. Jeter and Shivakumar (1999), and Kang (2005), apply the criteria of significance and standard error. Bartov, Tsui, and Gul (2001), consider the standard deviations of the parameters, which are much lower in the cross-sectional regression.

Ye (2006), compensates for the non-homogeneity of a cross-sectional sample by adding controls for firm-specific business fundamentals to the model of normal accruals. He shows that a pooled regression (Fama and

---

[22] This approach adjusts the measure of earnings management to the median measure in a portfolio of firms. The portfolio is chosen by a variable that is found to be correlated with both the earnings management measure and the partitioning variable dictated by the research design (such as lagged rate of return on assets, standard deviation of total accruals).

[23] The customary minimum (median) cutoff number is eight (ten).

MacBeth (1973)), with his chosen fundamentals, attains a higher R^2 than the cross-sectional model that slices the sample by year and industry only. Restricting the observations to the period after the statement of cash flows became mandatory, Ye's 1987–2003 sample numbers 75,348 observations.

10.2.2.3 Measurement Errors

Contaminated data poses a problem because if total accruals are measured with an error, the measurement of DA may also be erroneous. To some extent, this issue is unavoidable, as research relies on public data that is not always complete. For example, the depreciation expense is an aggregate of the depreciation of assets of different ages. Kaplan (1985), observes that the depreciation of older assets is less likely to be managed.

10.2.2.3.1 The Effect of Measurement Errors on Estimating DA

Several authors (McNichols and Wilson, 1988; Kang and Sivaramakrishnan, 1995; Hansen, 1999; McNichols, 2000; Hribar and Collins, 2002, table 3) have employed a linear model to detect earnings management around an event that is measured by a partitioning variable, **PART**,[24]

$$DA = \alpha + \beta \, \textbf{PART} + \varepsilon, \qquad (10.23)$$

where

DA	=	discretionary accruals according to the Jones model (typically deflated by lagged total assets);
PART	=	a dummy variable partitioning the data into two groups for which earnings management predictions are specified by the researcher; it takes the value of zero or one;
ε	=	an error term that is independently and identically normally distributed.

PART equals one in firm-years during which earnings management allegedly takes place (the "event period") and zero during other firm-years (the "estimation period"). Hence, average discretionary accruals are α if **PART** =0 and $\alpha + \beta$ if **PART** =1.

We use ODA to denote the directional accruals estimated based on observable variables. If there is a measurement error in ODA, denoted by ME (i.e., ODA= DA–ME), the regression estimates

---

[24] To provide a general commentary, we ignore issues of whether this is a pooled regression or any other research design by not incorporating subscripts for either firm (i) or year (t). The extension to a specific design is immediate.

$$\text{ODA} = \hat{\alpha} + \hat{\beta}\ \textbf{PART} + v, \tag{10.24}$$

where

$$v = \text{ME} + \varepsilon. \tag{10.25}$$

As Hansen observes, "Since measurement error in discretionary accrual models is substantial, the usefulness of these models hinges critically on whether or not they are biased" (1999, p. 2). If the partitioning variable, **PART**, and the measurement error, ME, are uncorrelated, the regression yields unbiased estimates. If not, $\hat{\beta}$ will be biased because

$$\hat{\beta} = \beta + \frac{\text{Cov}(\textbf{PART}, v)}{\text{Var}(\textbf{PART})}.^{25} \tag{10.26}$$

When the sign of the covariance of **PART** with measurement errors is the opposite of the sign of the true coefficient, the researcher might reach erroneous conclusions.

> To interpret accruals-based tests as evidence that earnings management did not occur, one must be confident that the discretionary accrual proxy is sufficiently sensitive to reflect it. To interpret accruals-based tests as evidence that earnings management occurred, one must be confident that measurement error in the discretionary accrual proxy is not correlated with the partitioning variable in the study's research design. (McNichols, 2000, p. 320)

---

[25] Algebraic manipulation shows that the bias can also be written as

$\rho_{v,\text{PART}}\ \dfrac{\sigma_v}{\sigma_{\text{PART}}}$, where ρ is the correlation coefficient between the two variables and σ is the standard error (the square root of the variance).

10.2.2.3.2 A Remedy: Different Methods of Calculating Accruals[26]

The contaminated data issue is also affected by the researcher's definition of accruals. Two mutually exclusive approaches prevail[27]:

1. The balance-sheet approach (BA): total accruals are the change in non-cash current assets (Compustat item #4 minus #1) less the change in current liabilities, excluding the current portion of long-term debt (Compustat item #5 minus #34), less depreciation (Compustat item #14).[28]

2. The statement-of-cash-flows approach (CA): total accruals are the difference between income before extraordinary items and discontinued operations (Compustat item #123) and cash from operations (Compustat item #308).

Both approaches deflate the regressors by lagged assets (Compustat item #6).

The two approaches might yield different figures for a number of reasons. First, BA includes non-current accruals, other than depreciation, such as accruals from discontinued operations. Second, the balance sheet does not articulate with the income statement.[29]

Hribar and Collins (2002), identify three main events that may give rise to these divergences: mergers and acquisitions (M&A), divestitures, and foreign currency translations. M&A and divestitures give rise to invest-

---

[26] Econometrically, the Instrumental Variables approach (IV) provides a solution to the case in which the regressor is correlated with the error term. Kang and Sivaramakrishnan (1995), compare OLS with IV and the Generalized Method of Moments procedure (GMM). They are not concerned with the Jones model. Still, it is worth noting that they find that both IV and GMM reduce the scope of type I and type II errors (when accruals are injected by the authors in a magnitude that approximates 2% of beginning net total assets) and that GMM dominates IV. For example, the type II error of erroneously accepting the null hypothesis of no earnings management is detected in 47% of the firms (z-statistic 19.26) under GMM as compared to 34% under IV (z-statistic 12.84) and 23% under the Jones model (z-statistic 8.25). Similar conclusions are reported in Kang (2005), a study that is discussed in Chap. 11.

[27] The research largely focuses on working-capital accruals plus depreciation. To the best of our knowledge, one exception is Richardson, Tuna, and Wu (2002), who find that the non-working capital accruals are useful in predicting the likelihood of SEC enforcement actions.

[28] Jones also subtracts from accruals the change in income taxes payable (Compustat item # 71).

[29] The balance sheet articulates with the income statement when the change in owner's equity from internal sources net of dividends equals the net income (loss) in the income statement.

ment activity in the statement of cash flows, but they are likely to affect working capital as well. When M&A increase working-capital accruals, they introduce a positive bias into the estimation of normal accruals and a negative bias into the estimation of discretionary accruals. Divestitures have the opposite effect. Foreign currency translations are recognized in comprehensive income on the balance sheet. They thus have no effect on earnings reported in the income statement. The bias in the estimation of BA depends on whether the dollar strengthens or weakens. Note that this list is not comprehensive. For example, another source of difference between BA and CA is reclassification, such as moving an item from above the line to the "discontinued operations" part of the income statement, which is below the line.

CA yields a lower measurement error than BA (Bahnson, Miller, and Budge, 1996; Baber and Kang, 2001; Hribar and Collins, 2002). Hribar and Collins examine a sample of 14,558 firm-years over the period 1988–1997. Univariate tests of samples of 2991 firm/years with acquisition activity, 1,277 firm/year with discontinued operations (a surrogate for divestitures), and 2,812 firm/years with foreign currency translations, as compared to 8,203 firm/years with none of these three (non-articulate) events, indicate that BA introduces a bias into measurement of accruals. In the M&A-, discontinued operations-, and foreign currency-subsample, the error in estimated accruals under the balance-sheet approach equals 64.34, 19.85, and 24.66%, respectively, of earnings before extraordinary items for 25% of the firm-years, as compared to 25.19% in the subsample of firms without a non-articulate event. Multivariate analysis shows that M&A induce a positive bias of 1.48% of lagged total assets, discontinued operations introduce a negative bias of –1.56% of lagged total assets, and foreign currency translations introduce a negative bias of –0.49% of lagged total assets. If the merger is large (i.e., it increases current sales by more than 50%), the bias introduced by M&A increases to 2.39% of lagged total assets.

The implications for earnings management research is that some results reported in Part 2 might be attributable to measurement errors. Hribar and Collins note, for example, that a finding that write-offs coincide with earnings being managed downward may be an artifact of the positive correlation between write-offs, which are motivated by restructuring and discontinued operations and discontinued operations (see Rees, Gill, and Gore, 1996, who find earnings management of about 3% of total assets). Similarly, discontinued operations by firms in distress may bias the test for downward earnings management for such firms (Perry and Williams, 1994; DeFond and Subramanyam, 1998).

Young (1999), provides further insight into the importance of omitted variables. He examines the relationship between expected discretionary accruals and cash flows, growth in sales, asset intensity (measured as the ratio of net fixed assets to market capitalization), average life of fixed assets (measured as the ratio of the gross value of fixed assets to the depreciation expense), leverage (measured as the ratio of long-term debt to total shareholders' equity), directors' total equity as a percentage of total equity, size (the natural log of lagged sales), and an indicator variable for smoothing (which takes the value of one if the NDA of a given firm exceeds the median lagged NDA of the industry to which it belongs). The first four controls are conjectured to be omitted variables that induce bias in the estimates. The last three control for incentives for earnings management and are assumed to be orthogonal to the first four. Young shows that all the variables contribute to variation in abnormal accruals and are significant.

For a further discussion of the properties of accruals measured by the different approaches, consult Sloan (1996), and Bradshaw, Richardson, and Sloan (2001). The accruals measured by the balance-sheet approach "tend to be fairly constant over time and account for little of the variation in total accruals..." (Bradshaw, Richardson, and Sloan, p. 51).

10.2.2.4 Omitted Variables

To the extent that F-statistics and R^2 indicate how well the Jones model fits the data, the evidence is that it does not include all relevant regressors.

For example, in the sample we employ above, the R^2 of the regressions of current accruals is distributed as in Fig. 10.8.

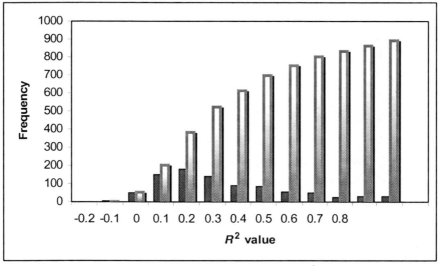

Fig. 10.8 The frequency (and cumulative frequency) of R^2

Note that the R^2 of 151 observations (16.87% out of 895) are zero, and 382 (42.68%) lie between –0.1 and 0.1. An obvious explanation is that some variables that explain TA are omitted.[30]

Dechow, Hutton, and Sweeney (1995), elaborate on the omitted variables issue. Consider their linear test of earnings management:

$$\text{DA}_t = \alpha + \beta\,\textbf{PART}_t + \sum_k \gamma_k X_{kt} + \varepsilon_t, \tag{10.27}$$

where

DA	=	discretionary accruals, typically deflated by lagged total assets;
PART	=	a dummy variable partitioning the data into two groups for which earnings management predictions are specified by the researcher;
X_{kt}	=	Other relevant variables influencing discretionary accruals; $k=1,2,\dots,K$;
ε	=	An error term that is assumed to be independently and identically normally distributed.

If no variable is omitted and **PART** equals one in firm-years in the "event period" and zero in the "estimation period," the average DA are

---

[30] We report the results for current accruals only. Given the difficulty with depreciation noted above, we do not expect better results for the total accruals model.

$\alpha+\sum_k \gamma_k X_{kt}$ if $\beta=0$ and $\alpha+\beta+\sum_k \gamma_k X_{kt}$ if $\beta=1$. As before, the null hypothesis is that $\beta=0$.

If variables are omitted, the estimated coefficient will be biased when the partition variable is correlated with them even if discretionary accruals are estimated correctly because the regression is

$$\mathrm{DA}_{it}=\hat{\alpha}_{it} + \hat{\beta}_{it}\,\mathbf{PART} + v_t, \qquad (10.28)$$

where

$$v_t = \sum_k \gamma_k X_{kt} + \varepsilon_t. \qquad (10.29)$$

Note that there is no subscript i on the noise terms by virtue of our assumption that the error terms are identically distributed.

Hence, $\hat{\beta}_{it} = \beta_{it} + \sum_k \delta_{k,\mathrm{PART}}\gamma_k$, where $\delta_{k,\mathrm{PART}}$ is the regression

coefficient of **PART** in a regression of the kth omitted variable on **PART** (Maddala, 1988, p. 123). If $\delta_{k,\mathrm{PART}}=0$, the coefficient of **PART** is unbiased. Yet the omission of the additional variables, $\sum_k \gamma_k X_{kt}$, could weaken the power of the test because it inflates the prediction error and reduces R^2 and the t-statistics.

An obvious omitted variable is expenses. Kang (2005), observes, "[C]hanges in expenses are positively correlated with changes in revenues, but negatively correlated with the dependent variable. Thus, the omission of expense can bias the coefficient of ΔREV downward" (p. 19).

In essence, the omitted variables issue is merely part of the broader issue of model misspecification. Hence, in the following subsection, we discuss the two together.

10.2.3 The Tests of the Efficiency of the Jones Model

When omitted variables are correlated with **PART** or the linear model is misspecified, DA are measured with one of two errors:

Type I error: an erroneous rejection of the null hypothesis that firms do not manage earnings.

Type II error: an erroneous acceptance of the null hypothesis that firms do not manage earnings.

Klein (2002b), summarizes,

> Any test of earnings management is a joint test of (1) earnings management and (2) the expected accruals model used. Acceptance or rejection of the null hypothesis of no earnings management cannot be disentangled from the key methodological issue of how well the chosen

expected accruals model separates total accruals into its unexpected (abnormal) and expected components. (p. 381)

10.2.3.1 Type I Error

The research checks for type I error in samples wherein earnings management is unlikely to take place. If the Jones approach is efficient, its test results will not reject the null hypothesis (of no earnings management).

Two such candidate samples have been considered:

- Firms with extreme performance (Dechow, Sloan, and Sweeney, 1995; Kothari, Leone, and Wasley, 2005).
- Random samples (Dechow, Sloan, and Sweeney, 1995; Kang and Sivaramakrishnan, 1995; Bartov, Tsui, and Gul, 2001; Kothari, Leone, and Wasley, 2005).

Accruals of firms with extreme performance

In this test, the sample is composed of firms with extreme performance. The motivation is that abnormal accruals may be related to the performance and not to earnings management. Hence, if the Jones model is efficient, it does not classify extreme normal accruals as discretionary.

To illustrate, consider a case in which the firm does not manage accruals, so that DA = 0, but the relationship between non-discretionary accruals (NDA) and the change in sales is captured by a non-linear function f. That is, after deflating all variables by lagged assets, non-discretionary accruals, NDA, discretionary accruals, DA, and total accruals, TAC, are as follows:

$$\text{NDA} = a_0 + f(\Delta\text{Sales}) + a_2 \text{ PP\&E};\tag{10.30}$$

$$\text{DA} = 0;\tag{10.31}$$

$$\text{TAC} = \text{NDA} + \text{DA} = a_0 + f(\Delta\text{Sales}) + a_2 \text{ PP\&E}.\tag{10.32}$$

Assume that sales are a random variable, so that by Taylor's series around the expected sales, $E[\text{Sales}]$,

$$f(\text{Sales}) \cong f(E[\Delta\text{Sales}]) +$$

$$+ f'(\Delta\text{Sales} - E[\Delta\text{Sales}]) + \frac{1}{2} f''(\Delta\text{Sales} - E[\Delta\text{Sales}])^2.\tag{10.33}$$

Observe that if the relationship between accruals and performance were linear, the terms in the second row of Eq. 10.33 would be zero. To simplify presentation, suppose that sales in the "estimation period" are normal and approximate expected sales. Consequently, an unbiased estimate of the coefficient of the change in sales regressor is $f(\Delta Sales) = f(E[\Delta Sales])$. Now suppose that performance in the "event period" is so extreme as to create a gap between change in sales, $[\Delta Sales]$, and the expected change in sales, $E[\Delta Sales]$. By (10.33), the estimated discretionary accruals are

$$\hat{DA} = TAC - \hat{NDA} \cong$$

$$f'(\Delta Sales - E[\Delta Sales]) + \frac{1}{2} f''(\Delta Sales - E[\Delta Sales])^2 \qquad (10.34)$$

Figure 10.9 illustrates the argument.

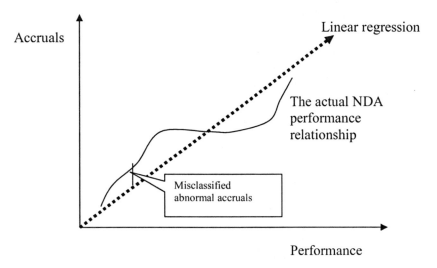

Fig. 10.9 The non-linear relationships between normal accruals and extreme performance

We note that a critical issue here is the non-linearity of the accruals model. Non-linearity has been duly noted by other researchers as well (Kang and Sivaramakrishnan, 1995; Jeter and Shivakumar, 1999). (Jones, who also was concerned with non-linearity, reported that scatter plots of the residuals of the regressions for her sample firms did not exhibit a non-linear relation between abnormal accruals and changes in revenues.)

Dechow, Sloan, and Sweeney (1995), construct their sample of 168,771 firm-years from Compustat industrial files with necessary data between 1950 and 1999. They select firm-years that have either extreme earnings performance or extreme cash from operations performance.[31] This test as-

---

[31] Kothari, Leone, and Wasley (2005), also use stratified random samples based on mutually exclusive criteria. An example of such a sample construction is collecting randomly selected stocks from an extreme quartile of stocks ranked on

sumes that the average firm in a sample of firms with extreme performance does not manage earnings. The procedure is as follows:

1. All observations are deflated by lagged assets.
2. All firm-years are ranked by either performance measure.
3. For each measure, firm-years are assigned in equal numbers to decile portfolios based on their ordered rank. Each portfolio contains about 17,000 firm-years.
4. Samples of 1,000 firm-years are randomly selected from the highest and the lowest portfolios for each performance measure, so long as each firm has at least 10 years of history available.[32]

This procedure yields four portfolios of extreme performance, which can be LOW or HIGH. The evaluation of the Jones model now hinges on the number of times the null hypothesis is rejected at the 5% level of significance (upper or lower one-tailed test). The results indicate that the Jones model erroneously identifies normal accruals in high-performance firms as discretionary.[33] Hence, it is likely that the Jones model is indeed misspecified because of the non-linear relationship between normal accruals and performance.

The solutions

Two solutions are offered in the literature. If extreme performance may erroneously lead the researcher to classify abnormal accruals as discretionary, then he should add a control for performance. Jeter and Shivakumar (1999), add cash flows deflated by lagged assets. Starting with 390,880 firm-quarters between 1984 and 1994, they classify 1,000 randomly selected firm-quarters into quintiles based on their cash flow from operations. They show a monotonic relationship between discretionary accruals

---

the basis of their book-to-market ratio (or large versus small firms, growth versus value stock, high versus low earnings yield, high versus low past sales growth, high versus low cash flow from operations, high versus low earnings per share (EPS)).

[32] The firms classified as having extreme performance indeed have exceptional performance. That is, if performance is LOW (HIGH), the trend in the 11-year window is that the performance declines (increases) over time before the event year and then rises (declines) again. See Dechow, Sloan, and Sweeney (1995, figure 1, p. 207).

[33] The rejection rates for low performance are 2.7 and 0.7%, which are lower than the test-specified rejection rates of 5 and 1%, respectively. Similarly, the rejection rates for high performance are 16.6 and 5.4%, which exceed the test-specified rejection rates of 5 and 1%, respectively.
Kothari, Leone, and Wasley (2005, table 3), reach similar conclusions. For example, in the low EP portfolio, the rejection rate for the Jones model in their tests is 68%.

and cash flows (low cash flows yield negative DA and high cash flows yield high DA). When they add their control, the differences between the quintiles vanish (see their tables 6 and 7). We discuss this issue again in Chap. 11.

The second solution is to abandon linear regression, instead, matching firms with others by industry and a performance criterion. The advantage to this approach is that successful matching applies to any functional relationship between performance and accruals. The caveat of such a procedure is that "...the success of the matched-firm approach hinges on the precision with which matching can be done and the homogeneity in the relation between performance and accruals for the matched firm and the sample firm" (Kothari, Leone, and Wasley, 2005, p. 170). Kothari, Leone, and Wasley argue that if the matched firms manage earning, there is an increased chance of type II error (see their discussion on pp. 170–171).[34]

Ye (2006), addresses the issue of detecting non-existent DA when performance is extreme by selecting a sample of firms with total assets, revenues, and PP&E all greater than $1 million in an effort to eliminate unusual observations (which chops off the low end of performance). He finds that two variables are non-linear: ROA and revenue growth. Winsorizing high values of ROA and revenue growth to the 0.1–0.3 range and the 0.05–0.5 range, respectively, solves the non-linearity problem.

Accruals of random samples

If firms do not manage earnings during the estimation period, the average firm represents the population. If they do manage earnings, but different firms manage earnings in different directions, then the average firm does not manage earnings (so long as firms are selected randomly and the sample size is sufficiently large). If the Jones model then detects earnings management, type I error can be suspected.

Dechow, Sloan, and Sweeney (1995), select a random sample of 1,000 firm-years from 168,771 firm-years obtained from the Compustat industrial files, choosing firms that have at least ten observations between 1950 and 1991 (for the estimation period); this selection is sequential and with-

---

[34] Matching based on a single criterion may identify similar firms that are de facto quite different. The solution is to use a hierarchy of matching criteria and apply them lexicographically. That is, all firms matched first, say on ROA, then, all matched firms on ROA are then matched on size, and so on. The problem is that the order of the criteria matters, which casts doubt on this selection process. For a study that overcomes the problematic use of lexicographic matching procedures, consult Li and Zhao (2005), who propose a propensity score that combines the criteria into a single measure.

out replacement.[35] They run a regression of discretionary accruals as the dependent variable, DA = α + β **PART** + ε, on a randomly chosen partition variable as the independent variable. Given this procedure, the expectation is that discretionary accruals ought to be zero.[36] Their findings indicate that neither the Jones model nor three others—Healy's model, DeAngelo's model, and Dechow and Sloan's Industry model—reject the null hypothesis. The Jones model outperforms the other, three because although the mean abnormal accruals of all models are close to zero, the Jones model's standard error is the smallest (0.092, compared to 0.195, 0.281, and 0.211, respectively). The Jones model is more efficient.

As mentioned above, the underlying assumption of this procedure is that even if firms manage earnings, they do it in opposite directions so that the average firm in a large enough sample does not. Yet is there any proof of such symmetry between income-increasing and income-decreasing earnings management? As anecdotal evidence, consider Davis-Hodder, Mayew, McAnally, and Weaver (2004). They explore the accuracy of parameters disclosed in calculating the fair value of employees' stock options. Examining hand-collected employee stock options (ESO) from 1995 through 1998 for a sample of S&P 1,500 firms, they find that the average firm decreased the stated fair value, reporting a fair value of $9.98 per share instead of the $11.43 per share that presumably would have been reported had the firm not attempted to manage earnings (in order to meet a benchmark). Only 25% of the firms deviated from benchmarks to increase reported, ESO fair values. Additional examples involve studies that indicate asymmetry between profits and losses (e.g., Barua Legoria, and Moffitt, 2006; Jacob and Jorgensen, 2007). In sum, then, the assumption that earnings management is offset in a sufficiently large sample requires further scrutiny.

10.2.3.2   *Type II Errors*

Researchers can check the Jones model for type II error by using a sample in which earnings management is known to take place.

Two such kinds of samples have been considered:

---

[35] Kothari, Leone, and Wasley (2005), select 250 samples of 100 firms each, with replacement. They report that the standard deviation is reduced when the random samples comprise 200 or 300 firms.

[36] The Jones model's mean (median) coefficient is 0.001 (−0.001), which is close enough to zero. Yet all other models have a mean (median) of 0.002 (Healy: − 0.001, DeAngelo: 0.001, and Dechow and Sloan: 0.000), which is also close to zero (see table 1).

- Samples of firms that are known to violate GAAP because they are subject to enforcement actions by the SEC, for example, the 32-firm sample of Dechow, Hutton, and Sweeney (1995), and the 64-firm sample of Beneish (1997).
- Random samples in which the researcher introduces deliberately managed accruals See, for example, Dechow, Hutton, and Sweeney (1995), Kang and Sivaramakrishnan (1995), Jeter and Shivakumar (1999), Peasnell, Pope, and Young (1999), and Kothari, Leone, and Wasley (2005).[37]

GAAP violators

Beneish (1997), studies a sample of 64 firms that violated GAAP, selecting firms with large accruals that did not report GAAP violations as a control group. In general, firms that violate GAAP tend to be relatively young firms that, once revealed as GAAP violators, report a large and negative reversal of accruals. Evidence that GAAP violators have large accruals is supported in other studies as well (e.g., Dechow, Sloan, and Sweeney, 1996 Bradshaw, Richardson, and Sloan, 2001[38]).[39] To test the Jones model, Beneish chooses as a control group firms with large accruals because "large discretionary accruals could result not only from earnings management but also from exogenous influences on firms' performance or from the effects of strategic operating decisions that are not motivated by the desire to artificially increase reported earnings" (p. 273).

Beneish finds that selecting firms in the top decile of Jones's discretionary accruals every year between 1983 and 1992 identified 59 of 64 GAAP violators, but the Jones model successfully predicted only 15 GAAP violators before the restatement. (A firm is classified as forecasted to be a vio-

---

[37] A related methodology is to assign randomly discretionary accruals to a predetermined sample (see, e.g., Elgers, Pfeiffer, and Porter, 2003, who use this methodology to evaluate whether the result of DeFond and Park, 1994, of anticipatory smoothing is not attributable to a mechanical error).

[38] Bradshaw, Richardson, and Sloan show that firms with unusually high working-capital accruals are more likely to experience declines in subsequent earnings performance.

[39] The United States Government Accountability Office, formerly the General Accounting Office (GAO), provides a free database of restatements (GAO-03-395R Financial Statement Restatement Database), and there has been a flurry of research activity into firms that have made restatements. GAO-03-395R covers 919 restatements between January 1, 1997, and June 30, 2002, and includes the name of each restating company, its stock ticker symbol, the market on which the stock was trading at the time of the announcement, the date of the announcement, the entity that prompted the restatement, and the reason(s) for the restatement; see GAO-03-395R Financial Statement Restatement Database.

lator if the prediction error from the accruals model was significant at least at the 5% level.) Dechow, Sloan, and Sweeney (1995), provide similar results.

This test of type II error is subject to criticism if there is a "pecking order" in achieving target earnings. Earnings management through accruals is likely to have been taking place even before the violation of GAAP. Hence, firms that violate GAAP are likely to run out of their reserves of accruals. The accruals in the estimation period, then, are probably already "abnormal accruals," which recast their abnormal accruals in the event period as normal. Beneish (1997), comments,

> [T]he actions of GAAP violators were extreme in the sense of the lengths they went to report higher earnings (e.g., recording fictitious transactions), but not necessarily in the sense of the magnitude of discretionary accruals. That is, although GAAP violators are more likely to have had consecutive positive accruals in years leading to and including the year of GAAP violation, their accruals were lower than those of aggressive accruers in the year of violation. (p. 292)

Random samples with deliberate manipulation

Dechow Hutton, and Sweeney (1995), choose samples of 1,000 randomly selected firm-years and introduce a fixed and known amount of accrual manipulation. Dechow, Hutton, and Sweeney find that the Jones model outperforms the Healy and DeAngelo models, but the Jones model classifies discretionary accruals as non-discretionary. The Jones model is able to yield abnormal accruals only when earnings management is 5% of total assets or higher. Their tests are based on the regression output and the z-statistics.

10.2.3.3 Additional Approaches to Testing the Relative Efficiency of the Jones Model

An important point in the evaluation of the Jones model goes beyond the issue of its susceptibility to type I and type II errors. Rather, of great importance is how it performs relative to the alternatives. On the one hand, Dechow, Sloan, and Sweeney (1995), and Bartov, Tsui, and Gul (2001), as well as others, provide compelling evidence that the Jones model outperforms the naïve models of Healy and DeAngelo, as well as Dechow and Sloan's Industry Model. Other research, however, indicates that no accruals model (sc., the Healy, DeAngelo, and Jones models) outperforms some other arbitrary procedure for detecting earnings management: Guay, Kothari, and Watts (1996), find that there is a high correlation between the discretionary accruals for all models. When accruals are randomly decomposed between discretionary and non-discretionary, however, they observe an equally high correlation. They note, "Overall, the high correlation between accrual components from the Jones and the modified Jones models … and the results based on random decomposition of accruals incline us to conclude that all five models estimate discretionary accruals with considerable imprecision" (p. 95).   Similarly, Thomas and Zhang (2000), find that the discretionary accruals models presented above, including the Jones model, are less accurate than a naïve model that predicts that discretionary accruals equal –5% of total assets for all firms and years. An alternative test is the relative persistence of normal accruals (Thomas and Zhang, 2000; Kothari, Leone, and Wasley, 2005; Ye, 2006). Intuitively, normal accruals are expected to be more persistent than abnormal accruals.

11 Modifications to the Jones Model and Alternative Methodologies

In Chap. 10, we elaborated on type I and type II errors in the results of the Jones model's tests. The consensus in the literature nowadays is that the major concern lies with the type I error (Bernard and Skinner, 1996; Healy, 1996; Dechow, Richardson, and Tuna, 2003; Kothari, Leone, and Wasley, 2005), which indicates incorrectly that earnings management has occurred. McNichols (2000), reasons that type II error is less urgent because editors reject studies with "weak" results.

This concern raises two independent questions. How can we improve the Jones model to reduce these errors? Are there alternative tests of earnings management that can corroborate the results of the Jones model? This chapter is organized around these two questions.

11.1 Improved Jones Models

The choice of the normal accruals in the Jones model is logical. It relates accruals to changes in "revenues" and "property, plant, and equipment" (PP&E). The former determine changes in working-capital accruals, such as accounts receivable, inventory, and accounts payable. The latter determine the accrual of the depreciation expense.

In what follows, we discuss the following improvements to the Jones model:

1. The modified Jones model of Dechow, Sloan, and Sweeney (1995).
2. The forward-looking model of Dechow, Richardson, and Tuna (2003).
3. Three performance-adjusted models:
   (a) The components model of Kang and Sivaramakrishnan (1995);
   (b) The cash-flows model of Dechow and Dichev (2002);
   (c) The linear performance-matching Jones model of Kothari, Leone, and Wasley (2005);
4. The synthesis model of Ye (2006).

11.1.1 The Modified Jones Model

Dechow, Sloan, and Sweeney (1995), present a *modified Jones model*. Its novelty is the treatment of accounts receivable. If the firm does not manage earnings in the estimation period and manages accounts receivable in the event period, then accruals of credit sales are normal in the estimation period and abnormal in the event period. The modified model recognizes this difference in time-series analysis by making the following adjustment: The first stage of estimating normal accruals is similar to the Jones model. In the second stage (the *event* period), normal accruals, NDA, are computed by multiplying the estimated coefficient of the change in sales by the change in cash sales (the change in revenues minus the change in accounts receivable) instead of the change in sales. The NDA of firm i in the event period p are computed as follows:

$$\text{NDA}_{ip} = \hat{\alpha}_i\,[1/A_{ip-1}] + \hat{\beta}_{1i}\,[(\Delta \text{REV}_{ip} - \Delta \text{AR}_{ip})/A_{ip-1}] + \hat{\beta}_{2i}\,[\text{PPE}_{ip}/A_{ip-1}], \quad (11.1)$$

where

NDA_{ip}	=	normal, non-discretionary accruals of firm i in period p;
A_{ip-1}	=	lagged assets of firm i;
REV	=	revenues;
AR	=	accounts receivable;
PPE	=	PP&E;
Δ	=	change;
$\hat{\beta}_{1i}$	=	the coefficient of total revenues in the estimation period. It is estimated from the regression of accruals on ΔREV_i and PPE_i.

On the face of it, the modified Jones model is inconsistent because the model of normal accruals is applied differently in the two stages. The concern that managed credit sales bias the estimate of normal accruals in the event period can be addressed by considering cash revenues in both stages, as done in cross-sectional tests. Using cash sales also lets one avoid the simultaneity problem caused by having accounts receivable in both the regressor (revenues) and the regressand (total accruals).

To grasp the implication of the differential treatment of accounts receivable, we construct two simple examples.

Suppose that the firm makes all sales at the end of the year and that all its costs, except for the bad-debt expense, are fixed (so that the intertemporal change in expenses is zero). When the firm does not manage earnings, its credit policy allows customers to purchase 20% on credit to be paid in full in the next accounting period. The bad-debt expense is correctly estimated as 10% of credit sales. That is, every dollar of credit sale boosts earnings by 90 cents and accruals by 18 cents. Hence, the accrued balance of accounts receivable net of the allowance for uncollectible accounts is 18% of sales [20%(100%–10%)]. We assume that uncollectible accounts receivable are written off in the following period. The estimation of the intensity of accruals by the Jones model correctly yields the 18% intensity; that is, $\hat{\beta}_{1i} = 0.18$.

Consider two cases. In the first, the firm manages earnings by allowing all customers to purchase 100% on credit; as a result, sales increase by $40, from $100 to $140 (in the normal business cycle sales increase by $10 each year). In the second, sales again increase to $140, but this occurs because of an industry boom, and the firm further boosts earnings by eliminating the bad-debt expense. Table 11.1 summarizes the DA of the Jones and the modified Jones models.

Table 11.1 Examples

		Example 1: The firm boosts earnings by managing sales	Example 2: The firm boosts earnings by eliminating the bad-debt expense
	The example	The firm increases sales to $140 (instead of $110) by relaxing its credit policy from 20% credit to 100% credit on all sales	Sales increase to $140 without an attempt to manage earnings. The firm manages earnings by recording zero bad-debt expense
1	The reported accruals in the event period	+ $108.0 $(140 \times 100\% \times 0.9 - 100 \times 18\%)$	+ $10.0 $(20\% \times 140 - 18\% \times 100)$
2	The unmanaged accruals in the event period (NDA)	$1.80 $(110 - 100) \times 18\%$	$7.20 $(140 - 100) \times 18\%$
3 =(1)–(2)	The "true" DA (3)=(1)–(2)	+ $106.20 $(108.0 - 1.80)$	+ $2.80 $(10 - 7.20)$
4	The Jones model's DA[a]	+ $100.80 $(108.0 - 18\% \times 40)$	+ $2.80 $(10.0 - 18\% \times 40)$
5	The modified Jones model's DA[b]	+ $122.40 $(108.0 - 18\%(-80)$	+ $4.24 $(10.0 - 18\% \times 32)$

[a] The change in sales in both cases is 140–100=40
[b] The change in cash sales in case 1 is $140 × 0 –$100 × 0.8= –$80; in case 2, it is 0.8 × ($140–$100)= $32

As these two examples illustrate, both models detect the earnings management attempts and in the right direction. The Jones model captures the manipulation of the bad-debt expense correctly but underestimates managed earnings when sales are manipulated. The modified Jones model overestimates the magnitude of earnings management in both examples.[1] Our examples suggest that the modified Jones model is less susceptible to type II error than the Jones model.

The modified Jones model is widely used. In cross-sectional analysis, the change in the accounts receivable is subtracted from the change in revenues for the estimation of the parameters of normal accruals (see, e.g., Subramanyam, 1996; DeFond and Park, 1997; Dechow, Richardson, and Tuna, 2003; Kothari, Leone, and Wasley, 2005). That is, the difference between the two versions of the Jones model affects both stages of the earnings management detection procedure: estimation of normal accruals and identification of the abnormal accruals. The following definitions summarize the model.

> *Definitions:* The **time-series modified Jones model** follows the first stage of the Jones model, but it estimates DA in the event period as follows:
>
> $$N\hat{D}A_{ip}/A_{ip-1} = \hat{\alpha}_i [1/A_{ip-1}] + \hat{\beta}_{1i} [(\Delta REV_{ip} - \Delta AR_{ip})/A_{ip-1}] + \hat{\beta}_{2i} [PPE_{ip}/A_{ip-1}],$$
>
> where ΔAR is the change in accounts receivable.
>
> The **cross-sectional modified Jones model** replaces the changes in revenues with the changes in cash revenues, $\Delta REV - \Delta AR$, for the estimation of both normal accruals and DA.

We end this subsection with the following comment. The issue of measurement errors is more complicated in the modified Jones model when one employs the balance-sheet approach (see Chap. 10). The measurement error also resides in the change in the accounts receivable regressor, in contrast to the Jones model, where it affects the regressand only.[2]

---

[1] This result is not unique to our examples. Kang (2005, p. 10), also observes that using cash sales when the estimator of normal accruals considers both cash and credit sales, REV, leads to a biased estimated coefficient: "[Managed accruals are overstated when receivables are increasing (which usually follows an increase in sales), and understated when receivables are decreasing."

[2] The econometric issue here is twofold. First, measurement error in one of the regressors in a multiple regression framework biases the coefficients of all other variables as well. Second, a simultaneity problem arises since accounts receivable appears both in the regressor and in the regressand. See the discussion in Chap. 10.

Hribar and Collins (2002), show that this bias is positive with mergers and acquisitions and negative with divestitures.[3]

11.1.2 The Forward-Looking Model

The forward-looking model is given in Dechow, Richardson, and Tuna (2003). This model includes three innovations: a separation of NDA from the DA in credit sales, a control for lagged accruals, and a control for growth.

The first innovation treats some credit sales as non-discretionary in the event period as well. Dechow, Richardson, and Tuna regress the change in accounts receivable, ΔREC, on the change in sales, ΔSales (both variables are deflated by lagged assets):

$$\Delta REC = a + k\,\Delta Sales + \varepsilon, \qquad (11.2)$$

where

ΔREC   = the change in accounts receivable (deflated by lagged assets);

ΔSales   = the change in sales (deflated by lagged assets);

k = the coefficient of the change in sales.

The parameter, k, measures the sensitivity of the change in non-discretionary accounts receivable to sales. Hence, $k=1$ if 100% of the change in accounts receivable is non-discretionary and $k=0$ if all the change is discretionary. k times sales separates NDA from DA in the accounts receivable. This *adapted* Jones model adds back the non-discretionary accounts receivable, $k\Delta$Sales, to the change in cash sales, ΔSales – ΔAR, which yields [ΔSales – ΔAR] + $k\Delta$Sales = (1+k)ΔSales – ΔAR.

Dechow, Richardson, and Tuna find that k takes values between 0 and 0.392, with an average of 0.07 (median of 0.068), in their 637 cross-sectional regressions, obtained from all two-digit SIC Compustat firms that were not financial institutions in the 1998–2000 period.

The second innovation is the addition of lagged accruals. Prior studies had pointed out the value of including lagged accruals in the regression (Kang and Sivaramakrishnan, 1995; Beneish, 1997; Chambers, 1999; Nwaeze, 2001). Beneish (1997, p. 296), states, "[T]he evidence presented

---

[3] Since Collins and Hribar (2000), report that the estimates of DA computed under the Jones and the modified Jones models are correlated at 0.99 with a balance-sheet approach, and 0.97 using the cash-flow approach, they conclude that this concern is minor.

thus far indicates that ... the accruals model's ability could be enhanced by adding lagged total accruals...."[4]

Past accruals control for reversals as discussed in the Introduction to Part 4. Dechow, Richardson, and Tuna report that this innovation increases the adjusted R^2 to 17.2%. The model without this control (i.e., with the first innovation only) has an adjusted R^2 of 9.3%, compared with 9.2% for the modified Jones model.

The third innovation reflects the fact that some abnormal accruals arise from changes in business decisions (Healy, 1996). If sales are expected to grow, inventory has to be built up to supply the forthcoming additional demand. This, in turn, increases current NDA (see Appendix of Chap. 9). A failure to recognize the demand for higher levels of inventory would lead to erroneously classifying NDA as DA. Hence, Dechow, Richardson, and Tuna control for growth in sales. They measure it as the ratio of sales in the following period to sales in the current period minus one. The NDA model thus incorporates a forward-looking variable. They report that the inclusion of this innovation further increases R^2 to 20%.

An alternative view of growth in sales is that growth is a characteristic of the firm.[5] McNichols (2000), notes that young firms are characterized by high growth and by high normal accruals. A failure to take into account these features might lead to erroneously classifying NDA as DA. McNichols measures growth as the median of analysts' long-term earnings growth forecasts (reported by I/B/E/S) in the last month of the fiscal year. The regression of DA on the rate of returns on assets (ROA) and the growth variable yields a significant positive association between DA and growth.[6]

---

[4] Beneish (1997), offers an approach to predicting earnings management that has been used in later research (see, e.g., Catanach and Rhoades, 2003).

[5] A common measure of expected growth is the book-to-market ratio.

[6] McNichols runs the following regression:

$DA_i = \alpha_0 + \alpha_1 ROA + \alpha_2 GROWTH + \varepsilon_1$,

where DA_i is the discretionary accrual estimate from either the Jones model or the modified Jones model, ROA is the rate of return on assets, and GROWTH is the median of analysts' long-term earnings growth forecasts (reported by I/B/E/S) in the last month of the respective fiscal year. She finds that growth is positively and significantly correlated with the estimated DA. In her 1988–1998 sample of Compustat firms that did not engage in mergers or acquisitions, the mean GROWTH is 17.04%, with a median of 15.0%. Without ROA, α_2 is 0.0426 (t-statistic 7.942) for the Jones model and 0.0577 (t-statistic 10.284) for the modified Jones model. With ROA, α_2 is 0.0473 (t-statistic 7.837) for the Jones model and 0.0668 (t-statistic 10.151) for the modified Jones model.

The following definition summarizes the cross-sectional forward-looking Jones model.

> *Definition:* The **cross-sectional forward-looking Jones model** estimates NDA with the following equation:
>
> $$TACC_{it} = \alpha + \beta_1((1+k)\Delta Sales - \Delta AR) + \beta_2 PPE + \beta_3 TACC_{it-1} + \beta_4 GR\_sales_{it+1},$$
>
> where
>
> | | | |
> |---|---|---|
> | $TACC_{it}$ | = | firm i's total accruals in the current year, scaled by year $t-1$ total assets; |
> | k | = | the slope coefficient from a regression of ΔAR on $\Delta Sales$; |
> | $\Delta Sales$ | = | the change in sales, scaled by year $t-1$ total assets; |
> | ΔAR | = | the change in accounts receivable, scaled by year $t-1$ total assets; |
> | PPE | = | property, plant, and equipment; |
> | $TACC_{it-1}$ | = | firm i's total accruals from the prior year, scaled by year $t-2$ total assets; |
> | GR_sales_{it+1} | = | The change in firm i's sales from year t to $t+1$, scaled by year t sales. |

11.1.3 The Performance-Adjusted Models

As discussed in Chap. 10, accruals are related to performance (McNichols and Wilson, 1988; Dechow, Sloan, and Sweeney, 1995; Kasznik, 1999). In her review of the research on earnings management, McNichols (2000), states,

> [R]esearchers comparing firms that differ in earnings performance or growth characteristics may well observe (or not observe) differences in estimated discretionary accruals *that relate to the performance characteristics* of these firms rather than their incentives to manage earnings. (p. 333, emphasis added)

Performance affects the estimation of earnings management because NDA may be erroneously classified as DA when performance is abnormal and the relationship between accruals and performance is non-linear. Some events discussed in Part 2 of this book are correlated with performance: compensation, insider trading, initial public offerings and seasoned equity offerings, management buyouts, and so on. The association between these events and earnings management therefore may be spurious, because of the relationship between accruals and performance.

In this section, we detail the improvements to the Jones model that deal with the effect of performance on DA. We start with Kang and Sivaramakrishnan (1995), who decompose the accruals into revenues, expenses, and depreciation. We then discuss Dechow and Dichev (2002), who suggest the incorporation of cash flows as a proxy for the quality of earnings. Next, we consider Kothari, Leone, and Wasley (2005), who add lagged return on assets to control for the non-linear effect of performance on accruals. Finally, we present a performance-matching procedure that abandons the linear OLS model altogether.[7]

11.1.3.1 The Competing-Component Model

Kang and Sivaramakrishnan (1995), present a competing-component model. Unlike the other models presented in this chapter, this model does not refine the Jones model. Rather, it contributes to the literature by pointing at neglected elements of the Jones model. It differs from the Jones model in three respects.

First, transactions and assets are matched to the working-capital accruals that originate from them:
- Revenues, REV, which determine the accounts receivable accruals, AR;
- Expenses, EXP, which determine the inventory accruals, INV, other non-cash current asset accruals, OCA, and current liability accruals, CL. These accruals are aggregated into one measure, APB, where APB= INV+ OCA−CL; and
- Gross PP&E, GPPE, which determines the depreciation expense, DEP.

Second, the model takes into account the behavior of the accruals over time. That is, in the absence of earnings management (which is denoted by stars on the unmanaged accrual), the following relationships are assumed:

$$\frac{AR_t^*}{REV_t^*} = \phi_{AR} \frac{AR_{t-1}^*}{REV_{t-1}^*} + v_{AR}, \qquad (11.3a)$$

$$\frac{APB_t^*}{EXP_t^*} = \phi_{APB} \frac{APB_{t-1}^*}{EXP_{t-1}^*} + v_{APB}, \qquad (11.3b)$$

---

[7] Prior studies that advocate abandoning OLS are Kang and Sivaramakrishnan (1995), and Kang (2005).

$$\frac{\overset{*}{DEP}_t}{\overset{*}{GPPE}_t} = \phi\, DEP\, \frac{\overset{*}{DEP}_{t-1}}{\overset{*}{GPPE}_{t-1}} + \nu_{DEP}, \tag{11.3c}$$

where ν is the error term. These relationships are explained by the policies that generate accruals from transactions. Since accounts receivable arise from credit sales, the previous period's credit policy predicts the credit policy of this period. The components that arise from expenses, APB, reflect the suppliers' credit policy, as given in the previous period. The intensity of depreciation depends on the firm's depreciation policies. The third difference is that all variables are ending balances rather than changes in balances.

Kang and Sivaramakrishnan deal with the error in variables, omitted variables, and simultaneity problems (see Chap. 10)[8] by applying the instrumental variables (IV) approach and the generalized method of moments procedure (GMM) rather than the OLS. Running simulations, they find that both IV and GMM reduce the scope of type I and type II errors (type II error is measured after adding manipulated accruals that approximate 2% of beginning net total assets in the designated event period) and that GMM dominates IV. For example, the type II error is detected in 47% of the firms (z-statistic 19.26) under GMM, as compared to 34% under IV (z-statistic 12.84) and 23% under the Jones model (z-statistic 8.25).

The advantage of Kang and Sivaramakrishnan's approach is twofold. First, the separation between revenues and expenses reduces the misspecification error when the credit policies for revenues and expenses are not perfectly related. Kang (2005, pp. 6–7), observes that the Jones model makes the assumption

> that change in current assets and current liabilities are both driven
> by changes in revenue. This assumption seems restrictive because cur-

---

[8] Kang and Sivaramakrishnan (1995), were the first to publicly recognize this problem. They state,
> [A] simultaneity problem arises because both the regressors and the regressand are jointly determined by the constraints imposed by GAAP and double-entry bookkeeping. We note that these constraints are independent of both the EM [earnings management] or EIV [error-in-variable] problems. For example, suppose that the relation between unmanaged income and unmanaged accruals is given by NA=γ_0 + γ_1Income+ w. This relation is constrained by the identity: income = NA +Cashflows, so that $E(w\,|\,\text{Income}) \neq 0$. As a result, OLS estimation applied to this example would yield inconsistent coefficient estimates with incorrect standard errors. (p. 355)

rent liabilities such as [account] payable are more likely to be related to expenses than to revenues. ... The omission of expenses potentially explains why the Jones model often produces a bias toward finding positive managed accruals in an economic upswing (e.g., when earnings increase) and conversely in an economic downsizing.[9]

The following summarizes Kang and Sivaramakrishnan's model:

$$\mathrm{AB}_{i,t} = \phi_0 + \phi_{\mathrm{AR}} \left[\frac{\mathrm{AR}_{t-1}^*}{\mathrm{REV}_{t-1}^*} \mathrm{REV}_{i,t} \right] + \phi_{\mathrm{APB}} \left[\frac{\mathrm{APB}_{t-1}^*}{\mathrm{EXP}_{t-1}^*} \mathrm{EXP}_{i,t} \right] + \phi_{\mathrm{DEP}} \left[\frac{\mathrm{DEP}_{t-1}^*}{\mathrm{GPPE}_{t-1}^*} \mathrm{GPPE}_{i,t} \right] + \varepsilon_{i,t},$$

where $\mathrm{AB}_{i,t}$ are the unmanaged accrued balances of firm i at the end of period t and $\varepsilon_{i,t}$ is white noise.

This study was followed with considerable interest.[10] Kang (2005), provides the missing link between this model and the Jones model by studying earnings management in a sample of 1,502 Compustat firm-years of firms suspected of having incentives to avoid reporting losses (matched with 1,451 out of 5,370 firms not suspected of avoiding loss) between 1978 and 1996. His results confirm that the IV approach is superior to the Jones model and that the Jones model is prone to both to type I and type II errors.

11.1.3.2 The Cash-Flows Jones Model

Given that the financial analysis literature advocates detecting earnings management by comparing the patterns of accruals and cash flows (e.g., Palepu, Healy, and Bernard, 2003), cash flows seem a natural candidate for a performance control (e.g., Dechow, Sloan, and Sweeney, 1995; Rees, Gill, and Gore, 1996; Jeter and Shivakumar, 1999; Zarowin, 2002; Park and Park, 2004; Cohen, Dey, and Lys, 2005a; Francis, LaFond, Olsson, and Schipper, 2005; Myers, Myers, and Skinner, 2006; Ye, 2006).[11]

To illustrate the Jones model with such a control, consider Jeter and Shivakumar (1999), who adapt the Jones model as follows:

$$\frac{\mathrm{NDA}_t}{A_{t-1}} = \beta_0 + \beta_1 \frac{\Delta \mathrm{REV}}{A_{t-1}} + \beta_2 \frac{\mathrm{PPE}}{A_{t-1}} + \sum_{j=3}^{7} \beta_j \times \mathbf{I}_{j-2} \times \frac{\mathrm{CFO}}{A_{t-1}}, \qquad (11.4)$$

---

[9] For an illustration of the bias, consult Kang (2005), footnote 8 and figure 1.

[10] See http://scholar.google.com.

[11] In some studies, cash flows are used as a measure of unmanaged earnings in robustness checks of the Jones model (e.g., DeFond and Park, 1994). Given the accruals nature of accounting earnings, as discussed in the Introduction to Part 4, cash flows can represent unmanaged accounting earnings under quite restricted conditions. So, this approach has not gained much popularity.

where the additional variables are cash flows from operations, CFO, and the indicator function I_{j-2}, which takes the value of 1 if the firm's CFO places it in the $j-2$ quintile and zero otherwise.

Since cash flows are defined as the difference between earnings before extraordinary items and accruals, including contemporaneous cash flows as a regressor may induce a simultaneity problem, especially if the research design uses the statement of cash-flows approach to calculate accruals. Thus, until Dechow and Dichev (2002), most studies did not control for this performance measure.

Dechow and Dichev (2002), focus on the quality of earnings. They make the argument that the quality of accruals depends on their mistake in predicting cash flows, since accruals separate the timing of cash flows from their accounting recognition.

To illustrate, consider a firm with a credit policy that requires customers to pay an advance of a fraction b of sales; a fraction $1-a-b$ is paid when the goods are delivered, and the remaining fraction a is paid in the following quarter. The firm pays all expenses, E, in cash. The cash flows, CF_t, earnings, X_t, and accruals, ACC_t, as a function of the stream of sales, S_{t-1}, S_t, S_{t+1}, are as follows:

$$CF_t = bS_{t+1} + [1 - a - b]S_t + aS_{t-1} - E_t = [S_t - E_t] - a\Delta S_t + b\Delta S_{t+1}, \quad (11.5a)$$

$$X_t = S_t - E_t, \text{ and} \quad (11.5b)$$

$$ACC_t = a\Delta S_t - b\Delta S_{t+1}, \quad (11.5c)$$

where $\Delta S_k = S_k - S_{k-1}$, $k = t, t + 1$.

A discrepancy between the accounting recognition and total cash flows over three periods ($t-1$, t, and $t+1$) might occur because of an unexpected return of merchandise sold in period $t-1$ or an unanticipated bad debt discovered on date $t+1$. In these cases, accruals include mistakes because total accruals are different from zero (see the Introduction to Part 4). Unexpected returns in period t ($t+1$) of sales made in period $t-1$ (t) imply that $-a\Delta S_t$ ($[1 - a - b]S_t$) is inflated. Accruals are erroneous, and thus of lower quality.

By Eq. 11.5c, accrued balances in period t match cash inflows in period $t-1$ due to the reversal of period $t-1$ unearned revenues (b), cash inflows in period $t+1$ due to reversal of period t accounts receivable (a), and cash inflows in period t due to period t cash sales ($1-a-b$). That is, accruals in period t are correlated with cash flows in three periods, $t-1$, t, and $t+1$. Dechow and Dichev run the following firm-level, time-series regression:

$$\Delta WC_t = b_0 + b_1 CF_{t-1} + b_2 CF_t + b_3 CF_{t+1} + \varepsilon_t, \tag{11.6}$$

where

ΔWC_t = the change in working capital, measured as the sum of the change in accounts receivable (Compustat #302) + the change in inventory (Compustat #303) minus the change in accounts payable (Compustat #304) minus the change in tax payable (Compustat #305) plus the change in other net assets net of liabilities (Compustat #307), with all variables scaled by average assets;

CF_t = cash flows from operations (Compustat #308);

ε = an error term that is used to measure the quality of earnings;

The residuals from this regression are used as the measure of the quality of earnings and accruals. Examining how a firm's characteristics affect the quality of earnings, they obtain three key findings: The quality of accruals decreases in total accruals, firm size, and the volatility of sales, cash flows, and accruals; these results are explained by the increased chance of being wrong when accruals are high. The quality of accruals is decreasing in the length of the operating cycle, which is 360/(sales/average accounts receivable)+360/(cost of goods sold/average inventory). The intuition of this result is immediate to the extent that the quality of accruals is influenced by uncertainty: the longer the cycle, the greater the likelihood of making mistakes in the estimation and recognition of accruals. The greater the frequency with which the firm reports losses, the lower the quality of its accruals, since the error in accruals is correlated with shocks, such as restructuring charges. Their most interesting discovery is that in a regression of the quality of accruals on a firm's characteristics—frequency of reporting losses, average operating cycle, standard deviation of sales, and size—the adjusted R^2 is 0.61. When the independent variables in the regression are only the standard deviation of accruals and the standard deviation of earnings, the adjusted R^2 jumps to 0.79. As they conclude, "[A] simple practical way to gauge the quality of accruals is to assess the volatility of both earnings and accruals" (p. 49).

In her discussion of Dechow and Dichev's paper, McNichols (2002), compares Dechow and Dichev's model with two others: the Jones model and a model that combines (11.6) with the Jones model, namely

$$\Delta WC_t = b_0 + b_1 CF_{t-1} + b_2 CF_t + b_3 CF_{t+1} + b_4 \Delta sales + b_5 PPE + \varepsilon_t. \tag{11.7}$$

In a sample of 15,015 firm-year observations with available data from Compustat with SIC codes 2000-3999 for the years 1988–1998, after excluding companies with mergers, acquisitions, or discontinued operations,

McNichols notes that the R^2 of the Jones model and Eq. 11.6 as a stand-alone (NDA are measured as in Dechow and Dichev's study) is 0.073 and 0.2011, respectively. The R^2 jumps to 0.30, when these two models are combined as in Eq. 11.7. Furthermore, the coefficients of the change in sales, b_4, and PPE, b_5, increase when the Jones model is modified by controlling for the history of cash flows: b_4 increases from 0.08 to 0.096 (the corresponding t-statistics are 33.74 and 45.93), and b_5 increases from – 0.005 to –0.002 (corresponding t-statistics of –5.57 and –3.32). McNichols's findings suggest the use of cash flows to control for performance in the Jones model.

11.1.3.3 The Performance-Matching Model

Kothari, Leone, and Wasley (2005), develop a performance-matching model. Their motivation is to address the non-linear relationship between normal accruals and performance:

> For statistical as well as economic reasons, we expect the mapping current performance into future performance, or the mapping of performance into returns, to be non-linear (e.g., Brooks and Buckmaster, 1976; Beaver et al., 1979; Freeman and Tse, 1992; Basu, 1997; Watts, 2003a, b).… Unless a discretionary accrual model, like the Jones or modified-Jones model, is improvised to address non-linearities, we do not expect the regression approach to be effective at controlling for non-zero estimated discretionary accruals in stratified-random samples. (pp. 169–170)

They offer two different approaches. The first involves matching similar firms, which alleviates the need to use an OLS estimate of DA. They detect earnings management by comparing the accruals of firms that are otherwise almost identical. The second, the linear-performance-matching model, embodies two modifications of the Jones and the modified Jones models: an intercept, and an additional control for the lagged rate of return on assets, ROA_{t-1}. They also use the contemporaneous ROA (see their table 1), but since later studies used only the lagged ROA, we restrict our attention to this variable.

Because the first term in the Jones model is the reciprocal of lagged assets, econometrically, the Jones model does not have an intercept. Deflating by lagged assets is meant to mitigate heteroskedasticity. Finding that heteroskedasticity is still an issue, Kothari, Leone, and Wasley also include an intercept to mitigate it. They find that an intercept yields higher symmetry around zero discretionary accruals, which enhances the power of tests for type I error. They report that excluding the intercept increases rejection rates by more than 20% over those reported for models including an intercept (see their table 3, panel A).

> The *linear-performance-matched Jones model* is
>
> $$\text{ND}\hat{A}_{ip}/A_{ip-1} = \alpha_0 + \hat{\alpha}_i\,[1/A_{ip-1}] + \hat{\beta}_{1i}\,[\Delta\text{REV}_{ip} - \Delta\text{AR}_{ip}\,/A_{ip-1}]$$
>
> $$+ \hat{\beta}_{2i}\,[\text{PPE}_{ip}/A_{ip-1}] + \delta_1\,\text{ROA}_{i,p-1},$$
>
> where α_0 is a constant and $\text{ROA}_{i,p-1}$ is the lagged rate of return on assets.

Kothari, Leone, and Wasley start with a sample of 122,798 observations from 1962 to 1999 of Compustat firms with sufficient data (i.e., at least 10 firms in the industry, and total accruals that do not exceed total assets) to construct 250 samples of 100 firms each. They find that having an ROA in the regression reduces discretionary accruals when they expect the null hypothesis of no earnings management to hold. For example, the DAs from the Jones and the modified Jones models without performance matching are –0.31 and –0.61, respectively, but with $\text{ROA}_{i,t-1}$ they are 0.08 and –0.14, respectively. Kothari, Leone, and Wasley observe that the standard error of the DAs increases with the lagged $\text{ROA}_{i,t-1}$. They propose the following test for substantiating the efficiency of their model:

> In non-random samples, total accruals themselves are likely to be correlated, which can lead to serially correlated estimates of discretionary accruals. The serial correlation in total accruals arises due to economic/operating reasons (e.g., actions by management such as expanding receivables or inventories in periods of growth). A major objective of the discretionary accrual models like the Jones model is to filter out non-discretionary accruals from total accruals to obtain estimates of discretionary accruals that have a zero mean and are serially uncorrelated as expected under the null hypothesis of no earnings management. (p. 179)

This model has become quite popular because it yields stronger results than the Jones model. Ye (2006), for example, reports an out-of-sample R^2 of 4.9%, as compared to an R^2 of 3.8% for the Jones model. When the test is executed for current accruals alone (see Chap. 10), the R^2 are higher, 8.09% for the Jones model and 11.13% for the performance-matched model. We describe Ye's study in the next section.

11.1.4 The Business Model: A Synthesis

Improvements to the Jones model discussed so far have involved adding controls to account for the persistence of accruals and growth, incorporating business fundamentals such as the historical rates, and applying research methods beyond the linear regression model.

These developments raise two questions: What is the most efficient way to incorporate all these modifications? How do we fine-tune the additional variables in order to enhance the efficiency of the modeling of normal accruals?

Ye's (2006) study provides an answer to these questions. Ye examines the following model:

$$
\begin{aligned}
TA_{i,t} = & \underset{\text{Non-zero}}{INT} + \underset{\text{The Jones}}{(\beta_0 + \beta_1 \Delta REV_{i,t} + \beta_2 PPE_{i,t})/A_{i,t-1}} + \underset{\text{Performance control}}{\beta_4 ROA_{i,t-1}} + \\
& \text{intercept} \qquad\qquad \text{model} \qquad\qquad \text{of Kothari et al.}
\end{aligned}
$$

$$
\underset{\substack{\text{Abnormal lagged} \\ \text{accruals deflated by sales}}}{\beta_5 NCWC_{i,t-1} - \beta_6 \overline{NCWC}_{i,t}} + \underset{\substack{\text{Working capital} \\ \text{intensity}}}{\beta_7 NCWC_{i,t-1} \times \Delta REV_{i,t}} + \underset{\substack{\text{Depreciation} \\ \text{rate}}}{\beta_8 dep_{i,t-1}} +
$$

$$
\underset{\substack{\text{Historical depreciation} \\ \text{for current assets}}}{\beta_9 dep_{i,t-1} PPE_{i,t}}, \tag{11.8}
$$

where

TA	=	total accruals;
INT	=	intercept;
ΔREV	=	chance in sales;
PPE	=	property, plant and equipment;
A	=	total assets;
ROA	=	rate of return on assets.
NCWC	=	non-cash working capital (current assets minus current liabilities [excluding the current portion of long-term debt] and cash), deflated by lagged assets;
$\overline{NCWC}$	=	normal non-cash working capital,

$$
\overline{NCWC}_{i,t} = \frac{1}{3} \sum_{k=2}^{4} NCWC_{i,t-k}.
$$

dep	=	depreciation rate: the depreciation expense divided by PPE;
i, t	=	indexes, i for firm and t for year.

Ye extends the linear-performance-matched model of Kothari, Leone, and Wasley (2005), by adding abnormal past accruals, the intensity of working capital, as discussed below, and expected depreciation, as well as the depreciation rate (for econometric reasons, to ensure that β_9 is indeed unbiased).

Ye evaluates the model in a battery of tests. The results reported are based on a sample of 75,348 firm-years in the annual Compustat 2004 (industrial, research, and full coverage) for 1987–2003. His selection criteria are as follows: available data; total assets, revenues, and PP&E, that all exceed $1M; and depreciation that does not exceed 33% of PP&E. The second criterion is a safeguard against the problematic non-linear relationship between extreme performance and accruals, which Ye further addresses by winsorizing ROA and change in sales. The third criterion eliminates unusual observations.

Abnormal lagged accruals: Lagged accruals, $NCWC_{i,t-1}$, are replaced with *abnormal* past accruals, $NCWC_{i,t-1} - \overline{NCWC_{it}}$. Econometrically, to test that abnormal accruals as well as lagged accruals matter, Ye separates the components of this variable and shows that their coefficients have approximately the same magnitude, but with a different sign. For current accruals, the coefficients are • 10.29 on NCWC ($t = 22.6$) and +10.55 on $\overline{NCWC_{it}}$ ($t = 22.6$).[12]

Working-capital intensity: To separate current accruals from the long-term depreciation accruals, Ye adds the firm's specific business fundamentals, $NCWC_{i,t-1} \times \Delta REV_{i,t}$. This variable controls for growth in sales, a variable whose significance was established by McNichols (2000), and Dechow, Richardson, and Tuna (2003). Consider the following two relationships, one inspired by Kang and Sivaramakrishnan and the other from an efficiency criterion:

$$\frac{NCWC_{it}}{\Delta REV_{it}} = \frac{NCWC_{i,t-1}}{\Delta REV_{i,t-1}}, \qquad \text{(NCWC intensity)}[13]$$

$$GROWTH = \frac{\Delta rev_{i,t-1}}{Sales_{i,t-1}}, \qquad \text{(Growth)}$$

---

[12] We report the results obtained by calculating accruals from the statement of cash flows. Ye also reports results for accruals derived from the balance sheet. Qualitatively, they are similar.

[13] Note that NCWC is the total accruals as measured by the balance sheet approach (see Chap. 10) and REV are sales. Hence, this condition is a requirement for stationarity in the relationships between accruals and the change in sales over time; an assumption that agrees with the time-series research design.

$$\text{ASSET UTILIZATION} = \frac{\text{Sales}_{i,t-1}}{A_{i,t-1}}, \qquad \text{(Efficiency)}$$

where, in order to be consistent with the notation in Ye's study, rev is revenues that are not divided by the beginning-of-the-period total assets, A. The product of GROWTH and EFFICIENCY is $\Delta REVi,t-1$, and the product of $\Delta REVi,t-1$ and NCWC is Ye's variable. Ye postulates that the coefficient of this variable ought to be positive because it reflects an increase in accruals when an increase in revenues is associated with a corresponding increase in working-capital accruals. Indeed, Ye shows that this is a significantly positive variable; its coefficient when the dependent variable is current accruals is 25.50 ($t=41.6$).

Depreciation: Similar to Kang and Sivaramakrishnan, as detailed above, Ye applies the historical depreciation rate, $\text{dep}_{i,t-1}$, to calculate the current expected deprecation, $\text{dep}_{i,t-1} \times \text{PPE}_{it}$. When accruals are calculated using the statement of cash-flows approach, the coefficient of depreciation is significantly negative, -56.63 ($t=39.6$).

Ye assembles the pieces of the various revised Jones models into a single model. Besides this valuable synthesis, Ye makes a contribution in two main regards. First, once we start departing from the Jones model, a boundless number of possibilities arise. Hence, the question is not what to add, but when to stop adding. Ye provides a significant insight, as he shows that even limited tweaking—by separating the dynamic of the working-capital accruals from that of depreciation—enhances the power of the Jones model. Second, as discussed in Chap. 10, although a cross-sectional analysis is to be preferred because it provides a richer sample size, such analysis suppresses firm-specific parameters, which creates a demand for identifying the "specific functional form linking accruals to past performance in the cross-section" (Kothari, Leone, and Wasley, 2005, p. 166). Ye's three additional firm-specific business fundamental variables accomplish that.

11.2 Alternative Methodologies for Detecting Earnings Management

Three major alternative methodologies have been employed for detecting earnings management:

- Analyzing a single income-statement item, or a portfolio of accounting treatments that are based on assumptions that require making judgments.

- Examining the distribution of firms' earnings—the distributional method.
- Examining the distribution of the second digit of the decimal in earnings per share (EPS).

Some researchers employ a combination of methodologies, using a score of earnings management measures rather than examining each measure separately (e.g., Leuz, Nanda, and Wysocki, 2003; Cohen, Dey, and Lys, 2005a). We present the combination methodology in the section that describes the single-account approach to indicate how the single-account approach can be extended.

11.2.1 Analysis of a Single Account

11.2.1.1 The Method

This approaches focuses on a single income-statement item, chosen because it has a material impact on reported earnings and can be manipulated legally within the boundaries of GAAP, since it is based on estimates: for example, write-offs (Strong and Meyer, 1987; Elliott and Shaw, 1988; Elliott and Hanna, 1996; Francis, Hanna, and Vincent, 1996; Rees, Gill, and Gore, 1996; Bunsis, 1997; Alciatore, Dee, Easton, and Spear, 1998; Bartov, Lindahl, and Ricks, 1998; Press and Dowdell, 2004; Dey, Cohen, and Lys, 2005a); the bad-debt expense, in the income statements of publishers (McNichols and Wilson, 1988); and loss reserves, in the income statements of property and casualty insurance companies (see Chap. 4).[14]

An examination of a single account rather than total accruals can be effective because the researcher can understand the accounting model and what the unmanaged expense ought to be. Since a major issue in earnings management studies is the unobservability of the unmanaged accounting numbers, having a correct model of the unmanaged expense is an advantage in formulating and interpreting a model. One disadvantage is that if the non-discretionary component of a given single account is large relative to the discretionary component, the former might "drown" the latter, which yields a type II error (McNichols and Wilson, 1988). Another criticism is that this methodology is too weak to detect earnings management by using

---

[14] Marquardt and Wiedman (2004a), Cohen, Dey, and Lys (2005a), and Roychowdhuri (2006), adopt a different tactics: They assume that earnings management takes place and then explore which individual accounts are used for that purpose.

a portfolio of accruals. We are reluctant to join in this criticism because it seems a matter of common sense that finding earnings management in one account supports earnings management in total accruals as well, though the absence of earnings management in one account does not imply that there is no earnings management in others.

Finally, note that some studies employ portfolios of accounting treatments (e.g., Healy and Palepu, 1990, and the studies that follow the "positive accounting theory" school) and that in some cases the single income-statement item is itself an aggregate item. For example, Dhaliwal, Gleason, and Mills (2004), observe that an examination of the components of the deferred tax expense, such as the allowance for valuation, might provide mixed results on the occurrence of earnings management, but studying the tax expense in total provides conclusive evidence.

We illustrate the application of the single-item approach with the study of McNichols and Wilson (1988).

11.2.1.2 *McNichols and Wilson (1988)*

McNichols and Wilson examine one accrual account—the provision for bad debts. This focus restricts their sample to industries where such an expense is material. The sample includes 289 firm-years from the 1967–1985 period, from printing and publishing (SIC 27, 37 firms), non-durable wholesale goods (SIC 50, 51 firms), and business services (SIC 73, 29 firms). The mean ratio of receivables to total assets is 28.7% in the sample, as compared to 22.3% for the Compustat population as a whole.

McNichols and Wilson explore the association between the abnormal expense and earnings (deflated by end-of-the-period assets to yield ROA), given the incentives of managers who receive earnings-based bonuses to manage earnings through the bad-debt expense. They test whether firms smooth earnings via this expense (the smoothing hypothesis) or whether, similar to the dynamics in Healy (1985), they take a bath when earnings are either extremely low or extremely high (the bonus hypothesis).

The managed accrual is the residual, $resprov_t$, of the following regression:

$$\text{Prov}_t = \alpha_0 + \alpha_1 \text{BgBl}_t + \alpha_2 \text{Write-off}_t + \alpha_3 \text{Write-off}_{t+1} + resprov_t, \quad (11.10)$$

where
Prov_t	=	the provision for bad debt, deflated by period-t sales;
BgBl_t	=	the beginning balance in the allowance for bad debts of period t, deflated by period-t sales;
Write-off_j	=	write-offs for period j, deflated by period-t sales, $j=t,t+1$;

resprov$_t$ =   the prediction error, which by design is orthogonal to the regressors;

The research design assumes that managers have perfect foresight of future write-offs, so that the unmanaged estimated ending allowance equals the actual, Write-off$_{t+1}$. In other words, prediction errors are attributable to earnings management. The median of the discretionary accruals is denoted by μ.

Since McNichols and Wilson deflate earnings by assets, the ROA statistic classifies firms by portfolios of high, medium, and low, determined on the basis of the deviation of their ROA from the benchmark. Initially, they consider four benchmarks: zero, industry average ROA, the return on the firm's average ROA over the sample period, and the firm's prior-year ROA. McNichols and Wilson choose two, changes in ROA and the deviation of ROA from the firm's mean ROA (see their table 5) based on their stronger correlation with the compensation data for firms' top four officers. For each of these two benchmark ROA, they rank observations according to their deviations from the benchmark. Firms in the top (bottom) decile are considered firms with unusually HIGH (LOW) earnings. Observations in deciles 2–9 are used to form a comparison sample, denoted by MID.[15]

Denoting by μ the median residual provision for bad debt, they perform three tests:

Test 1:

$\mu_{\text{HIGH}} = \mu_{\text{MID}}$ versus $\mu_{\text{HIGH}} > \mu_{\text{MID}}$
(consistent with both smoothing and bonus hypotheses)

Test 2:

$\mu_{\text{LOW}} = \mu_{\text{MID}}$ versus $\mu_{\text{LOW}} \neq \mu_{\text{MID}}$
(the smoothing hypothesis implies μLOW $< \mu$MID, and the bonus hypothesis implies μLOW $>\mu$MID)

Test 3:

$\mu_{\text{HIGH,LOW}} = \mu_{\text{MID}}$ versus $\mu_{\text{HIGH,LOW}} \neq \mu_{\text{MID}}$
(the bonus hypothesis predicts that firms manage earnings downward for both high and low earnings)

---

[15] "What distinguishes our approach is not so much that we focus on a single accrual, but that we use GAAP related to this account to develop a discretionary accrual proxy" (p. 2).

The findings support the tests' alternative hypotheses. Their table 7 reports the results when accruals are partitioned based on the deviation of return on assets from the firm's mean return on assets. It shows that the median provision in the first and the tenth deciles is positive, 0.001 in each, while in deciles 2–9 it is negative. The corresponding Wilcoxon z-statistics of tests 1, 2, and 3 are 4.90 (significant at the 0.009 level, one-tail test), 2.02 (significant at the 0.05 level, two-tail test), and 4.64 (significant at the 0.001 level, one-tail test), respectively. That is, the results are consistent with both the smoothing and the bonus hypotheses.

It is interesting to note that when the discretionary accruals are measured as Healy's total accruals measure, the results are weaker, as only test 1's alternative result is established. The median of total accruals is – 0.032 in the first decile and –0.005 in the tenth decile, and all other deciles also have negative total accruals, with the exception of decile 7, with 0.001 total accruals. The corresponding Wilcoxon z-statistics of tests 1, 2, and 3 are –3.78 (significant at the 0.009 level, one-tail test), 1.30 (insignificant), and –1.62 (insignificant), respectively.

This methodology can be enriched by combining it with other methodologies. Cohen, Dey, and Lys (2005a), observe that "focusing on a single measure may not be the right approach" (p. 15). They examine the following measures:

1. The cross-sectional modified Jones DA.
2. The ratio of the absolute value of total accruals to the absolute value of cash flows from operations.
3. The ratio of the change in accounts receivable to the change in sales.
4. The ratio of the change in inventories to the change in sales.
5. The value of special items for the period scaled by the total assets at the beginning of the period.

The first metric captures abnormal accruals, the second captures smoothing, and the next two capture unusual sales activity. For example, under channel stuffing, accounts receivable increase relative to sales, and under "bill and hold" transactions, inventory does not decrease with an increase in sales. The final measure captures classificatory earnings management, which occurs when items are moved into or from the special items category (see Chap. 2). In contrast to other studies that use different methodologies to compare results, Cohen, Dey, and Lys aggregate these measures by performing a principal factor analysis for each firm-quarter. They thus have the added advantage that their score "is likely to capture the overall level of earnings management in a firm more effectively than any of the single measures" (p. 15).

In contrast to the approach that aggregates a few measures for earnings management, Ibrahim (2005), proposes to decompose accruals. Ibrahim assumes that components of accruals will be managed in a consistent fashion, for example, to achieve positive income manipulation a manager chooses to use positive accounts receivable manipulation (to increase revenues and ultimately income) and negative accounts payable manipulation (to reduce expenses and increase income). She then proposes a ratio that captures the relationship between the components of discretionary accruals: the absolute value of the sum of the discretionary accrual components divided by the sum of the absolute values of the non-discretionary accrual components. This methodology is shown to increase the power of earnings management tests but with limited improvement in specification.

11.2.2 The Distributional Approach

We described this method in Chaps. 4 and 5, where we outlined incentives to meet benchmarks. There, the approach assumes that unmanaged earnings have a Gaussian distribution, and the evidence for earnings management is the deviation of observed earnings from this distribution.

In this subsection, we outline an alternative test, based on Burgstahler and Dichev (1997a). The mechanics of this alternative are based on the assumption that the cross-sectional distributions of unmanaged changes in earnings (and levels of unmanaged earnings) are relatively smooth: the expected number of observations in a small interval around zero equals the average of the number of observations in the two immediately adjacent intervals. The test statistic is the ratio of the difference between the actual and the expected number of observations over the estimated standard deviation of the difference. Under the null hypothesis of no earnings management, these standardized differences approximate the standard normal distribution (zero mean and standard deviation of 1). De facto, however, since the null hypothesis of smoothness might not hold at zero, the standardized differences for the interval immediately to the left and immediately to the right of zero are not independent. The test for a discontinuity at zero therefore is based on one difference, either left or right. Burgstahler and Dichev's test results yield a standardized difference for the interval immediately to the left (right) of zero of -8.00 (5.88), where they employ intervals of widths of 0.0025 in their sample of 64,466 firm-year observations for the period 1977–1994.

11.2.3 Rounding EPS

Earnings per share, EPS, are expressed as a decimal with two digits after the period, $zz.xy$. Companies can affect the perceived EPS by manipulating y so that the EPS can be rounded either up or down according to whether they wish to inflate or deflate reported EPS. As with the other methods, earnings management is detected by comparing the (distribution of the) actual object of earnings management with the hypothesized distribution absent earnings management. In this case, researchers test the distribution of y.

Inspired by Carslaw (1988), Thomas (1989), considers a hypothesized distribution that follows the mathematical rule of

$$\Pr(y \le y_0) = \sum_{x=1}^{9} \left(\log_{10}\left(x + \frac{y_0 + 1}{10} \right) - \log_{10}\left(x + \frac{y_0}{10} \right) \right).$$

It is not symmetric over all numbers, and it is less likely to produce zero than most other numbers (Table 11.2).

Table 11.2 The cumulative frequency of the digits

Y_0	Probability	Cumulative probability
0	0.120	0.120
1	0.114	0.234
2	0.229	0.342
3	0.218	0.447
4	0.329	0.547
5	0.315	0.644
6	0.422	0.737
7	0.405	0.827
8	0.510	0.915
9	0.490	1.000

Thomas partitions his sample into two: 68,738 firm-years with positive net income (profit firms) and 11,359 firm-years with losses (loss firms). The evidence suggests that profit firms round numbers up when $y=8$ or 9 because the frequency of reports with $y=0$ is higher than the probability per the mathematical rule, and the frequency of $y=8$ or 9 is lower.[16] Loss firms present the opposite pattern. The frequency of $y=9$ is higher than the frequency of $y=0$, but the magnitude of the deviation from the mathematical rule is weaker for loss firms. Further analysis of firms with good news (relative to prior-year earnings) and firms with bad news provides additional evidence of the unusual patterns of the digits. Earnings per share,

---

[16] Thomas also examines the first digit, x. He finds that profit firms exhibit a frequency of numbers with $x=1$ and $y=0$ that is higher than expected, while the frequency of numbers with $x=9$ and $y=9$ is lower.

however, seem to be based on rounding up the third number after the decimal point.

Studies that employ a similar methodology include Das and Zhang (2003), who consider U.S. firms, and Kinnunen and Koskela (2003), who conduct an international study. Das and Zhang examine the first digit after the decimal point (our x). They too find opposing patterns of behavior for profit and loss firms, indicating that both round EPS, by reporting more or less than 4, $x=4$, respectively. Since Thomas shows that the mathematical rule for unmanaged decimals is unlikely to apply to EPS, they choose a binomial test, where the unmanaged probability of having numbers less than 5 is significantly different from 50%. They bridge the gap between this and other distributional methodologies and the accruals methodology. Specifically, in their 103,944 firm-quarter observations between 1989 and 1998, they examine the frequency of rounding up for firms that meet analysts' forecasts, report small profits of 1 cent, and report the same EPS as in the same fiscal quarter of the previous year. They capture accruals management through working-capital accruals, since they reason that earnings management has a short window and that other accruals are either too large or beyond the ability of management to manage. Their evidence supports the notion that firms do indeed round the numbers to manage earnings. At present, we are aware of ongoing efforts to improve the Jones model and the methods to estimate earnings management (see e.g., Dopuch, Mashruwala, Seethamraju, and Zach. 2006).

Summary and Postscript

> The stock market awakened in 2002 to discover that it no longer had numbers it could trust. Securities issuers, oriented toward shareholder value enhancement by the corporate culture of 1990s, had been adopting aggressive, even fraudulent treatments to enhance reported earnings, and their auditors had been doing nothing to stop them. (Bratton, 2004, p. 2)

Earnings management has interested regulators (Levitt, 1998, 1999, 2000; Turner and Godwin, 1999; Barth, 2000; Turner, 2001a; Glassman, 2002, 2006a; Breeden, 2003[1]; Cox, 2006), practitioners and the press (Griffiths, 1986, 1995; O'Glove, 1987; Jameson, 1988; Kellogg and Kellogg, 1991; Naser, 1993; Pijper, 1994; Blake and Salas, 1996; Smith, 1996; Mulford and Comiskey, 1996; Schonfeld, 1998; McBarnet and Whelan, 1999; Loomis, 1999; Vickers, 1999; Collingwood, 2001; Miller and Bahnson, 2002; Schilit, 2002),[2] and academics.

Overview of the Book

In the first part of the book, we dwelt on why earnings are important enough that they are the object of manipulation and then defined earnings management. Our definition is, Earnings management is a collection of managerial decisions that result in not reporting the true short-term earnings as known to management.

Earnings management can be

- Beneficial: it signals long-term value;
- Pernicious: it conceals short- or long-term value;
- Neutral: it reveals the short-term truth.

---

[1] *Restoring trust* was composed by Richard Breeden, a former chief commissioner of the SEC, in his capacity as a corporate monitor of the bankrupt WorldCom, since renamed MCI.

[2] For additional references to newspapers, consult Teoh, Welch, and Wong (1998a).

The managed earnings result from taking production or investment actions before earnings are realized, or making accounting choices that affect the earnings numbers and their interpretation after the true earnings are realized.

We next reviewed the empirical literature. The following table summarizes the categories of earnings management classified around the key players in the accounting scene: management, plain-vanilla users, and gatekeepers; it also identifies the key papers regarding each.

Providers of Earnings numbers	Receivers of Earnings' information	
Senior management	Plain users[a]	Gatekeepers[b]
• Compensation (Healy, 1985) • Insider trading (Park and Park, 2004) • Turnover (Murphy and Zimmerman, 1993) • Management buyout (Wu, 1997)	• Beating benchmarks (DeGeorge, Patel, and Zeckhauser, 1999) • IPOs, seasoned equity offerings and new listings (Teoh, Welch, and Wong, 1998b) • Mergers and acquisitions (Erickson and Wang, 1999) • Bond covenants (Beneish, 1997) • Regulation (Aharony, Jevons Lee, and Wong, 2000) • Tax (Phillips, Pincus, and Rego, 2003) • Regulated industries such as insurance companies and banks (Beaver, McNichols, and Nelson, 2000) • Employees (Peltier-Rivest, 1999) • Suppliers and competitors (Peltier-Rivest, 2002)	• Meeting or beating analysts' expectations (Bartov, Tsui, and Gul, 2002) • Institutional owners (Bushee, 1998) • Governance (Klein, 2002b) • Auditors (Nelson, Elliott, and Tarpley, 2003) • Press (Miller, 2005)

[a] Suppliers, investors, employees, consumers, creditors, regulators
[b] Boards of directors, analysts, investment banks, credit agencies, auditors, attorneys, the press

In the third part, we discussed the main contributions of the analytical research, organizing it around four themes: the capital market, governance, product or market competition, and regulation. In the fourth part, we presented the mechanics of the empirical research and highlighted the different methods and metrics used to detect earnings management.

Lessons

We hope to leave the readers with several lessons. First, the most regrettable change in earnings management in this century is that earnings management has received an ugly connotation in the wake of large accounting scandals. In a report published on October 15, 2005, in the *New York Times*, Jenny Anderson and Landon Thomas noted, "The relentless pressure that chief executives face in feeding the appetites of impatient investors, combined with the calculus that better earnings equal a higher stock price and a richer trove of options, in some cases cause a chief executive to cross a certain ethical, if not legal, line." Our definition above indicates that earnings management at times is beneficial, serving to signal value and reduce the information asymmetry between the firm and its constituency.

Pernicious earnings management is costly to shareholders because the firm pays taxes on phantom earnings (Erickson, Hanlon, and Maydew, 2004), is bleeded by class action suits and penalties collected by the SEC and Department of Justice (e.g., Ronen and Yaari, 2002; Karpoff, Lee, and Martin, 2007a), and leads to distortion in resource allocation (Kedia and Phillippon, 2005). It may be costly to managers too because they lose reputational capital (Desai, Hogan, and Wilkins, 2006). Neural earnings management has no cash flows effect (Stein, 1989; Johnson and Schwartz, 2005), and beneficial earnings management enhances shareholders' value by reducing information asymmetry between firm and investors and by reducing agency cost (e.g., Demski, 1998; Arya, Glover, and Sunder, 2003; Ronen and Yaari, 2007).

Second, the discussion in Part 3 makes it clear that there is a friction between financial statement analysis and research regarding the economics of earnings management. The examples we offer of the effect of competition on earnings management are novel. The empirical research pays no attention to competition in product markets and other facets of business strategy, in that it assumes that controlling for industry and year in the regression analysis is sufficient to control for all these aspects.[3]

Third, we do not have yet a consensus methodology that perfectly overcomes the challenge posed by the fact that unmanaged earnings are unobservable. Although the work of Ye (2006), who added firm-specific business fundamentals to the Jones model, seems promising, the researchers continue to use tools that might be too weak (Dechow and Skinner, 2000).

Related Research

We cover a great deal of work in our book. Did we leave any line of research out? The answer is yes. We do not consider **earnings management in not-for-profit organizations** (e.g., Chase and Coffman, 1994; Krishnan, Yetman, and Yetman, 2002; Mensah, Considine, and Oakes 1994; Leone, and Van Horn, 2003; Jones and Roberts, 2006; Ranjani, Yetman, and Yetman, 2006; Keating, Parsons, and Roberts, 2007). Nor have we devoted attention to the substantial literature on **disclosure** and the interaction of disclosure and earnings management (Ajinkya and Gift, 1984; Atiase, 1985; Hoskins, Hughes, and Ricks, 1986; Darrough, 1993; Dontoh, 1989; Darrough and Stoughton, 1990; Gibbins, Richardson, and Waterhouse, 1990; Ruland, Tung, and Georege, 1990; Feltham, Gigler, and Hughes, 1992; Alles and Lundholm, 1993; Newman and Sansing, 1993; Ziv, 1993; Ali, Ronen, and Li, 1994; Antle, Demski, and Ryan, 1994; Botosan, 1997; Bamber and Cheon, 1998; Admati and Pfleiderer, 2000; Boot and Thakor, 2000; Schrand and Walther, 2000; Aerts, 2001; Lobo and Zhou, 2001; Begley and Feltham, 2002; Botosan and Plumlee, 2002; Boo and Simnett, 2002; Chen, DeFond, and Park, 2002; Lundholm and Myers, 2002; Hutton, Miller, and Skinner, 2003; Leone and Van Horn, 2003; Dobler, 2004; Fischer and Verrecchia, 2004; Einhorn, 2005, 2007; Wasley and Wu, 2005; Baginski, Hassell, and Kimbrough, 2006; Byard, Li, and Weintrop, 2006; Cao, Wasley, and Wu, 2006; Hoje and Kim, 2007; Langberg and Sivaramakrishnan, 2006).

Moreover, we have paid scant attention to the large body of **international** evidence from outside the United States (e.g., Walsh, Craig, and Clarke, 1991; Whittred and Chan, 1992; Ashari, Koh, Tan, and Wong, 1994; Sheikholeslami, 1994; Blake and Salas, 1996; Booth, Kallunki, and Martikainen, 1996, 1997; Gore, Taib, and Taylor, 1999; Eddey and Taylor,

---

[3] The economic repercussions of earnings management (on firm-level investment) are studied in Kedia and Philippon, 2005, and McNichols and Stubben, 2005.

1999; Herrmann and Tatsuo, 1996; Kasanen, Kinnunen, and Niskanen, 1996; Saudagaran and Sepe, 1996; Marsden and Wong, 1998; Culvenor, Godfrey, and Byrne, 1999; Kallunki and Martikainen, 1999; Kinnunen, Keloharju, Kasanen, and Niskanen, 1999; Magnan, Nadeau, and Cormier, 1999; Pierce-Brown and Steele, 1999; Pope and Walker, 1999; Aharony, Jevons Lee, and Wong, 2000; Garza, Okumura, and Kunimura, 2000; Land and Lang, 2002; Rahman and Bakar, 2002; Gabrielsen, Gramlich, and Plenborg, 2002; Gul, Srinidhi, and Shieh, 2002; Loh and Tan, 2002; Poitras, Wilkins, and Kwan, 2002; Wells, 2002; Yeo, Tan, Ho, and Chen, 2002; Bowman and Navissi, 2003; Chen, Lee, and Li, 2003; Liu and Zhou, 2003; Ming and Wong, 2003; Bushman, Piotroski, and Smith, 2004; Chen and Yuan, 2004; Haw, Hu, Hwang, and Wu, 2004; Jaime and Albornoz, 2004; Song, Jihe, and Windram, 2004; Melis, 2004; Riahi-Belkaoui, 2004; Jong, DeJong, Merterns, and Roosenboom, 2005; Lobo and Zhou, 2005; Pastor and Poveda, 2005; Peasnell, Pope, and Young, 2005; Ashbaugh, LaFond, and Lang, 2006; Ben and Zeghal, 2006; Burgstahler, Hail, and Leuz, 2006; Chen, Elder, and Hsieh, 2007; Beuselinck, Deloof, and Manigart, 2007).

We mention these omissions because we are aware of the future research opportunities available in these fronts that are likely to enrich our knowledge and understanding of the earnings management phenomena. We hope that the readers understand that this omission is an expression of our bounded rationality limitations, not a malicious or pernicious omission.

Bibliography

Abarbanell, Jeffery S. and Victor Bernard. 1992. Tests of analysts' overreaction/underreaction to earnings information as an explanation for anomalous stock price behavior. *Journal of Finance*, 47, 3 (July): 1181–1207.

Abarbanell, Jeffery S. and Brian J. Bushee. 1997. Fundamental analysis, future earnings, and stock prices. *Journal of Accounting Research*, 35, 1 (Spring): 1–24.

Abarbanell, Jeffery S. William N. Lanen, and Robert E. Verrecchia. 1995. Analysts' forecasts as proxies for investor beliefs in empirical research. *Journal of Accounting and Economics*, 20, 1 (July): 31–60.

Abarbanell, Jeffery S., and Reuven Lehavy. 2002. Differences in commercial database reported earnings: Implications for empirical research. SSRN.com/abstract=228918.

Abarbanell, Jeffery S. and Reuven Lehavy. 2003a. Can stock recommendations predict earnings management and analysts' earnings forecast errors? *Journal of Accounting Research*, 41, 1 (March): 1–31.

Abarbanell, Jeffery S. and Reuven Lehavy. 2003b. Biased forecasts or biased earnings? The role of reported earnings in explaining apparent bias and over/under reaction in analysts' earnings forecasts. *Journal of Accounting and Economics*, 36, 1–3: 105–146.

Abbott, Lawrence J. and S. Susan Parker. 2000. Audit committee characteristics and auditor selection. *Auditing: A Journal of Practice and Theory*, 19, 2 (Fall): 47–66.

Abbott, Lawrence J. and S.Susan Parker. 2001. Audit committee characteristics and auditor selection: Evidence from auditor switches. *Research in Accounting Regulation*, 15: 151–166.

Abbott, Lawrence, Susan Parker, and Gary F. Peters. 2004. Audit committee characteristics and restatements. *Auditing: A Journal of Practice and Theory*, 23, 1 (March): 69–87.

Abbott, Lawrence, Susan Parker, and Gary F. Peters. 2006. Earnings management, litigation risk, and asymmetric audit fee responses. *Auditing: A Journal of Practice and Theory*, 25, 1 (May): 85–98.

Abbott, Lawrence J., Susan Parker, Gary F. Peters, and Kannan Raghunandan. 2001. An investigation of the impact of audit committee characteristics on the relative magnitude of non-audit service purchases. SSRN.com/abstract=285151.

Abbott, Lawrence, Susan Parker, Gary F. Peters, and K. Raghunandan. 2003. An empirical investigation of audit fees, non-audit fees and audit committees. *Contemporary Accounting Research*, 20, 2: 215–234.

Abbott, Lawrence, Susan Parker, Gary F. Peters, and Dasaratha V. Rama. 2004. Audit, nonaudit, and information technology fees: Some empirical evidence. *Accounting and the Public Interest*, 3, 1: 1–21.

Abbott, Lawrence, Susan Parker, Gary F. Peters, and Dasaratha V. Rama. 2005. Corporate governance, audit quality and the Sarbanes-Oxley Act: Evidence from internal audit outsourcing. SSRN.com/abstract=759864.

Abdel-khalik, Ahmed Rashad. 2002. Reforming corporate governance post Enron: Share-holders' board of trustees and the auditor. *Journal of Accounting and Public Policy*, 21, 2 (Summer): 97–103.

Abdel-khalik, Ahmed Rashad. 2006. An empirical analysis of CEO risk aversion and the propensity to smooth earnings volatility. SSRN.com/abstract=926912.

Aboody, David. 1996. Recognition versus disclosure in the oil and gas industry. *Journal of Accounting Research*, 34, 3 (Supplement): 21–32.

Aboody, David, Mary E. Barth, and Ron Kasznik. 2004a. SFAS 123 stock-based compensation expense and equity market values. *The Accounting Review*, 79, 2 (April): 251–275.

Aboody, David, Mary E. Barth, and Ron Kasznik. 2004b. Firms' voluntary recognition of stock-based compensation expense. *Journal of Accounting Research*, 42, 2 (May): 123–150.

Aboody, David and Ron Kasznik. 2000. CEO stock option awards and the timing of corporate voluntary disclosure. *Journal of Accounting and Economics*, 29, 1 (February): 73–100.

Aboody, David Ron Kasznik, and Michael Williams. 2000. Purchase versus pooling in stock-for-stock acquisitions: Why do firms care? *Journal of Accounting and Economics*, 29, 3 (June): 261–286.

Abowd, John M. and David S. Kaplan. 1999. Executive compensation: Six questions that need answering. NBER Working Paper No. 7124.

Adams, Renée B. 2005. What do boards do? Evidence from board committee and director compensation data. EFA 2005 Moscow Meeting Paper. SSRN.com/abstract=397401.

Adams, Renée B., Heitor Almeida, and Daniel Ferreira. 2005. Powerful CEOs and their impact on corporate performance. *Review of Financial Studies*, 18, 4 (January): 1403–1432.

Adams, Renée B. and Daniel Ferreira. 2004. Do directors perform for pay? Working Paper, Stockholm School of Economics.

Adams, Renée and Daniel Ferreira. 2007. A theory of friendly boards. *Journal of Finance*, 62, 1 (February): 217–250.

Adams, Renée B. and Hamid Mehran. 2005. Corporate performance, board structure and its determinants in the banking industry. EFA 2005 Moscow Meeting Paper SSRN.com/abstract=302593.

Adams, Renée B., and João A.C. Santos. 2006. Identifying the effect of managerial control on firm performance. *Journal of Accounting and Economics*, 41, 1–2 (April): 55–85.

Adiel, Ron. 1996. Reinsurance and the management of regulatory ratios and taxes in the property—casualty insurance industry. *Journal of Accounting and Economics*, 22, 1–3 (August–December): 207–240.

Admati, Anat R. and Paul Pfleiderer. 2000. Forcing firms to talk: Financial disclosure regulation and externalities. *Review of Financial Studies*, 13, 3 (Fall): 479–519.

Admati, Anat R., Paul Pfleiderer, and Josef Zechner. 1994. Large shareholder activism, risk sharing, and financial market equilibrium. *Journal of Political Economy*, 102, 6 (December): 1097–1130.

Aerts, Walter. 2001. Inertia in the attributional content of annual accounting narratives. *European Accounting Review*, 10, 1 (March): 3–32.

Affleck-Graves, John, Carolyn M. Callahan, and Niranjan Chipalkatti. 2002. Earnings predictability, information asymmetry, and market liquidity. *Journal of Accounting Research*, 40, 3 (June): 561–583.

Aggarwal, Rajesh K. and Dhananjay Nanda. 2004. Access, common agency, and board size. SSRN.com/abstract=571801.

Aggarwal, Rajesh. K. and Andrew A. Samwick. 1999. The other side of the tradeoff: The impact of risk on executive compensation. *Journal of Political Economy*, 107, 1 (February): 65–105.

Aggarwal, Rajesh K. and Andrew A. Samwick. 2006. Empire-builders and shirkers: Investment, firm performance, and managerial incentives. *Journal of Corporate Finance*, 12, 3 (June): 489–515.

Aggarwal, Reena and Rohan G. Williamson. 2006. Did new regulations target the relevant corporate governance attributes? SSRN.com/abstract=859264.

Aghion, Philippe, Patrick Bolton, and Jean J. Tirole. 2004. Exit options in corporate finance: Liquidity versus incentives. *Review of Finance*, 8, 3 (September): 327–353.

Aghion, Philippe, Mathias Dewatripont, and Patrick Rey. 1994. Renegotiation design with unverifiable information. *Econometrica*, 62, 2 (March): 257–282.

Aghion, Philippe and Jean J. Tirole. 1997. Formal and real authority in organizations. *Journal of Political Economy*, 105, 1 (February): 1–29.

Agrawal, Anup and Sahiba Chadha. 2005. Corporate governance and accounting scandals. *Journal of Law and Economics*, 48, 2 (October): 371–406.

Agrawal, Anup, Sahiba Chadha, and Mark A. Chen. 2006. Who is afraid of Reg FD? The behavior and performance of sell-side analysts following the SEC's Fair Disclosure rules. *The Journal of Business*, 79, 6 (November): 2811–2834.

Agrawal, Anup and Mark A. Chen. 2006. Analysts conflicts and research quality. Working Paper, University of Alabama and University of Maryland.

Agrawal, Anup and Tommy Cooper. 2007. Insider trading before accounting scandals. SSRN.com/abstract=929413.

Agrawal, Anand and Sanjay Fuloria. 2004. Corporate governance for competitive credibility. *Journal of Social Science*, 9, 3: 185–194.

Agrawal, Anup, Jeffrey F. Jaffe, and Jonathan M. Karpoff. 1999. Management turnover and governance changes following the revelation of fraud. *Journal of Law and Economic*, 42, 1 (April): 309–342.

Agrawal, Anup and Charles R. Knoeber. 1996. Firm performance and mechanisms to control agency problems between managers and shareholders. *Journal of Financial and Quantitative Analysis*, 31, 3 (September): 377–397.

Agrawal, Anup and Charles R. Knoeber. 2001. Do some outside directors play a political role? *The Journal of Law and Economics*, 44, 1 (April): 179–198.

Agrawal, Anup, Charles, R. Knoeber, and Theofanis Tsoulouhas. 2006. Are outsiders handicapped in CEO successions? *Journal of Corporate Finance*, 12 (June): 619–644.

Agrawal, Anup and Gershon N. Mandelker. 1987. Managerial incentives and corporate investment and financing decisions. *Journal of Finance*, 42, 4 (September): 823–837.

Agrawal, Anup and Gershon N. Mandelker. 1990. Large shareholders and the monitoring of managers: The case of antitakeover charter amendments. *Journal of Financial and Quantitative Analysis*, 25, 2: 143–161.

Aharoni, Amram and Joshua Ronen. 1989. The choice among accounting alternatives and management compensation: Effects of corporate tax. *The Accounting Review*, 64, 1 (January): 69–86.

Aharony, Joseph, Chi-Wen Jevons Lee, and T.J. Wong. 2000. Financial packaging of IPO firms in China. *Journal of Accounting Research*, 38, 1 (Spring): 103–126.

Aharony, Joseph, C. Lin, and Martin Loeb. 1993. Initial public offerings, accounting choices, and earnings management. *Contemporary Accounting Research*, 10, 1 (Fall): 61–81.

Ahdieh, Robert B. 2005. From "federalization" to "mixed governance" in corporate law: A defense of Sarbanes-Oxley. *Buffalo Law Review* (September). SSRN.com/abstract=834386.

Ahmed, Anwer S. 1994. Accounting earnings and future economic rents: An empirical analysis. *Journal of Accounting and Economics*, 17, 3 (May): 377–400.

Ahmed, Anwer S., Bruce K. Billings, and Richard M. Morton. 2004. Extreme accruals, earnings quality, and investor mispricing. SSRN.com/abstract=544984.

Ahmed, Anwer S., Bruce K. Billings, Richard M. Morton, and Mary S. Stanford-Harris. 2002. The role of accounting conservatism in mitigating bondholder–shareholder conflicts over dividend policy and in reducing debt costs. *The Accounting Review*, 77, 4 (October): 867–890.

Ahmed, Anwer S., Scott Duellman, and Ahmed M. Abdel-Meguid. 2006. Auditor independence, corporate governance and abnormal accruals. SSRN.com/abstract=887364.

Ahmed, Anwer S., Gerald J. Lobo, and Jian Zhou. 2006. Job security and income smoothing: An empirical test of the Fudenberg and Tirole (1995) model. SSRN.com/abstract=248288.

Ahmed, Anwer S., Khalid Nainar, and Jian Zhou. 2005. Do analysts' forecasts fully reflect the information in accruals? *Canadian Journal of Administrative Sciences*, 22, 4 (December): 329–342.

Ahmed, Anwer S. and Carolyn Takeda. 1995. Stock market valuation of gains and losses on commercial banks' investment securities: An empirical analysis. *Journal of Accounting and Economics*, 20, 2 (September): 207–225.

Ahmed, Anwer S., Carolyn Takeda, and Shawn Thomas. 1999. Bank loan loss provisions: A reexamination of capital management, earnings management and signaling effects. *Journal of Accounting and Economics*, 28, 1 (November): 1–25.

Ahmed, Zeeshan. 2005. An investigation of firm's earnings management practices around product recalls. A Ph.D. dissertation. Mississippi State University.

AICPA. 1994. *Improving Business Reporting—A Customer Focus. Meeting the Needs of Investors and Creditors (Comprehensive Report of the Special Committee on Financial Reporting).* New York: American Institute of Certified Public Accountants.

Aier, Jagadison K., Joseph Comprix, Matthew T. Gunlock, and Deanna Lee. 2005. The financial expertise of CFOs and accounting restatements. *Accounting Horizons*, 19, 3 (September): 123–135.

AIMR. 1993. *Financial Reporting in the 1990s and Beyond.* A position paper of the Association for Investment Management and Research (AIMR), prepared by P.H. Knutson.

Ajinkya, Bipin B., Rowland K. Atiase, and Michael J. Gift. 1991. Volume of trading and the dispersion in financial analysts' earnings forecasts. *The Accounting Review*, 66, 2 (April): 389–401.

Ajinkya, Bipin B., Sanjeev Bhojraj, and Partha Sengupta. 2003. The governance role of institutional investors and outsider directors on the properties of management earnings forecasts. 14th annual conference on financial economics and accounting (FEA). SSRN.com/abstract=488107.

Ajinkya, Bipin B. and Michael J. Gift. 1984. Corporate managers' earnings forecasts and symmetrical adjustments of market expectations. *Journal of Accounting Research*, 22, 2 (Fall): 425–444.

Akerlof, George A. 1970. The market for "lemons": Quality uncertainty and the market mechanism. *Quarterly Journal of Economics*, 84, 3 (August): 488–500.

Albrecht, David W. and Fredrick M. Richardson. 1990. Income smoothing by economy sector. *The Journal of Business Finance and Accounting*, 17, 5 (Winter): 713–730.

Albuquerque, Rui A. and Jianjun Miao. 2006. CEO power, compensation, and governance. SSRN.com/abstract=922700.

Alchian, Armen A. and Harold Demsetz. 1972. Production, information costs, and economic organization. *American Economic Review*, 62, 5 (December): 777–795.

Alciatore, Mimi, Carol Callaway Dee, Peter Easton, and Nasser Spear. 1998. Asset write downs: A decade of research. *Journal of Accounting Literature*, 17: 1–39.

Alciatore, Mimi, Peter Easton, and Nasser Spear. 2000. Accounting for the impairment of long-lived assets: Evidence from the petroleum industry. *Journal of Accounting and Economics*, 29, 2 (April): 151–172.

Alexander, Janet C. 1991. Do the merits matter? A study of settlements in securities class actions. *Stanford Law Review*, 43 (February): 497–598.

Ali, Ashiq. 1994. The incremental information content of earnings, working capital from operations, and cash flows. *Journal of Accounting Research*, 32, 1 (Spring): 61–74.

Ali, Ashiq, Lee Seok Hwang, and Mark A. Trombley. 2000. Accruals and future stock returns: Tests of the naïve investor hypothesis. *Journal of Accounting, Auditing and Finance*, 15, 2 (Spring): 161–181.

Ali, Ashiq, April Klein, and James Rosenfeld. 1992. Analysts' use of information about permanent and transitory earnings components in forecasting annual EPS. *The Accounting Review*, 67, 1 (January): 183–198.

Ali, Ashiq and Krishna R. Kumar. 1994. The magnitudes of financial statement effects and accounting choice: The case of the adoption of SFAS 87. *Journal of Accounting and Economics*, 18, 1 (July): 89–114.

Ali, Ashiq, Joshua Ronen, and Shu-Hsing Li. 1994. Discretionary disclosures in response to intra-industry information transfers. *Journal of Accounting, Auditing and Finance*, 9, 2 (Spring): 265–282.

Alka, Arora and Alam Pervaiz. 2001. The dual role of accounting earnings: Contracting and valuation. *Journal of Corporate Communications*, 3 (October): 3. http://www.corpcomm.org.

Allaire Yvan and Mihaela Firsirotu. 2005. *Beyond Monks and Minow : From Fiduciary to Value Creating Governance (Series on Strategy and Governance).* Montreal, Canada: Forstrat-International-Press.

Allee, Kristian D., Neil Bhattacharya, Ervin L. Black, and Theodore E. Christensen. 2006. Pro forma disclosure and investor sophistication: External validation of experimental evidence using archival data. SSRN.com/abstract=483823.

Allen, Franklin. 1985a. Repeated principal–agent relationships with lending and borrowing. *Economics Letters*, 17, 1–2: 27–31.

Allen, Franklin. 1985b. Repeated principal–agent contracts with lending and borrowing. *Economic Letters*, 17, 1: 27–31.

Allen, Franklin and Roni Michaely. 1995. Dividend Policy. In Robert A. Jarrow, Vojislav Maksimovic, and William T. Ziemba eds. *Handbook in Operations Research and Management Science, 9: Finance.* New York: Elsevier Science. Chapter 25: 783–837.

Alles, Michael, and Russell J. Lundholm. 1993. On the optimality of public signals in the presence of private information. *The Accounting Review*, 68, 1 (January): 93–112.

Allgood, Sam and Kathleen A. Farrell. 2003. The match between CEO and firm. *The Journal of Business*, 76, 2 (April): 317–341.

Almazam, Andres, Jay C. Hartzell, and Laura T. Starks. 2005. Active institutional shareholders and costs of monitoring: Evidence from executive compensation. Working Paper, University of Texas.

Altamuro, Jennifer, Anne Beatty, and Joseph Peter Weber. 2005. Earnings management and earnings informativeness: Evidence from SEC Staff Accounting Bulletin (SAB) 101. *The Accounting Review*, 20, 2 (April): 373–401.

Altinkilic, Oya and Robert S. Hansen. 2003. Discounting and underpricing in seasoned equity offers. *Journal of Financial Economics*, 69, 2 (August): 285–323.

American Accounting Association. 1966. *A Statement of Basic Accounting Theory.* Prepared by a committee: Norton M. Bedford, R. Lee Brummet, Neil C. Churchill, Paul E. Fertig, Russell H. Morrison, Roland F. Salmonson, George H. Sorter, Lawrence L. Vance, and Charles T. Zlatkovich, Chairman.

Amershi, Amin H., Joel Demski, and John Fellingham. 1985. Sequential Bayesian analysis in accounting settings. *Contemporary Accounting Research*, 1, 2 (Spring): 176–192.

Amershi, Amin H., Joel Demski, and Mark Wolfson. 1982. Strategic behavior and regulation research in accounting. *Journal of Accounting and Public Policy*, 1, 1 (Autumn): 19–32.

Amershi, Amin H. and Shyam Sunder. 1987. Failure of stock prices to discipline managers in a rational expectations economy. *Journal of Accounting Research*, 25, 2 (Autumn): 177–195.

Amir, Eli and Elizabeth Gordon. 1996. Firms' choice of estimation parameters: Empirical evidence from SFAS No. 106. *Journal of Accounting, Auditing and Finance*, 11, 3 (Summer): 427–448.

Amir, Eli, Yanling Guan, and Gilad Livne. 2005. The effects of auditor independence on cost of public debt. SSRN.com/abstract=781844.

Amir, Eli and Joshua Livnat. 1996. Multiperiod analysis of adoption motives: The case of SFAS 106. *The Accounting Review*, 71, 4 (October): 539 –553.

Amir, Eli and Joshua Livnat. 1997. Adoption choices of SFAS 106: Implications for financial analysis. *Journal of Financial Statement Analysis*, 2, 2 (Winter): 51–60.

Amir, Eli and Amir Ziv. 1997a. Recognition, disclosure, or delay: Timing the adoption of SFAS 106. *Journal of Accounting Research*, 35, 1 (Spring): 61–81.

Amir, Eli and Amir Ziv. 1997b. Economic consequences of alternative adoption rules for new accounting standards. *Contemporary Accounting Research*, 14, 3 (Fall): 543–568.

Amoah, Nana. 2006. Auditor characteristics, board structure, and the likelihood of auditor initiated restatements. Working Paper, Morgan State University.

Amzaleg, Yaron, Uri Ben-Zion, and Ahron Rosenfeld. 2002. On the role of institutional investors in corporate governance: Evidence from voting of mutual funds in Israel. SSRN.com/abstract=746024.

Anand, Anita I. 2005. An analysis of enabling vs. mandatory corporate governance structures post Sarbanes-Oxley. *Delaware Journal of Corporate Law*, 31, 1: 229–252. SSRN.com/abstract=718341.

Anderson, Kirsten L., Daniel N. Deli, and Stuart L. Gillan. 2006. Boards of directors, audit committees, and the information content of earnings. Weinberg Center for Corporate Governance Working Paper No. 2003–04. SSRN.com/abstract=444241.

Anderson, Kirsten L. and Tery Lombardi Yohn. 2002. The effect of 10-k restatements on firm value, information asymmetries and investors' reliance on earnings. SSRN.com/abstract=332380.

Anderson, Lynne Ann. 2005. Sarbanes-Oxley's protection of employee whistleblowers impacts the financial services industry. *Journal of Taxation and Regulation of Financial Institutions*, 19, 1 (September/October). SSRN.com/abstract=876996.

Anderson, Ronald C., Sattar A. Mansi, and David M. Reeb. 2003. Founding family ownership and the agency cost of debt. *Journal of Financial Economics*, 68, 2 (May): 263–285.

Anderson, Ronald C., Sattar A. Mansi, and David M. Reeb. 2004. Board characteristics, accounting report integrity, and the cost of debt. *Journal of Accounting and Economics*, 37, 3 (September): 315–342.

Anderson, Ronald C. and David M. Reeb. 2003a. Family ownership, corporate diversification, and firm leverage. *The Journal of Law and Economics*, 46, 2 (October): 653–684.

Anderson, Ronald C. and David M. Reeb. 2003b. Founding family ownership and firm performance: Evidence from S&P 500. *Journal of Finance*, 58, 3 (June): 1301–1327.

Anderson, Ronald C. and David M. Reeb. 2004. Board composition: Balancing family influence in S&P 500 Firms. *Administrative Science Quarterly*, 49, 2 (June): 209–237.

Anonymous. 2003. Reforms: Watching the watchdogs. *Consumer reports publication* (March): 68.

Anthony, Joseph and Kathy R. Petroni. 1997. Accounting estimation disclosures and firm valuation in the property-casualty insurance industry. *Journal of Accounting, Auditing and Finance*, 12, 3 (Summer): 257–281.

Antle, Rick. 1982. The auditor as an economic agent. *Journal of Accounting Research*, 20, 2 (Autumn): 503–527.

Antle, Rick. 1984. Auditor independence. *Journal of Accounting Research*, 22, 1 (Spring): 1–20.

Antle, Rick and Joel Demski. 1989. Revenue recognition. *Contemporary Accounting Research*, 5, 2 (Spring): 423–451.

Antle, Rick, Joel Demski, and Stephen G. Ryan. 1994. Multiple sources of information, valuation, and accounting earnings. *Journal of Accounting, Auditing and Finance*, 9, 4 (Fall): 675–696.

Antle, Rick and Frøystein Gjesdal. 2001. Dividend covenants and income measurement. *Review of Accounting Studies*, 6, 1 (March): 53–76.

Antle, Rick, Elizabeth Gordon, Ganapathi Narayanamoorthy, and Ling Zhou. 2006. The joint determination of audit fees, non-audit fees, and abnormal accruals. *Review of Quantitative Finance and Accounting*, 27, 3 (November): 235–266.

Antle, Rick and Barry Nalebuff. 1991. Conservatism and auditor–client negotiations. *Journal of Accounting Research*, 29 (Supplement): 31–54.

Antle, Rick and Abbie Smith. 1985. Measuring executive compensation: Methods and an application. *Journal of Accounting Research*, 23, 1 (Spring): 296–325.

Archambeault, Deborah and Todd DeZoort. 2001. Auditor opinion shopping and the audit committee: An analysis of suspicious auditor switches. *International Journal of Auditing* 5, 1 (March): 33–52.

Arya, Anil, Hans Frimor, and Brian Mittendorf. 2003. Pouring money down the drain? How sunk investments and signing bonuses can improve employee incentives. *Topics in Economic Analysis & Policy*, 3, 1 (January): 1–14.

Arya, Anil, Jonathan Glover, and Pierre Jinghong Liang. 2004. Intertemporal aggregation and incentives. *European Accounting Review*, 13, 4 (December): 643–657.

Arya, Anil, Jonathan Glover, Brian Mittendorf, and Ganapathi Narayanamoorthy. 2005. Unintended consequences of regulating disclosures: The case of Regulation Fair Disclosure. *Journal of Accounting and Public Policy*, 24, 3 (May-June): 243–252.

Arya, Anil, Jonathan Glover, and Shyam Sunder. 1998. Earnings management and the revelation principle. *Review of Accounting Studies*, 3, 1–2 (March): 7–34.

Arya, Anil, Jonathan Glover, and Shyam Sunder. 2003. Are unmanaged earnings always better for shareholders? *The Accounting Horizon*, 17 (Supplement): 111–116.

Arya, Anil and Brian Mittendorf. 2004. Offering stock options to gauge managerial talent. *Journal of Accounting and Economics*, 40, 1–3 (December): 189–210.

Arya, Anil and Brian Mittendorf. 2007. The interaction among disclosure, competition between firms, and analyst following. *Journal of Accounting and Economics*, 43, 2–3:321–339.

Arya, Anil, Peter Woodlock, and Richard A. Young. 1992. Managerial reporting discretion and the truthfulness of disclosures. *Economics Letters*, 39, 2 (June): 163–168.

Ascioglu, Asli N., Shantaram Hegde, and John B. McDermott. 2005. Auditor compensation, disclosure quality, and market liquidity: Evidence from the stock market. *Journal of Accounting and Economics*, 24, 4 (July–August): 325–354.

Ashari, Nasuhiyah, Hian Chye Koh, Soh Leng Tan, and Wei Har Wong. 1994. Factors affecting income smoothing among listed companies in Singapore. *Accounting and Business Research*, 24, 96 (Autumn): 291–301.

Ashbaugh, Hollis, Ryan LaFond, and Brian H. Mayhew. 2003. Do nonaudit services compromise auditor independence? Further evidence. *The Accounting Review*, 78, 3 (July): 611–639.

Ashbaugh-Skaife, Hollis, Daniel W. Collins, and William R. Kinney, Jr. 2006. The discovery and reporting of internal control deficiencies prior to SOX-mandated audits. McCombs Working Paper No. ACC-02-05. SSRN.com/abstract=694681.

Ashbaugh-Skaife, Hollis, Daniel W. Collins, and Ryan LaFond. 2006. The effects of corporate governance on firms' credit ratings. *Journal of Accounting and Economics*, 42, 1–2 (October): 203–243.

Ashbaugh-Skaife, Hollis, Ryan LaFond, and Mark Lang. 2006. The effects of governance on smoothing and smoothing consequences: International evidence. Working Paper, University of North Carolina.

Asquith, Paul, Anne Beatty, and Joseph Peter Weber. 2005. Performance pricing in bank debt contracts. *Journal of Accounting and Economics,* 40, 1–3 (December): 101–128.

Asquith, Paul, Robert Gertner, and David Scharfstein. 1994. Anatomy of financial distress: An examination of junk-bond issuers. *Quarterly Journal of Economics*, 109, 3 (August): 625–658.

Asquith, Paul, Paul M. Healy, and Krishna G. Palepu. 1989. Earnings and stock splits. *The Accounting Review*, 64, 3 (July): 387–403.

Asquith, Paul, Michael B. Mikhail, and Andrea Au. 2005. Information content of equity analyst reports. *Journal of Financial Economics*, 75, 2 (February): 245–282.

Asquith, Paul and David Mullins. 1983. The impact of initiating dividend payments on shareholders' wealth. *The Journal of Business*, 56, 1 (January): 77–96.

Asthana Sharad. 1999. Determinants of funding strategies and actuarial choices for defined-benefit pension plans. *Contemporary Accounting Research*, 16, 1 (Spring): 39–74.

Asthana, Sharad, Steven Balsam, and Sungsoo Kim. 2004. The effect of Enron, Andersen, and Sarbanes-Oxley on the market for audit services. SSRN.com/abstract=560963.

Atiase, Rowland K. 1985. Predisclosure information, firm capitalization, and security price behavior around earnings announcements. *Journal of Accounting Research*, 23, 1 (Spring): 21–36.

Atwood, T.J. and Hong Xie. 2005. The market mispricing of special items and accruals: One anomaly or two? SSRN.com/abstract=734803.

Ausubel, Lawrence M. 1990. Insider trading in rational expectations economy. *American Economic Review*, 80, 5 (December): 1022–1041.

Ayers, Benjamin C., John (Xuefeng) Jiang, and Eric Yeung. 2006. Discretionary accruals and earnings management: An analysis of pseudo earnings targets. *The Accounting Review*, 81, 3 (May): 617–652.

Ayers, Benjamin C., Craig E. Lefanowicz, and John R. Robinson. 2002. Do firms purchase the pooling method? *Review of Accounting Studies*, 7, 1 (March): 5–32.

Ayres, Frances L. 1994. Perceptions of earnings quality: What managers need to know. *Management Accounting*, 75, 9 (March): 27–29.

Baber, William R., Shuping Chen, and Sok-Hyon Kang. 2006. Stock price reaction to evidence of earnings management: Implications for supplementary financial disclosure. *Review of Accounting Studies*, 11, 1 (March): 5–19.

Baber, William R., Patricia M. Fairfield, and James A. Haggard. 1991. The effect of concern about reported income on discretionary spending decisions: The case of research and development. *The Accounting Review*, 66, 4 (October): 818–829.

Baber, William R., Surya N. Janakiraman, and Sok-Hyon Kang. 1996. Investment opportunities and the structure of executive compensation. *Journal of Accounting and Economics*, 21, 3 (June): 297–318.

Baber, William R. and Sok-Hyon Kang. 2001. Stock price reactions to on-target earnings announcements: Implications for earnings management. SSRN.com/abstract=275275.

Baber, William R. and Sok-Hyon Kang. 2002a. The impact of split adjusting and rounding on analysts' forecast error calculations. *Accounting Horizons*, 16, 4 (December): 277–289.

Baber, William R. and Sok-Hyon Kang. 2002b. Is meeting the consensus EPS good news or bad news? A Working Paper. SSRN.com/abstract=303579.

Baber, William R. and Sok-Hyon Kang. 2003. Does the stock market ignore earnings management? Evidence from earnings announcements. A paper presented in the seminar of the Department of Accounting at University of Maryland, October.

Baber, William R., Sok-Hyon Kang, and Lihong Liang. 2005. Strong boards, management entrenchment, and accounting restatement. SSRN.com/abstract=760324.

Baber, William R., Sok-Hyon Kang, and Krishna R. Kumar. 1998. Accounting earnings and executive compensation: The role of earnings persistence. *Journal of Accounting and Economics*, 25, 2 (May): 169–193.

Bachar, Joseph. 1989. Auditing quality, signaling, and underwriting contracts. *Contemporary Accounting Research*, 6, 1 (Fall): 216–241.

Backer, Larry Catá. 2002. The Sarbanes Oxley Act: Federalizing norms for officer, lawyer and accountant behavior. *St. John Law Review*, 76, 4 (October): 897–952.

Backer, Larry Catá. 2004. Surveillance and control: Privatizing and nationalizing corporate monitoring after Sarbanes-Oxley. *Michigan State Law Review*, 2 (Summer): 327–440.

Badertscher, Brad, John D. Phillips, Morton P.K. Pincus, and Sonja O. Rego. 2006a. Tax implications of earnings management activities: Evidence from restatements. Working Paper.

Badertscher, Brad, John D. Phillips, Morton P.K. Pincus, and Sonja O. Rego. 2006b. Do firms manage earnings downward in a book-tax conforming manner? SSRN.com/abstract=921422.

Bae, Benjamin B. and Heibatollah Sami. 2005. The effect of potential environmental liabilities on earnings response coefficients. *Journal of Accounting, Auditing and Finance*, 20, 1 (Winter): 43–70.

Baginski, Stephen P. 1987. Intraindustry information transfers associated with management forecast of earnings. *Journal of Accounting Research*, 25, 2 (Spring): 196–216.

Baginski, Stephen P., Edward J. Conrad, and John M. Hassell. 1993. The effects of management forecast precision on equity pricing and the assessment of earnings uncertainty. *The Accounting Review*, 68, 4 (October): 913–927.

Baginski, Stephen P. and John M. Hassell. 1990. The market interpretation of management earnings forecasts as a predictor of subsequent financial analyst forecast revision. *The Accounting Review*, 65, 1 (January): 175–190.

Baginski, Stephen P. and John M. Hassell. 1997. Determinants of management forecast precision. *The Accounting Review*, 72, 2 (April): 303–312.

Baginski, Stephen P., John M. Hassell, and William A. Hillison. 2000. Voluntary casual disclosures: Tendencies and capital market reaction. *Review of Quantitative Finance and Accounting*, 15, 4 (December): 371–389.

Baginski, Stephen P., John M. Hassell, and Michael D. Kimbrough. 2002. The effect of legal environment on voluntary disclosure: Evidence from management earnings forecasts issued in U.S. and Canadian markets. *The Accounting Review*, 77, 1 (January): 25–50.

Baginski, Stephen P., John M. Hassell, and Michael D. Kimbrough. 2004. Why do managers explain their earnings forecasts? *Journal of Accounting Research*, 42, 1 (March): 1–29.

Baginski, Stephen P., John M. Hassell, and Michael D. Kimbrough. 2006. The effect of macro information environment change on the quality of management earnings forecasts. SSRN.com/abstract=926361.

Baginski, Stephen P., John M. Hassell, and John D. Neill. 1999. Predicting subsequent management forecasting behavior at the date of an initial public offering. *Review of Quantitative Finance and Accounting*, 12, 1 (January): 5–21.

Bagnoli, Mark, Messod D. Beneish, and Susan G. Watts. 1999. Whispers forecasts of quarterly earnings per share. *Journal of Accounting and Economics*, 28, 1 (November): 27–50.

Bagnoli, Mark, William Kross, and Susan G. Watts. 2002. The information in management's expected earnings report date: A day late, a penny short. *Journal of Accounting Research*, 40, 5 (December): 1275–1296.

Bagnoli, Mark, Stanley Levine, and Susan Watts. 2005a. Analyst estimation revision clusters and corporate events, Part I. *Annals of Finance*, 1, 3 (August): 245–265.

Bagnoli, Mark, Stanley Levine, and Susan Watts. 2005b. Analyst estimation revision clusters and corporate events, Part II. *Annals of Finance* 1, 4 (October): 379–393.

Bagnoli, Mark and Susan G. Watts. 2000. The effect of relative performance on earnings management: A game-theoretic approach. *Journal of Accounting and Public Policy*, 19, 4-5 (Winter): 377–397.

Bagnoli, Mark and Susan G. Watts. 2005. Conservative accounting choices. *Management Science*, 51, 5 (May): 786–801.

Bahnson, Paul R., Paul Miller, and Bruce Budge. 1996. Nonarticulation in cash flow statements and implications for education, research, and practice. *Accounting Horizons,* 10, 4 (December): 1–15.

Baik, Bok and Guohua Jiang. 2006. The use of management forecasts to dampen analysts' expectations. *Journal of Accounting and Public Policy*, 25, 5 (September-October): 531–553.

Bailey, Warren, Haitao Li, Connie Mao, and Rui Zhong. 2003. Regulation Fair Disclosure and earnings information: Market, analyst, and corporate responses. *Journal of Finance*, 58, 6 (December): 2487–2514.

Baiman, Stanley and Joel S. Demski. 1980. Variance analysis procedures as motivational devices. *Management Science*, 26, 8 (August): 840–848.

Baiman, Stanley and John H. Evans III. 1983. Pre-decision information and participative management control systems. *Journal of Accounting Research*, 21, 2 (Fall): 371–395.

Baiman, Stanley, John H. Evans III, and Nandu J. Nagarajan. 1991. Collusion in auditing. *Journal of Accounting Research*, 29, 1 (Spring): 1–18.

Baiman, Stanley, John H. Evans, and James Noel. 1987. Optimal contracts with a utility-maximizing auditor. *Journal of Accounting Research*, 25, 2 (Fall): 217–244.

Baiman, Stanley and Robert E. Verrecchia. 1995. Earnings and price-based compensation contracts in the presence of discretionary trading and incomplete contracting. *Journal of Accounting and Economics*, 20, 1 (July): 93–121.

Baiman, Stanley and Robert E. Verrecchia. 1996. The relation among capital markets, financial disclosure, production efficiency, and insider trading. *Journal of Accounting Research*, 34, 1 (Spring): 1–22.

Bainbridge, Stephen M. 2001. The law and economics of insider trading: A comprehensive primer. SSRN.com/abstract=261277.

Bainbridge, Stephen M. 2002. The board of directors as nexus of contracts: A critique of Gulati, Klein & Zolt's "Connected Contracts" model. UCLA School of Law Research Paper No. 02-05. SSRN.com/abstract=299743.

Bainbridge, Stephen M. 2005. Shareholder activism and institutional investors. UCLA School of Law, Law-Econ Research Paper 05-20. SSRN.com/abstract=796227.

Bainbridge, Stephen M. 2006. Sarbanes-Oxley: Legislating in haste, repenting in leisure. UCLA School of Law, Law-Econ Research Paper No. 06-14. SSRN.com/abstract=899593.

Bainbridge, Stephen M. and Christina J. Johnson. 2004. Managerialism, legal ethics, and Sarbanes-Oxley Section 307. *Michigan State Law Review*, 2: 299-326. SSRN.com/abstract=434721.

Baker, Alisa. 2006. *The Stock Option Book*. The National Center for Employee Ownership.

Baker, Malcolm P. and Paul A. Gompers. 2003. The determinants of board structure at the initial public offering. *The Journal of Law and Economics*, 46, 2 (October): 569–598.

Baker, Terry A. 1999. Options reporting and the political costs of CEO pay. *Journal of Accounting, Auditing and Finance*, 14, 2 (Spring): 125–145.

Baker, Terry A., Denton Collins, and Austin L. Reitenga. 2003. Stock option compensation and earnings management incentives. *Journal of Accounting, Auditing and Finance*, 18, 4 (Fall): 557–582.

Balachandran, Sudhakar and Partha S. Mohanram. 2006. Conservatism and the value relevance of accounting information. Working Paper, Columbia University.

Balatbat, Maria C.A. 2006. Discussion of explaining the short and long-term IPO anomalies in the US by R&D. *Journal of Business Finance and Accounting*, 33, 3-4 (April): 580–586.

Baldenius, Tim, Nahum Melumad, and Amir Ziv. 2002. Monitoring in multiagent organizations. *Contemporary Accounting Research*, 19, 4 (Winter): 483–511.

Baldenius, Tim and Amir Ziv. 2003. Performance evaluation and corporate income taxes in a sequential delegation setting. *Journal of Accounting Studies*, 8, 2-3 (June): 283–309.

Ball, Ray and Eli Bartov. 1996. How naive is the stock market's use of earnings information? *Journal of Accounting and Economics*, 11, 3 (July): 319–337.

Ball, Ray and Philip Brown. 1968. An empirical evaluation of accounting numbers. *Journal of Accounting Research*, 6, 2 (Fall): 159–175.

Ball, Ray, S.P. Kothari, and Ashok Robin. 2000. The effect of international institutional factors on properties of accounting earnings. *Journal of Accounting and Economics*, 29, 1 (February): 1–51.

Ball, Ray. 2001. Infrastructure requirements for an economically efficient system of public financial reporting and disclosure. Brookings-Wharton Papers on Financial Services (2001): 127–182.

Ball, Ray and Lakshmanan Shivakumar. 2006. Earnings quality at initial public offerings. SSRN.com/abstract=918421.

Balsam, Steven. 1998. Discretionary accounting choices and CEO compensation. *Contemporary Accounting Research*, 15, 3 (Fall): 229–252.

Balsam, Steven. 2002. *An Introduction to Executive Compensation*. New york: Academic Press.

Balsam, Steven, Eli Bartov, and Carol Marquardt. 2002. Accruals management, investor sophistication, and equity valuation: Evidence from 10-Q filings. *Journal of Accounting Research*, 40, 4 (September): 987–1012.

Balsam, Steven, Huajing Chen, and Srinivasan Sankaraguruswamy. 2003. Earnings management prior to stock option grants. SSRN.com/abstract=378440.

Balsam, Steven, Robert Halperin, and Haim A. Mozes. 1997. Tax costs and nontax benefits: The case of incentive stock options. *Journal of the American Taxation Association*, 19, 2 (Fall): 19–37.

Balsam, Steven, In-Mu Haw, and Steven B. Lilien. 1995. Mandated accounting changes and managerial discretion. *Journal of Accounting and Economics*, 20, 1 (July): 3–29.

Balsam, Steven, Jagan Krishnan, and Joon S. Yang. 2003. Auditor industry specialization and earnings quality. *Auditing: A Journal of Practice and Theory*, 22, 2 (September): 71–97.

Balsam, Steven, Haim A. Mozes, and Harry A. Newman. 2003. Managing pro forma stock option expense under SFAS 123. *Accounting Horizons*, 17, 1 (March): 31–45.

Balsam, Steven and Qin Jennifer Yin. 2005. Explaining firm willingness to forfeit tax deductions under Internal Revenue Code Section 162 (m): The million-dollar cap. *Journal of Accounting and Public Policy*, 24, 4 (July/August): 300–324.

Bamber, Linda Smith and Youngsoon Susan Cheon. 1998. Discretionary management earnings forecast disclosures: Antecedents and outcomes associated with forecast venue and forecast specificity choices. *Journal of Accounting Research*, 36, 2 (Fall): 167–190.

Bange, Mary M. and Werner F.M. De-Bondt. 1998. R&D budgets and corporate earnings targets. *Journal of Corporate Finance: Contracting, Governance and Organization*, 4, 2 (June): 153–184.

Banker, Rajiv D. and Srikat R. Datar. 1989. Sensitivity, precision, and linear aggregation of signals for performance evaluation. *Journal of Accounting Research*, 27, 1 (Spring): 21–39.

Banks, E. 2004. *Corporate Governance, Financial Responsibility, Controls and Ethics.* Palgrave Macmillan, Basingstoke, New York.

Bannister, James W. and Harry A. Newman. 1996. Accrual usage to manage earnings toward financial analysts' forecasts. *Review of Quantitative Finance and Accounting*, 7, 3 (November): 259–278.

Barber, Brad M. and John D. Lyon. 1996. Detecting abnormal operating performance: The empirical power and specification of test statistics. *Journal of Financial Economics*, 41, 3 (July): 359–399.

Barclay, Michael J., Dan Gode, and S.P. Kothari. 2000. Matching delivered performance. *Journal of Contemporary Accounting and Economics*, 1, 1 (June): 1–25.

Barnea, Amir, Joshua Ronen, and Simcha Sadan. 1976. Classificatory smoothing of income with extraordinary items. *The Accounting Review*, 51, 1 (January): 110–122.

Barone, Gerhard J. and Matthew J. Magilke. 2006. A re-examination of the naive-investor hypothesis in accruals mispricing: The role of cash flows. SSRN.com/abstract=886093.

Barrett, Edgar M., Victor L. Bernard, and Carol A. Frost. 1989. The role of debt covenants in assessing the economic consequences of limiting capitalization of exploration costs. *The Accounting Review*, 64, 4 (October): 788–808.

Barrett, Matthew J. 2003. New opportunities for obtaining and using litigation reserves and disclosures. *Ohio State Law Journal*, 64: 1183-1195. SSRN.com/abstract=794830.

Barron, Orie, Donal Byard, C. Kile, and E. Riedl. 2002. High-technology intangibles and analysts' forecasts. *Journal of Accounting Research*, 40, 2 (May): 289–312.

Barron, Orie, Donal Byard, and Oliver Kim. 2002. Changes in analysts' information around earnings announcements. *The Accounting Review*, 77, 4 (October): 821–846.

Barron, Orie, Oliver Kim, Steve Lim, and Douglas Stevens. 1998. Using analysts' forecasts to measure properties of analysts' information environment. *The Accounting Review*, 73, 4 (October): 421–433.

Barry, Christopher B. and Robert H. Jennings. 1992. Information and diversity of analyst opinion. *Journal of Financial and Quantitative Analysis*, 27, 2 (June): 169–183.

Barth, Mary E. 2000. Valuation-based accounting research: Implications for financial reporting and opportunities for future research. *Accounting and Finance*, 40, 1 (March): 7–32.

Barth, Mary E., William H. Beaver, John R.M. Hand, and Wayne R. Landsman. 1999. Accruals, cash flows, and equity values. *Review of Accounting Studies*, 4, 3-4 (December): 205–229.

Barth, Mary E., William H. Beaver, and Wayne R. Landsman. 2001. The relevance of the value relevance literature for financial accounting standard setting: Another view. *Journal of Accounting and Economics*, 31, 1-3 (September): 77–104.

Barth, Mary E., William H. Beaver, and Mark Wolfson. 1990. Components of earnings and the structure of bank share prices. *Financial Analysts Journal*, 46, 3 (May-June): 53–60.

Barth, Mary E., Donald P. Cram, and Karen K. Nelson. 2001. Accruals and prediction of future cash flows. *The Accounting Review*, 76, 1 (January): 27–58.

Barth, Mary E., John A. Elliott, and Mark W. Finn. 1999. Market rewards associated with patterns of increasing earnings. *Journal of Accounting Research*, 37, 2 (Autumn): 387–413.

Barth, Mary E. and Amy Hutton. 2000. Differential information environments: Effects on cost of capital and reflection in share prices of recognized and disclosed accounting amounts. SSRN.com/abstract=55488.

Barth, Mary, Ron Kasznik, and Maureen McNichols. 2001. Analyst coverage and intangible assets. *Journal of Accounting Research*, 39, 1 (June): 1–34.

Barton, Jan. 2001. Does the use of financial derivatives affect earnings management decisions? *The Accounting Review*, 76, 1 (January): 1–26.

Barton, Jan and Molly Mercer. 2004. To blame or not to blame: Analysts' reactions to external explanations for poor financial performance. *Journal of Accounting and Economics*, 39, 3 (September): 509–533.

Barton, Jan and Paul J. Simko. 2002. The balance sheet as an earnings management constraint. *The Accounting Review*, 77 (Supplement): 1–27.

Barton, Jan and Gregory Waymire. 2004. Investor protection under unregulated financial reporting. *Journal of Accounting and Economics*, 38, 1-3 (December): 65–116.

Bartov, Eli. 1991. Open-market stock repurchases as signals for earnings and risk changes. *Journal of Accounting and Economics*, 14, 3 (September): 275–294.

Bartov, Eli. 1992. Patterns of unexpected earnings as an explanation for post-announcement drift. *The Accounting Review*, 67, 3 (July): 610–622.

Bartov, Eli. 1993. The timing of asset sales and earnings manipulation. *The Accounting Review*, 68, 4 (October): 840–855.

Bartov, Eli and Daniel A. Cohen. 2007. Mechanisms to meet/beat analyst earnings expectations in the pre- and post-Sarbanes-Oxley Eras. NYU Law and Economics Research Paper No. 07-18. SSRN.com/abstract=954857.

Bartov, Eli, Dan Givoly, and Carla Hayn. 2002. The rewards to meeting or beating earnings expectations. *Journal of Accounting and Economics*, 33, 2 (June): 173–204.

Bartov, Eli, Ferdinand A. Gul, and Judy S.L. Tsui. 2000. Discretionary-accruals models and audit qualifications. *Journal of Accounting and Economics*, 30, 3 (December): 421–452.

Bartov, Eli, Ferdinand A. Gul, and Judy S.L. Tsui. 2002. The rewards to meeting or beating earnings expectations. *Journal of Accounting and Economics*, 33, 2 (June): 173–204.

Bartov, Eli, Frederick W. Lindahl, and William E. Ricks. 1998. Stock price behavior around announcements of write-offs. *Review of Accounting Studies*, 3, 4 (December): 327–346.

Bartov, Eli and Partha S. Mohanram. 2004. Private information, earnings manipulation, and executive stock option exercises. *The Accounting Review*, 79, 4 (October): 889–920.

Bartov, Eli, Partha S. Mohanram, and Doron Nissim. 2003. Stock option expense, forward-looking information, and implied volatilities of traded options. Working Paper, NYU and Columbia.

Bartov, Eli, Partha S. Mohanram, and Chanddrakanth Seethamraju. 2002. Valuation of internet stock–An IPO perspective. *Journal of Accounting Research*, 40, 2 (May): 321–346.

Bartov, Eli, Stephen G. Lynn, and Joshua Ronen. 1999. Return-earnings regressions: a mismeasured earnings expectations perspective. Working paper, New York University.

Bartov, Eli, Suresh Radhakrishnan, and Itzhak Krinsky. 2000. Investor sophistication and patterns in stock returns. *The Accounting Review*, 75, 1 (January): 43–63.

Barua, Abhijit, Joseph Legoria, and Jacquelyn Sue Moffitt. 2006. Accruals management to achieve earnings benchmarks: A comparison of pre-managed profit and loss firms. *Journal of Business Finance and Accounting*, 33, 5-6 (June-July): 653–670.

Baryh, Loretta, Peter DaDalt, and Varda Yaari. 2007. Earnings management and insider trading around seasoned equity offerings. Mid-Atlantic Regional Meeting Paper, Parsippany, NJ.

Barzel, Yoram, Michel A. Habib, and D. Bruce Johnsen. 2006. Prevention is better than cure: The role of IPO syndicates in precluding information acquisition. *The Journal of Business*, 79, 6 (November): 2911–2923.

Basu, Sudipta. 1995. Conservatism and the asymmetric timeliness of earnings. Ph.D. thesis, University of Rochester.

Basu, Sudipta. 1997. The conservatism principle and the asymmetric timeliness of earnings. *Journal of Accounting and Economics*, 24, 1 (December): 3–37.

Basu, Sudipta. 2004. What do we learn from two new accounting-based stock market anomalies? *Journal of Accounting and Economics*, 38 (December): 333–348.

Basu, Sudipta, Lee-Seok Hwang, and Ching-Lih Jan. 2002. Differences in conservatism between big eight and non-big eight auditors. Sudipta_Basu@bus.emory.edu.

Basu, Sudipta and Stanimir Markov. 2004. Loss function assumptions in rational expectations tests on financial analysts' earnings forecasts. *Journal of Accounting and Economics*, 38, 1-3 (December): 171–203.

Bathala, Chenchuramaiah T. and Ramesh P. Rao. 1995. The determinants of board composition: An agency theory perspective. *Managerial and Decision Economics*, 16, 1 (January–February): 59–69.

Bauman, Jeffery D. 1979. Rule 10b-5 and the corporation's affirmative duty to disclose. *The Georgetown Law Journal*, 67: 935–990.

Bauman, Christine C., Mark P. Bauman, and Robert F. Halsey. 2001. Do firms use the deferred tax asset valuation allowance to manage earnings? *Journal of the American Taxation Association*, 23 (Supplement): 27–48.

Bauman, Mark P., Mike Braswell, and Kenneth W. Shaw. 2006. The numbers game: How do managers compensated with stock options meet analysts' earnings forecasts? *Research in Accounting Regulation*, 18: 3–18.

Bauman, Mark P. and Kenneth W. Shaw. 2006. Stock option compensation and the likelihood of meeting analysts' quarterly earnings targets. *Review of Quantitative Finance and Accounting*, 26, 3 (May): 301–319.

Beale, Linda M. 2004. Putting SEC heat on audit firms and corporate tax shelters: Responding to tax risk with sunshine, shame and strict liability. *Journal of Corporation Law*, 29 (Winter): 219. SSRN.com/abstract=464761.

Beasley, Mark S. 1996. An empirical analysis of the relation between the board of director composition and financial statement fraud. *The Accounting Review*, 71, 4 (October): 443–465.

Beasley, Mark S., Joseph V. Carcello, Dana R. Hermanson, and Paul D. Lapides. 2000. Fraudulent financial reporting: Consideration of industry traits and corporate governance mechanism. *Accounting Horizons*, 14, 4 (December): 441-454

Beasley, Mark S. and Kathy R. Petroni. 1998. Board independence and audit firm type. SSRN.com/abstract=137582.

Beattie, Vivien, Stephen Brown, David Ewers, Brian John, Stuart Manson, Dylan Thomas, and Michael Turner. 1994. Extraordinary items and income smoothing: A positive accounting approach. *Journal of Business Finance and Accounting*, 21, 6 (September): 791–811.

Beattie, Vivien, Stella Fearnley, and Richard Brandt. 2004. Grounded theory model of auditor–client negotiations. *International Journal of Auditing*, 8, 1 (March): 1–19.

Beatty, Anne, Sandra Chamberlain, and Joseph Magliolo. 1995. Managing financial reports of commercial banks: The influence of taxes regulatory capital, and earnings. *Journal of Accounting Research*, 33, 2 (Fall): 231–261.

Beatty, Anne L. and David G. Harris. 1999. The effect of taxes, agency costs and information asymmetry on earnings management: A comparison of public and private firms. *Review of Accounting Studies*, 4, 3-4 (December): 299–326.

Beatty, Anne, Bin Ke, and Kathy Petroni. 2002. Earnings management to avoid earnings declines across publicly and privately held banks. *The Accounting Review*, 77, 3 (July): 547–570.

Beatty, Anne, Krishnamoorthy Ramesh, and Joseph Peter Weber. 2002. The importance of accounting changes in debt contracts: The cost of flexibility in covenant calculations. *Journal of Accounting and Economics*, 33, 2 (June): 205–227.

Beatty, Anne and Robert Verrecchia. 1989. The effect of mandated accounting change on the capitalization process. *Contemporary Accounting Research*, 5, 2 (Spring): 472–493.

Beatty, Anne and Joseph Peter Weber. 2000. Performance pricing in debt contracts. SSRN.com/abstract=249172.

Beatty, Anne and Joseph Peter Weber. 2003. The effects of debt contracting on voluntary accounting methods changes. *The Accounting Review*, 78, 1 (January): 119–142.

Beatty, Randolph P. and Edward J. Zajac. 1994. Managerial incentives, monitoring, and risk bearing: A study of executive compensation, ownership, and board structure in initial public offerings. *Administrative Science Quarterly*, 39, 2 (June): 313–335.

Beaulieu, Philip and Alan Reinstein. 2006. The effect of accounting research on the beliefs of practitioners: The case of auditor independence. A paper presented in the 2006 Auditing Midyear Conference, Los Angeles, CA.

Beaver, W.H. 1998. *Financial Reporting and Accounting Revolution*. Third edition. New Jersey: Prentice-Hall (Contemporary topics in accounting series).

Beaver, William, Carol Eger, Stephen Ryan, and Mark Wolfson. 1989. Financial reporting and the structure of bank share prices. *Journal of Accounting Research*, 27, 2 (Fall): 157–178.

Beaver, William H. and Ellen E. Engel. 1996. Discretionary behavior with respect to allowances for loan losses and the behavior of security prices. *Journal of Accounting and Economics*, 22, 1-3 (August–December): 177–206.

Beaver, William H., Maureen F. McNichols, and Karen Kristine Nelson. 2000. Do firms issuing equity manage their earnings? Evidence from the property-casualty insurance industry. SSRN.com/abstract=203408.

Beaver, William H., Maureen F. McNichols, and Karen Kristine Nelson. 2003. Management of the loss reserve accrual and the distribution of earnings in the property-casualty insurance industry. *Journal of Accounting and Economics*, 35, 3 (August): 347–376.

Beaver, William H., Maureen F. McNichols, and Karen Kristine Nelson. 2004. An alternative interpretation of the discontinuity in earnings distributions. 14th Annual Conference on Financial Economics and Accounting (FEA). AAA 2004 Annual Meeting, Orlando, L. SSRN.com/abstract=384580.

Beaver, William H. and Stephen Ryan. 2000. Biases and lags in book value and their effects on the ability of the book-to-market ratio to predict book return on equity. *Journal of Accounting Research*, 38, 1 (Spring): 127–148.

Beaver, William H. and Stephen Ryan. 2005. Conditional and unconditional conservatism: Concepts and modeling. *Review of Accounting Studies*, 10, 2-3 (September): 269–309.

Bebchuk, Lucian Arye. 2002. Asymmetric information and the choice of corporate governance arrangements. Harvard Law and Economics Discussion Paper No. 398.
SSRN.com/abstract=327842.

Bebchuk, Lucian Arye. 2003. The case for empowering shareholders. Berkeley Program
in Law & Economics, Working Paper Series, Working Paper No. 1085.

Bebchuk, Lucian Arye. 2005a. The case for increasing shareholder power. *Harvard Law
Review*, 118, 3 (January): 833–914.

Bebchuk, Lucian Arye. 2005b. The myth of the shareholder franchise. Harvard Law and
Economics Discussion Paper No. 565. SSRN.com/abstract=829804.

Bebchuk, Lucian Arye. 2007. Letting shareholders set the rules. *Harvard Law Review*,
119: 1784-1813, 2006. A revised version is available at SSRN:
SSRN.com/abstract=891823.

Bebchuk, Lucian Arye and Oren Bar-Gill. 2003. Misreporting corporate performance.
Harvard Law and Economics Discussion Paper No. 400. SSRN.com/abstract=354141.

Bebchuk, Lucian Arye and Alma Cohen. 2005. The cost of entrenched boards. *Journal of
Financial Economics*, 78, 2 (November): 409–433.

Bebchuk, Lucian Arye, Alma Cohen, and Allen Ferrell. 2004. What matters in corporate
governance? Harvard Law and Economics Discussion Paper No. 491.
SSRN.com/abstract=593423.

Bebchuk, Lucian Arye and Chaim Fershtman. 1991. The effect of insider trading on insiders' reactions to opportunities to "waste" corporate value. NBER Technical Working
Paper No. 95.

Bebchuk, Lucian Arye and Chaim Fershtman. 1993. The effects of insider trading on insiders' effort in good and bad times. *European Journal of Economic Theory*, 9, 4
(November): 469–481.

Bebchuk, Lucian Arye and Chaim Fershtman. 1994. Insider trading and the managerial
choice among risky projects. *Journal of Financial and Quantitative Analysis*, 29, 1
(March): 1–14.

Bebchuk, Lucian Arye and Jesse M. Fried. 2003. Executive compensation as an agency
problem. *Journal of Economic Perspectives*, 17, 3 (Summer): 71–93.

Bebchuk, Lucian Arye and Jesse M. Fried. 2004. *Pay Without Performance: The Unful-
filled Promise of Executive Compensation.*[1] Boston: Harvard University Press.

Bebchuk, Lucian Arye, Jesse M. Fried, and David I. Walker. 2002. Managerial power and
rent extraction in the design of executive compensation. *The University of Chicago
Law Review*, 69, 3 (Summer): 751–847.

Bebchuk, Lucian Arye, Yaniv Grinstein, and Urs C. Peyer. 2006. Lucky CEOs. Harvard
Law and Economics Discussion Paper No. 566. SSRN.com/abstract=945392.

Bebchuk, Lucian Arye and Oliver D. Hart. 2001. Takeover bids vs. proxy fights in contests
for corporate control. Harvard Law and Economics Discussion Paper No. 336, and
ECGI—Finance Working Paper No. 04/2002. SSRN.com/abstract=290584.

Bebchuk, Lucian Arye, Reinier H. Kraakman, and George G. Triantis. 2000. Stock pyra-
mids, cross-ownership, and dual class equity: The creation and agency costs of separating control from cash flow rights. Published in *Concentrated Corporate Ownership*,
R. Morck, ed. 445-460. SSRN.com/abstract=147590.

Bebchuk, Lucian Arye and Lars. A. Stole. 1993. Do short-term objectives lead to under- or
overinvestment in long-term projects? *Journal of Finance*, 48, 2 (June): 719–729.

---

[1] Part I: The Official View and its Limits is available at http://ssrn.com/abstract=537783.
Part II: Power and Pay is available at http://ssrn.com/abstract=537810. Part III: The De-
coupling of Pay from Performance is available at http://ssrn.com/abstract=546105. Part
IV: Going Forward is available at http://ssrn.com/abstract=546107.

Becht, Marco, Patrick Bolton, and Ailsa Roell. 2003. Corporate governance and control. In George M. Constantinides, Milton Harris, and Réne Stulz, eds., *Handbook of the Economics of Finance*, Volume 1. Amsterdam: North Holland. Ch. 1.

Becker, Connie, Mark DeFond, James J. Jiambalvo, and K.R. Subramanyam. 1998. The effect of audit quality on earnings management. *Contemporary Accounting Research*, 15, 1 (Spring): 1–24.

Bédard, Jean. 2006. Sarbanes Oxley internal control requirements and earnings quality. SSRN.com/abstract=926271.

Bédard, Jean, Sonda Marrakchi Chtourou, and Lucie Courteau. 2004. The effect of audit committee expertise, independence, and activity on aggressive earnings management. *Auditing: A Journal of Practice and Theory*, 23, 2 (September): 13–35.

Begley, Joy. 1990. Debt covenants and accounting choice. *Journal of Accounting and Economics*, 12, 1-3 (January): 125–139.

Begley, Joy and Gerald A. Feltham. 2002. The relation between market values, earnings forecasts, and reported earnings. *Contemporary Accounting Research*, 19, 1 (Spring): 1–48.

Begley, Joy and Paul E. Fischer. 1998. Is there information in an earnings announcement delay? *Review of Accounting Studies*, 3, 4 (December): 347–363.

Behn, Bruce K., Albert L. Nagy, and Richard A. Riley, Jr. 2002. The association between stock/compensation mix and earnings usefulness. SSRN.com/abstract=301659.

Beidleman, Carl R. 1973. Income smoothing: The role of management. *The Accounting Review*, 48, 4 (October): 653–667.

Beiner, Stefan, Wolfgang Drobertz, Frank Schmid, and Heinz Zimmerman. 2003. Is board size an independent corporate governance mechanism? *Kyklos*, 57, 3 (August): 327–356.

Belkaoui, Ahmed. 1983. Accrual accounting and cash accounting: Relative merits of derived accounting indicator numbers. *Journal of Business Finance and Accounting*, 10, 2 (Summer): 299–312.

Belkaoui, Ahmed and Ronald D. Picur. 1984. The smoothing of income numbers: Some empirical evidence on systematic differences between core and periphery industrial sectors. *Journal of Business Finance and Accounting*, 11, 4 (Winter): 527–545.

Belkhir, Mohamed. 2004. Board of directors size and performance in banking. SSRN.com/abstract=604505.

Ben, Othman Hakim and Daniel Zeghal. 2006. A study of earnings-management motives in the Anglo-American and Euro-Continental accounting models: The Canadian and French cases. *The International Journal of Accounting*, 41, 4 (December): 406–435.

Benabou, Roland and Guy Laroque. 1992. Using privileged information to manipulate markets: insiders, gurus, and credibility. *Quarterly Journal of Economics*, 107, 3 (August): 921–958.

Beneish, Messod Daniel. 1997. Detecting GAAP violations: Implications for assessing earnings management among firms with extreme financial performance. *Journal of Accounting and Public Policy*, 16, 3 (Fall): 271–309.

Beneish, Messod Daniel. 1998a. A call for paper: Earnings management. *Journal of Accounting and Public Policy*, 17, 1 (Spring): 85–88.

Beneish, Messod Daniel. 1998b. Discussion of "Are accruals during initial public offerings opportunistic?" *Review of Accounting Studies*, 3, 1-2 (March): 209–221.

Beneish, Messod Daniel. 1999a. Incentives and penalties related to earnings overstatements that violate GAAP. *The Accounting Review*, 74, 4 (October): 425–458.

Beneish, Messod Daniel. 1999b. The detection of earnings manipulation. *Financial Analysts Journal*, 55, 5 (September/October): 24–36.

Beneish, Messod Daniel. 1999c. A note on Wiedman's (1999) instructional case: Detecting earnings manipulation. *Issues in Accounting Education*, 14, 2 (May): 369–370.

Beneish, Messod Daniel. 2001. Earnings management: A perspective. *Managerial Finance*, 27, 12 (December): 3–17.

Beneish, Messod Daniel, Mary Brooke Billings, and Leslie D. Hodder. 2006. Internal control weaknesses and information uncertainty. SSRN.com/abstract=896192.

Beneish, Messod Daniel Patrick E. Hopkins and Ivo Ph. Jansen. 2001. Do auditor resignations convey information about continuing audit clients? SSRN.com/abstract=268953.

Beneish, Messod Daniel and Craig D. Nichols. 2005. Earnings quality and future returns: The relation between accruals and the probability of earnings manipulation. SSRN.com/abstract=725162.

Beneish, Messod Daniel and Craig D. Nichols. 2006. The long and short of the accrual anomaly. SSRN.com/abstract=920101.

Beneish, Messod Daniel and Eric G. Press. 1993. Costs of technical violation of accounting-based debt covenants. *The Accounting Review*, 68, 2 (April): 233–257.

Beneish, Messod Daniel and Eric G. Press. 1995a. The resolution of technical default. *The Accounting Review*, 70, 2 (April): 337–353.

Beneish, Messod Daniel and Eric G. Press. 1995b. Interrelation among events of default. *Contemporary Accounting Research*, 12, 1 (Fall): 57–84.

Beneish, Messod Daniel, Eric G. Press, and Mark E. Vargus. 2005. The effect of the threat of litigation on insider trading and earnings management. Working Paper, Indiana University.

Beneish, Messod Daniel and Mark E. Vargus. 2002. Insider trading, earnings quality, and accrual mispricing. *The Accounting Review*, 77, 4 (October): 755–791.

Bennedsen, Morten, Hans Christian Kongsted, and Kasper Meisner Nielsen. 2004. Board size effects in closely held corporations. Working Paper, University of Copenhagen.

Bennedsen, Morton and Daniel Wolfenzon. 2000. The balance of power in closely held corporations. *Journal of Financial Economics*, 58, 1-2 (October): 113–139.

Bens, Daniel and Rock Johnson. 2006. Accounting discretion: Use of abuse? Restructuring charges —1989-1992. Working Paper.

Bens, Daniel and Steven Monahan. 2005. Altering investment decisions to manage financial reporting outcomes: Asset backed commercial paper conduits and FIN 46. Working Paper, University of Chicago.

Bens, Daniel, Venky Nagar, and Franco Wong. 2002. Real investment implications of employee stock option exercises. *Journal of Accounting Research*, 40, 2 (May): 359–393.

Benston, George J., Michael Bromwich, and Alfred Wagenhofer. 2006. Principles- versus rules-based accounting standards: The FASB's standard setting strategy. *Abacus*, 42, 2 (June): 165–188.

Benston, George J. and Al L. Hartgraves. 2002. Enron: What happened and what we can learn from it. *Journal of Accounting and Public Policy*, 21, 2 (Summer): 105–127.

Beresford, Dennis R. 1988. The "balancing act" in setting accounting standards. *Accounting Horizons*, 1, 1 (March): 1–7.

Beresford, Dennis R. 1991. Standard setting process in trouble (again). *Accounting Horizons*, 5, 2 (June): 94–96.

Beresford, Dennis R. 1993. Frustrations of a standard setter. *Accounting Horizons*, 7, 4 (December): 70–76.

Beresford, Dennis R. 1995. How should the FASB be judged? *Accounting Horizons*, 9, 2 (June): 56–61.

Beresford, Dennis R. 1997. How to succeed as a standard setter by trying really hard. *Accounting Horizons*, 11, 3 (September): 79–90.

Beresford, Dennis, R. 2001. Congress looks at accounting for business combinations. *Accounting Horizons*, 15, 1 (March): 73–86.

Beresford, Dennis R. and Todd Johnson. 1995. Interactions between the FASB and the Academic Community. Accounting Horizons, 9, 4 (December): 108–117.

Bergstresser, Daniel, Mihir A. Desai, and Joshua Rauh. 2005. Earnings manipulation, pension assumptions and managerial investment decisions. SSRN.com/abstract=557084.

Bergstresser, Daniel and Thomas Philippon. 2006. CEO incentives and earnings management. Journal of Financial Economics, 80, 3 (June): 511–529.

Berle Jr., Adolf A. and Gardiner C. Means. [1932] 1935. The Modern Corporation and Private Property. New York: Macmillan.

Bernard, Victor L. and H. Nejat Seyhun. 1997. Does post earnings announcements drift in stock prices reflect a market inefficiency? A stochastic dominance approach. Review of Quantitative Finance and Accounting, 9, 1 (July): 17–34.

Bernard, Victor L. and Douglas J. Skinner. 1996. What motivates managers' choice of discretionary accruals? Journal of Accounting and Economics, 22, 1-3 (August-December): 313–325.

Bernard, Victor L. and Jacob K. Thomas. 1989. Post-earnings-announcement drift: Delayed price response or risk premium? Journal of Accounting Research, 27, 3 (Supplement): 1–36.

Bernhardt Dan and Murillo Campello. 2003. The dynamics of earnings forecast management. SSRN.com/abstract=379263.

Bernile, Gennaro, Gregg A. Jarrell, and Howard Mulcahey. 2006. The effect of the options backdating scandal on the stock-price performance of 110 accused companies. SSRN.com/abstract=952524.

Berry, Tammy K., John Bizjak, Michael L. Lemmon, and Lalitha Naveen. 2006. Organizational complexity and CEO labor markets: Evidence from diversified firms. Journal of Corporate Finance, 12, 4 (September): 797–817.

Berry, Tammy K., L. Paige Fields, and Michael S. Wilkins. 2006. The interaction among multiple governance mechanisms in young newly public firms. Journal of Corporate Finance, 12, 3 (June): 449–466.

Bertrand, Marianne and Sendhil Mullainathan. 2000. Agents with and without principals. American Economic Review, 90, 2 (May): 203–208.

Bethel, Jennifer E., Julia Porter Liebeskind, and Tim Opler. 1998. Block share purchases and corporate performance. Journal of Finance, 53, 2 (April): 605–634.

Bettis, J. Carr, Jeffrey L. Coles, and Michael L. Lemmon. 2000. Corporate policies restricting trading by insiders. Journal of Financial Economics, 57, 2 (August): 191–220.

Beuselinck, Christof, Marc Deloof, and Sophie Manigart. 2007. Private equity involvement and earnings quality. SSRN.com/abstract=483522.

Bewley, Kathryn, Janne Chung, Susan McCracken, and Peggy Ng. 2006. Auditor dismissals: An examination using evidence from Andersen's demise. A Paper Presented at the 2006 Auditing Midyear Conference, Los Angeles, CA.

Bhagat, Sanjai and Bernard Black. 1999. The uncertain relationship between board composition and rirm performance. Business Lawyer, 54: 921–963.

Bhagat, Sanjai, John Bizjack, and Jeffrey L. Coles. 1998. The shareholder wealth implications of corporate lawsuits. Financial Management, 27, 4 (Winter): 5–28.

Bhagat, Sanjai and Bernard S. Black. 2002. The non-correlation between board independence and long-term firm performance. Journal of Corporation Law, 27: 231-273. SSRN.com/abstract=133808.

Bhagat, Sanjai, Bernard S. Black, and Margaret M. Blair. 2004. Relational investing and firm performance. Journal of Financial Research, 27, 1 (Spring): 1–30.

Bhagat, Sanjai, Dennis C. Carey, and Charles M. Elson. 1998. Director ownership, corporate performance, and management turnover. SSRN.com/abstract=134488.

Bhagat, Sanjai and Richard H. Jefferies, Jr. 2005. *The Econometrics of Corporate Governance Studies*. Boston, MA: MIT Press.

Bharati, Rakesh, Manoj Gupta, and Prasad Nanisetty. 1998. Are dividends smoothed signals of earnings asymmetry? An empirical investigation. *International Journal of Business*, 3, 2 (Fall): 1–18.

Bharath, Sreedhar T., Jayanthi Sunder, and Shyam V. Sunder. 2004. Accounting quality and debt contracting. SSRN.com/abstract=545364.

Bhat, Vasanthakumar N. 1996. Banks and income smoothing: An empirical analysis. *Applied Financial Economics*, 6, 6 (December): 505–510.

Bhattacharya, Nilabhra Neil, Ervin L. Black, Theodore E. Christensen, and Chad R. Larson. 2003. Assessing the relative informativeness and permanence of pro forma earnings and GAAP operating earnings. *Journal of Accounting and Economics*, 36, 1-3 (December): 285–319.

Bhattacharya, Nilabhra Neil, Ervin L. Black, Theodore E. Christensen, and Rick D. Mergenthaler. 2004. Empirical evidence on recent trends in pro forma reporting. *Accounting Horizons*, 18, 1 (March): 27–43.

Bhattacharya, Nilabhra Neil, Ervin L. Black, Theodore E. Christensen, and Rick D. Mergenthaler. 2007. Who trades on pro forma earnings information? *The Accounting Review*, 82, 3(May): 581–620.

Bhattacharya, Somnath and Ronald F. Premuroso. 2006. Is there a relationship between firm performance, corporate governance, and a firm's decision to form a technology committee? SSRN.com/abstract=932143.

Bhattacharya, Sudipto. 1979. Imperfect information, dividend policy, and the "bird in the hand" fallacy. *Bell Journal of Economics*, 10, 1 (Spring): 259–270.

Bhattacharya, Uptal, Hazem Daouk, and Michael Welker. 2003. The world pricing of earnings opacity. *The Accounting Review*, 78, 3 (July): 641–678.

Bhattacharya, Utpal, Peter Groznik, and Bruce Haslem. 2003. Is CEO certification credible? *Regulation*, 26, 3 (Fall): 8–10.

Bhattacharya, Utpal, Peter Groznik, and Bruce Haslem. 2004. Is CEO certification of earnings numbers value-relevant? SSRN.com/abstract=332621.

Bhattacharya, Uptal and Murugappa (Murgie) Krishnan. 1999. To believe or not to believe. *Journal of Financial Markets*, 2, 1 (February): 69–98.

Bhattacharya, Uptal and Matthew Spiegel. 1991. Insiders, outsiders, and market breakdowns. *Review of Financial Studies*, 4, 2 (Summer): 255–282.

Bhojraj, Sanjeev, Paul Hribar, and Marc Picconi. 2003. Making sense of cents: An examination of firms that marginally miss or beat analyst's forecasts. SSRN.com/abstract=418100.

Bhojraj, Sanjeev and Partha Sengupta. 2003. Effect of corporate governance on bond ratings and yields: The role of institutional investors and outside directors. *The Journal of Business*, 76, 3 (July): 455–475.

Bhushan, Ravi. 1989. Firms characteristics and analyst following. *Journal of Accounting and Economics*, 11, 2-3 (July): 255–274.

Billings, Bruce K. and Richard M. Morton. 2001. Book to-market components, future security returns, and errors in expected future earnings. *Journal of Accounting Research*, 39, 2 (September): 197–219.

Bishop, Marguerite L. and Elizabeth A. Eccher. 2000. Do markets remember accounting changes? An examination of subsequent years. SSRN.com/abstract=218448.

Bitner, Larry N. and Robert C. Dolan. 1996. Assessing the relationship between income smoothing and the value of the firm. *Quarterly Journal of Business and Economics*, 35, 1 (Winter): 16–35.

Bizjak, John M., James A. Brickley, and Jeffrey L. Coles. 1993. Stock-based incentive compensation and investment behavior. *Journal of Accounting and Economics*, 16, 1-3 (January/April/July): 349–372.

Bizjak, John M., Michael L. Lemmon, and Ryan J. Whitby. 2006. Option backdating and board interlocks. SSRN.com/abstract=946787.

Blacconiere, Walter G., James R. Frederickson, Marilyn F. Johnson, and Melissa F. Lewis. 2003. Voluntary disclosures that disavow mandatory disclosures: The case of stock options. Working Paper, Indiana University.

Black, Bernard S. 2002. Shareholder activism and corporate governance in the United States. *The New Palgrave Dictionary of Economics and the Law* (1998), 3: 459-465. SSRN.com/abstract=45100.

Black, Ervin L., Thomas A. Carnes, Michael Mosebach, and Susan E. Moyer. 2004. Regulatory monitoring as a substitute for debt covenants. *Journal of Accounting and Economics*, 37, 3 (September): 367–391.

Black, Ervin L., Thomas A. Carnes, and Vernon J. Richardson. 2000. The value relevance of multiple occurrences of nonrecurring item. *Review of Quantitative Finance and Accounting*, 15, 4 (December): 391–411.

Black, Ervin L. and Brian W. McCulloch. 2003. Earnings management relations of accruals components: A multi-period setting. SSRN.com/abstract=476164.

Blackwell, David W., Thomas R. Noland, and Drew B. Winters. 1998. The value of auditor assurance: Evidence from loan pricing. *Journal of Accounting Research*, 36, 1 (Spring): 57–70.

Blair, Margaret M. 1995. *Ownership and Control: Rethinking Corporate Governance for the Twenty-First Century.* Washington, DC: Brookings Institution Press.

Blake, John and Oriol A. Salas. 1996. Creative accounting is not just an English disease. *Management Accounting*, 74, 9 (October): 54–56.

Block, Stanley. 1999. The role of nonaffiliated outside directors in monitoring the firm and the effect on shareholder wealth. *Journal of Financial and Strategic Decisions*, 12, 1 (Spring): 1–8.

Block, Stanley. 2003. The latest movement to going private: An empirical study. *Journal of Applied Finance*, 14, 1 (Spring/Summer): 36–44.

Blonigen, Bruce A. and Rossitza B. Wooster. 2003. CEO turnover and foreign market participation. SSRN.com/abstract=385040. NBER Working Paper 9527.

Bloomfield, Robert J. 2002. The "incomplete revelation hypothesis" and financial reporting. Accounting Horizons, 16, 3 (September): 233–243.

Blue Ribbon Committee (BRC). 1999. *Report and Recommendations of the Blue Ribbon Committee on Improving the Effectiveness of Corporate Audit Committees.* New York, NY: New York Stock Exchange and National Association of Security Dealers.

Blumberg Cane, Marilyn and Sarah Smith Kelleher. 2004. Bring on 'da noise: The SEC's proposals concerning professional conduct for attorneys under Sarbanes-Oxley. *Delaware Journal of Corporate Law*, 28, 2. SSRN.com/abstract=574081.

Boehmer, Ekkehart, Eric Kelley, and Christo Pirinsky. 2005. Institutional investors and the informational efficiency of prices. Working Paper, Texas A&M University.

Bolliger, Guido and Manuel Kast. 2004. Executive compensation and analyst guidance: The link between CEO compensation and expectations management. EFA 2003 Annual Conference Paper. SSRN.com/abstract=555221.

Bolton, Patrick and David Scharfstein. 1990. A theory of predation based on agency problems in financial contracting. *American Economic Review*, 80, 1 (March): 93–106.

Bolton, Patrick, Jose A. Scheinkman, and Wei Xiong. 2006. Executive compensation and short-termist behavior in speculative markets. *Review of Economic Studies*, 73, 3 (July): 577–610.

Bonner, Sarah, Zoe-Vonna Palmrose, and Susan Young. 1998. Fraud type and auditor litigation: An analysis of the SEC Accounting and Auditing Enforcement Releases. *The Accounting Review*, 73, 4 (October): 503–532.

Boo, Elfred and Roger Simnett. 2002. The information content of management's prospective comments in financially distressed companies: A note. *Abacus*, 38, 2 (June): 280–295.

Boone, Audra L., Laura Casares Field, Jonathan M. Karpoff, and Charu G. Raheja. 2004. The determinants of corporate board size and composition: An empirical analysis. AFA 2005 Philadelphia Meeting. SSRN.com/abstract=605762.

Boot, Arnoud W.A. and Anjan V. Thakor. 2000. The many faces of information disclosure. *Review of Financial Studies*, 14, 4 (October): 1021–1057.

Booth, Geoffrey G., Juha-Pekka Kallunki, and Teppo Martikainen. 1996. Post-announcement drift and income smoothing: Finnish evidence. *Journal of Business Finance and Accounting*, 23, 8 (October): 1197–1212.

Booth, Geoffrey G., Juha-Pekka Kallunki, and Teppo Martikainen. 1997. Delayed price response to the announcements of earnings and its components in Finland. *European Accounting Review*, 6, 3 (September): 377–392.

Booth, James R. and Daniel N. Deli. 1996. Factors affecting the number of outside directorships held by CEOs. *Journal of Financial Economics*, 40, 1 (January): 81–104.

Booth, Richard A. 2005. Executive compensation, corporate governance, and the partner-manager. *University of Illinois Law Review*, 1 (June): 269–302.

Borch, Karl. 1962. Equilibrium in reinsurance market. *Econometrica*, 30, 3 (July): 424–444.

Borden, Michael. 2007. The role of financial journalists in corporate governance. *Fordham Journal of Corporate and Financial Law*, 12, 2 (March): 311–369.

Border, Kim C. and Joel Sobel. 1987. Samurai accountant: A theory of auditing and plunder. *Review of Economics Studies*, 54, 180 (October): 525–540.

Borokhovich, Kenneth A., Kelly R. Brunarski, Maura S. Donahue, and Yvette S. Harman. 2006. The importance of board quality in the event of a CEO death. *The Financial Review*, 41, 3 (August): 307–337.

Borokhovich, Kenneth A., Kelly Brunarski, Yvette S. Harman, and Robert Parrino. 2006. Variation in the monitoring incentives of outside stockholders. *Journal of Law and Economics*, 49, 2 (October): 651–680.

Borokhovich, Kenneth A., Robert Parrino, and Teresa Trapani. 1996. Outside directors and CEO selection. *Journal of Financial and Quantitative Analysis*, 31, 3 (September): 337–355.

Botosan, Christine. 1997. Disclosure level and the cost of equity capital. *The Accounting Review*, 72, 3 (July): 323–349.

Botosan, Christine and Marlene Plumlee. 2002. A re-examination of disclosure level and the expected cost of equity capital. *Journal of Accounting Research*, 40, 1 (March): 21–40.

Boumosleh, Anwar and David Reeb. 2005. The governance role of corporate insiders. http://ssrn.com/abstract=674082.

Bowen, Robert N., David Burgstahler, and Lane A. Daley. 1987. The incremental information content of accruals versus cash flows. *The Accounting Review*, 62, 4 (October): 723–748.

Bowen, Robert, Angela K. Davis, and Dawn Matsumoto. 2005. Emphasis on pro forma versus GAAP earnings in quarterly press releases: Determinants, SEC intervention, and market reactions. *The Accounting Review*, 80, 4 (October): 1001–1038.

Bowen, Robert, Angela K. Davis, and Shivaram Rajgopal. 2002. Determinants of revenue-reporting practices for internet firms. *Contemporary Accounting Research*, 19, 4 (Winter): 523–562.

Bowen, Robert M., Larry DuCharme, and D.J. Shores. 1995. Stakeholders' implicit claims and accounting method choice. *Journal of Accounting and Economics*, 20, 3 (December): 255–295.

Bowen, Robert M., Shivaram Rajgopal, and Mohan Venkatachalam. 2004. Accounting discretion, corporate governance and firm performance. SSRN.com/abstract=367940.

Bowman, Robert G. and Farshid Navissi. 2003. Earnings management and abnormal returns: Evidence from the 1970-1972 price control regulations. *Accounting and Finance*, 43, 1 (March): 1–19.

Boyer, Carol Marie, Stephen J. Ciccone, and Wei N. Zhang. 2004. Insider trading and earnings reporting: Evidence of managerial optimism or opportunism? SSRN.com/abstract=426500. In *Advances in Investment Analysts and Portfolio Management*, volume. 8.

Boylan, Richard T. and Bente Villadsen. 1998. Contracting and income smoothing in an infinite agency model. Working Paper, Washington University. Olin Working Paper Series OLIN-97-16. SSRN.com/abstract=68848.

Boynton IV, Charles E., Paul S. Dobbins, and George A. Plesko. 1992. Earnings management and the corporate alternative minimum tax. *Journal of Accounting Research*, 30, 3 (Supplement): 131–153.

Bradbury, Michael E. 1992. Voluntary semiannual earnings disclosures, earnings volatility, unexpected earnings, and firm size. *Journal of Accounting Research*, 30, 1 (Spring): 137–145.

Bradbury, Michael E., Yuen Teen Mak, and S.M. Tan. 2004. Board characteristics, audit committee characteristics and abnormal accruals. SSRN.com/abstract=535764.

Bradshaw, Mark T. 2003. A discussion of "Assessing the relative informativeness and permanence of pro forma earnings and GAAP operating earnings." *Journal of Accounting and Economics*, 36, 1-3 (December): 321–335.

Bradshaw, Mark T. 2004. How do analysts use their earnings forecasts in generating stock recommendations? *The Accounting Review*, 79, 1 (January): 25–50.

Bradshaw, Mark T., Scott A. Richardson, and Richard G. Sloan. 2001. Do analysts and auditors use information in accruals? *Journal of Accounting Research*, 39, 1 (June): 45–74.

Bradshaw, Mark T., Scott A. Richardson, and Richard G. Sloan. 2006. The relation between corporate financing activities, analysts' forecasts and stock returns. *Journal of Accounting and Economics*, 42, 1-2 (October): 53–85.

Bradshaw, Mark T. and Richard G. Sloan. 2002. GAAP versus the Street: An empirical assessment of two alternative definitions of earnings. *Journal of Accounting Research*, 40, 1 (March): 41–66.

Brandenburger, Adam and Ben Polak. 1996. When managers cover their posteriors: Making the decisions the market wants to see. *The RAND Journal of Economics*, 27, 3 (Autumn): 523–541.

Branson, Douglas M. 2006. Too many bells? Too many whistles? Corporate governance in the post Enron, post WorldCom era. SSRN.com/abstract=887176.

Bratton, William W. 2004. Enron, Sarbanes-Oxley and accounting: Rules versus standards versus rents. *Villanova Law Review*, 48, 4. SSRN.com/abstract=399120.

Brayshaw, R.E. and Ahmed E.K. Eldin. 1989. The smoothing hypotheses and the role of exchange differences. *Journal of Business Finance and Accounting*, 16, 5 (Winter): 621–633.

Brazel, Joseph F. and Elizabeth Webb. 2006. CEO compensation and the seasoned equity offering decision. *Managerial and Decision Economics*, 27, 5 (July-August): 363–378.

Breeden, Richard C. 2003. Restoring trust. Report to the Hon. Jed S. Rakoff the United States District Court for the Southern District of New York on corporate governance for the future of MCI, Inc. http://www.sec.gov/spotlight/worldcom/wcomreport0803.pdf.

Brennan, Michael J. and Patricia J. Hughes. 1991. Stock prices and the supply of information. *Journal of Finance*, 46, 5 (December): 1665–1691.

Brennan, Michael J. and Avanidhar Subrahmanyam. 1995. Investment analysis and price formation in securities markets. *Journal of Financial Economics*, 38, 3 (July): 361–381.

Brennan, Michael J. and Claudia Tamarowski. 2000. Investor relations, liquidity, and stock prices. *Journal of Applied Corporate Finance*, 12, 4 (Winter): 26–37.

Brenner, Menachem, Rangarajan K. Sundaram, and David Yermack. 2000. Altering the terms of executive stock options. *Journal of Financial Economics*, 57, 1 (July): 103–128.

Breton, Gaéton and Richard J. Taffler. 1995. Creative accounting and investment analyst response. *Accounting and Business Research*, 25, 8 (Spring): 81–92.

Brick, Ivan E., Oded Palmon, and John K. Wald. 2006. CEO compensation, director compensation, and firm performance: Evidence of cronyism? *Journal of Corporate Finance*, 12, 3 (June): 403–423.

Bricker, Robert and Julia Grant. 2001. Surprise! Analyst responses to unexpected earnings. *Journal of Corporate Communications*, 3. http://69.171.137.25:85/articles/surprise103101.pdf.

Brickley, James A. 2003. Empirical research on CEO turnover and firm-performance: A discussion. *Journal of Accounting and Economics*, 36, 1-3 (December): 227–233.

Brickley, James A., Jeffrey L. Coles, and Gregg Jarrel. 1997. Leadership structure: Separating the CEO and the chairman of the board. *Journal of Corporate Finance*, 3, 3 (June): 189–220.

Brickley, James A., Jeffrey L. Coles, and James S. Linck. 1999. What happens to CEOs after they retire? New evidence on career concerns, horizon problems, and CEO incentives. *Journal of Financial Economics*, 52, 3 (June): 341–377.

Brickley, James A., Jeffrey L. Coles, and Rory L. Terry. 1994. Outside directors and the adoption of poison pills. *Journal of Financial Economics*, 35, 3 (June): 371–390.

Brickley, James A., Ronald C. Lease, and Clifford W. Smith. 1988. Ownership structure and voting on antitakeover amendments. *Journal of Financial Economics*, 20, 1 (March): 267–291.

Brickey, Kathleen F. 2003. From Enron to WorldCom and beyond: Life and crime after Sarbanes-Oxley. *Washington University Law Quarterly*, 81. SSRN.com/abstract=447100.

Bris, Arturo, Salvatore Cantale, and George P. Nishiotis. 2005. A breakdown of the valuation effects of international cross-listing. Yale ICF Working Paper No. 05-30. SSRN.com/abstract=868485.

Brochet, Francois. 2007. Information content of insider trades: Before and after the Sarbanes-Oxley Act. Working Paper, New York University.

Brochet, Francois and Zhan Gao. 2004. Managerial entrenchment and earnings smoothing. Working Paper, New York University.

Bronson, Scott N., Joseph V. Carcello, Carl W. Hollingswoth, and Terry L. Neal. 2006. Are fully independent audit committees really necessary? A paper presented in the 2006 Auditing Midyear Conference, Los Angeles, CA.

Brooks, LeRoy D. and Dale A. Buckmaster. 1976. Further evidence of the time series properties of accounting income. *Journal of Finance*, 31, 5 (December): 1359–1373.

Brooks, Robert E., Don M. Chance, and Brandon N. Cline. 2006. Private information and the exercise of executive stock options. SSRN.com/abstract=804564.

Broshko, Erinn B. and Kai Li. 2006. Corporate governance requirements in Canada and the United States: A legal and empirical comparison of the principles-based and rules-based approaches. SSRN.com/abstract=892708.

Brown, Helen L. 2003. The effects of engagement risks and experience in auditor–client negotiations. Working Paper, University of Wisconsin-Madison.

Brown, Lawrence D. 1993. Earnings forecasting research: Its implications for capital markets research. *International Journal of Forecasting*, 9, 3 (November): 295–320.

Brown, Lawrence D. 1998. Managerial behavior and the bias in analysts' earnings forecasts. SSRN.com/abstract=113508.

Brown, Lawrence D. 2001. A temporal analysis of earnings surprises: Profits versus losses. *Journal of Accounting Research*, 39, 2 (September): 221–241.

Brown, Lawrence D. and Marcus K. Caylor. 2005. A temporal analysis of quarterly earnings thresholds: Propensities and valuation consequences. *The Accounting Review*, 80, 2 (April): 423–440.

Brown, Lawrence D. and Marcus L. Caylor. 2006. Corporate governance and firm valuation. *Journal of Accounting and Public Policy*, 25, 4 (July-August): 409–434.

Brown, Lawrence D. and Ngo H. Higgins. 2001. Managing earnings surprises in the US versus 12 other countries. *Journal of Accounting and Public Policy*, 20, 4 (Winter): 373–398.

Brown, Lawrence D. and Kwon-Jung Kim. 1993. The association between nonearnings disclosures by small firms and positive abnormal returns. *The Accounting Review*, 68, 3 (July): 668–680.

Brown, Lawrence D. and Emad Mohd. 2003. The predictive value of analyst characteristics. *Journal of Accounting, Auditing and Finance*, 18, 4 (Fall): 625–647.

Brown, Lawrence D. and Kumar N. Sivakumar. 2003. Comparing the quality of two earnings measures. *Review of Accounting Studies*, 8, 4 (December): 561–572.

Brown, Stephen. 2004. The impact of pension assumptions on firm value. SSRN.com/abstract=596666.

Brown, Stephen, Stephen A. Hillegeist, and Kin Lo. 2004. Conference calls and information asymmetry. *Journal of Accounting and Economics*, 37, 3 (September): 343–366.

Brown, Stephen, Stephen A. Hillegeist, and Kin Lo. 2006. The effect of meeting or missing earnings expectations on information asymmetry. SSRN.com/abstract=922128.

Brown, Stephen, Kin Lo, and Thomas Lys. 1999. Use of R^2 in accounting research: Measuring changes in value relevance over the last four decades. *Journal of Accounting and Economics*, 28, 2 (January): 83–115.

Browne, Mark J., Yu-Luen Ma, and Ping Wang. 2004. Stock options and reserve errors. Working paper, University of Wisconsin-Madison.

Bruns, William J. and Kenneth A. Merchant. 1990. The dangerous morality of managing earnings. *Management Accounting*, 72, 2 (August): 22–25.

Bryan, Daniel M., Carol Liu, and Samuel L. Tiras. 2004. The influence of independent and effective audit committees on earnings quality. SSRN.com/abstract=488082.

Bryan, Daniel Varda M., Samuel L. Tiras, and Clark M. Wheatley. 2005. Do going concern opinions serve as early warnings of financial collapse? Working Paper, State University of New York at Buffalo.

Bryan, Stephen H., Lee-Seok Hwang, and Steven Lilien. 2000. CEO stock-based compensation: An empirical analysis of incentive-intensity, relative mix, and economic determinants. *The Journal of Business*, 73, 4 (October): 661–693.

Bryan, Stephen H., and Steven B. Lilien. 2005. Characteristics of firms with material weaknesses in internal control: An assessment of Section 404 of Sarbanes Oxley. SSRN.com/abstract=682363.

Bryan, Stephen, Robert Nash, and Ajay Patel. 2006. Can the agency costs of debt and equity explain the changes in executive compensation during the 1990s? *Journal of Corporate Finance*, 12, 3 (June): 516–535.

Bryant-Kutcher, Lisa, Emma Yan Peng, and Kristina Zvinakis. 2005. Timeliness and quality of 10-K filings: The impact of the accelerated filing deadline. SSRN.com/abstract=735583.

Buchheit, Steve and Mark Kohlbeck. 2002. Having earnings announcements lost information content? *Journal of Accounting, Auditing and Finance*, 17, 2 (Spring): 137–153.

Buckmaster, Dale A. 2001. In Gary Previs and Robert J. Bricker eds., *Development of the Income Smoothing Literature 1893-1998: A Focus on the United States*. Studies in the Development of Accounting Thought, Volume 4. Elsevier.

Buffet, Warren. 2003. Letter to the shareholders. http://www.berkshirehathaway.com/letters/2003ltr.pdf

Bunsis, Howard. 1997. A description and market analysis of write-off announcements. *Journal of Business Finance and Accounting*, 24, 9-10 (October-December): 1385–1400.

Burgstahler, David and Ilia Dichev. 1997a. Earnings management to avoid earnings decreases and losses. *Journal of Accounting and Economics*, 24, 1 (December): 99–126.

Burgstahler, David and Ilia Dichev. 1997b. Earnings, adaptation and equity value. *The Accounting Review*, 72, 2 (April): 187–215.

Burgstahler, David and Michael J. Eames. 2003. Earnings management to avoid losses and earnings decreases: Are analysts fooled? *Contemporary Accounting Research*, 20, 2 (Summer): 253–294.

Burgstahler, David and Michael J. Eames. 2006. Management of earnings and analysts' forecasts to achieve zero and small positive earnings surprises. *Journal of Business Finance and Accounting*, 33, 5-6 (June/July): 633–652.

Burgstahler, David, L. Hail, and Christian Leuz. 2006. The importance of reporting incentives: Earnings management in European private and public firms. *The Accounting Review*, 81, 5 (October): 983–1016.

Burgstahler, David, James Jiambalvo, and Terry Shevlin. 2002. Do stock prices fully reflect the implications of special items for future earnings? *Journal of Accounting Research*, 40, 3 (June): 585–612.

Burilovich, Linda S. and Susan C. Kattelus. 1997. Auditors' influence on earnings management: Evidence from the alternative minimum tax. *Journal of Applied Business Research*, 13, 2 (Spring): 9–22.

Burns, Natasha and Simi Kedia. 2006. The impact of performance-based compensation on misreporting. *Journal of Financial Economics*, 79, 1 (January): 35–67.

Bushee, Brian J. 1998. The influence of institutional investors on myopic R&D investment behavior. *The Accounting Review*, 73, 3 (July): 305–333.

Bushee, Brian J., John E. Core, Wayne R. Guay, and Jihae Wee. 2007. The role of the business press as an information intermediary. SSRN.com/abstract=955021.

Bushee, Brian J. and Christian Leuz. 2005. Economic consequences of SEC disclosure regulation: Evidence from the OTC bulletin board. *Journal of Accounting and Economics*, 39, 2 (June): 233–264.

Bushee, Brian J., Dawn A. Matsumoto, and Gregory S. Miller. 2003. Open versus closed conference calls: The determinants and effects of broadening access to disclosure. *Journal of Accounting and Economics*, 34, 1–3 (January): 149–180.

Bushee, Brian J. and Christopher F. Noe. 2000. Disclosure quality, institutional investors, and stock return volatility. *Journal of Accounting Research*, 38 (Supplement): 171–202.

Bushman, Robert M. 1991. Public disclosure and the structure of private information markets. *Journal of Accounting Research*, 29, 2 (Autumn): 261–276.

Bushman, Robert, Qi Chen, Ellen Engel, and Abbie J. Smith. 2004. Financial accounting information, organizational complexity and corporate governance systems. *Journal of Accounting and Economics*, 37, 2 (June): 167–201.

Bushman, Robert M., Ellen Engel, Jenifer Milliron, and Abbie J. Smith. 1998. An empirical investigation of trends in the absolute and relative use of earnings in determining CEO cash compensation. SSRN.com/abstract=130910 .

Bushman, Robert M., Ellen Engel, Jennifer C. Milliron, and Abbie J. Smith. 2000. An analysis of the relation between the stewardship and valuation roles of earnings. SSRN.com/abstract=221548.

Bushman, Robert M. and Raffi J. Indjejikian. 1993. Accounting income, stock price, and managerial compensation. *Journal of Accounting and Economics*, 16, 1-3 (January-July): 3–23.

Bushman, Robert M. and Raffi Indjejikian. 1995. Voluntary disclosures and the trading behavior of corporate insiders. *Journal of Accounting Research*, 33, 2 (Autumn): 293–316.

Bushman, Robert M., Raffi Indjejikian, and Abbie Smith. 1996. CEO compensation: The role of individual performance evaluation. *Journal of Accounting and Economics*, 21, 2 (April): 161–193.

Bushman, Robert M. and Joseph Piotroski. 2006. Financial reporting incentives for conservative accounting: The influence of legal and political institutions. *Journal of Accounting and Economics*, 42, 1-2 (October): 107–148.

Bushman, Robert M., Joseph Piotroski, and Abbie J. Smith. 2004. What determines corporate transparency? *Journal of Accounting Research*, 42, 2 (May): 207–252.

Bushman, Robert M. and Abbie J. Smith. 2001. Financial accounting information and corporate governance. *Journal of Accounting and Economics*, 32, 1-3 (December): 237–333.

Bushman, Robert M. and Abbie J. Smith. 2003. Transparency, financial accounting information, and corporate governance. *Economic Policy Review*, 9, 1 (April): 65–87.

Butler, Henry N. and Larry E. Ribstein. 2006. The Sarbanes-Oxley Debacle: How to fix it and what we've learned. Prepared for American Enterprise Institute. The Liability Project.

Butler, Marty, Arthur Kraft, and Ira S. Weiss. 2007. The effect of reporting frequency on the timeliness of earnings: The cases of voluntary and mandatory interim reports. *Journal of Accounting and Economics*, 43, 2–3 (July): 181–217.

Butler, Marty, Andrew J. Leone, and Michael Willenborg. 2004. An empirical analysis of auditor reporting and its association with abnormal accruals. *Journal of Accounting and Economics*, 37, 2 (June): 139–165.

Butler, Stephen A. and Harry A. Newman. 1989. Agency control mechanisms, effectiveness and decision making in an executive's final year with a firm. *Journal of Institutional and Theoretical Economics*, 145: 451–464.

Byard, Donal, Ying Li, and Joseph Weintrop. 2006. Corporate governance and the quality of financial analysts' information. *Journal of Accounting and Public Policy*, 25, 5 (September-October): 609–625.

Byard, Donal and Kenneth W. Shaw. 2003a. Corporate disclosure quality and properties of analysts' information environment. *Journal of Accounting, Auditing and Finance* 18, 3 (Summer): 355–378.

Byard, Donal and Kenneth W. Shaw. 2003b. The informational role of financial analysts: Interpreting public disclosures. *Journal of Financial Transformation*, 11 (August): 143–148.

Byrd, John W. and Kent A. Hickman. 1992. Do outside directors monitor managers? Evidence from tender offer bids. *Journal of Financial Economics*, 32, 2 (October): 195–221.

Byrd, John, Marilyn F. Johnson, and Susan L. Porter. 1998. Discretion in financial reporting: The voluntary disclosure of compensation peer groups in proxy statement performance graphs. *Contemporary Accounting Research*, 15, 1 (Spring): 25–52.

Cahan, Steven F. 1992. The effect of antitrust investigations on discretionary accruals: A refined test of the political-cost hypothesis. *The Accounting Review*, 67, 1 (January): 77–95 .

Cahan, Steven F., Betty M. Chavis, and Richard G. Elmendorf. 1997. Earnings management of chemical firms in response to political costs from environmental legislation. *Journal of Accounting, Auditing and Finance*, 12, 1 (Winter): 37–65.

Cahan, Steven F. and Wei Zhang. 2006. After Enron: Auditor conservatism and ex-Andersen clients. *The Accounting Review*, 81, 1 (January): 49–82.

Cai, Jie. 2007. Executive stock option exercises: Good timing or backdating. SSRN.com/abstract=951693.

Calegari, Michael J. 2000. The effect of tax accounting rules on capital structure and discretionary accruals. *Journal of Accounting and Economics*, 30, 1 (August): 1–31.

Callaghan, Sandra Renfro, Jane P. Saly, and Chandra Subramaniam. 2004. The timing of option repricing. *Journal of Finance*, 59, 4 (August): 1651–1676.

Callen, Jeffrey L., Joshua Livnat, and Dan Segal. 2006. The information content of SEC filings and information environment: A variance decomposition analysis. *The Accounting Review*, 81, 5 (October): 1017–1043.

Callen, Jeffrey L. and Dan Segal. 2004. Do accruals drive firm-level stock returns? A variance decomposition analysis. *Journal of Accounting Research*, 42, 3 (June): 527-560 .

Campos, Roel C. 2005. Remarks before the Committee on Banking, Housing, and Urban Affairs United States Senate. http://www.sec.gov/news/speech/spch072605rcc.htm.

Cao, Yan, Charles E. Wasley, and Joanna Shuang Wu. 2006. The impact of forecast ambiguity and forecast bias on the credibility of management cash flow forecasts. Simon School Working Paper No. FR 06-01. SSRN.com/abstract=874106.

Carcello, Joseph V., Roger H. Hermanson, and N.T. McGrath. 1992. Audit quality attributes: The perceptions of partners, preparers, and financial statement users. *Auditing: A Journal of Practice and Theory*, 11, 2 (Fall): 1–15.

Carcello, Joseph V. and Albert L. Nagy. 2002. Auditor industry specialization and fraudulent financial reporting. Proceedings of the 2002 Deloitte & Touche.

Carcello, Joseph V. and Terry L. Neale. 2000. Audit committee characteristics and auditor reporting. *The Accounting Review*, 75, 4 (October): 453 - 467.

Carcello, Joseph V. and Terry L. Neale. 2003. Audit committee composition and auditor dismissals following "new" going concern reports. *The Accounting Review*, 78, 1 (January): 95–117.

Carlson, S.J. and C.T. Bathala. 1997. Ownership differences and firms' income smoothing behavior. *Journal of Business Finance and Accounting*, 24, 2 (March): 179–196.

Carney, William J. 2006. The costs of being public after Sarbanes-Oxley: The irony of 'going private. Emory Law and Economics Research Paper No. 05–4. *Emory Law Journal*, 55: 141. SSRN.com/abstract=896564.

Carpenter, Jennifer and Barbara Remmers. 2001. Executive stock option exercises and inside information. *The Journal of Business*, 74, 4 (October): 513–534.

Carpenter, Mason A. and James D. Westphal. 2001. The strategic context of external network ties: Examining the impact of director appointments on board involvement in strategic decision making. *Academy of Management Journal*, 44, 4 (August): 639–660.

Carpenter, Tina D. and Jane L. Reimers. 2001. Unethical and fraudulent financial reporting: Applying the theory of planned behavior. *Journal of Business Ethics*, 60, 2 (August): 115–129.

Carslaw, Charles A.P.N. 1988. Anomalies in income numbers: Evidence of goal Varda(-) oriented behavior. *The Accounting Review*, 63, 2 (April): 321–327.

Carter, Mary Ellen, and Luann J. Lynch. 2001. An examination of executive stock option repricing. *Journal of Financial Economics*, 61, 2 (August): 207–225.

Carter, Mary Ellen and Luann J. Lynch. 2003. The consequences of the FASB's 1998 proposal on accounting for stock option repricing. *Journal of Accounting and Economics*, 35, 1 (April): 51–72.

Carter, Mary Ellen, Luann J. Lynch, and Sarah L. Center Zechman. 2006. The relation between executive compensation and earnings management: Changes in the post-Sarbanes-Oxley era. AAA 2006 Management Accounting Section (MAS). SSRN.com/abstract=770327.

Catanach, Anthony H. and Shelley C. Rhoades. 2003. Enron: A financial reporting failure? *Villanova Law Review*, 48, 4: 1057. SSRN.com/abstract=418920.

Caton, Gary L. and Jeremy Goh. 2003. Are all rivals affected equally by bond rating downgrades? *Review of Quantitative Finance and Accounting*, 20, 1 (January): 49–62.

Chai, Mary L. and Samuel Tung. 2002. The effect of earnings-announcement timing on earnings management. *Journal of Business Finance and* Accounting, 29, 9-10 (November/December): 1337–1354.

Chalmers, John M.R., Larry Y. Dann, and Jarrad Harford. 2002. Managerial opportunism? Evidence from directors' and officers' insurance purchases. *The Journal of Finance*, 57, 2 (April): 609–636.

Chambers, Dennis J. 1999. Earnings management and capital market misallocation. SSRN.com/abstract=198790.

Chambers, Dennis J., Robert N. Freeman, and Adam S. Koch. 2005. The effect of risk on price responses to unexpected earnings. *Journal of Accounting, Auditing and Finance*, 20, 4 (Fall): 461–482.

Chambers, Dennis, Ross Jennings, and Robert B. Thompson II. 2003. Managerial discretion and accounting for research and development costs. *Journal of Accounting, Auditing and Finance*, 18, 1 (Winter): 79–113.

Chan, Kam C., Barbara R. Farrell, and Picheng Lee. 2006. Earnings management and return–earnings association of firms reporting material internal control weaknesses under Section 404 of the Sarbanes-Oxley Act. Working Paper, Pace University.

Chan, Konan, Louis K.C. Chan, Narasimhan Jegadeesh, and Joseph Lakonishok. 2004. Earnings quality and stock returns. *The Journal of Business*, 79, 3 (May): 1041–1082.

Chan, Konan, John W. Cooney, Joonghyuk Kim, and Ajai K. Singh. 2003. The IPO Derby: Are there consistent losers and winners on this track? AFA 2004 San Diego Meeting, EFMA 2003 Helsinki Meeting. SSRN.com/abstract=392002.

Chan, Louis K.R., Jason Karceski, and Josef Lakonishok. 2003. Analysts' conflict of interests and biases in earnings forecasts. AFA 2004 San Diego Meeting; EFMA 2003, Helsinki Meeting. SSRN.com/abstract=392004.

Chandler III, William B. and Leo E. Strine, Jr. 2002. The new federalism of the American corporate governance system: Preliminary reflections of two residents of one small state. SSRN.com/abstract=367720.

Chaney, Paul K. and Debra Coleman Jeter. 1992. The effect of size on the magnitude of long-window earnings response coefficients. *Contemporary Accounting Research*, 8, 2 (Spring): 540–560.

Chaney, Paul K., Debra Coleman Jeter, and Craig M. Lewis. 1998. The use of accruals in income smoothing: A permanent earnings hypothesis. *Advances in Quantitative Analysis of Finance and Accounting* (old series), 6: 103–135.

Chaney, Paul K. and Craig M. Lewis. 1995. Earnings management and firm valuation under asymmetric information. *Journal of Corporate Finance: Contracting, Governance, and Organization*, 1, 3-4 (April): 319–345.

Chaney, Paul K. and Craig M. Lewis. 1998. Income smoothing and underperformance in initial public offerings. *Journal of Corporate Finance: Contracting, Governance, and Organization*, 4, 1 (March): 1–29.

Chaney, P. and Kirk L. Philipich. 2002. Shredded reputation: The cost of audit failure. *Journal of Accounting Research*, 40, 4 (September): 1221–1245.

Chang, Charles, Daouk Hazem, and Varda (Albert) Wang, Albert. 2006. Does the oil market learn about analyst accuracy? SSRN.com/abstract=931704.

Chang, Wen-Jing, Ling-Tai Lynette Chou, and Hsiou-wei William Lin. 2006. The effect of dismissal threat on auditor independence. A paper presented in the 2006 Auditing Midyear Conference, Los Angeles, CA.

Charitou, Andreas and Christodoulos Louca. 2003. Earnings management by foreign firms preceding their listing in U.S. stock exchanges. EFMA 2003 Helsinki Meeting.

Charitou, Andreas, Lampertidis Neophytos, and Lenos Trigeorgis. 2004. Managerial discretion, institutional ownership and monitoring preceding bankruptcy. EFMA 2004 Basel Meeting Paper. SSRN.com/abstract=486865.

Chase, Bruce W. and Edward N. Coffman. 1994. Choice of accounting method by not-for-profit institutions accounting for investments by colleges and universities. *Journal of Accounting and Economics*, 18, 2 (September): 233–243.

Chauvin, Keith W. and Catherine Shenoy. 2001. Stock price decreases prior to executive stock option grants. *Journal of Corporate Finance*, 7, 1 (March): 53–76.

Chen, Ken Y., Randal J. Elder, and Yung-Ming Hsieh. 2007. Corporate governance and earnings management: The implications of corporate governance best-practice principles for Taiwanese listed companies. *Journal of Contemporary Accounting and Economics*, forthcoming. SSRN.com/abstract=981926.

Chen, Kevin C.W. and Chi-Wen Jevons Lee. 1995. Executive bonus plans and accounting trade-offs: The case of oil and gas industry, 1985-86. *The Accounting Review*, 70, 1 (January): 91–111.

Chen, Kevin C.W. and K.C. John Wei. 1993. Creditors' decisions to waive violations of accounting-based debt covenants. *The Accounting Review*, 68, 2 (April): 218–232.

Chen, Kevin C.W., and Hongqui Yuan. 2004. Earnings management and capital resource allocation: Evidence form China's accounting based regulation of rights issues. *The Accounting Review*, 79, 3 (July) 645–665.

Chen, Peter and Lane Daley. 1996. Regulatory capital, tax, and earnings management effects on loan loss accruals in the Canadian banking industry. *Contemporary Accounting Research*, 13, 1 (Spring): 91–128.

Chen, Qi and Wei Jiang. 2006. Analysts' weighting of private and public information. *The Review of Financial Studies*, 19, 1 (April): 319–355.

Chen, Shuping 2003. Why do managers fail to meet their own forecasts? 14th Annual Conference on Financial Economics and Accounting (FEA). SSRN.com/abstract=490562.

Chen, Shuping, Mark L. DeFond, and Chul W. Park. 2002. Voluntary disclosure of balance sheet information in quarterly earnings announcements. *Journal of Accounting and Economics*, 33, 2 (June): 229–251.

Chen, Shuping, and Dawn Matsumoto. 2006. Favorable versus unfavorable recommendations: The impact on analyst access to management-provided information. *Journal of Accounting Research*, 44, 4 (September): 57–689.

Chen, Xia, Qiang Cheng, and Kin Lo. 2006. Are analyst research and corporate disclosures complements or substitutes? SSRN.com/abstract=917919.

Chen, Xiao, Chi-Wen Jevons Lee, and Jing Li. 2003. Chinese tango: Government assisted earnings management. SSRN.com/abstract=408800.

Chen, Yeh-Ning. 2004. Debt seniority and the lenders' incentive to monitor: Why isn't trade credit senior? EFA 2004 Maastricht Meeting Paper, 2244. SSRN.com/abstract=559009.

Cheng, Agnes C.S., William S. Hopewood, and James C. McKewon. 1992. Non-linearity and specification problems in unexpected earnings response regression model. *The Accounting Review*, 67, 3 (July): 579–598.

Cheng, Agnes C.S. and Austin L. Reitenga. 2006. Characteristics of institutional investors and discretionary accruals. SSRN.com/abstract=277717. *The Journal of Applied Business Research*, forthcoming.

Cheng, Agnes C.S. and Wayne B. Thomas. 2006. Evidence of the abnormal accrual anomaly incremental to operating cash flows. *The Accounting Review*, 81, 5 (October): 1151–1167.

Cheng, Qiang. 2005. The role of analysts' forecasts in accounting-based valuation: A critical evaluation. *Review of Accounting Studies*, 10, 1 (March): 5–31.

Cheng, Qiang and Kin Lo. 2006. Insider trading and voluntary disclosures. *Journal of Accounting Research*, 44, 5 (December): 815–848.

Cheng, Qiang and Terry Warfield. 2005. Equity incentives and earnings management. *The Accounting Review*, 80, 2 (April): 441–476.

Cheng, T.Y. and Michael Firth. 2000. An empirical analysis of the bias and rationality of profit forecasts published in new issue prospectuses. *Journal of Business Finance and Accounting*, 27, 3-4 (April/May): 423–446.

Cheung, Sheran C. and Itzhak Krinsky. 1994. Information asymmetry and the underpricing of initial public offerings: Further empirical evidence. *Journal of Business Finance and Accounting*, 21, 5 (July): 739–747.

Chevis, Gia Marie, Somnath Das, and K. Sivaramakrishnan. 2001. An empirical analysis of firms that meet or exceed analysts' earnings forecasts. SSRN.com/abstract=268628.

Chhaochharia, Vidhi and Yaniv Grinstein. 2005. Corporate governance and firm valuevarda (:or -) - the impact of the 2002 governance rules. AFA 2006 Boston Meeting Paper. SSRN.com/abstract=556990.

Chi, Wuchun and Huichi Huang. 2006. Discretionary accruals, audit-firm tenure and auditor tenure: An empirical case in Taiwan. Working Paper.

Chidambaran, N.K. and Ivan E. Brick. 2005. Board monitoring and firm risk. EFA 2005 Moscow Meeting Paper. SSRN.com/abstract=677123.

Chidambaran, N.K. and Kose John. 1999. Managerial compensation and the efficiency of large shareholder monitoring. New York University, Center for Law and Business, Working Paper 99-006. SSRN.com/abstract=164503.

Chidambaran, N.K. and Kose John. 2003. Managerial compensation, voluntary disclosure, and large shareholder monitoring. Working Paper, New York University.

Chidambaran, Nenmara K., and Nagpurnanand R. Prabhala. 2003. Executive stock option repricing, internal governance mechanisms, and management turnover. *Journal of Financial Economics*, 69, 1 (July): 153–189.

Ching, Ken, Michael Firth, and Oliver M. Rui. 2002. Earnings management, corporate governance and the market for seasoned equity offerings. SSRN.com/abstract=337880.

Chng, Chee-Kiong. 2002. Board independence and the shielding of CEO pay from unusual transactions. Working Paper, National University of Singapore.

Choi, Byeonghee Ben, BuRyung Brian Lee, and Eric G. Press. 2002. Differences in the value relevance of earnings in knowledge-based and traditional industries. SSRN.com/abstract=350320.

Choi, Jay Pil, Eirik G. Kristiansen, and Jae Hyon Nahm. 2007. Communication of soft information to lenders: Credibility and reputation. SSRN.com/abstract=976886.

Choi, Stephen. 2005. Do the merits matter less after the Private Securities Litigation Reform Act? American Law and Economics Association Annual Meeting: 25–50.

Choi, Sung K. and Debra C. Jeter. 1992. The effects of qualified audit opinions on earnings response coefficients. The Journal of Accounting and Economics, 5, 2-3 (June-September): 229–247.

Choi, Tae H. 2004. Characteristics of firms that persistently meet or beat analysts' forecasts. KDI School of Public Policy & Management Paper No. 04-17. SSRN.com/abstract=635104.

Chou, De-Wai, Michael Gombola, and Feng-Ying Liu. 2006. Earnings management and stock performance of reverse leveraged buyouts. Journal of Financial and Quantitative Analysis, 41, 2 (June): 407–438.

Chou, De-Wai and Jane-Raung Philip Lin. 2003. False signals from stock repurchase announcements: Evidence from earnings management and analysts' forecast revisions. SSRN.com/abstract=471122.

Christensen, John A. and Joel S. Demski. 2003. Accounting Theory: An Information Content Perspective. McGraw-Hill Irwin.

Christensen, Peter Ove, Joel S. Demski, and Hans Frimor. 2002. Accounting policies in agencies with moral hazard and renegotiation. Journal of Accounting Research, 40, 4 (September) 2002: 1071–1090.

Christensen, Peter Ove and Jerald A. Feltham. 1993. Communication in multiperiod agencies with production and financial decisions. Contemporary Accounting Research, 9, 2 (Spring): 706–744.

Christensen, Peter Ove and Jerald A. Feltham. 2000. Market performance measures and disclosure of private management information in capital markets. Review of Accounting Studies, 5, 4 (December): 301–329.

Christensen, Peter Ove and Jerald A. Feltham. 2002. Economics of Information, Volume I: Information in Markets. New York, LLC: Springer-Verlag.

Christensen, Peter Ove and Jerald A. Feltham. 2005. Economics of Information, Volume II: Performance Evaluation. New York, LLC: Springer-Verlag.

Christensen, Theodore E., Robert E. Hoyt, and Jeffrey S. Paterson. 1999. Ex ante incentives for earnings management and the informativeness of earnings. Journal of Business Finance and Accounting, 26, 7-8 (September-October): 807–832.

Christie, Andrew A. 1987. On cross-sectional analysis in accounting research. Journal of Accounting and Economics, 9, 3 (December): 231–258.

Christie, Andrew A. 1990. Aggregation of test statistics: An evaluation of the evidence on contracting and size hypotheses. Journal of Accounting and Economics, 12, 1-3 (January): 15–36.

Christie, Andrew A. and Jerold L. Zimmerman. 1994. Efficient and opportunistic choices of accounting procedures: Corporate control contexts. The Accounting Review, 69, 4 (October): 539–566.

Chtourou, Sonda Marrakchi, Jean Bédard, and Lucie Courteau. 2001. Corporate governance and earnings management. SSRN.com/abstract=275053.

Chung, Hyeesoo and Sanjay Kallapur. 2003. Client importance, non audit services, and abnormal accruals. The Accounting Review, 78, 4 (October): 931–955.

Chung, Kwang-Hyun, Rudolph A. Jacob, and Ya B. Tang. 2003. Earnings management by firms announcing earnings after SEC filing. International Advances in Economic Research, 9, 2 (May): 152–162.

Chung, Richard, Michael Firth, and Jeong-Bon Kim. 2002. Institutional monitoring and opportunistic earnings management. *Journal of Corporate Finance: Contracting, Governance and Organization*, 8, 1 (January): 29–48.

Ciccone, Stephen J. 2002. GAAP versus street earnings: Making earnings look higher and smoother. SSRN.com/abstract=319320.

Clarke, Jonathan, Stephen P. Ferris, Narayanan Jayaraman, and Jinsoo Lee. 2006. Are analysts recommendations biased? Evidence from corporate bankruptcies. *Journal of Financial and Quantitative Analysis*, 41, 1 (March): 169–196.

Clarke, Richard N. 1983. Collusion and incentives for information sharing. *Bell Journal of Economics*, 14, 2 (Autumn): 383–394.

Clark, Robert Charles. 2005. Corporate governance changes in the wake of the Sarbanes-Oxley Act: A morality tale for policymakers too. Harvard Law and Economics Discussion Paper No. 525. SSRN.com/abstract=808244.

Clarkson, Peter M., Jennifer L. Rao, and Gordon D. Richardson. 1994. The voluntary inclusion of forecasts in the MD&A Section of annual reports. *Contemporary Accounting Research*, 11, 2 (Fall): 423–450.

Clearfield, Andrew Mark. 2005. With friends like these, who needs enemies? The structure of the investment industry and its reluctance to exercise governance oversight. *Corporate Governance: An International Review*, 13, 2 (March): 114–121.

Clinch, Greg and Joseph Magliolo. 1993. CEO compensation and components of earnings in bank holding companies. *Journal of Accounting and Economics*, 16, 1-3 (January-July): 241–272.

Cloyd, Bryan C. 1995. The effects of financial accounting conformity on recommendations of tax preparers. *The Journal of the American Taxation Association*, 17, 2 (Fall): 50–70.

Cloyd, Bryan, C., Jamie Pratt and Toby Stock. 1996. The use of financial accounting choice to support aggressive tax positions: Public and private firms. *Journal of Accounting Research*, 34, 1 (Spring): 23–43.

Coase, Ronald H. 1937. The nature of the firm. *Economica*, New Series, 4, 16. (November): 386–405.

Coffee, John C. 1991. Liquidity versus control: The institutional investor as corporate monitor. *Columbia Law Review*, 91, 6 (October): 1277–1368.

Coffee, John C. 2001. The acquiescent gatekeeper: Reputational intermediaries, auditor independence and the governance of accounting. Columbia Law and Economics Working Paper 191. SSRN.com/abstract=270944.

Coffee, John C. 2002. Understanding Enron: It's about the gatekeepers, stupid. SSRN.com/abstract=325240.

Coffee, John C. 2003a. Gatekeeper failure and reform: The challenge of fashioning relevant reforms. Columbia Law and Economics Working Paper No. 237. SSRN.com/abstract=447940.

Coffee, John C. 2003b. What caused Enron? A capsule social and economic history of the 1990's. Columbia Law and Economics Working Paper No. 214. SSRN.com/abstract=373581.

Coffee, John C. 2003c. Ensuring independence, promoting investor confidence: Governance of the New York Stock Exchange as a quasi-public entity. A testimony before the Subcommittee of U.S. House of Representatives on Capital Markets, Insurance and Government Sponsored Enterprises of the Committee on Financial Services.

Coffee, John C. 2005. A theory of corporate scandals: Why the U.S. and Europe differ Varda(?). *Oxford Review of Economic Policy*, 21, 2: 198–211.

Coglianese, Cary and Michael L. Michael. 2006. After the scandals: Changing relationships in corporate governance. KSG Working Paper No. RWP06-024. SSRN.com/abstract=911653.

Cohen, Daniel A., Aiyesha Dey, and Thomas Z. Lys. 2005a. Trends in earnings management and informativeness of earnings announcements in the pre- and post-Sarbanes Oxley periods. SSRN.com/abstract=658782.

Cohen, Daniel A., Aiyesha Dey, and Thomas Lys. 2005b. The Sarbanes Oxley Act of 2002: Implications for compensation structure and risk-taking incentives of CEOs. SSRN.com/abstract=568483.

Cohen, Daniel A., Rebecca N. Hann, and Maria Ogneva. 2007. Another look at GAAP versus the street: An empirical assessment of measurement error bias. *Review of Accounting Studies*, 2–3 (September): 271–303.

Cohen, Jeffrey, Ganesh Krishnamoorthy, and Arnold Wright. 2002. Corporate governance and the audit process. *Contemporary Accounting Research*, 19, 4 (Winter): 573–594.

Cohen, Jeffrey, Ganesh Krishnamoorthy, and Arnold Wright. 2004. Corporate governance mosaic and financial reporting quality. *The Journal of Accounting Literature*, 23: 87–152.

Cohen, Randolph B., Brian J. Hall, and Luis M. Viceira. 2000. Do executive stock options encourage risk-taking? Working Paper, Harvard University.

Coles, Jeffrey L., Michael L. Lemmon, and Lalitha Naveen. 2003. A comparison of profitability and CEO turnover sensitivity in large private and public firms. SSRN.com/abstract=391103.

Coles, Jeffrey L., Michael Hertzel, and Swaminathan Kalpathy. 2006. Earnings management around employee stock option reissues. *Journal of Accounting and Economics*, 41, 1-2 (April): 173–200.

Coles, Jeffrey L., Naveen D. Daniel, and Lalitha Naveen. 2006a. Managerial incentives and risk-taking. *Journal of Financial Economics*, 79, 2 (February): 431–468.

Coles, Jeffrey L., Naveen D. Daniel, and Lalitha Naveen. 2006b. Boards: Does one size fits all? *Journal of Financial Economics*, forthcoming.

Coles, Jeffrey L. and Chun Keung Hoi. 2003. New evidence on the market for directors: Board membership and Pennsylvania Senate Bill 1310. *Journal of Finance*, 58, 1 (February): 197–230.

Coller, Maribeth and Julia L. Higgs. 1997. Firm valuation and accounting for employee stock options. *Financial Analysts Journal*, 53, 1 (January/February): 26–34.

Coller, Maribeth and Teri Lombardi Yohn. 1997. Management forecasts and information asymmetry: An examination of bid-ask spreads. *Journal of Accounting Research*, 35, 2 (Autumn): 181–191.

Collingwood, Harris. 2001. The earnings game: Everybody plays, nobody wins. *Harvard Business Review*, 79, 6 (June): 65–74.

Collins, Daniel W. and Linda DeAngelo. 1990. Accounting information and corporate governance: Market and analyst reactions to earnings of firms engaged in proxy contests. *Journal of Accounting and Economics*, 13, 3 (October): 213–247.

Collins, Daniel W., Guojin Gong, and Paul Hribar. 2003. Investor sophistication and the mispricing of accruals. *Review of Accounting Studies*, 8, 2-3 (June): 251–276.

Collins, Daniel W., Guojin Gong, and Haidan Li. 2005. The effect of the Sarbanes-Oxley Act on the timing manipulation of CEO stock option awards. SSRN.com/abstract=850564.

Collins, Daniel W. Guojin Gong, and Haidan Li. 2006. Corporate governance and backdating of executive stock options. SSRN.com/abstract=934881.

Collins, Daniel W., and Paul Hribar. 2000. Earnings-based and accrual-based market anomalies: One effect or two? *Journal of Accounting and Economics* 29, 1 (February): 101–123.

Collins, Daniel W., Edward L. Maydew, and Ira S. Weiss. 1997. Changes in the value-relevance of earnings and book values over the past forty years. *Journal of Accounting and Economics*, 24, 1 (December): 39–67.

Collins, Denton, Austin L. Reitenga, and Juan Manuel Sanchez. 2005. Managerial consequences of earnings restatements. SSRN.com/abstract=771564.

Collins, Julie, Deen Kemsley, and Mark Lang. 1998. Cross-jurisdictional income shifting and earnings valuation. *Journal of Accounting Research*, 36, 2 (Autumn): 209–229.

Collins, Julie H., Douglas A. Shackelford, and James M. Wahlen. 1995. Bank differences in the coordination of regulatory capital, earnings and taxes. *Journal of Accounting Research*, 33, 2 (Autumn): 263–291.

Committee of Governmental Affairs of the US Senate. 2002. The Role of the Board of Directors in Enron's Collapse. Report 107-70. http://news.findlaw.com/hdocs/docs/enron/senpsi70802rpt.pdf.

Comprix, Joseph, Lillian Mills, and Andrew Schmidt. 2004. Bias in quarterly effective tax rate estimates: Implications for earnings management and analysts' forecasts. Working Paper, Arizona State University and University of Arizona.

Comprix, Joseph and Karl A. Muller III. 2006. Asymmetric treatment of reported pension expense and income amounts in CEO cash compensation calculations. *Journal of Accounting and Economics*, 42, 3 (December): 385–416.

Constantinou, Constantina, William Forbes, and Len Skerratt. 2000. Analyst underreaction to past information about earnings: Reporting, processing or plain old misspecification bias. Working Paper.

Conyon, Martin J. and Annita Florou. 2004. Does governance quality mitigate horizon effects? Investment patterns surrounding CEO departures. SSRN.com/abstract=545982.

Conyon, Martin J. and Mark R. Muldoon. 2006. The small world of corporate boards. *Journal of Business Finance and Accounting*, 33, 9-10 (November/December): 1321–1343.

Conyon, Martin J. and Laura E. Read. 2006. A model of the supply of executives for outside directorships. *Journal of Corporate Finance*, 12, 3 (June): 645–659.

Cook, Kirsten A., George Ryan Huston, and Thomas C. Omer. 2006. Earnings management through effective tax rates: The effects of tax planning investment and the Sarbanes-Oxley Act of 2002. SSRN.com/abstract=897749.

Core, John E. 2001. A review of the empirical disclosure literature: Discussion. *Journal of Accounting and Economics*, 31, 1-3 (September): 441–456.

Core, John E. 2006. Discussion of "An analysis of the theories and explanations offered for the mispricing of accruals and accrual components." *Journal of Accounting Research*, 44, 2 (May): 341–350.

Core, John E. and Wayne R. Guay. 1999. The use of equity grants to manage optimal equity incentive levels. *Journal of Accounting and Economics*, 28, 2 (December): 151–184.

Core, John E. and Wayne R. Guay. 2001. Stock option plans for non-executive employees. *Journal of Financial Economics*, 61, 2 (August): 253–287.

Core, John E. and Wayne R. Guay. 2002a. The other side of the trade-off: The impact of risk on executive compensation, a revised comment. SSRN.com/abstract=292955.

Core, John E. and Wayne R. Guay. 2002b. Estimating the value of employee stock option portfolios and their sensitivities to price and volatility. *Journal of Accounting Research*, 40, 4 (June): 613–630.

Core, John E., Wayne R. Guay, and David F. Larcker. 2003. Executive equity compensation and incentives: A survey. *Economic Policy Review*, 9, 1 (April): 27–50.

Core, John E., Wayne R. Guay, Scott A. Richardson, and Rodrogi S. Verdi. 2006. Stock market anomalies: What can we learn from repurchases and insider trading? *Review of Accounting Studies*, 11, 1 (March): 49–70.

Core, John E., Wayne R. Guay, and Tjomme O. Rusticus. 2006. Does weak governance cause weak stock returns? An examination of firm operating performance and analysts' expectations. *Journal of Finance*, 61, 2 (April): 655–687.

Core, John E., Wayne R. Guay, and Robert E. Verrecchia. 2003. Price versus non-price performance measures in optimal CEO compensation contracts. *The Accounting Review*, 78, 4 (October): 957–981.

Core, John E., Robert W. Holthausen, and David F. Larcker. 1999. Corporate governance, chief executive officer compensation, and firm performance. *Journal of Financial Economics*, 51, 3 (March): 371–406.

Core, John E. and Jun Qian. 2001. Option-like contracts for innovation and production. SSRN.com/abstract=207968.

Core, John E. and Catherine M. Schrand. 1999. The effect of accounting-based debt covenants on equity valuation. *Journal of Accounting and Economics*, 27, 1 (February): 1–34.

Cotter, James F. and Sarah W. Peck. 2001. The structure of debt and active equity investors: The case of the buyout specialist. *Journal of Financial Economics,* 59, 1 (January): 101–147.

Cotter, James F., Anil Shivdasani, and Marc Zenner. 1997. Do independent directors enhance target shareholder wealth during tender offers? *Journal of Financial Economics*, 43, 2 (February): 195–218.

Cotter, Julie, Irem A. Tuna, and Peter D. Wysocki. 2006. Expectations management and beatable targets: How do analysts react –o explicit earnings guidance? *Contemporary Accounting Research*, 23, 3 (Autumn): 593–624.

Cotter, Julie and Susan Young. 2004. Do analysts anticipate accounting fraud? Working Paper, Emory University.

Coughlan, Anne T. and Ronald M. Schmidt. 1985. Executive compensation, management turnover, and firm performance. *Journal of Accounting and Economics*, 7, 1-3 (April): 43–66.

Coulton, Jeff, Sarah Taylor, and Stephen Taylor. 2005. Is "benchmark beating" by Australian firms evidence of earnings management? *Accounting and Finance*, 45, 4 (December): 553–576.

Cowen, Amanda, Boris Groysberg, and Paul Healy. 2006. Which types of analyst firms are more optimistic? *Journal of Accounting and Economics*, 41, 1-2 (April): 119–146.

Cox, Christopher. 2006. *A Message from the Chairman*. Securities and Exchange Commission 2006 Performance and Accountability Report. http://www.sec.gov/about/secpar/secpar2006.pdf#chairman.

Cox, Clifford. 1985. Further evidence on the representativeness of management earnings forecasts. *The Accounting Review*, 60, 4 (October): 692–701.

Craig, Russell and Paul Walsh. 1989. Adjustments for "extraordinary items" in smoothing reported profit of listed Australian companies: Some empirical evidence. *Journal of Business Finance and Accounting*, 16, 2 (Spring): 229–245.

Crainer, Stuart. 2004. Interview: Robert A.G. Monks. *Business Strategy Review*, 15, 2 (June): 34-36. SSRN.com/abstract=551168.

Craswell, Allen T., Jere R. Francis, and Stephen L. Taylor. 1995. Auditor brand name reputations and industry specializations. *Journal of Accounting and Economics*, 20, 3 (December): 297–322.

Craswell, Allen, Donald J. Stokes, and Janet Laughton. 2002. Auditor independence and fee dependence. *Journal of Accounting and Economics*, 33, 2 (June): 253–275.

Crawford, Vincent P. and Joel Sobel. 1982. Strategic information transmission. *Econometrica*, 50, 6 (November): 579–594.

Cremers, Martijn, Joost Driessen, Pascal Maenhout, and David Weinbaum. 2005. Does skin in the game matter? Director incentives and governance in the mutual fund industry. http://faculty.insead.edu/maenhout/research/PDF/weinbaum.pdf.

Crocker, Keith, J. and Steven Huddart. 2006. An optimal contracting approach to earnings management. Working Paper, Pennsylvania State University.

Crocker, Keith, J., and Joel Slemrod. 2006. The economics of earnings manipulation and managerial compensation. SSRN.com/abstract=938971.

Cross, Frank B. and Robert A. Prentice. 2006. Economies, capital markets, and securities law. University of Texas Law, Law and Economics Research Paper No. 73. SSRN.com/abstract=908927.

Culvenor, Jane, Jayne M. Godfrey, and Graeme Byrne. 1999. Modeling total accruals in international environment: The impact of alternative measures of PPE. *Journal of International Accounting, Auditing and Taxation,* 8, 2: 289–313.

Cuñat, Vicente and Maria Guadalupe. 2005. Managerial compensation and product market competition. *Journal of the European Economic Association*, 3, 5 (September): 1058–1082.

Cunningham, Lawrence A. 2003. The Sarbanes-Oxley yawn: Heavy rhetoric, light reform (and it might just work). *University of Connecticut Law Review*, 36: 915-988: 1698–1735.

Cunningham, Lawrence A. 2006. Too big to fail: Moral hazard in auditing and the need to restructure the industry before it unravels. *Columbia Law Review*, 106. SSRN.com/abstract=928482.

Cyert, Richard M. 1997. The executive compensation controversy. A lecture given at Latrobe, Pennsylvania, on October 29, 1997 as the 39th lecturer in the Alex G. McKenna Economic Education Series. http://facweb.stvincent.edu/Academics/cepe/Articles/Cyert.htm.

Cyert, Richard, Sok-Hyon Kang, and Praveen Kumar. 2002. Corporate governance, take-overs, and top-management compensation: Theory and evidence. *Management Science*, 48, 4 (April): 453–469.

DaDalt, Peter and Speros Margetis. 2007. The intra-industry contagion effects of earnings restatements. Temporary title. Working Paper.

Dallas, Lynne. 2002. The new managerialism and diversity on corporate boards of directors. *Tulane Law Review*, 76. SSRN.com/abstract=313425.

Dalton, Dan R., Catherine. M. Daily, Jonathan L. Johnson, and Alan E. Ellstrand. 1999. Number of directors and financial performance: A meta-analysis. *Academy of Management Journal*, 42, 6 (December): 674–686.

Daneilson, Morris G. and Jonathan M. Karpoff. 1998. On the uses of corporate governance provisions. *Journal of Corporate Finance*, 4, 4 (December): 347–371.

Daneshfar, Alireza and Daniel Zeghal. 2001. Earnings management and the stock price environment. Working Paper, University of New Haven and University of Ottawa.

Dann, Larry Y., Diane Del Guercio, and Megan Partch. 2003. Governance and boards of directors in closed-end investment companies. EFA 2002 Berlin Meeting Paper; and Tuck-JFE Contemporary Corporate Governance Conference. SSRN.com/abstract=236105.

Dann, Larry Y., Ronald W. Masulis, and David Mayers. 1992. Repurchase tender offers and earnings information. *Journal of Accounting and Economics*, 14, 3 (September): 217–251.

Danos, Paul and John W. Eichenseher. 1981. Audit industry dynamics: Factors affecting changes in client-industry market shares. *Journal of Accounting Research*, 20, 2 (Autumn): 604–616.

Danos, Paul and John W. Eichenseher. 1986. Long-term trends toward seller concentration in the U.S. audit market. *The Accounting Review*, 61, 4 (October): 633–650.

Daouk, Hazem, Charles M.C. Lee, and David Ng. 2006. Capital market governance: How do security laws affect market performance? *Journal of Corporate Finance*, 12, 3 (June): 560–593.

Darrough, Masako N. 1993. Disclosure policy and competition: Côurnot vs. Bertrand. *The Accounting Review*, 68, 3 (July): 534–561.

Darrough, Masako N. and Srinivasan Rangan. 2005. Do insiders manipulate earnings when they sell their shares in an initial public offering? *Journal of Accounting Research*, 43, 1 (March): 1–33.

Darrough, Masako N. and Neal M. Stoughton. 1990. Financial disclosure policy in an entry game. *Journal of Accounting and Economics*, 12, 1-3 (January): 219–243.

Das, Sonnath, Carolyn B. Levine, and Siva Sivaramakrishnan. 1998. Earnings predictability and bias in analysts' earnings forecasts. *The Accounting Review*, 73, 2 (April): 277–294.

Das, Somnath and Pervin K. Shroff. 2002. Fourth quarter reversals in earnings changes and earnings management. SSRN.com/abstract=308441.

Das, Somnath and Huai Zhang. 2003. Rounding-up in reported EPS, behavioral thresholds, and earnings management. *Journal of Accounting and Economics*, 35, 1 (April): 31–50.

Datar, Srikant M., Gerald A. Feltham, and John S. Hughes. 1991. The role of audits and audit quality in valuing new issues. *Journal of Accounting and Economics*, 14, 1-2 (March): 3–49.

Datar, Srikant, Susan Cohen Kulp, and Richard A. Lambert. 2001. Balancing performance measures. *Journal of Accounting Research*, 39, 1 (June): 75–92.

Davidson, Wallace N., Pornsit Jiraporn, and Peter J. DaDalt. 2006. Causes and consequences of audit shopping: An analysis of auditor opinions, earnings management, and auditor changes. *Quarterly Journal of Business and Economics*, 45, 1/2 (Winter/Spring): 69–87.

Davidson, Wallace N. III, Biao Xie, and Weihong Xu. 2004. Market reaction to voluntary announcements of audit committee appointments: The effect of financial expertise. *Journal of Accounting and Public Policy*, 23, 3 (July-August): 279–293.

Davis, Angela. 2002. The value relevance of revenue for internet firms: Does reporting grossed-up or barter revenue make a difference? *Journal of Accounting Research*, 40, 2 (May): 445–477.

Davis, Larry R., Billy Soo, and Greg Trompeter. 2006. Auditor tenure and the ability to meet or beat earnings forecasts. A paper presented in the 2006 Auditing Midyear Conference, Los Angeles, CA.

Davis-Hodder, Leslie, William Mayew, Mary Lea McAnally, and Constance D. Weaver. 2004. Using valuation model inputs to manage employee stock option disclosures. SSRN.com/abstract=537222.

De, Sankar and Pradyot K. Sen. 2002. Legal liabilities, audit accuracy and the market for audit services. *Journal of Business Finance and Accounting*, 29, 3-4 (April/May): 353–410.

De Franco, Gus, Yuyan Guan, and Hai Lu. 2005. The wealth change and redistribution effects of Sarbanes-Oxley internal control disclosures. SSRN.com/abstract=706701.

De Miguel, Alberto, Julio Pindado, and Chabela de la Torre. 2003. How do managerial entrenchment and expropriation affect control mechanisms? SSRN.com/abstract=475981.

DeAngelo, Linda Elizabeth. 1982. Mandated successful efforts and auditor choice. *Journal of Accounting and Economics*, 4, 3 (December): 171–203.

DeAngelo, Harry and Linda Elizabeth DeAngelo. 1991. Union negotiations and corporate policy: A study of labor concessions in the domestic steel industry during the 1980s. *Journal of Financial Economics*, 30, 1 (November): 3–43.

DeAngelo, Harry, Linda Elizabeth DeAngelo, and Edward Rice. 1984. Going private: Minority freezeouts and stockholders wealth. *The Journal of Law and Economics*, 27, 2 (October): 367-401.

DeAngelo, Harry, Linda Elizabeth DeAngelo, and Douglas J. Skinner. 1994. Accounting choice in troubled companies. *Journal of Accounting and Economics*, 17, 1-2 (January): 113–143.

DeAngelo, Harry, Linda Elizabeth DeAngelo, and Douglas J. Skinner. 1996. Reversal of fortune: Dividend signaling and the disappearance of sustained earnings growth. *Journal of Financial Economics*, 40, 3 (March): 341–371.

DeAngelo, Harry, Linda Elizabeth DeAngelo, and Douglas J. Skinner. 2004. Are dividends disappearing? Dividend concentration and the consolidation of earning. *Journal of Financial Economics*, 72, 3 (June): 425–456.

DeAngelo, Linda Elizabeth. 1981a. Auditor independence, "low-balling," and disclosure regulation. *Journal of Accounting and Economics*, 3, 2 (August): 113–127.

DeAngelo, Linda Elizabeth. 1981b. Auditor size and audit quality. *Journal of Accounting and Economics*, 3, 3 (December): 183–199.

DeAngelo, Linda Elizabeth 1986. Accounting numbers as market valuation substitutes: A study of management buyouts of public stockholders. *The Accounting Review*, 61, 3 (July): 400–420.

DeAngelo, Linda Elizabeth. 1988a. Managerial competition, information costs, and corporate governance: The use of accounting performance measures in proxy contests. *Journal of Accounting and Economics*, 10, 1 (January): 3–36.

DeAngelo, Linda Elizabeth. 1988b. Discussion of evidence of earnings management from the provision for bad debts. *Journal of Accounting Research*, 26 (Supplement): 32–40.

DeAngelo, Linda Elizabeth. 1990. Equity valuation and corporate control. *The Accounting Review*, 65, 1 (January): 93–112.

DeZoort, Todd F., Dana R. Hermanson, Deborah S. Archambeault, and Scott A. Reed. 2002. Audit committee effectiveness: A synthesis of the empirical audit committee literature. *Journal of Accounting Literature*, 21: 38–75.

DeZoort Todd F. and Steven E. Salterio. 2001. The effects of corporate governance experience and financial-reporting and audit knowledge on audit committee member judgments. *Auditing: A Journal of Practice and Theory*, 20, 2 (September): 31–47.

Dechow, Patricia M. 1994. Accounting earnings and cash flows as measures of firm performance: The role of accounting accruals. *Journal of Accounting and Economics*, 18, 1 (July): 3–42.

Dechow, Patricia M. 2006. Asymmetric sensitivity of CEO cash compensation to stock returns: A discussion. *Journal of Accounting and Economics*, 42, 1-2 (October): 193–202.

Dechow, Patricia M. and Ilia D. Dichev. 2002. The quality of accruals and earnings: The role of accrual estimation errors. *The Accounting Review*, 77 (Supplement): 35–59.

Dechow, Patricia M. and Weili Ge. 2006. The persistence of earnings and cash flows and the role of special items: Implications for the accrual anomaly. *Review of Accounting Studies*, 11, 2-3 (September): 253–296.

Dechow, Patricia M., Mark R. Huson, and Richard G. Sloan. 1994. The effect of restructuring charges on executives' cash compensation. *The Accounting Review*, 69, 1 (January): 138–156.

Dechow, Patricia M., Amy P. Hutton, Lisa B. Meulbroek, and Richard G. Sloan 2001. Short-sellers, fundamental analysis and stock returns. *Journal of Financial Economics*, 61, 1 (July): 77–106.

Dechow, Patricia M., Amy P. Hutton, and Richard G. Sloan. 1996. Economic consequences of accounting for stock-based compensation. *Journal of Accounting Research*, 34 (Supplement): 1–20.

Dechow, Patricia M., Amy P. Hutton, and Richard G. Sloan. 2000. The relation between analysts' forecasts of long-term earnings growth and stock price performance following equity offerings. *Contemporary Accounting Research*, 17, 1 (Spring): 1–32.

Dechow, Patricia M., S.P. Kothari, and Ross L. Watts. 1998. The relation between earnings and cash flows. *Journal of Accounting and Economics*, 25, 2 (May): 133–168.

Dechow, Patricia M., Scott Anthony Richardson, and Richard G. Sloan. 2006. The persistence and pricing of the cash component of earnings. Working paper. University of Pennsylvania.

Dechow, Patricia M., Scott Anthony Richardson, and Irem A. Tuna. 2000. Are benchmark beaters doing anything wrong? SSRN.com/abstract=222552.

Dechow, Patricia M., Scott Anthony Richardson, and Irem A. Tuna. 2003. Why are earnings kinky? An examination of the earnings management explanation. *Review of Accounting Studies*, 8 (June-September): 355–384.

Dechow, Patricia M., Jowell Sabino, and Richard G. Sloan. 1998. Implications of nondiscretionary accruals for earnings management and market-based research. Working Paper, University of Michigan.

Dechow, Patricia M. and Catherine M. Schrand. 2004. *Earnings Quality*. Research Foundation of CFA Institute.

Dechow, Patricia M. and Douglas J. Skinner. 2000. Earnings management, reconciling the views of accounting academics, practitioners, and regulators. *Accounting Horizons*, 14, 2 (June): 235–250.

Dechow, Patricia M. and Richard Sloan. 1991. Executive incentives and the horizon problem: An empirical investigation. *Journal of Accounting and Economics*, 14, 1 (March): 51–89.

Dechow, Patricia, Richard Sloan, and Amy P. Sweeney. 1995. Detecting earnings management. *The Accounting Review*, 70, 2 (April): 193–225.

Dechow, Patricia M., Richard G. Sloan, and Amy P. Sweeney. 1996. Causes and consequences of earnings manipulation: An analysis of firms subject to enforcement actions by the SEC. *Contemporary Accounting Research*, 13, 1 (Spring): 1–36.

DeFond, Mark L. 2002. Discussion of "The balance sheet as an earnings management constraint." *The Accounting Review*, 77 (Supplement): 29–33.

DeFond, Mark L., Michael Ettredge, and David B. Smith. 1997. An investigation of auditor resignations. *Research in Accounting Regulation*, 11: 25–45.

DeFond, Mark L. and Jere R. Francis. 2005. Audit research after Sarbanes-Oxley. *Auditing: A Journal of Practice and Theory*, 24, Supplement (May): 5–30.

DeFond, Mark L., Rebecca N. Hann, and Xuesong Hu. 2005. Does the market value financial expertise on audit committees of boards of directors? *Journal of Accounting Research*, 43, 2 (May): 153-193. SSRN.com/abstract=498822.

DeFond, Mark L. and Mingyi Hung. 2003. An empirical analysis of analysts' cash flow forecasts. *Journal of Accounting and Economics*, 35, 1 (April): 73–100.

DeFond, Mark L., and James Jiambalvo. 1991. Incidence and circumstances of accounting errors. *The Accounting Review*, 66, 3 (July): 643–655.

DeFond, Mark L. and James Jiambalvo. 1993. Factors related to auditor–client disagreements over income-increasing accounting methods. *Contemporary Accounting Research*, 9, 2 (Spring): 415–431.

DeFond, Mark L. and James Jiambalvo. 1994. Debt covenant violation and manipulation of accruals. *Journal of Accounting and Economics*, 17, 1-2 (January): 145–176.

DeFond, Mark L. and Chul W. Park. 1997. Smoothing income in anticipation of future earnings. *Journal of Accounting and Economics*, 23, 2 (July): 115–139.

DeFond, Mark L. and Chul W. Park. 1999. The effect of competition on CEO turnover. *Journal of Accounting and Economics*, 27, 1 (February): 33–56.

DeFond, Mark L. and Chul W. Park. 2001. The reversal of abnormal accruals and the market valuation of earnings surprise. *The Accounting Review*, 76, 3 (July): 375–404.

DeFond, Mark L., K. Raghunandan, and K.R. Subramanyam. 2002. Do non-audit service fees impair auditor independence? Evidence from going concern audit opinions. *Journal of Accounting Research*, 40, 4 (September): 1247–1274.

DeFond, Mark L. and K.R. Subramanyam. 1998. Auditor changes and discretionary accruals. *Journal of Accounting and Economics*, 25, 1 (February): 35–67.

DeGeorge, François, Yuan Ding, Thomas Jeanjean, and Hervé Stolowy. 2004. Do financial analysts curb earnings management? International evidence. Working Paper, HEC Paris.

DeGeorge, Francois, Jayendu Patel, and Richard Zeckhauser. 1999. Earnings management to exceed thresholds. *The Journal of Business*, 72, 1 (January): 1–33.

Deli, Daniel and James Booth. 2006. Managerial incentives and audit fees: Evidence from the mutual fund industry. A paper presented in the Auditing Midyear Conference, Los Angeles, CA.

Deloitte and Touche. 2005. *Under Control: Sustaining Compliance with Sar banes-Oxley in Year Two and Beyond.*

DeMarzo, Peter M., Michael J. Fishman, and Kathleen M. Hagerty. 1998. The optimal enforcement of insiders trading regulations. *Journal of Political Economy*, 106, 3 (June): 602–633.

Demers, Elizabeth A. and Philip Joos. 2006. IPO failure risk. Simon School. Working Paper No. FR 05-07. SSRN.com/abstract=656542.

Demougin, Dominique and C. Claude Fluet. 1998. Mechanism sufficient statistic in the risk-neutral agency problem. *Journal of Institutional and Theoretical Economics*, 154, 4 (December): 622–639.

Demougin, Dominique and Claude Fluet. 2001. Monitoring versus incentives. *European Economic Review*, 45, 9 (October): 1741–1764.

Dempsey, Jayendu S., Herbert G. Hunt, and Nicholas W. Schrodder. 1993. Earnings management and corporate ownership structure: An examination of extraordinary item reporting. *Journal of Business Finance and Accounting*, 20, 4 (June): 479–500.

Demsetz, Harold and Kenneth Lehn. 1985. The structure of corporate ownership: Causes and consequences. *Journal of Political Economy*, 93, 6 (December): 1155–1177.

Demski, Joel S. 1973. The general impossibility of normative accounting standards. *The Accounting Review*, 48, 4 (October): 718–723.

Demski, Joel. 1994. *Managerial Uses of Accounting Information*. Boston: Kluwer.

Demski, Joel S. 1998. Performance measure manipulation. *Contemporary Accounting Research*, 15, 3 (Fall): 261–285.

Demski, Joel S. 2002. Enron et al.—A comment. *Journal of Accounting and Public Policy*, 21, 2 (Summer): 129–130.

Demski, Joel S. 2003. Corporate conflicts of interest. *Journal of Economic Perspectives*, 17, 2 (June): 51–72.

Demski, Joel S. 2004. Endogenous expectations. *The Accounting Review*, 79, 2 (April): 519–539.

Demski, Joel S. and Ronald A. Dye. 1999. Risk, return, and moral hazard. *Journal of Accounting Research*, 37, 1 (Spring): 27–55.

Demski, Joel S., Stephen A. FirzGerald, Yuri Ijiri, Yumi Ijiri, and Haijin Lin. 2006. Quantum information and accounting information: Their salient features and conceptual applications. *Journal of Accounting and Public Policy*, 25, 4 (July-August): 435–464.

Demski, Joel S. and Hans Frimor. 1999. Performance measure garbling under renegotiation in multi-period agencies. *Journal of Accounting Research*, 37 (Supplement): 187–214.

Demski, Joel S., Hans Frimor, and David E.M. Sappington. 2004. Efficient manipulation in a repeated setting. *Journal of Accounting Research*, 42, 1 (March): 31–49.

Demski, Joel S., James M. Patell, and Mark A. Wolfson. 1984. Decentralized choice of monitoring systems. *The Accounting Review*, 59, 1 (January): 16–34.

Demski, Joel S. and David E.M. Sappington. 1984. Optimal incentive contracts with multiple agents. *Journal of Economic Theory*, 33, 1 (June): 152–171.

Demski, Joel S. and David E.M. Sappington. 1987. Delegated expertise. *Journal of Accounting Research*, 25, 1 (Spring): 68–89.

Demski, Joel S. and David E.M. Sappington. 1990. Fully revealing income measurement. *The Accounting Review*, 65, 2 (April): 363–383.

Demski, Joel S. and David E.M. Sappington. 1992. Further thoughts on fully revealing income measurement. *The Accounting Review*, 67, 3 (July): 628–630.

Demski, Joel S. and David E.M. Sappington. 1999. Summarization with errors: A perspective on empirical investigations of agency relationships. *Management Accounting Research*, 10, 1 (March): 21–37.

Demski, Joel S., David E.M. Sappington, and Pablo T. Spiller. 1988. Incentive schemes with multiple agents and bankruptcy constraints. *Journal of Economic Theory*, 44, 1 (February): 156–167.

Denis, David J. and Diane K. Denis. 1995. Performance changes following top management dismissals. *Journal of Finance*, 50, 4 (September): 1029–1057.

Denis, David J., Diane K. Denis, and Atulya Sarin. 1997. Ownership structure and top executive turnover. *Journal of Financial Economics*, 45, 2 (August): 193–221.

Denis, David J., Paul Hanouna, and Atulya Sarin. 2006. Is there a dark side to incentive compensation? *Journal of Corporate Finance*, 12, 3 (June): 467–488.

Denis, David J. and Timothy A. Kruse. 2000. Managerial discipline and corporate restructuring following performance declines. *Journal of Financial Economics*, 55, 3 (March): 391–424.

Denis, David J. and Atulya Sarin. 1999. Ownership and board structures in publicly traded corporations. *Journal of Financial Economics*, 52, 2 (May): 187–223.

Denis, David J. and J.M. Serrano, 1996. Active investors and management turnover following unsuccessful control contests. *Journal of Financial Economics*, 40, 2 (February): 239–266.

Dennis, Patrick J. and Deon Strickland. 2002. Who blinks in volatile markets, individuals or institutions? *Journal of Finance,* 57, 5 (2002): 1923–1949.

Dennis, Steven A. and Donald J. Mullineaux. 2000. Syndicated loans. *Journal of Financial Intermediation*, 9, 4 (October): 404–426.

Dennis, Steven, Debarshi Nandy, and Ian G. Sharpe. 2000. The determinants of contract terms in bank revolving credit agreements. *Journal of Financial and Quantitative Analysis*, 35, 1 (March): 87–110.

Depamphilis, Donald. 2003. *Mergers, Acquisitions, and Other Restructuring Activities*. Second edition. New York: Academic Press.

DePree, Chauncey M. and Terry C. Grant. 1999. Earnings management and ethical decision making: Choices in accounting for security investments. *Issues in Accounting Education*, 14, 4 (November): 613–640.

Desai, Hemang, Chris E. Hogan, and Michael S. Wilkins. 2006. The reputational penalty for aggressive accounting: Earnings restatements and management turnover. *The Accounting Review*, 81, 1 (January): 83–112.

Desai, Hemang and Prem C. Jain. 2004. Long-run stock returns following Briloff's analyses. *Financial Analysts Journal*, 60, 2 (March/April): 47–56.

Desai, Hemang, Srinivasan Krishnamurthy, and Kumar Venkataraman. 2006. Do short sellers target firms with poor earnings quality? Evidence from earnings restatements. *Review of Accounting Studies*, 11, 1 (March): 71–90.

Desai, Hemang, Shivaram Rajgopal, and Mohan Venkatachalam. 2004. Value-glamour and accruals mispricing: One anomaly or two? *The Accounting Review*, 79, 2 (April): 355–385.

Desai, Hemang, K. Ramesh, Ramu S. Thiagarajan, and Bala V. Balachandran. 2002. An investigation of the informational role of short interest in the Nasdaq market. *The Journal of Finance*, 57, 5 (October): 2263–2287.

Desai, Mihir A. 2003. The divergence between book and tax income. Working Paper, Harvard University.

Deutsch, Yuval. 2005. The impact of board composition on firms' critical decisions: A meta-analytic review. *Journal of Management Review*, 31, 3 (June): 424–444.

Dey, Aiyesha. 2005. Corporate governance and financial reporting credibility. Working Paper, University of Chicago.

Dhaliwal, Dan S., M. Frankel, and K. Trezevant. 1994. The taxable and book income motivations for a LIFO layer liquidation. *Journal of Accounting Research*, 32, 2 (Autumn): 278–289.

Dhaliwal, Dan S., Christie A. Gleason, and Lillian Mills. 2004. Last-chance earnings management: Using the tax expense to meet analysts' forecasts. *Contemporary Accounting Research*, 21, 2 (Summer): 431–459.

Dhaliwal, Dan S. and Shiing-wu Wang. 1992. The effect of book income adjustment in the 1986 alternative minimum tax on corporate financial reporting. *Journal of Accounting and Economics*, 15, 1 (March): 7–26.

Dharan, Bala G. 2003. Earnings management with accruals and financial engineering. http://www.ruf.rice.edu/~bala/files/EM_and_financial_Engineering-the_accountants_world_ICFAI_02-2003.pdf.

Diamond, Douglas W. 1985. Optimal release of information by firms. *Journal of Finance*, 40, 4 (September): 1071–1094.

Dichev, Ilia D., Anne L. Beatty, and Joseph Peter Weber. 2002. The role and characteristics of accounting-based performance pricing in private debt contracts. SSRN.com/abstract=318399.

Dichev, Ilia D. and Douglas J. Skinner. 2002. Large-sample evidence on the debt covenants hypothesis. *Journal of Accounting Research*, 40, 4 (September): 1091–1123.

Dietrich, Richard J., Steven J. Kachelmeier, Don N. Kleinmuntz, and Thomas J. Linsmeier. 2001. Market efficiency, bounded rationality, and supplemental business reporting disclosures. *Journal of Accounting Research*, 39, 2 (September): 243–268.

DiGabriele, James A. and Alan B. Eisner. 2005. Putting the E back in P/E ratios. *The Valuation Examiner*, (December): 24–27.

DiGabriele, James A. and Aron A. Gottesman. 2006. The Sarbanes-Oxley Act and the private company discount: An empirical investigation. SSRN.com/abstract=908061.

Dilla, William N., Diane J. Janvrin, and Cynthia G. Jeffrey. 2006. The impact of non-GAAP earnings and interactive data displays on earnings and investment judgments. SSRN.com/abstract=920121.

Dionne, Georges and Thouraya Triki. 2004. On risk management determinants: What really matters? HEC Montreal Risk Management Chair Working Paper, No. 04-04. SSRN.com/abstract=558761.

Dlugosz, Jennifer, Rudiger Fahlenbrach, Paul A. Gompers, and Andrew Metrick. 2006. Large blocks of stock: Prevalence, size, and measurement. *Journal of Corporate Finance*, 12, 3 (June): 594–618.

Dobler, Michael. 2004. Credibility of Managerial Forecast Disclosure—Game Theory and Regulative Implications. Working Paper, University Munch.

Dontoh, Alex. 1989. Voluntary disclosure. *Journal of Accounting, Auditing and Finance*, 4, 4 (Fall) 480–511.

Dontoh, Alex. 1992. Discussion of "The effects of line-of-business reporting on competition in oligopoly settings". *Contemporary Accounting Research*, 9, 1 (Fall): 24–28.

Dontoh, Alex, Suresh Radhakrishnan, and Joshua Ronen. 2004. The declining value-relevance of accounting information and non-information-based trading: An empirical analysis. *Contemporary Accounting Research*, 21, 4 (Winter): 795–812.

Dontoh, Alex and Joshua Ronen. 1993. Information content of accounting announcements. *The Accounting Review*, 68, 4 (October): 857–869.

Dontoh, Alex, Joshua Ronen, and Bharat Sarath. 2003. On the rationality of the post announcement drift. *Review of Accounting Studies*, 8, 1 (March): 69–104.

Dontoh, Alex, Joshua Ronen, and Bharat Sarath. 2007. Financial statements insurance. Working Paper, New York University.

Doogar, Rajib and Robert F. Easley. 1998. Concentration without differentiation: A new look at the determinants of audit market concentration. *Journal of Accounting and Economics*, 25, 3 (June): 235–253.

Dopuch, Nicholas, Raj Mashruwala, Chandra Seethamraju, and Tzachi Zach. 2006. Accrual determinants, sales changes and their impact on empirical accrual models. Working Paper.

Dopuch, Nicholas, Chandra Seethamraju, and Weihong Xu. 2003. An empirical assessment of the credibility premium associated with meeting or beating both time-series earnings expectations and analysts' forecasts. SSRN.com/abstract=471622.

Dopuch, Nicholas, Chandra Seethamraju, and Weihong Xu. 2005. The pricing of accruals for profit and loss firms. SSRN.com/abstract=663514.

Dowdell, Thomas D. and Jagan Krishnan. 2004. Former audit firm personnel as CFOSs: Effect on earnings management. *Canadian Accounting Perspectives*, 3, 1 (Spring): 117–142.

Doyle, Jeffrey T., Weili Ge, and Sarah E. McVay. 2006. Determinants of weaknesses in internal control over financial reporting. SSRN.com/abstract=770465.

Doyle, Jeffrey T., Russell J. Lundhom, and and Mark T. –oliman. 2003. The predictive value of expenses excluded from "pro forma" earnings. *Review of Accounting Studies*, 8, 2–3 (June–September): 145–174.

Doyle, Jeffrey T., Maureen McNichols, and Mark T. Soliman. 2004. Do managers use pro forma earnings to exceed analyst forecasts? Working Paper, University of Michigan.

D'Souza, Julia, John Jacob, and K. Ramesh. 2000. The use of accounting flexibility to reduce labor renegotiation costs and manage earnings. *Journal of Accounting and Economics*, 30, 2 (October): 187–208.

DuCharme, Larry L., Paul H. Malatesta, and Stephen E. Sefcik. 2002. Earnings management, stock issuance, and shareholder lawsuits. *Journal of Financial Economics*, 71, 1 (January): 27–49.

DuCharme, Larry L., Paul H. Malatesta, and Stephen E. Sefcik. 2004. Earnings management: IPO valuation and subsequent performance. *Journal of Accounting, Auditing and Finance*, 16, 4 (Fall): 369–396.

Duemes, Rogier. 2003. The effect of firm risk and management ownership on board composition and ownership concentration. Working Paper, Maastricht University, The Netherlands.

Dugar, Amitabh and Siva Nathan. 1995. The effect of investment bank relationships on financial analysts' earnings forecasts and investment recommendations. *Contemporary Accounting Research*, 12, 1 (Fall): 131–160.

Dugar, Amitabh, and Siva Nathan. 1996. Analysts' research reports: Caveat emptor. *The Journal of Investing,* (Winter): 13–22.

Duke, Joanne C. and Herbert G. Hunt. 1990. An empirical examination of debt covenant restrictions and accounting-related debt proxies. *Journal of Accounting and Economics*, 12, 1–3 (January): 45–63.

Durtschi, Cindy and Peter D. Easton. 2005. Earnings management? The shapes of the frequency distributions of earnings metrics are not evidence ipso facto. *Journal of Accounting Research*, 43, 4 (September): 557–592.

Duru, Augustine, Sattar A. Mansi, and David M. Reeb. 2005. Earnings-based bonus plans and the agency costs of debt. *Journal of Accounting and Public Policy*, 24, 5 (September-October): 431–447.

Dutta, Sunil and Frank Gigler. 2002. The effect of earnings forecasts on earnings management. *Journal of Accounting Research*, 40, 3 (June): 631–656.

Dutta, Sunil and Brett Trueman. 2002. The interpretation of information and corporate disclosure strategies. *Review of Accounting Studies*, 7, 1 (March): 75–96.

Dyck, Alexander, Adair Morse, and Luigi Zingales. 2007. Who blows the whistle on corporate fraud? NBER Working Paper No. W12882.

Dyck, Alexander I.J. and Luigi Zingales. 2002. The corporate governance role of the media. CRSP Working Paper, 543. SSRN.com/abstract=335602.

Dye, Ronald A. 1983. Communication and post-decision information. *Journal of Accounting Research*, 21, 2 (Autumn): 514–533.

Dye, Ronald A. 1984a. Inside trading and incentives. *The Journal of Business*, 57, 3 (July): 295–313.

Dye, Ronald A. 1984b. The trouble with tournaments. *Economic Inquiry*, 22, 1: 147–149.

Dye, Ronald A. 1984c. Relative performance evaluation and project selection. *Journal of Accounting Research*, 30, 1 (Spring): 27–52.

Dye, Ronald A. 1985a. Disclosure of nonproprietary information. *Journal of Accounting Research*, 23, 1 (Spring): 123–145.

Dye, Ronald A. 1985b. Strategic accounting choice and the effects of alternative financial reporting requirements. *Journal of Accounting Research*, 23, 2 (Autumn): 123–145.

Dye, Ronald A. 1986a. Proprietary and nonproprietary disclosures. *The Journal of Business*, 59, 2 Part 1 (April): 331–366.

Dye, Ronald A. 1986b. Optimal monitoring policies in agencies. *RAND Journal of Economics*, 17, 3 (Autumn): 339–350.

Dye, Ronald A. 1988. Earnings management in an overlapping generations model. *Journal of Accounting Research*, 26, 2 (Autumn): 195–235.

Dye, Ronald A. 1991. Informationally motivated auditor replacement. *Journal of Accounting and Economics*, 14, 4 (December): 347–374.

Dye, Ronald A. 1998a. Discussion of "On the frequency, quality, and informational role of mandatory financial reports." *Journal of Accounting Research*, 36, 3 (Supplement): 149–160.

Dye, Ronald A. 1998b. Investor sophistication and voluntary disclosures. *Review of Accounting Studies*, 3, 3 (September): 261–287.

Dye, Ronald A. 2001. An Evaluation of "Essays on disclosure" and the disclosure literature in accounting. *Journal of Accounting and Economics*, 32, 1-3 (December): 181–235.

Dye, Ronald A. 2002. Classifications manipulation and Nash accounting standards. *Journal of Accounting Research*, 40, 4 (September): 1125–1163.

Dye, Ronald A. and Sri S. Sridhar. 1995. Industry-wide disclosure dynamics. *Journal of Accounting Research*, 33, 1 (Spring): 157–174.

Dye, Ronald A. and Sri S. Sridhar. 2004. Reliability-relevance trade-offs and the efficiency of aggregation. *Journal of Accounting Research*, 42, 1 (March): 51–88.

Dye, Ronald A. and Robert Verrecchia. 1995. Discretion vs. uniformity: Choices among GAAP. *The Accounting Review*, 70, 3 (July): 389–415.

Eades, Kenneth M. 1982. Empirical evidence on dividends as a signal of firm value. *Journal of Financial and Quantitative Analysis*, 17, 4 (November): 471–500.

Easley, David, Soeren Hvidkjaer, and Maureen O'Hara. 2002. Is information risk a determinant of asset returns? *Journal of Finance*, 57, 5 (October): 2185–2221.

Easley, David and Maureen O'Hara. 2004. Information and the cost of capital. *Journal of Finance*, 59, 4 (August): 1553–1583.

Easley, David, Maureen O'Hara, and J. Paperman. 1998. Financial analysts and information-based trade. *Journal of Financial Markets*, 1, 2 (August): 175–201.

Easterbrook, Frank H. 1985. Insider trading as an agency problem, in John W. Pratt and Richard J. Zeckhauser eds., *Principals and Agents: The Structure of Business*. Boston: Harvard Business Press.

Easterbrook, John C., and Stacey R. Nutt. 1999. Inefficiency in analysts' earnings forecasts: Systematic misreaction or systematic optimism? *Journal of Finance*, 54, 5 (October): 1777–1797.

Easterwood, Cynthia M. 1998. Takeovers and incentives for earnings management: An empirical analysis. *Journal of Applied Business Research*, 14, 1 (Winter): 29–48.

Easton, Peter D., Peter H. Eddey, and Trevor S. Harris. 1993. An investigation of revaluations of tangible long-lived assets. *Journal of Accounting Research*, 31 (Supplement): 1–38.

Easton, Peter D., and Trevor S. Harris. 1991. Earnings as an explanatory variable for returns. *Journal of Accounting Research*, 29, 1 (Spring): 19–36.

Easton, Peter D., Pervin K. Shroff, and Gary Taylor. 2000. Permanent and transitory earnings, accounting recording lag, and the earnings coefficient. *Review of Accounting Studies*, 5, 4 (December): 281–300.

Eddey, Peter D. and Stephen L. Taylor. 1999. Directors' recommendations on takeover bids and the management of earnings: Evidence from Australian takeovers. *Abacus*, 35, 1 (February): 29–45.

Efendi, Jap, Anup Srivastava, and Edward P. Swanson. 2006. Why do corporate managers misstate financial statements? The role of option compensation, corporate governance, and other factors. *Journal of Financial Economics*, 83, 3 (September): 667–708.

Eilifsen, Aasmund, Kjell Henry Knivsfla, and Frode Saettem. 1999. Earnings manipulation: Cost of capital versus tax. *European Accounting Review*, 8, 3 (September): 481–491.

Eilifsen, Aasmund and William F. Messier. 2000. The incidence and detection of misstatements: A review and integration of archival research. *Journal of Accounting Literature*, 19: 1–43.

Einhorn, Eti. 2005. The nature of the interaction between mandatory and voluntary disclosures. *Journal of Accounting Research*, 43, 4 (September): 593–622.

Einhorn, Eti. 2007. Voluntary disclosure under uncertainty about the reporting objective. *Journal of Accounting and Economics*, 43, 2–3 (July): 245–274.

Eisenberg, Theodore and Jonathan R. Macey. 2004. Was Arthur Andersen different? An empirical examination of major accounting firm audits of large clients. *Journal of Empirical Legal Studies*, 1, 2 (July): 263–300.

Eisenberg, Theodore S., Stefan Sundgren, and Martin T. Wells. 1998. Larger board size and decreasing firm value in small firms. *Journal of Financial Economics*, 48 (April): 35–54.

Eldenburg, Leslie, Benjamin E. Hermalin, Michael S. Weisbach, and Marta Wosinka. 2004. Governance, performance objectives and organizational form: Evidence from hospitals. *Journal of Corporate Finance*, 10, 4 (September): 527–548.

Eldridge, Susan W. and Burch T. Kealey. 2005. SOX costs: Auditor attestation under Section 404. SSRN.com/abstract=743285.

El-Gazzar, Samir M. 1993. Stock market effects of the closeness to debt covenant restrictions resulting from capitalization of leases. *The Accounting Review*, 68, 2 (April): 258–272.

El-Gazzar, Samir M. and Victor Pastena. 1990. Negotiated accounting rules in private financial contracts. *Journal of Accounting and Economics*, 12, 4 (March): 381–396.

El-Gazzar, Samir M. and Victor Pastena. 1991. Factors affecting the scope and initial tightness of covenant restrictions in private lending agreements. *Contemporary Accounting Research*, 8, 1 (Fall): 132–151.

Elgers, Pieter T., Mary H. Lo, and Ray J. Pfeiffer Jr. 2001. Delayed security price adjustments to financial analysts' forecasts of annual earnings. *The Accounting Review*, 76, 4 (October): 613–632.

Elgers, Pieter T., Ray J. Pfeiffer Jr., and Susan L. Porter. 2003. Anticipatory income smoothing: A re-examination. *Journal of Accounting and Economics*, 35, 3 (August): 405–422.

Elitzur, Ramy. 1995. A classroom exercise on executive incentive compensation schemes. *Managerial and Decision Economics*, 16, 6 (November): 649–652.

Elitzur, Ramy. 2007. The accounting art of war: A multi-period model of earning manipulation and insider trading. Working paper, University of Toronto.

Elitzur, Ramy and Arieh Gavious. 2003. Contracting, signaling, and moral hazard: A model of entrepreneurs, "angels," and venture capitalists. *Journal of Business Venturing*, 18, 6 (November): 709–725.

Elitzur, Ramy and Varda Yaari. 1995. Managerial equity holdings, insider trading and earnings management in multi-period contract. *Journal of Economic Organization and Behavior*, 26, 2 (March): 201–219.

Elliott, Brooke W. 2004. Emphasis and information display of non-GAAP earnings measures: Effects on professional and non-professional investor judgments and decisions. SSRN.com/abstract=497548.

Elliott, John A. and Douglas J. Hanna. 1996. Repeated accounting write-offs and the information content of earnings. *Journal of Accounting Research*, 34 (Supplement): 135–155.

Elliott, John A. and Wayne H. Shaw. 1988. Write-off as accounting procedures to manage perceptions. *Journal of Accounting Research*, 26 (Supplement): 91–119.

Ely, Kirsten M. 1991. Interindustry differences in the relation between compensation and firm performance variables. *Journal of Accounting Research*, 29, 1 (Spring): 37–58.

Elyasiani, Elyas, Lin Guo, and Liang Tang. 2002. The determinants of debt maturity at issuance: A system-based model. *Review of Quantitative Finance and Accounting*, 19, 4 (December): 351–377.

Engel Ellen, Rachel M. Hayes, and Xue Wang. 2003. CEO turnover and properties of accounting information. *Journal of Accounting and Economics*, 36, 1-3 (December): 197–226.

Engel, Ellen, Rachel M. Hayes, and Xue Wang. 2007. The Sarbanes-Oxley Act and firms' go-ing-private decisions. *Journal of Accounting and Economics*, 441 (September): 116–145.

Entwistle, Gary M., Glenn D. Feltham, and Chima Mbagwu. 2006. Financial reporting regulation and the reporting of pro forma earnings. *Accounting Horizons*, 20, 1 (March): 39–55.

Erickson, Merle, Michelle Hanlon, and Edward L. Maydew. 2004. How much will firms pay for earnings that do not exist? Evidence of taxes paid on allegedly fraudulent earn-ings. *The Accounting Review*, 79, 2 (April): 387–408.

Erickson, Merle, Michelle Hanlon, and Edward L. Maydew. 2006. Is there a link between executive compensation and accounting fraud? *Journal of Accounting Research*, 44, 1 (March): 113–144.

Erickson, Merle and Shiing-wu Wang. 1999. Earnings management by acquiring firms in stock for stock mergers. *Journal of Accounting and Economics*, 27, 2 (April): 149–176.

Ertimur, Yonca and Stephen R. Stubben. 2005. Analysts' incentives to issue revenue and cash flows forecasts. Working Paper, Stanford University.

Espahbodi, Hassan, Pouran Espahbodi, Zabihollah Rezaee, and Hassan Tehranian. 2002. Stock price reaction and value relevance of recognition versus disclosure: The case of stock-based compensation. *Journal of Accounting and Economics*, 33, 3 (August): 343–373.

Ettredge, Michael L., Jim Heintz, Chan Li, and Susan W. Scholz. 2006. Auditor realign-ments accompanying implementation of SOX 404 reporting requirements. SSRN.com/abstract=874836.

Ettredge, Michael L., SooYoung Kwon, and David Smith. 2002. Competitive harm and companies' positions on SFAS 131. *Journal of Accounting, Auditing, & Finance*, 17, 2 (Spring): 93–110.

Ettredge, Michael L., Chan Li, and Lili Sun. 2005. Internal control quality and audit delay in the SOX era. SSRN.com/abstract=794669.

Ettredge, Michael L., Chan Li, and Lili Sun. 2007. CFO turnover following adverse SOX 404 opinions. SSRN.com/abstract=959215.

Evans, John H. 1980. Optimal contracts with costly conditional auditing. *Journal of Ac-counting Research*, 18 (supplement): 108–128.

Evans, John H., Kyonghee Kim, and Nandu J. Nagarajan. 2006. Uncertainty, legal liability, and incentive contracts. *The Accounting Review*, 81, 5 (October): 1045–1071.

Evans, John H. and Sri S. Sridhar. 1996. Multiple control systems, accrual accounting, and earnings management. *Journal of Accounting Research*, 34, 1 (Spring): 45–65.

Ewert, Ralf and Alfred Wagenhofer. 2005. Economic effects of tightening accounting standards to restrict earnings management. *The Accounting Review*, 80, 4 (October): 1101–1124.

Fairchild, Lisa and Joanne Li. 2005. Director quality and firm performance. *The Financial Review*, 40, 2 (May): 257–279.

Fairfax, Lisa. 2002a. The Sarbanes-Oxley Act as confirmation of recent trends in director and officer fiduciary obligations. *St. John's Law Review*, 76 (Fall): 953-979. SSRN.com/abstract=921061.

Fairfax, Lisa. 2002b. Form over substance? Officer certification and the promise of en-hanced personal accountability under the Sarbanes-Oxley Act. *Rutgers Law Review*, 55, 1 (Fall): 1–64.

Fairfax, Lisa. 2005. Sarbanes-Oxley, corporate federalism, and the declining significance of federal reforms on state director independence standards. *Ohio Northern University Law Review*, 31: 381-417. SSRN.com/abstract=921036.

Fairfield, Patricia, Scott Whisenant, and Teri Lombardi Yohn. 2002. The differential persistence of accruals and cash flows for future operating income versus future profitability. *Review of Accounting Studies*, 8, 2-3 (June): 221–243.

Faleye, Olubunmi. 2004. Are large boards poor monitors? Evidence from CEO turnover. SSRN.com/abstract=498285.

Fama, Eugene F. 1980. Agency problems and the theory of the firm. *Journal of Political Economy*, 88, 2 (April): 288–307.

Fama, Eugene F. 1998. Market efficiency, long-term returns, and behavioral finance. *Journal of Financial Economics*, 49, 3 (September): 283–306.

Fama, Eugene F. and Kenneth French. 1995. Size and book-to-market factors in earnings and returns. *Journal of Finance*, 50, 1 (March): 131–155.

Fama, Eugene F. and Kenneth French. 2000. Forecasting profitability and earnings. *The Journal of Business*, 73, 2 (April): 161–175.

Fama, Eugene F. and Michael C. Jensen. 1983. Separation of ownership and control. *The Journal of Law and Economics*, 26, 2 (June): 301–325.

Fama, Eugene F. and James D. MacBeth. 1973. Risk, return, and equilibrium: Empirical tests. *Journal of Political Economy*, 81, 3 (May-June): 607–636.

Fan, Joseph P.H. and T.J. Wong. 2002. Corporate ownership structure and the informativeness of accounting earnings in East Asia. *Journal of Accounting and Economics*, 33, 3 (August): 401–425.

Fan, Qintao. 2007. Earnings management and ownership retention for initial public offering firms: Theory and evidence. *The Accounting Review*, 82, 1 (January): 27–64.

Farber, David B. 2005. Restoring trust after fraud: Does corporate governance matter? *The Accounting Review*, 80, 2 (April): 539–561.

Farinha, Jorge. 2003. Corporate governance: A survey of the literature. SSRN.com/abstract=470801.

Farrell, Kathleen A. and David A. Whidbee. 2003. Impact of firm performance expectations on CEO turnover and replacement decisions. *Journal of Accounting and Economics*, 36, 1-3 (December): 165–196.

Faure-Grimoud, Antoine and Denis Gromb. 2004. Public trading and Private incentives. *Review of Financial Study*, 17, 4 (Winter): 985–1014.

Fee, Edward C. and Charles J. Hadlock. 2004. Management turnover across the corporate hierarchy. *Journal of Accounting and Economics*, 37, 1 (February): 3–38.

Fellingham, John C., Paul D. Newman, and Young Soo Suh. 1985. Contracts without memory in agency models. *Journal of Economic Theory*, 37, 2 (December): 340–355.

Felo, Andrew J., Srinivasan Krishnamurthy, and Steven A. Solieri. 2003. Audit committee characteristics and the perceived quality of financial reporting: An empirical analysis. SSRN.com/abstract=401240.

Feltham, Gerald A., Frank B. Gigler, and John S. Hughes. 1992. The effects of line-of-business reporting on competition in oligopoly settings. *Contemporary Accounting Research*, 9, 1 (Fall): 1–23.

Feltham, Gerald A., John S. Hughes, and Dan A. Simunic. 1991. Empirical assessment of the impact of auditor quality on the valuation of new issues. *Journal of Accounting and Economics*, 14, 4 (December): 375–399.

Feltham, Gerald A., Raffi Indjejikian, and Dhananjay Nanda. 2006. Dynamic incentives and dual-purpose accounting. *Journal of Accounting and Economics*, 42, 3 (December): 417–437.

Feltham, Jerald A. and Jinhan Pae. 2000. Analysis of the impact of accounting accruals on earnings uncertainty and response coefficients. *Journal of Accounting, Auditing and Finance*, 15, 3 (Summer): 199–220.

Feltham, Jerald A. and Martin Wu. 2000. Public reports, information acquisition by investors, and management incentives. *Review of Accounting Studies*, 5, 2 (June): 155–190.

Feltham, Jerald A. and Martin Wu. 2001. Incentive efficiency of stock versus options. *Review of Accounting Studies*, 6, 1 (March): 7–28.

Feltham, Gerald A. and J.Z. Xie. 1992. Voluntary financial disclosure in an entry game
with continua of types. *Contemporary Accounting Research*, 9, 1 (Fall): 46–80.

Feltham, Gerald A. and Jim Xie. 1994. Performance measure congruity in multi-task
principal/agent relations. *The Accounting Review*, 69, 3 (July): 429–453.

Feng, Mei. 2004. A rational explanation for why managers meet or slightly beat earnings
forecasts. Working Paper, University of Michigan.

Fenn, George W. and Nellie Liang. 2001. Corporate payout policy and managerial stock
incentives. *Journal of Financial Economics*, 60, 1 (April): 45–72.

Ferguson, Michael J., Kevin C.K. Lam, and Grace M. Lee. 2002. Voluntary disclosure by
state-owned enterprises listed on the stock exchange of Hong Kong. *Journal of International Financial Management and Accounting*, 13, 2 (Summer): 125–152.

Fern, Richard H., Betty C. Brown, and Steven W. Dickey. 1994. An empirical test of po-
litically-motivated income smoothing in the oil refining industry. *Journal of Applied
Business Research*, 10, 1: (Winter): 92–100.

Feroz, Ehsan H., Kyungjoo Park, and Victor S. Pastena. 1991. The financial and market effects of the SEC's Accounting and Auditing Enforcement Releases. *Journal of Accounting Research*, 29, 3 (Supplement): 107–142.

Ferreira, Daniel and Marcelo Rezende. 2006. Corporate strategy and information disclosure. *RAND Journal of Economics*, forthcoming.

Ferri, Fabrizio. 2004. Structure of option repricings: Determinants and consequences.
EFMA 2004 Basel Meeting Paper; 14th Annual Conference on Financial Economics
and Accounting (FEA).

Ferri, Fabrizio. 2005. The structure of option repricings: Determinants and consequences.
A Ph.D. dissertation. New York University.

Ferris, Stephen P. and Murali Jagannathan. 2001. The incidence and determinants of multiple corporate directorships. *Applied Economics Letters*, 8, 1 (January), 31–35.

Ferris, Stephen P., Murali Jagannathan, and A.C. Pritchard. 2003. Too busy to mind the
business? Monitoring by directors with multiple board appointments. *Journal of Finance*, 58, 3 (June): 1087–1112.

Ferris, Stephen P., Robert M. Lawless, and Anil K. Makhija. 2001. Derivative lawsuits as a
corporate governance mechanism: Empirical evidence on board changes surrounding
filings, *Contracting and Organizations Research Institute*, Working Paper #2001-03,
University of Missouri-Columbia.

Ferris, Stephen P. and Adam C. Pritchard. 2001. Stock price reactions to securities fraud
class actions under the Private Securities Litigation Reform Act. Michigan Law and
Economics Research Paper 01-009. SSRN.com/abstract=288216.

Fershtman, Chaim and Kenneth L. Judd. 1987. Equilibrium incentives in oligopoly.
American Economic Review, 77, 5 (December): 927–940.

Fich, Eliezer M. 2005. Are some outside directors better than others? Evidence form director appointments by Fortune 1000 firms. *The Journal of Business*, 78, 5 (September): 1943–1971.

Fich, Eliezer M. and Anil Shivdasani. 2005. The impact of stock-option compensation for
outside directors on firm value. *The Journal of Business*, 78, 6 (November): 2229–2254.

Fich, Eliezer M. and Anil Shivdasani. 2006. Are busy boards effective monitors? *Journal
of Finance*, 61, 2 (April): 689- 724.

Fich, Eliezer M. and Lawrence J. White. 2001. Why do CEO's reciprocally sit on each
other boards? Working Paper, New York University.

Fields, Andrew M. and Phyllis Y. Keys. 2003. The emergence of corporate governance from Wall St. to Main St.: Outside directors, board diversity, earnings management, and managerial incentives to bear risk. *The Financial Review*, 38, 1 (February): 1–24.

Fields, Thomas D., Thomas Z. Lys, and Linda Vincent. 2001. Empirical research on accounting choice. *Journal of Accounting and Economics*, 31, 1-3 (September): 255–307.

Financial Accounting Standards Board. 1987. Statement of Financial Accounting Concepts, 1: *Objectives of Financial Reporting by Business Enterprises* (FASB, Stamford, CT).

Finger, Catherine A. 1994. The ability of earnings to predict future earnings and cash flows. *Journal of Accounting Research*, 32, 2 (Autumn): 210–223.

Firth, Michael and Andrew Smith. 1992. The accuracy of profit forecasts in initial public offering prospectuses. *Accounting and Business Research*, 22, 87 (Summer): 239–247.

Fisch, Gill E. and Caroline M. Jentile. 2003. The qualified legal compliance committee: Using the attorney conduct rules to restructure the board of directors. *Duke Law Journal*, 53: 517–584.

Fischer, Christopher. 2000. Why do companies go public? Empirical evidence from Germany's Neuer Market. SSRN.com/abstract=229529.

Fischer, Paul E. and Steven J. Huddart. 2005. Optimal contracting with endogenous social norms. SSRN.com/abstract=528842.

Fischer, Paul E. and Philip Stocken. 2004. Effect of investor speculation on earnings management. *Journal of Accounting Research*, 42, 5 (December): 843–870.

Fischer, Paul E. and Robert E. Verrecchia. 2000. Reporting bias. *The Accounting Review*, 75, 2 (April): 229–245.

Fischer, Paul E. and Robert E. Verrecchia. 2004. Disclosure bias. *Journal of Accounting and Economics*, 38, 1-3 (December): 223–250.

Fishman, Michael J. and Katherine M. Hagerty. 1989. Disclosure decisions by firms and the competition for price efficiency. *Journal of Finance*, 44, 3 (July): 633–646.

Fishman, Michael J. and Katherine M. Hagerty. 1992. Insider trading and the efficiency of stock prices. *RAND Journal of Economics*, 23, 1 (Spring): 106–122.

Fisman, Raymond J., Rakesh Khurana, and Matthew Rhodes-Kropf. 2005. Governance and CEO turnover: Do something or do the right thing? EFA 2005 Moscow Meeting Paper. SSRN.com/abstract=656085.

Fleischer, Victor. 2006. Options backdating, tax shelters, and corporate culture. University of Colorado Law Legal Studies Research Paper No. 06-38. SSRN.com/abstract=939914.

Forbes, Daniel P. and Frances J. Milliken. 1999. Cognition and corporate governance: Understanding boards of directors as strategic decision-making groups. *The Academy of Management Review*, 24, 3 (July): 489–505.

Foster, George. 1979. Briloff and the capital market. *Journal of Accounting Research*, 17, 1: (Spring): 262–274.

Foster, George. 1987. Rambo IX: Briloff and the capital market. *Journal of Accounting, Auditing and Finance*, 2, 4 (Fall): 409–430.

Foster, George, Chris Olsen, and Terry Shevlin. 1984. Earnings releases, anomalies, and the behavior of security returns. *The Accounting Review*, 59, 4 (October): 574–603.

Francis, Jennifer. 1990. Corporate compliance with debt covenants. *Journal of Accounting Research*, 28, 2 (Autumn): 326–347.

Francis, Jennifer. 1994. Discussion of lawsuits against auditors. *Journal of Accounting Research*, 32 (Supplement): 95–102.

Francis, Jennifer. 2001. Discussion of empirical research on accounting choice. *Journal of Accounting and Economics*, 31, 1-3 (September): 309–319.

Francis, Jennifer, Qi Chen, Donna R. Philbrick, and Richard H. Willis. 2004. *Security Analyst Independence*. Research Foundation of CFA Institute.

Francis, Jennifer, Douglas J. Hanna, and Linda Vincent. 1996. Causes and effects of discretionary asset write-offs. *Journal of Accounting Research*, 34, 1 (Spring): 117–134.

Francis, Jennifer, Ryan LaFond, Per Olsson, and Katherine Schipper. 2005. The market pricing of accruals quality. *Journal of Accounting and Economics*, 39, 2 (June): 295–327.

Francis, Jennifer, Dhananjay Nanda, and Xin Wang. 2006. Re-examining the effects of regulation fair disclosure using foreign listed firms to control for concurrent shocks. *Journal of Accounting and Economics*, 41, 3 (September): 271–292.

Francis, Jennifer and Donna Philbrick. 1993. Analysts' decisions as a product of a multi-task environment. *Journal of Accounting Research*, 31, 2 (Autumn): 216–230.

Francis, Jennifer, Donna Philbrick, and Katherine Schipper. 1994. Shareholder Litigation and Corporate Disclosures. *Journal of Accounting Research*, 32, 2 (Autumn): 137–164.

Francis, Jennifer, Katherine Schipper, and Linda Vincent. 2002. Earnings announcements and competing information. *Journal of Accounting and Economics*, 33 3 (August): 313–342.

Francis, Jennifer, Katherine Schipper, and Linda Vincent. 2003. The relative and incremental explanatory power of alternative (to earnings) performance measures for returns. *Contemporary Accounting Research*, 21, 1 (Spring): 121–164.

Francis, Jennifer and Leonard Soffer. 1997. The relative informativeness of analysts stocks' recommendations and earnings forecast revisions. *Journal of Accounting Research*, 35, 2 (Autumn): 193–211.

Francis, Jere R. 2006. Are auditors compromised by nonaudit services? Assessing the evidence. *Contemporary Accounting Research*, 23, 3 (Fall): 747–760.

Francis, Jere R. and Bin Ke. 2006. Disclosure of fees paid to auditors and the market valuation of earnings surprises. *Review of Accounting Studies*, 11, 4 (December): 495–523.

Francis, Jere R. and Jagan Krishnan. 1999. Accounting accruals and auditor reporting conservatism. *Contemporary Accounting Research*, 16, 1 (Spring): 135–165.

Francis, Jere R., Edward Maydew, and H. Sparks. 1999. The role of Big 6 Auditors in the credible reporting of accruals. *Auditing: A Journal of Practice and Theory*, 18, 2 (Fall): 17–34.

Francis, Jere R. and Daniel Simon. 1987. A test of audit pricing in the small-client segment of the U.S. audit market. *The Accounting Review*, 62, 1 (January): 145–157.

Francis, Jere R. and Dechun Wang. 2004. Investor protection, auditor conservatism and earnings quality: Are big 4 auditors conservative only in the United States? Working Paper, University of Toronto.

Francis, Jere R. and Earl R. Wilson. 1988. Auditor changes: A joint test of theories relating to agency costs and auditor differentiation. *The Accounting Review*, 63, 4 (October): 663–682.

Frank, Mary Margaret, Luann J. Lynch, and Sonja Olhoft Rego. 2004. Does aggressive financial reporting accompany aggressive tax reporting (and vice versa)? Working Paper, University of Iowa.

Frank, Mary Margaret and Sonja O. Rego. 2006. Do managers use the valuation allowance account to manage earnings around certain earnings targets? *Journal of the American Taxation Association*, 28, 1 (Spring): 43–65.

Frankel, Richard M., Marilyn F. Johnson, and Karen K. Nelson. 2002. The relation between auditors' fees for non-audit services and earnings management. *The Accounting Review*, special issue on quality of earnings, 77, 4 (October): 71–105.

Frankel, Richard M., S.P. Kothari, and Joseph Peter Weber. 2006. Determinants of the informativeness analyst research. *Journal of Accounting and Economics*, 41, 1-2 (April): 29–54.

Frankel, Richard M. and M.C. Lee. 1998. Accounting valuation, market expectation, and cross-sectional stock returns. *Journal of Accounting and Economics*, 25, 3 (June): 283–319.

Frankel, Richard M. and Xu Li. 2004. Characteristics of a firm's information environment and the information asymmetry between insiders and outsiders. *Journal of Accounting and Economics*, 37, 2 (June): 229–259.

Frankel, Richard M., Maureen McNichols, and Peter Wilson. 1995. Discretionary disclosure and external financing. *The Accounting Review*, 70, 1 (January): 135–150.

Frankel, Richard M., Sarah E. McVay, and Mark T. Soliman. 2006. Street earnings and board independence. Working Paper, New York University.

Frankel, Richard M. and Sugata Roychowdhury. 2006. Testing the clientele effect: An explanation for non-GAAP earnings adjustments used to compute I/B/E/S earnings. SSRN.com/abstract=833304.

Frankel, Tamar. 2006. Using Sarbanes-Oxley Act to reward honest corporations. Boston University School of Law Working Paper No. 06-08. SSRN.com/abstract=897783.

Frederickson, James R., Frank D. Hodge, and Jamie H. Pratt. 2006. The evolution of stock option accounting: Disclosure, voluntary recognition, mandated recognition, and management disavowals. *The Accounting Review*, 81, 5 (October): 1073–1093.

Frederickson, James R. and Jeffrey S. Miller. 2004. Pro Forma earnings disclosures: Do analysts and nonprofessional investors react differently? *The Accounting Review*, 79, 3 (July): 667–686.

Freeman, Robert N. and Senyo Y. Tse. 1992. A nonlinear model of security price responses to unexpected earnings. *Journal of Accounting Research*, 30, 2 (Autumn): 185–209.

Freixas, Xavier, Roger Guesnerie, and Jean J. Tirole. 1985. Planning under incomplete information and the ratchet effect. *Review of Economic Studies*, 52, 2 (April): 173–191.

Friebel, Guido, and Sergei M. Guriev. 2005. Earnings manipulation and incentives in firms. EFA 2005 Moscow Meeting Paper. SSRN.com/abstract=637221.

Fried, Dov. 1984. Incentives for information production and disclosure in duopolistic environment. *Quarterly Journal of Economics*, 99, 2 (May): 367–381.

Friedlan, John. 1994. Accounting choices of issuers of initial public offerings. *Contemporary Accounting Research*, 11, 1 (Summer): 1–31.

Froot, Kenneth A., Andre F. Perold, and Jeremy C. Stein. 1992. Shareholder trading practices and corporate investment horizons. *Journal of Applied Corporate Finance*, 5, 2 (Summer) 42–58.

Froot, Kenneth A., David S. Scharfstein, and Jeremy C. Stein. 1991. Risk management: Coordinating corporate investment and financing policies. *Journal of Finance*, 48, 5 (December): 1629–1658.

Frost, Carol A. and Victor L. Bernard. 1989. The role of debt covenants in assessing the economic consequences of limiting capitalization of exploration costs. *The Accounting Review*, 64, 4 (October): 788–808.

Frost, Carol A. and Grace Pownall. 1994. Accounting disclosure practices in the United States and the United Kingdom. *Journal of Accounting Research*, 32, 1 (Spring): 75–102.

Fudenberg, Drew, Bengt Holmström, and Paul Milgrom. 1990. Short-term contracts and long-term agency relationships. *Journal of Economic Theory*, 51, 1 (June): 1–31.

Fudenberg, Drew and David Kreps. 1987. Reputation in the simultaneous play of multiple opponents. *The Review of Economics Studies*, 54, 4 (October): 541–568.

Fudenberg, Drew and Jean J. Tirole. 1986. A "signal-jamming" theory of predation. *RAND Journal of Economics*, 17, 3 (Autumn): 366–376.

Fudenberg, Drew and Jean J. Tirole. 1995. A theory of income and dividend smoothing based on incumbency rents. *Journal of Political Economy*, 103, 1 (February): 75–93.

Fuller, Joseph. 2004. So, why be public? *Directors and Boards (Winter)*. SSRN.com/abstract=499942.

Gabrielsen, Gorm, Jeffrey D. Gramlich, and Thomas Plenborg. 2002. Managerial ownership, information content of earnings, and discretionary accruals in a non-US Setting. *Journal of Business Finance and Accounting*, 29, 7-8 (September/October): 967–988.

Gal-Or, Esther. 1985. Information sharing in oligopoly. *Econometrica*, 53, 2 (March): 329–343.

Galbraith, Craig S. and Gregory B. Merrill. 1996. The politics of forecasting: Managing the truth. *California Management Review*, 38, 2 (Winter): 29–43.

Gale, Douglas and Martin Hellwig. 1985. Incentive-compatible debt contracts: The one-period problem. *Review of Economic Studies*, 52, 4 (October): 647–663.

Galindo, Raquel. 2005. The echoing effects of the Sarbanes-Oxley Act: Are the high costs of its implementation worth it. SSRN.com/abstract=728439.

Gao, Pengjie and Ronald E. Shrieves. 2002. Earnings management and executive compensation: A case of overdose of option and underdose of salary? A paper presented in the EFA Berlin Meeting. SSRN.com/abstract=302843.

Gao, Yanmin. 2006. Is more monitoring better? AAA 2006 Financial Accounting and Reporting Section (FARS) Meeting. SSRN.com/abstract=815025.

Garrie, Daniel and Matthew Armstrong. 2006. Electronic discovery and the challenge posted by the Sarbanes Oxley Act. *UCLA Journal of Law and Technology*, forthcoming.

Garrod, Neil. 2002. Environmental contingencies and sustainable modes of corporate governance. SSRN.com/abstract=215951.

Garza, Gomez Xavier, Masashi Okumura, and Michio Kunimura. 2000. Discretionary accrual models and the accounting process. *Kobe Economic and Business Review*, 45: 103-135. SSRN.com/abstract=209073.

Garvey Gerald, T., Simon Grant, and Stephen P. King. 1999. Myopic corporate behaviour with optimal management incentives. *Journal of Industrial Economics*, 47, 2 (June) 231–250.

Gasparino, Charles. 2005. *Blood on the Street,* New York: Free Press.

Gaver, Jennifer J. 1998. Discussion of "Discretionary accounting choices and CEO compensation." *Contemporary Accounting Research,* 15, 3 (Fall): 253–260.

Gaver, Jennifer J. and Kenneth M. Gaver. 1993. Additional evidence on the association between the investment opportunity set and corporate financing, dividend, and compensation polices. *Journal of Accounting and Economics*, 16, 1-3 (April): 125–160.

Gaver, Jennifer J. and Kenneth M. Gaver. 1998. The stock market reaction to performance plan adoptions. *The Accounting Review*, 67, 1 (January): 172–182.

Gaver, Jennifer J., Kenneth M. Gaver, and Jeffrey R. Austin. 1995. Additional evidence on bonus plans and income management. *Journal of Accounting and Economics*, 19, 1 (February): 3–28.

Gaver, Jennifer J. and Jeffrey S. Paterson. 2000. Earnings management under changing regulatory regimes: State accreditation in the insurance industry. *Journal of Accounting and Public Policy*, 19, 4-5 (Winter): 399–420.

Gaver, Jennifer J. and Jeffrey S. Paterson. 2001. The association between external monitoring and earnings management in the property-casualty insurance industry. *Journal of Accounting Research*, 39, 2 (September): 269–282.

Gaver, Jennifer J. and Jeffrey S. Paterson. 2004. Do insurers manipulate loss reserves to mask solvency problems? *Journal of Accounting and Economics*, 37, 3 (September): 393–416.

Gavious, Arieh, Joshua Ronen, and Varda Yaari. 2002. Valuation and growth rate manipulation. *Asian-Pacific Journal of Accounting and Economics*, 9, 3 (June): 87–104.

Ge, Weili and Sarah E. McVay. 2005. The disclosure of material weaknesses in internal control after the Sarbanes-Oxley Act. *Accounting Horizons*, 19, 3 (September): 137–158.

Géczy, Christopher C., Bernadette A. Minton, and Catherine Schrand. 2006. The use of multiple risk management strategies: Evidence from the natural gas industry. *The Journal of Risk*, 8, 3 (Spring): 19–54.

Geiger, Marshall A., David S. Marshall, and Brendan T. O'Connell. 2005. The auditor to client revolving door and earnings management. *Journal of Accounting, Auditing and Finance*, 20, 1 (Winter): 1–26.

Geiger, Marshall A. and David S. North. 2006. Does hiring a new CFO change things? An investigation of changes in discretionary accruals. *The Accounting Review*, 81, 4 (July): 781–809.

Gelb, David S. and Paul Zarowin. 2002. Corporate disclosure policy and the informativeness of stock price. *Review of Accounting Studies*, 7, 1 (March): 33–52.

Gerety, Mason and Kenneth Lehn. 1997. The causes and consequences of financial fraud. *Managerial and Decision Economics*, 18, 7-8 (November/December): 587–599.

Gertner, Robert and Steven N. Kaplan. 1998. The value maximizing board. *Corporate Governance Today*, the Sloan Project on Corporate Governance at Columbia Law School.

Ghose, Anindya. 2006. Information disclosure and regulatory compliance: Economic issues and research directions. SSRN.com/abstract=921770.

Ghosh, Aloke, Sanjay Kallapur, and Doocheol Moon. 2006. Provision of non-audit services by auditors: Economic efficiency or managerial opportunism? Working Paper, Baruch College.

Ghosh, Aloke and Martien Jan Peter Lubberink. 2006. Timeliness and mandated disclosures on internal controls under Section 404. SSRN.com/abstract=931896.

Ghosh, Aloke and Doocheol Moon. 2005. Auditor tenure and perceptions of audit quality. *The Accounting Review*, 80, 2 (April): 585–612.

Gibbins, Michael, Susan McCracken, and Steve Salterio. 2005. Negotiations over accounting issues: The congruency of audit partner and chief financial officer recalls. *Auditing: A Journal of Practice and Theory*, 24 (Supplement): 171–193.

Gibbins, Michael, Alan J. Richardson, and John Waterhouse. 1990. The management of corporate financial disclosure: Opportunism, ritualism, policies, and processes. *Journal of Accounting Research*, 32 (Spring): 75–102.

Gibbins, Michael, Alan J. Richardson, and John Waterhouse. 1992. *The Management of Financial Disclosure: Theory and Perspectives*. The Canadian Certified General Accountants' Research Foundation. Research Monograph Number 20.

Gibbons, Robert and Kevin J. Murphy. 1992a. Does executive compensation affect investment? *Journal of Applied Corporate Finance*, 5, 2 (June): 99–109.

Gibbons, Robert and Kevin J. Murphy. 1992b. Optimal incentive contracts in the presence of career concerns: Theory and evidence. *Journal of Political Economy*, 100, 3 (June): 468–505.

Gigler, Frank. 1994. Self-enforcing voluntary disclosures. *Journal of Accounting Research*, 32, 2 (Autumn): 224–241.

Gigler, Frank B. and Thomas Hemmer. 2001. Conservatism, optimal disclosure policy, and the timeliness of financial reports. *The Accounting Review*, 76, 4 (October): 471–493.

Gigler, Frank B. and Thomas Hemmer. 2002. Informational costs and benefits of creating separately identifiable operating segments. *Journal of Accounting and Economics*, 33, 1 (February): 69–90.

Gigler, Frank B. and Thomas Hemmer. 2004. On the value of transparency in agencies with renegotiation. *Journal of Accounting Research*, 42, 5 (December): 871–893.

Gigler, Frank B. and Mark Penno. 1995. Imperfect competition in audit market and its effect on the demand for audit-related services. *The Accounting Review*, 70, 2 (April): 317–336.

Gilkeson, James H. and Mitchell Stengel. 1999. Factors influencing a firm's adoption of new reporting requirements: SFAS 122 and mortgage servicers. Economics Working Paper 99-2. University of Central Florida. www.occ.treas.gov/ftp/workpaper/wp99-2.pdf.

Gillan, Kayla J. 2003. A journey of thousand miles. A speech given in the Annual Meeting of the National Association of State Boards of Accountancy. http://www.pcaobus.org/News_and_Events/Events/2003/Speech/10-27_Gillan.aspx.

Gillan, Stuart L. 2006. Recent developments in corporate governance: An overview. *Journal of Corporate Finance*, 12, 3 (June): 381–402.

Gillan, Stuart L., Jay C. Hartzell, and Laura T. Starks. 2003. Explaining corporate governance: Boards, bylaws, and charter provisions. Weinberg Center for Corporate Governance Working Paper, NYU.

Gillan, Stuart L. and Laura T. Starks. 1998. A survey of shareholder activism: Motivation and empirical evidence. *Contemporary Finance Digest*, 2, 3 (Autumn): 10–34.

Gillan, Stuart L. and Laura T. Starks. 2000. Corporate governance proposals and shareholder activism: The role of institutional investors. *Journal of Financial Economics*, 57, 2 (August): 275–305.

Gillan, Stuart L. and Laura T. Starks. 2003. Corporate governance, corporate ownership, and the role of institutional investors: A global perspective. *Journal of Applied Finance*, 13, 2, (Fall/Winter): 4–22.

Gillan, Stuart L. and Laura T. Starks. 2007. The evolution of shareholder activism in the United States. *Journal of Applied Corporate Finance*, 19, 1 (Winter): 55–73.

Gilson, Stuart C. 1989. Management turnover and financial distress. *Journal of Financial Economics*, 25, 2 (December): 241–262.

Gilson, Stuart C. 1990. Bankruptcy, boards, banks, and blockholders: Evidence on changes in corporate ownership and control when firms default. *Journal of Financial Economics*, 27, 2 (October): 355–387.

Gilson, Stuart C. and Michael R. Vetsuypens. 1993. CEO compensation in financially distressed firms: An empirical analysis. *Journal of Finance*, 48, 2 (June): 425–458.

Gilson, Stuart C. and Jerold B. Warner. 1998. Private versus public debt: Evidence from firms that replace bank loans with junk bonds. SSRN.com/abstract=140093.

Givoly, Dan and Carla Hayn. 2000. The changing time-series properties of earnings, cash flows and accruals: Has financial reporting become more conservative? *Journal of Accounting and Economics*, 29, 3 (June): 287–320.

Givoly, Dan and Carla Hayn. 2002. Rising conservatism: Implications for financial analysis. *Financial Analysts Journal*, 58, 1 (January/February): 56–74.

Givoly, Dan, Carla Hayn, and Ashok Natarajan. 2007. Measuring reporting conservatism. *The Accounting Review*, 82, 1 (January): 65–106.

Givoly, Dan, Joshua Ronen, and Alan Schiff. 1978. Does audit involvement affect the quality of interim report numbers? *Journal of Accounting, Auditing, and Finance*, 1, 4 (Summer): 361–372.

Gjesdal, Froystein. 1981. Accounting for stewardship. *Journal of Accounting Research*, 19, 1 (Spring): 208–231.

Gjesdal, Froystein. 1989. Piecewise linear incentive schemes. In Seppo Honkapohja ed., *Information and Incentives in Organizations*. Base, UK: Blackwell. Ch. 2.

Glassman, Cynthia. 2002. Sarbanes-Oxley and the idea of "good" governance. A speech given at the American Society of Corporate Secretaries, Washington DC, September 27. http://www.sec.gov/news/speech/spch586.htm.

Glassman, Cynthia. 2006a. Corporate governance in the United States. Remarks before the ECGI/ALI 2006 Transatlantic Corporate Governance Conference, Brussels, Belgium, June 27.

Glassman, Cynthia. 2006b. Observations of an economist commissioner on leaving the SEC. A speech given at National Economists Club, Washington, DC, July 6. http://www.sec.gov/news/speech/2006/spch070606cag.htm.

Gleason, Cristi A. and Lillian F. Mills. 2004. Evidence of differing market responses to meeting or beating targets through tax expense management. SSRN.com/abstract=521962.

Gleason, Cristi A. and Lillian F. Mills. 2006. Do audit-provided tax services compromise auditor independence with respect to tax expense? Working Paper, University of Iowa and University of Texas.

Glosten, Lawrence R. and Paul R. Milgrom. 1985. Bid, ask, and transaction prices in a specialist market with heterogeneously informed traders. *Journal of Financial Economics*, 14, 1 (March): 71–100.

Godfrey, Jayne M. and Kerrie L. Jones. 1999. Political cost influences on income smoothing via extraordinary items classification. *Accounting and Finance*, 39, 3 (November): 229–253.

Godfrey, Jayne M., Paul R. Mather, and Alan L. Ramsay. 2003. Earnings and impression management in financial reports: The case of CEO changes. *Abacus*, 39, 1 (February): 95–123.

Goel, Anand Mohan and Anjan V. Thakor. 2003. Why do firms smooth earnings? *The Journal of Business*, 76, 1 (January): 151–192.

Goel, Anand M. and Anjan V. Thakor. 2007. Overconfidence, CEO selection, and corporate governance. AFA 2007 Chicago Meeting Paper. SSRN.com/abstract=890274.

Goldman, Eitan and Steven L. Slezak. 2006. An equilibrium model of incentive contracts in the presence of information manipulation. *Journal of Financial Economics*, 80, 3 (June): 603–626.

Gompers, Paul A., Joy L. Ishii, and Andrew Metrick. 2003. Corporate governance and equity prices. *The Quarterly Journal of Economics*, 118, 1 (February) 107–155.

Gompers, Paul A. and Andrew Metrick. 2001. Institutional investors and equity prices. *Quarterly Journal of Economics*, 116, 1 (February): 229–259.

Gonedes, Nicholas J. 1972. Income-smoothing behavior under selected stochastic processes. *The Journal of Business*, 45, 4 (October): 570–584.

Gong, Goujin, Henock Louis, and Amy X. Sun. 2007. Earnings management and firm performance following open-market repurchases. *Journal of Finance*, forthcoming.

Gooch, Roxanne and Robert C. Lipe. 2003. An empirical comparison of grant-date and exercise-date measurements in employee stock option accounting. Working Paper, University of Oklahoma.

Gopalakrishnan,V. and Mohinder Parkash. 1995. Borrower and lender perceptions of accounting information in corporate lending agreements. *Accounting Horizons*, 9, 1 (March): 13–26.

Gordon, Elizabeth A. and Elaine Henry. 2005. Related party transactions and earnings management. SSRN.com/abstract=662234.

Gordon, Elizabeth A., Elaine Henry, and Darius Palia. 2004. Related party transactions: Associations with corporate governance and firm value. EFA 2004 Maastricht Meeting Paper No. 4377. SSRN.com/abstract=558983.

Gordon, Jeffrey N. 2003. Governance failures of the Enron board and the new information order of Sarbanes-Oxley. Columbia Law and Economics Working Paper No. 216; Harvard Law and Economics Discussion Paper No. 416. SSRN.com/abstract=391363.

Gordon, Lawrence A., Martin P. Loeb, William Lucyshyn, and Tashfeen Sohail. 2006. The impact of the Sarbanes-Oxley Act on the corporate disclosures of information security activities. *Journal of Accounting and Public Policy,* 25, 5 (September-October): 503–530.

Gordon, Myron J. 1964. Postulates, principles and research in accounting. *The Accounting Review* 39, 2 (April): 251–263.

Gore, Pelham, Fauziah M. Taib, and Paul, A. Taylor. 1999. Accounting for goodwill: What factors influence management preferences. SSRN.com/abstract=144608.

Gorton, Gary B. and George G. Pennacchi. 1995. Banks and loan sales: Marketing non-marketable assets. *Journal of Monetary Economics*, 35, 3 (June): 389–411.

Goyal, Vidham K. and Chul W. Park. 2002. Board leadership structure and CEO turnover. *Journal of Corporate Finance*, 8, 1 (January): 49–66.

Grace, Elizabeth V. 1990. Property-liability insurer reserve errors: A theoretical and empirical analysis. *Journal of Risk and Insurance*, 57, 1 (March): 28–46.

Graham, John R. 1999. Herding among investment newsletters: Theory and evidence. *The Journal of Finance*, 54, 1 (February): 237–268.

Graham, John R., Campbell R. Harvey, and Shiva Rajgopal. 2005. The economic implications of corporate financial reporting. *Journal of Accounting and Economics*, 40, 1-3 (December): 3–73.

Gramlich, Jeffrey D. 1991. The effect of the alternative minimum tax book income adjustment on accrual decisions. *The Journal of the American Taxation Association*, 13, 1 (Spring): 36–56.

Gramlich, Jeffrey D. 1992. Discussion of earnings management and the corporate alternative minimum tax. *Journal of Accounting Research,* 30 (Supplement): 154–160.

Gramlich, Jeffrey D., M.L. McAnally, and J. Thomas. 2001. Balance sheet management: The case of short-term obligations reclassified as long term debt. *Journal of Accounting Research*, 39, 2 (September): 283–295.

Grant, Julia, Garen Markarian, and Antonio Parbonetti. 2007. CEO risk-related incentives and income smoothing. SSRN.com/abstract=975266.

Gray, Robert. 2004. The allowance for loan ˈlosses and earnings management. SSRN.com/abstract=598482.

Gary, Robert P. and Frank L. Clarke. 2004. A methodology for calculating the allowance for loan losses in commercial banks. *Abacus*, 40, 3 (October): 321–341.

Green, Edward J. 1984. On the difficulty of eliciting summary information. *Journal of Economic Theory*, 32, 2 (April): 228–245.

Green, Jerry and Jean-Jacques Laffont. 1986. Partially verifiable information and mechanism design. *Review of Economics Studies*, 53, 3 (July): 447–456.

Greenawalt, Mary Brady and Joseph F. Sinkey. 1988. Bank loan-loss provisions and income smoothing hypothesis: An empirical analysis, 1976-84. *Journal of Financial Services Research*, 1, 4 (December): 301–318.

Grˈegoire, Philippe. 2004. Insider trading and voluntary disclosure. Working Paper, Lakehead University.

Griffin, Paul A. 1996. Financial and stock price performance following shareholder litigation. *Journal of Financial Statement Analysis*, 2, 1 (Fall): 5–22.

Griffin, Paul A. 2003. A league of their own? Financial analysts' responses to restatements and corrective disclosures. *Journal of Accounting, Auditing and Finance*, 18, 4 (Fall): 479–518.

Griffin, Paul, Joseph A. Grundfest, and Michael A. Perino. 2004. Stock price response to news of securities fraud litigation: An analysis of sequential and conditional information. *Abacus*, 40, 1 (February): 21–48.

Griffin, Paul A. and David H. Lont. 2005a. Taking the oath: Investor response to SEC certification under Sarbanes-Oxley. *Contemporary Journal of Accounting and Economics*, 1, 1 (June): 27–63.

Griffin, Paul A. and David H. Lont. 2005b. The effects of auditor dismissals and resignations on audit fees: Evidence based on SEC disclosures under Sarbanes-Oxley. SSRN.com/abstract=669682.

Griffiths, Ian. 1986. *Creative Accounting*. London: Unwin Paperback.

Griffiths, Ian. 1995. *New Creative Accounting: How to Make Your Profits What You Want Them To Be*. London: Macmillan.

Grossman, Sanford J. 1981. The informational role of warranties and private disclosure about product quality. *The Journal of Law and Economics*, 24, 3 (June): 461–483.

Grossman, Sanford J. and Oliver Hart. 1983. An analysis of the principal–agent problem. *Econometrica*, 51, 1 (January): 7–45.

Grullon, Gustavo and Roni Michaely. 2004. The information content of share repurchase programs. *Journal of Finance*, 59, 2 (April): 651–680.

Gu, Zhaoyang and Ting Chen. 2004. Analysts' treatment of nonrecurring items in street earnings. *Journal of Accounting and Economics*, 38, 1-3 (December): 129–170.

Gu, Zhaoyang, Chi-Wen Jevons Lee, and Joshua G. Rosett. 2003. Measuring the pervasiveness of earnings management from quarterly accrual volatility. SSRN.com/abstract=305764.

Guay, Wayne R. 1999. The sensitivity of CEO wealth to equity risk: An analysis of the magnitude and determinants. *Journal of Financial Economics*, 53, 1 (July): 43 –71.

Guay, Wayne R. 2002. Discussion of "real investment implications of employee stock option exercises." *Journal of Accounting Research*, 40, 2 (May): 395–406.

Guay, Wayne, S.P. Kothari, and Ross Watts. 1996. A market-based evaluation of discretionary accrual models. *Journal of Accounting Research*, 34 (Supplement): 83–105.

Guay, Wayne R. and Baljit K. Sidhu. 1996. The role of short-versus long-term accruals: A re-assessment and extension. Working Paper, Rochester University. Simon School of Business Working Paper, FR 95–27.

Guenther, David A. 1994. Earnings management in response to corporate tax rate changes. Evidence from the 1986 Tax Reform Act. *The Accounting Review*, 69, 1 (January): 230–243.

Guidry, Flora, Andrew J. Leone, and Steve Rock. 1999. Earnings-based bonus plans and earnings management by business-unit managers. *Journal of Accounting and Economics*, 26, 1-3 (January): 113–142.

Gul, Ferdinand A., and Judy S.L. Tsui. 2001. Free cash flow, debt monitoring and audit pricing: Further evidence on the role of director equity ownership. *Auditing: A Journal of Practice and Theory*, 20, 2 (September): 71–84.

Gul, Ferdinand A., Charles Jieping Chen, and Judy S.L. Tsui. 2003. Discretionary accounting accruals, managers' incentives, and audit fees. *Contemporary Accounting Research*, 20, 3 (Fall): 441–464.

Gul, Ferdinand A. and Simon Y.K. Fung. 2004. Investor protection, cross listings and opportunistic earnings management. Working Paper, City University of Hong Kong.

Gul, Ferdinand A. and Kam-Wah Lai. 2002. Insider entrenchment, board leadership structure and market perceptions of earnings management. SSRN.com/abstract=304399.

Gul, Ferdinand A., S. Leung, and Bin Srinidhi, 2000. Efficient management of earnings to
signal growth opportunities–an empirical investigation. Working Paper, City University
of Hong Kong.

Gul, Ferdinand A., Sidney Leung, and Bin Srinidhi. 2002. The effect of investment opportunity set and debt level on earnings–returns relationship and the pricing of discretionary accruals. SSRN.com/abstract=236080.

Gul, Ferdinand, A., Bin Srinidhi, and Tony Shieh. 2002. The Asian financial crisis, accounting conservatism and audit fees: Evidence from Hong Kong.
SSRN.com/abstract=315062.

Gul, Ferdinand A., Judy S.L. Tsui, Xijia Su, and Rong Min. 2002. Legal protection, enforceability and tests of the debt hypothesis: An international study.
SSRN.com/abstract=304539.

Gumport, M.A. 2006. The next, great, corporate scandal: Potential liability of corporations
engaged in open market, 10B-18 buybacks; a minority view; case histories; summary of
published studies; direction of future research. SSRN.com/abstract=927111.

Gunny, Katherine. 2005. What are the consequences of real earnings management?
SSRN.com/abstract=816025.

Gunther, Marc. 2004. *Faith and Fortune: The Quiet Revolution to Reform American Business*. Crown Business books.

Gupta, Parveen, P. and Tim Leech. 2006. Making Sarbanes-Oxley 404 work: Reducing
cost, increasing effectiveness. *International Journal of Disclosure and Governance*, 3,
1 (March): 27–48.

Gupta, Parveen P. and Nandu Nayar. 2006. Market reaction to control deficiency disclosures under the Sarbanes-Oxley Act: The early evidence. A paper presented at the Auditing Section 2006 Midyear Conference, January 12-14, 2006 Los Angeles, CA.

Guttman, Ilan, Ohad Kadan, and Eugene Kandel. 2006. A rational expectations theory of
kinks in financial reporting. *The Accounting Review*, 81, 4 (July): 811–848.

Haas, Max. 2000. Earnings management in two-period principal–agent models. Discussion paper series in economics and management. German Economic Association of
Business Administration, Discussion Paper No. 00–02.

Hackenbrack, Karl E. and Chris D. Hogan. 2002. Market response to earnings surprises
conditional on reasons for an auditor change. *Contemporary Accounting Research*, 19,
2 (Summer): 197–223.

Hall, Brian J. 1999. The design of multi-year stock options plans. *Journal of Applied Corporate Finance*, 12, 2 (Summer): 97–102.

Hall, Brian J. and Jeffrey B. Liebman. 1998. Are CEOs really paid like bureaucrats?
Quarterly Journal of Economics, 113, 3 (August): 653–691.

Hall, Brian J. and Kevin J. Murphy. 2002. Stock options for undiversified executives.
Journal of Accounting and Economics, 33, 1 (February): 3–42.

Hall, Steven C. 1994. Dividend restrictions and accounting choices. *Journal of Accounting, Auditing and Finance*, 9, 3 (Summer): 447–463.

Hall, Steven and William W. Stammerjohan. 1997. Damage awards and earnings management in the oil industry. *The Accounting Review*, 72, 1 (January): 47–65.

Hallock, Kevin F. 1997. Reciprocally interlocking boards of directors and executive
compensation. *Journal of Financial and Quantitative Analysis*, 32, 3 (September):
331–344.

Hallock, Kevin F. and Paul Oyer. 1999. The timeliness of performance information in determining executive compensation. *Journal of Corporate Finance*, 5, 4 (December):
303–321.

Hammersley, Jacqueline S., Linda A. Myers, and Catherine Shakespeare. 2005. Market reactions to the disclosure of internal control weaknesses and to the characteristics of those weaknesses under Section 302 of the Sarbanes-Oxley Act of 2002. SSRN.com/abstract=830848.

Han, Jerry C.Y. and Shiing-wu Wang. 1998. Political costs and earnings management of oil companies during the 1990 Persian Gulf crisis. *The Accounting Review*, 73, 1 (January): 103–117.

Han, Jerry C.Y. and John J. Wild. 1990. Unexpected earnings and intraindustry information transfers: Further evidence. *Journal of Accounting Research*, 28, 1 (Spring): 211–219.

Han, Jerry C.Y. and John J. Wild. 1991. Stock-price behavior associated with managers' earnings and revenue forecasts. *Journal of Accounting Research*, 29, 1 (Spring): 79–95.

Hand, John R.M. 1989. Did firms undertake debt-equity swaps for an accounting paper profit or true financial gain? *The Accounting Review*, 64, 4 (October): 587–623.

Hand, John R.M. 1990. A test of the extended functional fixation hypothesis. *The Accounting Review*, 65, 4 (October): 739–763.

Hand, John R.M. 2005. The value relevance of financial statements in the venture capital market. *The Accounting Review*, 80, 2 (April): 613–648.

Hand, John R.M. and Terrance R. Skantz. 1997. The economic determinants of accounting choices: The unique case of equity carve-outs under SAB 51. *Journal of Accounting and Economics*, 24, 2 (December): 175–203.

Haniffa, R.M. and Terry E. Cooke. 2002. Culture, corporate governance and disclosure in Malaysian corporations. *Abacus*, 38, 3 (October): 317–349.

Hanlon, Michelle. 2005. The persistence and pricing of earnings, accruals, and cash flows when firms have large book-tax differences. *The Accounting Review*, 80, 1 (January): 137–166.

Hanlon, Michelle, Shivaram Rajgopal, and Terry Shevlin. 2003. Are executive stock options associated with future earnings? *Journal of Accounting and Economics,* 36, 1-3 (December): 3–43.

Hann, Rebecca, Yvonne Lu, and K.R. Subramanyam. 2007. Uniformity versus flexibility: Evidence from pricing of the pension obligation. *The Accounting Review*, 82, 1 (January): 107–137.

Hansen, Gary S. and Charles W. Hill. 1991. Are institutional investors myopic? A time-series study of four technology-driven industries. *Strategic Management Journal*, 12, 1(January): 1–16.

Hansen, Glen A. 1999. Bias and measurement error in discretionary accrual models. SSRN.com/abstract=192748.

Hansen, James C. 2004. Additional evidence on discretionary accrual levels of benchmark beaters. Working Paper, University of Illinois at Chicago. AAA 2004 Annual Meeting Paper, Orlando, FL.

Harford, Jarrad. 2003. Takeover bids and target directors' incentives: The impact of a bid on directors' wealth and board seats. *Journal of Financial Economics*, 69, 1 (July): 51–83.

Harris, Mary Stanford. 1998. The association between competition and managers, business segment reporting decisions. *Journal of Accounting Research*, 26, 1 (Spring): 111–128.

Harris, Milton. 1987. *Dynamic Economic Analysis*. New York: Oxford University Press.

Harris, Milton and Arthur Raviv. 1978. Some results on incentive contracts with applications to education and employment, health insurance, and law enforcement. *The American Economic Review*, 68, 1 (March): 20–30.

Harris, Milton and Arthur Raviv. 1979. Optimal incentive contracts with imperfect information. *Journal of Economic Theory*, 20, 2 (April): 231–259.

Harris, Milton and Arthur Raviv. 1990. Capital structure and the informational role of debt. *Journal of Finance*, 45, 2 (June): 321–349.

Harris, Milton and Arthur Raviv. 1991. The theory of capital structure. *Journal of Finance*, 46, 1 (March): 297–355.

Harris, Milton and Arthur Raviv. 1992. Financial contracting theory. Jean J. Laffont, ed., In *Advances in Economic Theory*, ed. Cambridge University Press.

Harris, Milton and Arthur Raviv. 2005. A theory of board control and size. Working Paper, University of Chicago and Northwestern University. Working Paper, Northwestern University.

Harsanyi, John C. 1973. Games with randomly disturbed payoffs: A new rationale for mixed-strategy equilibrium points. *International Journal of Game Theory*, 2, 1 (December): 1–23.

Harsanyi, John C. and Reinhard Selten. 1988. *Equilibrium Selection in Games*. MIT Press.

Hart, Oliver. 1983a. The market mechanism as an incentive scheme. *Bell Journal of Economics*, 14, 2 (Autumn): 366–382.

Hart, Oliver. 1983b. Optimal labour contracts under asymmetric information: An introduction. *Review of Economic Studies*, 50, 1 (January): 1-35. Reprinted in Sherwin Rosen, ed., *Implicit Contract Theory*. Edward Elgar Publishing Ltd, 1994.

Hart, Oliver. 1995a. Corporate governance: Some theory and implications. *The Economic Journal*, 105, 430 (May): 678–689.

Hart, Oliver. 1995b. *Firms, Contracts, and Financial Structure*. Oxford: Oxford University Press.

Hart, Oliver. 2001. Financial contracting. *Journal of Economic Literature*, 39: 1079–1100.

Hart, Oliver and Bengt Holmström. 1985. *The Theory of Contracts*. In Truman F. Bewley, ed., *Advances in Economic Theory*. *Fifth World Congress*. Econometric Society Monprgran. Ch 3: 71–156.

Hartman, Thomas E. 2005. The cost of being public in the era of SOX. Foley & Lardner LLP.

Hartzell, Jay C. and Laura T. Starks. 2003. Institutional investors and executive compensation. *Journal of Finance*, 58, 6 (December): 2351–2374.

HassabElnaby, Hassan R. 2006. Waiving technical default: The role of agency costs and bank regulations. *Journal of Business Finance and Accounting*, 33, 9-10 (November/December): 1368–1389.

HassabElnaby, Hassan R., Michael Mosebach, and Scott Whisenant. 2005. The effect of technical default cost on discretionary accounting decisions. SSRN.com/abstract=660802.

Hassell, John M., Robert H. Jennings, and Dennis J. Lasser. 1988. Management earnings forecasts: Their usefulness as a source of firm-specific information to security analysts. *Journal of Financial Research*, 11, 4 (Winter): 303–319.

Hatfield, H.R. 1927. *Accounting: Its Principles and Problems*. Scholar Books Co. Houston, TX.

Hatfield, Richard C., Scott B. Jackson, and Scott D. Vandervelde. 2006. The effect of auditor rotation and client pressures on proposed audit adjustments. Working Paper, University of Texas at San Antonio.

Haw, In-Mu, Bingbing Hu, Lee-Seok Hwang, and Woody Wu. 2004. Ultimate ownership, income management, and legal and extra-legal institutions. *Journal of Accounting Research*, 42, 2 (May): 423–462.

Hayes, Rachel M. 1998. The impact of trading commission incentives on analysts' stock coverage decisions and earnings forecasts. *Journal of Accounting Research*, 36, 2 (Autumn): 299–320.

Hayes, Rachel M. and Russell J. Lundholm. 1996. Segment reporting to the capital market in the presence of a competitor. *Journal of Accounting Research*, 34, 2 (Autumn): 261–279.

Hayes, Rachel M. Paul E. Oyer, and Scott Schaefer. 2005. Co-worker complementarity and the stability of top management teams. Working Paper, Stanford University.

Hayn, Carla. 1995. The information content of losses. *Journal of Accounting and Economics*, 20, 2 (September): 125–153.

He, Frank, Bin Srinidhi, Xijia Su, and Ferdinand A. Gul. 2003. Earnings management by changing R&D expenditure: Evidence on the role of CEO stock compensation. SSRN.com/abstract=459040.

Healy, Paul M. 1985. The effect of bonus schemes on accounting decisions. *Journal of Accounting and Economics*, 7, 1-3 (April): 85–107.

Healy, Paul M. 1996. Discussion of a market-based evaluation of discretionary accrual models. *Journal of Accounting Research*, 34, 3 (Supplement): 107–115.

Healy, Paul M. 1999. Discussion of earnings-based bonus plans and earnings management by business unit managers. *Journal of Accounting and Economics*, 26, 1-3 (January): 143–147.

Healy, Paul M., Amy P. Hutton, and Krishna G. Palepu. 1999. Stock performance and intermediation changes surrounding sustained increases in disclosure. *Contemporary Accounting Research*, 16, 3 (Fall): 485–520.

Healy, Paul M., Sok-Hyon Kang, and Krishna G. Palepu. 1987. The effect of accounting procedure changes on CEO's cash salary and bonus compensation. *Journal of Accounting and Economics*, 9, 1 (April): 7–34.

Healy, Paul M. and Krishna G. Palepu. 1988. Earnings information conveyed by dividend initiations and omissions. *Journal of Financial Economics*, 21, 2 (September): 149–175.

Healy, Paul M. and Krishna G. Palepu. 1989. How investors interpret changes in corporate financial policy. *Journal of Applied Corporate Finance*, 2, 3 (September): 59–64.

Healy, Paul M. and Krishna G. Palepu. 1990. Effectiveness of accounting-based dividend covenants. *Journal of Accounting and Economics*, 12, 1-3 (January): 97–123.

Healy, Paul M. and Krishna G. Palepu. 1993. The effect of firms' financial disclosure strategies on stock prices. *Accounting Horizons*, 7, 1 (March): 1–11.

Healy, Paul M. and Krishna G. Palepu. 1995. The challenges of investor communication: The case of CUC International, Inc. *Journal of Financial Economics*, 38, 2 (June): 111–141.

Healy, Paul M. and Krishna G. Palepu. 2001. Information asymmetry, corporate disclosure and the capital markets: A review of the empirical disclosure literature. *Journal of Accounting and Economics*, 31, 1-3 (September): 405–440.

Healy, Paul M. and Krishna G. Palepu. 2003. The fall of Enron. *Journal of Economics Perspectives*, 17, 2 (Spring): 3–26.

Healy, Paul M. and James Michael Wahlen. 1999. A review of the earnings management literature and its implications for standard setting. *Accounting Horizons*, 13 , 4 (December): 365–383.

Heflin, Frank and Charles Hsu. 2005. The impact of the SEC's regulation of non-GAAP disclosures. SSRN.com/abstract=494882.

Heflin, Frank, Sing S. Kwon, and John J. Wild. 2002. Accounting choices: Variation in managerial opportunism. *Journal of Business Finance and Accounting*, 29, 7/8 (September): 1047–1078.

Heflin, Frank, K.R. Subramanyam, and Yuan Zhang. 2003. Regulation FD and the financial information environment: Early evidence. *The Accounting Review*, 78, 1 (January): 1–37.

Helland, Eric. 2006. Reputational penalties and the merits of class-action securities litigation. *Journal of Law and Economics*, 49, 2 (October): 365–396.

Helland, Eric and Michael E. Sykuta. 2005. Who's monitoring the monitor? Do outside directors protect shareholders' interests? *Financial Review*, 40, 2, (May): 155–172.

Hellman, Niclass. 1999. Earnings manipulation: Cost of capital versus tax. A commentary. *European Accounting Review*, 8, 3 (September): 493–497.

Hemmer, Thomas, Oliver Kim, and Robert E. Verrecchia. 1999. Introducing convexity into optimal compensation contracts. *Journal of Accounting and Economics*, 28, 3 (December): 307–327.

Heninger, William G. 2001. The association between auditor litigation and abnormal accruals. *The Accounting Review*, 76, 1 (January): 76–111.

Henning, Peter J. 2004. Sarbanes-Oxley Act Section 307 and corporate counsel: Who better to prevent corporate crime? *Buffalo Criminal Law Review*, 8: 101. SSRN.com/abstract=642561.

Hepworth, Samuel R. 1953. Periodic income smoothing. *The Accounting Review*, 28, 1 (January): 32–39.

Hermalin, Benjamin E. and Michael L. Katz. 1991. Moral hazard and verifiability: The effects of renegotiation in agencies. *Econometrica*, 59, 6 (November): 1735–1753.

Hermalin, Benjamin E. and Michael S. Weisbach. 1998. Endogenously chosen boards of directors and their monitoring of the CEO. *American Economic Review*, 88, 1 (March): 96–118.

Hermalin, Benjamin E. and Michael S. Weisbach. 2003. Boards of directors as an endogenously determined institution: A survey of the economic literature. *Economic Policy Review*, 9, 1 (April): 1–20.

Hermalin, Benjamin E. and Michael S. Weisbach. 2007. Transparency and corporate governance. SSRN.com/abstract=958628.

Heron, Randall A. and Erik Lie. 2002. Operating performance and the method of payment in takeovers. *Journal of Financial and Quantitative Analysis*, 37, 1 (March): 137–155.

Heron, Randall A. and Erik Lie. 2006. What fraction of stock option grants to top executives have been backdated or manipulated? http://www.issproxy.com/pdf/OptionsBackdatingStudy071406.pdf.

Heron, Randall A. and Erik Lie. 2007. Does backdating explain the stock price pattern around executive stock option grants? *Journal of Financial Economics*, 83, 2 (February): 271–295.

Herrmann, Don R. and Inoue Tatsuo. 1996. Income smoothing and incentives by operating condition: An empirical test using depreciation changes in Japan. *Journal of International Accounting, Auditing and Taxation*, 5, 2: 161–177.

Hertig, Gerard. 2005. On-going board reforms: One-size-fits-all and regulatory capture. ECGI–Law Working Paper No. 25/2005. SSRN.com/abstract=676417.

Hertz, Kathleen. 2006. The impact of SOX on auditor resignations and dismissals. Working Paper, University of Washington.

Hertzel, Michael and Prem Jain. 1991. Earnings and risk changes around stock repurchase tender offers. *Journal of Accounting and Economics*, 14, 3 (September): 253–274.

Hilary, Gilles and Clive Steven Lennox. 2005. The credibility of self-regulation: Evidence from the accounting profession's peer review program. *Journal of Accounting and Economics*, 40, 1-3 (December): 211–229.

Himmelberg, Charles P., Glenn R. Hubbard, and Darius Palia. 1999. Understanding the determinants of managerial ownership and the link between ownership and performance. *Journal of Financial Economics*, 53, 3 (September): 353–384.

Hirschey, Mark and Vernon J. Richardson. 2002. Information content of accounting good-will numbers. *Journal of Accounting and Public Policy*, 21, 3 (Autumn): 173–191.

Hirshleifer, David A. and Yoon Suh. 1992. Risk, managerial effort, and project choice. *Journal of Financial Intermediation*, 2, 3 (September): 308–345.

Hirshleifer, David A. and Siew Hong Teoh. 2003. Limited attention, information disclosure, and financial reporting. *Journal of Accounting and Economics*, 36, 1-3 (December): 337–386.

Hirst, Eric D. 2006. Discussion of "Cherry picking, disclosure quality, and comprehensive income reporting choices: The case of property-liability insurers." *Contemporary Accounting Research*, 23, 3 (Fall): 693–700.

Hirst, Eric D. and Patrick E. Hopkins. 1998. Comprehensive income reporting and analysts' valuation judgments. *Journal of Accounting Research*, 36 (Supplement): 47–75.

Hirst, Eric D., Patrick E. Hopkins, and James M. Wahlen. 2004. Fair values, income measurement, and bank analysts' risk valuation judgments. *The Accounting Review*, 79, 2 (April): 453–472.

Hirst, Eric D., Lisa L. Koonce, and Jeffrey Miller. 1999. The joint effect of management's prior forecast accuracy and the form of its financial forecasts on investor judgments. *Journal of Accounting Research*, 37 (Supplement): 101–124.

Hirst, Eric D., Lisa L. Koonce, and Shankar Venkataraman. 2006. Management earnings forecasts: A review and framework. SSRN.com/abstract=921583.

Ho, Yueh-Fang. 2003. Three essays on seasoned equity offerings. Ph.D. dissertation. Drexel University.

Hochberg, Yael V. 2005. Venture capital and corporate governance in the newly public firm. Working Paper, Northwestern University.

Hochberg, Yael V., Yigal S. Newman, and Michael A. Rierson. 2003. Information in the time-series dynamics of earnings management: Evidence from insider trading and firm returns. Working Paper, Northwestern University.

Hochberg, V. Yael, Paola Sapienza, and Annette Vissing-Jørgensen. 2006. A lobbying approach to evaluating the Sarbanes-Oxley Act of 2002. Working Paper, Northwestern University.

Holland, Kevin E. and Richard H.G. Jackson. 2004. Earnings management and deferred tax. *Accounting and Business Research*, 34, 2: 101–123.

Hollie, Dana, Joshua Livnat, and Benjamin Segal. 2004. "Oops, our earnings were indeed preliminary": Market reactions to companies that subsequently file different earnings with the SEC. http://pages.stern.nyu.edu/~jlivnat/jpm%20submission.pdf.

Holmström, Bengt R. 1979. Moral hazard and observability. *The Bell Journal of Economics*, 10, 1 (Spring): 74–91.

Holmström, Bengt R. 1999. Managerial incentive problems: A dynamic perspective. *Review of Economic Studies,* 66, 1 (January), 169–182.

Holmström, Bengt R. and Steven N. Kaplan. 2001. Corporate governance and merger activity in the U.S.: Making sense of the 1980s and 1990s. *The Journal of Economic Perspectives*, 15, 2 (Spring): 121–144.

Holmström, Bengt R. and Steven N. Kaplan. 2003. The State of U.S. corporate governance. What's right and what's wrong? Finance Working Paper 23/2003, European Corporate Governance Institute. A 2004 revision is available at http://www.aei-brookings.org/admin/authorpdfs/page.php?id=319.

Holmström, Bengt R. and Paul Milgrom. 1987. Aggregation and linearity in the provision of intertemporal incentives. *Econometrica*, 55, 2 (March): 303–328.

Holmström, Bengt and Jean J. Tirole. 1993. Market liquidity and performance monitoring. *Journal of Political Economy*, 101, 4 (August): 678–709.

Holthausen, Robert W. 1990. Accounting method choice: Opportunistic behavior, efficient contracting, and information perspectives. *Journal of Accounting and Economics*, 12, 1-3 (January): 207–218.

Holthausen, Robert W. and David F. Larcker. 1996. The financial performance of reverse leveraged buyouts. *Journal of Financial Economics*, 42, 3 (November): 293–332.

Holthausen, Robert W., David F. Larcker, and Richard G. Sloan. 1995. Annual bonus schemes and the manipulation of earnings. *Journal of Accounting and Economics*, 19, 1 (February): 29–74.

Holthausen, Robert W. and Richard W. Leftwich. 1983. The economic consequences of accounting choice implications of costly contracting and monitoring. *Journal of Accounting and Economics*, 5: 77–117.

Holthausen, Robert W. and Ross L. Watts. 2001. The relevance of the value-relevance literature for financial accounting standard setting. *Journal of Accounting and Economics*, 31, 1-3 (September): 3–75.

Hong, Harrison. 2003. Seeing through the seers of Wall Street: Analysts' career concerns and biased forecasts. Working Paper, Stanford University and Princeton University.

Hong, Harrison, Jeffrey D. Kubik, and Amit Solomon. 2000. Security analysts' career concerns and herding of earnings forecasts. *RAND Journal of Economics*, 31, 1 (Spring): 121–144.

Hoogendoorn, Martin N. 1985. Income smoothing. A paper presented Erasmus University. 8503/ACC.

Hopkins, Patrick E., Richard W. Houston, and Michael F. Peters. 2000. Purchase, pooling, and equity analysts' valuation judgments. *The Accounting Review*, 75, 3 (July): 257–281.

Hoskins, Robert E., John S. Hughes, and William E. Ricks. 1986. Evidence on the incremental information content of additional firm disclosures made concurrently with earnings. *Journal of Accounting Research*, 24 (Supplement): 1–36.

Hotchkiss, Edith S. and Deon Strickland. 2003. Does shareholder composition matter? Evidence from the market reaction to corporate earnings announcements. *Journal of Finance*, 58, 4 (August): 1469–1498.

Houston, Joel F., Baruch Lev, and Jennifer W. Tucker. 2006. To guide or not to guide? Causes and consequences of stopping and subsequently resuming quarterly earnings guidance. Working Paper, University of Florida, New York University.

Hribar, Paul and Dan Collins. 2002. Errors in estimating accruals: Implications for empirical research. *Journal of Accounting Research*, 40, 1 (March): 105–134.

Hribar, Paul and Nicole Thorne Jenkins. 2004. The effect of accounting restatements on earnings revisions and the estimated cost of capital. *Review of Accounting Studies*, 9, 2-3 (June-September): 337–356.

Hribar, Paul, Nicole Thorne Jenkins, and W. Bruce Johnson. 2006. Stock repurchases as an earnings management device. *Journal of Accounting and Economics*, 41, 1-2 (April): 3–27.

Hsieh, Jim, Lilian Ng, and Qingghai Wang. 2005. Analyst stock recommendations and insider trading activities. A revised paper presented in the FMA 2004 Annual Meeting, New Orleans.

Hsu, Charles. 2004. Strategic choices of street earnings and earnings perceptions management. Ph.D. dissertation. Purdue University.

Hsu, Peter C. 2004. Going private—A response to an increased regulatory burden? SSRN.com/abstract=619501.

Huang, Wenli. 2005. Executive stock options and risk-taking. Working Paper, University of Califronia at Berkeley.

Hubbard, Glenn R., Kenneth N. Kuttner, and Darius N. Palia. 2002. Are there bank effects in borrowers' costs of funds? Evidence from a matched sample of borrowers and banks. *The Journal of Business*, 75, 4 (October): 559–581.

Huddart, Steven J. 1993. The effect of a large shareholder on corporate value. *Management Science*, 39, 11 (November): 1407–1421.

Huddart, Steven J., Bin Ke, and Charles Shi. 2007. Jeopardy, non-public information, and insider trading around SEC 10-K and 10-Q filings. *Journal of Accounting and Economics*, 43, 1 (March): 3–36.

Huddart, Steven J. and Mark Lang. 1996. Employee stock option exercises: An empirical analysis. *Journal of Accounting and Economics*, 21, 1 (February): 5–43.

Huddart, Steven J. and Mark Lang. 2003. *Information* distribution within firms: Evidence from stock option exercises. *Journal of Accounting and Economics*, 34, 1-3 (January): 3–31.

Huddart, Steven J. and Henock Louis. 2006. Stock returns, earnings management, and insider selling during the 1990s stock market bubble. SSRN.com/abstract=912214.

Hughes, Patricia J. 1986. Signaling by direct disclosure under asymmetric information. *Journal of Accounting and Economics*, 8, 2 (June): 119–142.

Hughes, Patricia J. and Mandira Sankar. 2006. The quality of discretionary disclosure under litigation risk. *Journal of Accounting, Auditing and Finance*, 21, 1 (Winter): 55–81.

Hughes, Patricia J., Eduardo S. Schwartz, and John Fellingham. 1988. The LIFO/FIFO choice: An asymmetric information approach. *Journal of Accounting Research*, 26, 3 (Supplement): 41–63.

Hui, Loi Teck and Quek Kia Fatt. 2007. Strategic organizational conditions for risks reduction and earnings management: A combined strategy and auditing paradigm. *Accounting Forum*, 31, 2 (June): 179–201.

Huijgen, Carel and Martien Lubberink. 2005. Earnings conservatism, litigation and contracting: The case of cross-listed firms. *Journal of Business Finance and Accounting*, 32, 7–8 (September): 1275–1309.

Hunt, Alister, Susan E. Moyer, and Terry Shevlin. 1996. Managing interacting accounting measures to meet multiple objectives: A study of LIFO firms. *Journal of Accounting and Economics*, 21, 3 (June): 339–374.

Hunt, Alister, Susan E. Moyer, and Terry Shevlin. 2000. Earnings volatility, earnings management, and equity value. Working Paper, University of Washington.

Hunton, James E., Robert Libby, and Cheri L. Mazza. 2006. Financial reporting transparency and earnings management. *The Accounting Review*, 81, 1 (January): 135–158.

Huson, Mark R., Paul H. Malatesta, and Robert Parrino. 1997. Managerial succession and firm performance. *Journal of Financial Economics*, 74, 2 (November): 237–275.

Huson, Mark R., Robert Parrino, and Laura T. Starks. 2001. Internal monitoring mechanisms and CEO turnover: A long-term perspective. *Journal of Finance*, 56, 6 (December): 2265–2297.

Hutton, Amy, Gregory Miller, and Douglas Skinner. 2003. The role of supplementary statements with management earnings forecasts. *Journal of Accounting Research*, 41, 5 (December), 867–890.

Hwang, Lee-Seok and Stephen G. Ryan. 2000. The varied nature and pricing implications of discretionary behavior: Big baths, loss avoidance and sugarbowling. Working Paper, Baruch College and New York University.

Hyeesoo, Chung and Sanjay Kallapur. 2003. Client importance, non-audit fees, and abnormal accruals. *The Accounting Review*, 78, 4 (October): 931–955.

Ibrahim, Salma. 2005. An alternative measure to detect intentional earnings management through discretionary accruals. Ph.D. dissertation. University of Maryland.

Ikenberry, David L. and S. Ramnath. 2002. Underreaction to self-selected news events: The case of stock splits. *The Review of Financial Studies*, 15, 2 (March): 489–526.

Ikenberry, David L., Graeme Rankine, and Earl K. Stice. 1996. What do stock splits really signal? *Journal of Financial and Quantitative Analysis*, 31, 3 (September): 357–375.

Indjejikian, Raffi J. 1991. The impact of costly information interpretation on firm disclosure decisions. *Journal of Accounting Research*, 29, 2 (Autumn): 277–301.

Indjejikian, Raffi J. and Dhananjay (DJ) Nanda. 1999. Dynamic incentives and responsibility accounting. *Journal of Accounting and Economics*, 27, 2 (April): 177–201.

Indjejikian, Raffi J. and Dhananjay (DJ) Nanda. 2002. Executive target bonuses and what they imply about performance standards. *The Accounting Review*, 77, 4 (October): 755–792.

Ingley, C.B. and N.T. van der Walt. 2004. Corporate governance, institutional investors and conflicts of interest. *Corporate Governance: An International Review*, 12, 4 (October): 534–551.

Innes, Robert D. 1990. Limited liability and incentive contracting with ex-ante action choices. *Journal of Economic Theory*, 52, 1 (October): 45–67.

Institutional Shareholders Services. 2005. Post-season report: *Corporate Governance at Crossroads*. http://www.issproxy.com/pdf/2005PostSeasonReportFINAL.pdf.

Irving, Jim. 2006. The information content of internal controls legislation: Evidence from material weakness disclosures. AAA 2006 Annual Meeting Paper, Washington, DC.

Ittner, Christopher D., Richard A. Lambert, and David F. Larcker. 2003. The structure and performance consequences of equity grants to employees of new economy firms. *Journal of Accounting and Economics*, 34 ,1–3 (January): 89–127.

Ittner, Christopher D., David F. Larcker, and Madhav V. Rajan. 1997. The choice of performance measures in annual bonus contracts. *The Accounting Review*, 72, 2 (April): 231–255.

Jacob, John and Bjorn N. Jorgensen. 2007. Earnings management and accounting income aggregation. *Journal of Accounting and Economics*, 43, 2–3 (July): 369–390.

Jaffe, Jeffery. 1974. Special information and insider trading. *The Journal of Business*, 47, 3 (July): 410–428.

Jaggi, Bikki and Ferdinand A. Gul. 1999. An analysis of joint effects of investment opportunity set, free cash flows and size on corporate debt policy. *Review of Quantitative Finance and Accounting*, 12, 4 (June): 371–381.

Jaggi, Bikki and Picheng Lee. 2002. Earnings management response to debt covenant violations and debt restructuring. *Journal of Accounting, Auditing and Finance*, 17, 4 (Fall): 295–324.

Jaggi, Bikki and Alexander Sannella. 1995. The association between the accuracy of management earnings forecasts and discretionary accounting changes. *Journal of Accounting, Auditing and Finance*, 10, 1 (Winter): 1–21.

Jaggi, Bikki and Lili Sun. 2006. Financial distress and earnings management: Effectiveness of independent audit committees. Whitcomb Center for Research in Financial Services (WCRFS): 06-31. A paper presented in the 2006 Auditing Midyear Conference, Los Angeles, CA.

Jagolinzer, Alan and Darren T. Roulstone. 2004. Corporate restrictions on insider trading around earnings announcements. Working Paper, Stanford.

Jaime, Jose J. Alcarria and Belen Hill De Albornoz Moguer. 2004. Specification and power of cross-sectional abnormal working capital accruals models in the Spanish context. *European Accounting Review*, 13, 1 (May): 73–104.

Jain, Neelan and Leonard J. Mirman. 1999. Insider trading with correlated signals. *Economics Letters*, 65, 1 (October): 105–113.

Jain, Pankaj K., Jang-Chul Kim, and Zabihollah Rezaee. 2006. Trends and determinants of market liquidity in the pre- and post-Sarbanes-Oxley Act periods. 14th Annual Conference on Financial Economics and Accounting (FEA). SSRN.com/abstract=488142.

Jain, Pankaj K. and Zabihollah Rezaee. 2004. The Sarbanes-Oxley Act of 2002 and accounting conservatism. SSRN.com/abstract=554643.

Jameson, M. 1988. *A Practical Guide to Creative Accounting.* London: Kogan Page.

Janakiraman, Surya N., Suresh Radhakrishnan, and Rafal Szwejkowski. 2006. Regulation fair disclosure and analysts' first-forecast horizon. SSRN.com/abstract=898624.

Janes, Troy D. 2003. Accruals, financial distress, and debt covenants. Working Paper, American University.

Jayaraman, Nayrayanan, Charles Mulford, and Lei Wedge. 2005. Management turnover in anticipation of SEC enforcement actions for accounting fraud. Working Paper.

Jegadeesh, Narasimhan and Joshua Livnat. 2006. Post-earnings-announcement drift: The role of revenue surprises. *Financial Analysts Journal, –.*

Jeng, Leslie A., Andrew Metrick, and Richard R. Zeckhauser. 2001. The profits to insider trading: A performance-evaluation perspective. NBER working paper No. 6913.

Jenkins, Thorne N. and Morton Pincus. 1998. LIFO versus FIFO: Updating what we have learned. Working Paper, University of Iowa.

Jensen, Michael. 2006. Should we stay or should we go? Accountability, status anxiety, and client defections. *Administrative Science Quarterly*, 51, 1 (March): 97–128.

Jensen, Michael C. 1986. Agency cost and free cash flows, corporate finance and takeovers. *American Economic Review*, 76, 2 (May): 323–339.

Jensen, Michael C. 2000. The modern industrial revolution, exit, and the failure of internal control systems. *Theory of the Firm.* Cambridge, MA: Harvard University Press (An earlier version published in *Journal of Finance*, July 1993).

Jensen, Michael C. 2001. Paying people to lie: The truth about the budgeting process. Harvard NOM Research Paper No. 01-03, and HBS Working Paper No. 01–072.

Jensen, Michael C. 2004. Agency costs of overvalued equity. Center for Public Leadership. Working Paper, Harvard University.

Jensen, Michael C. 2005a. Managers and capital markets: Issues in managing the tensions between two cultures (PowerPoint slides). Harvard NOM Working Paper No. 05-14, Kalmbach Lecture, University of Rochester, and University of Chicago Finance Seminar. SSRN.com/abstract=723382.

Jensen, Michael C. 2005b. The puzzling state of low-integrity relations between managers and capital markets (PowerPoint slides). SSRN.com/abstract=783604.

Jensen, Michael C. and William H. Meckling. 1976. Theory of the firm: Managerial behavior, agency costs and ownership structure. *Journal of Financial Economics*, 3, 4 (October): 305–360.

Jensen, Michael C. and Kevin J. Murphy. 1990a. Performance pay and top-management incentives. *Journal of Political Economy*, 98, 2 (April): 225–264.

Jensen, Michael C. and Kevin J. Murphy. 1990b. CEO incentives: It's not how much you pay. It's how. *Journal of Applied Corporate Finance*, 3, 3 (Fall): 36–49. Reprinted in Michael C. Jensen, *Foundations of Organizational Strategy.* Boston, MA: Harvard University Press.

Jensen, Michael C., Kevin J. Murphy, and Wruck, Eric G. 2004. Remuneration: Where we've been, how we got to here, what are the problems, and how to fix them. Harvard NOM Working Paper No. 04-28, ECGI—Finance Working Paper No. 44/2004. SSRN.com/abstract=561305.

Jenter, Dirk C. 2001. Understanding high-powered incentives. Harvard NOM Working Paper No. 01-06, EFMA 2001 Lugano Meeting Paper. SSRN.com/abstract=269420.

Jenter, Dirk C. 2005. Market timing and managerial portfolio decisions. *Journal of Finance*, 60, 4 (August): 1903–1949.

Jenter, Dirk C. Katharina Lewellen, and Jerold B. Warner. 2006. Security issue timing: What do managers know, and when do they know it. NBER Working Paper No. W12724.

Jeter, Debra C. and Lakshmanan Shivakumar. 1999. Cross-sectional estimation of abnormal accruals using quarterly and annual data. Effectiveness in detecting event-specific earnings management. *Accounting and Business Research*, 29, 4 (Autumn): 299–319.

Jevons Lee, Chi-Wen, Yue Li, and Heng Yue. 2006. Performance, growth and earnings management. *Review of Accounting Studies*, 11, 2-3 (September): 305–334.

Jewitt, Ian. 1988. Justifying the first-order approach to principal–agent problem. *Econometrica*, 56, 5 (September): 1177–1190.

Jiambalvo, James. 1996. Discussion of causes and consequences of earnings manipulation: An analysis of firms subject to enforcement actions by the SEC. *Contemporary Accounting Research*, 13, 1 (Spring): 37–47.

Jiambalvo, James, Shivaram Rajgopal, and Mohan Venkatachalam. 2002. Institutional ownership and the extent to which stock prices reflect future earnings. *Contemporary Accounting Research*, 19, 1 (Spring): 117–145.

Jiraporn, Pornsit, Peter DaDalt, Wallace Davidson, and Yixi Ning. 2007. To bust to show up? An analysis of directors' absences. Working Paper, Pennsylvania State University—Great Valley.

Jiraporn, Pornsit, Young Sang Kim, and Ike Mathur. 2004. Does corporate diversification exacerbate or mitigate earnings management? An empirical analysis. SSRN.com/abstract=879803.

Jiraporn, Pornsit, Gary Miller, Soon Suk Yoon, and Young Sang Kim. 2006. Is earnings management opportunistic or beneficial? An agency theory perspective. SSRN.com/abstract=917941.

Jo, Hoje, Yong H. Kim, and Yongtae Kim. 2005. Earnings management and CEO cash compensation. *International Journal of Finance*, forthcoming.

Jo, Hoje and Yongtae Kim. 2006. Disclosure frequency and earnings management. *Journal of Financial Economics*, 84, 2(May): 561–590.

Joe, Jennifer J. 2003. Why press coverage of a client influences the audit opinion. *Journal of Accounting Research*, 41, 1 (March): 109–134.

John, Kose and Teresa John. 1993. Top-management compensation and capital structure. *Journal of Finance*, 48, 3 (July): 949–974.

John, Kose Teresa John, and Joshua Ronen. 1996. Corporate taxes, choice among accounting alternatives, and information content of earnings. *Journal of Accounting, Auditing and Finance*, 11, 2 (Spring): 163–181.

John, Kose and Lemma W. Senbet. 1998. Corporate governance and board effectiveness. *Journal of Banking and Finance*, 22, 4 (May): 371–401.

Johnson, Bruce W. and Thomas Lys. 1990. The market for audit services: Evidence from voluntary auditor changes. *Journal of Accounting and Economics*, 12, 1-3 (January): 281–308.

Johnson, Bruce W. and William C. Schwartz. 2005. Are investors misled by "pro forma" earnings? *Contemporary Accounting Research*, 22, 4 (Winter): 915–963.

Johnson, Jonathan L., Catherine M. Daily, and Alan E. Ellstrand. 1996. Board of directors: A review and research agenda. *Journal of Management*, 22, 3 (Fall): 409–438.

Johnson, Marilyn, Ron Kasznik, and K. Nelson. 2000. Shareholder wealth effects of the Private Securities Litigation Reform Act of 1995. *Review of Financial Studies*, 5, 3 (September): 217–233.

Johnson, Marilyn, Ron Kasznik, and K. Nelson. 2001. The impact of securities litigation reform on the disclosure of forward-looking information by high technology firms. *Journal of Accounting Research*, 39, 2 (September): 297–327.

Johnson, Marilyn, Karen K. Nelson, and Adam C. Pritchard. 2007. Do the merits matter more? Class actions under the Private Securities Litigation Reform Act. *The Journal of Law, Economics, and Organization*, 23, 3(Oct): 627–652.

Johnson, Shane A., Harley E. Ryan, and Yisong Sam Tian. 2003. Executive compensation and corporate fraud. SSRN.com/abstract=395960.

Johnson, Van E., Inder K. Khurana, and Kenneth Reynolds. 2002. Audit-firm tenure and the quality of financial reports. *Contemporary Accounting Research*, 19, 4 (Winter): 637–660.

Johnston, Derek. 2006. Managing stock option expense: The manipulation of option-pricing model assumptions. *Contemporary Accounting Research*, 23, 2 (Summer): 395–425.

Jolls, Christine. 1998. Stock repurchases and incentive compensation. NBER Working Paper No. 6467.

Jones, Christopher and Andrea Roberts. 2006. Management of financial information in charitable organizations: The case of joint cost allocations. *The Accounting Review*, 81, 1 (January): 159–178.

Jones, Jennifer J. 1991. Earnings management during import relief investigations. *Journal of Accounting Research*, 29, 2 (Autumn): 193–228.

Jong, Abe De, Douglas V. DeJong, Gerard Merterns, and Peter Roosenboom. 2005. Royal ahold: A failure of corporate governance and an accounting scandal. Working Paper 2005–57, Tilburg University.

Jordan, Charles E., Stanley J. Clark, and Robert E. Smith. 1997-1998. Earnings management under SFAS 115: Evidence from the insurance industry. *Journal of Applied Business Research*, 14, 1 (Winter): 49–56.

Jorion, Philippe, Charles Shi, and Sanjian Zhang. 2005. Tightening credit standards: Fact or fiction. Working Paper, Washington University.

Jung, Boochun, Shiva Sivaramakrishnan, and Naomi S. Soderstrom. 2006. Informational effects of Regulation Fair Disclosure on equity analysts' responses to debt rating changes. SSRN.com/abstract=907487.

Jung, Woon-Oh and Young K. Kwon. 1998. Disclosure when the market is unsure of information endowment of managers. *Journal of Accounting Research*, 26, 1 (Spring): 146–153.

Kadan, Ohad and Jun Yang. 2006. Exeutive stock options and earnings management: A theoretical and empirical analysis. Working Paper, Washington University.

Kahn, Charles and Andrew Winton. 1998. Ownership structure, speculation, and shareholder intervention. *Journal of Finance*, 53, 1 (February): 99–129.

Kalay, Avner. 1982. Stockholder–bondholder conflict and dividend constraints. *Journal of Financial Economics*, 10, 2 (July): 211–233.

Kallunki, Juha-Pekka and Minna Martikainen. 1999. Do firms use industry-wide targets when managing earnings? Finnish evidence. *The International Journal of Accounting*, 34, 2 (June): 249–259.

Kallunki, Juha-Pekka, and Minna Martikainen. 2003. Earnings management as a predictor of future profitability of Finish firms. *European Accounting Review*, 12, 2 (July): 311–325.

Kallunki, Juha-Pekka and Teppo Martikainen. 1999. Financial failures and managers' accounting responses: Finnish evidence. *Journal of Multinational Financial Management*, 9, 1 (January): 15–26.

Kamar, Ehud, Pinar Karaca-Mandic, and Eric L. Talley. 2005. Going-private decisions and the Sarbanes-Oxley Act of 2002: A cross-country analysis. Working Paper, University of California at Berkeley.

Kanagaretnam, Kiridaran, Gerald J. Lobo, and Dong-Hoon Yang. 2004. Joint tests of signaling and income smoothing through bank loan loss provisions. *Contemporary Accounting Research*, 21, 4 (Winter): 843–884.

Kang, Sok-Hyon. 2005. A conceptual and empirical evaluation of accrual prediction models. SSRN.com/abstract=147259.

Kang, Sok-Hyon and K. Sivaramakrishnan. 1995. Issues in testing earnings management and an instrumental variable approach. *Journal of Accounting Research*, 33, 2 (Autumn): 353–367.

Kaplan, Robert. 1985. Evidence of the effect of bonus schemes on accounting procedure on accruals decisions. *Journal of Accounting and Economics*, 7, 1-3 (April) 109–113.

Kaplan, Steven. 1989. The effects of management buyouts on operating performance and value. *Journal of Financial Economics*, 24, 2 (October): 217–254.

Kaplan, Steven. 1991. The staying power of leveraged buyouts. *Journal of Financial Economics*, 29, 2 (October): 287–313.

Kaplan, Steven. 2001a. Ethically related judgments by observers of earnings management. *Journal of Business Ethics*, 32, 4 (August): 285–298.

Kaplan, Steven. 2001b. Further evidence on the ethics of managing earnings: An examination of the ethically related judgments of shareholders and non-shareholders. *Journal of Accounting and Public Policy*, 20, 1 (Spring): 27–44.

Kaplan, Steven N. and David Reishus. 1990. Outside directors and corporate performance. *Journal of Financial Economics*, 27, 2 (October): 389–410.

Karmel, Roberta S. 2004. Should a duty to the corporation be imposed on institutional shareholders? Brooklyn Law School, Public Law Research Paper No. 11. SSRN.com/abstract=546642.

Karmel, Roberta S. 2005. Realizing the dream of William O. Douglas—The Securities and Exchange Commission takes charge of corporate governance. *Delaware Journal of Corporate Law*, 30, 1: 79-144. SSRN.com/abstract=758644.

Karpoff, Jonathan M. 1998. The impact of shareholder activism on target companies: A survey of empirical findings. Working Paper, University of Washington.

Karpoff, Jonathan M., Scott D. Lee, and Gerald S. Martin. 2007a. The cost to firms of cooking the books. SSRN.com/abstract=652121.

Karpoff, Jonathan M., Scott D. Lee, and Gerald S. Martin. 2007b. The consequences to managers for financial misrepresentation. SSRN.com/abstract=972607.

Karuna, Christo. 2004. The effect of product-market competition on managerial incentives in compensation contracts. Working Paper.

Kasanen, Earo, Juha Kinnunen, and Jyrki Niskanen. 1996. Dividend-based earnings management. *Journal of Accounting and Economics*, 22, 1-3 (August-December): 283–312.

Kasznik, Ron. 1999. On the association between voluntary disclosure and earnings management. *Journal of Accounting Research*, 37, 1 (Spring): 57–81.

Kasznik, Ron 2003. Discussion of "Information distribution within firms: Evidence from stock option exercises." *Journal of Accounting and Economics*, 34, 1-3 (January): 33–41.

Kasznik, Ron and Baruch Lev. 1995. To warn or not to warn: Management disclosures in the face of an earnings surprise. *The Accounting Review*, 70, 1 (January): 113–134.

Kasznik, Ron and Maureen F. McNichols. 2002. Does meeting earnings expectations matter? Evidence from analyst forecast revisions and share prices. *Journal of Accounting Research*, 40, 3 (June): 727–759.

Ke, Bin. 2001. Why do CEOs of publicly traded firms prefer reporting small increases in earnings and long duration of consecutive earnings increases? SSRN.com/abstract=250308.

Ke, Bin, Steven Huddart, and Kathy Petroni. 2003. What insiders know about future earnings and how they use it: Evidence from insider trades. *Journal of Accounting and Economics*, 35, 3 (August): 315–346.

Ke, Bin, Kathy Ruby Petroni, and Assem M. Safieddine. 1999. Ownership concentration and sensitivity of executive pay to accounting performance measures: Evidence from publicly and privately-held insurance companies. *Journal of Accounting and Economics*, 28, 2 (December): 185–209.

Ke, Bin and Yong Yu. 2006. The effect of issuing biased earnings forecasts on analysts' access to management and survival. *Journal of Accounting Research*, 44, 5 (December): 965–999.

Keating, Elizabeth K., Linda Parsons, and Andrea Alston Roberts. 2007. Misreporting fundraising: How do nonprofit organizations account for telemarketing campaigns? SSRN.com/abstract=960091.

Keating, Scott A. and Jerold L. Zimmerman. 1999. Depreciation policy changes: Tax, earnings management, and investment opportunity incentives. *Journal of Accounting and Economics*, 28, 3 (December): 359–389.

Kedia, Simi and Thomas Philippon. 2005. The economics of fraudulent accounting. AFA 2006 Boston Meeting Paper. SSRN.com/abstract=687225.

Kellogg, Irvin and Loren B. Kellogg. 1991. *Fraud, Window Dressing, and Negligence in Financial Statements*. Shepard's Commercial Law Series.

Kellogg, Robert L. 1984. Accounting activities, security prices, and class action lawsuits. *Journal of Accounting and Economics*, 6, 3 (December): 185–204.

Kelly, Stacie O., Ping-Sheng Koh, and Yen H. Tong. 2004. Governance structures and abnormal accruals characteristics. Working Paper, The University of Queensland.

Kerstein, Joseph J. and Atul Rai. 2005. Intra-year shifts in the earnings distribution and implications for earnings management. AAA 2006 Financial Accounting and Reporting Section (FARS) Meeting Paper. SSRN.com/abstract=817365.

Key, Kimberly Galligan. 1997. Political cost incentives for earnings management in the cable television industry. *Journal of Accounting and Economics*, 23, 3 (November): 309–337.

Keys, Phyllis and Joanne Li. 2005. Evidence on the market for professional directorship. *The Journal of Financial Research*, 28, 4 (December): 575–589.

Khurana, Inder K. and K.K. Raman. 2004. Litigation risk and the financial reporting credibility of big 4 versus non-big 4 audits: Evidence from Anglo-American countries. *The Accounting Review*, 79, 2 (April): 473–495.

Kile, Charles, Grace Pownall, and Gregory Waymire. 1998. How frequently do managers disclose prospective earnings information? *Journal of Financial Statement Analysis*, 3, 3 (Spring): 5–16.

Kim, Irene. 2002. An analysis of the market reward and torpedo effect of firms that consistently meet expectations. European Financial Management and Marketing Association 2002 Meeting Paper. SSRN/com/abstract=314381.

Kim, Irene. 2006. Directors' and officers' insurance and opportunism in accounting choice. Working Paper, Duke University.

Kim, Jeong-Bon, Richard Chung, and Michael Firth. 2003. Audit conservatism, asymmetric monitoring, and earnings management. *Contemporary Accounting Research*, 20, 2 (Summer): 323–359.

Kim, Kyonghee. 2005. Large shareholder turnover and CEO compensation. Working Paper, University of Pittsburgh.

Kim, Oliver. 1993. Disagreement among shareholders over a firm's disclosure policy. *Journal of Finance*, 48, 2 (June): 747–760.

Kim, Oliver, Steve C. Lim, and Kenneth Shaw. 2001. The inefficiency of the mean analyst forecast as a summary forecast of earnings. *Journal of Accounting Research*, 39, 2 (September): 329–335.

Kim, Oliver and Yoon S. Suh. 1993. Incentive efficiency of compensation based on accounting and market performance. *Journal of Accounting and Economics*, 16, 1-3 (January-July): 25–53.

Kim, Oliver and Robert Verrecchia. 2001. The relation among disclosure, returns, and trading volume information. *The Accounting Review*, 76, 4 (October): 633–654.

Kim, Yongtae and Myung Seok Park. 2005. Pricing of seasoned equity offers and earnings management. *Journal of Financial and Quantitative Analysis*, 40, 2 (June): 435–463.

Kim, Yongtae and Myung Seok Park. 2006. Market uncertainty and disclosure of internal control deficiencies under the Sarbanes-Oxley Act. AAA 2006 Annual Meeting Paper, Washington, DC.

King, Ronald, Grace Pownall, and Gregory Waymire. 1990. Expectations adjustment via timely management forecasts: Review, synthesis, and suggestions for future research. *Journal of Accounting Literature*, 9: 113–144.

King, Ronald, Grace Pownall, and Gregory Waymire. 1992. Corporate disclosure and price discovery associated with NYSE temporary trading halts. *Contemporary Accounting Research*, 8, 2 (Spring): 509–531.

Kinney, William, David Burgstahler, and Roger Martin. 2002. Earnings surprise "materiality" as measured by stock returns. *Journal of Accounting Research*, 40, 5 (December): 1297–1329.

Kinney, William R. and Roger Martin. 1994. Does auditing reduce bias in financial reporting? A review of audit-related adjustment studies. *Auditing: A Journal of Practice and Theory,* 13, 1 (Spring): 149–156.

Kinney, William R., Zoe-Vonna Palmrose, and Susan Scholz. 2004. Auditor independence, non-audit services, and restatements: Was the U.S. government right? *Journal of Accounting Research*, 42, 3 (June): 561–588.

Kinnunen, Juha, Marti Keloharju, Eero Kasanen, and Jyrki Niskanen. 1999. Earnings management and expected dividend increases around seasoned share issues: Evidence from Finland. *Scandinavian Journal of Management*, 16, 2 (June): 209–228.

Kinnunen, Juha and Markku Koskela. 2003. Who is Miss World in cosmetic earnings management? A cross-sectional comparison of small upward rounding of net income numbers among eighteen countries. *Journal of International Accounting Research*, 2, 1: 39–68.

Kirby, Alison J. 1988. Trade associations as information exchange mechanisms. *RAND Journal of Economics*, 19, 1 (Spring): 37–57.

Kirchmaier, Tom and Mariano Selvaggi. 2006. The dark side of "good" corporate governance: Compliance-fuelled book-cooking activities. FMG Discussion Paper No. 559. SSRN.com/abstract=895362.

Kirschenheiter, Michael and Nahum Melumad. 2000. Can "big bath" and earnings smoothing co-exist as equilibrium financial reporting strategies? *Journal of Accounting Research*, 40, 3 (June): 761–796.

Klassen, Kenneth J. 1997. The impact of insider ownership concentration on the trade-off between financial and tax reporting. *The Accounting Review*, 72, 3 (July): 455–474.

Klausner, Michael D. 2001. Institutional shareholders' split personality on corporate governance: Active in proxies, passive in IPOs. Stanford Law and Economics Olin Working Paper, No.225. SSRN.com/abstract=292083.

Klein, April. 1998. Firm performance and board committee structure. *The Journal of Law and Economics*, 41, 1 (April): 275–303.

Klein, April. 2002a. Economic determinants of audit committee independence. *The Accounting Review*, 77, 2 (April): 435–452.

Klein, April. 2002b. Audit committee, board of director characteristics, and earnings management. *Journal of Accounting and Economics*, 33, 3 (August): 375–400.

Klein, April. 2003. Likely effects of stock exchange governance proposals and Sarbanes-Oxley on corporate boards and financial reporting. *Accounting Horizons*, 17, 4 (December): 343–355.

Koch, Timothy W. and Larry D. Wall. 2006. The use of accruals to manage reported earnings: Theory and evidence. Federal Reserves Bank of Atlanta. SSRN.com/abstract=252756.

Kofman, Fred and Jacques Lawarree. 1993. Collusion in hierarchical agency. *Econometrica*, 61, 3 (May): 629–656.

Koh, Kevin, Dawn A. Matsumoto, and Shivaram Rajgopal. 2007. Meeting or beating analyst expectations in the post-scandals world: Changes in stock market rewards and managerial actions. SSRN.com/abstract=879831.

Kolasinski, Adam and S.P. Kothari. 2004. Investment banking and analyst objectivity: Evidence from forecasts and recommendations of analysts affiliated with M&A advisors. MIT Sloan School of Management Working Paper No. 4467-04. SSRN.com/abstract=499068.

Kole, Stacey R. and Kenneth M. Lehn. 1999. Deregulation and the adaptation of governance structure: The case of the U.S. airline. *Journal of Financial Economics*, 52, 1 (April): 79–117.

Kolev, Kain, Carol Marquardt, and Sarah McVay. 2007. SEC scrutiny and the evolution of non-GAAP reporting. *Acccounting Review*, forthcoming.

Korczak, Adriana. 2004. Managerial ownership and informativeness of accounting numbers in a European emerging market. Working Paper, European University Viadrina Frankfurt.

Kothari, S.P. 2001. Capital markets research in accounting. *Journal of Accounting and Economics*, 31, 1-3 (September): 105–231.

Kothari, S.P., Andrew L. Leone, and Charles E. Wasley. 2005. Performance matched discretionary accrual measures. *Journal of Accounting and Economics*, 39, 1 (February): 163–197.

Kothari, S.P., Thomas Lys, Clifford W. Smith, and Ross L. Watts. 1988. Auditor liability and information disclosure. *Journal of Accounting, Auditing and Finance*, 3, 4 (Fall): 307–339.

Kren, Leslie and Bruce A. Leauby. 2001. The effect of FAS 106 on chief executive compensation. *Advances in Public Interest Accounting* 8.

Kreps, David M. 1990. *Game Theory and Economic Modeling*. Clarendon Lectures in Economics. Oxford: Clarendon Press.

Krishnan, Gopal V. 2003a. Audit quality and the pricing of discretionary accruals. *Auditing: A Journal of Practice and Theory*, 22, 1 (March): 109–126.

Krishnan, Gopal V. 2003b. Does big 6 auditor industry expertise constrain earnings management? *Accounting Horizons*, 17 (Supplement): 1–16.

Krishnan, Gopal V. 2005a. Did Houston clients of Arthur Andersen recognize publicly available bad news in a timely fashion? *Contemporary Accounting Research*, 22, 1 (Spring): 165–193.

Krishnan, Gopal V. 2005b. The association between big 6 auditor industry expertise and the asymmetric timeliness of earnings. *Journal of Accounting, Auditing and Finance*, 20, 3 (Summer): 209–228.

Krishnan, Gopal V. and Ferdinand A. Gul. 2002. Has audit quality declined? Evidence from the pricing of discretionary accruals. SSRN.com/abstract=304392.

Krishnan, Gopal V. and Gnanakumar Visvanathan. 2005a. Reporting internal control deficiencies in the post-Sarbanes-Oxley era: The role of auditors and corporate governance. SSRN.com/abstract=646925,

Krishnan, Gopal V. and Gnanakumar Visvanathan . 2005b. Does the SOX definition of an accounting expert matter? The association between audit committee director's expertise and conservatism. SSRN.com/abstract=866884.

Krishnan, Jagan and Jayanthi Krishnan. 1997. Litigation risk and auditor resignations. *The Accounting Review*, 72, 4 (October): 539–560.

Krishnan, Jayanthi, Heibatollah Sami, and Yinqi Zhang. 2005. Does the provision of nonaudit services affect investor perceptions of auditor independence? *Auditing: A Journal of Practice and Theory*, 24, 2 (November): 111-135 .

Krishnan, Ranjani. 2005. The effect of changes in regulation and competition on firms' demand for accounting information. *The Accounting Review*, 80, 1 (January): 269–287.

Krishnan, Ranjani, Michelle H. Yetman, and Robert J. Yetman. 2002. Financial disclosure management by nonprofit organizations. Working Paper, University of Iowa.

Krishnaswami, Sudha, Paul A. Spindtand, and Venkat R. Subramaniam. 1999. Information asymmetry, monitoring, and the placement structure of corporate debt. *Journal of Financial Economics*, 51, 3 (March): 407–434.

Krull, Linda K. 2004. Permanently reinvested foreign earnings, taxes, and earnings management. *The Accounting Review*, 79, 3 (July): 745–767.

Kumar, Krishna R. and Gnanakumar Visvanathan. 2003. The information content of the deferred tax valuation allowance. *The Accounting Review*, 78, 2 (April): 471–490.

Kumar, Praveen and Shiva Sivaramakrishnan. 2002. Optimal incentive structures for the board of directors: A hierarchical agency framework. SSRN.com/abstract=339180.

Kwon, Young K. 2005. Accounting conservatism and managerial incentives. *Management Science*, 51, 11 (November): 1626–1632.

Kwon, Young K., D. Paul Newman, and Yoon S. Suh. 2001. The demand for accounting conservatism for management control. *Review of Accounting Studies,* 6 (March): 29–51.

La Porta, Rafael, Josef Lakonishok, Andrei Shleifer, and Robert W. Vishny. 1997. Good news for value stocks: Further evidence on market efficiency. *Journal of Finance*, 52, 2 (June): 859–874.

La Porta, Rafael, Florencio Lopez-De-Silanes, and Andrei Shleifer. 1999. Corporate ownership around the world. *Journal of Finance*, 54, 2 (April): 471–517.

La Porta, Rafael, Florencio Lopez-De-Silanes, Andrei Shleifer, and Robert Vishny. 2002. Investor protection and corporate valuation. *Journal of Finance*, 57, 3 (June): 1147–1170.

Laffont, Jean-Jacques, and Eric S. Maskin. 1990. The efficient market hypothesis and insider trading on the stock market. *Journal of Political Economy*, 98, 1 (February): 70–93.

Lai, Kam Wah. 2003. The Sarbanes-Oxley Act and auditor independence: Preliminary evidence from audit opinion and discretionary accruals. SSRN.com/abstract=438280.

Lakonishok, Josef and Inmoo Lee. 2001. Are insider trades informative? *Review of Financial Studies*, 14, 1 (Spring): 79–111.

Lakonishok, Josef, Andrei Shleifer, and Robert W. Vishny. 1992. The impact of institutional trading on stock prices. *Journal of Financial Economics*, 32, 1 (August): 23–43.

Lakonishok, Josef, Andrei Shleifer, Richard H. Thaler, and Robert W. Vishny. 1991. Window dressing by pension fund managers. *American Economic Reuiew Papers and Proceedings,* 81: 227–231.

Lambert, Richard A. 1983. Long term contracts and moral hazard. *The Bell Journal of Economics*, 14, 2 (Autumn): 441–452.

Lambert, Richard A. 1984. Income smoothing as rational equilibrium behavior. *The Accounting Review*, 59, 4 (October): 604–618.

Lambert, Richard A. 1986. Executive effort and selection of risky projects. *The RAND Journal of Economics*, 17, 1 (Spring): 77–88.

Lambert, Richard A. 1993. The use of accounting and security price measures of performance in managerial compensation contract: A discussion. *Journal of Accounting and Economics*, 16, 1-3 (January): 101–123.

Lambert, Richard A. 1999. Discussion of performance measure garbling under renegotiation in multi-period agencies. *Journal of Accounting Research*, 37 (Supplement): 215–221.

Lambert, Richard A. 2001. Contracting theory and accounting. *Journal of Accounting and Economics*, 32, 1-3 (December): 3–87.

Lambert, Richard A. 2003. Discussion of "Limited attention, information disclosure, and financial reporting." *Journal of Accounting and Economics*, 36, 1-3 (December): 387–400.

Lambert, Richard A., William N. Lanen, and David F. Larcker. 1989. Executive stock option plans and corporate dividend policy. *Journal of Financial and Quantitative Analysis*, 24, 4 (December): 409–425.

Lambert, Richard A. and David F. Larcker. 1987. An analysis of the use of accounting and market measures of performance in executive compensation contracts. *Journal of Accounting Research*, 25 (Supplement): 85–125.

Lambert, Richard A. and David F. Larcker. 2004. Stock options, restricted stock, and incentives. SSRN.com/abstract=527822.

Lambert, Richard A., David F. Larcker, and Robert Verrecchia. 1991. Portfolio considerations in valuing executive compensation. *Journal of Accounting Research*, 29, 1 (Spring): 129–149.

Lamont, Owen. 1998. Earnings and expected returns. *The Journal of Finance*, 53, 5 (October): 1563–1587.

Land, Judy and Mark H. Lang. 2002. Empirical evidence on the evolution of international earnings. *The Accounting Review*, 77, 4 (October): 115–133.

Lander, Guy P. 2004. *What is Sarbanes-Oxley?* New York: McGraw-Hill.

Landsman, Wayne R., Karen K. Nelson, and Brian Robert Rountree. 2006. An empirical analysis of Big N auditor switches: Evidence from the pre- and post-Enron eras. SSRN.com/abstract=899544.

Lang, Mark. 1991. Time-varying stock price response to earnings induced by uncertainty about the time-series process of earnings. *Journal of Accounting Research*, 29, 2 (Autumn): 229–257.

Lang, Mark H., Karl V. Lins, and Darius P. Miller. 2003. ADRs, analysts, and accuracy: Does cross listing in the U.S. improve a firm's information environment and increase market value? *Journal of Accounting Research*, 41, 2 (May): 317–345.

Lang, Mark H., Karl V. Lins, and Darius P. Miller. 2004. Concentrated control, analyst following, and valuation: Do analysts matter most when investors are protected least? *Journal of Accounting Research*, 42, 3 (June): 589–623.

Lang, Mark and Russel J. Lundholm. 1993. Cross-sectional determinants of analysts ratings of corporate disclosures. *Journal of Accounting Research*, 31, 2 (Autumn): 246–271.

Lang, Mark and Russell J. Lundholm. 1996. Corporate disclosure policy and analyst behavior. *The Accounting Review*, 71, 4 (October): 467–492.

Lang, Mark and Muareen McNichols. 1997. Institutional trading and corporate performance. Working Paper No. 1460, Stanford University.

Lang, Mark, Jana Smith Raedy, and Wendy M. Wilson. 2006. Earnings quality and cross listing: Are reconciled earnings comparable to US earnings? *Journal of Accounting and Economics*, 42, 1-2 (October): 255–283.

Langberg, Nisan and Shiva Sivaramakrishnan. 2006. Analyst coverage and conservatism: Implications for the precision of voluntary disclosures. SSRN.com/abstract=909549.

Langevoort, Donald C. 2003. Managing the "expectations gap" in investor protection: The SEC and the post-Enron reform agenda. *Villanova Law Review*, 48, 4: 1139. SSRN.com/abstract=474721.

Larcker, David F. and Scott A. Richardson. 2004. Fees paid to audit firms, accrual choices, and corporate governance. *Journal of Accounting Research*, 42, 3 (June): 625–658.

Larcker, David F., Scott A. Richardson, Andrew Seary, and Irem A. Tuna. 2005. Back door links between directors and executive compensation. SSRN.com/abstract=671063.

Larcker, David F., Scott A. Richardson, and Irem A. Tuna. 2005. How important is corporate governance? SSRN.com/abstract=595821.

Larrymore, Norris L., Pu Liu, and James N. Rimbey. 2006. Asymmetric information and bond rating downgrade announcements. Working Paper, Quinnipiac University and University of Arkansas.

Latane, Henry A. and Charles P. Jones. 1979. Standardized unexpected earnings–1971-1977. *Journal of Finance*, 34, 3 (June): 717–724.

Latham, Mark. 2005. Vote your stock. http://www.corpmon.com/VoteYourStock.pdf.

Lavelle, Louis. 2002. Commentary: When directors join CEOs at the trough. *Business Week*, June 17.

Lee, Chun I., Stuart Rosenstein, Nanda Rangan, and Wallace N. Davidson. 1992. Board composition and shareholder wealth. The case of management buyouts. *Financial Management*, 21, 1 (Spring): 58–72.

Lee, Ho Young, Vivek Mande, and Richard Ortman. 2004. The effect of audit committee and board of director independence on auditor resignation. *Auditing: A Journal of Practice and Theory*, 23, 2 (September): 131–146.

Lee, Susan. 2002. A market remedy. *Wall Street Journal*, July 10.

Lee, Yen-Jung, Kathy Ruby Petroni, and Min Shen. 2006. Cherry picking, disclosure quality, and comprehensive income reporting choices: The case of property-liability insurers. *Contemporary Accounting Research*, 23, 3 (Fall): 655–692.

Lefwich, Robert. 1983. Accounting information in private markets: Evidence from private lending agreements. *The Accounting Review*, 58, 1 (January): 23–42.

Lehavy, Reuven and Lawrence Revsine. 1994. Adopting timing: An examination of SFAS 106 choices. Working Paper, Northwestern University.

Lehn, Kenneth and Anil K. Makhija. 1997. EVA, accounting profits, and CEO turnover. An empirical examination 1985–1994. *Journal of Applied Corporate Finance*, 10, 2 (Fall): 90–97.

Lehn, Kenneth, Sukesh Patro, and Mengxin Zhao. 2005. Determinants of the size and structure of corporate boards: 1935-2000. SSRN.com/abstract=470675.

Lehn, Kenneth and Mengxin Zhao. 2004. CEO turnover after acquisitions: Do bad bidders get fired? SSRN.com/abstract=562502.

Leland, Hayne E. 1992. Insider trading: Should it be prohibited? *Journal of Political Economy*, 100, 4 (August): 859–887.

Leland, Hayne E. and David Pyle. 1977. Informational asymmetries, financial structure, and financial intermediation. *Journal of Finance*, 32, 2 (May): 371–387.

Lemke, Kenneth W. and Michael J. Page. 1992. Economic determinants of accounting policy choice: The case of current cost accounting in the U.K. *Journal of Accounting and Economics*, 15, 1 (March): 87–114.

Lennox, Clive S. 2005. Audit quality and executive officers' affiliations with CPA firms. *Journal of Accounting and Economics*, 39, 2 (June): 201–231.

Lennox, Clive S. and Chul W. Park. 2006. The informativeness of earnings and management's issuance of earnings forecasts. *Journal of Accounting and Economics*, 42, 3 (December): 439–458.

Leon, Gregory C. 2006. Stigmata: The stain of Sarbanes-Oxley on U.S. capital markets. GWU Law School Public Law Research Paper No. 224. SSRN.com/abstract=921394.

Leone, Andrew J. and Steve Rock. 2002. Empirical tests of budget ratcheting and its effect on managers' discretionary accrual choices. *Journal of Accounting and Economics*, 33, 1 (February): 43–67.

Leone, Andrew J. and Lawrence Van Horn. 2003. Earnings management in not-for-profit institutions: Evidence from hospitals. SSRN.com/abstract=146610.

Leone, Andrew J., Joanna Shuang Wu, and Jerold L. Zimmerman. 2005. Asymmetric Sensitivity of CEO Cash Compensation to Stock Returns. Simon School, University of Rochester, Research Paper No. FR 06-04. SSRN.com/abstract=510603.

Leone, Andrew J. Joanna Shuang Wu, and Jerold L. Zimmerman. 2006. Asymmetric sensitivity of CEO cash compensation to stock returns. *Journal of Accounting and Economics*, 42, 1-2 (October): 167–192.

Leuz, Christian, Dhananjay J. Nanda, and Peter David Wysocki. 2003. Earnings management and investor protection: An intentional comparison. *Journal of Financial Economics*, 69, 3 (September): 505–527.

Leuz, Christian, Alexander J. Triantis, and Tracy Yue Wang. 2006. Why do firms go dark? Causes and economic consequences of voluntary SEC deregistrations. AFA 2006 Boston Meeting Paper. SSRN.com/abstract=592421.

Leuz, Christian and Robert E. Verrecchia. 2000. The economic consequences of increased disclosure. *Journal of Accounting Research*, 38, 3 (Supplement): 91–124.

Lev, Baruch. 1989. On the usefulness of earnings and earnings research: Lessons and directions from two decades of empirical research. *Journal of Accounting Research*, 27, 3 (Supplement): 153–192.

Lev, Baruch. 2003. Corporate earnings: Facts and fiction. *Journal of Economic Perspectives*, 17, 2 (Summer): 27–50.

Lev, Baruch and Stephen H. Penman. 1990. Voluntary forecast disclosure, nondisclosure, and stock prices. *Journal of Accounting Research*, 28, 1 (Spring): 49–76.

Levi, Shai. 2005. Voluntary disclosure of accruals in earnings press releases and the pricing of accruals. SSRN.com/abstract=772306.

Levitt, Arthur. 1998. The numbers game. A speech delivered at the NYU Center for Law and Business, New York, N.Y. http://www.sec.gov/spch220.txt. Printed in *Take on the Street: What Wall Street and Corporate America Don't Want You to Know: What You Can Do to Fight Back* (with Paula Dwyer). New York: Pantheon Books.

Levitt, Arthur. 1999. Quality information: The lifeblood of our markets. Unpublished remarks. Available at http://www.sec.gov.news.speeches/spch304.txt.

Levitt, Arthur. 2000. Renewing the covenant with investors. A speech given at New York University Center for Law and Business on May 10. http://www.sec.gov/news/speech/spch370.htm.

Levitt, Arthur. 2002. *Take on the Street: What Wall Street and Corporate America Don't Want You to Know.* Pantheon.

Lewellen, Wilbur, Taewoo Park, and Byung T. Ro. 1995. Executive stock options compensation: The corporate reporting decision. *Managerial and Decision Economics*, 16, 6 (November/December): 633–647.

Lewellen, Wilbur G., Taewoo Park, and Byung T. Ro. 1996. Self-serving behavior in managers' discretionary information disclosure decisions. *Journal of Accounting and Economics*, 21, 2 (April) : 227–251.

Li, Chan and Qian Wang. 2006.   SOX 4O4 assessments and financial reporting errors. SSRN.com/abstract=926180.

Li, Haidan, Morton P.K. Pincus, and Sonja O. Rego. 2006.   Market reaction to events surrounding the Sarbanes-Oxley Act of 2002: Overall and as a function of earnings management. SSRN.com/abstract=475163.

Li, Jinliang, Lu Zhang, and Jian Zhou. 2005.   Earnings management and delisting risk: The case of IPO firms.   Simon School Working Paper FR 05-05.   SSRN.com/abstract=641021.

Li, Oliver, Zhen Hong Xie, and Weihong Xu. 2005.   Heterogeneous valuation of accruals and trading volume.   SSRN.com/abstract=493043.

Li, Si. 2003.   Stock-based incentives, corporate governance, and managers' fraudulent stock price manipulation. A Ph.D. dissertation. Duke University.

Li, Xianghong and Shelly Zhao. 2005.   Propensity score matching and abnormal performance after seasoned equity offerings.   AFA 2004 San Diego Meeting Paper. SSRN.com/abstract=451740.

Li, Yue and Bruce J. McConomy. 2004.   Simultaneous signaling in IPOs via management earnings forecasts and retained ownership: An empirical analysis of the substitution effect. *Journal of Accounting, Auditing and Finance*, 19, 1 (Winter): 1–28.

Liang, Pierre J. 2000.   Accounting recognition, moral hazard, and communication. *Contemporary Accounting Research*, 17, 3 (Fall): 457–490.

Liang, Pierre Jinghong. 2004.   Equilibrium earnings management, incentive contracts, and accounting standards. *Contemporary Accounting Research*, 21, 3 (Fall): 685–718.

Libby, Robert and William R. Kinney. 2000.   Does mandated audit communication reduce opportunistic corrections to manage earnings to forecasts? *The Accounting Review*, 75, 4 (October): 383–404.

Libby, Robert, Market W. Nelson, and James E. Hunton. 2006.   Recognition v. disclosure, auditor tolerance for misstatement, and the reliability of stock-compensation and lease information. *Journal of Accounting Research*, 44, 3 (June): 533–560.

Liberty, Susan E. and Jerold L. Zimmerman. 1986.   Labor unions contract negotiations and accounting choices. *The Accounting Review*, 61, 4 (October): 692–712.Lie, Erik. 2005. On the timing of CEO stock option awards. *Management Science*, 51, 5 (May): 802–812.Lim, Stephen and Zoltan Matolscy. 1999.   Earnings management of firms subjected to product price controls. *Accounting and Finance*, 39, 2 (July): 131–150.

Lim, Steve C. and Steven Lusgarten. 2002.   Testing for income smoothing using the backing out method. A review of specification issues. *Review of Quantitative Finance and Accounting*, 19, 3 (November): 273–290.

Lim, Terence. 2001.   Rationality and analysts' forecast bias. *Journal of Finance*, 56, 1 (February): 369–385.

Lin, Hsiou-Wie. and Maureen McNichols. 1998.   Underwriting relationships, analysts' earnings forecasts and investment recommendations. *Journal of Accounting and Economics*, 25, 1 (February): 101–127.

Lin, Jane-Raung Philip. 2003.   The long-run underperformance of post-listing stock returns: The evidence of earnings management. AFA 2003 Meeting Paper, Washington, DC. SSRN.com/abstract=341740.

Lin, Shu, Suresh Radhakrishnan, and Lixin (Nancy) Su. 2006.   Earnings management and guidance for meeting or beating analysts' earnings forecasts.   SSRN.com/abstract=928182.

Lin, Zhi-Xing and Michael S.H. Shih. 2002.   Earnings management in economic downturns and adjacent periods: Evidence from the 1990-1991 recession.   SSRN.com/abstract=331400.

Lin, Zhi-Xing and Michael S.H. Shih. 2006. Does the stock market see a zero or small positive earnings surprise as a red flag? SSRN.com/abstract=929943.

Linck, James S., Jeffry M. Netter, and Tina Yang. 2006. Effects and unintended consequences of the Sarbanes-Oxley Act on corporate boards. AFA 2006 Boston Meeting Paper. SSRN.com/abstract=687496.

Lipton, Martin and Jay Lorsch. 1992. A modest proposal for improved corporate governance. *Business Lawyer*, 48, 1: 59–77.

Litvak, Kate. 2006. The effect of the Sarbanes-Oxley Act on non-US companies cross-listed in the US. University of Texas Law, Law and Econ Research Paper No. 55. SSRN.com/abstract=876624.

Liu, Carol. 2004. The influence of audit committee oversight on corporate disclosure. Working Paper, University of Waterloo.

Liu, Chi-Chun and Stephen Ryan. 2006. Income smoothing over the business cycle: Changes in banks' coordinated management of provisions for loan losses and loan charge-offs from the pre-1990 bust to the 1990s boom. *The Accounting Review*, 81, 2 (March): 421–441.

Liu, Qiao and Joe Zhou Lu. 2003. Earnings management to tunnel: Evidence from China's listed companies. EFMA 2004 Basel Meeting Paper. SSRN.com/abstract=349880.

Liu, Ti and Stephen Paul Green. 2004. China's informal stock market: How it developed, how it works and how it might grow. SSRN.com/abstract=504043.

Liu, Yang and Paul H. Malatesta. 2006. Credit ratings and the pricing of seasoned equity offerings. Working Paper, University of Washington.

Livnat, Joshua. 2003. Differential persistence of extremely negative and positive earnings surprises: Implications for the post-earnings-announcement drift. SSRN.com/abstract=42100.

Livnat, Joshua and Richard R. Mendenhall. 2006. Comparing the post-earnings announcement drift for surprises calculated from analyst and time series forecasts. *Journal of Accounting Research*, 44, 1 (March): 177–205.

Lobo, Gerald J. and Jian Zhou. 2001. Disclosure quality and earnings management. *Asia-Pacific Journal of Accounting and Economics*, 8, 1 (June): 1–20.

Lobo, Gerald J., and Jian Zhou. 2005. To swear early or not to swear early? An empirical investigation of factors affecting CEOs' decisions. *Journal of Accounting and Public Policy*, 24, 2 (March-April): 153–160.

Lobo, Gerald J. and Jian Zhou. 2006. Did conservatism in financial reporting increase after the Sarbanes-Oxley Act? Initial evidence. *Accounting Horizons*, 20, 1 (March): 57–73.

Lock, Mark S., Mansi Sattar, and William F. Maxwell. 2005. Does corporate governance matter to bondholders? *Journal of Financial and Quantitative Analysis*, 40, 4 (December): 693–719.

Loh, Alfred L.C. and Tin Hoe Tan. 2002. Assets write-offs–managerial incentives and macroeconomic factors. *Abacus*, 38, 1 (February): 134–151.

Loomis, C.J. 1999. Lies, damned lies, and managed earnings. *Fortune*, 140, 3 (August 2): 74–92.

Lopez, Thomas J. and Lynn Rees. 2002a. The effect of beating and missing analysts' forecasts on the information content of unexpected earnings. *Journal of Accounting, Auditing, and Finance*, 17, 2 (Summer): 155–184.

Lopez, Thomas J. and Lynn Rees. 2002b. The effect of beating and missing analysts' forecasts on the information content of unexpected earnings. *Journal of Accounting, Auditing, and Finance* 17, 2 (Spring): 155–184.

Lopez-De-Silanes, Florencio. 2005. Overview of current research. Working paper, University of Califronia at Berkely.

Lord, Richard A. and Yoshie Saito. 2004. Interrelationships between components of managerial compensation and firm characteristics. Working paper, Montclair State University and Temple University. AAA 2004 Annual Meeting Paper, Orlando, FL .

Lougee, Barbara and Carol Marquardt. 2004. Earnings quality and strategic disclosure: An empirical examination of "pro forma" Earnings. *The Accounting Review*, 79, 3 (July): 769–795.

Loughran, Tim and Jay R. Ritter. 1997. The operating performance of firms conducting seasoned equity offerings. *Journal of Finance*, 52, 5 (December): 1823–1850.

Louis, Henock. 2004. Earnings management and the market performance of acquiring firms. *Journal of Financial Economics*, 74, 1 (October): 121–148.

Louis, Henock. 2005. Acquirers' abnormal returns and the non-big 4 auditor clientele effect. *Journal of Accounting and Economics*, 40, 1-3 (December): 75–99.

Louis, Henock, Jennifer Joe, and Dahlia Robinson. 2005. Managers' and investors' responses to media exposure of board ineffectiveness. SSRN.com/abstract=714501.

Louis, Henock and Dahlia Robinson. 2005. Do managers credibly use accruals to signal private information? Evidence from the pricing of discretionary accruals around stock splits. *Journal of Accounting and Economics*, 39, 2 (June): 361–380.

Louis, Henock, Dahlia Robinson, and Andrew M. Sbaraglia. 2006. An integrated analysis of the association between accrual disclosure and the abnormal accrual anomaly. SSRN.com/abstract=785148.

Lu, J. 2000. The valuation allowance for deferred tax assets and earnings management. Working Paper, University of Southern California.

Lu, Tong. 2006. Does opinion shopping impair auditor independence and audit quality? *Journal of Accounting Research*, 44, 3 (June): 561–584.

Lu, Yvonne Y. 2003. Earnings management and securities litigation. Working Paper, University of California at Berkeley.

Lubberink, Martien and Carel Huijgen. 2000. A wealth based explanation for earnings conservatism. SSRN.com/abstract=253854.

Lundholm, Russell J. 1988. Price-signals relations in the presence of correlated public and private information. *Journal of Accounting Research*, 26, 1 (Spring): 107–118.

Lundholm, Russell J. 1991. Public signals and the equilibrium allocation of private information. *Journal of Accounting Research*, 29, 2 (Autumn): 322–349.

Lundholm, Russell J. 1999. Reporting on the past: A new approach to improving accounting today. *Accounting Horizons*, 13, 4 (December): 315–322.

Lundholm, Russell J. and Linda A. Myers. 2002. Bringing the future forward: The effect of disclosure on the returns–earnings relation. *Journal of Accounting Research*, 40, 3 (June): 809–839.

Luo, Yuanzhi. 2005. Do insiders learn from outsiders? Evidence from mergers and acquisitions. *Journal of Finance*, 60, 4 (August): 1951–1982.

Lys, Thomas and Ross Watts. 1994. Lawsuits against auditors. *Journal of Accounting Research*, 32 (Supplement): 65–93.

Ma, Ching-To. 1988. Unique implementation of incentive contracts with many agents. *Review of Economics Studies*, 55, 4 (October): 555–572.

Ma, Christopher K. 1988. Loan loss reserves and income smoothing: The experience in the US banking industry. *Journal of Business Finance and Accounting*, 15, 4 (Winter): 487–497.

MacAvoy, Paul and Ira M. Millstein. 1999. The active board of directors and its effect on the performance of the large publicly traded corporation. *Journal of Applied Corporate Finance*, 11, 4 (Winter): 8–20.

Maddala, G.S. 1998. Introduction to Econometrics. London: Collier McMillan Publishers.

Magee, Robert P. and Mein Chiun Tseng. 1990. Audit pricing and independence. *The Accounting Review*, 65, 2 (April): 315–336.

Magnan, Michel and Denis Cormier. 1997. The impact of forward-looking financial data in IPOs on the quality of financial reporting. *Journal of Financial Statement Analysis*, 3, 2 (Winter): 6–17.

Magnan, Michel, Cathy Nadeau, and Denis Cormier. 1999. Earnings management during antidumping investigations: Analysis and implications. *Canadian Journal of Administrative Science*, 16, 2 (June) 149–162.

Maines, Laureen A. and Linda S. McDaniel. 2000. Effects of comprehensive income characteristics on nonprofessional investors' judgments: The role of financial-statement presentation format. *The Accounting Review*, 75, 2 (April): 179–207.

Mak, Yuen Teen and Yuanto Kusnadi. 2002. Size really matters: Further evidence on the negative relationship between board size and firm value. NUS Business School Working Paper. SSRN.com/abstract=303505.

Makar, Stephen D. and Pervaiz Alam. 1998. Earnings management and antitrust investigations: Political cost over business cycles. *Journal of Business Finance and Accounting*, 25, 5-6 (June/July): 701–720.

Maksimovic, Vojislav and Sheridan Titman. 1991. Financial policy and reputation for product quality. Review of Financial Studies, 4, 1 (Spring): 175–200.

Malcomson, James M. and Frans Spinnewyn. 1988. The multiperiod principal–agent problem. *Review of Economic Studies*, 55, 3 (July): 391–407.

Malmendier, Ulrike and Geoffrey Alan Tate. 2005. Superstar CEOs. 7th Annual Texas Finance Festival Paper. SSRN.com/abstract=709861.

Malmquist, David H. 1990. Efficient contracting and the choice of accounting method in the oil and gas industry. *Journal of Accounting and Economics*, 12, 1-3 (January): 173–205.

Manne, Henry G. 1966. *Insider Trading and the Stock Market*. New York: Free Press.

Mansi, Sattar A., William F. Maxwell, and Darius P. Miller. 2004. Does auditor quality and tenure matter to investors? Evidence from the bond market. *Journal of Accounting Research*, 40, 4 (September): 755–793.

Manzon Jr., Gil B. 1992. Earnings management of firms subject to the alternative minimum tax. *The Journal of American Taxation Association*, 14, 2 (Fall): 86–111.

Markelevich, Ariel, Rani Hoitash, and Charles A. Barragato. 2005. Auditor fees, abnormal fees and audit quality before and after the Sarbanes-Oxley Act. SSRN.com/abstract=646681.

Marks, Erin. 2004. The Sarbanes-Oxley Act: Costs and trade offs relating to international application and convergence. *Research in Accounting Regulation*, 17: 233–266.

Marosi, Andras and Nadia Ziad Massoud. 2004. Why do firms go dark? SSRN.com/abstract=570421.

Marquardt, Carol A. 2002. The cost of employee stock option grants: An empirical analysis. *Journal of Accounting Research*, 40, 4 (September): 1191–1217.

Marquardt, Carol A. and Christine I. Wiedman. 2004a. How are earnings managed? An examination of specific accruals. *Contemporary Accounting Research*, 21, 4 (Summer): 461–491.

Marquardt, Carol A. and Christine I. Wiedman. 2004b. The effect of earnings management on the value relevance of accounting information. *Journal of Business Finance and Accounting*, 31, 3/4 (April/May): 297–332.

Marquardt, Carol A. and Christine I. Wiedman. 2005. Earnings management through transaction structuring: Contingent convertible debt and diluted EPS. *Journal of Accounting Research*, 43, 2 (May): 205–243.

Marquardt, Carol A., Christine I. Wiedman, and Michael Welker. 1998. Voluntary disclosure, information asymmetry, and insider selling through secondary equity offerings. *Contemporary Accounting Research*, 15, 4 (Winter): 505–537.

Marques, Ana Christina. 2006. SEC interventions and the frequency and usefulness of non-GAAP financial measures. *Review of Accounting Studies*, 11, 4 (December): 549–574.

Marsden, Alastair and Jilnaught Wong. 1998. The impact of taxation on the earnings management of New Zealand electric power boards. *The Pacific Accounting Review*, 10, 2 (December): 1–31.

Mashruwala, Christina, Shivaram Rajgopal, and Terry Shevlin. 2006. Why is the accruals anomaly not arbitraged away? The role of idiosyncratic risk and transaction costs. *Journal of Accounting and Economics*, 42, 1-2 (October): 3–33.

Mason, Lori and Mir A. Zaman. 2004. Insider trading and motivations for earnings management. A paper presented in 2004 FMA Conference, Zurich Switzerland.

Matsumoto, Dawn A. 2002. Management's incentives to avoid negative earnings surprises. *The Accounting Review*, 77, 3 (July): 483–514.

Matsunaga, Steve R. and Chul W. Park. 2001. The effect of missing a quarterly earnings benchmark on the CEO's annual bonus. *The Accounting Review*, 76, 3 (July): 313–332.

Matsunaga, Steve R., Terry S. Shevlin, and D. Shores. 1992. Disqualifying dispositions of incentive stock options: Tax benefits versus financial reporting costs. *Journal of Accounting Research*, 30, 3 (Supplement): 37–76.

Matthews, Steven A. 2001. Renegotiating moral-hazard contracts under limited liability and monotonicity. *Journal of Economic Theory*, 97, 1 (March): 1–29.

Maug, Ernest. 1998. Large shareholders as monitors: Is there a trade-off between liquidity and control? *Journal of Finance*, 53, 1 (February): 65–98.

Maug, Ernst G. and Kristian Rydqvist. 2006. Do shareholders vote strategically? Voting behavior, proposal screening, and majority rules. Mannheim Finance Working Paper No. 2006-15. SSRN.com/abstract=471362.

May, Don O. 1995. Do managerial motives influence firm risk reduction strategies? *Journal of Finance*, 50, 4 (September): 1291–1308.

Maydew, Edward L. 1997. Tax-induced earnings management by firms with net operating losses. *Journal of Accounting Research*, 35, 1 (Spring): 83–96.

Maydew, Edward L. 2001. Empirical tax research in accounting: A discussion. *Journal of Accounting and Economics*, 31, 1-3 (September): 398–403.

Mayers, David, Anil Shivdasani, and Clifford W. Smith. 1997. Board composition and corporate control: Evidence from the insurance industry. *The Journal of Business*, 70, 1 (January): 33–62.

Mayew, William J. 2006. Evidence of management discrimination among analysts during earnings conference calls. SSRN.com/abstract=924417.

Mayhew, Brian W. and Joel E. Pike. 2004. Does investor selection of auditors enhance auditor independence? *The Accounting Review*, 79, 3 (July): 797–822.

McAnally, Mary Lea, Anup Srivastava, and Connie D. Weaver. 2006. Executive stock options, missed earnings targets and earnings management: Evidence from book-tax differences. AAA 2007 Financial Accounting & Reporting Section (FARS) Meeting Paper. SSRN.com/abstract=925584.

McBarnet, Doreen and Christopher Whelan. 1999. *Creative Accounting and the Cross-Eyed Javelin Thrower*. New York: Wiley.

McConnell, John J. and Henri Servaes. 1990. Additional evidence on equity ownership and corporate value. *Journal of Financial Economics*, 27, 2 (October): 595–612.

McConomy, Bruce J. and Merridee L. Bujaki. 2002. Corporate governance: Factors influencing voluntary disclosure by publicly traded Canadian firms. *Canadian Accounting Perspectives*, 1, 2 (Fall): 105–139.

McCulloch, Brian W. 1998a. Multi-period incentives and alternative dials for earnings management. Working Paper. SSRN.com/abstract=121531.

McCulloch, Brian W. 1998b. Relations among components of accruals under earnings management. SSRN.com/abstract=131455.

McDaniel, Linda, Roger D. Martin, and Laureen A. Maines. 2002. Evaluating financial reporting quality: The effects of financial expertise vs. financial literacy. *The Accounting Review*, 77, 1 (January): 139–167.

McDonnell, Brett H. 2004. SOX appeals. *Michigan State University—DCL Law Review*. SSRN.com/abstract=497422.

McInnis, John M. and Daniel W. Collins. 2006. Do cash flow forecasts deter earnings management? SSRN.com/abstract=922770.

McNeil, Chris, Greg Niehaus, and Eric Powers. 2004. Management turnover in subsidiaries of conglomerates versus stand-alone firms. *Journal of Financial Economics*, 72, 1 (April) 2004: 63–96.

McNichols, Maureen F. 1989. Evidence of informational asymmetries from management earnings forecasts and stock returns. *The Accounting Review*, 64, 1 (January), 1–27.

McNichols, Maureen F. 2000. Research design issues in earnings management studies. *Journal of Accounting and Public Policy*, 19, 4-5 (Winter): 313–345.

McNichols, Maureen F. 2002. Discussion of the quality of accruals and earnings: The role of accrual estimation error. *The Accounting Review*, 77 (Supplement): 61–69.

McNichols, Maureen F. and Stephen R. Stubben. 2005. Does earnings management affect firms' investment decisions? Working Paper, Stanford University.

McNichols, Maureen F. and Peter G. Wilson. 1988. Evidence of earnings management from the provision for bad debts. *Journal of Accounting Research*, 26, 3 (Supplement): 1–40.

McVay, Sarah Elizabeth. 2006. Earnings management using classification shifting: An examination of core earnings and special items. *The Accounting Review*, 81, 3 (May): 501–531.

McVay, Sarah Elizabeth, Venky Nagar, and Vicki Wei Tang. 2006. Trading incentives to meet earnings thresholds. *Review of Accounting Studies*, 11, 4 (December): 575–598.

McWilliams, Victoria B. and Nilanjan Sen. 1997. Board monitoring and antitakeover amendments. *Journal of Financial and Quantitative Analysis*, 32, 4 (December): 491–505.

Melendrez, Kevin, William C. Schwartz Jr., and Mark A. Trombley. 2005. How does the market value accrual and cash flow surprises? SSRN.com/abstract=676651.

Melis, Andrea. 2004. Corporate governance failures. To what extent is Parmalat a particularly Italian case? *Corporate Governance: An International Review*, 13, 4 (July): 478–488.

Mendenhall, Richard R., William D. Nichols, and Krishna G. Palepu. 1988. Bad news and differential market reactions to announcements of earlier-quarters versus fourth-quarter earnings. *Journal of Accounting Research*, 26, 3 (Supplement): 63–91.

Menon, Krishnagopal and Joanne Deahl Williams. 1994. The use of audit committees for monitoring. *Journal of Accounting and Public Policy*, 13, 2 (Summer): 121–139.

Menon, Krishnagopal and Joanne Deahl Williams. 2004. Former audit partners and abnormal accruals. *The Accounting Review*, 79, 4 (October): 1095–1118.

Mensah, Yaw M., Judith M. Considine, and Leslie Oakes. 1994. Statutory insolvency regulations and earnings management in the prepaid health-care industry. *The Accounting Review*, 69, 1 (January): 70–95.

Merchant, Kenneth A. 1990. The effects of financial controls on data manipulation and management myopia. *Accounting Organizations and Society*, 15, 4: 297–313.

Merchant, Kenneth A. and Joanne Rockness. 1994. The ethics of managing earnings: An empirical investigation. *Journal of Accounting and Public Policy*, 13, 1 (Spring): 79–94.

Mest, David P. and Elizabeth Plummer. 2003. Analysts' rationality and forecast bias: Evidence from sales forecasts. *Review of Quantitative Finance and Accounting*, 21, 2 (September): 103–122.

Meth, Bracha. 1996. Reduction of outcome variance: Optimality and incentives. *Contemporary Accounting Research*, 13, 1 (Spring): 309–328.

Meulbroek, Lisa. 2001. The efficiency of equity-linked compensation: Understanding the full cost of awarding executive stock options. *Financial Management*, 30, 2 (Summer): 5–30.

Meuwissen, Roger, Frank Moers, Erik Peek, and Ann Vanstraelen. 2004. The influence of auditor independence regulation on earnings quality: An empirical analysis of firms cross-listed in the U.S. SSRN.com/abstract=552001.

Michaely, Roni and Michael R. Roberts. 2006. Dividend smoothing, agency costs, and information asymmetry: Lessons from the dividend policies of private firms. SSRN.com/abstract=927802.

Michaely, Roni and Kent L. Womack. 1999. Conflict of interest and the credibility of underwriter analyst recommendations. *The Review of Financial Studies*, 12, 4 (Special): 653–686.

Michaud, Dennis Wright and Kate A. Magaram. 2006. Recent technical papers on corporate governance. SSRN.com/abstract=895520.

Michelson, Stuart E., James Jordan-Wagner, and Charles H. Wootton. 1995. A market based analysis of income smoothing. *Journal of Business Finance and Accounting*, 22, 8 (December): 1179–1193.

Mikhail, Michael B. 1999. Coordination of earnings, regulatory capital and taxes in private and public companies. SSRN.com/abstract=165010.

Mikhail, Michael B., Beverly R.Walther, and Richard H. Willis. 1999. Does forecast accuracy matter to security analysts? *The Accounting Review*, 74, 2 (April): 185–200.

Mikhail, Michael B., Beverly R.Walther, and Richard H. Willis. 2003. The effect of experience on security analyst underreaction. *Journal of Accounting and Economics*, 35, 1 (April): 101–116.

Mikhail, Michael B., Beverly R. Walther, and Richard H. Willis. 2004. Earnings surprises and the cost of equity capital. SSRN.com/abstract=504662.

Mikkelson, Wayne H. and Magen M. Partch. 1997. The decline of takeovers and disciplinary managerial turnover. *Journal of Financial Economics*, 44, 2 (May): 205–228.

Milgrom, Paul R. 1981. Good news and bad news: Representation theorems and applications. *Bell Journal of Economics*, 12, 2 (Autumn): 380–391.

Milgrom, Paul R. and John Roberts. 1986. Relying on the information of interested parties. *RAND Journal of Economics*, 17, 1 (Spring): 18–32.

Milgrom, Paul R. and John Roberts. 1992. *Economics, Organization, and Management*. Englewood Cliffs, New Jersey: Prentice-Hall.

Miller, Gregory S. 2002. Earnings performance and discretionary disclosure. *Journal of Accounting Research*, 40, 1 (March): 173-204. .

Miller, Gregory S. 2005. The press as a watchdog for accounting fraud. SSRN.com/abstract=484423.

Miller, Gregory S. and Joseph D. Piotroski. 2000. Forward-looking earnings statements: Determinants and market response. SSRN.com/abstract=238593.

Miller, Gregory and Douglas Skinner. 1998. Determinants of the valuation allowance for deferred tax assets under SFAS 109. *The Accounting Review*, 73, 2 (April): 213–233.

Miller, Merton H. and Kevin Rock. 1985. Dividend policy under asymmetric information. *Journal of Finance*, 40, 4 (September): 1031–1051.

Miller, Paul B.W. and Paul R. Bahnson. 2002. *Quality Financial Reporting*, New York: McGraw-Hill.

Mills, Lilian F. 1998. Book-tax differences and Internal Revenue Service adjustments. *Journal of Accounting Research,* 36, 2 (Autumn): 343–356.

Mills, Lilian F. and Kaye J. Newberry. 2001. The influence of tax and nontax costs on book-tax reporting differences: Public and private firms. *Journal of the American Taxation Association,* 23, 1 (Spring): 1–19.

Mills, Lilian F. and Richard Sansing. 2000. Strategic tax and financial reporting decisions: Theory and evidence. *Contemporary Accounting Research,* 17, 1 (Spring): 85–106.

Ming, Jian Jane and T.J. Wong. 2003. Earnings management and tunneling through related party transactions: Evidence from Chinese corporate groups. EFA 2003 Annual Conference Paper 549. SSRN.com/abstract=424888.

Mitchell, Lawrence E. 2003. The Sarbanes-Oxley Act and the reinvention of corporate governance? *Villanova Law Review,* 48, 4: 1189. SSRN.com/abstract=474761.

Mitchell, Mark L. and Erik Stafford. 2000. Managerial decisions and long-term stock price performance. *The Journal of Business,* 73, 3 (July): 287–329.

Mitra, Santanu and Mahmud Hossain. 2006. Ownership composition and nonaudit service fees. A paper presented in the auditing midyear conference, Los Angeles, CA.

Mittendorf, Brian and Yun Zhang. 2005. The role of biased earnings guidance in creating a healthy tension between managers and analysts. *The Accounting Review,* 80, 4 (October): 1193–1209.

Moberly, Richard. 2006. Sarbanes-Oxley's structural model to encourage corporate whistle-blowers. *Brigham Young University Law Review,* 1107. SSRN.com/abstract=902941.

Moehrle, Stephen R. 2002. Do firms use restructuring charge reversals to meet earnings targets? *The Accounting Review,* 77, 2 (July): 397–413.

Mohanram, Partha S. 1999. How do young firms choose among different modes of investor communications? SSRN.com/abstract=151021.

Mohanram, Partha S. and Shyam V. Sunder. 2004. How has Regulation Fair Disclosure affected the functioning of financial analysts? SSRN.com/abstract=297933.

Mohd, Emad. 2005. Financial analysts turnover. A paper presented at the Annual Meeting of the Canadian Academic Accounting Association, Quebec City, Canada.

Mohrman, MaryBeth. 1993. Debt contracts and FAS No. 19: A test of the debt covenant hypothesis. *The Accounting Review,* 68, 2 (April): 273–288.

Mohrman, MaryBeth. 1996. The use of Fixed GAAP provisions in debt contracts. *Accounting Horizons,* 10, 3 (September): 78–91.

Monahan, Steven J. 2005. Conservatism, growth and the role of accounting numbers in the equity valuation process. *Review of Accounting Studies,* 10, 2-3 (September): 227–260.

Monahan, Steven J. 2006. Discussion of "Why do managers voluntarily issue cash flows forecasts?" *Journal of Accounting Research,* 44, 2 (May): 431–436.

Monks, Robert A.G. and Nell Minow. 2004. *Corporate Governance.* Third Edition. Oxford: Blackwell.

Monsen, Joseph R. and Anthony Downs. 1965. A theory of large managerial firms. *Journal of Political Economy,* 73, 3 (June): 221–236.

Mookherjee, Dilip. 1984. Optimal incentives schemes with many agents. *The Review of Economic Studies,* 51, 3 (July): 433–446.

Moore, Don A., Philip E. Tetlock, Lloyd Tanlu, and Max H. Bazerman. 2006. Conflicts of interest and the case of auditor independence: Moral seduction and strategic issue cycling. *The Academy of Management Review,* 31, 1: 10–29.

Morsfield, Suzanne G. and Christine E. Tan. 2006. Do venture capitalists influence the decision to manage earnings in initial public offerings? *The Accounting Review,* 81, 5 (October): 1119–1150.

Moses, Douglas O. 1987. Income smoothing and incentives: Empirical tests using accounting changes. *The Accounting Review,* 62, 2 (April): 358–377.

Moyen, Nathalie. 2000. Investment distortions caused by debt financing. SSRN.com/abstract=237088.

Moyer, Susan E. 1990. Capital adequacy ratio regulations and accounting choices in commercial banks. *Journal of Accounting and Economics*, 13, 2 (July): 123–154.

Mozes, Haim A. 1997. The implications of a LIFO liquidation for future gross margins. *Journal of Financial Statement Analysis*, 2, 4 (Summer): 39–51.

Mulford, Charles W. and Eugene E. Comiskey. 1996. *Financial Warnings*. New York: Wiley.

Mulford, Charles W. and Eugene E. Comiskey. 2002. The financial numbers game: detecting creative accounting practices. New York: Wiley.

Muller, Karl A. 1999. An examination of the voluntary recognition of acquired brand names in the United Kingdom. *Journal of Accounting and Economics*, 26, 1-3 (January): 179–191.

Munzig, Peter Grosvenor. 2003. Enron and the economics of corporate governance. Working Paper. A Ph.D. dissertation. Stanford University.

Murphy, Kevin J. 1985. Corporate performance and managerial remuneration: An empirical analysis. *Journal of Accounting and Economics*, 7, 1-3 (April): 11–42.

Murphy, Kevin J. 1996. Reporting choice and the 1992 proxy disclosure rules. *Journal of Accounting, Auditing and Finance*, 11, 3 (Summer): 497–515.

Murphy, Kevin J. 1998. Performance standards in incentive contracts. *Journal of Accounting and Economics*, 30, 3 (December): 245–278.

Murphy, Kevin J. 1999. Executive compensation. In Orley Ashenfelter and David Card, eds., *Handbook of Labor Economics*, Volume 3B. Amsterdam: North Holland. Ch. 38: 2485–2563.

Murphy, Kevin J. and Jerold Zimmerman. 1993. Financial performance surrounding CEO turnover. *Journal of Accounting and Economics*, 16, 1-3 (January-July): 273–315.

Muscarella, Chris J. and Michael R. Vetsuypens. 1990. Efficiency and organizational structure: A study of reverse LBOs. *Journal of Finance*, 45, 6 (December): 1389–1413.

Myers, James, Linda A. Myers, and Thomas C. Omer. 2003. Exploring the term of the auditor–client relationship and the quality of earnings: A case for mandatory auditor rotation? *The Accounting Review*, 78, 3 (July): 779–799.

Myers, James N., Linda A. Myers, and Douglas J. Skinner, 2006. Earnings momentum and earnings management. SSRN.com/abstract=741244.

Myers, Stewart C. 1991. Signaling and accounting information. MIT working Paper.

Myers, Stewart C. and Nicholas Majluf. 1984. Corporate financing and investment decisions when firms have information that investors do not have. *Journal of Financial Economics*, 13, 2 (June): 187–221.

Myerson, Roger. 1979. Incentive compatibility and the bargaining problem. *Econometrica*, 47, 1 (January): 61–73.

Myerson, Roger. 1991. *Game Theory: Analysis of Conflict*. Cambridge, MA: Harvard University Press.

Nagar, Venky. 2002. Delegation and incentive compensation. *The Accounting Review*, 77, 2 (April): 379–396.

Nagar, Venky and Paolo Petacchi. 2005. An economy-level model of earnings management with endogenous enforcement. SSRN.com/abstract=806684.

Nagar, Venky, Kathy Petroni, and Daniel Wolfenzon. 2002. Governance problems in close corporations. Working Paper, New York University.

Nagarajan, Nandu J. and Sri S. Sridhar. 1996. Corporate responses to segment disclosure requirements. *Journal of Accounting and Economics*, 21, 2 (April): 253–275.

Nam, Seunghan and Joshua Ronen. 2007. Information transfer effects of senior executives' migrations and subsequent write-offs. Working Paper, Rutgers Business School and Leonard N. Stern School of Business.

Narayanan, M.P. 1985. Managerial incentives for short-term results. *Journal of Finance*, 40, 5 (December): 1469–1484.

Narayanan, M.P. 1996. Form of compensation and managerial decision horizon. *Journal of Financial and Quantitative Analysis*, 31, 4 (December): 467–491.

Narayanan, M.P. and Nejat H. Seyhun. 2006. The dating game: do managers designate option grant dates to increase their compensation? SSRN.com/abstract=896164.

Narayanan, M.P., Cindy A. Schipani, and H. Nejat Seyhun. 2006. The economic impact of backdating of executive stock options. *The Michigan Law Review*, 105, 8 (June): 1597–1641.

Narayanan, M.P. and Nejat H. Seyhun. 2005. Effect of Sarbanes-Oxley Act on the influencing of executive compensation. SSRN.com/abstract=852964.

Narayanan, Ranga. 2000. Insider trading and the voluntary disclosure of information by firms. *Journal of Banking and Finance*, 24, 3 (March): 395–425.

Narayanan, V.G. and Antonio Davila. 1998. Using delegation and control systems to mitigate the trade-off between the performance-evaluation and belief-revision uses of accounting signals. *Journal of Accounting and Economics*, 25, 3 (June): 255–282.

Naser, Kamal H.M. 1993. *Creative Financial Reporting: Its Nature and Use*. Hemel Hempstead: Prentice-Hall.

Nash, John. 1950. The bargaining problem. *Econometrica*, 18, 2 (April): 155–162.

Natarajan, Ramachandran. 1996. Stewardship value of earnings components: Additional evidence on the determinants of executive compensation. *The Accounting Review*, 71, 1 (January): 1–22.

Natarajan, Ramachandran. 2004. Informativeness of performance measures in the presence of reporting discretion. *Journal of Accounting, Auditing and Finance*, 19, 1 (Winter): 61–83.

Navissi, Farshid. 1999. Earnings management under price regulation. *Contemporary Accounting Research*, 16, 2 (Summer): 281–304.

Ndubizu, Gordian A. 2007. Do cross-border listing firms manage earnings or seize a window of opportunity? *The Accounting Review*, July, forthcoming.

Ndubizu Gordian A., and Yongtao Hong. 2007. Is earnings management at the cross-listing period informative? Working paper, Drexel University.

Neill, John D., Susan G. Pourciau, and Thomas F. Schaefer. 1995. Accounting method choice and IPO valuation. *Accounting Horizons*, 9, 3 (September): 68–80.

Nelson, Mark. 2006. Response. Ameliorating conflicts of interests in auditing: Effects of recent reforms on auditors and their clients. *The Academy of Management Review*, 31, 1: 30–42.

Nelson, Mark W., John A. Elliott, and Robin L. Tarpley. 2002. Evidence from auditors about managers' and auditors' earnings management decisions. *The Accounting Review*, 77 (Supplement): 175–202.

Nelson, Mark W., John A. Elliott, and Robin L. Tarpley. 2003. How are earnings managed: Examples from auditors. *Accounting Horizons*, 17 (Supplement): 17–35.

Newkirk, Thomas C. and Melissa A. Robertson. 1998. Insider trading—A U.S. perspective. A speech given at the 16th International Symposium on Economic Crime. Jesus College, Cambridge, England. http://www.sec.gov/news/speech/speecharchive/1998/spch221.htm.

Newman, Paul. 1988. Discussion of "An explanation for accounting income smoothing". *Journal of Accounting Research*, 26, 3 (Supplement): 140–143.

Newman, Paul. 1998. Discussion of "Performance measure manipulation." *Contemporary Accounting Research*, 15, 3 (Fall): 287–290.

Newman, Paul and Richard Sansing. 1993. Disclosure policies with multiple users. *Journal of Accounting Research*, 31, 1 (Spring): 92–112.

Nichols, Donald R. and David B. Smith. 1983. Auditor credibility and auditor changes. *Journal of Accounting Research*, 21, 2 (Autumn): 534–544.

Nichols, Nancy, Sid B. Gray, and Donna L. Street. 2005. Pro forma adjustments to GAAP earnings: An analysis of specific adjustments, materiality, and SEC action. *Research in Accounting Regulation*, 18: 29–52.

Nicolaisen, Donald T. 2004. Keynote speech at 11th Annual Midwestern Financial Reporting Symposium. http://www.sec.gov/news/speech/spch100704dtn.htm.

Niehaus, Greg and Greg Roth. 1999. Insider trading, equity issues, and CEO turnover in firms subject to securities class actions. *Financial Management*, 28, 4 (Winter): 52–72.

Niskanen, William A. (ed.) 2005. *After Enron: Lessons for Public Policy*. Lanham, MD: Rowman & Littlefield Publishers, Inc.

Nissim, Doron and Stephen H. Penman. 2001. Ratio analysis and equity valuation: From research to practice. *Review of Accounting Studies*, 6, 1 (March): 109–154.

Niu, Flora. 2006. Corporate governance and the quality of accounting earnings: A Canadian perspective. AAA 2006 Annual Meeting Paper, Washington, DC.

Noe, Christopher F. 1999. Voluntary disclosures and insider transactions. *Journal of Accounting and Economics*, 27, 3 (July): 305–326.

Noe, Thomas H. 1997. Insider trading and the problem of corporate agency. *Journal of Law, Economics, and Organization*, 13, 2 (October): 287–318.

Noe, Thomas H. 2002. Investor activism and financial market structure. *Review of Financial Studies*, 15, 1 (Spring): 289–318.

Noe, Thomas H. 2003. Tunnel-proofing the executive suite: Transparency, temptation, and the design of executive compensation. SSRN.com/abstract=453961.

Nofsinger, John R. and Kenneth A. Kim. 2003. *Infectious Greed: Restoring Confidence in America's Companies*. Upper Saddle River, NJ: Prentice-Hall.

Nofsinger, John R. and Richard W. Sias. 1999. Herding and feedback trading by institutional and individual investors. *Journal of Finance*, 54, 6 (December): 2263–2295.

Nohel, Tom and Steven K. Todd. 2002. Compensation for managers with career concerns: The role of stock option in optimal contracts. SSRN.com/abstract=299991.

Nwaeze, Emeka T. 2001. The adjustment process of accruals: Empirical evidence and implication for accrual research. *Review of Quantitative Finance and Accounting*, 17, 2 (September): 187–211.

O'Brien, Patricia and Ravi Bhushan. 1990. Analyst following and institutional ownership. *Journal of Accounting Research*, 28, 3 (Supplement): 55–82.

O'Brien, Patricia C., Maureen F. McNichols, and Hsiou-Wei Lin. 2005. Analyst impartiality and investment banking relationships. *Journal of Accounting Research*, 43, 4 (September): 623–650.

O'Connell, Brendan T. 2004. Enron.Con: "He that filches from me my good name...makes me poor indeed." *Critical Perspectives on Accounting*, 15, 6-7 (August): 733–749.

O'Connor, Sean M. 2002. The inevitability of Enron and the impossibility of "auditor independence" under the current audit system. SSRN.com/abstract=303181.

Oded, Jacob and Yu Wang. 2005. Large shareholders' activism and corporate valuation. Working paper, Boston University.

Odegaard, Bernt Arne and Øyvind Bøhren. 2003. Governance and performance revisited. ECGI-Finance Working Paper No. 28/2003; EFA 2003 Annual Conference Paper No. 252. SSRN.com/abstract=423461.

OECD. 2004. *OECD Principles of Corporate Governance.* Organization for Economic Co-Operation and Development.

Oesterle, Dale A. 2006. The high cost of IPOs depresses venture capital in the United States. Ohio State Public Law Working Paper No. 75. SSRN.com/abstract=923572.

Ofek, Eli and David Yermack. 2000. Taking stock: Equity-based compensation and the evolution of managerial ownership. *Journal of Finance,* 55, 3 (June): 1367–1384.

Ofer, Aharon and Daniel Siegel. 1987. Corporate financial policy, information, and market expectations: An empirical investigation of dividends. *Journal of Finance,* 42, 4 (September): 889–911.

O'glove, Thornton L. (with R. Sobel). 1987. *Quality of Earnings: The Investor's Guide to How Much Money a Company is Really Making.* New York: Free Press.

Ogneva, Maria, K.R. Subramanyam, and Kannan Raghunandan. 2006. Internal control weakness and cost of equity: Evidence from SOX section 404 disclosures. AAA 2006 Financial Accounting and Reporting Section (FARS) Meeting Paper. SSRN.com/abstract=766104.

Omer, Thomas C., Jean C. Bédard, and Diana Falsetta. 2006. Auditor-provided tax services: The effects of a changing regulatory environment. *The Accounting Review,* 81, 5 (October): 1095–1117.

Oswald, Dennis R. and Paul Zarowin. 2005. Capitalization vs. expensing of R&D and earnings management. Working Paper, Stanford University.

Owers, James E., Chen-Miao Lin, and Ronald C. Rogers. 2004. The informational content and valuation ramifications of earnings restatements. *International Business and Economics Research Journal,* 1, 5: 71–84.

Oyer, Paul. 1998. Fiscal year ends and non-linear incentive contracts: The effect on business seasonality. *Quarterly Journal of Economics,* 113, 1 (February): 149–185.

Pacharn, Parunahana. 2003. Optimal incentive contracts with accounting method choice. SSRN.com/abstract=438563.

Pae, Jinhan, Daniel B. Thornton, and Michael Welker. 2005. The link between earnings conservatism and the price-to-book ratio. *Contemporary Accounting Research,* 22, 3 (Fall): 693–717.

Pae, Sunil. 2002. Discretionary disclosure, efficiency, and signal informativeness. *Journal of Accounting and Economics,* 33, 3 (August): 279–311.

Palepu, Krishna G., Paul M. Healy, and Victor Bernard. 2003. *Business Analysis and Valuation: Using Financial Statements.* Belmont, CA: SouthWestern College Publishing.

Palmon, Oded and John K. Wald. 2002. Are two heads better than one? The impact of changes in management structure on performance by firm size. *Journal of Corporate Finance,* 8, 3 (July): 213–226.

Palmrose, Zoe-Vonna. 1988. An analysis of auditor litigation and audit service quality. *The Accounting Review,* 63, 1 (January): 55–73.

Palmrose, Zoe-Vonna, Vernon Richardson, and Susan Scholz. 2004. Determinants of market reactions to restatement announcements. *Journal of Accounting and Economics,* 37, 1 (February): 59–89.

Palmrose, Zoe-Vonna and Susan W. Scholz. 2004. The circumstances and legal consequences of non-GAAP reporting: Evidence from restatements. *Contemporary Accounting Research,* 21, 1 (Spring): 139–180.

Papanastasopoulos, George A., Dimitrios D. Thomakos, and Tao Wang. 2007. The implications of retained and distributed earnings for future profitability and market mispricing. SSRN.com/abstract=882108.

Paredes, Troy A. 2003. Blinded by the light: Information overload and its consequences for securities regulation. *Washington University Law Quarterly.* SSRN.com/abstract=413180.

Parfet, William U. 2000. Accounting subjectivity and earnings management: A preparer perspective. *Accounting Horizons*, 14, 4 (December): 481–488.

Park, Eun-Soo. 1995. Incentives contracting under limited liability. *Journal of Economics and Management Strategy*, 4, 3 (September): 477–490.

Park, Myung Seok and Taewoo Park. 2004. Insider sales and earnings management. *Journal of Accounting and Public Policy*, 23, 5 (September-October): 381–411.

Parker, Susan S. 1997. The effect of audit committees on financial reporting. A Ph.D. dissertation. University of Oregon.

Parrino, Robert, Richard Sias, and Laura T. Starks. 2003. Voting with their feet: Institutional ownership changes around forced CEO turnover. *Journal of Financial Economics*, 68, 1 (April): 3–46.

Pastena, Victor and Joshua Ronen. 1979. Some hypotheses on the pattern of management informal disclosures. *Journal of Accounting Research*, 17, 2 (Autumn): 550–564.

Pastor, María Jesús, and Francisco Poveda. 2005. Earnings management as an explanation of the equity issue puzzle. *IVIE* Working paper, 2005–04.

Paton, William Andrew. 1922. *Accounting Theory*. Houston, TX: Scholars Book, Co.

Paul, Donna. 2001. Board composition and corrective action: Evidence from corporate responses to bad acquisition bids. Working Paper, Babson College.

Pavlik, Ellen L., Thomas W. Scott, and Peter Tiessen. 1993. Executive compensation: Issues and research. *Journal of Accounting Literature*, 12: 131–189.

Payne, Jeff A. and Sean W.G. Robb. 2000. Earnings management: The effect of ex-ante earnings expectations. *Journal of Accounting, Auditing and Finance*, 15, 4 (Fall): 371–392.

Peasnell, K.V., Peter F. Pope, and Stephen Young. 1999. Detecting earnings management using abnormal accruals model. Working Paper, Lancaster University.

Peasnell, K.V., Peter F. Pope, and Stephen Young. 2005. Board monitoring and earnings management: Do outside directors influence abnormal accruals? *Journal of Business Finance and Accounting*, 32, 7-8 (September): 1311–1346.

Peltier-Rivest, Dominic. 1999. The determinants of accounting choices in troubled companies. *Quarterly Journal of Business and Economics*, 38, 4 (Autumn): 28–44.

Peltier-Rivest, Dominic. 2002. Implicit claim incentives on the accounting choices of troubled companies. *Journal of Forensic Accounting*, III, 2 (December): 165–184.

Peltier-Rivest, Dominic and Steve Swirsky. 2000. Earnings management in healthy firms. *Quarterly Journal of Business and Economics*, 39, 4 (Autumn): 21–37.

Peng, Lin and Alisa A. Röell. 2006. Executive pay, earnings manipulation and shareholder litigation. AFA 2005 Meeting Paper. SSRN.com/abstract=488148.

Penman, Stephen H. 1980. An empirical investigation of the voluntary disclosure of corporate earnings forecasts. *Journal of Accounting Research*, 18, 1 (Spring): 132–160.

Penman, Stephen H. and Xiao-Jun Zhang. 2002. Accounting conservatism, the quality of earnings, and stock returns. *The Accounting Review*, 77, 2 (April): 237–264.

Penno, Mark. 1987. Accrual accounting in a principal–agent setting. Working paper, University of Chicago.

Perino, Michael A. 2003. American corporate reform abroad: Sarbanes-Oxley and the foreign private issuer. *European Business Organization Law Review*, 4, 2(October): 213–244.

Perino, Michael A. 2006. Enron's legislative aftermath: Some reflections on the deterrence aspects of the Sarbanes-Oxley Act of 2002. Columbia Law and Economics Working Paper No. 212; St. John's Legal Studies Research Paper. SSRN.com/abstract=350540.

Perry, Susan E. and Thomas H. Williams. 1994. Earnings management preceding management buyout offers. *Journal of Accounting and Economics*, 18, 2 (September): 157–179.

Perry, Tod. 2000. Incentive compensation for outside directors and CEO turnover. Presented at Tuck-JFE Contemporary Corporate Governance Conference. SSRN.com/abstract=236033.

Perry, Tod and Urs Peyer. 2005. Board seat accumulation by executives: A shareholder's perspective. *Journal of Finance*, 60, 4 (August): 2083–2123.

Perry, Tod and Anil Shivdasani. 2005. Do boards affect performance? Evidence from corporate restructuring. *The Journal of Business*, 78, 4 (July): 1403-1432 .

Perry, Tod and Marc Zenner. 2001. Pay for performance? Government regulation and the structure of compensation contracts. *Journal of Financial Economics*, 62, 3 (December): 453–488.

Persons, Obeua S. 2006. The effects of fraud and lawsuit revelation on U.S. executive turnover and compensation. *Journal of Business Ethics*, 64, 4 (April): 405–419.

Petroni, Ruby K. 1992. Optimistic reporting in the property-casualty insurance industry. *Journal of Accounting and Economics*, 15, 4 (December): 485–508.

Petroni, Kathy and Mark Beasley. 1996. Errors in accounting estimates and their relation to audit firm type. *Journal of Accounting Research*, 34, 1 (Spring): 151–171.

Petroni, Kathy R., Stephen G. Ryan, and James M. Wahlen. 2000. Discretionary and non-discretionary revisions of loss reserves by property-casualty insurers: Differential implications for future profitability, risk and market value. *Review of Accounting Studies*, 5, 2 (June): 95–125.

Pfeiffer, Ray J. and Pieter T. Elgers. 1999. Controlling for lagged stock price responses in pricing regressions: An application to the pricing of cash flows and accruals. *Journal of Accounting Research*, 37, 1 (Spring): 239–247.

Pfeiffer, Ray J., Pieter T. Elgers, May H. Lo, and Lynn L. Rees. 1998. Additional evidence on the incremental information content of cash flows and accruals: The impact of errors in measuring market expectations. *The Accounting Review*, 73, 3 (July): 373–385.

Phillips, John D., Morton P.K. Pincus, and Sonja O. Rego. 2003. Earnings management: New evidence based deferred tax expense. *The Accounting Review*, 78, 2 (April): 491–521.

Phillips, John D., Morton P.K. Pincus, Sonja O. Rego, and Huishan, Wan. 2004. Decomposing changes in deferred tax assets and liabilities to isolate earnings management activities. *The Journal of the American Taxation Association*, 26 (Supplement): 43–66.

Pierce-Brown, Rhoda and Tony Steele. 1999. The economics of accounting for growth. *Accounting and Business Research*, 29, 2 (Spring): 157–173.

Pijper, Trevor. 1994. *Creative Accounting: The Effectiveness of Financial Reporting in the UK*. London: Macmillan.

Pincus, Morton and Sivaram Rajgopal. 2002. The interaction between accrual management and hedging: Evidence from oil and gas firms. *The Accounting Review*, 77, 1 (January): 127–160.

Pincus, Morton, Sivaram Rajgopal, and Mohan Venkatachal. 2007. The accrual anomaly: International evidence. *The Accounting Review*, 82, 1 (January): 169–203.

Piotroski, Joseph D. and Darren T. Roulstone. 2005. Do insider trades reflect both contrarian beliefs and superior knowledge about future cash flow realizations? *Journal of Accounting and Economics*, 39, 1 (February): 55–81.

Poitras, Geoffrey, Trevor Wilkins, and Yoke Shang Kwan. 2002. The timing of asset sales: Evidence of earnings management? *Journal of Business Finance and Accounting*, 29, 7/8 (August/September): 903–934.

Pope, Peter F. and Martin Walker. 1999. International differences in the timeliness, conservatism and classification of earnings. *Journal of Accounting Research*, 37, 3 (Supplement): 53–87.

Potter, Gordon. 1992. Accounting earnings announcements, institutional investor concentration, and common stock returns. *Journal of Accounting Research*, 30, 1 (Spring): 146–155.

Povel, Paul, Rajdeep Singh, and Andrew Winton. 2005. Booms, busts, and fraud. Working Paper, University of Minnesota.

Pozen, Robert. 2004. Can European companies escape U.S. listings? Harvard Law and Economics Discussion Paper, 464. SSRN.com/abstract=511942.

Prendergast, Canice. 2000. What trade-off of risk and incentives? *The American Economic Review*, 90, 2 (May): 421–425.

Prendergast, Canice. 2002. The tenuous trade-off between risk and incentives. *Journal of Political Economy*, 110, 5 (October): 1071- 1102.

PricewaterhouseCoopers LLP. 2000. *Securities Litigation Study*.

Pourciau, Susan. 1993. Earnings management and nonroutine executive changes. *Journal of Accounting and Economics*, 16, 1-3 (January-July): 317–336.

Pownell, Grace, Charles Wasley, and Gregory Waymire. 1993. The stock price effect of alternative types of management earnings forecasts. *The Accounting Review*, 68, 4 (October): 896–912.

Pownall, Grace and Gregory Waymire. 1989. Voluntary disclosure credibility and securities prices: Evidence from management earnings forecasts. *Journal of Accounting Research*, 27, 2 (Autumn): 227–245.

Press, Eric G. and Thomas D. Dowdell. 2004. The impact of SEC scrutiny on financial statement reporting of in-process research and development expense. *Journal of Accounting and Public Policy*, 23, 3 (May-June): 227–244.

Press, Eric G. and Joseph B. Weintrop. 1990. Accounting-based constraints in public and private debt agreements: Their associations with leverage and impact on accounting choice. *Journal of Accounting and Economics*, 12, 1-3 (January): 65–95.

Price, Renée. 1999. Voluntary earnings disclosures in uniform franchise offering circulars. *Journal of Accounting and Economics*, 28, 3 (December): 391–423.

Puffer, Sheila M. and Joseph B. Weintrop. 1991. Corporate performance and CEO turnover: The role of performance expectation. *Administrative Science Quarterly*, 36, 1 (March): 1–19.

Raghunandan K. and Dasaratha Rama. 2006. SOX Section 404 material weakness disclosures and audit fees. *Auditing: A Journal of Practice and Theory*, 25, 1 (May): 99–114.

Raheja, Charu G. 2005. Determinants of board size and composition: A theory of corporate boards. *Journal of Financial and Quantitative Analysis*, 40, 2 (June): 283–306.

Rahman, Rashidah Abdul and Afidah Abu Bakar. 2002. Earnings management and acquiring firms preceding acquisitions in Malaysia. Working Paper presented at 2002 APFA/PACAP/FMA Finance International Conference, Tokyo, Japan.

Raith, Michael A. 1996. A general model of information sharing in oligopoly. *Journal of Economic Theory*, 71, 1 (October): 260–288.

Raith, Michael A. 2003. Competition, risk and managerial incentives. *American Economic Review*, 93, 4 (September): 1425–1436.

Rajan, Madhav V. and Bharat Sarath. 1996. Limits to voluntary disclosure in efficient markets. *Journal of Accounting, Auditing and Finance*, 11, 3 (Summer): 361–387.

Rajgopal, Shivaram and Terry Shevlin. 2002. Empirical evidence on the relation between stock option compensation and risk taking. *Journal of Accounting and Economics*, 33, 2 (June): 145–171.

Rajgopal, Shivaram and Mohan Venkatachalam. 1997. The role of institutional investors in corporate governance: An empirical investigation. SSRN.com/abstract=130901.

Rajgopal, Shivaram, Mohan Venkatachalam, and Suresh Kotha. 2002. Managerial actions, stock returns, and earnings: The case of business-to-business internet firms. *Journal of Accounting Research*, 40, 2 (May): 529–556.

Rama, Dasaratha V. and William J. Read. 2006. Resignations by the big 4 and the market for audit services. *Accounting Horizons*, 20, 2 (June): 97–109.

Ramakrishnan, Ram. 1998. Valuation of permanent, transitory, and price-irrelevant components of reported earnings. *Journal of Accounting, Auditing and Finance*, 13, 3 (Summer): 301–336.

Ramakrishnan, Ram and Anjan V. Thakor. 1982. Moral hazard, agency costs, and asset prices in a competitive equilibrium. *Journal of Financial and Quantitative Analysis*, 17, 4 (November): 503–532.

Ramakrishnan, Ram and Anjan V. Thakor. 1984. The valuation of assets under moral hazard. *Journal of Finance*, 39, 1 (March): 229–238.

Ramasastry, Ambarish, Kose John, and Joseph Williams. 1987. Efficient signaling with dividends and investments. *Journal of Finance*, 42, 2 (June): 321–343.

Ramsay, Ian Malcolm, Geof Stapledon, and Kenneth Fong. 2000. Corporate governance: The perspective of Australian institutional shareholders. *Company and Securities Law Journal*, 18, 2 (March): 110–142.

Ramesh, K. and Lawrence Revsine. 2000. The effects of regulatory and contracting costs on banks' choice of accounting method for other postretirement employee benefits. *Journal of Accounting and Economics*, 30, 2 (October): 159–186.

Rangan, Srinivasan. 1998. Earnings management and the performance of seasoned equity offerings. *Journal of Financial Economics*, 50, 1 (October): 101–122.

Ranjani, Krishnan, Michelle H. Yetman, and Robert J. Yetman. 2006. Expense misreporting in nonprofit organizations. *The Accounting Review*, 81, 2 (March): 399–420.

Rao, Gita R. 1993. The relation between stock returns and earnings: A study of newly-public firms. Working Paper, New York University.

Rauterkus, Stephanie Yatest and Kyojil "Roy" Song. 2003. Auditor's reputation, equity offerings, and firm size: The case of Arthur Andersen. Working Paper.

Rayburn, Judy. 1986. The association of operating cash flows and accruals with security returns. *Journal of Accounting Research*, 24 (Supplement): 112–133.

Rayburn, Judy and Stefanie Lenway. 1992. An investigation of the behavior of accruals in the semiconductor industry. *Contemporary Accounting Research*, 9, 3 (Fall): 237–251.

Rees, Lynn L. 2005. Abnormal returns from predicting earnings thresholds. *Review of Accounting Studies*, 10, 4 (December): 465–496.

Rees, Lynn L., Susan Gill, and Richard Gore. 1996. An investigation of asset write-downs and concurrent abnormal accruals. *Journal of Accounting Research*, 34 (Supplement): 157–169.

Rees, Lynn L. and Shiva Sivaramkrishnan. 2006. The effect of meeting or beating revenue forecasts on the association between quarterly returns and earnings forecast errors. *Contemporary Accounting Research*, 24, 1(Spring): 259–290.

Reichelstein, Stephen. 2000. Providing managerial incentives: Cash flows versus accrual accounting. *Journal of Accounting Research*, 38, 2 (Autumn): 243–270.

Reingold, Daniel and Jennifer Reingold. 2006. *Confessions of a Wall Street Analyst*: A true story of inside Information and Corruption in the Stock Market. New York: Harper Collins.

Reitenga, Austin, Steve Buchheit, Qin Jennifer Yin, and Terry Baker. 2002. CEO bonus pay, tax policy, and earnings management. *Journal of the American Taxation Association*, 24, 2 (Supplement): 1–25.

Reitenga, Austin L. and Michael G. Tearney. 2003. Mandatory CEO retirements, discretionary accruals, and corporate governance mechanisms. *Journal of Accounting, Auditing and Finance*, 18, 2 (Spring): 255–280.

Revsine, Lawrence. 1991. The selective financial misrepresentation hypothesis. *Accounting Horizons*, 5, 4 (December): 16–27.

Revsine, Lawrence. 2002. Enron: Sad but inevitable. *Journal of Accounting and Public Policy*, 21, 2 (Summer) 137–145.

Reynolds, Kenneth J. and Jere R. Francis. 2000. Does size matter? The influence of large clients on office-level auditor reporting decisions. *Journal of Accounting and Economics*, 30, 3 (December): 375–400.

Reynolds, Kenneth J., D. Deis, and Jere R. Francis. 2004. Professional service fees and auditor objectivity. *Auditing: A Journal of Practice and Theory*, 23, 1 (Spring): 29–52.

Rezaee, Zabihollah and Pankaj K. Jain. 2006. The Sarbanes-Oxley Act of 2002 and security market behavior: Early evidence. *Contemporary Accounting Research*, 23, 3 (Fall): 629–654.

Riahi-Belkaoui, Ahmed. 2004. What is puzzling with this picture? The determinants of earnings opacity internationally. SSRN.com/abstract=483983.

Ribstein, Larry E. 2002. Market vs. regulatory responses to corporate fraud: A critique of the Sarbanes-Oxley Act of 2002. *Journal of Corporation Law*, 28 (September): 1–74.

Ribstein, Larry E. 2003. International implications of Sarbanes-Oxley: Raising the rent on U.S. law. *Journal of Corporate Law Studies*, 3, 2: 299–327.

Ribstein, Larry E. 2005. Sarbanes-Oxley after three years. Illinois Law & Economics Research Paper No. LE05-016. SSRN.com/abstract=746884.

Richardson, Scott A. 2003. Earnings quality and short sellers. *The Accounting Horizons*, 17 (Supplement): 49–61.

Richardson, Scott Anthony. 2005. Discussion of "consequences of financial reporting failure for outside directors: Evidence from accounting restatements and audit committee members." *Journal of Accounting Research*, 43, 2 (May): 335–342.

Richardson, Scott A., Richard G. Sloan, Mark T. Soliman, and Irem A. Tuna. 2005. Accruals reliability, earnings persistence and stock prices. *Journal of Accounting and Economics*, 39, 3 (September): 437–485.

Richardson, Scott Anthony, Richard G. Sloan, Mark T. Soliman, and Irem A. Tuna. 2006. The implications of accounting distortions and growth for accruals and profitability. *The Accounting Review*, 81, 3 (May): 713–743.

Richardson, Scott Anthony, Siew Hong Teoh, and Peter D. Wysocki. 2004. The walkdown to beatable analyst forecasts: The role of equity issuance and insider trading incentives. *Contemporary Accounting Research*, 21, 4 (Winter): 885–924.

Richardson, Scott Anthony, Irem A. Tuna, and Min Wu. 2002. Predicting earnings management: The case of restatements. SSRN.com/abstract=338681.

Richardson, Vernon J. 2000. Information asymmetry and earnings management: Some evidence. *Review of Quantitative Finance and Accounting*, 15, 4 (December): 325–347.

Richardson, Vernon J. and James F. Waegelein. 2002. The influence of long-term performance plans on earnings management and firm performance. *Review of Quantitative Finance and Accounting*, 18, 2 (March): 161–183.

Riedl, Edward J. 2004. An examination of long-lived asset impairments. *The Accounting Review*, 79, 3 (July): 823–852.

Riedl, Edward J. and Suraj Srinivasan. 2006. The strategic reporting of special items: Does management presentation reflect underlying firm performance or opportunism? SSRN.com/abstract=923898.

Ritter, Jay R. 1998. Initial public offerings. *Contemporary Finance Digest*, 2, 1 (Spring): 5–30.

Ritter, Jay R. and Ivo Welch. 2002. A review of IPO activity, pricing, and allocations. *The Journal of Finance*, 57, 4 (August): 1795–1828.

Robb, Sean W.G. 1998. The effect of analysts' forecasts on earnings management in financial institutions. *Journal of Financial Research*, 21, 3 (Fall): 315–331.

Roberts, Gordon S. and Kamphol Panyagometh. 2003. Private information, agency problems and determinants of loan syndications. SSRN.com/abstract=310003.

Roberts, Michael R. and Sudheer Chava. 2006. Is financial contracting costly? An empirical analysis of debt covenants and corporate investment. AFA 2007 Chicago Meeting Paper. SSRN.com/abstract=854324.

Roe, Mark J. 1991. A political theory of American corporate finance. *Columbia Law Review*, 91 (January): 10-67. Working Paper, Columbia University.

Rogerson, William. 1985a. Repeated moral hazard. *Econometrica*, 53, 1 (January): 69–76.

Rogerson, William. 1985b. The first-order approach to principal–agent problems. *Econometrica*, 53, 6 (December): 1357–1367.

Romano, Roberta. 1991. The shareholder suit: Litigation without foundation? *Journal of Law, Economics, and Organization*, 7, 1 (Spring): 55–87.

Romano, Roberta. 2001. Less is more: Making institutional investor activism a valuable mechanism of corporate governance. *Yale Journal on Regulation*, 18, 2 (Summer): 174–251.

Romano, Roberta. 2005. The Sarbanes-Oxley Act and the making of quack corporate governance. *Yale Law Journal* (June). SSRN.com/abstract=749524.

Ronen, Joshua. 1979. The dual role of accounting: A financial economic perspective. In Amsterdam: James L. Bicksler, ed. Handbook of Financial Economics. North-Holland. 415–454.

Ronen, Joshua. 2002a. Market solution to the accounting crisis. *New York Times*, March 8, 2002, Section A, 21.

Ronen, Joshua. 2002b. Policy reforms in the aftermath of accounting scandals. *Journal of Accounting and Public Policy*, 21, 4-5 (Summer): 281–286.

Ronen, Joshua. 2002c. Post-Enron reform: Financial statement insurance, and GAAP revisited. *Stanford Journal of Law, Business & Finance*, 8, 1 (Autumn): 1–30.

Ronen, Joshua, and Kenneth A. Sagat. 2007. The public auditor as an insurer of client restatements: A radical proposal for reform. *Journal of Accounting, Auditing and Finance,* forthcoming.

Ronen, Joshua, Joseph Tzur, and Varda Lewinstein Yaari. 2006. The effect of directors' equity incentives on earnings management. *Journal of Accounting and Public Policy*, 25, 4 (July-August): 359–389.

Ronen, Joshua, Joseph Tzur, and Varda Lewinstein Yaari. 2007. Legal insider trading, CEO's incentives, and quality of earnings. *Corporate Governance and Control*, 4 (Spring): 210–219.

Ronen, Joshua. 2005. Accounting for share-based payments. SSRN.com/abstract=934437.

Ronen, Joshua and Arnold Berman. 2004. Musing on post Enron reforms. *Journal of Accounting, Auditing and Finance,* 19, 3 (Summer): 331–342.

Ronen, Joshua and Seunghan Nam. 2007. Information transfer effects of senior executives' migrations and subsequent write-offs. SSRN.com/abstract=649141.

Ronen, Joshua and Simcha Sadan. 1975. Classificatory smoothing: Alternative income models. *Journal of Accounting Research*, 13, 1 (Spring): 133–149.

Ronen, Joshua and Simcha Sadan. 1981. *Smoothing Income Numbers: Objectives, Means, and Implications*. Reading, MA: Addison-Wesley.

Ronen, Joshua, Simcha Sadan, and Charles Snow. 1977. Income smoothing—A review. *The Accounting Journal*, 1, 1 (Spring): 11–26.

Ronen, Joshua, and Varda Lewinstein Yaari. 1993. The disclosure policy of the firm in an efficient market. *Review of Quantitative Finance and Accounting*, 3, 3 (September): 311-324 .

Ronen, Joshua, and Varda L. Yaari. 2001. Limited-liability contracts with earnings management. SSRN.com/abstract=255274. AAA 2001 Annual Meeting Paper, Atlanta, Georgia.

Ronen, Joshua, and Varda Lewinstein Yaari. 2002. Incentives for voluntary disclosure. *Journal of Financial Markets*, 5, 3 (July): 349–390.

Ronen, Joshua and Varda Lewinstein Yaari. 2007. Demand for the truth in principal–agent relationships. *Review of Accounting Studies*, 12, 1 (March): 125–153.

Ronen, Tavy and Varda Lewinstein Yaari. 2002. On the tension between full revelation and earnings management: A reconsideration of the revelation principle. *Journal of Accounting, Auditing and Finance*, 17, 4 (Fall): 273–294.

Ronen, Tavy, Joshua Ronen, and Varda Lewinstein Yaari. 2003. The effect of voluntary disclosure and preemptive preannouncements on earnings response coefficients (ERC) when firms manage earnings. *Journal of Accounting, Auditing and Finance*, 18, 3 (Summer): 379–410.

Roosenboom, Peter, Tjalling van der Goot, and Gerard Mertens. 2002. Earnings management and the fortunes of IPOs: A tale of two forms. Working Paper, Tilburg University.

Roosenboom, Peter, Tjalling van der Goot, and Gerard Mertens. 2003. Earnings management and initial public offerings: Evidence from the Netherlands. *The International Journal of Accounting*, 38, 3 (Autumn): 243–266.

Rose, Paul. 2005. Balancing public market benefits and burdens for smaller companies post-Sarbanes-Oxley. *Willamette Law Review*, 41, 3 (Summer). SSRN.com/abstract=668062.

Rosenstein, Stuart and Jeffrey G. Wyatt. 1990a. Outside directors, board independence and shareholder wealth. *Journal of Financial Economics*, 26, 2 (August): 175–191.

Rosenstein, Stuart and Jeffrey G. Wyatt. 1990b. Inside directors, board independence, and shareholder wealth. *Journal of Financial Economics*, 44, 2 (May): 229–250.

Rosner, Rebecca L. 2003. Earnings manipulation in failing firms. *Contemporary Accounting Research*, 20, 2 (Summer): 361–408.

Roulstone, Darren T. 2003. The relation between insider-trading restrictions and executive compensation. *Journal of Accounting Research*, 41, 3 (June): 525–551.

Roychowdhury, Sugata. 2006. Earnings management through real activities manipulation. *Journal of Accounting and Economics*, 42, 3 (December): 335–370.

Roychowdhury, Sugata and Ross L. Watts. 2007. Asymmetric timeliness of earnings, market-to-book and conservatism in financial reporting. *Journal of Accounting and Economics*, 44, 1–2 (September): 2–31.

Rubinstein, Ariel and Menachem Yaari. 1983. Repeated insurance contracts and moral hazard. *Journal of Economic Theory*, 30, 1 (June): 74–97.

Ruddock, Caitlin, M.S. and Sarah J. Taylor. 2006. Non-audit services and earnings conservatism: Is auditor independence impaired? *Contemporary Accounting Research*, 23, 3 (Autumn): 701–746.

Ruland, William, Samuel Tung, and Nashwa E. Georege. 1990. Factors associated with the disclosure of managers' forecasts. *The Accounting Review*, 65, 3 (July): 710–721.

Russ, Tobert W. 2005. SEC regulation of corporate 10K filing dates: The effect on earnings management and market recognition. A Ph.D. dissertation. Marietta College.

Ryan, Stephen G., Baruch Itamar Lev, and Min Wu. 2006. Rewriting earnings history. SSRN.com/abstract=878690.

Ryan, Stephen G. and Paul Zarowin. 2003. Why has the contemporaneous linear returns–earnings relation declined? *The Accounting Review*, 78, 2 (April): 523–553.

Safdar, Irfan. 2003. Stock option exercise, earnings management, and abnormal stock returns. Simon Business School Working Paper FR 03-31. SSRN.com/abstract=468561.

Sainty, Barbara J., Gary K. Taylor, and David D. Williams. 2002. Investors dissatisfaction toward auditors. *Journal of Accounting, Auditing and Finance*, 17, 2 (Spring): 111–136.

Salmon, Walter J. 1993. Crisis prevention: How to gear up your board? The fight for good governance. *Harvard Business Review* (January/February): 68–83.

Sankar, Mandira Roy. 1995. Disclosure of predecision information in a duopoly. *Contemporary Accounting Research*, 11, 2 (Spring): 829–859.

Sankar, Mandira Roy. 1999. The impact of alternative forms of earnings management on the return–earnings relation. SSRN.com/abstract=146732.

Sankar, Mandira Roy and K.R. Subramanyam. 2001. Reporting discretion and private information communication through earnings. *Journal of Accounting Research*, 39, 2 (Fall): 365–386.

Sansing, Richard C. 1992. Accounting and the credibility of management forecasts. *Contemporary Accounting Research*, 9, 1 (Fall): 33–45.

Santaló, Juan. 2002. Substitution between product market competition and financial managerial incentives. Working Paper, University of Chicago.

Santos, Joao A.C. 1998. Commerical banks in the securities business: A review. *Journal of Financial Services Research*, 14, 1 (July): 35–60.

Sappington, David E.M. 1983. Limited liability contracts between principal and agent. *Journal of Economic Theory*, 29, 1 (February): 1–21.

Sappington, David E.M. 1991. Incentives in principal–agent relationships. *Journal of Economic Perspectives*, 5, 2 (Spring): 45–66.

Sarath, Bharat and Ramachandran Nagarajan. 1996. Unobservable risk preferences and value of information in financial markets with adverse selection. *Journal of Accounting, Auditing and Finance*, 11, 2 (Spring): 197–222.

Sarbanes-Oxley Act of July 2002. Public Company Accounting Reform and Investor Protection Act of 2002.

Saudagaran, Shahrokh M. and James F. Sepe. 1996. Replication of Moses' income smoothing test with Canadian and UK data: A note. *Journal of Business Finance and Accounting*, 23, 8 (October): 1219–1222.

Saul, Ralph S. 1996. Commentary: What ails the accounting profession? *Accounting Horizons*, 10, 2 (June): 131-137.

Sawicki, Julia. 2005. Are insider trades and earnings management related? SSRN.com/abstract=740864.

Schadler, Fredrick P. and Timothy L. Manuel. 1994. Underwriter choice and announcement effects for seasoned equity offerings. *Journal of Financial and Strategic Decisions*, 7, 2 (Summer): 53–65.

Scharfstein, David S. 1988. Product-market competition and managerial slack. *Rand Journal of Economics*, 19 (Spring): 147–155.

Schelleman, Caren and Robert W. Knechel. 2005. The impact of potential earnings management on the pricing and production of audit services. www.isarhq.org/papers/Schelleman.doc.

Schilit, Howard M. 2002. *Financial Shenanigans: How to Detect Accounting Gimmicks and Fraud in Financial Reports.* Second edition. New York: McGraw Hill (1st edition 1993).

Schipper, Katherine. 1989. Commentary on earnings management. *Accounting Horizons*, 3, 4 (December): 91–102.

Schipper, Katherine and Linda Vincent. 2003. Earnings quality. *Accounting Horizons* (Earnings Quality Supplement): 97–110.

Schloetzer, Jason D. 2006. Arthur Andersen, SOX Section 404 and auditor turnover: Theory and evidence. SSRN.com/abstract=870586.

Schmidt, Klaus M. 1997. Managerial incentives and product market competition. *The Review of Economic Studies*, 64, 2 (April): 191–213.

Schøler, Finn. 2005. Earnings management to avoid earnings decreases and losses. Working Paper. Financial Reporting Research Group, Working Paper No. 2005-03, Aarhus School of Business.

Scholes, Myron S., Peter G. Wilson, and Mark A. Wolfson 1992. Firms responses to anticipated reductions in tax rates: The Tax Reform Act of 1986. *Journal of Accounting Research*, 30 (Supplement): 161–185.

Schonfeld, E. 1998. The guidance game. *Fortune*, December 21: 256–257.

Schrand, Catherine M. 2004. Discussion of firms' voluntary recognition of stock-based compensation expense. *Journal of Accounting Research*, 42, 2: 151–158.

Schrand, Catherine M. and Robert E. Verrecchia. 2002. Disclosure choice and cost of capital: Evidence from underpricing in initial public offerings. SSRN.com/abstract=316824.

Schrand, Catherine M. and Beverly R. Walther. 2000. Strategic benchmarks in earnings announcements: The selective disclosure of prior-period components. *The Accounting Review*, 75, 2 (April): 151–177.

Schrand, Catherine M. and Franco M.H. Wong. 2003. Earnings management using the valuation allowance for deferred tax assets under SFAS 109. *Contemporary Accounting Research*, 20, 3 (Fall): 579–611.

Schuetze, W. 2000. A speech given in the session: SEC Issues/Concerns in the New Millennium. The 2000 Annual Meeting of the American Accounting Association, Philadelphia, PA, Sunday, August 13.

Schwartz, Rachel. 1997. Legal regimes, audit quality and investment. *The Accounting Review*, 72, 3 (July): 385–406.

Schwarzkopf, David L. and Hugh M. Miller. 2005. Early evidence of how Sarbanes-Oxley implementation affects individuals and their workplace relationships. *Business and Society Review*, 110, 1 (February): 21–45.

Scott, William R. 1997. *Financial Accounting Theory*. Second edition. Upper Saddle River, NJ: Prentice Hall.

Scott, William R. 2003. *Financial Accounting Theory*. Third edition. Upper Saddle River, NJ: Prentice Hall.

Securities and Exchange Rule 14a-8 in Release 34-40018, dated May 21, 1998. Securities and Exchange Commission.

Seetharaman, Ananth, Ferdinand A. Gul, and Stephen G. Lynn. 2002. Litigation risk and audit fees: Evidence from UK firms cross-listed on US markets. *Journal of Accounting and Economics*, 33, 1 (February): 91–115.

Seida, Jim A. and William F. Wempe. 2004. Investors' and managers' reactions to corporate inversion transactions. Working Paper, University of Notre Dame, Indiana, and Texas Christian University, Forth Worth, Texas.

Selective Disclosure and Insider Trading, Securities and Exchange Commission, 17 CFR Parts 240, 243, and 249. Release Nos. 33-7881, 34-43154, IC-24599, File S7-31-99 RIN 3235-AH82.

Selten, Reinhard. 1965. Spieltheoretische behandlung eines oligopolmodels mit nachfragetragheit. *Zeitschrift für die Gesamte Staatswissenschaft*, 121: 301–324.

Selten, Reinhard. 1975. Reexamination of the perfectness concept for equilibrium points in extensive games. *International Journal of Game Theory*, 4, 1 (March): 25–55.

Seyhun, Nejat H. 1988. *Investment Intelligence from Insider Trading.* Cambridge, MA: MIT Press.

Seyhun, Nejat H. 1992. The effectiveness of the insider trading sanctions. *The Journal of Law and Economics*, 35, 1 (April): 149–182.

Seyhun, Nejat H. 2000. *Investor Intelligence from Insider Trading.* Cambridge, MA: The MIT Press.

Seyhun, Nejat H., and Michael Bradley. 1997. Corporate bankruptcy and insider trading. *The Journal of Business*, 70, 2 (April): 189–216.

Shackelford, Douglas A. 1996. Earnings, regulatory capital, and tax management. *Journal of Accounting and Economics*, 22, 1-3 (August-December): 241–247.

Shackelford, Douglas A. 1999. Discussion of "The effects of taxes, agency costs and information asymmetry on earnings management: A comparison of public and private firms." *Review of Accounting Studies*, 4, 3-4 (December): 327–329.

Shackelford, Douglas A. and Terry Shevlin. 2001. Empirical tax research in accounting. *Journal of Accounting and Economics*, 31, 1-3 (September): 321–387.

Shafer, William E. 2002. Effects of materiality, risk, and ethical perceptions on fraudulent reporting by financial executives. *Journal of Business Ethics*, 38, 3 (July): 241–260.

Shah, Atul K. 1996. Creative compliance in financial reporting: *Accounting Organizations and Society*, 21, 1 (January): 23–39.

Shane, Philip B., Naomi S. Soderstrom, and SungWook Yoon. 2001. Earnings and price discovery in the post-Reg. FD information environment: A preliminary analysis SSRN.com/abstract=291082.

Shang, Alfred. 2003. Earnings management and institutional ownership. Working Paper, Harvard University.

Shapiro, Amy. 2005. Who pays the auditor calls the tune? Auditing regulation and clients' incentives. *Seton Hall Law Review*, 30, Book 3 (June): 1030–1095.

Shapiro, Carl. 1986. Exchange of cost information in oligopoly. *Review of Economic Studies*, 53, 3 (July): 433–446.

Shareholder Proposal. Staff legal bulletin 14B (CF). 2004. Securities and Exchange Commission. (September 15). http://www.sec.gov/interps/legal/cfslb14b.htm.

Shavell, Steven. 1979. Risk sharing and incentives in the principal and agent relationship. *Bell Journal of Economics*, 10, 1 (Spring): 55–73.

Sheikh, Aamer. 2001. The effect of ratcheting performance standards on CEO compensation. Working Paper, University of Georgia.

Sheikholeslami, Mehdi. 1994. The impact of foreign stock exchange listing on income smoothing: Evidence from Japanese firms. *International Journal of Management*, 11, 2 (June): 737–742.

Sherman, Anne E. 2000. IPOS and long term relationships: An advantage of book building. *Review of Financial Studies*, 13, 3 (Autumn): 697–714.

Shiller Robert and John Pound. 1989. Survey evidence on the diffusion of interest and information among investors. *Journal of Economic Behavior and Organizations*, 12, 1 (August): 44–66.

Shin, Jae Yong. 2004. Stock-based versus cash compensation: Does the correlation between earnings and stock returns matter? Working Paper, University of Wisconsin—Madison. AAA 2004 Meeting Paper, Orlando, FL.

Shin, Hyun Song. 2006. Disclosure risk and price drift. *Journal of Accounting Research*, 44, 2 (May): 351–380.

Shivakumar, Lakshmanan M. 2000. Do firms mislead investors by overstating earnings before seasoned equity offerings? *Journal of Accounting and Economics*, 29, 3 (June): 339–371.

Shivdasani, Anil. 1993. Board composition, ownership structure, and hostile takeovers. *Journal of Accounting and Economics*, 16, 1-3 (January-July): 167–198.

Shivdasani, Anil and David Yermack. 1999. CEO involvement in the selection of new board members: An empirical analysis. *Journal of Finance*, 54, 5 (October): 1829–1853.

Shleifer, Andrei. 2000. *Inefficient Markets: An Introduction to Behavioral Finance,* Oxford: Oxford University Press.

Shleifer, Andrei and Robert Vishny. 1986. Large shareholders and corporate control. *Journal of Political Economy*, 94, 3 (June): 461–488.

Shleifer, Andrei and Robert Vishny. 1990. Equilibrium short horizons of investors and firms. *American Economic Review*, 80, 2 (May): 148–153.

Shleifer, Andrei and Robert Vishny. 1997. A survey of corporate governance. *Journal of Finance*, 52, 2 (June): 737–783.

Shroff, Pervin K. 1995. Determinants of the returns–earnings correlation. *Contemporary Accounting Research*, 12, 1 (Fall): 41–55.

Shroff, Pervin K. 1999. The variability of earnings and non-earnings information and earnings prediction. *Journal of Business Finance and Accounting*, 26, 7-8 (September): 863–882.

Shroff, Pervin K. 2002. The relation between aggregate earnings and security returns over long intervals. *Contemporary Accounting Research*, 19, 1 (Spring): 147–164.

Shroff, Pervin K., Ramgopal Venkataraman, and Baohua Xin. 2004. Leaders and followers among security analysts: Analysis of impact and accuracy. 14th Annual Conference on Financial Economics and Accounting (FEA). SSRN.com/abstract=487902.

Shroff, Pervin K., Ramgopal Venkataraman, and Suning Zhang. 2004. The conservatism principle and the asymmetric timeliness of earnings: An event-based approach. A Working Paper, University of Minnesota. AAA 2004 Annual Meeting, Orlando, FL. SSRN.com/abstract=437144.

Shu, Susan Zhan. 2000. Auditor resignations: Clientele effects and legal liability. *Journal of Accounting and Economics*, 29, 2 (April): 173–205.

Shubik, Martin. 2002. Accounting and economic theory. Yale SOM Working Paper No. AC-16. SSRN.com/abstract=344421.

Sias, Richard. 1996. Volatility and the institutional investor. *Financial Analysts Journal*, 52, 21 (April/May): 13–20.

Sidak, J. Gregory. 2003. The failure of good intentions: The WorldCom fraud and the collapse of American telecommunications after deregulation. *Yale Journal on Regulation*, 20: 207. SSRN.com/abstract=335180.

Sidhu, Baljit K., Tom M. Smith, and Robert E. Whaley. 2006. Regulation Fair Disclosure and the cost of adverse selection. SSRN.com/abstract=917850.

Singer, Zvi. 2007. Discretionary financial reporting: Items manipulated by IPO firms, and investors' increased awareness. SSRN.com/abstract=898644.

Singh, Manohar and Wallace N. Davidson III. 2003. Agency costs, ownership structure and corporate governance mechanisms. *Journal of Banking and Finance*, 27, 5 (May): 793–816.

Singh, Ravi. 2005. Board independence and the design of executive compensation. EFA 2005 Moscow Meeting Paper. SSRN.com/abstract=673741.

Sinha, Nishi and John S. Watts. 2001. Economic consequences of the declining relevance of financial reports. *Journal of Accounting Research*, 39, 3 (December): 663–681.

Sivaramakrishnan, K. 1994. Information asymmetry, participation, and long-term contracts. *Management Science*, 40, 10 (October): 1228–1244.

Skinner, Douglas J. 1990. Options markets and the information content of accounting earnings releases. *Journal of Accounting and Economics*, 13, 3 (October): 191–211.

Skinner, Douglas J. 1993. The investment opportunity set and accounting procedure choice: Preliminary evidence. *Journal of Accounting and Economics*, 16, 4 (October): 407–445.

Skinner, Douglas J. 1994. Why firms voluntarily disclose bad news? *Journal of Accounting Research*, 32, 1 (Spring): 38–61.

Skinner, Douglas J. 1997. Earnings disclosures and stockholder lawsuits. *Journal of Accounting and Economics*, 23, 3 (November): 249–282.

Skinner, Douglas J. and Richard G. Sloan. 2002. Earnings surprises, growth expectations and stock returns or don't let an earnings torpedo sink your portfolio. *Review of Accounting Studies*, 7, 2-3 (June): 289–312.

Skousen, Fred K., Steven M. Glover, and Douglas F. Prawitt. 2005. *An Introduction to Corporate Governance and the SEC.* Thompson South-Western.

Sloan, Richard G. 1993. Accounting earnings and top executive compensation. *Journal of Accounting and Economics*, 16, 1-3 (January-July): 55–100.

Sloan, Richard G. 1996. Do stock prices fully reflect information in accruals and cash flows about future earnings? *The Accounting Review*, 71, 3 (July): 289–315.

Sloan, Richard G. 1999. Discussion of "Accruals, cash flows and equity values." *Review of Accounting Studies*, 4, 3-4 (December): 231–234.

Sloan, Richard G. 2001. Financial accounting and corporate governance: A discussion. *Journal of Accounting and Economics*, 32, 1-3 (December): 335–347.

Slovin, Myron B., Marie E. Sushka, and Carl D. Hudson. 1990. External monitoring and its effect on seasoned common stock issues. *Journal of Accounting and Economics*, 12, 4 (March): 397–417.

Smith, Abbie. 1990. Corporate ownership structure and performance: The case of management buyouts. *Journal of Financial Economics*, 27, 1 (September): 143–164.

Smith, Abbie. 1993. Earnings and management incentives: Comments. *Journal of Accounting and Economics*, 16, 1-3 (January-July): 289–303.

Smith, Clifford W. 1993. A perspective on accounting-based debt covenant violations. *The Accounting Review*, 68, 2 (April): 289–303.

Smith, Clifford W. and Jerold B. Warner. 1979. On financial contracting: An analysis of bond covenants. *Journal of Financial Economics*, 7, 2 (June): 117-161 .

Smith, Clifford W. and Ross L. Watts. 1992. The investment opportunity set and corporate financing, dividend, and compensation polices. *Journal of Financial Economics*, 32, 3 (December): 263–292.

Smith, Geoffrey Peter. 2006. A look at the impact of US regulation on cross-listed firms. SSRN.com/abstract=931051.

Smith, James A. and Zabihollal Rezaee. 1995. Earnings management by the early adopters of SFAS 106. *International Advances in Economic Research*, 1, 4 (November): 426–430.

Smith, Rebecca and John R. Emshwiller. 2003. 24 Days: *How Two WALL STREET JOURNAL Reporters Uncovered The Lies That Destroyed Faith in Corporate America?* Harper Business, Harper Collins.

Smith, Roy C. and Ingo Wlater. 2006. Four years after Enron: Assessing the financial-market regulatory cleanup. *The Independent Review*, 11, 1 (Summer): 53–66.

Smith, Terry. 1996. *Accounting for growth—Stripping the camouflage from company accounts.* Second edition. London: Century Business.

Soffer, Leonard C., Ramu S. Thiagarajan, and Beverly R. Walther. 2000. Earnings preannouncements strategies. *Review of Accounting Studies*, 5, 1 (March): 5–26.

Song, Chang Soon. 2004. Are interest rate swaps used to manage banks' earnings? Working Paper, Michigan State University.

Song, Jihe and Brian Windram. 2004. Benchmarking audit committee effectiveness in financial reporting. *International Journal of Auditing*, 8, 3 (November): 195–205.

Spagnolo, Giancarlo. 2000. Stock-related compensation and product-market competition. *The RAND Journal of Economics*, 31, 1 (Spring): 22–42.

Spathis, C.H., M. Doumpos, and C. Zopounidis. 2002. Detecting falsified financial statements: A comparative study using multicriteria analysis and multivariate statistical techniques. *European Accounting Review*, 11, 3 (September): 509–535.

Spear, Stephen E. and Sanjay Srivastava. 1987. On repeated moral hazard with discounting. *The Review of Economic Studies*, 54, 4 (October): 599–618.

Spira, Laura F. 1999. Ceremonies of governance: Perspectives on the role of the audit committee. *Journal of Management and Governance*, 3, 3 (September): 231–260.

Srinidhi, Bin and Ferdinand A. Gul. 2006. The differential effects of auditors' non-audit and audit fees on accrual quality. *Contemporary Accounting Research*, 24, 2 (Summer): 595–629.

Srinidhi, Bin, Joshua Ronen, and A.J. Maindiratta. 2001. Market imperfections as the cause of accounting income smoothing—the case of differential capital access. *Review of Quantitative Finance and Accounting*, 17, 3 (November): 283–300.

Srinivasan, Suraj. 2005. Consequences of financial reporting failure for outside directors: Evidence from accounting restatements. *Journal of Accounting Research*, 43, 2 (May): 291–334.

Stadtmann, Georg and Markus F. Wissmann. 2005. SOX around the world—Corporate transparency and risk management disclosure of foreign issuers in the United States. SSRN.com/abstract=858884.

Stammerjohan, William W. and Steven C. Hall. 2003. Legal costs and accounting choices: Another test of the litigation hypothesis. *Journal of Business Finance and Accounting*, 30, 5/6 (June/July): 829–862.

Standard & Poor's. 2002. Standard & Poor's Corporate Governance Scores - Criteria, methodology and definitions. http://www2.standardandpoors.com/servlet/Satellite?pagename=sp/sp_article/ArticleTemplate&c=sp_article&cid=1021558139012&s=&ig=&b=2&dct=24.

Stein, Jeremy C. 1988. Takeover threats and managerial myopia. *Journal of Political Economy*, 96, 1 (February): 61–80.

Stein, Jeremy C. 1989. Efficient capital markets, inefficient firms: A model of myopic corporate behavior. *Quarterly Journal of Economics*, 104, 4 (November): 655–669.

Stickel, Scott E. 1991. Common stock returns surrounding earnings forecast revisions: More puzzling evidence. *The Accounting Review*, 66, 2 (April) :402–416.

Stiglitz, Joseph E. 1969. A re-examination of the Modigliani–Miller Theorem. *The American Economic Review*, 59, 5 (December): 784–793.

Stiglitz, Joseph E. 2003. *The Roaring Nineties*. New York: W.W. Norton & Company. Ch. 5: 115–139.

Stocken, Philip C. 2000. Credibility of voluntary disclosure. *RAND Journal of Economics*, 31, 2 (Summer): 359–374.

Stolowy, Herve and Gaetan Breton. 2000. Accounts manipulation: A literature review and proposed conceptual framework. *Review of Accounting and Finance*, 3, 1: 5–66.

Strahan, Philip E. 1998. Securities class actions, corporate governance and managerial agency problems. Working Paper, Federal Reserve Bank of New York.

Strobl, Günter. 2004. Managerial compensation, market liquidity, and the overinvestment problem. Working Paper, University of Pennsylvania.

Strong, John S. and John R. Meyer. 1987. Asset writedowns: Managerial incentives and security returns. *Journal of Finance*, 42, 3 (June): 643–661.

Stubben, Stephen R. 2006. Do firms use discretionary revenues to meet earnings and revenue targets? Working Paper, Stanford University.

Stuerke, Pamela S. 2005. Financial analysts as users of accounting information: A study of financial analysts' forecast revision activity after earnings announcements. *International Journal of Managerial Finance*, 1, 1 (April): 8–24.

Subrahmanyam, Avanidhar. 2003. Disclosure, intelligence, and financial markets: Some perspectives. http://www.stern.nyu.edu/fin/pdfs/seminars/033w-asubrahmanyam_paper.pdf.

Subramanian, Guhan. 2005. Fixing freezeouts. *Yale Law Journal*, 155, 2: 2–70.

Subramanyam, K.R. 1996. The pricing of discretionary accruals. *Journal of Accounting and Economics*, 22, 1-3 (August-December): 249–281.

Subramanyam, K.R. and John J. Wild. 1996. Going-concern status, earnings persistence, and informativeness of earnings. *Contemporary Accounting Research*, 13, 1 (Spring): 251–273.

Suh, Yoon S. 1990. Communication and income smoothing through accounting method choice. *Management Science*, 36, 6 (June): 704–729.

Suijs, Jeroen. 2005. Voluntary disclosure of bad news. *Journal of Business Finance and Accounting*, 32, 7/8 (September/October): 1423–1436.

Suk, In-Ho. 2005. Persistence in meeting/beating earnings thresholds and strategic earnings reporting policy. Working Paper, Purdue University.

Sullivan, Richard J. and Kenneth Spong. 2004. Managerial wealth, ownership structure, and risk in commercial banks. SSRN.com/abstract=558684.

Summers, Scott L. and John T. Sweeney. 1998. Fraudulently misstated financial statements and insider trading: An empirical analysis. *The Accounting Review*, 73, 1 (January): 131–146.

Sun, Yan. 2003. Analysis of accrual mispricing. www.olin.wustl.edu/fs/acadseminars/downloadPDF.cfm?recNum=40868.

Sunder, Shyam. 1996. Security markets and accounting standards: Lessons from research. Working Paper, Yale University.

Sunder, Shyam. 1997. *Theory of Accounting and Control.* Cincinnati: Southwest College Publishing.

Sunder, Shyam. 1999. Classical stewardship, and market perspectives on accounting: A synthesis. In Shyam Sunder and Hidetoshi Yamaji, eds., *The Japanese Style of Business Accounting.* Westport, CT: Quorum Books: 17–31.

Sunder, Shyam. 2002. Management control, expectations, common knowledge, and culture. *Journal of Management Accounting Rese*arch, 14, 1: 173–187.

Sunder, Shyam. 2004. Contract theory and strategic management: Balancing expectations and actions. Working Paper, Yale University.

Swaminathan, Siva and Joseph Weintrop. 1991. The information content of earnings, revenues, and expenses. *Journal of Accounting Research*, 29, 2 (Autumn): 418–427.

Sweeney, Amy P. 1994. Debt-covenant violations and manager's accounting responses. *Journal of Accounting and Economics*, 17, 3 (May): 281–308.

Tan, Hun-Tong, Robert Libby, and James E. Hunton. 2002. Analysts' reactions to earnings preannouncement strategies. *Journal of Accounting Research*, 40, 1 (March): 223–246.

Tan, Hwee-Cheng and Karim Jamal. 2006. Effect of accounting discretion on ability of managers to smooth earnings. *Journal of Accounting and Public Policy*, 25, 5 (September-October): 554–573.

Taplin, Ross, Greg Tower, and Phil Hancock. 2002. Disclosure (discernibility) and compliance of accounting policies: Asia-Pacific evidence. *Accounting Forum*, 26, 2 (June): 172-190

Tasker, Sarah C. 1998. Bridging the information gap: Quarterly conference calls as a medium of voluntary disclosure. *Review of Accounting Studies*, 3, 1-2 (March): 137–167.

Taylor, Sarah J. and Stephen L. Taylor. 2004. Earnings conservatism in a continuous disclosure environment: Empirical evidence. Working Paper, University of Melbourne and University of South Wales, Australia. AAA 2004 Annual Meeting Paper, Orlando, FL.

Teets, Walter R. 1994. A note on the frequency of negative earnings–returns relations in the Antle-Demski-Ryan Model. *Journal of Accounting, Auditing and Finance*, 9, 4 (Fall): 697–702.

Teo, Melvyn. 2000. Strategic interactions between sell-side analysts and the firms they cover. SSRN.com/abstract=258028.

Teoh, Siew Hong, Ivo Welch, and T.J. Wong. 1998a. Earnings management and the underperformance of seasoned equity offerings. *Journal of Financial Economics*, 50, 1 (October): 63–99.

Teoh, Siew H., Ivo Welch, and T.J. Wong. 1998b. Earnings management and the long-run market performance of initial public offerings. *Journal of Finance*, 53, 6 (December): 1935–1974.

Teoh, Siew Hong and T.J. Wong. 1993. Perceived auditor quality and the earnings response coefficient. *The Accounting Review*, 68, 2 (April): 346–366.

Teoh, Siew Hong and T.J. Wong. 2002. Why new issues and high-accrual firms underperform: The role of analysts' credulity. *The Review of Financial Studies*, 15, 3 (July): 869–900.

Teoh, Siew Hong, T.J. Wong, and Gita Rao. 1998. Are accruals during initial public offerings opportunistic? *Review of Accounting Studies*, 3, 1-2 (March): 175–208.

Thaler, Richard H. 1994. *Quasi Rational Economics*, New York: Russell Sage Foundation.

Thomas, Jacob K. 1989. Unusual patterns in reported earnings. *The Accounting Review*, 64, 4 (October): 773–787.

Thomas, Jacob K. and Huai Zhang. 2002. Inventory changes and future returns. *Review of Accounting Studies*, 7, 2-3 (June): 163–187.

Thomas, Jacob K. and X.J. Zhang. 2000. Identifying unexpected accruals: A comparison of current approaches. *Journal of Accounting and Public Policy*, 19, 4-5 (Winter): 347–376.

Thomas, Randall S. and Kenneth J. Martin. 1999. The effect of shareholder proposals in executive compensation. *University of Cincinnati Law Review*, 67: 1021–1081.

Tippett, Elizabeth Chika. 2006. The promise of compelled whistleblowing: What the corporate governance provisions of Sarbanes Oxley mean for employment law. SSRN.com/abstract=930226.

Tirole, Jean J. 1988. *The Theory of Industrial Organization*. Reading MA: MIT Press.

Tirole, Jean J. 2002. Corporate governance. *Econometrica*, 69, 1 (January): 1–35.

Titman, Sheridan and Brett Trueman. 1986. Information quality and the valuation of new issues. *Journal of Accounting and Economics*, 8, 2 (June): 159–172.

Townsend, Robert M. 1979. Optimal contracts and competitive markets with costly state verification. *Journal of Economic Theory*, 21, 2 (October): 265–293.

Townsend, Robert M. 1982. Optimal multiperiod contracts and the gain from enduring relationships under private information. *The Journal of Political Economy*, 90, 6 (December): 1166–1186.

Trueman, Brett. 1990. Theories of earnings announcement timing. *Journal of Accounting and Economics*, 13, 3 (October): 285–301.

Trueman, Brett. 1996. The impact of analyst following on stock prices and the implications for firms' disclosure policies. *Journal of Accounting, Auditing and Finance*, 11, 3 (Summer): 333–354.

Trueman, Brett. 1997. Managerial disclosures and shareholder litigation. *Review of Accounting Studies*, 2, 2 (June): 181–199.

Trueman, Brett and Sheridan Titman. 1988. An explanation for accounting income smoothing. *Journal of Accounting Research*, 29, 3 (Supplement): 127–139.

Tsoulouhas, Theofanis, Charles R. Knoeber, and Anup Agrawal. 2007. Contests to become CEO: Incentives, selection and handicaps. *Economic Theory*, 30, 2 (February): 195–221.

Tucker, Jennifer W. and Paul Zarowin. 2006. Does income smoothing improve earnings informativeness? *The Accounting Review*, 81, 1 (January): 251–270.

Tufano, Peter and Matthew Sevick. 1997. Board structure and fee-setting in the U.S. mutual fund industry. *Journal of Financial Economics*, 46, 3 (December): 321–355.

Turner, Lynn E. 2001a. *The Accounting Profession's Obligation to Global Investors: Quality Investor Information through Quality Audits.* April 6. http://www.sec.gov/news/speech/spch480.htm.

Turner, Lynn E. 2001b. *The State of Financial Reporting Today. An Unfinished Chapter III.* June 21. http://www.sec.gov/news/speech/spch508.htm.

Turner, Lynn E. 2001c. *Independence: A Covenant for the Ages.* June 28. http://www.sec.gov/news/speech/spch504.htm.

Turner, Lynn E. and Joseph H. Godwin. 1999. Auditing, earnings management, and international accounting-issues at the Securities and Exchange Commission. *Accounting Horizons*, 13, 3 (September): 281–287.

Tweedie, David and Geoffrey Whittington. 1990. Financial reporting: Current problems and their implications for systematic reform. *Accounting and Business Research*, 21, 81 (Winter): 87–102.

Tzur, Joseph and Varda (Lewinstein) Yaari. 1994. Management's reporting strategy and the imperfection of the capital market. *Managerial and Decision Economics*, 15, 1 (January): 57–61.

Tzur, Joseph and Varda (Lewinstein) Yaari. 1999. Microstructure of firm's disclosure. *Review of Quantitative Finance and Accounting*, 13, 4 (December): 367–391.

United States General Accounting Office. 2002. Financial Statement Restatements: Trends, Market Impacts, Regulatory Responses and Remaining Challenges. A Report to the Chairman, Committee on Banking, Housing and Urban Affairs, U.S. Senate. GAO-03-138 (October).

Uzun, Hatice, Samuel H. Szewczyk, and Raj R. Varma. 2004. Board composition and corporate fraud. *Financial Analysts Journal*, 60, 3 (May/June): 33–43.

Vafeas, Nikos. 1999a. Board meeting frequency and firm performance. *Journal of Financial Economics*, 53, 1 (July): 113–142.

Vafeas, Nikos. 1999b. The nature of board nominating committees and their role in corporate governance. *Journal of Business Finance and Accounting*, 26, 1/2 (January-March): 199–225.

Vafeas, Nikos. 2000. Board structure and the informativeness of earnings. *Journal of Accounting and Public Policy*, 19, 2 (June): 139–160.

Vafeas, Nikos. 2003. Length of board tenure and outside director independence. *Journal of Business Finance and Accounting*, 30, 7-8 (September/October): 1043–1064.

Vafeas, Nikos. 2005. Audit committees, boards, and the quality of reported earnings. *Contemporary Accounting Research*, 22, 4 (Winter): 1093–1122.

Vafeas, Nikos, Adamos Vlittis, Philippos Katranis, and Kanalis Ockree. 2003. Earnings management around share repurchases: A note. *Abacus*, 39, 2 (June): 262–272.

Van Damme, Eric. 1987. *Stability and Perfection of Nash Equilibria.* Berlin: Springer-Verlag.

Vance, Stanley C. 1983. *Corporate Leadership: Boards, Directors, and Strategy.* New York: McGraw-Hill.

Vancil, Richard F. 1987. *Passing the Baton: Managing the Process of CEO Succession.* Boston: Harvard Business School Press.

Venugopalan, Raghu. 2004. Conservatism in accounting: Good or bad? Working Paper, University of Chicago.

Vermaelen, Theo. 1981. Common stock repurchases and market signaling: An Empirical study. *Journal of Financial Economics*, 9, 2 (June): 139–183.

Vermeer, Thomas, E. 2005. Do CEO/CFO certifications provide a signal of credible financial reporting? *Research in Accounting Regulation*, 18: 163–176.

Verrecchia, Robert E. 1982. The use of mathematical models in financial accounting. *Journal of Accounting Research*, 20 (Supplement): 1–42.

Verrecchia, Robert E. 1983. Discretionary disclosure. *Journal of Accounting and Economics*, 5: 179–194.

Verrecchia, Robert E. 1986. Managerial discretion in the choice among financial reporting alternatives. *Journal of Accounting and Economics*, 8, 3 (October): 175–195.

Verrecchia, Robert E. 1990a. Endogenous proprietary costs through firm interdependence. *Journal of Accounting and Economics*, 12, 1-3 (January): 245–250.

Verrecchia, Robert E. 1990b. Information quality and discretionary disclosure. *Journal of Accounting and Economics*, 12, 4 (March): 365–380.

Verrecchia, Robert E. 2001. Essays on disclosure. *Journal of Accounting and Economics*, 32, 1-3 (December): 97–180.

Verrecchia, Robert E. and Joseph Peter Weber. 2005. Redacted disclosure. SSRN.com/abstract=875888.

Vickers, Marcia. 1999. Ho-hum, another earnings surprise. *Business Week*, May 24: 83–84.

Visvanathan, Gnanakumar. 1998. Deferred tax valuation allowances and earnings management. *Journal of Financial statements Analysis*, 3, 4 (Summary): 6–15.

Wagenhofer, Alfred. 1990. Voluntary disclosure with a strategic opponent. *Journal of Accounting and Economics*, 12, 4 (March): 341–363.

Wahlen, James M. 1994. The nature of information in commercial bank loan loss disclosures. *The Accounting Review*, 69, 3 (July): 455–478.

Wall, Larry D. and Pamela P. Peterson. 1996. Banks' responses to binding regulatory capital requirements. *Economic Review,* Federal Reserve Bank of Atlanta.

Walker, David. 2006. Some observations on the stock option backdating scandal of 2006. The Boston University School of Law Working Paper 06-31. SSRN.com/abstract=929702.

Walsh, Pauk, Russell Craig, and Frank Clarke. 1991. "Big bath accounting" using extraordinary items adjustments: Australian empirical evidence. *Journal of Business Finance and Accounting*, 18, 2 (January): 173–189.

Walther, Beverly R. 1997. Investor sophistication and market earnings expectations. *Journal of Accounting Research*, 35, 2 (Autumn): 157–192.

Wan-Hussin, Wan Nordin, and Noraizan Ripain. 2003. IPO profit guarantees and income smoothing. SSRN.com/abstract=411380.

Wang, Hefei. 2006. Pooling the good and the bad: A theory of reputation acquisition of stock analysts. SSRN.com/abstract=887156.

Wang, Shiing-wu and Jerry Han. 1998. Political costs and earnings management of oil companies in the 1990 Persian Gulf crisis. *The Accounting Review*, 73, 1 (January): 103–117.

Wang, Tracy Yue. 2004. Investment, shareholder monitoring, and the economics of corporate securities fraud. Working Paper, University of Maryland.

Wang, Zhemin and Thomas H. Williams. 1994. Accounting income smoothing and stockholder wealth. *Journal of Applied Business Research*, 10, 3 (Summer): 96–110.

Warfield, Terry D. and Thomas J. Linsmeier. 1992. Tax planning, earnings management, and the differential information content of bank earnings components. *The Accounting Review*, 67, 3 (July): 546–562.

Warfield, Terry D. and John J. Wild. 1992. Accounting recognition and the relevance of earnings as an explanatory variable for returns. *The Accounting Review*, 67, 4 (October): 821–842.

Warfield, Terry D., John J. Wild, and Kenneth L. Wild. 1995. Managerial ownership, accounting choices, and informativeness of earnings. *Journal of Accounting and Economics*, 20, 1 (July): 61–91.

Warner, Jerold B., Ross L. Watts, and Karen H. Wruck. 1988. Stock prices and top management changes. *Journal of Financial Economics*, 20: 461–492.

Warther, Vincent A. 1998. Board effectiveness and board dissent: A model of the board's relationship to management and shareholders. *Journal of Corporate Finance: Contracting, Governance & Organization*, 4, 1 (March): 53–70.

Wasley, Charles, E. and Joanna Shuang Wu. 2005. Why do managers voluntarily issue cash flow forecasts? *Journal of Accounting Research*, 44, 2 (May): 389–429.

Wasley Charles and Joanna Shuang Wu. 2006. Why do managers voluntarily issue cash flows forecasts? *Journal of Accounting Research*, 44, 2 (May): 389–429.

Wasserman, Craig M. 2005. Dear Prudence: Finding a proper balance in the post-Enron regulatory and enforcement arena. Yale Law & Economics Research Paper No. 325. SSRN.com/abstract=879300.

Wasserman, Noam, Nitin Nohria, and Bharat N. Anand. 2001. When does leadership matter? The contingent opportunities view of CEO leadership. Strategy Unit Working Paper, 02-04, Harvard Business School Working Paper 01-063. SSRN.com/abstract=278652.

Watts, Ross L. 2003a. Conservatism in accounting part I: Explanations and implications. *Accounting Horizons*, 17, 3 (September): 207–221.

Welch, Ivo. 1996. Herding among security analysts. John E. Anderson Graduate School of Management at UCLA Publishing.

Watts, Ross L. 2003b. Conservatism in accounting part II: Evidence and research opportunities. *Accounting Horizons*, 17, 4 (December): 287–301.

Watts, Ross, L. and Sugata Roychowdhury. 2005. Asymmetric timeliness of earnings, market-to-book and conservatism in financial reporting. MIT Sloan Research Paper No. 4550-05. SSRN.com/abstract=638001.

Watts, Ross L. and Jerold L. Zimmerman. 1978. Towards a positive theory of the determination of accounting standards. *The Accounting Review*, 53, 1 (January): 112–134.

Watts, Ross L. and Jerold L. Zimmerman. 1986. *Positive Accounting Theory.* Englewood Cliffs: Prentice Hall.

Watts, Ross L. and Jerold L. Zimmerman. 1990. Positive accounting theory: A ten year perspective. *The Accounting Review*, 65, 1 (January): 131–156.

Waymire, Gregory. 1984. Additional evidence on the information content of management earnings forecasts. *Journal of Accounting Research*, 22, 2 (Autumn): 703–718.

Waymire, Gregory. 1986. Additional evidence on the accuracy of analyst forecasts before and after voluntary management earnings forecasts. *The Accounting Review*, 61, 1 (January): 129–141.

Wayne, Leslie. 2003. Creative deal or highflying pork? *New York Times*, 4/20/2003.

Weber, Margaret Liebenow. 2004. Executive equity incentives, earnings management and corporate governance. Ph.D. dissertation. The University of Texas at Austin.

Wei, K.C. John and Feixue Xie. 2005. Earnings management, corporate investments, and stock returns. SSRN.com/abstract=685113.

Weisbach, Michael S. 1988. Outside directors and CEO turnover. *Journal of Financial Economics*, 20, 1 (March): 431–460.

Weisbach, Michael S. 1995. CEO turnover and the firm's investment decisions. *Journal of Financial Economics*, 37, 2 (February): 159–188.

Weisbenner, Scott J. 2000. Corporate share repurchases in the 1990s: What role do stock options play? The Federal Reserve Board.

Welch, Ivo. 1992. Sequential sales, learnings, and cascades. *Journal of Finance*, 47, 2 (June): 695–732.

Welch, Ivo. 2000. Herding among security analysts. *Journal of Financial Market*, 58, 3 (December): 369–396.

Welch, Jack and John A. Bryne. 2001. *Jack: Straight from the Gut.* New York: Warner Books, Inc.

Wells, Peter. 2002. Earnings management surrounding CEO changes. *Accounting and Finance*, 42, 2 (June): 169–193.

Werhane, Patricia H., Jenny Mead, and Cindy Eddins Collier. 2006. HealthSouth (C): The Trial. UVA-E-0275. SSRN.com/abstract=908774.

Westphal, James D. 1999. Collaboration in the boardroom: The consequences of social ties in the CEO/board relationship. *Academy of Management Journal*, 42, 2 (March): 7–24.

Westmore, Jill L. and John R. Brick. 1994. Loan loss provisions of commercial banks and adequate disclosure: A note. *Journal of Economics and Business*, 46, 4 (October): 299–305.

Westport Tippett and Elizabeth Chika. 2006. The promise of compelled whistleblowing: What the corporate governance provisions of Sarbanes-Oxley mean for employment law. SSRN.com/abstract=930226.

White, Gerald I., Ashwinpaul C. Sondhi, and Dov Fried. 1998. *The Analysis and Use of Financial Statements*. Second edition. New York: Wiley.

Whittred, Greg and Yoke Kai Chan. 1992. Asset revaluation and the mitigation of undervaluation. *Abacus*, 28, 1 (March): 58-73 .

Wiedman, Christine I. 1999. Instructional case: Detecting earnings manipulation: *Issues in Accounting Education*, 14, 1 (February): 145–176.

Willekens, Marleen. 2003. Auditor reporting conservatism as a defense mechanism against increased post-Enron litigation risk. Working Paper, Katholeike Universiteit at Leuven.

Willett, Roger J., Yeo Hwan Kim, and Jee In Jang. 2002. Default risk as a factor affecting the earnings response coefficient. SSRN.com/abstract=300350.

Williams, Jan. 2006. An empirical examination of the management strategies used by firms to meet or beat analysts' forecasts: Pre and post Regulation FD and Sarbanes Oxley Act. A Ph.D. dissertation. Morgan State University.

Williams, Jan, Peter DaDalt, Wei Liang Sun, and Varda Yaari. 2006. Has regulation changed the market's reward for meeting or beating expectations? In M. Neelan, ed., *Focus on Accounting and Finance,* Hauppauge, NY: Nova Publishers.

Williamson, Oliver E. 1985. *The Economic Institutions of Capitalism*, New York: Free Press.

Williamson, Oliver E. 1996. *The Mechanisms of Governance*. Oxford: Oxford University Press.

Wilson, Thomas E. and Richard A. Grimlund. 1990. An examination of the importance of an auditor's reputation. *Auditing: A Journal of Practice and Theory*, 9, 2 (Spring): 43–59.

Winton, Andrew. 1993. Limitation of liability and the ownership structure of the firm. *Journal of Finance,* 48, 2 (June): 487–512.

Wojcik, Dariusz, Gordon Leslie Clark, and Rob Bauer. 2004. Corporate governance and cross-listing: Evidence from European companies. SSRN.com/abstract=593364.

Wolnizer, P.W. 1995. Are audit committees red herrings? *Abacus*, 31, 1 (March): 45–66.

Wright, David W. 1999. Evidence on the relation between corporate governance characteristics and the quality of financial reporting. SSRN.com/abstract=10138.

Wu, Min. 2002. Earnings restatements: A capital market perspective. Working Paper, New York University.

Wu, Woody Y. 1997. Management buyouts and earnings management. *Journal of Accounting, Auditing and Finance*, 12, 4 (Fall): 373–389.

Wu, Yilin. 2000. "Honey, CalPERS shrunk the board." SSRN.com/abstract=235295.

Wysocki, Peter D. 2004. Discussion of ultimate ownership, income management, and legal and extra-legal institutions. *Journal of Accounting Research*, 42, 2 (May): 463–474.

Xie, Biao, Wallace N. Davidson III, and Peter J. DaDalt. 2003. Earnings management and corporate governance: The roles of the board and the audit committee. *Journal of Corporate Finance*, 9, 3 (June): 295–316.

Xie, Hong. 2001. The mispricing of discretionary accruals. *The Accounting Review*, 76, 3 (July): 357–373.

Xue, Yanfeng. 2003. Information content of earnings management: Evidence from managing earnings to exceed thresholds. SSRN.com/abstract=582601.

Yaari, Hila, Peter DaDalt, Joshua Ronen, and Varda Yaari. 2007. An accruals conundrum in earnings management research. Work in process.

Yaari, Varda. 1991. On hoarding in contract theory. *Economics Letters*, 35, 1 (January): 21–25.

Yaari, Varda. 1993. A taxonomy of disclosure policies. *Journal of Economics and Business*, 45, 5 (December): 361–374.

Yaari, Varda. 2005. Smoothing, conservative smoothing, and truth telling. CAAA 2005 Annual Meeting, Quebec, Canada, 2005, and AAA 2005 Meeting, San Francisco, CA. SSRN.com/abstract=754886.

Yan, Xiong. 2006. Earnings management and its measurement: A theoretical perspective. *Journal of American Academy of Business*, 9, 1 (March): 214–219.

Ye, Jianming. 2006. Accounting accruals and tests of earnings management. Working Paper, Baruch College.

Yeo, Gillian H.H., Patricia M.S. Tan, Kim Wai Ho, and Sheng-Syan Chen. 2002. Corporate ownership structure and the informativeness of earnings. *Journal of Business Finance and Accounting*, 29, 7/8 (September/October): 1023–1046.

Yeo, Gillian-Hian-Heng and David A. Zeibart. 1995. The effect of self-selection bias on the testing of a stock price reaction to management's earnings forecasts. *Review of Quantitative Finance and Accounting*, 5, 1 (March): 5–25.

Yermack, David. 1995. Do corporations award CEO stock options effectively? *Journal of Financial Economics*, 39, 2-3 (October-November): 237–269.

Yermack, David. 1996. Higher market valuation of companies with a small board of directors. *Journal of Financial Economics*, 40, 2 (February): 185–211.

Yermack, David. 1997. Good timing: CEO stock option awards and company news announcements. *Journal of Finance*, 52, 2 (June): 449–477.

Yermack, David. 1998. Companies' modest claims about the value of CEO stock option awards. *Review of Quantitative Finance and Accounting*, 10, 2 (March): 207–226.

Yermack, David. 2004. Remuneration, retention, and reputation incentives for outside directors. *Journal of Finance*, 59, 5 (October): 2281–2308.

Yermack, David. 2006a. Flights of fancy: Corporate jets, CEO perquisites, and inferior shareholder returns. *Journal of Financial Economics*, 80, 1 (April): 211–242.

Yermack, David. 2006b. Golden handshakes: Separation pay for retired and dismissed CEOs. *Journal of Accounting and Economics*, 41, 3 (September): 237–256.

Young, Richard A. 2000. Discussion of "Accounting recognition, moral hazard, and communication." *Contemporary Accounting Research*, 17, 3 (Fall): 491–496.

Young, Steven. 1999. Systematic measurement error in the estimation of discretionary accruals: An evaluation of alternative modeling procedures. *Journal of Business Finance and Accounting*, 26, 7-8 (September-October): 833–862.

Young, Stewart M. 2004. Whistleblowing in a foreign key: The consistency of ethics regulation under Sarbanes-Oxley with the WTO GATS provisions. *Denver Journal of International Law and Policy*, 32, 1: 55–85. SSRN.com/abstract=586821.

Zach, Tzachi. 2003. Inside the "accrual anomaly." Working Paper, Washington University.

Zacharias, Fred C. 2004. Lawyers as gatekeepers. *San Diego Law Review*, 41, issue 3, p. 1387. SSRN.com/abstract=591655.

Zajac, Edward J. 1990. CEO selection, succession, compensation and firm performance: A theoretical integration and empirical analysis. *Strategic Management Journal*, 11, 3 (March): 217–230.

Zajac, Edward J. and James D. Westphal. 2004. The costs and benefits of managerial incentives and monitoring in large U.S. corporations: When is more not better? *Strategic Management Journal*, 15, Special Issue: Competitive Organizational Behavior (Winter): 121–142.

Zang, Y. Amy. 2007. Evidence on the tradeoff between real manipulation and accrual manipulation. Working Paper, University of Rochester.

Zarowin, Paul. 2002. Does income smoothing make stock prices more informative? Working Paper, New York University. SSRN.com/abstract=315099.

Zeff, Stephen A. 1978. The rise of economic consequences. *The Journal of Accountancy* (December): 56–63.

Zeff, Stephen A. 1993. The politics of accounting standards. *Economic Aziendale*, 12, 2 (August): 123–142.

Zhang, Hua Jessie. 2003. Reputation and monitoring ability in loan syndications. Working Paper, York University.

Zhang, Huai. 2000. How rational is the stock market towards properties of analyst consensus forecasts? A Ph.D. dissertation. Columbia University.

Zhang, Ivy Xiying. 2005. Economic consequences of the Sarbanes-Oxley Act of 2002. Working Paper, University of Rochester.

Zhang, Ping. 1999. A bargaining model of auditor reporting. *Contemporary Accounting Research*, 16, 1 (Spring): 167–184.

Zhang, Yan, Jian Zhou, and Nan Zhou. 2006. Audit committee quality, auditor independence, and internal control weaknesses. SSRN.com/abstract=925732.

Zhou, Jian and Ken Y. Chen. 2004. Audit committee, board characteristics and earnings management by commercial banks. Working Paper, SUNY at Binghamton and National Cheng Kung University.

Zhou, Jian and Randal J. Elder. 2004. Audit quality and earnings management by seasoned equity offering firms. *Asia-Pacific Journal of Accounting and Economics*, 11, 2 (August): 95–120.

Zhou, Xianming. 2001. Understanding the determinants of managerial ownership and the link between ownership and performance: Comment. *Journal of Financial Economics*, 62, 3 (December): 559–571.

Zingales, Luigi. 1998. Peter Newman, Ed., *Corporate Governance. The New Palgrave Dictionary of Economics and the Law*, New York: Stockton Press.

Zingales, Luigi. 2006. Is the U.S. capital market losing its competitive edge? The Initiative on Global Financial Markets. Working Paper No. 1.

Ziv, Amir. 1993. Information sharing in oligopoly: The truth-telling problem. *RAND Journal of Economics*, 24, 3 (Autumn): 455–465.

Ziv, Amir. 1998. Discussion of "Earnings management and the revelation principle." *Review of Accounting Studies*, 3, 1-2 (March): 35–40.

Zou, Xiaopeng and Xuejie Chen. 2002. Earnings management of Chinese listed firms: A survey of empirical studies. Special reports.

Index

Breinigsville, PA USA
29 January 2010
231604BV00004B/8/A